Ethnocultural Perspectives on Disaster and Trauma

Foundations, Issues, and Applications

International and Cultural Psychology Series
Series Editor: **Anthony Marsella**, *University of Hawaii, Honolulu, Hawaii*

A Continuation Order Plan is available for this series. A continuation order will bring delivery of each new volume immediately upon publication. Volumes are billed only upon actual shipment. For further information please contact the publisher.

Ethnocultural Perspectives on Disaster and Trauma

Foundations, Issues, and Applications

Edited by

Anthony J. Marsella
University of Hawaii
Honolulu, Hawaii

Jeannette L. Johnson
Friends Research Institute
Baltimore, Maryland

Patricia Watson
National Center for PTSD
White River Junction, Vermont

Jan Gryczynski
Friends Research Institute
Baltimore, Maryland

 Springer

Anthony J. Marsella
Alpharetta, GA, USA
8925 Nesbit Lakes Drive
Alpharetta 30022
marsella@hawaii.edu

ISBN: 978-0-387-73284-8   e-ISBN: 978-0-387-73285-5

Library of Congress Control Number: 2007933090

Printed on acid-free paper

9 8 7 6 5 4 3 2 1

springer.com

To those who have fallen before the destructive forces of earth, water, wind, and fire . . .
And to those who have risen from the ashes, mud, and debris . . .
And from their loss, sorrow, and suffering to survive . . .
To recover . . .
And to rebuild lives for yet another day.

Contents

Section III Appendices

Preface

The past decade, more than any other period in our history, has brought home the terrible human, social, and economic consequences of natural and human-made disasters. Media images and headlines of fires, mudslides, hurricanes, floods, and terrorism became part of daily life across the world. No sooner did one disaster pass than another occurred, each time reminding us of the horrors of human suffering and victimization that are part of natural and human-made disasters. The words associated with disasters (i.e., the lexicon – see Appendix A) became familiar to all of us and are no longer restricted to professional vocabularies and discussions. Numerous public and private disaster agencies and organizations (e.g., FEMA, Red Cross, Salvation Army, CARE, International Rescue Committee, Doctors Without Borders, Department of Homeland Security) gained widespread recognition and familiarity, and their acronyms now dot the news media on a regular basis.

During this period, donations and appropriations from private citizens and from national and international organizations to assist in post-disaster healing and rehabilitation reached record amounts, and massive supplies and materials were transported to disaster sites by governmental and private agencies (e.g., NGOs). Volunteers joined professional responders in record numbers working on the frontlines to bring comfort and care. Through all of this, however, what remains at the core of each disaster is the enormous human cost that has been exacted – the tragic deaths, the destructive injuries, the psychic scars in survivors, the enduring and permanently inscribed memories of the terrible experiences involved during the crisis, and the efforts to survive and to rebuild.

Before our eyes, we witnessed buildings being toppled and destroyed, houses razed by fire and flood, roads crushed or swept away, and trees torn from their roots and tossed together in heaping piles of refuse and debris. But, it is in the faces and the minds of the survivors that the true impact of disasters is to be found; it is in the empty stare of an old man still in shock, in the tear-stained cheeks of an orphaned child, in the horror-filled eyes of a mother holding a lifeless child. It is in these images that the toll of disasters must be measured for almost all else can be rebuilt and restored. It is the human cost that is most important, and it is the human cost that most needs our understanding, concern, and healing. More than survival is at stake – we are faced with struggles for hope, purpose, and meaning.

This volume grew from efforts at the National Center for Post-Traumatic Stress Disorder (NC-PTSD) and the Substance Abuse and Mental Health Services Administration (SAMHSA) to better understand, assist, and respond to the human experience of natural and man-made disasters. In a series of meetings that began in 2004 involving Centers for Disease Control (CDC), NC-PTSD, SAMHSA, and other private and public agencies, efforts were made to identify critical issues and concerns involved in preparing for and responding to disasters. Among these issues and concerns was the recognition that even the best of intentions in providing disaster services was insufficient and inadequate because of a failure or inability to understand the diverse human experiences involved in disasters as a result of ethnocultural and racial variations.

We are not speaking here specifically of the apparent racism and classism following Hurricane Katrina when the entire world watched in horror as local and national government agencies failed to respond to the thousands of poor Black Americans and White Americans that were abandoned in cordoned areas of New Orleans. Nor are we speaking here of the widespread humanitarian response to the tragic Asian Tsunami of December 2004, when we watched in horror as tidal waves destroyed lives and villages across Southeast Asia only to find in later months that many of our efforts were ineffective in addressing the vast psychological, social, and economic needs of the region because of a failure to grasp the cultural context of the victim's lives and their unique construction of the events.

Rather, we are speaking here of the simple fact that disasters bring together victims and responders of varying ethnocultural and racial backgrounds that may limit or even impair the delivery of disaster services. In the case of medical services, a broken arm, a punctured lung, or a burned face may be treated and healed by providers often independent of the cultural or racial backgrounds of the victim and physician. But, when it comes to the complex and demanding responsibility of assisting a victim who under the pressures of disaster trauma has deteriorated to the point of psychosis or total helplessness, we are faced with a different and more pressing need for an understanding, appreciation, and sensitivity to the cultural and racial backgrounds of those involved. It is at this point – when we refer to mental health – that racial and cultural differences become critical because of the issues of communication, the nature and meaning of health and illness, treatment preferences and reluctance, and the complex social, ethical, and administrative considerations involved. Figure 1 displays the dynamics of cultural interactions in disasters (see Marsella & Christopher, 2004).

Every disaster brings together people from differing cultural traditions and ways of life. This is especially true in the case of developing nations when local aid and resources are typically limited and international assistance is required. Much as an ethnic culture has its reality assumptions, values, leaders, social structure, communication patterns, and ways of knowing and adjusting to meet the needs and challenges of life, a disaster generates a similar culture

Figure 1.   Cultural Encounters in Disasters

milieu and context, but this time the situation is increasingly complex because of the addition of outsiders (i.e., other world views) and the pressing burden of the disaster.

Disasters also have complex global political implications for individuals, societies, and nations because of the problematic cultural encounters that occur when victims and service providers from contrasting cultural traditions must work with one another. Michael Wessells, one of the most active and knowledgeable disaster professionals in psychology, identified the problems that can emerge when Western disaster professionals intervene in developing countries. He writes:

> In emergency situations, psychologists hired by NGOs or UN agencies often play a lead role in defining the situation, identifying the psychological dimensions of the problems, and suggesting interventions . . . . Viewed as experts, they tacitly carry the imprimatur of Western science and Western psychology, regarded globally as embodying the highest standards of research, education, training, and practice . . . . Unfortunately, the dynamics of the situation invite a tyranny of Western expertise. The multitude of problems involved usually stems not from any conspiracy or conscious intent but rather from hidden power dynamics and the tacit assumption that Western knowledge trumps local knowledge . . . . Local communities have specific methods and tools for healing such as rituals, ceremonies, and practices of remembrance. Since they are grounded in the beliefs, values, and traditions of the local culture, they are both culturally appropriate and more sustainable than methods brought in from the outside
>
> (Wessells, 1999, pp. 274–275).

Consider this rather simple case example from Taiwan in which a woman found Western oriented counseling efforts to be not only unacceptable to her, but also ineffective. Lin (2000) pointed out that "talk therapy" approaches were not effective among some Taiwanese natural disaster victims, but victims did find satisfaction in traditional religious practices (Shou-Jing). She writes the following of one victim:

> "I do not know how to communicate with the experts. He told me that I have some kind of disease in my mind but I think I am okay. He kept asking me

to express my feelings toward the earthquake, but I feel embarrassed if I tell people my own feelings . . . . I went to a Master in the temporary temple and she taught me how to deal with the situation. How to calm my anxieties through worship and helping others. How to accept grief as an arrangement of the gods. You know that our people have done so many wrong things."

(Lin, 2000, pp. 10–11)

There are countless examples of the good intentions of disasters responders resulting in increased problems for disaster victims because of failures to grasp the significance of cultural differences in the provision of services. Amidst the countless panoramas of traumas that are part of any disaster, the rendering of care must be responsive to the cultural context of suffering. This means showing sensitivity to the situational and historical dimensions of the disaster including racial, religious, socio-economic, and political aspects. For example, the response to Hurricane Katrina victims revealed that there were far more complications involved than the sheer provision of shelter, housing, food, and medical care. Following Hurricane Katrina there was an acute and painful revelation of racism and cultural insensitivities and biases as victims struggled for survival amidst local and national governmental policies and practices that were painfully oblivious to the socioeconomic disadvantage of the victims.

In the following chapters, disaster responders – professional and volunteer – will find some background knowledge and information that may prevent the problem of "good intentions gone awry" by offering insights into the cultural and racial backgrounds and contexts of different minority groups within the United States. This volume does not cover all minority groups since this would be impossible. However, the volume does address a sampling of major minority groups, and in doing so, it does provide a framework for improving disasters policies and practices by calling attention to every disaster victim's cultural and personal uniqueness, and the need to respond to this so we may go beyond simple assistance to healing and the restoration of hope and meaning.

To this end, the editors developed a prototypical chapter outline that requested knowledge about critical topical areas that might be useful for increasing responder competencies, sensitivities, and effectiveness with regard to working with particular ethnocultural groups. The chapter outline prototype then became the basis for each ethnocultural group. At that point, the editors identified chapter authors interested in the task and capable of meeting the assignment. The result of these efforts, of course, is this volume, a substantive source of information and insights regarding selected ethnocultural groups (i.e., ethnocultural minorities) and in possible disasters contexts.

In developing the standard chapter information protocol, the editors asked themselves what knowledge might be useful in increasing and improving responder services. It was decided that "formulaic" clinical information

would be far less important than information that would enable the responder to grasp the historical and situational complexities of assisting a specific
ethnocultural group (i.e., to know and to understand the group in its uniqueness and similarities) amidst a disaster context. The editors asked each chapter
author(s) to provide information about ten major topics including: **(1) population demographics** (e.g., number, age distribution, gender distribution,
primary locations, background demographics such as religion and education,
and ethnic customs. In addition, the chapter authors were asked to provide
information about **(2) ten key historical events** that have shaped identity and
behavior arranged in a chronology and **(3) ten key values** associated with
the ethnic group. To this array of information, editors also asked for information about **(4) communication styles, (5) valid assessment instruments,
(6) special disorder considerations**, especially "culture-specific" disorders,
and **(7) special therapies and healing considerations** including concerns
for **(8) medications and therapies**. Lastly, the editors requested information
regarding **(9) disasters and trauma insights** on ethnocultural groups' inclinations to respond to disasters with particular patterns of individual or group
behavior, and **(10) special recommendations for improving services**. While
there is some variation in coverage within the topics, the material across the
chapters is similar in basic format.

In our opinion, the response of the invited chapter authors to meeting the
task before them was exceptional as the volume's contents will demonstrate.
The reader – be they professional or lay person – will find a substantive
overview of knowledge about selected ethnocultural groups that should
enhance and increase their technical, personal, and professional skills and
behaviors. Perhaps, above all, the material will be cause for the responder to
appreciate the complexities of rendering human services and assistances to
diverse populations during crisis situations.

The editors designed the volume to have three different but mutually supporting sections. **Section I** is to provide basic and essential information on
disasters and critical ethnocultural considerations. In **Chapter 1**, the editors introduce the reader to basic terminology (e.g., culture, disaster, disaster
parameters) and the need to appreciate and support cultural variation and
diversity during disaster responses. **Chapter 2**, written by Fran Norris, is a
reprint of a publication distributed by the National Center for PTSD in the
face of the pressing need for information about cultural considerations in
disasters following the South Asia Tsunami. The chapter offers a brief but
relatively comprehensive summary of research publications on ethnic variations in disaster responses. While the chapter does not critique the research
in meeting cultural research requirements, it does raise important questions
and considerations about the cultural encounter.

Section II constitutes the heart of the volume and its major contribution
to the field. In **Section II**, expert writers belonging to different American
ethnocultural minority groups prepared chapters on their respective groups

using the ten discussion criteria cited previously as guidelines for their comments. This resulted in nine chapters filled with useful information about the different groups. **Chapter 3** focuses on African Americans. It was written by Steve Carswell, a sociologist, and Melissa Carswell, a psychologist. Their complimentary expertise in research and clinical practice results in an enlightening presentation regarding disaster service delivery considerations for African Americans. As is well known, African Americans do not constitute a homogenous group because of widespread differences in income, education, social class, urban vs. rural living, and ancestral histories. Yet, in spite of these profound differences, the Carswells offer the reader a portrayal of African American culture, history, and behavior patterns that is filled with insights and suggestions that will be informative and useful. **Chapter 4**, American Indians, was written by a group of scholars and practitioners led by Jeannette Johnson, a developmental psychologist with a long history of involvement in the American Indian community. She was joined in her efforts by Julie Baldwin, Rodney C. Haring, Shelly A. Wiechelt, Susan Roth, Jan Gryczynski, and Henry Lozano. In spite of the enormous variations in American Indian tribes and their respective cultures, the chapter authors managed to provide a careful and informative discussion of material for consideration in disasters.

In **Chapter 5**, Naji Abi-Hashem, an Arab American psychologist with a successful history of clinical practice and research regarding Arab Americans, offers a detailed discussion of Arab American culture and behavior patterns. Among American ethnic minority groups, Arab Americans have often been ignored in favor of the more populous groups. As a result, little is known about this growing community which is now faced with considerable challenges due to the current Middle Eastern crisis. Abi-Hashem's comments provide a thorough introduction to this recent group of arrivals to America's shores. B. J. Prashantham, an Asian Indian psychologist practicing in the Pacific Northwest area, authored **Chapter 6** on Asian Indians with comments on related South Asian groups. Like Arab Americans, Asian Indians have frequently been ignored in the minority group literature. Yet, given the new economic, political, and social attachments of the US to India and the increasing Asian Indian population in the US, it is essential that we expand our understanding and regard for this culture whose civilization is more than 4000 years old.

Chapter 7 was written by G. Rita Dudely-Grant and Wayne Etheridge, two resident psychologists from the Virgin Islands with considerable experience working with Caribbean Island Black populations. Their chapter offers rich insight into the cultural complexities of the Caribbean Blacks who inhabit these fabled islands in the sun. Behind the tourist facade so often associated with the Caribbean, one finds both a history and current life context that requires understanding and admiration for the adaptation skills of the diverse peoples of this region. **Chapter 8**, Chinese Americans, prepared by Fred Leong and Szu-Hui Lee, offers the reader a detailed presentation of Chinese culture. Chinese laborers did much to build the American West through generational sacrifices of difficult work and poor living conditions. The Chinese civilization is thousands of years old, with an extraordinarily complex culture shaped to a large extent by the teachings of the great sages Confucius, Buddha, and Lao Tze (Taoism). Understanding Chinese Americans requires a grasp of their history and their culture's capacity to promote survival and success amidst new settings.

In **Chapter 9**, Laurie McCubbin, Michele Ishikawa, and Hamilton McCubbin lead the reader through the rich cultural beliefs and practices of the indigenous people of Hawaii (Kanaka Maole), whose very existence was once threatened by the many Westerners who came to their idyllic shores as whalers, missionaries, business people, and military conquerors. What emerges from their writing is a moving story of a lifestyle that was at odds with Western ways of life and that remains even today as tourists flock to the Islands to see their beauty and to encounter a culture that goes far beyond the commercialized hula dancing, luaus, and lei-bedecked airport greeters. The growing populations of Mexican, Caribbean, and other Latin Americans in the US are discussed in **Chapter 10** by Patricia Arredondo, Veronica Bordes, and Freddy Paniagua, prominent psychologists of Hispanic heritage whose writings and public leadership activities have established them as respected voices for their culture's members. Within the first few pages of their chapter, readers are made aware of the heterogeneity and diversity of this population that is often erroneously lumped together as a single group. The information provided by the chapter authors will enrich the reader's understanding of the wonderful shared cultural traditions and ways of life that characterize these groups.

In **Chapter 11**, Aaron Kaplan and Uyen Kim Huynh, both clinical psychologists, discuss one of the newest arrivals to America's shores, the Vietnamese. As is well known, the tragedies of the ill-fated Vietnam War resulted in the forced departure of hundreds of thousands of Vietnamese people. Their journey to the US and other countries of asylum and refuge were filled with as many horrors as the land they left behind. Yet, they endured the brutalities of pirates at sea and the burdens of life in refugee camps throughout South East Asia to begin a new life in a strange land. Their cultural resiliency is testimony to the critical role that culture plays in impacting adaptation and adjustment amidst the turmoil of starting a new life.

Lastly, **Chapter 12**, written by John Wilson, a leading trauma theorist and prolific publisher on the psychology of trauma, offers a rich and sensitive journey into the meaning and implications of the trauma experience, and the complexities of understanding trauma across cultures. The chapter raises serious questions about the cultural variations in trauma and the necessity of using care and sensitivity when treating people from different cultural traditions.

The appendices included at the end of the volume in **Section III** make an additional contribution to the reader's knowledge and skills regarding disasters. These appendices were selected on the basis of their capacity to enhance the disaster worker's abilities by increasing their familiarity and mastery of the many disaster terms and organizations. Appendix A summarizes specific terms used by disaster-response professionals. Appendix B augments the material through careful and meticulous summaries of the empirical research. Finally, Appendix C calls attention to the stresses associated with being a disaster worker.

In brief, this volume offers the reader a unique of combination of chapters on basic disaster concepts, knowledge, and skills, as well as essential information on specific ethnocultural and racial groups. This combination is unduplicated in the research and professional literature and in the training and educational arenas. We feel confident that a careful reading of this volume will provide the reader with a much improved and expanded competency to deal with members of different ethnocultural groups throught the disaster cycle. To the disaster worker seeking to better understand the behavior and needs of disaster victims from different ethnocultural traditions, we say, this volume is the beginning of a lifelong journey into cultural understanding and cultural competency.

The Editors: Anthony J. Marsella, Jeannette L. Johnson, Patricia Watson, & Jan Gryczynski

References

Lin, S.-P. (2000). Why counseling, why not shou-jing? Why shou-jing, why not counseling? *Cross-Cultural Psychology Bulletin, 34*(3), 10–15.

Marsella, A. J., & Christopher, M. A. (2004). Ethnocultural considerations in disasters: An overview of research, issues, and directions. *Psychiatric Clinics of North America, 27*(30), 521–539.

Wessells, M. (1999). Culture, power and community: Intercultural approaches to psychosocial assistance and healing. In K. Nader, N. Dubrow, & B. Stamm (Eds.), *Honoring differences. Cultural issues in the treatment of trauma and loss.* Philadelphia: Bruner/Mazel.

Acknowledgments

The editors would like to express their deep appreciation to the authors who contributed chapters to this volume. It was a pleasure to work with such an informed and talented group of scholars and practitioners. Each one approached the task before them with an admirable and welcome dedication that revealed a personal commitment to humanitarian assistance and disaster management. Within a very short time, it became clear to us as editors that each author not only grasped the importance of providing information about their particular ethnic minority group, but also a passionate concern for making sure that this information would enhance and improve the quality of services offered to each group in future disasters.

In addition, the editors would like to express a special appreciation to Dr. Fran Norris, Research Psychologist, National Center for PTSD, and Professor at the Department of Psychiatry, Dartmouth University Medical School. Dr. Norris is considered by many to be the foremost scientist and professional in the area of ethnocultural studies of PTSD and related trauma disorders. Her publications are now considered essential reading. Dr. Norris gave her permission to include two of her publications in this volume to help broaden the coverage of empirical research on disasters and trauma. The editors would also like to thank Matthew Friedman, M.D., Director, and the staff at the National Center for PTSD in White River Junction, Vermont for the many services they rendered in bringing this volume to publication and distribution.

Special thanks is also extended to staff members at SAMHSA whose vision of the importance of ethnocultural considerations for disasters resulted in a conference and workshop from which this volume emerged. The staff at SAMHSA has been a source of continued support for this project and for a score of efforts to increase ethnocultural and racial sensitivity in service provision and knowledge development.

Lastly, the editors would like to thank Ms. Sharon Panulla, Senior Editor, Psychology Books, and Ms. Anna Tobias, Associate Editor, Psychology Books, Springer SBM Publications, New York, for their continual support and assistance throughout the completion of this volume. Their combination of patience, humor, and monitoring helped bring the volume to completion. We are grateful.

The Editors

Contributors

Volume Editors

Jan Gryczynski, M.A.,
Research Associate, Friends Research Institute, Inc., Social Research Center. Baltimore, MD.

Jeannette L. Johnson, Ph.D.,
Senior Research Scientist, Friends Research Institute, Inc., Social Research Center. Baltimore, MD.

Anthony J. Marsella, Ph.D., D.H.C.
Professor Emeritus, Department of Psychology, University of Hawaii. Honolulu, HI.

Patricia Watson, Ph.D.,
Deputy Director, Education and Clinical Networking, National Center for PTSD. White River Junction, VT.

Promoting Disaster Recovery

Margarita Alegria,
Director, Center for Multicultural Mental Health Research and Professor, Department of Psychiatry, Harvard Medical School. Boston, MA.

Fran H. Norris,
Research Professor, Department of Psychiatry, Dartmouth Medical School and the National Center for PTSD. White River Junction, VT.

African Americans

Melissa A. Carswell, Psy.D.,
Neuropsychologist, The Neurology Center. Rockville, MD. Postdoctoral Fellow, Hospital of the University of Pennsylvania. Philadelphia, PA.

Steven B. Carswell, Ph.D.,
Senior Research Scientist, Friends Research Institute, Inc., Social Research Center. Baltimore, MD.

American Indians

Julie Baldwin, Ph.D.,
University of South Florida, Department of Community and Family Health, College of Public Health. Tampa, FL.

Jan Gryczynski, M.A.,
Friends Research Institute, Inc., Social Research Center. Baltimore, MD.

Rodney C. Haring, M.S.W., Ph.D.,
University of Buffalo, School of Social Work. Buffalo, NY.

Jeannette L. Johnson, Ph.D.,
Senior Research Scientist, Friends Research Institute, Inc., Social Research Center. Baltimore, MD.

Henry Lozano,
Corporation for National and Community Service. Forest Falls, CA.

Susan Roth, B.S.,
LifeLines Community Native American Program. Baltimore, MD.

Shelly A. Wiechelt, Ph.D.,
University of Maryland, Baltimore County, Baltimore, MD.

Arab Americans and Middle Eastern Populations

Naji Abi-Hashem, Ph.D., DABPS, BCETS,
Clinical & Cultural Psychologist, Visiting Scholar at the Fuller Theological Seminary, Pasedena, and the Graduate Theological Union in Berkely, California; Seattle, Washington; and Beirut, Lebanon. Mercer Island, WA

Asian Indians

B. J. Prashantham, D. P. C.,
Director, Pacific Consulting Services. Bellevue, WA.

Caribbean Blacks

G. Rita Dudley-Grant, Ph.D., MPH,
Clinical Director, Virgin Islands Behavioral Services. Christiansted, Virgin Islands.

Wayne Etheridge, Ph.D.,
School Psychologist, Virgin Islands Department of Education. St. Croix, Virgin Islands.

Chinese Americans

Frederick T. L. Leong, Ph.D.,
Professor of Psychology, Director of Counseling/Psychology Program. University of Tennessee. Knoxville, TN.

Szu-Hui Lee, Ph.D.,
Assistant Professor, Department of Psychology, Ohio State University. Columbus, OH.

Hawaiian Americans

Michele E. Ishikawa,
Washington State University. Pullman, WA.

Hamilton I. McCubbin, Ph.D.,
Professor, Department of Family Studies, University of Hawaii. Honolulu, HI.

Laurie D. McCubbin, Ph.D.,
Assistant Professor, Washington State University. Pullman, WA.

Latin Americans (Mexican and Central American)

Patricia Arredondo, Ph.D.,
Professor and Program Leader, Department of Counseling, Arizona State University. Tucson, AZ.

Veronica Bordes, M.A.,
Research Assistant, Department of Counseling, Arizona State University. Tucson, AZ.

Freddy A. Paniagua, Ph.D.,
Professor, Department of Psychiatry and Behavioral Sciences, University of Texas Medical Branch. Galveston, TX.

Vietnamese Americans

Aaron S. Kaplan, Ph.D.,
Chief Psychologist, Waikiki Health Center. Honolulu, HI.

Uyen Kim Huynh, Ph.D.,
Clinical Psychologist, Association for the Help of Retarded Children,
Department of Traumatic Brain Injury. New York, NY.

Culture, Disasters, and Trauma-related Disorders

John P. Wilson, Ph.D.,
Professor, Department of Psychology, Cleveland State University.
Cleveland, OH.

Appendix A

Antony Marsella, Ph.D.,
Professor Emeritus, Department of Psychology, University of Hawaii.
Honollulu, HI.

Appendix B

Fran Norris, Ph.D.,
Research Professor, Department of Psychiatry, Dartmouth Medical School
and the National Center for PTSD. White River Junction, VT.

Appendix C

Juliian D. Ford, Ph.D.,
National Center for PTSD. White River Junction, VT.

Patricia Watson, Ph.D.,
Deputy Director, Education and Clinical Networking, National Center for
PTSD. White River Junction, VT.

Bruce H. Young, LCSW,
Chief Psychologist, National Center for PTSD. Palo Alto, CA.

Section I

Background and Foundations

Chapter 1

Essential Concepts and Foundations

Anthony J. Marsella, Jeannette L. Johnson,
Patricia Watson, and Jan Gryczynski

A monkey and a fish were caught in a terrible flood and were being swept downstream amidst torrents of water and debris. The monkey spied a branch from an overhanging tree and pulled himself to safety from the swirling water. Then, wanting to help his friend the fish, he reached into the water and pulled the fish from the water onto branch. The moral of the story is clear: *Good intentions are not enough. If you wish to help the fish, you must understand its nature.*

Ancient Chinese Fable

INTRODUCTION

The Complexities of Disasters

And so it is with disasters! Good intentions, though essential, are not enough. To help the victims of disasters, we must understand who they are and what they need from their own perspective. To do so, it is essential we understand, respect, and use their culture in our efforts. While it is axiomatic that emergency care is essential for the saving of human lives and the prevention of disease and disorder, it must also be understood that the cycle of a disaster extends far beyond the acute phases to short-term, mid-term, and long-term recovery, rebuilding, and prevention phases. While there are obvious variations in cultural factors that should optimally be considered in the acute and emergency phases (e.g., familiarity with medical care, compliance with treatments, food variations, security needs, communications patterns), many of the cultural determinants of responses to disasters emerge in the subsequent phases involving rehabilitation, rebuilding and reconstruction.

The World Health Organization (WHO) has called attention to the risks of rendering disaster assistance without a full understanding of the complex cultural contexts of a disaster. They wrote the following about the post-disaster situation in Aceh, Indonesia following the South East Asia Tsunami of December, 2004:

> "The disaster has been invested with religious meaning and is under-standable, and manageable, in that context. As a result, the prevalence of trauma-related psychiatric disorder may be substantially less than that which would be expected based on the international literature. Attempts from out-side Aceh to "train" various community leaders in how they might respond to widespread psychological distress at a community level, using western con-structs of community reconstruction and development, may be misguided and will probably be unwelcome. The religious construction of meaning sur-rounding the disaster may mean that efforts to deal with psychological and social consequences of the disaster in ways that are not consonant with such religious and cultural values and beliefs (e.g., trauma-focused counselling, psychiatric approaches) will be both ineffective and unacceptable. Control of rehabilitation and reconstruction from outside Aceh, including from Jakarta but particularly by international agencies and organizations, may result in many problems. The Acehnese may wish to see outsiders leave Aceh earlier rather than later. There may be a rise in tensions and there is the possibility of a serious deterioration of the security situation, particularly for foreigners (WHO, 2005, p. 4)."

It is now clear that disaster mental health workers must demonstrate cul-tural competencies to be effective in their work. These competencies must include a broad area of knowledge and skills. To help advance the field in this area, the editors proposed to develop a field guidebook that will help disaster mental health workers have quick and easy access to basic information about different ethnocultural populations that may be disaster victims.

This guidebook is at best a beginning – a first step – for understanding the complex relations between culture, disasters, and trauma – an introduction that can help increase sensitivity to the importance ethnocultural factors play in shaping the nature, meaning, and responses of people from different eth-nocultural traditions to the burdens and tragedies that disasters impose upon human lives.

The preparation of this guidebook stemmed from the growing recogni-tion that responses to disasters often failed to consider the variations in the cultural world-views, values, and lifestyle preferences of disaster victims. Too often, the assistance that is rendered is based upon a preconceived set of assumptions and policies rooted within the Western cultural traditions of the providers, especially ideas about how one must construe a disaster and what is necessary for recovery and rehabilitation from a disaster's impact.

But, as the fable states, good intentions, no matter how noble in thought and purpose, may often end up causing more problems because they fail to understand the lives and context of the very people they are intended to assist.

In the present volume, chapter authors offer basic introductions to the cultures of a sample of ethnocultural and racial minority groups in the United States with the idea that the material offered can inform disaster workers in planning and providing assistance. The idea is quite simple. If disaster response workers can better understand the cultural context of a disaster – that is to say, the context that emerges as the culture of the victims and the culture of the workers encounter one another within the circumstances of the disaster – more effective services can be offered. What is especially critical here is that the emergent disaster culture that arises from the complex and unique interactions of the responders, the victims, and the disaster parameters (e.g., type, location, extent) can be a source of strength and resiliency in dealing with the traumas, or it can contribute to the problems.

The Concept of Culture

The term culture in these instances can be defined in the following way:

> Culture is shared learned behavior and meanings that are socially trans-ferred in various life-activity settings for purposes of individual and collec-tive adjustment and adaptation. Cultures can be (1) transitory (i.e., situational even for a few minutes) or (2) enduring (e.g., ethnocultural life styles), and in all instances are (3) dynamic (i.e., constantly subject to change and modification). Cultures are represented (4) internally (i.e., values, beliefs, attitudes, axioms, orientations, epistemologies, consciousness levels, per-ceptions, expectations, personhood) and (5) externally (i.e., artifacts, roles, institutions, social structures). Cultures (6) shape and construct our reali-ties (i.e., they contribute to our world views, perceptions, orientations) with ideas, morals, and preferences (Marsella, 2005, p. 657).

This definition points out that cultures can be temporary or transitory as well as relatively enduring. But, more importantly, the definition calls attention to the fact that culture constructs our realities and shapes the way we per-ceive and experience reality. Cultures differ in the ways they codify and know reality. There are cultural variations in the use and emphasis of words, feel-ings, and images, as well as visceral, proprioceptive, and skeletal means for handling "reality" content and processes. In the mediation process, it is crit-ical to attend to the vocabulary of emotion. Among the words that I have learned to attend to as a therapist are the following: absolve, acceptance, apology, exonerate, forgiveness, healing, heart, images, meaning, memories, pain, pardon, reconciliation, regret, remorse, repentance, self, sorrow, and trauma. Understanding the subjective experience of a cultural construction of reality requires sensitivity to the heavy metaphorical basis of some languages because metaphors provide immediate, poetic sensory constructions of reality awareness (Marsella, 1985).

In some cultures (e.g., embedded, contextualized, field dependent), communication is based on relational negotiation in which there are presumptions of interpersonal sensitivities, hierarchy, and roles. There is a strong emphasis on reading non-verbal cues and "what is not said," as much as what is said. Indeed, the very nature of the self in this cultural milieu can be considered unindividuated (e.g., relational, collateral, diffuse) in which self as process and self as object become fused (Marsella, 1985). We cite this material to emphasize the importance of recognizing the profound variations that may exist when parties with different cultural constructions of world-views may be in conflict and may be in need of mediation or negotiation. The differences in the emphasis on verbal versus non-verbal cues, concepts of justice and related terms such as forgiveness, retribution, apology, revenge, and a host of other emotion and image laden ideas, become critical in building trust and reconciliation. What is involved is not only what we know, but how we know it, what it means and implies to us, and how we can translate our experience for others to understand and value (Marsella, 2005).

Another critical ethnocultural consideration is the extent of the victim populations' acculturation or ethnic identification level. For example, in an isolated community (e.g., 2005 Pakistan border earthquake), the inhabitants lived in relative isolation from the world and continued Middle Eastern and Muslim life styles that were centuries old. There was little or no acculturation to "contemporary" urban cultures in the region and certainly not to Western cultures. Thus, even the best intentioned efforts to assist can become problematic encounters, especially with regard to communications, gender dynamics and relationship patterns, priorities for recovery, and acceptance of certain kinds of assistance. This means that responders must be acutely aware of the attachment and commitment of the victim to a particular cultural life style and world view.

Bracken and Petty (1998) argue that Western relief workers often assume universality in the application of their humanitarian efforts because of the ethnocentricity that is fostered by the obvious power of science and technology. Bracken & Petty write:

> The challenge to Western NGOs and other agencies dealing with refugees and other victims of violence around the world is to establish ways of supporting people through times of suffering by listening and hearing their different voices in a way that does not impose an alien order. It is a challenge which demands that we work with a spirit of humility about what we can offer and an acceptance that there is no quick fix or magic bullet that will rid people everywhere of the suffering brought by violence
>
> (Bracken & Petty, 1998, p. 58).

Disasters

The term "disaster" refers to an occurrence of some events that cause widespread damage and destruction. Related terms include catastrophes and calamities. Sometimes there is a preference for the term "complex humanitarian disasters or emergencies." This term is often used in wartime situations when there is a breakdown or collapse of societal resources including medical, agricultural, commercial/economic, political, military, and so forth. In general, disasters are divided into two different types or categories based upon the cause. Natural disasters are those associated with "natural" acts over which there may be no human control other than the preventive or anticipatory responses to the event. In some instances there are warnings and in others there is a sudden onset. Human-made disasters are those associated with human-related accidents, violence, and failures in safety and security systems (e.g., nuclear meltdown in Chernobyl, USSR; poisonous fume leakages from Union Carbide Plant in Bhopal, India; the 9/11 terrorist attack). Of course, a disaster can have both natural and human-made components. Hurricane Katrina was itself a natural meteorological event, but the devastation of New Orleans was greatly exacerbated by failure of the human-built levee system and the inadequate post-disaster government response. Table 1.1 lists examples of these two types of disasters.

Cultural Competence

The term cultural competence has emerged in the last decade as a popular way to encourage helping professionals to acquire knowledge and skills

Table 1.1.   Disaster Types

Natural Disasters	Human-caused Disasters
Avalanches	Accidents in Communities or Work Sites
Catastrophic Disasters (i.e., Massive destruction)	Ecological Destruction (e.g., Acid Rain, Global Warming)
Droughts	
Earthquakes	Nuclear Leaks and Meltdowns
Floods	Oil Spills (Wells and Ships)
Hurricanes	Secondary Disasters (e.g., unemployment, violence, rioting)
Ice and Hail Storms	
Insects (e.g., Locusts)	Terrorist Attacks
Mudslides	Toxic Waste Spills
Tsunami (Tidal Wave)	Transportation Accidents (e.g., Air, Sea, Train)
Typhoons	War and Civil Destruction Acts
Volcanic Eruptions	

that will enable them to function competently within the cultural context of the people they are serving. The idea behind this is quite simple: In order to provide effective services, it is essential that you understand the lived experience of the client/patient/victim. Failing to do so can lead to errors in assessment, diagnosis, and treatment, increasing problems rather than helping to resolve them. There are now a number of professional codes regarding cultural competence, and many professional organizations (e.g., American Psychological Association) have established ethical policies and practice guidelines that consider the absence of cultural competence to be a potential legal liability. The content of cultural competence can vary across organizations. Table 1.2 provides a substantive list of cultural competencies that can be aspired to by disaster workers. Marsella and Christopher (2004) call for formal cross-cultural training for disaster professionals.

The Disaster Experience

Like any event, the parameters of a disaster can account for its costs and consequences including such parameters as perceived attribution of responsibility,

Table 1.2.   Multicultural Competencies

---

1. Knowledge of the history of victims and manifestations of such issues as oppression, prejudice, marginalization, and their psychological sequelae.
2. Knowledge that family structures, gender roles, values, and beliefs differ across cultures and affect personality formation, developmental outcomes, and manifestations of mental and physical illness.
3. Knowledge of how cultural variables influence the etiology and manifestation of mental illness.
4. Knowledge of values, help seeking norms, and world views of groups to be treated.
5. Ability to evaluate emic (internal) and etic (external) hypotheses.
6. Ability to design and implement non-biased treatment plans.
7. Ability to initiate and explore differences between the therapist and client, and to incorporate these into treatment.
8. Knowledge of culture-specific disorders and diagnostic categories.
9. Knowledge of culture-specific assessment procedures and tools.
10. Ability to establish rapport and convey empathy.
11. Knowledge of how to assess variables of special relevance to identified groups (e.g., cultural orientation, acculturation, culture shock, discrimination).
12. Ability to ascertain effects of therapist-client language differences on assessment and treatment.
13. Ability to modify assessment tools for use with specified groups.
14. Ability to explain results in a culturally-sensitive and contextual way.
15. Ability to assess one's own multicultural competence.
16. Ability to critique epistemologies, concepts, methods, instruments, and results based on assumptions related to a group and to propose alternatives.
17. Knowledge of how psychological theory, methods of inquiry, and professional practices are culturally embedded.
18. Ability to thoughtfully critique multicultural approaches in mental health.

Source: Adapted from Hansen, Pepitone-Arreola-Rockwell, and Greene (2000).

sense of control and predictability, and even availability of resources for recovery and prevention. In the case of Hurricane Katrina, the massive human costs and consequences were intensified by the perceptions of helplessness due to the inadequate local, state, and national emergency care. Many of the victims' problems were raised to new levels of severity by the conclusion that they had intentionally been abandoned because of race and poverty. Also, in the case of Hurricane Katrina, the losses extended beyond individual and family tragedies to the loss of an entire city, and with it a sense of collective and personal identity related to location. Lost were housing, schools, churches, jobs, transportation, and all human services. It was cataclysmic in its implications for the immediate and long-term efforts of disasters responders.

The Costs and Consequences of Disasters

Of course, all these disasters can extend into each other, compounding the actual disaster crisis. For example, earthquakes can cause floods, fires, mudslides, and even volcanic eruptions. These, in turn, could cause human-related disasters such as toxic waste spills or even transportation accidents. There is widespread agreement that the number of disasters and the intensity of their consequences are increasing because of a number of factors including population concentrations in high risk areas and the destruction of certain natural protections through such acts as forest clearing and dam building for water control. An international gathering of experts on quality control in disaster management wrote:

> "Disasters continue to increase in frequency and severity worldwide. The costs associated with these catastrophes continue to skyrocket in an unanticipated manner. These costs can be quantified in human, economic, and intangible terms. Human costs generally are computed on the basis of numbers of persons killed. More than 800,000 persons were killed in Rwanda, the floods in China have consumed >300,000 and >400,000 in Bangladesh. More than 25,000 deaths resulted from the Armenia earthquake, there are 20,000 or more persons missing or dead from Hurricanes Georges and Mitch, and >5,000 died from the Great Hanshin-Awaji earthquake, to mention only a few. However, the number of deaths does not represent the only human costs. Thousands of persons are injured physically and/or emotionally as a result of such events, and the effects will continue long after worldwide attention has disappeared; many persons will remain incapacitated for the rest of their lives, including the many children left without families and with terrifying memories and nightmares.
>
> Recent estimates of economic costs are astounding. Estimates of the economic costs associated include [US] $5-billion for Kobe earthquake; and $30-billion for Hurricane Andrew in Florida. Often, the economic costs do not correlate with the number of deaths; for example, there were only 33 deaths directly attributable to the Northridge earthquake, but the disaster was [at the time] the most costly in the history of the United States. Furthermore, cost estimates do not include the aid provided by external

governments, United Nations agencies, and non-governmental agencies that provide humanitarian assistance during the acute and reconstruction phases of disasters or to those costs associated with loss of production. For example, 80% of the production capacity of Honduras has been lost following Hurricane Mitch. Currently, it is estimated that disasters in the USA alone consume more than $1-billion per day! Other costs are more intangible and their value cannot be estimated in quantitative terms. They include the loss of confidence in governments, fear for security, and loss of trust in fellow human beings. In some nations, such as the component states of Africa, disasters now are an everyday occurrence and are ongoing.

   Often, the risks associated with natural hazards are augmented by human actions. Deforestation leads to flooding, mudslides, and/or drought. "Development" of societies presents new risks, i.e., construction of dams over well-defined fault lines. Inter-human conflicts result in hundreds of thousands of displaced persons and refugees, in addition to thousands or hundreds of thousands of deaths and injuries

                              (Task Force on Quality Control of Disaster Management,
                                            2003, Executive Summary, p. 1)."

It is also important to understand that disasters have many political implications that can lead to governmental collapse and instability. They often reveal, as was the case for Hurricane Katrina, a side to society that was hidden or denied by governmental officials. This political dimension is becoming a major concern as failures of governments to meet victims' needs can result in mobilizations of national and international anger. This is now the case in Pakistan where the government has failed to respond adequately to the tragic earthquake of October 8, 2005 in the Kashmir-Pakistan border area. Under these circumstances, terrorism can be born out of desperation and anger, and government leaders can become vilified and criticized for inept leadership.

Disaster Phases and Culture

Disasters are best understood as a complex cycle of phases rather than a discrete event. The different phases represent varying needs for victims and responsibilities for disaster service providers. According to Marsella and Christopher (2004), the disaster cycle can be divided into different phases, each of which raises important cultural considerations.

   1. **Pre-Disaster Context:** What are the life circumstances of a location and people prior to the occurrence of a disaster, especially with regard to human, technical, and social resources? What is the prior history of disasters for the people and location? People and sites with existing high stress levels face a new threat under unique conditions of vulnerability and risk. Does the victim's culture have a history of disaster exposures, and how have they responded?
   2. **Disaster Threat and Warning:** How much time is there between recognition that a disaster will occur and its onset? This period involves the

possibility of preparation and the mobilization of resources. However, disasters often occur with little warning. This is true for both natural and human-made disasters. What constitutes an acceptable cultural preparation effort for the victim culture? Will victims alter previous perceptions, habits, and activities and engage in prevention? Do they have the resources necessary for effective responses? Do they believe that their efforts will help prevent difficulties? Do they trust the warning sources?

3. **Disaster Event and Impact:** What kind of disaster has occurred – natural or human-made? How extensive is the destruction? How available are technical, social, and economic coping resources? What are the victims' perceptions of the causes and nature of the disaster? Do these differ from those of the disaster workers?

4. **Acute or Immediate Response:** What is the first response? What resources are available? Is the community response organized and effective? Is the victim culture prepared and willing to respond effectively? Do the victims have needed resources or must they rely on external and possibly "alien" assistance?

5. **Reconstruction Response:** After the acute phase, are the local, national, and international resources present for reconstruction, rebuilding and rehabilitation? If so, how will they be implemented? It is interesting that even years after the end of a disaster, the site may still be in turmoil and distress because of failed recovery efforts.

6. **Learning and Prevention Response:** Although frequently little attention is given to this phase, it does constitute an important element in the disaster cycle. Too often, disasters occur in the same location and to the same people. Thus, efforts to develop a prevention dimension to mitigate future problems can be very helpful. This means giving attention to human and technical resources through training and preparation. Does the victim culture accept and sustain prevention efforts? How does it view prevention?

Disasters and Mental Health: The Pressing Challenges

Even as we respond to the massive immediate medical and social needs of victims to emerge from the disaster, it is essential that we recognize and respond to the massive psychological and cultural needs of the disaster with equal if not greater determination, effectiveness, and resources. Taylor and Frazier (1981 – cited in The New South Wales Institute of Psychiatry's Disaster Mental Health Response Handbook, 2000, p. 11) suggested that there are many victims in the course of disasters, including the following:

Primary Victims: Maximum exposure to catastrophic event;
Secondary Victims: Grieving relatives and friends of primary victims;

Third Level Victims:	Rescue and recovery personnel in need of help to maintain their functional efficiency and to cope with their traumatic effects afterwards;
Fourth Level Victims:	The community involved with the disaster, including those who converge, who offer help, and who share the felt sense of grief and loss;
Fifth Level Victims:	People, who though not directly involved, may still experience states of distress and disturbance;
Sixth Level Victims:	Those, who but for chance, would have been primary victims, who persuaded others to the course that made them victims, and those who may be vicariously involved.

What is notable about this classification is that it calls attention to the fact that disasters impact far more people than those immediately involved. Disasters exact complex combinations of physical, psychological, economic and moral costs and consequences that extend far beyond the crisis period to a broad range of people, agencies, and even nations. The NSW Disaster Response Handbook (2000), a volume that the editors consider to be among the best educational and training resources available, also calls attention to the array of stressors that emerge in the course of a disaster, either alone or in combination with one another including:

1. Threat to life and an encounter with death
2. Feelings of helplessness and powerlessness
3. Loss (i.e., loved ones, home, possessions)
4. Dislocation (i.e., separation from people and location)
5. Feeling responsible (i.e., could have done more)
6. Inescapable horror (e.g., being trapped, tortured)
7. Human malevolence (e.g., result of deliberate human actions).

It is clear from these comments and observations that disasters represent major challenges to our individual and collective human health and well being, and that our responses to them must be informed by the very best knowledge available for intervening and preventing destructive outcomes. All of this points to the important purpose of this volume which is to provide a resource for informing and educating professional and lay responders to the ethnocultural variations and diversity they will encounter in disasters, and the need to develop competencies for acknowledging and mediating these variations rather than denying or distorting them.

Essentially, this volume will provide the reader with a substantive introduction to the history, background, and cultural traditions and practices of some major American ethnic minority groups whose ways of life are often profoundly different than those of the reader. As noted in the beginning of this chapter, we do not doubt the good intentions of the disaster worker. But we do feel compelled to call attention to the old adage that "good intentions are not enough." Failing to understand the way of life of the disaster victim can often lead to an exacerbation and compounding of problems. Thus, we encourage disaster workers – professionals and volunteers – to read carefully the volume's chapters and to pursue further education in the area of ethnocultural diversity and its implications for rendering human services.

References

Bracken, P., & Petty, C. (1998). *Rethinking the trauma of war.* London, UK: Free Association Books.

Hansen, N. D., Pepitone-Arreola-Rockwell, F., & Greene, A. F. (2000). Multicultural *competence:* Criteria and case examples. *Professional Psychology Research and Practice, 31*(6), 652–660.

Marsella, A. J. (1985). Culture, self, and mental disorder. In A. J. Marsella, G. DeVos, & F. Hsu (Eds.), *Culture and self.* NY/London: Tavistock Publications.

Marsella, A. J. (2005). Culture and conflict: Understanding and negotiating different cultural constructions of reality. *International Journal of Intercultural Relations, 29,* 651–673.

Marsella, A. J., & Christopher, M. A. (2004). Ethnocultural considerations in disasters: An overview of research, issues, and directions. *Psychiatric Clinics of North America, 27*(30), 521–539.

New South Wales Institute of Psychiatry. (2000). *Disaster response handbook.* NSW, Australia (Locked Bag 7118), Parramatta BC NSW, Australia 2150. ISBN: 07347 32139.

Task Force on Quality Control of Disaster Management. (2003, April). Health disaster management: Guidelines for evaluation and research in the Utstein Style: Executive summary. Accessed on April 22, 2007 at: http://pdm.medicine.wisc.edu/executiv2.htm [see also *Prehospital & Disaster Medicine, 17* Supplement 3; 2003]

World Health Organization. (2005). *WHO Recommendations for Mental Health in Aceh,* Department of Mental Health and Substance Abuse. World Health Organization: Geneva, Switzerland (Report by B. Saraceno, H. Minas, & S. Indradjaya)

Chapter 2

Promoting Disaster Recovery in Ethnic-Minority Individuals and Communities

Fran H. Norris and Margarita Alegría

People who identify as African American, Native American, Asian American, or Hispanic/Latino accounted for 30% of the U.S. population in 2000 and are projected to account for almost 40% of the population in 2025 (U.S. Department of Health and Human Services [DHHS], 2001). The mental health system in general and the disaster mental health system in particular are challenged to meet the needs of this increasingly diverse population. The issues are complex because the effects of ethnicity and culture are pervasive. They may influence the need for help, the availability of help, comfort in seeking help, and the appropriateness of that help. In this chapter, we review the evidence regarding each of these points to draw conclusions regarding how to promote disaster recovery in ethnic-minority individuals and communities.

NEED FOR MENTAL HEALTH SERVICES

Ethnicity and the Epidemiology of Mental Disorders

Consistent with the Surgeon General's Report, *Mental Health: Culture, Race, and Ethnicity* (DHHS, 2001), need is defined here as the prevalence of psychiatric disorder or elevated distress in the population. Prevalence rates are clearly imperfect measures of need, but they may serve reasonably as

Originally published in *Interventions Following Mass Violence and Disasters* (Richie, E. C., Watson, P. J., & Friedman, M. J., Eds.), pp. 319–342. Reprinted with permission.

population-level markers of relative need for help. The inclusion of elevated levels of distress allows us to examine whether immigrants, particularly those who are less acculturated, are more likely to express their reactions to disaster by higher levels of distress, including cultural idioms, such as *ataque de nervios* or *neurasthenia*. Because research has pointed to posttraumatic stress disorder (PTSD) and depression as the two most likely adverse psychological consequences of disasters (Norris, Friedman, et al., 2002), we paid particular attention to the epidemiology of these two conditions. Findings from disaster research are best interpreted in light of the general epidemiology of mental disorders.

Holzer and Copeland (2000) presented a useful review of the role of ethnicity in the epidemiology of mental disorders in the United States and presented results from reanalyses of data from the Epidemiologic Catchment Area Survey (ECA) and the National Comorbidity Survey (NCS), two well-known national studies. In rank order, annual prevalence rates of major depressive disorder (MDD) were highest for Hispanics (4.0%, ECA; 14.1%, NCS), next highest for non-Hispanic whites (3.6%; 10.2%), some-what lower but not very different for African Americans (3.2%; 8.4%), and lowest for Asian Americans (2.5%; 6.3%). More recent results of the National Comorbidity Survey Replication (NCS-R) indicate no ethnic differences in the rates of MDD between Hispanics and non-Hispanic whites (Kessler et al., 2003), but lower odds ratios for non-Hispanic blacks (odds ratio = 0.6, 95% confidence interval = 0.5–0.8). Perhaps because they composed the smallest subsample in the ECA and NCS, results were least consistent for Native Americans; their rate of MDD was lowest in the ECA (1.9%) but equivalent to that of African Americans in the NCS (8.5%).

These national surveys are supplemented by studies of particular or more localized populations. The Washington Needs Assessment Household Survey (WANAHS, also described by Holzer and Copeland, 2000) included over 1,000 Native Americans and, in this case, their MDD rate was the highest of all groups (11.7%, compared to 7.9% of white Americans). The Chinese American Psychiatric Epidemiology Study (CAPES; Takeuchi et al., 1998) replicated findings showing that Asian Americans had lower than average MDD prevalence rates. In the Mexican American Prevalence Study (MAPS; Vega et al., 1998), rates of MDD were comparable to those seen in the NCS but varied by place of birth, being higher for U.S.-born Mexican Americans than for Mexican-born participants. In general, researchers find that recent Latino and Asian immigrants tend to experience better physical and mental health outcomes than more established Latino and Asian residents (Takeuchi et al., 1998; Vega et al., 1998). Whether these outcomes can be attributed to selection processes or to acculturation into American lifestyles is open to conjecture. Overall, the available data on the need for mental health care suggest that prevalence rates of depression are similar or lower among ethnic minorities than among white Americans.

Estimating the relative vulnerability of culturally diverse groups to trauma is more challenging. The PTSD measure used in the ECA is generally considered to have been insensitive to the disorder regardless of ethnicity (e.g., Solomon & Canino, 1990). The NCS did not detect ethnic differences in the prevalence of PTSD (Kessler, Somnega, Bromet, Hughes, & Nelson, 1995), nor did Norris (1992) in a survey of black and white residents of four midsize southeastern cities. CAPES found extraordinarily low rates of PTSD (1.1% of men and 2.2% of women reported by Norris, Foster, & Weisshaar, 2002, with the assistance and permission of CAPES investigators). MAPS, unfortunately, did not assess PTSD, but an epidemiological study of PTSD in Mexico (Norris, Murphy, Baker, Perilla, et al., 2003) found the lifetime prevalence of PTSD (11% after and 13% before the criterion of functional impairment was applied) to be substantially higher there than in the United States (8%). Using data from the National Vietnam Veterans Readjustment Survey (NVVRS), Ortega and Rosenheck (2000) found Puerto Rican and Mexican American veterans, but not other Hispanic veterans, to have higher probabilities of PTSD and more severe symptoms than non-Hispanic white veterans.

The Detroit Area Survey of Trauma (Breslau et al., 1998) showed African Americans to be at increased risk for PTSD relative to whites, but this effect dropped out when central city residence was controlled. Innercity Americans are disproportionately exposed to community violence (Osofsky, 1997; Parson, 1997). These findings suggest that more than minority status, living in urban inner cities with high exposure to community violence might pose increased risk for PTSD.

Limitations of the Epidemiological Research

Altogether, research on the epidemiology of depression and PTSD among American minorities is inadequate. The NCS Hispanic, Asian, and Native American samples were small in size, heterogeneous in terms of national origin, and limited to English-speaking persons. Supplementary surveys provided good data for specific subpopulations but can be generalized past them only with the utmost caution. The results quite obviously do not apply to the various smaller populations of Asian, African, Latino, and European refugees who live in the United States precisely because of violence and trauma in their home countries. Moreover, a number of investigators have argued that health data should be disaggregated by using subethnic groups (e.g., African Caribbean within the African Americans in the United States) because of considerable differences within groups (e.g., Srinivasan & Guillermo, 2000). For example, whereas Asian Americans as a group may appear similar to whites on a number of health-related and socioeconomic indicators, such statistics disguise higher rates of health problems and poverty among Asian American subgroups, such as the Vietnamese. These studies point to the complexity of understanding diverse subgroup process and the need to distinguish the impact of culture from minority status or poverty.

In addition to sampling, assessment raises a host of challenges. There is evidence to suggest that responses to screener items in diagnostic batteries may vary as a function of ethnicity/race, gender, education, and socioeconomic status of the respondent (Alegría & McGuire, 2003). A strict focus on traditional diagnoses may cause the clinician to miss "culture-bound syndromes" and somaticized distress (Kirmayer; 1996; Norris, Weisshaar, et al., 2001). Zheng and colleagues (1997) provided an excellent example of this in their research on *neurasthenia*, a condition that is recognized among Chinese Americans and is characterized by fatigue or weakness accompanied by an array of physical and psychological complaints, such as diffuse pains, gastrointestinal problems, memory loss, irritability, and sleep problems. Over half of those meeting criteria for neurasthenia did not meet criteria for any DSM-III-R (American Psychiatric Association, 1987) diagnoses. Another example is *ataques de nervios*. In a Puerto Rican disaster study, 14% of the sample reported experiencing these acute episodes of emotional upset and loss of control, although the rate of disaster specific PTSD was quite low (Guarnaccia, Canino, Rubio-Stipec, & Bravo, 1993). With these caveats, the available data appear to suggest that Latinos most consistently show elevated mental health needs and that black and white Americans do not consistently differ. Data for Asian and Native Americans are too sparse, contradictory, or both to draw any comparative conclusions.

Ethnicity, Culture, and Disaster Recovery

Despite a few exceptions, most disaster studies that have examined the effects of ethnicity on outcomes have found that minority ethnic groups fare worse than persons who are of majority group status (Bolton & Klenow, 1988; Galea et al., 2002; Garrison et al., 1995; Green et al., 1990; March, Amaya-Jackson, Terry, & Costanzo, 1997; Palinkas, Downs, Petterson, & Russell, 1993; Perilla, Norris, & Lavizzo, 2002; Webster, McDonald, Lewin, & Carr, 1995). A few noncomparative studies have similarly shown that postdisaster stress was quite high in particular ethnic communities (Chen, Chung, Chen, Fang, Chen, & Chen, 2003; Hough et al., 1990; Thiel de Bocanegra and Brickman, 2004). Ethnic differences in posttraumatic stress may point to effects of various risk factors, such as low socioeconomic status, chronic adversities, and differential exposure to the event itself that have little to do with culture per se. Nonetheless, culture can also shape the experience and consequences of disaster exposure.

Palinkas and colleagues' (1993) study of the aftermath of the *Exxon Valdez* spill is a case in point. The investigation revealed significant differences between Native Alaskans and others in rates of postdisaster major depression, generalized anxiety, and PTSD that were not explained by exposure alone. The spill interrupted subsistence activities, and these disruptions had greater impact on natives because they feared losing long-held traditions that defined their culture and community.

Perilla and colleagues (2002) explicitly tested whether *differential exposure* or *differential vulnerability* best explained their results showing that Latinos and non-Hispanic blacks were more adversely affected by Hurricane Andrew than were non-Hispanic whites. Consistent with the differential exposure hypothesis, non-Hispanic whites were less often personally traumatized and far less exposed to neighborhood-level trauma than the other groups. The severity of their exposure accounted for much of minority group members' higher posttraumatic stress. However, the interaction of trauma and ethnicity indicated that differential vulnerability also would have to be considered, and, in fact, some of minorities' disproportionate distress was explained by their higher levels of fatalism and acculturative stress. Fatalism refers to beliefs that fate plays a disproportionate role in life circumstances and that events are not under a person's control. Perilla and colleagues' findings are consistent with a large literature showing that external control is a risk factor for poor psychological outcomes following stressful life events (leading to increase vulnerability). It is reasonable to speculate that the intergroup tensions manifested in acculturative stress could exacerbate the effects of other stressors like job disruption or homelessness caused by a disaster. Theoretically, it was important to demonstrate that differential exposure and vulnerability can work in tandem and are not necessarily rival explanations.

Thiel de Bocanegra and Brickman's (2004) study was important for documenting the potential of disasters to affect the mental health of Asian Americans. In this sample of Chinese Americans seeking financial assistance after the September 11 terrorist attacks, 22% showed a pattern of symptoms consistent with PTSD, a rate strikingly higher than the presumed base rate of PTSD in this population. An additional study of Chinese Americans living in Chinatown, New York City, found that more than half of community residents reported one or more symptoms of psychological distress immediately following the event, but less than 4% received counseling from a mental health professional during the 5-month period after the disaster (Chen et al., 2003).

Also pertinent to this discussion are findings showing that culture shapes the effects of other important variables, such as gender and age, on postdisaster mental health outcomes. Norris, Perilla, Ibañez, and Murphy (2001) found that being of Mexican culture exacerbated gender differences and African American culture attenuated them. Webster and colleagues (1995) also found that sex differences in the effects of the Newcastle earthquake in Australia were greatest within the non-English-speaking immigrant portion of their sample. Norris, Kaniasty, Inman, Conrad, and Murphy (2002) examined age effects in three disaster-stricken samples. Among Americans, age had a curvilinear relation with PTSD such that middle-age respondents were most distressed. This was consistent with the other findings from the United States (Norris, Friedman, et al., 2002). Among Mexicans, however, age had a linear and negative relation with PTSD such that younger people were most distressed. Forming yet a third pattern, age had a linear and positive relation with PTSD in Poland, such that older people were most distressed after the disaster. The authors interpreted the findings in light of anthropological research showing that the family life cycle is different in each of these societies. For our purposes here, the important lesson from this comparison is that there was no one consistent effect of disaster by age; rather, it depended on the cultural and historical context of the population and the country variance of social roles played at various ages (see also Chen et al., 2003).

USE OF MENTAL HEALTH SERVICES

Ethnic Disparities in Service Use

There are striking disparities for minorities in use of mental health services. To begin with, minorities in the United States are less likely than whites to seek mental health treatment until symptoms are more severe and less likely to seek treatment from mental health specialists, as they are more inclined to turn to primary care or to use informal sources of support (DHHS, 2001; Vega & Alegría, 2001). The disparities appear to hold specifically for PTSD as well as for mental disorders in general (Koenen, Goodwin, Struening, Hellman, & Guardino, 2003). There is substantial evidence that patients' views about health care differ by race, ethnicity, socioeconomic status, language, and literacy levels (Blendon et al., 1995; Carrasquillo, Ovar, Brennan, & Burstin, 1999).

Availability and Accessibility of Services

A number of explanations for these disparities have been offered, including insurance (Hargraves & Hadley, 2003) and inadequate detection of problems (Borowsky et al., 2000). The threshold for what is considered distressing or impairing may have strong cultural determinants, thereby producing an effect on reporting and ascertaimnent of symptoms that could have a bearing on diagnosis and detection. In many Hispanic and Asian cultures, communication in the absence of a relationship is not accepted or proper. Many immigrants have difficulties communicating in English or fear immigration or legal authorities, leading them to never receive care (Castaneda, 1994). Sue, Fujino, Hu, and Takeuchi (1991) concluded that an important cause of underutilization is the limited availability of culturally competent psychotherapists and culturally responsive services. Altogether, these facts point to a general problem in the availability and accessibility of mental health care for American minorities.

Help-Seeking Comfort, Stigma, and Mistrust

It is difficult to isolate *help seeking* from *help receiving* in most of the literature. It is often assumed that minorities possess more negative attitudes about seeking help because of the findings showing that they receive less help than white Americans. However, the issue for minorities is not help seeking per se. Kaniasty and Norris (2000) studied ethnic differences in help-seeking comfort after Hurricane Andrew. All ethnic groups reported feeling most comfortable requesting help from family, somewhat less comfortable seeking help from friends, and the least comfortable seeking help from outsiders (which would include formal sources). Overall, minorities held more rather than less positive views about seeking help from other people, and this effect was more rather than less pronounced for outsiders. If these findings at first seem surprising, they actually are in accord with cross-cultural descriptions noting the greater value that white Americans place on self-reliance. Still, most people prefer receiving help from natural, informal sources.

Of course, the preceding results did not specifically address willingness to acknowledge a mental illness and to seek professional help for that problem. The Surgeon General's Report (SGR) (DHHS, 2001) identified stigma as a critical barrier to the use of mental health services. Stigma refers to a cluster of negative attitudes and beliefs that motivate the general public to fear, reject, avoid, and discriminate against people with mental illness. People with mental problems internalize public attitudes and conceal symptoms to avoid embarrassment or shame. Stigma is pervasive in American society and prevalent among white Americans as well as among minority groups.

Mistrust is a somewhat different issue than stigma. As reviewed in the SGR, African Americans and Latinos are more likely to feel that a health provider has judged them unfairly and to be afraid of mental health treatment. Allen (1996) argued that shame and guilt were especially common in African American PTSD patients who may be hypersensitive to outsiders, including therapists, if they seem to stand in harsh judgment of them. Minorities also appear to have greater concerns around side effects and addiction potential of medication (Cooper-Patrick et al., 1997). For these and other issues of trust, even when offered, minorities may be less likely to opt for receiving evidence-based treatments such as antidepressant medication or specialty psychiatric care (Miranda & Cooper, 2002; Wang, Bergland, & Kessler, 2000; Young, Klap, Shebourne, & Wells, 2001). More research is needed, but at present the data suggest that (1) stigma is a pervasive problem in America and (2) mistrust exacerbates its effects among minorities.

Promoting Service Use in the Aftermath of Disasters

The SGR noted that such negative attitudes could be addressed through public education efforts that are tailored to the languages, needs, and cultures of ethnic minorities. They proposed that one way to advance these efforts would be to involve representatives from the community in the design, planning, and implementation of services. On the basis of results from refugee programs, they concluded that successful programs do aggressive outreach and furnish a familiar and welcoming atmosphere (DHHS, 2001, p. 166). Disaster mental health services begin with critical assumptions (Flynn, 1994; Norris et al., Chapter 18, this volume) that match these recommendations quite well. First, crisis counseling programs assume that disaster victims are normal people responding normally to abnormal situations and therefore that services should be directed at normalizing individuals' experience and distress. By normalizing distress and help seeking, disaster services afford atypical opportunities to destigmatize mental health care. Second, crisis counseling programs assume that people prefer natural sources of assistance and therefore that services should be provided in schools, churches, and places of work. Third, these programs assume that people who need help the most may not necessarily seek it and therefore that services must assume a proactive posture to reach out to vulnerable groups.

There are few data that document whether these principles actually help to reduce disparities in service use. However, some data from Project Liberty in New York provide tentative support for the hypothesis that minorities are as likely as others to seek and receive care when other barriers are reduced (stigma, mistrust) or eliminated (cost). The ethnic breakdown of crisis counseling recipients matched the demographics of New York quite well (Felton, 2002). Moreover, in a diverse sample of 800 adults receiving crisis counseling services, and with the intensity of psychological reactions controlled, African American and white clients were equally willing to accept a referral to "enhanced services" (treatment). Hispanic ethnicity actually increased the likelihood that the referral was accepted (Norris, Donahue, Felton, Watson, & Hamblen, 2004).

Although Project Liberty was generally successful in reaching out to minority communities in the aftermath of 9/11, there was room for improvement (Norris et al., Chapter 18, this volume). Sometimes trust was difficult to establish. Most often mentioned was the difficulty in engaging the Muslim community. Sometimes hostilities were encountered in communities that had a multitude of predisaster problems and histories of neglect (Battery Park and Harlem were mentioned as two good examples in New York) but were overcome by involving community members in generating strategies and solutions.

APPROPRIATENESS OF MENTAL HEALTH SERVICES

Shortcomings of the Evidence Base for Minorities

The challenge for serving American minorities is to be both scientifically and culturally appropriate. The SGR concluded that the evidence base regarding effective treatments for minorities has remained quite poor (DHHS, 2001). Although effective treatments are available for many mental disorders, they are not being translated into community settings and are not being provided to everyone who comes in for care. The gap between research and practice is worse for minorities. The evidence base is meager but improving for trauma and PTSD. Zoellner, Feeny, Fitzgibbons, and Foa (1999) found no ethnic differences in completion rates and achieved equivalent results for 60 white and 35 black female assault victims who had been randomly assigned to active cognitive-behavioral treatment (CBT) or waitlist control. Kataoka and colleagues (2003) showed that an eight-session CBT intervention for Latino students exposed to community violence produced significant declines in depression and PTSD symptoms compared to a wait-list control. Many more studies like these are needed to establish the efficacy of various treatment approaches.

Ethnic Disparities in Quality of Care

A few studies have raised concerns about the overall quality of care being received by minority clients in community settings. Even after entering care, minorities face a higher risk of being misdiagnosed. This may be due to minorities being more likely to seek help in primary care as opposed to specialty care, where about one-third to one-half of patients with mental disorders remain undiagnosed (Williams et al., 1999). But even in psychiatric evaluation in emergency rooms, minorities are at greater risk of non-detection of mental disorders (e.g., Borowsky et al., 2000).

In many studies in the United States, members of minority groups are found to receive inferior health care compared to white patients. Using data from a large-scale survey, Wang and colleagues (2000) examined proportions receiving care that could be considered consistent with evidence-based treatment recommendations. This was defined operationally as attending at least four therapy sessions plus receiving medication or attending eight sessions in the absence of medication. African Americans were much less likely than white Americans to have received such care. Similarly, Young and colleagues (2001) showed that Latinos were less likely than non-Hispanic whites to receive treatment that was in accord with evidence-based guidelines.

Inappropriate prescription of medication is a source of significant concern. Clinicians in psychiatric emergency services prescribe both more and higher doses of oral and injectable antipsychotic medications to African Americans than to whites (Segel, Bola, & Watson, 1996), even when research recommends lower dosages to African Americans due to their slower metabolizing of some antidepressants and antipsychotic medications (Bradford & Kirlin, 1998). African Americans are less likely than whites to receive an antidepressant when their depression is first diagnosed and less likely to receive newer selective serotonin reuptake inhibitors (SSRIs), once medicated (Melfi, Croghan, Hanna, & Robinson, 2000).

Some studies suggest that retention and outcomes are superior when clients and clinicians are matched ethnically (Sue et al., 1991), but the crux of the matter may be *cognitive match*—that is, the congruence between therapist and client conceptions (Sue, 1998). One central dimension of care is the physician's or clinician's ability to communicate with the patient. The diagnostic formulation and treatment of mental disorders rely to a large degree on verbal communication between patient and physician about symptoms, the understanding of the possible causes of the problem, and the proper assessment of its impact on functioning. Miscommunication can lead to misdiagnosis, mismatch between the patient and the provider's expectation about treatment, and poor adherence to treatment. The assessment process is thus especially important when treating non-English-speaking populations.

Frameworks for Cultural Competence

The adoption of cultural competence as an overriding principle of services for minority populations is based in the premise that caregiver's or agencies' understanding of a person's cultural background and experience facilitates a better match of services and thus more effective care and improved client outcomes. Siegel and colleagues (2000) provided a series of indicators that may serve to establish the performance of the agency or system in providing culturally competent services. Some of the indicators include consumer and family involvement in the design of services, training of staff in cultural competence, and number of services adapted for cultural or racial groups.

In recent years, various recommendations have appeared for creating culturally competent mental health services. Cultural competence refers to the behaviors, attitudes, skills, and policies that help mental health caregivers to work effectively and efficiently across cultures (New York State Office of Mental Health, 1997). Of these, the best known is the *Outline for Cultural Formulation* published in the appendix of DSM-IV (American Psychiatric Association, 1994). The process of applying DSM criteria across cultures involves several steps: (1) assessing the cultural identify of the client, including his or her degree of involvement with the culture of origin and host culture; (2) exploring cultural explanations for the individual's symptoms, including his or her perception of their cause; (3) exploring cultural factors related to the psychosocial environment and level of functioning, with particular attention to social stressors and social support and the role of religion and kin networks in the person's life; (4) identifying cultural elements in the relationship between the individual and clinician, such as differences between them in language and heritage; and (5) creating an overall formulation of diagnosis and care. The formulation has been criticized for not going far enough (e.g., Lopez & Guarnaccia, 2000), but it nonetheless represents a tremendous step forward for multicultural care.

Around the same time, the American Psychological Association (1993) established benchmarks for cultural competency. The competent provider is characterized by an awareness of his or her own assumptions and values, a respect for the worldviews of clients, and the ability to develop culturally appropriate interventions. Knowledge, beliefs, and attitudes must all be considered. Yet, there is evidence suggesting that clinician bias and stereotyping play a role in medical decision making. For example, broadly adopted stereotypes of Asian Americans as "problem free" may lead providers to miss an individual's mental health problems (Takeuchi & Uehara, 1996).

Fortunately, certain goals of psychotherapy can reasonably be assumed to be universal, such as the removal of distressing symptoms and communication of empathy (Draguns, 1996). Beyond these goals, standard practices are likely to need some adaptation across cultures. Vega (1992) summarized the challenges well by noting that "off-the-shelf" intervention materials are difficult to use in diverse settings because they are unknowingly embedded with cultural expectations and unsubstantiated assumptions about such issues as time orientation, social and occupational commitments, family structure, and gender roles. These issues are overlooked by interventionists with surprising regularity. Intervention materials, levels of respondent burden, and assessment protocols must be carefully reviewed by community judges before a program can be piloted and evaluated in the targeted community or population.

Sue (1998) advised that an important component is *scientific mindedness*, saying, "By scientific mindedness, I am referring to therapists who form hypotheses rather than make premature conclusions about the status of culturally different clients, who develop creative ways to test hypotheses, and who act on the basis of acquired data" (p. 445). Sue continued by noting:

> A good clinician who is uncertain of the cultural meaning of a symptom should engage in hypothesis testing. For example, if the symptom is a reflection of a psychotic episode rather than a culturally influenced characteristic, one would expect (a) the client to manifest other psychotic symptoms, (b) other individuals in the culture to be unfamiliar with the symptom, or (c) experts in the culture to indicate that the symptom is unusual in that culture. (p. 446)

However, this type of assessment might be particularly difficult to implement in the absence of cultural psychiatric liaisons, such as the ones proposed by Kirmayer and Young (1999).

On the basis of many years of experience working with traumatized refugees, Kinzie (2001) advised cross-cultural treatment programs to incorporate several key elements. These elements appear to apply to postdisaster clinical settings quite well. Such programs need to be able to treat major disorders in addition to PTSD because of high rates of comorbidity (e.g., depression and substance abuse) in some populations. Programs must address language needs, and they must be easy to access and perceived as credible. In addition, according to Kinzie, the program must have linkages with other services, integrate care for both physical and mental disorders, create mechanisms for feedback and advice, and be staffed by competent clinicians and bilingual mental health workers who can create bridges between the patient and professional staff.

Social Functioning as an Organizing Principle for Multicultural Interventions

Draguns (1996) speculated that cultural dimensions, especially individualism–collectivism, provided clues for the content of multicultural interventions. He reasoned that in individualist cultures that emphasize independence, it is appropriate for self-actualization to serve as the ultimate goal of psychological interventions, whereas in collectivistic cultures that emphasize interdependence, it would be more fitting to aim for the attainment of harmonious social relationships. Both objectives are inherently desirable; it is only their respective prominence that would differ given the cultural identify of the client. We agree with these points and would like to elaborate further on their implications for the content of multicultural postdisaster interventions. Individualist and collectivist cultures subsume strikingly different constructions of self (Markus & Kitayama, 1994). In collectivist cultures, such as found across most of Latin America and Asia, the self is unbounded and fundamentally interrelated with others. The goal is not to become autonomous but to fulfill and create obligation and, in general, to become part of various interpersonal relationships. In an important cross-cultural study, Kitayama, Markus, and Matsumoto (1995) distinguished between socially engaged emotions (e.g., feelings of closeness), socially disengaged emotions (e.g., pride), and generic emotions (e.g., happiness). They found that socially engaged emotions were more strongly related to emotional states than were socially disengaged emotions among the Japanese, whereas the reverse was true in the United States.

This finding is of particular interest for our purposes because perceptions of belonging and being cared for are critical to the well being of disaster victims (see Kaniasty & Norris, 2004, for a review of the literature on disasters and social support). Across a variety of settings both within and outside the United States, Kaniasty and Norris have shown that disasters exert their adverse impact on psychological distress both directly and indirectly, through disruptions of social relationships and expectations of support. This disruption of social supports occurs just when the need for them is at its highest. A disaster is an excellent example of a community event that alters the quantity and quality of social interactions. Because disasters affect entire indigenous networks, the need for support may simply exceed its availability, causing expectations of support to be violated. Relocation and job loss remove important others from victims' supportive environments. There are fewer opportunities for companionship and leisure. Physical fatigue, emotional irritability, and scarcity of resources augment the potential for interpersonal conflicts and social withdrawal. Interactions that are apparently supportive may be seen quite differently when one's obligations to help others in the network are taken into account; reciprocity is highly valued in many cultures. Furthermore, it needs to be recognized that disaster recovery can be a long process. The heightened level of helping and concern evident initially cannot be expected to last for the full length of the recovery process. Nor are supportive resources distributed equitably. Following several disasters, it has been found that disaster victims who had fewer economic resources or were members of ethnic minority groups received less emotional support than did their comparably affected counterparts who had greater economic resources or were members of ethnic majority groups (Kaniasty & Norris, 1995). Socially and economically disadvantaged groups are frequently too overburdened to provide ample help to other members in time of additional need.

From this research, a clear and deceptively simple recommendation for culturally responsive postdisaster interventions can be drawn. This is always to remember that *the individual is embedded in a broader familial, interpersonal, and social context.* (See Hobfoll, 1998, for an exceptional elaboration on this point.) The interventionist or practitioner must spend time assessing— and addressing—socially relevant cognitions and emotions as well as the person's social supports, network demands, and performed and expected social roles. On the positive side are constructs such as (1) perceptions of social support, social competence, belonging, and trust; (2) mutuality and marital satisfaction; and (3) social participation, sense of community, and communal mastery. On the negative side are constructs such as (4) withdrawal, loneliness, isolation, interpersonal estrangement, shame, and remorse; (5) familial obligations, caretaking burdens, and parenting stress; (6) domestic and other interpersonal conflicts; and (7) hostility, anger, societal alienation, perceptions of neglect, and acculturative stress. Broadly speaking, *the intervention goal is to enhance social functioning*, which indirectly addresses an important risk factor for chronic PTSD (Norris, Murphy, Baker, & Perilla, 2003).

Some previous recommendations in the multicultural treatment literature are consistent with our own. As Lindsey & Cuéllar (2000) noted, "African Americans will respond more favorably if therapy efforts are directed toward the environment or toward working with the extended family or toward spiritualistic and/or religious interventions or toward strengthening interdependency" (p. 199). They went on to say that cognitive therapy provides a good example. Similar recommendations to adjust cognitive-behavioral interventions to make them acceptable to Latino culture have been offered by Vera, Vila, and Alegría (2003). The therapist's techniques are essentially the same regardless of culture, but the client's explanatory models are culturally derived.

Community Action

To be culturally responsive in the aftermath of disasters, practitioners need to go beyond providing traditional services in nontraditonal settings and embrace novel approaches to meeting community needs. Solomon (2003) summarized this well:

> The major concern is in fostering natural resiliency. For many survivors, removing obstacles to self-help, or providing for basic needs such as food, shelter, education, and health care may be the only intervention needed. This type of secondary prevention may also involve reparations, provision of a safe and healthy recovery environment, and reunion of family and community members. The underlying goal is to empower victims to participate in their own recovery efforts so as to regain both a sense of control over their lives and an orientation toward the future. (p. 12)

Solomon went on to note, "Although professionals working in the mental health arena are seldom trained or prepared to work at a broader community level, the scale of these emergences may require abandoning dyadic interventions for those that can be implemented via community action using a public health approach" (p. 12). Somasundarum, Norris, Asukai, and Murthy (2003) and Hobfoll (1998) similarly advocated for community-level interventions that foster community competence and ownership of problems and solutions. Culturally based rituals and traditions sometimes can be used as the basis for innovative interventions (Manson, 1997; Nader, Dubrow, & Stamm, 1999). No one set of recommendations will apply to all communities cross-culturally, and activities must be developed from the "bottom up" to match the cultural context and needs of the group. Working collectively toward specific, achievable goals is helpful for many communities; community gatherings also help people to interpret and share their experiences and to establish social links (Somasundarum et al., 2003).

The evidence base supporting the effectiveness of community-oriented trauma programs is minimal, and building such a base is crucial for the advancement of culturally competent care. A few pilot studies are promising. For example, Weine and colleagues (2003) described the "Tea and Families Education and Support" intervention for Kosovar refugees. Three months after entering the program, participants demonstrated increases in knowledge about trauma and mental health, use of mental health services, perceived social support, and family hardiness.

RECOMMENDATIONS

Table 2.1 summarizes the following recommendations:

- *Assess community needs early and often.* Prior research indicates that minorities are at elevated risk for postdisaster mental health problems such as depression and PTSD. Small but important percentages will have mental health needs that predate the disaster. Assessment of needs in disaster-stricken communities is critical, and these assessments should

Table 2.1.   Guidelines for culturally sensitive postdisaster care

---

- *Assess community needs early and often.* Gaps in rates of recovery, awareness of services, and use of services can be noted and addressed.
- *Provide free and easily accessible services.* Minorities will be more likely to take advantage of services that are close to home, community-based, and offered in concert with other services and activities.
- *Work collaboratively and proactively to build trust and to engage minorities in care.* To reduce disparities in service use, practitioners must get out of the clinic into the community.
- *Validate and normalize distress.* Help seeking as well as symptoms can and should be normalized. Diagnosis of pathology should be deemphasized, relative to standard practice. An important task of the clinician is to help individuals identify and mobilize their natural resources.
- *Value interdependence as well as independence as an appropriate goal.* The intervention goal is to enhance social functioning, helping the person retain or resume his or her social roles.
- *Promote community action.* Novel and innovative strategies should be explored that involve minority communities in their own recovery by working toward specific, achievable goals.
- *Recognize that cultural competence is a process not an end-state.* Continuing education is key.
- *Advocate for, facilitate, or conduct treatment and evaluation research.* Researchers and practitioners should collaborate to test the efficacy and effectiveness of different intervention strategies for minority populations.
- *Leave a legacy.* Disasters create opportunities to educate the public, destigmatize mental health problems, and build trust between providers and minority communities.

---

oversample minority populations to determine the ways in which they were exposed and affected by the particular event. Because diagnoses may be less valid for minority persons and because they represent only the tip of the iceberg in any case, needs assessments should include a focus on experienced emotional distress and impaired functioning, especially social functioning. Valid needs assessments for culturally diverse populations also require information on contextual and cultural variables such as trauma exposure in the country of origin, losing of social ties, level of comfort in host society, and level of English-language proficiency. Gaining support among policy researchers is the notion of surveillance. Needs evolve. Repeating the needs assessment periodically will provide invaluable information about the extent to which minorities are recovering from the disaster, have recovered, or still require help. Gaps in rates of recovery, awareness of services, and use of services can be noted and addressed.

- *Provide free and easily accessible services.* Minorities often lack insurance and other means of paying for mental health services. They will be more likely to take advantage of services that are close to home, community-based, and offered in concert with other services and activities. This might translate in providing services in community-based organizations with sustainable relations with the minority community or offering services in schools or community facilities with easy access.

- *Work collaboratively and proactively to reduce stigma and mistrust and to engage minorities in care.* It should be anticipated at the outset that minority disaster victims, even those who have suffered intensely, will not necessarily seek professional mental health services, as they will tend to rely on families, friends, and other natural sources of help. Viewing this as an asset rather than a problem to be overcome reminds the interventionist to work collaboratively with natural helpers in the community, such as *promotoras* or paraprofessionals with experience and credibility in the community. To reduce disparities in service use, programs must build trust and be highly proactive; practitioners must get out of the clinic into the community. To the extent possible, programs should employ ethnic minority practitioners in the recruitment, retention in care, and recovery efforts. If such practitioners are scarce, they may serve the overall effort best in consultant, training, and supervisory roles. Local representatives of minority communities should be involved from the outset in preparing for and planning responses to disasters and terrorism.
- *Validate and normalize distress.* Over and over again, experienced disaster and trauma clinicians emphasize that some distress is a normal reaction to an abnormal event. But this does not mean that help cannot lessen that distress or hasten recovery. Help seeking as well as symptoms can and should be normalized. Diagnosis of pathology should be deemphasized, relative to standard practice. Even when highly stressed, most people possess strengths they can draw on, and an important task of the clinician is to help individuals identify and mobilize their natural resources. At the same time, education regarding when dependence solely on self-reliance can be harmful to overcoming one's mental health problems or emotional distress should also be a task of disaster service providers. Self-reliance ("can handle the problem on my own") is a strong barrier to mental health care (Ortega & Alegría, 2002).
- *Value interdependence as well as independence as an appropriate goal.* As noted previously, the individual is embedded in a broader familial, interpersonal, and social context. The practitioner must spend time assessing and addressing socially relevant cognitions and emotions. The intervention goal is to enhance social functioning, helping the person retain or resume his or her social roles.
- *Promote community action.* Novel and innovative strategies should be explored that involve minority communities in their own recovery by working toward specific, achievable goals. Social marketing, advocacy, community organizing, train-the-trainer models, and mentoring programs are but a few examples that can be explored. By assuming a consultant or facilitator role, practitioners can help communities make informed choices while still recognizing that the choices are the community's own. At the same time, finding out about successful community interventions with similar communities and populations

might help identify ingredients that can be used to enhance mainstream interventions.

- *Recognize that cultural competence is a process not an end-state.* Clinicians will only experience despair if they are expected to know everything that would be helpful about every culture that makes up the American whole. The importance of continuing education cannot be overstated.
- *Advocate for, facilitate, or conduct treatment and evaluation research.* There are still so few data on which to base recommendations for culturally responsive mental health care. Minorities will ultimately be better served if practitioners and researchers collaborate to test the efficacy and effectiveness of different intervention strategies.
- *Leave a legacy.* Notwithstanding the pain and stress they cause, disasters create opportunities to educate the public about trauma and mental health, to destigmatize mental health problems and mental health services, to build trust between service providers and minority communities, and to develop collaborative relationships that may serve the entire populace for years to come.

Acknowledgment

Preparation of this chapter was supported by Grant No. K02 MH63909 from the National Institute of Mental Health to Fran H. Norris.

References

Alegría, M., & McGuire, T. (2003). Rethinking a universal framework in the psychiatric symptom–disorder relationship. *Journal of Health and Social Behavior, 44*(3), 257–274.

Allen, I. (1996). PTSD among African Americans. In A. Marsella, M. Friedman, E. Gerrity, & R. Scurfield (Eds.), *Ethnocultural aspects of posttraumatic stress disorder: Issues, research, and clinical applications* (pp. 209–238). Washington, DC: American Psychiatric Association Press.

American Psychiatric Association. (1987). *Diagnostic and statistical manual of mental disorders* (3rd ed., rev.). Washington, DC: Author.

American Psychiatric Association. (1994). *Diagnostic and statistical manual of mental disorders* (4th ed.). Washington, DC: Author.

American Psychological Association. (1993). Guidelines for providers of psychological services to ethnic, linguistic, and culturally diverse populations. *American Psychologist, 48*, 45–48.

Blendon, R. J., Scheck, A. C., Donelan, K., Hill, C. A., Smith, M., Beatrice, D., et al. (1995). How white and African Americans view their health and social problems: Different experiences, different expectations. *Journal of the American Medical Association, 273*(4), 341–346.

Bolton, R., & Klenow, D. (1988). Older people in disaster: A comparison of Black and White victims. *International Journal of Aging and Human Development, 26*, 29–43.

Borowsky, S., Rubenstein, L., Meredith, L., Camp, P., Jackson-Triche, M., & Wells, K. (2000). Who is at risk of nondetection of mental health problems in primary care? *Journal of General Internal Medicine, 15*, 381–388.

Bradford, L. D., & Kirlin, W. G. (1998). Polymorphism of CYP2D6 in Black populations: Implications for psychopharmacology. *International Journal of Neuro-psychopharmacology, 1*(2), 173–185.

Breslau, N., Kessler, R., Chilcoat, H., Schulz, L., Davis, G., & Andreski, P. (1998). Trauma and posttraumatic stress disorder in the community: The 1996 Detroit Area Survey of Trauma. *Archives of General Psychiatry, 55,* 627–632.

Carrasquillo, O., Ovar, E. V., Brennan, T. A., & Burstin, H. R. (1999). Iimpact of language barriers on patient satisfaction in an emergency department. *Journal of General Internal Medicine, 14*(2), 82–87.

Castaneda, D. M. (1994). A research agenda for Mexican-American adolescent mental health. *Adolescence, 29*(113), 225–239.

Chen, H., Chung, H., Chen, T., Fang, L., & Chen, J.-P. (2003). The emotional distress in a community after the terrorist attack on the World Trade Center. *Community Mental Health Journal, 39,* 157–165.

Cooper-Patrick, L., Powe, N. R., Jenckes, M. W., Gonzales, J. J., Levine, D. M., & Ford, D. E. (1997). Identification of patient attitudes and preferences regarding treatment of depression. *Journal of General Internal Medicine, 12,* 431–438.

Draguns, J. (1996). Ethnocultural considerations in the treatment of PTSD: Therapy and service delivery. In A. Marsella, M. Friedman, E. Gerrity, & R. Scurfield (Eds.), *Ethnocultural aspects of PTSD: Issues, research, and clinical applications* (pp. 459–482). Washington, DC: American Psychiatric Association Press.

Felton, C. (2002). Project liberty: A public health response to New Yorkers' mental health needs arising from the World Trade Center terrorist attacks. *Journal of Urban Health, 79,* 429–433.

Flynn, B. (1994). Mental health services in large scale disasters: An overview of the Crisis Counseling Program. *NCPTSD Clinical Quarterly, 4,* 1–4.

Galea, S., Ahern, J., Resnick, H., Kilpatrick, D., Bucuvalas, M., Gold, J., et al. (2002). Psychological sequelae of the September 11 terrorist attacks in New York City. *New England Journal of Medicine, 346,* 982–987.

Garrison, C., Bryant, E., Addy, C., Spurrier, P., Freedy, J., & Kilpatrick, D. (1995). Post-traumatic stress disorder in adolescents after Hurricane Andrew. *Journal of the American Academy of Child and Adolescent Psychiatry, 34,* 1193–1201.

Green, B., Lindy, J., Grace, M., Gleser, G., Leonard, A., Korol, M., et al. (1990). Buffalo Creek survivors in the second decade. *American Journal of Orthopsychiatry, 60,* 43–54.

Guarnaccia, P., Canino, G., Rubio-Stipec, M., & Bravo, M. (1993). The prevalence of *ataques de nervios* in the Puerto Rico disaster study. *Journal of Nervous and Mental Disease, 181,* 157–165.

Hargraves, J. L., & Hadley, J. (2003). The contribution of insurance coverage and community resources to reducing racial/ethnic disparities in access to care. *Health Services Research, 38*(3), 809–829.

Hobfoll, S. (1998). *Stress, culture, and community: The psychology and philosophy of stress.* New York: Plenum Press.

Holzer, C., & Copeland, C. (2000). Race, ethnicity, and the epidemiology of mental disorders in adults. In I. Cuéllar & F. Paniagua (Eds.), *Handbook of multicultural mental health* (pp. 341–357). San Diego, CA: Academic Press.

Hough, R., Vega, W., Valle, R., Kolody, B., Griswold del Castillo, R., & Tarke, H. (1990). The prevalence of symptoms of posttraumatic stress disorder in the aftermath of the San Ysidro massacre. *Journal of Traumatic Stress, 3,* 71–92.

Kaniasty, K., & Norris, F. (1995). In search of altruistic community: Patterns of social support mobilization following Hurricane Hugo. *American Journal of Community Psychology, 23,* 447–477.

Kaniasty, K., & Norris, F. (2000). Help-seeking comfort and the receipt of help: The roles of context and ethnicity. *American Journal of Community Psychology, 28,* 545–582.

Kaniasty, K., & Norris, F. (2004). Social support in the aftermath of disasters, catastrophes, and acts of terrorism: Altruistic, overwhelmed, uncertain, antagonistic, and patriotic communities. In R. Ursano, A. Norwood, & C. Fullerton (Eds.), *Bioterrorism: Psychological and public health interventions* (pp. 200–229). Cambridge, UK: Cambridge University Press.

Kataoka, S., Stein, B., Jaycox, L., Wong, M., Escudero, P., Tu, W., et al. (2003). A school based mental health program for traumatized Latino immigrant children. *Journal of the Academy of Child and Adolescent Psychiatry, 42,* 311–318.

Kessler, R., Berglund, P., Demler, O., Jin, R., Koretz, D., Merikangas, K. R., et al. (2003). The epidemiology of major depressive disorder: Results from the National Comorbidity Survey Replication (NCS-R). *Journal of the American Medical Association, 289*(23), 3095–3105.

Kessler, R., Somnega, A., Bromet, E., Hughes, M., & Nelson, C. (1995). Posttraumatic stress disorder in the National Comorbidity Survey. *Archives of General Psychiatry, 52*, 1048–1060.

Kinzie. J. D. (2001). Cross-cultural treatment of PTSD. In J. P. Wilson, M. J. Friedman, & J. D. Lindy (Eds.), *Treating psychological trauma and PTSD* (pp. 255–277). New York: Guilford Press.

Kirmayer, L. (1996). Confusion of the senses: Implications of ethnocultural variations in somatoform and dissociative disorders for PTSD. In A. Marsella, M. Friedman, E. Gerrity, & R. Scurfield (Eds.), *Ethnocultural aspects of posttraumatic stress disorder: Issues, research, and clinical applications* (pp. 165–182). Washington, DC: American Psychiatric Association Press.

Kirmayer, L. J., & Young, A. (1999). Culture and context in the evolutionary concept of mental disorder. *Journal of Abnormal Psychology, 108*, 446–452.

Kitayama, S., Markus, H. R., & Matsumoto, H. (1995). Culture, self, and emotion: A cultural perspective on "self-conscious" emotions. In J. P. Tangney & K. W. Fischer (Eds.), *Self-conscious emotions: The psychology of shame, guilt, embarrassment, and pride* (pp. 439–464). New York: Guilford Press.

Koenen, K., Goodwin, R., Struening, E., Hellman, F., & Guardino, M. (2003). Post-traumatic stress disorder and treatment seeking in a national screening sample. *Journal of Traumatic Stress, 16*, 5–16.

Lindsey, M., & Cuéllar, I. (2000). Mental health assessment and treatment of African Americans: A multicultural perspective. In I. Cuéllar & F. Paniagua (Eds.), *Handbook of multicultural mental health* (pp. 195–209). San Diego, CA: Academic Press.

Lopez, S., & Guarnaccia, P. (2000). Cultural psychopathology: Uncovering the social world of mental illness. *Annual Review of Psychology, 51*, 571–598.

Manson, S. (1997). Cross-cultural and multiethnic assessment of trauma. In J. P. Wilson & T. M. Keane (Eds.), *Assessing psychological trauma and PTSD* (pp. 239–266). New York: Guilford Press.

March, J., Amaya-Jackson, L., Terry, R., & Costanzo, P. (1997). Posttraumatic symptomatology in children and adolescents after an industrial fire. *Journal of the American Academy of Child and Adolescent Psychiatry, 36*, 1080–1088.

Markus, H., & Kitayama, S. (1994). The cultural construction of self and emotion: Implications for social behavior. In S. Kitayama & H. Markus (Eds.), *Emotion and culture: Empirical studies of mutual influence* (pp. 89–130). Washington, DC: American Psychological Association.

Melfi, C. A., Croghan, T. W., Hanna, M. P., & Robinson, R. L. (2000). Racial variation in antidepressant treatment in a Medicaid population. *Journal of Clinical Psychiatry, 61*(1), 16–21.

Miranda, J., & Cooper, L. (2002). *Disparities in care for depression among primary care patients.* Unpublished manuscript.

Nader, K., Dubrow, N., & Stamm, B. (1999). *Honoring differences: Cultural issues in the treatment of trauma and loss.* Philadelphia: Brunner/Mazel.

New York State Office of Mental Health. (1997). *Crisis counseling guide to children and families in disasters.* Retrieved January 10, 2004, from www.omh.state.ny.us/omhweb/crisis/crisiscounseling.html

Norris, F. (1992). Epidemiology of trauma: Frequency and impact of different potentially traumatic events on different demographic groups. *Journal of Consulting and Clinical Psychology, 60*, 409–418.

Norris, F., Donahue, S., Felton, C., Watson, P., & Hamblen, J. (2004). *Making and monitoring referrals to clinical treatment: A psychometric analysis of Project Liberty's Adult Enhanced Services Referral Tool.* Manuscript under review.

Norris, F. H., Foster, J. D., & Weisshaar, D. L. (2002). The epidemiology of sex differences in PTSD across developmental, societal, and research contexts. In R. Kimerling, P. Ouimette, & J. Wolfe (Eds.), *Gender and PTSD* (pp. 3–42). New York: Guilford Press.

Norris, F., Friedman, M., Watson, P., Byrne, C., Diaz, E., & Kaniasty, K. (2002). 60,000 disaster victims speak, Part I: An empirical review of the empirical literature, 1981–2001. *Psychiatry, 65*, 207–239.

Norris, F., Kaniasty, K., Inman, G., Conrad, L, & Murphy, A. (2002). Placing age differences in cultural context: A comparison of the effects of age on PTSD after disasters in the U.S., Mexico, and Poland. *Journal of Clinical Geropsychology* [Special issue], *8*, 153–173.

Norris, F., Murphy, A., Baker, C., & Perilla, J. (2003). Severity, timing, and duration of reactions to trauma in the population: An example from Mexico. *Biological Psychiatry, 53*, 769–778.

Norris, F., Murphy, A., Baker, C., Perilla, J., Gutierrez-Rodriguez, F., & Gutierrez-Rodriguez, J. (2003). Epidemiology of trauma and posttraumatic stress disorder in Mexico. *Journal of Abnormal Psychology, 112*, 646–656.

Norris, F., Perilla, J., Ibañez G., & Murphy, A. (2001). Sex differences in symptoms of posttraumatic stress: Does culture play a role? *Journal of Traumatic Stress, 14*, 7–28.

Norris, F., Weisshaar, D., Kirk, L., Diaz, E., Murphy, A., & Ibañez, G. (2001). A qualitative analysis of PTSD symptoms among Mexican victims of disaster. *Journal of Traumatic Stress, 14*, 741–756.

Ortega, A., & Alegría, M. (2002). Self-reliance, mental health, need and the use of mental health care among Island Puerto Ricans. *Mental Health Services Research, 4*, 131–140.

Ortega, A., & Rosenheck R. (2000). Posttraumatic stress disorder among Hispanic Vietnam veterans. *American Journal of Psychiatry, 157*, 615–619.

Osofsky, J. D. (1997). Community-based approaches to violence prevention. *Journal of Developmental and Behavioral Pediatrics, 18(6)*, 405–407.

Palinkas, L., Downs, M., Petterson, J., & Russell, J. (1993). Social, cultural, and psychological impacts of the Exxon Valdez oil spill. *Human Organization, 52*, 1–13.

Parson, E. R. (1997). Postraumatic child therapy (P-TCT): Assessment of treatment factors in clinical work with inner-city children exposed to community violence. *Journal of Interpersonal Violence, 12*, 172–194.

Perilla, J., Norris, F., & Lavizzo, E. (2002). Ethnicity, culture, and disaster response: Identifying and explaining ethnic differences in PTSD six months after Hurricane Andrew. *Journal of Social and Clinical Psychology, 21*, 28–45.

Pynoos, R. S., Frederick, C., Nader, K., Arroyo, W., Steinberg, A., Eth, S., et al. (1987). Life threat and posttraumatic stress in school-age children. *Archives of General Psychiatry, 44(12)*, 1057–1063.

Segel, S. P., Bola, J. R., & Watson, M. A. (1996). Race, quality of care, and antipsychotic prescribing practices in psychiatric emergency services. *Psychiatric Services, 47*, 282–286.

Siegel, C., Davis-Chambers, E., Haugland, G., Bank, R., Aponte, C., & McCombs, H. (2000). Performance measures of cultural competency in mental health organizations. *Administration, Policy, and Mental Health, 28(2)*, 91–106.

Solomon, S. (2003). Introduction. In B. L. Green, M. J. Friedman, J. T. V. M. De Jong, S. D. Solomon, T. M. Keane, J. A. Fairbank, et al. (Eds.), *Trauma interventions in war and peace: Prevention, practice, and policy* (pp. 3–16). New York: Kluwer/Plenum Press.

Solomon, S., & Canino, G. (1990). The appropriateness of DSM-IIIR criteria for post-traumatic stress disorder. *Comprehensive Psychiatry, 31*, 227–237.

Somasundarum, D., Norris, F., Asukai, N., & Murthy, R. (2003). In B. L. Green, M. J. Friedman, J. T. V. M. De Jong, S. D. Solomon, T. M. Keane, J. A. Fairbank, et al. (Eds.), *Trauma interventions in war and peace: Prevention, practice, and policy* (pp. 291–318). New York: Kluwer/Plenum Press.

Srinivasan, S., & Guillermo, T. (2000). Toward improved health: disaggregating Asian American and Native Hawaiian/Pacific Islander data. *American Journal of Public Health, 90(11)*, 1731–1734.

Sue, S. (1998). In search of cultural competence in psychotherapy and counseling. *American Psychologist, 53*, 440–448.

Sue, S., Fujino, D., Hu, L., & Takeuchi, D. (1991). Community mental health services for ethnic minority groups: A test of the cultural responsiveness hypothesis. *Journal of Consulting and Clinical Psychology, 59*, 533–540.

Takeuchi, D., Chung, R., Lin, K., Shen, H., Kuraski, K., Chung, C., et al. (1998). Lifetime and twelve-month prevalence rates of major depressive episodes and dysthymis among Chinese Americans in Los Angeles. *American Journal of Psychiatry, 155*, 1407–1414.

Takeuchi, D., & Uehara, E. (1996). Ethnic minority mental health services: Current research and future conceptual directions. In B. L. Levin & J. Petrila (Eds.), *Mental health services: A public health perspective* (pp. 63–80). New York: Oxford University Press.

Thiel de Bocanegra, H., & Brickman, E. (2004). Mental health impact of the World Trade Center attacks on displaced Chinese workers. *Journal of Traumatic Stress, 17*, 55–62.

U.S. Department of Health and Human Services. (2001). *Mental health: Culture, race, and ethnicity—A supplement to Mental health: A report of the Surgeon General.* Rockville, MD: U.S. Department of Health and Human Services, Public Health Service, Office of the Surgeon General.

Vega, W. (1992). Theoretical and pragmatic implications of cultural diversity for community research. *American Journal of Community Psychology, 20*, 375–392.

Vega, W., & Alegría, M. (2001). Latino mental health and treatment in the United States. In M. Aguirre-Molina, C. Molina, & R. Zambrana (Eds.), *Health issues in the Latino community* (pp. 179–208). San Francisco: Jossey-Bass.

Vega, W., Kolody, B., Aguilar-Gaxiola, S., Alderette, E., Catalano, R., & Caraveo-Anduaga, J. (1998). Lifetime prevalence of DSM-III-R psychiatric disorders among urban and rural Mexican Americans in California. *Archives of General Psychiatry, 55*, 771–778.

Vera, M., Vila, D., & Alegría, M. (2003). Cognitive-behavioral therapy: Concepts, issues, and strategies for practice with racial/ethnic minorities. In G. Bernal, J. Trimble, A. Berlew, & F. Leong (Eds.), *Handbook of racial and ethnic minority psychology* (pp. 1–18). Thousand Oaks, CA: Sage.

Wang, P., Bergland, P., & Kessler, R. (2000). Recent care of common mental disorders in the United States. *Journal of General Internal Medicine, 15*, 284–292.

Webster, R., McDonald, R., Lewin, T., & Carr, V. (1995). Effects of a natural disaster on immigrants and host population. *Journal of Nervous and Mental Disease, 183*, 390–397.

Weine, S., Raina, D., Zhubi, M., Delesi, M., Husenl. D, Feetham, S., et al. (2003). The TAFES Multi-Family Group Intervention for Kosovar refugees: A feasibility study. *Journal of Nervous and Mental Disease, 191*, 100–107.

Williams, J. W. J., Rost, K., Dietrich, A. J., Ciotti, M. C., Zyzanski, S. J., & Cornell, J. (1999). Primary care physicians' approach to depressive disorders: Effects of physician specialty and practice structure. *Archives of Family Medicine, 8*, 58–67.

Young, A., Klap, R., Shebourne, C., & Wells, K. (2001). The quality of care for depression and anxiety disorders in the United States. *Archives of General Psychiatry, 58*, 55–61.

Zheng, Y., Lin, K., Takeuchi, D., Kurasaki, K., Wang, Y., & Cheung, F. (1997). An epidemiologic study of neurasthenia in Chinese-Americans in Los Angeles. *Comprehensive Psychiatry, 38*, 249–259.

Zoellner, L., Feeny, N., Fitzgibbons, L., & Foa, E. (1999). Response of American and Caucasian women to cognitive behavioral therapy for PTSD. *Behavior Therapy, 30*, 581–595.

Section II

Ethnocultural and Racial Group Considerations

Chapter 3

Meeting the Physical, Psychological, and Social Needs of African Americans Following a Disaster

Steven B. Carswell and Melissa A. Carswell[1]

INTRODUCTION

This chapter provides basic background information regarding individuals who either self-identify or are identified by people in the larger society as being members of the African American ethnocultural group. Although African Americans share many things in common with one another including similar historical experiences, cultural traits, and health considerations, great diversity exists among group members in terms of socioeconomic status, educational background, family structure, and individual reactions to racism (Boyd-Franklin, 2003; Sue & Sue, 2003). As with other ethnocultural groups, differences among group members may be just as varied as the differences between members of one ethnocultural group and another. Thus, one should be mindful of such considerations when making sweeping generalizations about group characteristics or attributes.

Bearing these considerations in mind, terms such as "in general," "many," or "some" will be used frequently throughout the course of this presentation when describing cultural and family characteristics, behavioral practices and patterns, and economic and health-related issues common to African Americans. However, it should be noted that regardless of ethnocultural group membership, individuals with comparable social, economic, and political backgrounds may hold or maintain similar values, beliefs, and lifestyles, which transcend ascribed ethnocultural affiliations (Lassiter, 1998).

---

[1] This chapter was written prior to the events of Hurricane Katrina in New Orleans, Louisiana. The reader may wish to consult some of the post-katrina literature on African Americans and disasters.

Nonetheless, although individual differences may exist among members of ethnocultural groups, and socioeconomic and political backgrounds may influence individual behavioral practices and patterns, it is generally true that distinct characteristics or attributes, similar ancestry or experiences, and/or cultural traits or traditions can be identified that distinguish members of one ethnocultural group from another. Acknowledging and understanding both the similarities and differences between members of varying ethnocultural groups, particularly in terms of disaster response, may provide disaster responders and mental health workers with a more complete understanding of the complex interrelationships that exist between culture and disasters. Such information may increase their awareness and sensitivity to the important role that cultural factors play in shaping the nature, meaning, and varied responses of ethnocultural group members during and immediately following a disaster. It is our hope that this type of information will assist them in being more effective in their work.

HISTORICAL AND POPULATION OVERVIEW

Group Identification

The term African American describes an ethnocultural group whose members identify their ancestry as being invariably linked to Africa. Group membership is comprised of individuals whose African ancestors arrived in the United States prior to slavery, who were themselves slaves or free Negroes, or who arrived sometime after slavery (Boyd-Franklin, 2003; Quarles, 1987). Throughout their history in America, members of this ethnocultural group have either self-identified or been identified by people in the larger society by the use of various terms, including but not limited to African, Negro, Colored, and Black. Currently, most group members prefer to be identified by terms such as Black or African American, Afro-American, Person of Color, Black Native American, Caribbean-American, and/or African (Lassiter, 1998). Recently, however, the term African American has emerged as the word of choice to identify group members, although, as stated above, other terms are still frequently used and may actually be preferred by some group members (Lassiter, 1998; Philogène, 1999).

For purposes of this presentation, the term African American will be used primarily when referring to members of this ethnocultural group, as the term "Black" generally refers to skin color and not an ethnic or cultural group. Moreover, the term "Black" is severely limiting when used to identify African Americans, as their gene pool is comprised of more than 100 racial strains, making skin color quite diverse among group members (Philogène, 1999; Purnell & Paulanka, 2005). In addition, African American is preferred in comparison to other terms such as "Afro-American" and "People of Color" as the term African in connection with American connotes the inextricable link

Table 3.1. Key Historical Dates (Chronology)

Date	Historical Event
1619	The first Africans to be forcibly settled as laborers in the North American British Colonies arrive in Jamestown, Virginia.
1857	The *Dred Scott* decision is handed down by the U.S. Supreme Court stating that no slave or descendant of a slave could be nor had ever been a U.S. citizen. This decision also denied Congress the power to restrict slavery in any Federal territory and contributed to tensions between the citizens of free and slave states just prior to the American Civil War.
1863	The Emancipation Proclamation freed slaves in those states rebelling against the Union.
1865	The Thirteenth Amendment to the Constitution abolished slavery as a legal institution in the U.S. or in any place subject to its jurisdiction.
1868	The Fourteenth Amendment to the Constitution granted citizenship to all persons born or naturalized in the United States and equal protection under the law.
1870	The Fifteenth Amendment to the Constitution granted Negroes the right to vote.
1896	The *Plessy vs. Ferguson* decision is handed down by the U.S. Supreme Court upholding the doctrine of "separate but equal," legalizing racial segregation in public facilities as long as such accommodations for blacks were equal to those of whites.
1909	The National Association for the Advancement of Colored People (NAACP) is founded by a multiracial group of activists to fight against social, economic, and political injustice for all persons.
1954	The *Brown vs. Board of Education of Topeka, Kansas* decision is handed down by the U.S. Supreme Court overturning *Plessy vs. Ferguson* by declaring the "separate but equal" doctrine unconstitutional regarding public education and requiring the desegregation of public schools across the U.S.
1957	The Southern Christian Leadership Conference (SCLC) is formed to fight for civil rights for all persons, to end segregation, and to carry out such fights through nonviolent mass action. Dr. Martin Luther King Jr. is elected the organization's first president.
1964	The Twenty-Fourth Amendment to the Constitution outlaws the use of the poll or any other tax to deny U.S. citizens the right to vote.
1964	President Lyndon B. Johnson signs into law The Civil Rights Act of 1964, which has been called the most important piece of civil rights legislation since reconstruction. This Act is intended to end discrimination based on race, color, religion, or national origin and gives federal law enforcement agencies the power to prevent racial discrimination in employment, voting, and the use of public facilities.
1968	Dr. Martin Luther King Jr. is assassinated in Memphis, Tennessee.
1991	President George H.W. Bush signs into law The Civil Rights Act of 1991 which strengthens existing civil rights laws and provides damages in cases of intentional employment discrimination.

(Source: Center for Substance Abuse Prevention [CSAP], 2001)

between individuals in this ethnocultural group and their ancestral homeland of Africa, while the term American pays homage to their heritage in America. Table 3.1 provides a timeline of key historical dates in African American history.

Historical Perspective and Population Demographics

Transported in a Dutch ship, the first Africans to be forcibly settled as laborers in the North American British Colonies arrived in Jamestown, Virginia in 1619. During the course of their subjugation, these twenty Africans were baptized by their captors and converted to Christianity. Under English law, which governed the colony of Virginia at the time, captured individuals destined to become slaves who had been converted to Christianity were no longer considered infidels and were to be free from a life of bondage. Thus, these twenty Africans were to become members of a previously established class of colonial laborers known as indentured servants (Quarles, 1987).

At the time, indentured servitude was one of many practices considered to be an acceptable, efficient, and effective method by which to meet the growing labor demands of the burgeoning colonies. Indentured servants generally worked for their masters for 4 years and at the end of their term of service they were owed clothing, a small sum of money, and/or a plot of land (Franklin, 1974). However, by the early 1700's, many plantation owners viewed this practice as being too costly and laborers too scarce to meet the labor requirements needed to adequately maintain and expand their plantations. Alternatively, around this time, the institution of slavery had grown in popularity and was perceived as being a more cost efficient method of securing and exploiting labor power (Quarles, 1987). As compared to the practice of indentured servitude, slavery provided far greater benefits and far fewer drawbacks to plantation owners in that slaves were not owed money or land for their work, could be provided only the barest necessities for sustenance, their services were for life, and they could be replaced either through purchase, trading, or sexual relations (Boyd-Franklin, 2003; Quarles, 1987).

As such, the practice of slavery flourished in the colonies during the antebellum period, particularly in the South, which derived much of its wealth from the cultivation of agricultural products that required enormous amounts of labor power. Over two and a half centuries later, around the time of the passage of the 13th Amendment to the Constitution in 1865, which abolished slavery as a legal institution in America, the number of Negroes living in the United States had swelled to approximately four million people with almost the entire population living and working in the South (Quarles, 1987).

Between 1910 and 1930, following the Civil War, Reconstruction, and the emergence of *Jim Crow* laws designed to permanently institutionalize second-class citizenship status upon Negroes in the South, African Americans began to leave this region of the country in record numbers making their way to the Northern and, to a lesser extent, Western regions in what came to be known as *The Great Migration* (Lemann, 1991; Woodward, 2002). During this period of time, approximately 1 $\frac{1}{2}$ million Negroes left the South spurred on by thoughts of escaping from racism and violence, enhanced job opportunities, better living conditions, obtaining political rights, becoming full or complete citizens, and fulfilling dreams of crafting better lives for themselves and their families (Lemann, 1991; Taulbert, 1995). What they soon came to realize, however, was that life outside the South was a mixed bag, full of opportunities and setbacks, promise and discouragement, as well as hope and hardship, and the unavoidable reality that racial prejudice and discrimination were not solely confined to the South (Quarles, 1987).

During the 1930s, the migration of Negroes to the North and West slowed, as fewer jobs were available throughout the country as a result of the Great Depression (Lemann, 1991; Wilson, 1980). However, Negro migration picked up again with the onset of American involvement in World War II as factory and agricultural workers were needed to meet the demands of a flourishing wartime economy (Quarles, 1987). In fact, by the early 1940s the number of Negroes living outside the South had grown to almost 25% of the population (Lemann, 1991), which was considerable when compared to the early 1900s when only 10% of the Negro population lived outside this region of the country (Wilson, 1980). By the 1950's, the number of Negroes living outside the South had increased significantly as more than 50% of the population lived in the Northern and, to a lesser extent, Western regions of the country (Woodward, 2002).

Not only were Negroes leaving the South in record numbers, they were increasingly becoming more urban as they tended to settle in large metropolitan areas (Quarles, 1987; Wilson, 1980). As a result of these evolving settlement patterns, the Negro population was transformed from one that was primarily rural in the 1890s (80% rural versus 20% urban) to one that had become predominately urban in the 1950s (62% urban versus 38% rural). By the 1960s, 73% of Blacks lived in urban areas and by the 1970s this number had grown to 81% (Wilson, 1980).

Over a sixty-year period, between 1910 and 1970, approximately six million African Americans migrated from the South to the North and other regions of the country (Eldridge & Thomas, 1964; United States Census Bureau, 1975). Beginning in the 1970s and continuing through the 1980s, however, the migration of African Americans to regions outside of the South began to reverse itself, as group members began making their way back to the South. Presently, although African Americans reside in various regions throughout the country, group members primarily live and work in the South (McKinnon, 2001; United States Census Bureau, 2003). Table 3.2 below provides general population characteristics for African Americans.

Economics

After adjusting for inflation, real median household income for African Americans in 2003 was approximately $29,689. In comparison, this amount made up only 62% of the real median household income of non-Hispanic White Americans, which was approximately $47,777, and this amount was also lower than the median household income for Hispanic or Latino

Table 3.2. African American General Population Characteristics African American alone or in combination, population survey information – 2000*

Total African American Population	36,419,434
Percent of Total U.S. Population	12.9
Region	
Northeast	6,556,909
South	19,528,231
Midwest	6,838,669
West	3,495,625
Primary State Locations	
New York	3,234,165
California	2,513,041
Texas	2,493,057
Florida	2,471,730
Georgia	2,393,425
Age Distribution	
Under 18 years	11,845,257
18 to 64 years	21,693,497
65 years and older	2,880,680
Gender Distribution	
Male	17,315,333
Female	19,104,101

Education**
Males & Females (15 + years of age)

High School or Less	16,089,000
Some College (no degree)	5,422,000
Associate Degree	1,692,000
Bachelor's Degree	2,769,000
Master's Degree	852,000
Professional Degree	143,000
Doctoral Degree	106,000

	Males (age 15+)	*Females (age 15+)*
High School or Less	7,540,000	8,549,000
Some College (no degree)	2,393,000	3,029,000
Associate Degree	638,000	1,054,000
Bachelor's Degree	1,188,000	1,581,000
Master's Degree	298,000	555,000
Professional Degree	66,000	77,000
Doctoral Degree	66,000	40,000

*(McKinnon, 2001) **(U.S. Census Bureau, 2003)

Americans, which was approximately $32,997 (DeNavas-Walt, Proctor, & Mills, 2004). [Note: Median household income is influenced by many factors such as household size and number of earners]. The poverty rate for African Americans in 2003 was approximately 24.3%, which equates to over 9 million people. In contrast, the poverty rate for non-Hispanic White Americans in 2003 was approximately 8.2%, which equates to over 15 million people, and for Hispanic or Latino Americans the poverty rate was approximately 22.5%, which equates to almost 9 million people (DeNavas-Walt et al., 2004).

Despite these economic disparities, the African American middle and upper classes have grown steadily since the late 1960s with more than one-third of African American households being members of these classes. Moreover, the number of African American households determined to be in the upper income bracket (i.e., those households making between $75,000 to $99,000) have increased nearly fourfold since 1967, constituting approximately 7% of the African American population. In addition, although real median household income for African Americans is lower than for non-Hispanic White Americans and Hispanic or Latino Americans, this number has increased substantially since 1967 – rising by nearly 47%. In contrast, real median household income for non-Hispanic White Americans rose approximately 31% over this same time period. Finally, between 1992 and 1997, the number of small businesses owned by African Americans rose approximately 33% from 621,000 to 823,499 (DeNavas-Walt et al., 2004; McKinnon, 2001).

For some African Americans, however, membership in higher social classes comes with a unique set of problems and challenges including stress, frustration, isolation, and guilt. Stress may be associated with their tenuous positions in such classes as they generally have fewer resources to fall back on during harsh economic times (Boyd-Franklin, 2003; Shapiro, 2004). Frustration may be related to real or perceived unfair work environments in which artificial "glass ceilings" based on racial characteristics impede or deny occupational opportunities and advancement (Boyd-Franklin, 2003; Cose, 1993). Isolation and guilt may result from being a member of only a small group of African Americans in such classes, or may be related to feelings of having "made it" while other group members struggle to survive within or move beyond their immediate class conditions (Ford, 1997; Sue & Sue, 2003). Because of such circumstances, some middle and upper class African Americans may feel that they occupy a marginal or tenuous position in American society, in that, acceptance by White Americans and assimilation into mainstream society is an ever evolving process which may lead to happiness, frustration, or uncertainty while such acceptance and assimilation may result in them becoming separated and/or ostracized by family or other group members (Boyd-Franklin, 2003; Cose, 1993; Sue & Sue, 2003).

Health Indicators

Compared to other ethnocultural groups, African Americans generally rank at or near the bottom on a significant number of health indicators (National Center for Health Statistics, 2004). A multitude of factors contribute to poor health outcomes among African Americans including individual and community factors, cultural barriers that discourage health-seeking behavior, discrimination, and a lack of access to health care (United States Commission on Civil Rights, 1999). [Specific information regarding relationships between these factors and health considerations for African Americans will be discussed later in this chapter in more detail.]

The percentage of African Americans without health insurance in 2003 was approximately 19.4%, which equates to over 7 million people. In contrast, the percentage of non-Hispanic White Americans without health insurance in 2003 was lower and was approximately 11.1%, which equates to over 21 million people, and for Hispanic or Latino Americans the percentage was approximately 32.7%, which equates to approximately 13 million people (DeNavas-Walt et al., 2004). In 2003, employer-based health insurance coverage was available to just over 49.6% of African Americans. In contrast, the percentage of non-Hispanic White Americans with employer-based health insurance coverage was approximately 66.3%, and for Hispanic or Latino Americans the percentage was approximately 41.5% (DeNavas-Walt et al., 2004). In 2003, Medicaid health insurance coverage (i.e., government health insurance coverage for people with low incomes and resources) for African Americans was approximately 24.7%. In contrast, the percentage of non-Hispanic White Americans with Medicaid health insurance coverage was approximately 8.3%, and for Hispanic or Latino Americans the percentage was approximately 21%.

In 2000–2002, infant mortality occurred at a rate of approximately 13.5 deaths per 1,000 live births among African Americans. In contrast, the infant mortality rate for non-Hispanic White Americans was 5.7 deaths per 1,000 live births, and for Hispanic or Latino Americans the rate was 5.5 deaths per 1,000 live births during this same period (National Center for Health Statistics, 2004). Research indicates that infant deaths among African Americans may be related to Sudden Infant Death Syndrome (SIDS), congenital abnormalities, pre-term/low birth weight, problems related to complications during pregnancy, and respiratory distress syndrome (Centers for Disease Control, 2005a).

In 2002, life expectancy rates for African American males and females were approximately 68.8 and 75.6 years, respectively. In contrast, life expectancy rates for non-Hispanic White American males and females were 75.1 and 80.3 years (National Center for Health Statistics, 2004). As of 2002, the ten leading causes of death for African Americans in the United States were: 1) cardiovascular disease, 2) cancer, 3) stroke, 4) diabetes, 5) unintentional injuries, 6) homicide, 7) HIV/AIDS, 8) chronic lower respiratory disease, 9) nephritis

Table 3.3. General Economic and Health Characteristics for African Americans and Other Groups Alone or in combination population survey information – 2003*

	African Americans	Non-Hispanic Whites	Hispanics or Latinos
Total Population (2000)**	36,419,434	216,930,975	35,305,818
Median Household Income	29,689	47,777	32,997
Number in Poverty	9,108,000	15,902,000	9,051,000
Poverty Rates (percent)	24.3	8.2	22.5
Number Uninsured	7,307,000	21,582,000	13,237,000
Uninsured Rates (percent)	19.4	11.1	32.7

*(DeNavas-Walt et al., 2004) **(McKinnon, 2001)

or kidney disease, and 10) septicemia or blood poisoning (National Center for Health Statistics, 2004). Table 3.3 provides general economic and health information for African Americans and other ethnocultural groups.

ETHNOCULTURAL CHARACTERISTICS

Family Characteristics

Similar to other ethnocultural groups, family members play a pivotal role in the lives of African Americans. While individual differences certainly exist, and socioeconomic and political backgrounds may influence attitudes and behaviors, in general, African American family members promote self-reliance, a strong work ethic, and the virtues of individual as well as educational achievement. African American family members typically emphasize to children the importance of conforming to parent-defined rules, being obedient, maintaining good behavior, and being respectful to elders. Emanating from such convictions is a fundamental belief that a firm parenting style, which includes both structure and discipline, is a necessary prerequisite to raise positive-minded, healthy children. African American family members may also display a strong tendency to be overprotective of their children, due to concerns regarding racism and discrimination, and attempt to act as buffers between them and members of the outside world. However, despite such concerns, African American parents generally instill in their children the mindset that most obstacles can be overcome through hard work, diligence, and the development of educational and career goals at an early age (Lewis & Looney, 1983; Sue & Sue, 2003).

The African American family structure often extends beyond the immediate nuclear configuration encompassing both extended family members (e.g., grandparents, aunts, cousins) and non-related persons or "fictive kin," who are also considered to be members of the family (Hatchett, Cochran, & Jackson, 1991; Hill, 1997). Generally speaking, such extended family members and fictive kin often provide support services to one another and, in some cases, willingly care for sick family members during times of need including assuming their responsibilities until such individuals recover sufficiently (Purnell & Paulanka, 2005). Strong kinship bonds between group members also frequently result in the adoption of orphaned or rejected children and the elderly by relatives and neighbors (Hill, 1997). Older adults, particularly grandmothers, are generally respected for their knowledge and insight and may play a significant role in the family by providing nurturing, childcare, and/or other support services to family members.

Recently, the support services typically provided by extended family members and fictive kin have been especially needed by many African American families as the percentage of families headed by single parents has been steadily increasing. For instance, in 1970 over 68% of African American families were headed by married couples, however, by 1980 this percentage had dropped to 56% and by 1994 this percentage had fallen to approximately 47% (United States Census Bureau, 1995). Among lower-class African American families the percentage headed by single parents, who are primarily women, has grown to over 70%. Moreover, single women account for nearly 60% of all childbirths among African American families, with the majority of these women being teenagers (Sue & Sue, 2003). As previously stated, extended family members and fictive kin often play a pivotal role in providing needed support services to family members during times of need. Research suggests that extended family networks are one of the many strengths found within the African American family structure (Billingsley, 1992; Dickerson, 1995; Hill, 1997). Other strengths of such families include an adaptability of family roles, strong kinship bonds, a strong work and achievement ethic, and a strong religious orientation (Billingsley, 1992; Hildebrand, Phenice, Gray, & Hines, 1996; McCollum, 1997).

Cultural Values / Ethnic Orientation

As a whole, Americans generally share many of the same basic cultural values; however, members of varying ethnocultural groups may hold certain values in higher esteem than others. Understanding those cultural values deemed important by ethnocultural group members may provide disaster response workers insight into individual perceptions, interpretations, and behaviors following a disaster.

African Americans may vary greatly in the degree to which they adopt mainstream cultural values. Moreover, they may also differ in terms of their adoption of those cultural values and traditions typically held in high regard by group members (Sue & Sue, 2003). In general, however, the following key cultural values are commonly held in high regard by most group members: 1) strong kinship bonds, 2) communal orientation, 3) strong religious orientation, 4) importance of traditions, 5) strong work ethic, 6) high individual and academic achievement, 7) respect for elders, 8) harmony with nature, 9) holistic thinking, and 10) adherence to mainstream American cultural norms and values (Billingsley, 1992; Dickerson, 1995; Hildebrand et al., 1996; Hill, 1997; McCollum, 1997).

As opposed to a mainstream American cultural orientation that tends to promote individualism and materialism, African Americans generally embrace a communal orientation, which is more social in nature and stresses unity, affectivity, and collective ownership (Scott, 2003). Such an orientation values the input and abilities of group members and the importance of group togetherness (Boykin, 1983, 1986; Jackson, McCullough, Gurin, & Broman, 1991). A strong religious orientation among African Americans is focused on the belief in a greater power than oneself, concern for the well-being and care of others, and the collective power of the group to help individuals improve their lives (Boykin, 1983). For most African Americans, the church is the epicenter of this collective orientation and where such beliefs are made manifest as, throughout their history in America, the church has played a key role in improving the lives of millions of African Americans by addressing the social, economic, and political needs of group members (Hill, 1997; Lincoln & Mamiya, 1990; Taylor & Chatters, 1991).

Religion

As stated above, the church is often an important institution in the African American community. Most group members believe that regular involvement in church activities is related to positive mental and physical health. Moreover, many African Americans believe in the power of prayer to overcome illness and to maintain a connection with God. As many African Americans consider themselves to be spiritual beings, God is considered to be the supreme healer while sickness may be an indication of separateness from God. Having faith in God is also viewed as a major source of inner strength (Purnell & Paulanka, 2005).

For most African Americans prayer is the primary vehicle by which they commune with God. Prayer also reflects and reaffirms their faith and trust in God. Some African Americans also believe that through prayer and faith some people have the ability to heal others who are sick by the "laying of hands" on those individuals. Moreover, some African Americans believe that during prayer and religious celebration the spirit of God may speak through them to others in a foreign tongue, commonly referred to as "speaking in tongues," at which time only they or another righteous person have the ability to interpret the meaning of such language (Purnell & Paulanka, 2005).

The predominant form of religious faith practiced by African Americans is Protestantism, one of the three major divisions in Christianity, which also includes Roman Catholicism and Eastern Orthodoxy. Historically, this term refers to the group of dissenters who separated from the Roman Catholic Church during the Reformation or those individuals who share similar doctrines or ideologies. Examples of the major denominations that encompass this faith include Anglicans, Baptists, Lutherans, Methodists, and Presbyterians (Boyd-Franklin, 1989). Examples of other religious faiths practiced by a significant number of African Americans include the Jehovah's Witnesses, Church of God in Christ, Seventh Day Adventist, Pentecostal, Apostolic, Roman Catholic, Islam, and Buddhism (Taylor & Chatters, 1991).

General Communication Styles

The primary language used by African Americans in the United States is Standard English. However, it has been suggested that some African Americans also use a version of this language that differs from Standard English in terms of grammar, pronunciation, and vocabulary (Baugh, 1983; Johnson, 1971). This different version or dialect has been referred to as African American Vernacular English (AAVE) (Louden, 2000). Clinicians should be aware of such considerations when providing treatment services and, if necessary, ask questions to clarify meanings of words not clearly understood or as a means to facilitate verbal communication between themselves and clients (Paniagua, 1998).

In general, African Americans tend to limit discussions of their feelings or opinions to trusted family members and friends. There is a strong belief in the importance of respecting the privacy of others. Moreover, issues that arise as a result of family problems or troubles may be viewed as private and not appropriate for discussion outside of the family context (Boyd-Franklin, 2003). [The expression passed down by elders to succeeding generations of African American children that both encapsulates and reinforces the importance of upholding such a belief is simply stated as follows: "*Do not air our dirty laundry in public.*"]

When speaking, some African Americans make regular use of body movements to assist them in expressing themselves, with speech tending to be both boisterous and dynamic (Johnson, 1971). However, during social interactions, some African Americans may be reluctant to maintain eye contact with individuals to whom they are speaking for a variety of reasons including showing respect for elders and authority figures in recognition of the authority-subordinate relationship. In some cases, this behavior may reflect historical survival considerations, particularly in the South as African Americans who looked Whites directly in the eyes may have been perceived as being disrespectful and subsequently beaten or killed for such actions, or because some group members may believe that direct eye contact conveys the unintended message of aggressiveness (Johnson, 1971; Wilson, 1996). When greeted, some African Americans prefer to be addressed formally and may take offense to the presumption of a close personal relationship if referred to solely by their first name. Also, some African Americans display a tendency toward being present-oriented, which may result in relaxed standards regarding time commitments (Purnell & Paulanka, 2005). [Some group members refer to such relaxed time standards as CP or "Colored People's" time.]

Food

Besides the obvious need for sustenance, African Americans use food to celebrate birthdays, holidays, and other special occasions (Purnell & Paulanka, 2005). Historical and cultural influences, including responses to racial and economic oppression as well as traditional African eating habits, have shaped the diet of African Americans in the United States. A common term that has been used to describe African American cuisine that emerged from southern roots is "soul food." This may include the following types of food: fried chicken, barbecued ribs, ham, salmon croquettes, grits, chitterlings, black-eyed peas and rice, various types of greens (including chard, collard, mustard, spinach and turnip), okra, sweet potatoes, yams, and corn bread with ham hocks and necks being used to provide seasoning to soups, beans, and boiled greens (Lassiter, 1998). For some African Americans, however, this food may not be preferred. For those group members that practice Islam or other religious faiths, or simply because of their own personal preference, the eating of pork or pork by-products is shunned (Purnell & Paulanka, 2005).

Holidays / Celebrations

Most African Americans participate in many of the same holidays, cultural events, and festivities as other Americans including Memorial Day, the Fourth of July, Thanksgiving, and Christmas. In addition to their participation in such events and activities, they may also take part in specific cultural festivities such as Juneteenth and/or Kwanzaa.

Although the Emancipation Proclamation freed slaves in 1863, this only occurred in those states that were rebelling against the Union. Thus, it was not until the passage of the 13th amendment to the Constitution in 1865 that slavery was completely abolished as a legal institution in the United States or in any place subject to its jurisdiction. Juneteenth pays homage to the day in which all remaining slaves throughout America were finally freed from bondage, which occurred on June 19, 1865. Kwanzaa is a celebration that focuses on the importance of traditional African values including family, community, and self-improvement. In addition, this event reaffirms the value of African American people as a whole, their ancestors, culture, and their contributions to American society.

HEALTH ISSUES AND SERVICE PROVISION

Health Considerations

African Americans are overrepresented among those individuals suffering from either chronic conditions or preventable diseases (Bowen-Reid & Harrell, 2002). Research suggests that consistent exposure to stress may be related to poor health outcomes among African Americans including high blood pressure, diabetes, hypertension, stroke, and heart disease (Anderson, McNeilly, & Myers, 1991; Harrell, Hall, & Taliaferro, 2003; Jackson et al., 1996; Krieger & Sidney, 1996). Other factors that may contribute to poor health outcomes among group members include racism and discrimination, cultural barriers that discourage health-seeking behavior and a lack of access to necessary health care services (United States Commission on Civil Rights, 1999).

Racism is grounded in the belief that individuals who are members of a particular racial/ethnic group are inherently superior or inferior to members of a different racial/ethnic group (Schaefer & Lamm, 1998). Discrimination is the behavioral manifestation of such beliefs through the denial of opportunities and equal rights to non-group members based on racial/ethnic considerations (Harrell, 2000; Schaefer & Lamm, 1998). Racism and discrimination occur in various ways and operate at many different levels in American society including individual, social, economic, and political (Jones, 1997). The effects of racism vary by individual experience but may include racism-related life events, vicarious racism experiences, daily racism microstressors, chronic contextual stress, and collective and transgenerational transmission of individual and group experiences (Harrell, 2000). With respect to African American health issues related to racism and discrimination, research suggests that preparation for, adjustment to, and/or coping with possible daily occurrences of such events may inflict a profound psychological toll on the African American psyche leading to higher levels of psychological distress and lower levels of both physical and psychological well-being (Brown et al., 2000; Williams, Yu, Jackson, & Anderson, 1997).

Attendant physical and psychological responses to racism and discrimination may be apparent or external including anger, hostility, or aggression, potentially leading to deadly non-apparent or internal physiological or psychological responses including increased cardiovascular activity, frustration, or depression (Clark, Anderson, Clark, & Williams, 1999; Cose, 1993; Scott, 2003). Other internal responses to such occurrences may include avoidant coping behaviors (avoidance or denial of such stressors), anxiety, hostility, and heart disease, as well as somatic symptoms such as headaches or chest pains (Bowen-Reid & Harrell, 2002; Clark et al., 1999; Cose, 1993). Also, for some group members, maladaptive coping strategies may be employed such as licit and illicit substance use/abuse, suicide, or homicide (Bowen-Reid & Harrell, 2002; Clark et al., 1999).

With respect to treatment services from health-care professionals, many African Americans as well as many members of other racial and ethnic minority groups, generally have a profoundly different experience within the health care system than non-Hispanic White Americans. African Americans are more likely to be uninsured (in part due to lower incomes) and even when insured at the same levels as non-Hispanic White Americans are likely to receive a lower standard of care for similar conditions or less care overall (Agency for Healthcare Research and Quality, 2004). For example, research results indicate that African Americans suffering from kidney disease are less likely to be referred to kidney transplant centers than non-Hispanic White Americans with similar health conditions. In such cases, following two to three years of dialysis treatment, only 35% of African American men, as compared to 60% of non-Hispanic White American men, and 31% of African American women, as compared to 56% of non-Hispanic White American women, were referred to such centers for kidney transplants (Congressional Black Caucus Foundation, 2005). Moreover, African Americans are also less likely to receive appropriate treatment for heart disease, as compared to non-Hispanic White Americans (Agency for Healthcare Research and Quality, 2004).

Health Considerations / Special Disorders

Acquired immunodeficiency syndrome (AIDS), a major public health pandemic affecting more than 42 million people worldwide, is caused by the human immunodeficiency virus (HIV). HIV is transmitted by blood, bodily fluid, and/or sexual contact with HIV-infected individuals. Typically, HIV-infected individuals are asymptomatic for many years (Karon, Fleming, Steketee, & DeCock, 2001). Ethnocultural minority populations, particularly African Americans, are disproportionately affected by the HIV/AIDS epidemic (DeNavas-Walt et al., 2004).

Although originally considered to be a disease primarily affecting white gay males, African Americans and other ethnocultural minority group members in the United States have been severely impacted by the HIV/AIDS pandemic, as evidenced by the exceedingly high infection and death rates within their communities over the last decade (Centers for Disease Control, 2001; Karon et al., 2001). Although African Americans comprise approximately 12% of the U.S. population, they account for over 50% of the total number of new cases of HIV infection reported in America (Centers for Disease Control, 2001). Moreover, AIDS claims the lives of thousands of African Americans each year and is the leading cause of death among African American women between 25–34 years of age and African American men between 35–44 years of age (National Center for Health Statistics, 2002). The death rates for African Americans from HIV/AIDS are more than seven times that for non-Hispanic White Americans (Centers for Disease Control, 2005b).

In the United States, adolescents and young adults are at increased risk of HIV infection as a result of their early initiation and participation in sexual activities; risky sexual behavior practices, including the failure to use condoms consistently; use of alcohol, tobacco, and other drugs; and injection drug use (Centers for Disease Control, 1998; Holtzman, Mathis, Kann, Collins, & Kolbe, 1995; Jemmott & Jemmott, 2000; Miller, Forehand, & Kotchick, 2000; Murphy, Rotheram-Borus, & Reid, 1998). It has been estimated that at least half of the newly reported cases of HIV infection occur among individuals under the age of 25, with the virus commonly spread through sexual transmission (Johnson, McCaul, & Klein, 2002; Rosenberg, Biggar, & Goedert, 1994). African American youth, in particular, are disproportionately affected by HIV/AIDS as they represent 67% of the HIV infections reported among youth between the ages of 13 to 19 and 49% of the AIDS cases reported among all youth in this same age group (Office of National AIDS Policy Report, 2000).

Among African Americans, the most common modes of transmission of HIV/AIDS are either through heterosexual contact or injection drug use. Sadly, survey findings suggest that many African Americans may be unaware of the fact that they are infected and, thus, may unwittingly infect other people. Thus, efforts to increase individual knowledge, prevention initiatives, and the means by which to access appropriate medical care are sorely needed. Moreover, community involvement is critical to assist those individuals at increased risk of contracting the virus to obtain needed health-care services (Karon et al., 2001).

Other health-related conditions that disproportionately affect African Americans include heart disease and cancer (Chatters, 1991; DeNavas-Walt et al., 2004). The death rates for African Americans from heart disease are 40 percent higher than for non-Hispanic White Americans and the death rates from all cancers are 30 percent higher for African Americans than for non-Hispanic White Americans (Centers for Disease Control, 2005c; National Center for Health Statistics, 1998). Research suggests that such health disparities among African Americans, as compared to non-Hispanic White Americans, may be related to individual health behaviors, genetic variations, cultural factors, economic inequities, and environmental factors (Centers for Disease Control, 2005c).

Also, as compared to non-Hispanic White Americans, African Americans are more likely to be victims of all types of crime, particularly violent crime (Council of Economic Advisers for the President's Initiative on Race, 1998). The largest disparity between the two groups with respect to all health issues is related to the disproportionately high number of homicide deaths to which African Americans fall victim to each year. To illustrate the magnitude of this disparity, in 1995 African Americans were *six times* more likely than non-Hispanic White Americans to be victims of a homicide-related death.

Research suggests that residential segregation may create and exacerbate environmental conditions that lead to violent crime. Moreover, high rates of concentrated poverty, male joblessness, and residential instability among African Americans may lead to high rates of violent crime and an increase in single-parent households. The combination of all of these factors may account for elevated levels of violent crime in African American neighborhoods (Sampson & Wilson, 1995). In addition, high rates of criminal victimization and exposure to violent crime, homicide, police harassment, and incarceration may have adverse physical and mental health consequences for African Americans. Indirect victimization through exposure to scenes of violence may also have adverse mental health effects for group members (Williams & Williams-Morris, 2000).

In addition to health and environmental events that impact African Americans, African American youth are at increased risk of negative physical and mental health outcomes. Adolescence is a tumultuous period for many African American youth, as they must overcome obstacles related to poverty, illiteracy, and racism. In addition, such youth are negatively affected by premature deaths related to homicides, suicides, and sexually related transmitted diseases. Homicides are the leading cause of death among African American youth between the ages of 15–24 (Thornton, Craft, Dahlberg, Lynch, & Baer, 2000). With respect to suicide, between 1980 and 1992, suicide rates increased to over twice that of other teenagers. Moreover, when African American youth engage in sexual relations, they are more likely than other teenage groups to contract a sexually transmitted disease (Harvey & Rauch, 1997). Finally, economic opportunities for such youth are severely limited as unemployment rates among African American youth typically range from 37%–50% (Harvey & Rauch, 1997; Sue & Sue, 2003).

Health Considerations / Communication Styles

Open and honest communication between patients and physicians is critical in the delivery of effective health care services. However, as compared to non-Hispanic White Americans, African Americans are more likely to report that their physicians were inconsiderate of their thoughts or feelings, that the information provided by such individuals was ambiguous or confusing, and that they were uncomfortable asking questions about their condition and/or the proposed treatment. African Americans are also more likely than non-Hispanic White Americans to report that during their visits to health-care facilities, employees treated them disrespectfully by speaking rudely to them, belittling them, or by simply ignoring them (Health Policy Institute, 2004).

As compared to non-Hispanic White Americans, African Americans are less likely to seek medical care and when treated may be hesitant to inform physicians of long-standing illnesses or health-related problems. The hesitancy of some African Americans to seek medical care and then to be less than forthcoming when such care is provided may stem from long-standing group beliefs that largely White health care providers lack understanding of cultural characteristics. As such, it is important for health care providers to keep in mind that patient health decisions may be influenced by a variety of factors, such as individual or group experiences, cultural characteristics, religious beliefs, acculturation, or mistrust of medicine (Health Policy Institute, 2004).

As a means of addressing health-related communication issues with respect to African Americans and other members of racial/ethnic minority groups, research findings suggest the implementation of the following practices: 1) Develop education programs that aim to increase patients' knowledge of and best methods to access and obtain needed health care services, 2) Provide culturally appropriate and relevant training and education to ethnocultural minority group members, through the use of community-based organizations, regarding common practices of health-care providers as well as necessary information that may help empower them during the treatment decision-making process; and 3) Develop or modify existing training procedures and manuals to provide cross-cultural education information to health-care providers regarding important cultural values, beliefs, behaviors, and practices of ethnocultural minority group members as well as relevant information to assist them in opening lines of communication with group members (Health Policy Institute, 2004).

Mental Health Care

Although approximately one-third of all Americans with a mental health illness or problem receive needed care, only 50% of African Americans receive such care as compared to non-Hispanic White Americans (United States Department of Health and Human Services, 1999). Those African Americans who seek mental health care services are more likely to use emergency services or seek care from a primary care physician rather than accessing a mental health provider directly, a fact that may contribute to their under-representation in outpatient mental health care settings and over-representation among inpatient hospitalizations (United States Department of Health and Human Services, 1999). In addition, African Americans are also less likely to receive mental health counseling or psychotherapy and are more likely to receive pharmacotherapy as compared to non-Hispanic White Americans (Richardson, Anderson, Flaherty, & Bell, 2003).

Research findings indicate that African Americans are over-represented among high-need populations, which may increase their risk for mental illnesses (Snowden, 2001). For example, in its annual survey of America's cities, the U.S. Conference of Mayors found that in 2003 approximately 49% of homeless individuals were African American (Ahmed & Toro, 2004; United States Conference of Mayors, 2003), and among those individuals in prisons or jail in that same year, the National Urban League reported that approximately 44% were African American males (National Urban League, 2003). Despite such adversities, however, research suggests that African Americans appear to have no greater rates of mental illness than do non-Hispanic White Americans (Neighbors, 1991; Robins & Reiger, 1991; Snowden, 2001).

In addition to an overrepresentation among high-need populations, African Americans are also faced with a multitude of barriers to mental health treatment which may contribute to an underutilization of mental health services including, but not limited to, limited access and availability of mental health services, poorer quality of services, lack of or inadequate health insurance (Snowden & Thomas, 2000), racism and discrimination that thwarts equitable service delivery and access to care, cultural mistrust of the medical and mental health community based upon a history of oppression and discrimination (Grier & Cobbs, 1968; Ridley, 1984), societal stigma associated with mental health problems (United States Department of Health and Human Services, 1999), the perception that treatment is intrusive, misdiagnosis and overrepresentation of African Americans among specific clinical populations and inpatient hospital admissions (Garb, 1997; Lindsey & Paul, 1989; Neighbors, Jackson, Campbell, & Williams, 1989), and lack of cultural awareness and sensitivity among mental health care workers (Swartz et al., 1998). Of those African Americans who do seek mental health treatment, they are more likely to deny or downplay mental health problems or difficulties, they are more likely to express their problems through physical or somatic complaints and symptoms, and once in treatment they are at increased risk for early termination (Snowden, 2001). As a result of these factors, African Americans tend to seek support during times of distress through more traditional sources of support including family members and friends, community elders, or through spiritual/religious guidance and counseling or prayer (Bowen-Reid & Harrell, 2002; Boyd-Franklin, 1989). Some research suggests that those individuals who maintain a strong spiritual orientation and attend church regularly tend to have fewer-stress-related physical and mental health problems (Williams, Larson, Buckler, Heckmann, & Pyle, 1991).

Research regarding mental health service utilization has also identified sociodemographic factors within the African American community that may impact service use. In general, females tend to seek mental health services more than males (McClennen & Glenn, 1997), young adults utilize services at a higher rate compared to older adults (Black, Rabins, German, McGuire, & Roca, 1997), and employed individuals and those with a higher education tend to access mental health care at higher rates (Scheffler & Miller, 1991). Moreover, based on their history of racism, discrimination, and oppression in the United States, African Americans may view mental health services as being undesirable and ineffective, particularly among those group members who continue to feel excluded and oppressed (Hines-Martin, 2002; Wallen, 1992). Such perceptions may be well-founded given the fact that ethnic and racial minorities in general still face social and economic inequities, increased rates of violence and poverty, and the continuous effects of racism and discrimination – all of which are stressful life events that place minorities at increased risk for mental health related problems (United States Department of Health and Human Services, 1999). Furthermore, research also suggests that the internalization of racist and mainstream cultural stereotypes by group members may adversely affect social and psychological functioning by increasing psychological distress (Fischer et al., 1996; Steele, 1997; Taylor, Henderson, & Jackson, 1991; Taylor & Jackson, 1991).

A study by Hines-Martin, Malone, Kim, and Brown-Piper (2003) identified and highlighted additional individual, environmental, and institutional barriers to mental health access and treatment among African Americans. Individual barriers may consist of a cultural mistrust of mental health providers; denial avoidance, or repression of problems; unwillingness to disclose problems; limited awareness of possible resources or strategies to seeking care; physical or cognitive limitations that impede the ability to seek care; economic obstacles; competing responsibilities that may minimize help-seeking behavior; and noncompliance or discontinuation of treatment. Environmental factors include being influenced by family or community members to seek help through more traditional means, such as seeking religious advice or pastoral counseling rather than direct mental health services, and the difficulties that may arise in terms of finding appropriate resources needed to receive treatment. Institutional barriers to treatment may include time limitations (i.e., length of time before care is available); capacity of providers to provide services; negative impact of cultural biases and attitudes of providers that may impede willingness to seek and/or accept care; and provisions to care that may inhibit access or use of mental health services.

Given the underutilization of mental health services by African Americans, recommendations to improve, increase, and provide adequate and appropriate care include: 1) improve knowledge, understanding, and incorporation of African American values and beliefs in treatment (Comas-Diaz, 1992; Mays & Albee, 1992), 2) improve cultural competence of mental health care providers, 3) through education and training, attempt to improve the ability of treatment providers to identify and make appropriate diagnoses, thereby, hopefully decreasing misdiagnosis and use of inappropriate treatments, 4) provide better education about available services and programs, 5) collaborate with community leaders and members to assist with mental health outreach efforts, 6) improve geographic availability of services, 7) integrate mental health care with primary care in order to improve direct access to needed care, 8) coordinate care to particular high-need and vulnerable populations within the community (i.e., homeless and incarcerated individuals), 9) improve and expand scientific research to better understand the mental health needs of African Americans, 10) through knowledge and information improve language and communication issues between providers and group members, and 11) incorporate spirituality and promote the strengths of African Americans within the context of therapy (i.e., positive ethnic identity, traditional values, role of the family, etc.) (United States Department of Health and Human Services, 1999).

In addition, as stated throughout, spirituality and religion are important factors in the lives of many African American family members providing emotional support and comfort in the face of oppression. Moreover, participation in religious activities affords individuals opportunities for self-expression, leadership, and community involvement (Hill, 1997). Thus, if a mental health worker becomes aware that family members maintain strong religious beliefs and/or are heavily involved in religious activities, they may want to enlist the aid of a religious leader (e.g., priest, pastor, or minister) to assist individuals in addressing mental health issues.

Valid Assessment Instruments

As a means to conduct effective assessments of ethnocultural group members, physicians and practitioners should be considerate of and attempt to understand members' personal and cultural histories and contexts. When providing treatment services they should be mindful of the fact that some group members may be less than forthcoming when providing health-care information, thus, they should thoroughly review patients' histories, discuss past or present health-related problems, and familiarize themselves with the possible treatment methods employed by ethnocultural group members, including self-care practices. They should also become familiar with the literature regarding potential problems and possible limitations related to the use of standardized testing measures with ethnocultural group members. In addition, they should attempt to identify culturally related strengths at the individual, interpersonal, and environmental levels and consider potential influences of culture on responses to standardized assessment questions and tests (Hays, 2001).

In general, when conducting assessments of African American mental-health issues, care should to taken to avoid focusing primarily on identifying individual pathologies. Instead, a more balanced approach that recognizes individual strengths, resilience, and resourcefulness should be considered. Assessments should attempt to understand health-care needs from a framework that takes into account cultural influences, including cultural strengths and barriers to treatment. Appropriate clinical instruments should also be utilized that account for specific cultural norms and values (Parham, 2002).

Special Therapies / Healers

Although most African Americans commonly consult mainstream health care professionals when seeking treatment for illness or sickness, some group members may also use home remedies or consult folk healers to treat some health-related conditions. In addition, some African Americans may view mainstream health care professionals as outsiders and therefore they may be cautious or suspicious of receiving health care services from such individuals (Purnell & Paulanka, 2005). Alternatively, folk medicines may be viewed as effective health remedies and folk healers as health-care specialists capable of providing necessary relief from the negative symptoms associated with medical and mental health problems (Baker & Lightfoot, 1993; Wilkinson & Spurlock, 1986).

Types of folk medicines used by some group members to treat or cure health-related illnesses include herbs, teas, or other natural substances. Folk healers may be consulted for the treatment and care of physical and mental health issues, particularly if spiritual factors are believed to be the underlying cause of such illnesses (Dana, 1993).

Folk practitioners may be spiritual leaders, grandparents, elders from the community, voodoo doctors, or priests. Regardless of socioeconomic status, some African Americans respect and value the abilities of such individuals and seek their assistance when addressing health-related problems. For those African Americans who consult such individuals, the most common type of folk healer contacted to assist them in treating illnesses or problems is the faith healer or spiritualist. Other types of folk healers include independent generalists who deal with physical, psychological, or spiritual problems that stem from "unnatural causes" (Snow, 1978) as well as specialized independents (e.g., midwives, herbalists, neighborhood prophets) who assist with childbirths, supply health remedies, counseling, prophesy, and prayer for health-related issues or problems. Faith healers, who generally function within groups such as religious organizations, include spiritualists, Voodoo or "Hoodoo" Priests or Priestesses, and Black Muslim or Black Hebrew Healers. To a lesser extent, particularly in the rural South, other specialized healers (e.g., bone-setters, blood-stoppers) may be consulted to treat physical ailments (Koss-Chioino, 2000).

Considerations for Medications / Therapies

It is important for physicians to be aware of ethnic differences in metabolism and those cultural factors that may impact the physiological and psychological effectiveness of medications (Hays, 2001). Results from ethnopsychopharmacology studies suggest that African Americans may metabolize antidepressant medications in such a way that makes them more sensitive to the adverse effects of such medications. These outcomes may be related to differential treatment providers and/or prescription practices as research suggests that when treated by primary care physicians, rather than psychiatrists for issues related to mental health, African Americans may receive poor or less effective mental health care services (Wang, Berglund, & Kessler, 2000).

Results from research studies also suggest that African Americans may respond to or metabolize alcohol, antihypertensives, beta-blockers, psychotropic drugs, and caffeine differently as compared to non-Hispanic White Americans (Kalow, 1991; Levy, 1993). In particular, some African Americans receiving services for mental health issues have displayed a higher incidence of extrapyramidal effects with haloperidol decanoate than non-Hispanic White Americans. Moreover, some group members have been found to be more susceptible to tri-cyclic antidepressant delirium, showing higher blood levels and faster therapeutic response than similarly treated non-Hispanic White Americans. As a result of these occurrences, some group members may also be more likely to experience toxic side effects more frequently than non-Hispanic White Americans. Being mindful of such considerations, African American clients receiving mental health services should be closely monitored for incidences of side effects related to tricyclics and other psychotropic medications.

Finally, some African Americans may view the use of medications as too impersonal when seeking treatment to address health-related issues. If medications are prescribed, it is important to discuss with group members their treatment expectations, as well as the potential benefits, shortcomings, and side effects related to the use of such medications (Paniagua, 1998). In addition to educating patients about the medicines they are prescribed, providers should make efforts to address any medication-related concerns that patients may have, such as the equivalency of generic and brand-name drugs or the importance of properly adhering to the dosing regimen.

Interventions / Approach

To more effectively meet the treatment needs of ethnocultural group members, health care professionals should be culturally competent – that is, they should be aware of varying cultural values and treatment approaches that may be culturally specific including being mindful of cultural communication styles, as they may impact therapeutic interactions with clients (Jones Warren, 2002). With respect to African Americans, health care professionals should be aware of the important role that religion and, in particular, religious organizations play in the lives of group members as they often provide support services during times of need. Group members may derive psychosocial resources and strength through affiliation with such organizations, as they may provide assistance in meeting health-care needs and support in combating the adverse consequences of racial discrimination. In addition, health care professionals should be aware of those health-related illnesses that disproportionately affect African Americans and the most commonly prescribed medications to treat such illnesses, possible contraindications, and side effects. Moreover, as suggested above, they should also be aware of the reluctance of some African Americans to follow prescribed treatment plans, as group members may take medications only "as needed" or deviate in other ways from directed treatment schedules (Purnell & Paulanka, 2005).

For many African Americans, informal support networks, including friends, neighbors, coworkers, and church members provide necessary assistance during times of need (Billingsley, 1992; Chatters, Taylor, & Neighbors, 1989). Members of such informal networks may provide support to group members in a number of different ways including helping individuals define the complexity and significance of a personal problem, moderating the effects of stress, and, when necessary, providing referrals to health-care providers (Doherty, 1992; Steinglass, 1992). As illustrated by the results of a study conducted by Neighbors and Jackson (1984), when seeking to obtain outside assistance to address problems or meet individual or family needs, a significant number of African Americans used informal help only (44%) or a combination of both informal and professional help (44%), whereas a small number (4%) used professional support only and some (8.7%) did not receive any outside assistance. As such, the results of this study appear to suggest that informal helpers function as a critical link for African Americans to social service agencies (Taylor, Burns Hardison, & Chatters, 1996; Taylor, Neighbors, & Broman, 1989).

Generally, with respect to those group members typically more likely to seek treatment for health-related issues, African American women are more likely than men to seek both informal and professional help; older respondents are less likely than younger respondents to seek informal help only; persons with physical health problems are more likely than persons with other types of problems to seek both informal and professional assistance, and those with emotional problems are less likely to seek help from either source (Neighbors & Jackson, 1996).

ISSUES IN DISASTER RELIEF

Special Considerations for Disasters / Trauma

Impoverished individuals are generally more susceptible to the harmful effects of disasters and suffer more long-term residual and negative effects than members of higher-income groups (Bolin & Stanford, 1998). These individuals typically lose a much larger percentage of their material assets and are generally less able to access necessary help following a disaster (Wisner, 1993). Barriers to obtaining assistance may be related to a lack of familiarity with and knowledge of how and where to obtain needed support services.

With respect to African Americans in particular, disaster relief workers should consider the fact that in 2003 approximately 9 million group members lived in poverty and over 7 million were without any health insurance. Additionally, when providing necessary support services to African Americans following a disaster, relief workers should be mindful that group members generally maintain strong connections in their communities and during times of crisis they are likely to turn to a community organization such as the church for needed assistance. Thus, disaster relief workers may want to consider coordinating their individual and community disaster relief efforts with community leaders and local churches.

Disaster relief workers should also be aware that although African American nuclear and extended family members are chiefly responsible for the welfare of the family, fictive kin may also play an important role in the lives of family members. Following a disaster, if such persons have been adversely impacted, many African American families may be left without their previous support networks. Therefore, helping individuals reunite with both family and fictive kin may be one way to reestablish such family connections and help to ensure mutual support.

In addition to the aforementioned factors, disaster relief workers should also be aware of some of the cultural grief responses of African Americans. For most African Americans, a person's death may not end their connection with that individual, particularly if they were a member of the family, a close friend, or good acquaintance. For example, it is not uncommon for some group members to attempt to communicate with the dead, especially if the deceased was a relative. Moreover, upon hearing of the death of a relative or close friend, it is not uncommon for some group members to respond by fainting. Generally, such reactions do not require medical attention but instead are more of an indication of a severe emotional shock after receipt of such information. Some African Americans may also internalize their grief and, thus, be less likely to express their emotions openly and publicly (Purnell & Paulanka, 2005).

Rural / Urban Considerations for Disaster Care

Although similar in many respects, differences between rural and urban African Americans may impact disaster relief efforts. Approximately one million African Americans live in rural areas in the United States and over 95% of these individuals live in the South. Such individuals may be particularly disadvantaged, as compared to group members living in urban areas, with respect to economic considerations, education, and health-care.

Analysis of demographic information indicates that approximately 30% of rural African American families live in poverty, which is almost three times the percentage of urban African American families. As compared to urban African American families, rural family median income is a little less than two-thirds of their urban counterparts. Moreover, on average, rural African Americans are less educated and have higher rates of unemployment than urban African Americans with approximately 60% of such individuals working in unskilled jobs. Finally, with respect to those rural African Americans who reside in the South, the quality of housing available to them is generally not as good as that found in other regions of the country (Dillman & Hobbs, 1982; Lawton, 1980; Phillips, 1996).

With respect to family characteristics, rural African American families are more likely to be comprised of both parents and have larger extended family networks than urban African American families. Many rural African American families residing in the South, in particular, have often lived in the same communities for generations and typically live closer to their relatives than members of African American families living in other regions of the country (Boyd-Franklin, 2003; Chatters & Taylor, 1993; Taylor & Chatters, 1991). As such, these families may have stronger family and social support networks than those African American families residing in other regions of the country.

In general, rural areas lack adequate medical providers and mental health care facilities to meet the needs of their residents. As such, individuals living in rural areas may have less access to health care, fewer community services and resources available to them and they may be more isolated from those community resources that are available than individuals living in urban communities (Hart, 1994). Individuals living in rural areas are more likely to suffer from higher rates of depression and anxiety, higher rates of alcohol abuse and dependence, and higher rates of infant mortality than residents of urban areas (American Psychological Association, 1999). Rural hospitals are also more likely to treat larger numbers of uninsured patients than urban hospitals as rural areas typically have higher percentages of self-employed and uninsured individuals than do urban areas (Urban Institute, 2001).

Regarding African American health considerations, in particular, research suggests that group members living in rural areas suffer from higher rates of diabetes and hypertension and maintain far less control over these conditions as compared to those members living in urban areas (Mainous, King, Garr, & Pearson, 2004). Moreover, group members who reside in rural areas have been found to display higher psychophysiologic symptoms, suffer from more depressive symptoms and demonstrate lower well-being as compared to urban African Americans (Neff, 1984; Neff & Husaini, 1987). Environmental factors may be related to both higher levels of depression and helplessness including exposure to chronic stressors related to poverty, prejudice, and discrimination rather than more acute stressors or life events. In addition, dissatisfaction with one's community appears to have a greater influence on mental distress among African Americans residing in rural areas than transient stress. However, among African Americans living in urban areas, life events are better predictors of depressive symptoms than community satisfaction. However, it is important to note that African Americans living in disadvantaged and often segregated urban environments face unique challenges as well, particularly in the erosion of social institutions (i.e., public schools), lack of economic opportunity, inadequate healthcare and social services within the community, and unequal access to available resources, to name a few.

For both rural and urban African Americans, strong social support networks were found to be associated with significant declines in depressive symptoms (Linn, Husaini, Whitten-Stovall, & Broomes, 1989). Moreover, low-income African Americans living in rural areas, in particular, are more likely to supplement prescribed medications with a variety of home remedies and herbs to treat ailments than similarly-situated group members living in urban areas. Finally, for both rural and urban African Americans, prayer is a commonly utilized method to treat illness and sickness along with seeking assistance from relatives, a significant other, or a religious figure (Snow, 1985).

Suggested Guidelines for Service Providers

Table 3.4 highlights a set of suggested guidelines to improve mental health care for African Americans in disaster contexts.

Table 3.4. Suggested Disaster Response Guidelines for Mental Health Care for African Americans

1. Improve knowledge, understanding, and incorporation of African American values and beliefs in treatment.
2. Improve cultural knowledge, awareness, and competence of disaster mental health care workers.
3. Through continued educational initiatives, provide training to improve the identification of appropriate diagnoses to decrease misdiagnosis and the use of inappropriate treatments.
4. Provide better education about available services and programs within the community.
5. Collaborate with community leaders and members to assist with mental health outreach efforts.
6. Improve the geographic and general availability of mental health services within the community.
7. Consider the integration of disaster mental health care response with primary care in order to improve direct access to needed mental health care services.
8. Coordinate mental health care to particularly high-need and vulnerable populations within the community, such as the homeless and incarcerated.
9. Through cultural knowledge and understanding, improve language and communication between providers and mental health consumers.
10. Incorporate spirituality where indicated and promote the strengths of African Americans within the context of mental health care delivery.
11. Improve and expand scientific research to better understand the mental health needs of African Americans.

(Source: Comas-Diaz, 1992; Mays & Albee, 1992; USDHHS, 1999).

References

Agency for Healthcare Research and Quality. (2004). *National healthcare disparities report*. Retrieved February 26, 2006, from http://www.ahrq.gov/qual/measurix.htm

Ahmed, S., & Toro, P. A. (2004). Homeless African Americans. In D. Levinson (Ed.), *Encyclopedia of homelessness*. Thousand Oaks, CA: Sage.

American Psychological Association. (1999). *An APA report: Executive summary of the behavioral health care needs of rural women*. Washington, DC: American Psychological Association. Retrieved January 18, 2005, from www.apa.org/rural/ruralwomen.pdf

Anderson, N. B., McNeilly, M., & Myers, H. (1991). Autonomic reactivity and hypertension in Blacks: A review and proposed model. *Ethnicity & Disease, 1*, 154–170.

Baker, F. M., & Lightfoot, O. B. (1993). Psychiatric care of ethnic elders. In A. C. Gaw (Ed.), *Culture, ethnicity, and mental illness* (pp. 517–552). Washington, DC: American Psychiatric Press.

Baugh, J. (1983). *Black street speech: Its history, structure and survival* (pp. 1–22). Austin: University of Texas Press.

Black, B. S., Rabins, P. V., German, P., McGuire, M., & Roca, R. (1997). Need and unmet need for mental health care among elderly public housing residents. *The Gerontologist, 37*, 717–728.

Billingsley, A. (1992). *Climbing Jacob's ladder: The enduring legacy of African American families*. New York: Simon & Schuster.

Bolin, R., & Stanford, L. (1998). The Northridge earthquake: Community-based approaches to unmet recovery needs. *Disasters, 22*, 21–38.

Bowen-Reid, T. L., & Harrell, J. P. (2002). Racist experiences and health outcomes: An examination of spirituality as a buffer. *Journal of Black Psychology, 28*, 18–36.

Boyd-Franklin, N. (1989). *Black families in therapy: A multisystems approach*. New York: Guilford Press.

Boyd-Franklin, N. (2003). *Black families in therapy: Understanding the African American experience* (2nd ed.). New York: Guilford.

Boykin, A. W. (1983). The academic performance of Afro-American children. In J. T. Spence (Ed.), *Achievement and achievement motives: Psychological and sociological approaches* (pp. 321–371). San Francisco: Freeman.

Boykin, A. W. (1986). The triple quandary and the schooling of Afro-American children. In U. Neiser (Ed.), *The school achievement of minority children: New perspectives* (pp. 57–92). Hillsdale, NJ: Lawrence Erlbaum.

Brown, T. N., Williams, D. R., Jackson, J. S., Neighbors, H. W., Torres, M., Sellers, S. L., et al. (2000). Being Black and feeling blue: The mental health consequences of racial discrimination. *Race & Society, 2*, 117–131.

Centers for Disease Control. (1998). Youth behavior surveillance – United States 1997. *Morbidity Weekly Report, 47*(SS-3), 1–89.

Centers for Disease Control. (2001). *HIV/AIDS Surveillance Report, 13* (No. 2), 1–44, Atlanta, GA: CDC.

Centers for Disease Control. (2005a). *Eliminate disparities in infant mortality.* Retrieved February 26, 2005, from www.cdc.gov/omh/AMH/factsheets/infant.htm

Centers for Disease Control. (2005b). *HIV among African Americans.* Retrieved February 26, 2005, from http://www.cdc.gov/hiv/pubs/Facts/afam.htm

Centers for Disease Control. (2005c). *Health disparities experienced by Blacks or African Americans – United States.* Retrieved April 13, 2005, from http://www.cdc.gov/mmwr/preview/mmwrhtml/mm5401a1.htm

Center for Substance Abuse Prevention (CSAP). (2001). *Assessing substance abuse and risk in African Americans* [Draft]. Unpublished manuscript. Department of Health and Human Services, Substance Abuse and Mental Health Services Administration.

Chatters, L. M. (1991). Physical health. In J. S. Jackson (Ed.), *Life in Black America* (pp. 199–220). Newbury Park, CA: Sage Publications.

Chatters, L. M., & Taylor, R. J. (1993). Intergenerational support: The provision of assistance to parents by adult children. In J. S. Jackson, L. M. Chatters, & R. J. Taylor (Eds.), *Again in Black America* (pp. 69–83). Newbury Park, CA: Sage.

Chatters, L. M., Taylor, R. J., & Neighbors, H. W. (1989). Size of informal helper network mobilized during a serious personal problem among Black Americans. *Journal of Marriage and the Family, 51*, 667–676.

Clark, R., Anderson, N. B., Clark, V. R., & Williams, D. R. (1999). Racism as a stressor for African Americans. *American Psychologist, 54*, 805–816.

Comas-Diaz, L. (1992). The future of psychotherapy with ethnic minorities. *Psychotherapy: Theory, Research and Practice, 29*, 88–94.

Congressional Black Caucus Foundation. (2005). *The health care divide – why race matters.* Retrieved January 8, 2005, from http://www.cbcfhealth.org/content/contentID/1041

Council of Economic Advisers for the President's Initiative on Race. (1998). *Changing America: Indicators of social and economic well-being by race and Hispanic origin.* Washington, DC: U.S. Government Printing Office.

Cose, E. (1993). *The rage of a privileged class.* New York: Harper Collins.

Dana, R. H. (1993). *Multicultural assessment perspectives for professional psychology.* Boston: Allyn & Bacon.

DeNavas-Walt, C., Proctor, D. B., & Mills, R. J. (2004). Income, poverty, and health insurance coverage in the United States: 2003. *Current Population Reports* (P60-226). U.S. Census Bureau, U.S. Department of Commerce, Economics and Statistics Administration. Washington, DC: U.S. Government Printing Office.

Dickerson, B. J. (1995). *African American single mothers: Understanding their lives and families.* Thousand Oaks, CA: Sage.

Dillman, D. A., & Hobbs, D. J. (Eds.). (1982). *Rural society in the United States: Issues for the 1980s.* Boulder, CO: Westview.

Doherty, W. J. (1992). Linkages between family theories and primary health care: In R. J. Sawa (Ed.), *Family health care* (pp. 30–39). Newbury Park, CA: Sage.

Eldridge, H. T., & Thomas, D. S. (1964). *Population, redistribution, and economic growth.* Philadelphia, PA: American Philosophical Society.

Fischer, C. S., Hout, M., Jankowski, M. S., Lucas, S. R., Swidler, A., & Voss, K. (1996). *Inequality by design: Cracking the bell curve myth.* Princeton, NJ: Princeton University Press.

Ford, D. Y. (1997). Counseling middle-class African Americans. In C. C. Lee (Ed.), *Multicultural issues in counseling* (pp. 81–108). Alexandria, VA: American Counseling Association.

Franklin, J. H. (1974). *From slavery to freedom: A history of Negro Americans* (4th ed.). New York: Knopf.

Garb, H. N. (1997). Race bias, social class bias, and gender bias in clinical judgement. *Clinical Psychology: Science and Practice, 4,* 99–120.

Grier, W. H., & Cobbs, P. M. (1968). *Black rage.* New York: Basic Books.

Hatchett, S. J., Cochran, D. L., & Jackson, J. S. (1991). Family life. In J. S. Jackson (Ed.), *Life in Black America* (pp. 46–83). Newbury Park, CA: Sage Publications.

Harrell, J. P. (2000). A mutildimensional conceptualization of racism-related stress: Implications for the well-being of people of color. *American Journal of Orthopsychiatry, 70,* 42–57.

Harrell, J. P., Hall, S., & Taliaferro, J. (2003). Physiological responses to racism and discrimination: An assessment of the evidence. *American Journal of Public Health, 93,* 243–248.

Hart, D. (1994). *All in the family.* Retrieved January 18, 2005, from http://www.ovpr.uga.edu/researchnews/94su/family.html

Harvey, A. R., & Rauch, J. B. (1997). A comprehensive Afrocentric rites of passage program for Black male adolescents. *Health and Social Work, 22,* 32–37.

Hays, P. A. (2001). *Addressing cultural complexities in practice: A framework for clinicians and counselors.* Washington, DC: American Psychological Association.

Health Policy Institute. (2004). *Understanding health disparities.* Columbus, OH: Health Policy Institute of Ohio.

Hildebrand, V., Phenice, L. A., Gray, M. M., & Hines, R. P. (1996). *Knowing and serving diverse families.* Englewood Cliffs, NJ: Prentice-Hall.

Hill, R. B. (1997). *The strengths of African American families: Twenty-five years later.* Washington, DC: R & B Publishers.

Hines-Martin, V. P. (2002). African American consumers: What should we know to meet their mental health needs? *Journal of the American Psychiatric Nurses Association, 8,* 188–193.

Hines-Martin, V., Malone, M., Kim, S., & Brown-Piper, A. (2003). Barriers to mental health care access in an African American population. *Issues in Mental Health Nursing, 24,* 237–256.

Holtzman, D., Mathis, M. P., Kann, L., Collins, J. F., & Kolbe, L. J. (1995). Trends in risk behaviours for HIV infection among U.S. high school students, 1989–1991. *AIDS Education and Prevention, 7,* 265–277.

Jackson, J. S., Brown, T. N., Williams, D. R., Torres, M., Sellers, S. L., & Brown, K. (1996). Racism and the physical and mental health status of African Americans: A thirteen year national panel study. *Ethnicity & Disease, 6,* 132–147.

Jackson, J. S., McCullough, W. R., Gurin, G., & Broman, C. L. (1991). Race identity. In J. S. Jackson (Ed.), *Life in Black America* (pp. 238–253). Newbury Park, CA: Sage Publications.

Jemmott, J. B., & Jemmott, L. S. (2000). HIV behavioral interventions for adolescents in community settings. In J. L. Peterson & R. J. DiClemente (Eds.), *Handbook of HIV Prevention* (pp. 103–127). New York: Plenum Publishers.

Johnson, K. (1971). *Black kinesics: Some nonverbal communication patters in Black culture.* In L. Samovar & R. Porter (Eds.), Intercultural communication: A reader (pp. 181–189). Belmont, CA: Wadsworth.

Johnson, R. J., McCaul, K. D., & Klein, W. M. P. (2002). Risk involvement and risk perception among adolescents and young adults. *Journal of Behavioral Medicine, 25,* 67–82.

Jones Warren, B. (2002). The interlocking paradigm of cultural competence: A best practice approach. *Journal of the American Psychiatric Nurses Association, 8*, 209–213.

Jones, J. M. (1997). *Prejudice and racism* (2nd ed.). New York: McGraw-Hill.

Kalow, W. (1991). Interethnic variation of drug metabolism. *Trends in Pharmacological Science, 12*, 102–107.

Karon, J. M., Fleming, P. L., Steketee, R. W., & DeCock, K. M. (2001). HIV in the United States at the turn of the century: An epidemic in transition. *American Journal of Public Health, 91*(7), 1060–1068.

Koss-Chioino, J. D. (2000). Traditional and folk approaches among ethnic minorities (pp. 149–166). In J. F. Aponte & J. Wohl (Eds.), *Psychological intervention and cultural diversity* (2nd ed.). Boston, MA: Allyn & Bacon.

Krieger, N., & Sidney, S. (1996). Racial discrimination and blood pressure: The CARDIA study of young Black and White adults. *American Journal of Public Health, 86*, 1370–1378.

Lassiter, S. M. (1998). *Cultures of color in America: A guide to family, religion, and health*. Westport, CT: Greenwood Press.

Lawton, M. P. (1980). *Environment and aging*. Pacific Grove, CA: Brooks/Cole.

Lemann, N. (1991). *The promised land: The great Black migration and how it changed America*. New York: Vintage Books.

Levy, R. A. (1993). *Ethnic & racial differences in response to medicines: Preserving individualized therapy in managed pharmaceutical programs*. Reston, VA: National Pharmaceutical Council.

Lewis, J., & Looney, J. (1983). *The long struggle: Well-functioning working-class Black families*. New York: Brunner/Mazel.

Lincoln, E. C., & Mamiya, L. H. (1990). *The Black church in the African American experience*. Durham, NC: Duke University Press.

Lindsey, K. P., & Paul, G. L. (1989). Involuntary commitment to public mental institutions: Issues involving the overrepresentation of Blacks and assessment of relevant functioning. *Psychological Bulletin, 106*, 171–183.

Linn, J. G., Husaini, B. A., Whitten-Stovall, R., & Broomes, L. R. (1989). Community satisfaction, life stress, social support, and mental health in rural and urban southern Black communities. *Journal of Community Psychology, 17*, 78–88.

Louden, M. L. (2000). African Americans and minority language maintenance in the United States. *Journal of Negro History, 85*(4), 223–240.

Mainous, A. G., King, D. E., Garr, D. R., & Pearson, W. S. (2004). Race, rural residence, and control of diabetes and hypertension. *Annals of Family Medicine, 2*, 563–568.

Mays, V. M., & Albee, G. W. (1992). Ethnic minorities and psychotherapy: A question of policy and matter of relevance. In D. K. Freedheim (Ed.), *History of psychotherapy: A century of change* (pp. 552–570). Washington, DC: American Psychological Association.

McClennen, J. C., & Glenn, R. T. (1997). Use of social services by African American families: A multivariate analysis. *Family Therapy, 24*, 39–53.

McCollum, V. J. C. (1997). Evolution of the African American family personality: Considerations for family therapy. *Journal of Multicultural Counseling and Development, 25*, 219–229.

McKinnon, J. (2001). The Black Population. *Census 2000 Brief* (C2KBR/01-5). U.S. Census Bureau, U.S. Department of Commerce, Economics and Statistics Administration.

Miller, K. S., Forehand, R., & Kotchick, B. A. (2000). Adolescent sexual behavior in two ethnic minority groups: A multisystem perspective. *Adolescence, 35*, 313–333.

Murphy, D. A., Rotheram-Borus, M. J., & Reid, H. M. (1998). Adolescent gender differences in HIV related sexual risk acts, social-cognitive factors and behavioral skills. *Journal of Adolescence, 21*, 197–208.

National Center for Health Statistics. (1998). *Health, United States: Socioeconomic status and health chartbook*. Hyattsville, MD: USDHHS.

National Center for Health Statistics. (2002). *National vital statistics report*. Hyattsville, MD: USDHHS.

National Center for Health Statistics. (2004). *Health, United States, 2004.* Hyattsville, MD: USDHHS.

National Urban League. (2003). *National urban league institute for opportunity and equality factbook: 1963–2003: Then and now.* New York: National Urban League.

Neff, J. A. (1984). Race differences in psychological distress: The effects of sex, urbanicity, and measurement strategy. *American Journal of Community Psychology, 12,* 337–357.

Neff, J. A., & Husaini, B. A. (1987). Urbanicity, race, and psychological distress. *Journal of Community Psychology, 15,* 520–536.

Neighbors, H. W. (1991). Mental health. In J. S. Jackson (Ed.), *Life in Black America* (pp. 221–237). Newbury Park, CA: Sage Publications.

Neighbors, H. W., & Jackson, J. S. (1996). Mental health in Black America: Psychosocial problems in help seeking behavior. In H. W. Neighbors & J. S. Jackson (Eds.), *Mental health in Black America* (pp. 1–13). Thousand Oaks, CA: Sage.

Neighbors, H. W., & Jackson, J. S. (1984). The use of informal and formal help: Four patterns of illness behavior in the Black community. *American Journal of Community Psychology, 12,* 629–644.

Neighbors, H. W., Jackson, J. S., Campbell, L., & Williams, D. (1989). The influence of racial factors on psychiatric diagnosis: A review and suggestions for research. *Community Mental Health Journal, 25,* 301–311.

Office of National AIDS Policy Report. (2000). *A generation at risk – youth agenda.* Retrieved February 26, 2005, from http://clinton4.gov/ONAP/youth/youth4.html

Paniagua, F. A. (1998). *Assessing and treating culturally diverse clients* (2nd ed.). Thousand Oaks, CA: Sage.

Parham, T. A. (2002). Counseling models for African Americans: The what and how of counseling. In T. A. Parham (Ed.), *Counseling persons of African descent* (pp. 100–118). Thousand Oaks, CA: Sage.

Phillips, G. Y. (1996). Stress and residential well-being. In H. W. Neighbors & J. J. Jackson (Eds.), *Mental Health in Black America* (pp. 27–44). Thousand Oaks, CA: Sage.

Philogène, G. (1999). *From Black to African American: A new social representation.* Westport, CT: Praeger.

Purnell, L. D., & Paulanka, B. J. (2005). *Guide to culturally competent health care.* Philadelphia: F. A. Davis Company.

Quarles, B. (1987). *The Negro in the making.* New York: MacMillan.

Richardson, J., Anderson, T., Flaherty, J., & Bell, C. (2003). The quality of mental health care for African Americans. *Culture, Medicine, and Psychiatry, 27,* 487–498.

Ridley, C. R. (1984). Clinical treatment of the nondisclosing Black client. *American Psychologist, 39,* 1234–1244.

Robins, L. N., & Reiger, D. A. (1991). *Psychiatric disorders in America: The epidemiologic catchment area study.* New York: Free Press.

Rosenberg, P., Biggar, R., & Goedert, J. (1994). Declining age at HIV infection in the United States. *New England Journal of Medicine, 330,* 789–790.

Sampson, R. J., & Wilson, W. J. (1995). Toward a theory of race, crime, and urban inequality. In J. Hagan & R. D. Peterson (Eds.), *Crime and inequality.* Stanford, CA: Stanford University Press.

Schaefer, R. T., & Lamm, R. P. (1998). *Sociology* (6th ed.). New York: McGraw-Hill.

Scheffler, R. M., & Miller, A. B. (1991). Differences in mental health service utilization among ethnic subpopulations. *International Journal of Law & Psychiatry, 14,* 363–376.

Scott, L. D. (2003). Cultural orientation and coping with perceived discrimination among African American Youth. *Journal of Black Psychology, 29,* 235–256.

Shapiro, T. M. (2004). *The hidden cost of being African American: How wealth perpetuates inequality.* New York: Oxford University Press.

Snow, L. (1978). Sorcerers, saints and charlatans: Black folk healers in urban America. *Culture, Medicine & Psychiatry, 2,* 69–106.

Snow, J. (1985). *Common health care beliefs and practices of Puerto Ricans, Haitians and low-income Blacks in the New York/New Jersey area*. Boston: John Snow Public Health Group, Inc.

Snowden, L. R. (2001). Barriers to effective mental health services for African Americans. *Mental Health Services Research, 3*, 181–187.

Snowden, L. R., & Thomas, K. (2000). Medicaid and African American outpatient mental health treatment. *Mental Health Services Research, 2*, 115–120.

Steele, C. M. (1997). A threat in the air: How stereotypes shape intellectual identity and performance. *American Psychologist, 52*, 613–629.

Steinglass, P. (1992). Family systems theory and medical illness. In R. J. Sawa (Ed.), *Family health care* (pp. 18–29). Newbury Park, CA: Sage.

Sue, D. W., & Sue, D. (2003). *Counseling the culturally diverse: Theory and practice* (4th ed.). New York: John Wiley & Sons.

Swartz, M. S., Wagner, H. R., Swanson, J. W., Burns, B. J., George, L. K., & Padgett, D. K. (1998). Comparing use of public and private mental health services: The enduring barriers of race and age. *Community Mental Health Journal, 34*, 133–144.

Taylor, R. J., & Chatters, L. M. (1991). Extended family networks of older Black adults. *Journal of Gerontology, 46*, S210–S217.

Taylor, J., & Jackson, B. B. (1991). Evaluation of a holistic model of mental health symptoms in African American women. *The Journal of Black Psychology, 18*, 19–45.

Taylor, J., Henderson, D., & Jackson, B. B. (1991). A holistic model for understanding and predicting depression in African American women. *Journal of Community Psychology, 19*, 306–320.

Taylor, R. J., Burns Hardison, C., & Chatters, L. M. (1996). Kin and nonkin as sources of informal assistance. In H. W. Neighbors & J. J. Jackson (Eds.), *Mental health in Black America* (pp. 130–145). Thousand Oaks, CA: Sage.

Taylor, R. J., Neighbors, H. W., & Broman, C. L. (1989). Evaluation by Black Americans of the social service encounter during a serious personal problem. *Social Work, 34*, 205–211.

Taulbert, C. L. (1995). *Once upon a time when we were colored*. New York: Penguin Books.

Thornton, T., Craft, C., Dahlberg, L., Lynch, B., & Baer, K. (2000). *Best practices of youth violence prevention: A sourcebook for community action*. Atlanta: CDC.

United States Census Bureau. (1995). *Population profile of the United States*. Washington, DC: U. S. Government Printing Office.

United States Census Bureau. (1975). *Historical statistics of the United States: Colonial times to 1970*. Washington, DC: U. S. Government Printing Office.

United States Census Bureau (2003). Table 3.1. Educational attainment of the population 15 years and over, by age, sex, race, and Hispanic origin: 2003. Internet release date: June 29, 2004.

U.S. Conference of Mayors. (2003). *A status report on hunger and homelessness in America's cities: 2003*. Retrieved February 26, 2005, from http://www.nul.org/news/2005/lockdown.pdf

United States Commission on Civil Rights. (1999). *Health care challenge: Acknowledging disparity, confronting discrimination, and ensuring equality* Vol. 1: The role of governmental and private health care programs and initiatives, 287.

United States Department of Health and Human Services. (1999). *Mental health: Culture, race, and ethnicity: Report of the surgeon general* (SMA-01-3613). Retrieved February 26, 2005, from http://www.mentalhealth.samhsa.gov/cre/toc.asp

Urban Institute. (2001). Supporting the rural health care safety net. Retrieved February 26, 2005, from http://newfederalism.urban.org/pdf/occa36.pdf

Wallen, J. (1992). Providing culturally appropriate mental health services for minorities. *Journal of Mental Health Administration, 19*, 288–295.

Wang, P. S., Berglund, P., & Kessler, R. C. (2000). Recent care of common mental disorders in the United States. *Journal of General Internal Medicine, 15*, 284–292.

Wilkinson, C. B., & Spurlock, J. (1986). Mental health of Black Americans. In C. B. Wilkinson (Ed.), *Ethnic psychiatry* (pp. 13–60). New York: Plenum Press.

Williams, D. R., Larson, D. B., Buckler, R. E., Heckmann, R. C., & Pyle, C. M. (1991). Religion and psychological distress in a community sample. *Social Science & Medicine, 32,* 1257–1262.

Williams, D. R., & Williams-Morris, R. (2000). Racism and mental health: The African American experience. *Ethnicity & Health, 5,* 243–268.

Williams, D. R., Yu, Y., Jackson, J. S., & Anderson, N. B. (1997). Racial differences in physical and mental health: Socio-economic status, stress and discrimination. *Journal of Health Psychology, 2,* 335–351.

Wilson, W. J. (1996). *When work disappears: The world view of the urban poor.* New York: Random House.

Wilson, W. J. (1980). *The declining significance of race.* Chicago, IL: University of Chicago Press.

Wisner, B. (1993). Disaster vulnerability: Scale, power and daily life. *Geo Journal, 30,* 127–140.

Woodward, C. V. (2002). *The strange career of Jim Crow: A commemorative edition.* New York: Oxford University Press.

Chapter 4

Essential Information for Disaster Management and Trauma Specialists Working with American Indians

Jeannette L. Johnson, Julie Baldwin, Rodney
C. Haring, Shelly A. Wiechelt, Susan Roth,
Jan Gryczynski, and Henry Lozano

¡'I request and require you to recognize the Church as your Mistress and as governess of the world and universe, and the High Priest, called the Pope, in her name, and His Majesty, king of Spain, in Her place, as Ruler and Lord King. And if you do not do this, with the help of God I shall come mightily against you, and I shall make war on you everywhere and in every way that I can, and I shall subject you to the yoke and obedience of the Church and His Majesty, and I shall seize your women and children, and I shall make them slaves to sell and dispose of as His Majesty commands, and I shall do all the evil and damage to you that I am able. And I insist that the deaths and destruction that result from this will be your fault." – The Requirement, a 16ᵗʰ Century statement read by Spanish troops to villages upon entry

(Ronald Wright, 1992, p. 65).

¡'If the Great Spirit had desired me to be a white man, he would have made me so in the first place. He put in your heart certain wishes and plans; in my heart he put other and different desires. Each man is good in the sight of the Great Spirit. It is not necessary, that eagles should be crows."

– Sitting Bull (Teton Sioux)

INTRODUCTION

The terms "American Indian" and "Native American" refer to those individuals whose ancestry stems from the indigenous inhabitants of the American continents. American Indians today are a diverse and culturally complex group, numbering at over four million and consisting of over 500 recognized tribes. In order to understand the issues surrounding modern American Indians, it is imperative to become familiar with the unique history and culture of this population, particularly with regards to the impact of over five centuries of interaction with the Western world. A working knowledge of American Indian history and culture can be an important asset for professionals who work with this population in times of disaster and trauma.

This chapter will provide the reader with a brief overview of American Indian history, demographics, and culture. The material should be useful for disaster responders and mental health professionals working with American Indians, particularly within the context of traumatic events. We begin by providing a brief synopsis of the consequences of American Indian contact with European people, examining current population statistics against this historical backdrop. We then guide the reader through an exploration of American Indian cultural values, traditions, and communication styles. Finally, we discuss the relevance of culture within the context of service provision and offer suggestions for working with the American Indian population in the aftermath of disasters or trauma.

AMERICAN INDIANS: A HISTORICAL SNAPSHOT

Upon arriving in North America, European settlers found a wide variety of geographically dispersed indigenous groups which were culturally and politically distinctive from one another. There is a lack of consensus on the precise numbers of the indigenous population prior to European contact, with estimates ranging from as low as 1 million to as high as 18 million (Snipp, 1992). It is estimated that by 1800, only 600,000 American Indians remained (Thornton, 1987), and the U.S. Census counted only 237,196 American Indians in 1900 (U.S. Census, 1937). Approximately two thirds of the American Indian population perished during the course of the nineteenth century. The decimation of North America's indigenous people is unparalleled – American Indians experienced a population decrease of as much as 98 percent during the first 400 years of European contact (Thornton, 1987).

The indigenous people of the American continents experienced massive devastation upon contact with European settlers. One of the major factors which contributed to the demise of Native civilizations was the introduction of new diseases (e.g., small pox) for which Native Americans had no acquired biological defenses (Snipp, 1992; Thornton, 1987). Epidemics spread quickly, and accounted for the bulk of the initial population decrease. The remainder of the population was threatened by wars and genocide (Snipp, 1992).

As Europeans spread throughout the lands of North America, clashes with the Native population became commonplace. From 1492 to approximately 1890, Native Americans endured a four hundred year military struggle that ended at Wounded Knee, South Dakota on December 29, 1890. This is considered to be the last battle of the Indian Wars. The "Indian Wars" were a series of military campaigns waged by the United States which sought to remove the American Indian presence from valuable lands on the North American continent, paving the way for continued westward expansion. As many as half a million American Indians died as a direct result of warfare with other tribes, colonists, and newly established governments (i.e., the U.S.) (Thornton, 1987). The federal government conceded to 30,000 American Indian casualties from their military efforts, but noted that this was likely an underestimate (Thornton, 1987, as cited in Snipp, 1992, p. 355). In contrast, the Department of Veteran's Affairs estimates only 1,000 battle deaths for U.S. servicemen between 1817 and 1898 (Department of Veteran's Affairs, 2002), though it is important to note that this number does not include civilian casualties and that there were military conflicts with American Indians prior to 1817.

While an accurate depiction of the historical record of early American Indian contact with the West is complicated by disagreements among scholars with regard to early American Indian population numbers and the precise effects of military conflicts in terms of numbers of people killed, it is clear that the combination of disease, war, and genocidal policies led to the near-extermination of American Indian cultures. In 1890, the "Indian Wars" were officially declared over as a result of the drastic reduction in the American Indian population (Stiffarm, 1992).

The widespread belief in the 18th and 19th centuries was that American Indians were inferior to Europeans. Labeling American Indians as "savages" and stripping them of their humanity offered fodder for war and justification for a variety of policies which attempted to extinguish the population – either through genocide or, later, through forced assimilation. Understanding how the American Indian was conceptualized during this time is important for understanding the context of the events which nearly destroyed the population. The words of William Blackmore (1869–1870), in a paper written during the Indian Wars and read to the Ethnological Society of London, convey how American Indians were viewed by Europeans and Americans at the time:

> ¡'... In the case of truth, however, it is necessary to present the [American] Indian as he really is – a degraded, brutal savage, devoid of either pity, feeling or mercy ..." (p. 288).

In describing the effects of American westward expansion, he goes on to write,

> ¡'The steady and resistless emigration of white men into the territories of the West, restricts [American] Indians yearly to still narrower limits, and, destroying the game, which in their normal state constituted their principal means of subsistence, reduces them to a state of semistarvation and desperation. The records of every tribe tell the same story of their gradual decrease and probable extinction" (p. 290).

Those American Indians that did not succumb to the deadly trinity of disease, war, and genocide faced additional struggles in the form of a myriad of harmful policies implemented by the United States. American Indians were prompted to relinquish their lands in numerous treaties which were subsequently not honored by the U.S. government. The Indian Removal Act of 1830 initiated a policy of forced removal of American Indians from their lands, placing them on reservations. The reservations were often located in inhospitable areas, and in many cases American Indians had to endure walking hundreds of miles to reach reservations west of the Mississippi River, with thousands dying in the course of these arduous journeys (i.e., "The Trail of Tears").

There were a series of initiatives that aimed not only at sequestering land, but also at eradicating American Indian culture. These policies were congruent with the idea that American Indians were inferior to whites, and reflect the dehumanization which this population has endured throughout much of its history. Perhaps one of the most far-reaching policies of forced assimilation has been that of boarding schools for American Indian children (Child, 1998).

Boarding schools, which were located far from reservations, were created for the purpose of removing American Indians from their culture and instilling in them the dominant (i.e., white) ideology. The Bureau of Indian Affairs (BIA) had the responsibility of overseeing the operations of the boarding schools, and some of the schools lacked standard amenities such as bedding or adequate food. Upon arriving at the institutions, children were forced to cut their hair short and were forbidden to wear Native clothing styles or speak their Native languages (Meriam, 1977; Carlisle Indian School, 2005). One of the first things that occurred at BIA boarding schools was an official name change. American Indian children were not allowed to keep their Indian names. Once the child's name was changed, it was enforced by school officials and they were not permitted to use their Indian names or risked punishment (Standing Bear, 1928).

American Indian children attending the BIA boarding schools were taught to discard their Native cultural identities and assimilate in the American mainstream. Below is a first hand account of the didactics at the Carlisle Indian school in Pennsylvania (for more information see Carlisle Indian school, 2005).

> ¡'They told us that Indian ways were bad. They said we must get civilized. I remember that word, too. It means ¡be like the white man.' I am willing to be like the white man, but I did not believe Indian ways were wrong. But they kept teaching us for seven years. And the books told how bad the Indians had been to the white men – burning their towns and killing their women and children. But I had seen white men do that to Indians. We all wore white man's clothes and ate white man's food and went to white man's churches and spoke white man's talk. And so after a while we also began to say Indians were bad. We laughed at our own people and their blankets and cooking pots and sacred societies and dances. I tried to learn the lessons – and after seven years I came home . . ." Sun Elk, from Taos Pueblo, telling of his experiences at Carlisle Indian School in 1890 (from Nabokov, 1991, p. 222).

The far-reaching attempts at separating American Indian children from their families and culture finally resulted in Congress passing the Indian Child Welfare Act in 1978 (Guerrero, 1979; Wares, Wedel, Rosenthal, & Dobrec, 1994). This law aimed to reconcile earlier efforts at removing American Indian children from their families, such as boarding schools and disproportionate foster care placement with non-Indian families. The Indian Child Welfare Act gives American Indian children priority placement with their family, then within their tribe, and finally by other Native Americans before attempting placement with non-Native families.

Throughout history, there has been a consistent effort by the U.S. government to encourage American Indians' dissociation from their culture and tribal identity (Officer, 1971). Some scholars have argued that the pattern of oppression which American Indians have endured contributes to the modern-day plights of the population (such as health disparities and social problems) in a phenomenon termed historical unresolved grief or generational trauma (see Brave Heart & DeBruyn, 1998; Brave Heart, 2004, 2005).

While the atrocities of the earlier era are no longer being perpetrated against the American Indian people, many still suffer from injustice and experience the effects of many centuries of maltreatment. Even in the 21st century, federal funding for American Indian programs has not been sufficient to meet the needs of the population. In 2003, the U.S. Commission on Civil Rights wrote,

> ¡'Thus, there persists a large deficit in funding Native American programs that needs to be paid to eliminate the backlog of unmet Native American needs, an essential predicate to raising their standards of living to that of other Americans. Native Americans living on tribal lands do not have access to the same services and programs available to other Americans, even though the government has a binding trust obligation to provide them" (p. ix, Executive Summary).

POPULATION DEMOGRAPHICS

Interpreting Population Data

There are a number of difficulties associated with assessing historical demographic data for American Indians. Data on race has been collected by the U.S. Census since 1790, but American Indians were not counted as a separate group until 1860. Prior to 1890, data collection was limited to those living in the general population and did not include individuals living in American Indian territories or reservations (thus producing inaccurate estimates of the Native American population). Alaska Natives have been counted since 1880, but were grouped in the American Indian category. It was not until the 1980 Census that data for Aleuts and Eskimos (Alaska Natives) were collected separately for all the states (Ogunwole, 2002). The current racial category of "American

Indian and Alaska Native" refers to people having ancestral origins in any of the indigenous peoples of the American continents (including Central America), and who maintain tribal affiliation or community attachment. It includes people who indicate their race or races by marking this category or writing in their principal or enrolled tribe, such as Rosebud Sioux, Chippewa, or Navajo.

Beginning in the year 2000, the U.S. Census altered its survey instructions to allow individuals to check as many boxes as apply to them in the race category. This change is particularly important in the case of Native Americans, as a significant proportion of the population is of mixed race. While the new practice on the Census has resulted in more sensitive and realistic measurement, the different operationalization of race renders direct comparisons with Census surveys in previous years difficult, and between-Census interpretations of race statistics should be approached with caution and an understanding of these measurement nuances.

We urge the reader to keep these considerations in mind when examining data on Native Americans in this chapter and in other sources. While the focus of this chapter is on American Indians, the demographic data presented here will include Alaska Natives unless otherwise noted. Moreover, some of the statistical tabulations by the U.S. Census Bureau report characteristics of American Indians/Alaska Natives alone (all data prior to 2000), while other data from 2000 onward may be describing American Indians/Alaska Natives who reported one race, or those who reported their race as American Indian/Alaska Native in combination with one or more races. With these evolving measurement and reporting practices, it is easy to get confused or draw inaccurate conclusions if one is not careful.

American Indians in the 21st Century

Despite the violent and turbulent history of American Indian contact with European peoples, this population has been rebounding since the early 1900's, with remarkable population growth since the 1950's (Snipp, 1992). According to the 2000 U.S. Census, 4.1 million Americans (1.5 percent of the total U.S. population) report their race as American Indian or Alaska Native. This includes 2.5 million people who report a sole race of American Indian or Alaska Native, as well as 1.6 million people who report American Indian and Alaska Native in combination with one or more other races (Table 4.1). The majority of mixed-race Native Americans identified their additional race as white (Ogunwole, 2002).

Sex and Age

The American Indian population is approximately evenly divided by sex, with males and females generally represented in comparable numbers irrespective of age group. American Indians and Alaska Natives are young compared to

Table 4.1.   American Indian and Alaska Native Population: 2000

Race	Number	Percent of total population
American Indian and Alaska Native alone or in combination with one or more other races	4,119,301	1.5
American Indian and Alaska Native alone	2,475,956	0.9
American Indian and Alaska Native in combination with one or more other races	1,643,345	0.6
• American Indian and Alaska Native: White	1,082,683	0.4
• American Indian and Alaska Native: Black or African American	182,494	0.1
• American Indian and Alaska Native: White, Black or African American	112,207	–
• American Indian and Alaska Native: Some other race	93,842	–
All other combinations including American Indian and Alaska Native	172,119	0.1

(Source: Ogunwole, 2002)

the general population, with a median age of 29 years – six years younger than the national median age. About one-third of American Indians are children under the age of 18, compared with about one-quarter for the total U.S. population (Ogunwole, 2006).

Education

American Indian and Alaska Native educational attainment is lower than that of the general population. In 2000, 71% of American Indians/Alaska Natives aged 25 and older reported having a high school diploma or GED, compared with 80% of the general population. The percentage of American Indians and Alaska Natives who reported having a four year college degree or higher (11.5%) was less than half the rate for the general population (24.4%). Educational attainment profiles for American Indians differ based on tribal groupings, with Navajo (37.3%), Lumbee (35.3%), and Apache (31.0%) tribes displaying the greatest proportion of individuals with less than a high school education (Ogunwole, 2006).

Employment

The labor force participation rate for American Indians is slightly lower than that of the total U.S. population, with a larger gap for men than for women. Table 4.2 shows the labor force participation rate by sex for American Indians and the general population, as well as American Indian representation in various occupation types contrasted with those of the general population. Alaska Natives are not grouped with American Indians for this data, though

Table 4.2. Occupational Sector Representation and Labor Force Participation

Occupational Sector		American Indian (%)		Total U.S. population (%)	
Management/Professional		25.2		33.6	
Service		20.4		14.9	
Sales and Office		23.9		26.7	
Farming/ Fishing/ Forestry		1.3		0.7	
Construction/ Extraction/ Maintenance		12.8		9.4	
Production/ Transportation/ Moving		16.4		14.6	
	Males	*Females*		*Males*	*Females*
Labor Force Participation Rate	65.6	56.8		70.7	57.5

(Source: Ogunwole, 2006)

the inclusion of Alaska Natives alters all statistics by less than 1 percent. The percentages are for the population in the labor force age 16 and older.

American Indians have significantly higher unemployment rates than the general population of the United States. In 2000, the unemployment rate for American Indians/Alaska Natives in the labor force ages 20–64 was 7.6%, whereas only 3.7% of the general population of the same age and status was unemployed (Clark & Weismantle, 2003).

Poverty and Income

American Indians have a significantly higher poverty rate than the general U.S. population. The median earnings in 1999 for American Indian (not including Alaska Native) male workers were $28,890, compared to $37,057 for all male workers in the United States. As is the case in the general population, American Indian females had lower median earnings than their male counterparts. American Indian females earned a median amount of $22,762 in 1999, compared with $27,194 for all female workers in the U.S. in the same year. It is important to note that the data above is for full-time workers who worked throughout the year (Ogunwole, 2006), and thus does not include part-time or temporary workers.

When family income is considered, those individuals identifying as American Indian/Alaska Native alone had a combined median family income of $33,144 in 1999. When American Indians who claimed an additional racial identification are included in the analysis, the median family income was slightly higher, $36,120. When one considers that the median family income for non-Hispanic whites during this time period was $54,698 (Annie E. Casey Foundation, 2003), it is clear that Native Americans face serious income disparities. Based on 1999 income, more than one in four American Indians fell below the official poverty line. The specific tribal groupings with the highest poverty rates were Sioux (38.9% in poverty), Navajo (37.0% in poverty), and Apache (33.9% in poverty) (Ogunwole, 2006).

Perhaps no other segment of society is more affected by poverty than children. In 1999, 9.3% of non-Hispanic white children across the United States were in poverty. The poverty rate for Native American children was much greater, with 31.9% of sole race Native American children living in poverty. South Dakota had the highest proportion of American Indian/Alaska Native children in poverty, with 54.3% compared with 10.8% for the state's non-Hispanic white children (Annie E. Casey Foundation, 2003). It is important to recognize, however, that lack of resources and economic opportunity may pose a problem for individuals and families even if they do not fall below the official poverty threshold.

Violence and Crime

Between 1992 and 2002, the average number of violent victimizations per 1,000 persons age 12 and over was higher for Native Americans than for any other race/ethnicity. The National Crime Victimization Survey (Perry, 2004) from the Bureau of Justice Statistics (BJS) reported that the rate of violent victimization for American Indians/Alaska Natives is well above that of other groups and more than twice as high as the national average.

The findings of this study included: 1) American Indians have higher violent victimization rates than the general population in all age groups; 2) Violent victimizations for Native Americans age 25–34 were 2.5 times the rate for the general population in the same age group; 3) an estimated 1 in 10 American Indians age 12 and older had been a victim of violent crime; 4) Between 1992–2001, the rate of violent victimization for Natives was twice as high as that of Blacks, the next highest group; 5) Non-Indians committed approximately 70 percent of the violence perpetrated against Indians; 6) Native American victims of violence were more likely than victims of other races to indicate that the offender had been drinking alcohol at the time of the incident (Perry, 2004).

In addition, data from the BJS study revealed that American Indians entering federal prisons were more than four times as likely as Blacks and more than 12 times as likely as Whites to be incarcerated for a violent offense in 2001. American Indians were significantly less likely to be incarcerated for drug-related offenses or crimes classified as "other" than Blacks, Whites, or Asians (Perry, 2004). In sum, the findings indicate that, across age, geographic location, gender, and social class, Native Americans experience substantially higher rates of violence than other Americans.

Health Disparities

American Indians face significant health disparities compared to the general population, with high rates of illness and early death from injuries and disease (Urban Indian Health Institute, 2004; Williams & Collins, 1995). Both reservation and urban-dwelling American Indians are an at-risk population for a number of health concerns (Grossman, Krieger, Sugarman, & Forquera, 1994; Urban Indian Health Institute, 2004). However, the effects of geographic location should not be underemphasized. In addition to the geographical health variations which are seen for the U.S. population as a whole, American Indians have the unique issue of dealing within a special health system – the Indian Health Service (IHS). Some reservation Indians may experience limited care as a result of an underfunded healthcare system (U.S. Commission on Civil Rights, 2004), while urban Indians can suffer from inadequate access to healthcare resources in urban communities (Burhansstipanov, 2000; Urban Indian Health Institute, 2004).

Native Americans have an estimated adult diabetes rate of 15.1%, and are over twice as likely to have diagnosed diabetes as non-Hispanic whites. American Indians living in the southern United States and Arizona are at greatest risk for diabetes (CDC, 2005a). Native Americans are also overrepresented in injury-related mortality (CDC, 2005b). Based on age-adjusted death rates, American Indians have the highest level of mortality from chronic liver disease and cirrhosis among all racial groups, and have the second highest death rates from diabetes after African Americans (USDHHS, 2003). Substance abuse and mental health are particularly important health issues facing American Indians today. Native Americans are at significantly higher risk for poor mental health outcomes, including depression, anxiety, substance abuse, and mental illness (Johnson & Cameron, 2001; USDHHS, 2005).

Even though the majority of American Indians live in urban areas, Federal health care policy toward them continues to focus largely on the needs of those living on reservations in rural areas (Forquera, 2001), although the healthcare system for reservation Indians lacks the necessary resources to meet their needs (U.S. Commission on Civil Rights, 2003, 2004). Attention to Native American health care began in the nineteenth century when contagious diseases such as smallpox threatened the once substantial populations of Native American people. In 1849, responsibility for Native American health was transferred from the War Department to the Bureau of Indian Affairs (BIA). The BIA oversaw the use of congressional appropriations for the establishment of health programs for Native Americans. Responsibility for Native American health has since endured many organizational transfers, and now resides with the Indian Health Service (IHS), an operating division of the Department of Health and Humans Services (DHHS). The IHS is the principal federal health care provider and health advocate for Indian people. Members of federally recognized Indian tribes and their descendants are eligible for services provided by the Indian Health Service. The IHS provides health care services to Native Americans on reservations, in rural communities and in urban areas. IHS services are delivered in three ways: through direct IHS services; through tribal services; or by contract with non-IHS service providers, as is most often the case in urban communities. Disaster response teams would probably need to work in coordination with IHS service agencies.

Substance Abuse

Alcohol, tobacco, and illicit drugs continue to be a problem in many American Indian communities. Native Americans have earlier onset of alcohol and other drug use, they use substances at significantly higher rates than the general population, and they are more likely to experience negative consequences as a result of substance use (CSAT, 1999; May & Moran, 1995). Alcohol is the leading substance of abuse, ranging from 47 percent for Native American treatment admissions in large central metropolitan areas to 76 percent in non-metropolitan areas without cities. Native admissions in large central metropolitan areas are almost three times more likely to report daily use of alcohol than similar admissions in non-metropolitan areas without cities (DASIS, 2005). The age-adjusted alcohol related mortality rate for American Indians is over 5 times that of the general population (Keppel, Pearcy, & Wagener, 2002).

Native Americans are more likely to have used an illicit drug in the past month compared with persons from other racial/ethnic groups (SAMHSA, 2003). In the 2005 National Survey on Drug Use and Health (SAMHSA, 2006), Native Americans displayed the highest rate of substance dependence or abuse among individuals 12 and older (Table 4.3).

Native American youth are at increased risk for drug and alcohol abuse. In 2005, the rate of current illicit drug use among youth ages 12–17 was highest for American Indian/Alaska Natives, twice the rate for the general population in the same age range. Native Americans age 12 and older reported the highest rate of heavy alcohol use and binge drinking within the last 30 days of the survey. Native Americans 12 and older also had the highest rate of tobacco use within the last 30 days when compared to all other racial groups. The rate of smokeless tobacco use by American Indian/Alaska Native adults showed a steep increase, from 3.6% in 2004 to 8.6% in 2005, with smokeless tobacco use by other racial/ethnic groups remaining essentially unchanged (SAMHSA, 2006).

Table 4.3.   Rates of Substance Dependence or Abuse by Race, Ages 12 and Older

American Indian/Alaska Native	21.0
Native Hawaiian/Pacific Islander	11.0
Two or more races	10.9
White	9.4
Hispanic	9.3
Black	8.5
Asian	4.5

(Source: SAMHSA, 2006)

Mental Health

American Indians are at disproportionate risk for the development of mental health disorders (Nelson, McCoy, Stetter, & Vanderwagen, 1992; USD-HHS, 2005). A report from the Surgeon General indicated that the high rate of mental illness for Native Americans may be attributable to, and exacerbated by, the other problems which plague this population – specifically homelessness, incarceration, substance abuse, stress, and trauma (USDHHS, 2005). One survey (SAMHSA, 2006) showed that American Indians and Alaska Natives were by far the most likely racial group to experience serious psychological distress (Table 4.4).

Depression and trauma are two of the most serious mental health problems facing Native Americans in the modern era. The effect of these mental disorders can be seen in suicide rates. The suicide rate for Native Americans is second only to that of whites (USDHHS, 2003). According to the Indian Health Service FY2005 Budget Justification, the highest suicide rate for the general population is found among individuals 74 and older. However, among Native Americans, the highest suicide rate is found in the 15 to 34 age group (IHS, 2005). The suicide rate for Native American youth ages 14–24 was twice that of the general population. The suicide rate for pre-teen Native American children is even more disturbing, at about three times that of the general population (Biggs, 2002).

Geographic Distribution

According to Census 2000, American Indians and Alaska Natives are geographically distributed as follows: 43% live in the West, 31% live in the South, 17% live in the Midwest, and 9% live in the Northeast. Sixty-two percent of American Indians/Alaska Natives live in just 11 states: California, Oklahoma, Arizona, Texas, New Mexico, New York, Washington, North Carolina, Michigan, Alaska, and Florida. California and Oklahoma combined comprise about 25 percent of the total American Indian population with 627,562 and 391,949 Native Americans, respectively (Ogunwole, 2002).

Table 4.4. Percentage Experiencing Serious Psychological Distress in the Past Year (Survey Conducted in 2005)

American Indian/Alaska Native	21.1
Two or more races	16.8
Hispanic	11.7
White	11.4
Black	10.7
Asian	7.2

(Source: SAMHSA, 2006)

Tribal Affiliation

The term "tribe" is commonly used to delineate distinct groups of aboriginal people who share social, cultural, and political ties. Among American Indians, the term tribe can be used interchangeably with confederacy, nation, band, community, village, and corporation. Although most Americans are familiar with a few tribal groups, like the Navajo, Sioux, Cherokee, Chippewa, Apache, and Hopi, few are aware of the many others. Tribal membership is determined by the enrollment criteria of the tribe from which Indian blood may be derived, and this varies with each tribe. Generally, if linkage to an identified tribal member is far removed, one would not qualify for membership. A person must belong to or be enrolled in a federally recognized tribe in order to be recognized as an Indian to receive special services. The Bureau of Indian Affairs issues a Certificate of Degree of Indian Blood (CDIB) to individuals enrolled in federally recognized tribes (Thornton, 1996). This is commonly referred to as blood quantum, and Indians with CDIB are sometimes referred to as card-carrying Indians. Tribal membership is typically limited to individuals who have at least one-fourth degree of Indian Blood, but there is considerable variation across tribes (Wilson, 1992; Thornton, 1996).

It is not necessary to be of 100 percent American Indian racial heritage to be recognized as Indian by the Federal Government. Thornton (1996) reports that in 1910 only 56.5 percent of American Indians were "full bloods", and that by 1930 the percentage had dropped to 46.3. This trend has continued for the past 70 years and is due in large part to high rates of marriage and childbearing between Indians and non-Indians.

Historically, the U.S. government has granted federal recognition through treaties, congressional acts, or administrative decisions within the executive branch, principally by the Department of Interior. Treaty making with Indian nations was suspended in 1871 and many tribes were never recognized by the Federal government. In addition, during the 1950s, Congress made several efforts to end Federal responsibility for American Indians. By 1961, these efforts were successful in terminating Federal recognition of 109 tribes (O'Brien, 1985). In the 1970s, efforts to reduce Federal responsibility were reversed, and Congress re-established Federal recognition of approximately 10 of the "terminated" tribes. In 1978, the Bureau of Indian Affairs established the Federal Acknowledgement Program, which defined procedures whereby tribes could apply for Federal recognition. To be recognized, tribes must document the existence of some form of tribal authority from historical times until the present. As of 1999, 14 tribes have received Federal recognition, 13 tribes have been denied, and 190 tribes were in various stages of the multi-year application process (BIA, 2003). By March of 2004, there were 291 groups seeking federal recognition as tribes (Peterson, 2004).

There are currently more than 550 federally recognized tribes and Alaska village groups in the United States. "Federally recognized" means these tribes and groups have a special, legal relationship with the U.S. government commonly referred to as a government-to-government relationship. A number of American Indian tribes do not have a federally recognized status, and thus are generally not eligible for BIA programs. Most of the BIA's services and programs, however, are limited to Indians living on or near Indian reservations, a situation which leaves a potential service vacuum for urban American Indians who either cannot access services in the community or are unwilling to utilize such services due to perceptions that they are not culturally appropriate.

In Census 2000, respondents were asked to report their tribal affiliations. Seventy-nine percent of respondents (approximately 2 million people) who identified as American Indian also specified a tribe. If the American Indian population who identified as one or more additional races is also considered, 74% (3.1 million people) specified a tribe. The largest tribal groups in terms of population size were Cherokee, Navajo, Latin American Indian, Choctaw, Sioux, and Chippewa, accounting for 40 percent of all respondents who reported a single race of American Indian/Alaska Native (Ogunwole, 2002). Table 4.5 shows the ten largest tribal groupings from Census 2000, along with population numbers for the American Indian/Alaska Native alone population and the population reporting American Indian alone or in any racial combination. It is clear from this data that the proportion of American Indians identifying as mixed-race varies considerably across tribal lines.

Reservations

For many, reservations are a fundamental part of American Indian identity (Snipp, 1996), despite the fact that most American Indians do not currently live on reservation land (Ogunwole, 2006). An Indian reservation is land reserved

Table 4.5. Ten Largest American Indian Tribal Groupings from Census 2000

Tribe	American Indian alone or in any combination	American Indian tribal grouping alone	Percent reporting American Indian and an additional race
Cherokee	729,533	281,069	63%
Navajo	298,197	269,202	9.8%
Latin American Indian	180,940	104,354	42.4%
Choctaw	158,774	87,349	45.0%
Sioux	153,360	108,272	29.5%
Chippewa	149,669	105,907	29.3%
Apache	96,833	57,060	41.1%
Blackfeet	85,750	27,104	68.4%
Iroquois	80,822	45,212	44.1%
Pueblo	74,085	59,53	19.7%

(Source: Ogunwole, 2002)

for a tribe because the tribe relinquished its other land areas to the U.S. through treaties. Reservations vary widely in size. The Navajo Reservation, for example, covers an area approximately the size of West Virginia, sprawling across 16 million acres over three states. Some reservations are much smaller, at less than 1,000 acres. The tribal government has jurisdiction on reservations (Forquera, 2001), and only federal and tribal laws are in effect for American Indians living on reservations. This is why many tribes have been able to open lucrative casinos on their reservations even when casinos are prohibited in the state. The Assimilative Crimes Act, however, automatically makes violations of state criminal law on reservations a federal offense.

The importance of cultural awareness and competency when working in reservations with close-knit Native American communities cannot be understated. Mental health and disaster response workers need to be aware of existing community and familial support structures, and attempts should be made to provide services with these frameworks in mind. Specifically, it is important to work collaboratively with the community and foster a participatory service environment. Involving tribal elders and other respected community leaders may provide opportunities for innovative service provision and the building of trust – a crucial element when working with this population. Trust may not come easily, and given the historical record some communities may be justified in their reluctance to accept external assistance. Good intentions, demonstrations of respect, a willingness to learn, and a working knowledge of American Indian culture will likely constitute the first vital steps to providing services which are accepted by the people.

Urban Indians

It is commonly believed that most American Indians live on reservation lands or rural environments. However, this is not the case. Rather, the majority of the Native American population now lives in urban areas (Forquera, 2001; Hirschfelder & Montano, 1993). Census 2000 data indicates that only 36 percent of American Indians and Alaska Natives currently live on reservations, or in other Census-defined tribal areas (Ogunwole, 2006). The concentration of many Native Americans in urban environments is in large part due to a range of historical policies which have encouraged (many times forcefully) American Indians to leave their reservations and settle in cities. Resettlement in the urban metropolis is consistent with early governmental policies of forced assimilation and attempts at destroying Native cultural bonds with land and community. An additional reason for the large number of city-dwelling Indians is the modern-day lack of economic opportunity on some reservations, a factor which prompts some to relocate to cities for financial reasons (Snipp, 1992).

The Indian population in most urban areas is composed of people from many different tribes. For example, Walker (1981) found members of 36 different tribes in his study of American Indians in Seattle. From Census 2000, the cities with the largest urban Indian populations were New York, Los Angeles, Phoenix, Anchorage, Tulsa, Oklahoma City, Albuquerque, Tucson, Chicago, San Antonio, Houston, Minneapolis, San Diego, Denver, San Jose, Fresno, Mesa, Dallas, Seattle, and Portland (Ogunwole, 2002). It is important to note that the migration of American Indians off of reservations and into urban areas does not necessarily indicate a disintegration of cultural identity. Indeed, American Indians have shown remarkable resilience in this regard, developing innovative methods of retaining their cultural values and practices in urban environments (Cheshire, 2001; Snipp, 1992).

The increase in the metropolis-bound American Indian population has not occurred by chance. Rather, policies of the Federal government directed at facilitating assimilation into the dominant culture are in large part responsible for the current geographical distribution of this population. The General Allotment Act of 1887 (also known as the Dawes Act) represented the pinnacle of an effort to switch communal reservation lands over to individual ownership, resulting in even greater displacement and disintegration of the American Indian people (Hirschfelder & Montano, 1993). Over two-thirds of Indian land had been given over to non-Indians by 1933 (Sorkin, 1978).

The fact that most American Indians now live in urban environments represents an extremely important and radical shift in the American Indian cultural landscape. Relationships with land and with nature are central to many Native cultures, and such a fundamental change in a people's environment can have numerous implications for individual psyches, communities, and collective identity.

Language

There is great diversity among Native American languages and today over 100 different American Indian languages exist, which is a vastly lower number than existed prior to European contact. Native American language classification is done geographically rather than linguistically because Native American languages do not belong to a single linguistic stock. Many Native American languages have died out, or are only spoken by tribal elders. Many of the Native American languages that remain are considered in danger of becoming extinct (Crawford, 1995).

Most linguists agree that while the grammatical structure of Native American languages varies considerably, none of the languages can be called primitive. Many Native American languages have complex grammars. The glottal stop is a common sound in some Native American languages. Vowel systems of some Native American languages are quite variable, and several languages have nasalized vowels, as with the Chickasaw tribe. During World War II, the Navajo language was used to create a secure and classified code to transmit military information in the Pacific for the Marines. To anyone not thoroughly trained, the Navajo syntax, dialects, and tonal qualities made it unintelligible. The Japanese were never able to decipher the Navajo code (Durrett, 1998).

Foods

Native Americans made significant contributions to the U.S. agricultural base; two-thirds of cultivated crops were given to the world by Native Americans. Fruits and vegetables such as sweet peppers, squash, corn, tomatoes, peanuts, green beans, kidney beans, paprika, cranberries, pecans, and even the potato were unknown to Europeans prior to arriving on the American continents. Because Native Americans covered such a huge land mass, many tribal foods were dependent upon geography and thus, it is difficult to characterize a typical Native American food. For example, many Pacific Northwest tribes were excellent fishermen and a staple of their diet was salmon. For the American Indians living in prairie lands, Buffalo became a staple of their diet. For tribes of wetlands, wild rice became a dietary staple. Fry bread (flat fried dough used as a base for many dishes, and also eaten alone as bread or dessert) can be seen throughout the southwest. Native Americans ate what the land grew, and for that reason, it was not uncommon to see stews of acorns, hickory nuts, blackberries, bristle grass, cattail, or any variety of plant. Despite these differences in food preferences, corn, beans, and squash remain an integral component of many Native American diets. Typically, Native Americans eat the same things non-Natives eat, but emphasize the natural foods of the area. Mutton is eaten in the southwest, salmon is eaten in the Northwest, and deer is eaten in the Midwest and northeast. However, many contemporary Native Americans eat more "mainstream" foods as well (see Berzok, 2005).

Entertainment

Choices of entertainment depend on opportunities. On reservations there are typically fewer entertainment opportunities than in the city, and the Native Americans living in large metropolitan areas generally do what everyone else does. Many Native Americans, however, have begun to take an active role in providing entertainment in the movie industry and publishing world. Writings from Native Americans have begun to influence contemporary society since the advent of what has been termed the "Native American renaissance" (see Peterson, 1999). Native American participation and visibility in the literary arts can be seen as a testament to the resilience of the culture (Kroeber, 1992). Movies, art, and books by and about Native Americans are also a growing refection of how they are influencing their own entertainment options.

Another important avenue of entertainment for Native Americans is powwows. Both urban and reservation Indians go to powwows, which is an

Anglicized Indian word derived from an Algonquian term "pau-wau" or "pauau" – a gathering of medicine men and/or spiritual leaders in reference to a religious ceremony. The history of the powwow is obscure and there is no exact written record of the first powwow. The roots of the powwow come from Pawnee religious ceremonies practiced in the 19th century, but the powwow was later embraced by the Omaha and other tribes. In the Dakotas, some powwows are still referred to as "Omaha Dances". Many modern-day powwows are not tribe-specific, but rather celebrate pan-Indian culture, borrowing ceremonies and dances from different tribes and incorporating them into the festivities. More traditional powwows may embrace the historical practices of the organizing tribe.

The powwow today is a derivative of early religious and warrior celebrations and now includes dancing, honoring, gift giving and feasting. Powwow dances are typically celebrations of family, clan and tribal membership and most dances are rooted in pride. At the center of a powwow is the drumming circle, composed typically of male elders and youth; the steady drumming serves as the heartbeat of the dance to keep the rhythm for the dancers. Dancing is circular, and dancers of all ages dance to the drum around the circle. Freedom of movement is allowed so that your body can keep to the rhythm of the drumming in its own way. Whirling, spinning, and tapping feet in time to the drumming is not uncommon, nor is it uncommon to dance using a slow, steady, repetitive pulse around and around the circle.

It is important to recognize that pow-wows and other traditional ceremonies have significance beyond mere entertainment. Rather, these practices can have both spiritual significance by incorporating traditional religious ceremonies or dances, and can act to solidify cultural or community cohesion among American Indians. Snipp (1992) identifies powwows, churches, Indian Centers, and bars as particularly important venues for American Indian social interaction and cultural expression.

KEY HISTORICAL EVENTS

Presenting an overview of the 500 years of American Indian interaction with the dominant society in the United States necessitates selectivity. Table 4.6 below draws from several sources (Driver, 1969; Hirschfelder & Montano, 1993; Jaimes, 1992; Nichols, 1986; Snipp, 1992; Thornton, 1987). The events highlighted in the chronology of Table 4.6 are not meant to present a complete history of the American Indian people, but rather a pattern of events that contributed to the situations American Indian people in the United States have faced. In such an abbreviated format, it is often more instructive to describe historical themes rather than a single event. Therefore, events or policies with broad impact for the entire American Indian population are emphasized over the history of specific tribes.

Table 4.6.   A Brief Chronology of Events in American Indian History

1492–1890	In 1492, Columbus lands on the Island of Hispaniola. The multi-national European invasions of the Americas shortly ensued. From 1492 to the late 1800's, the American Indian population suffer greatly as a result of genocidal policies, wars, and diseases brought by the Europeans for which they had no acquired immunity. A series of conflicts between European powers, the newly established government of the United States, and among different tribes results in the decimation of many American Indian people. Throughout this period, the United States implements a series of policies to remove Indians from their land.
1600's–1800's	Missionaries begin to flood the American continents to try to convert the American Indians to Christianity and "civilize the savages". In essence, this means forced assimilation, the infusion of the dominant ideology into the American Indian population, and the destruction of American Indian cultures. For some American Indians, resistance to the Christian faith results in torture and eventual execution.
1778	The Continental Congress makes the first treaty with an Indian tribe, the Delaware. This sets the stage for the signing of hundreds of treaties with various tribes throughout the next century. The primary aim of the treaties is land acquisition, and they are essentially a means for securing an orderly and peaceful transfer of land ownership. Scores of treaties are subsequently broken and altered as conditions change, such as when resources are discovered on land that was given to American Indian tribes in previous agreements. American Indians are caught at a disadvantage given that treaties are written in English and often use "fine print" that favors U.S. interests.
1787	Congress approves the Northwest Ordinance, a law which promises that land and property will not be taken from American Indians without their consent except in the case of "just and lawful wars". Several "just and lawful wars" soon follow.
c. 1800's–1890	A series of conflicts known as the "Indian Wars" are fought between the United States and various tribes. The precise beginning of the wars is difficult to ascertain, as military engagements with American Indians were commonplace during the period of American westward expansion. However, the Indian Wars came to an end at Wounded Knee, South Dakota with the massacre of over 200 Sioux American Indians.
1824	Congress establishes the Bureau of Indian Affairs (BIA) within the United States War Department, but the BIA is later transferred to the Department of the Interior. The BIA serves as the principal government agency for American Indian issues, and has jurisdiction over trade with American Indians, their removal from land deemed valuable, their protection from exploitation, and their concentration on reservations. The BIA evolved into a land-administering agency, a process speeded up by the Dawes Act of 1887, the Burke Act of 1906, and the Wheeler-Howard Act of 1934. Currently, the BIA manages and administers over 55 million acres of land held in trust by the U.S. government. The bureau also promotes agricultural and economic development and provides a health program, social services, and education to American Indians living on trust lands. In recent years, the BIA has received criticism for its mismanagement of American Indian funds.
1830	The Indian Removal Act is passed by Congress, mandating the removal of Indians to the west of the Mississippi River. The process of removal is often brutal, with whole tribes being forced to walk several hundred miles. Reservations are typically located on the least desirable land, and sustenance is therefore dependent on assistance from the Federal government. Thousands of American

(Continued)

Table 4.6.   (Continued)

	Indians die during the journey. The route they traversed and the journey itself became known as "The Trail of Tears" or, as a direct translation from Cherokee, "The Trail Where They Cried" (*"Nunna daul Tsuny"*).
1832	U.S. Supreme Court Chief Justice John Marshall recognizes the sovereignty of Indian tribes in the landmark case *Cherokee Nation v. Georgia*.
1871	Congress passes a law prohibiting further treaties with Indian tribes.
1876	The Battle of Little Big Horn takes place in Montana during the latter years of the Indian Wars. Chief Sitting Bull of the Sioux Indians defeats the overconfident Colonel Custer's army.
1879–mid 1900's	The Carlisle Indian School is founded. By 1889, there are 148 Indian Boarding Schools and 225 Indian Day Schools, and attendance by Indian children exceeds 20,000. The primary goal of this effort is acculturation of Indian children to White ways, often punishing them for speaking their tribal languages (Meriam, 1977).
1887	The General Allotment Act (Dawes Act) is passed in an effort to transfer communal tribal lands to individual ownership. The Dawes Act provided incentives for Indians to become farmers. The basic provisions of this Federal law were to distribute reservation land to individual Indian people. Each head of household was allotted 160 acres, although the amount of the allotment was amended to 80 acres after 1891. For each reservation, after all of the persons who were tribal members at that time had been assigned parcels of land, remaining reservation land was opened to homesteading by non-Indians. One of the most serious consequences of this law was the loss of Indian land and the subsequent erosion of the possibility for viable reservation based economic development. By 1934 more than two thirds of the Indian land base had passed into non-Indian hands (Sorkin, 1978).
1924	The American Indian Citizenship Act is passed, making all Indians citizens of the United States and giving them the right to vote, though not all states cooperate. It is not until 1948 that Arizona loses a lawsuit and Indians in that State gain the right to vote.
1934	The Indian Reorganization Act (Wheeler-Howard Act) is passed by Congress. This law ends allotment, recognizes the principle of self-determination, and provides a plan for organizing tribal governments along the lines of a Western model, with tribal presidents and council members being elected.
1948–1968	In the effort to increase and enhance the atomic weapons capabilities of the United States at the dawn of the Cold War, the government begins uranium mining and milling operations on the Navajo Nation. Over 2000 Navajos were employed in the uranium mining and milling industry, facing poor working conditions. Navajo workers faced long-term health and psychological consequences as a result of exposure to high levels of external radiation, radon, and high silica dust (see Markstrom & Charley, 2003).
1951–1980	The BIA Relocation Program is created to assist reservation Indians to relocate to select urban areas, promoting the continued migration of American Indians off reservation lands and into urban areas.
1968-1973	The American Indian Movement (AIM) is founded in Minneapolis, with chapters soon to follow in several cities. AIM is a Native American civil rights movement developed to encourage self-determination among Native Americans and to establish international recognition of their treaty rights. A group of Indian activists occupies Alcatraz Island in 1969 and thus serves as a catalyst for Indian activism across the United States. In 1973, AIM occupied Wounded Knee on the Pine Ridge reservation. After a 70-day siege by the FBI and tribal police, a violent confrontation ensued in which a church was burned, two

militants were killed, one FBI agent was paralyzed, and two FBI agents were killed. Among their demands was a review of more than 300 treaties between the Native Americans and the federal government that AIM alleged were broken. The leaders of the siege were subsequently brought to trial, but the case was dismissed on grounds of misconduct by the prosecution.

1978   The Indian Child Welfare Act is passed, providing priority placement of American Indian children in foster care with their family first, their tribe second, other Native Americans third, and finally non-Indians. The Act only applies to American Indians whose tribe has a federally recognized status.

1978   The American Indian Religious Freedom Act establishes a policy of preserving and protecting the inherent right to believe, express, and exercise the traditional religions of American Indians, Alaska Natives, and Native Hawaiians. The Act essentially counters a series of nineteenth and early twentieth century statutes that criminalized a range of indigenous practices, including, for example, the Sun Dance of the northern Plains tribes and the potlatch ceremonies of the northwestern tribes. The Bureau of Indian Affairs establishes a process by which Indian tribes can petition the government to seek federal recognition, outlining the criteria for eligibility. The process has been criticized as unreasonably strict and lengthy.

1990   President George H. W. Bush signs a joint Congressional resolution which designates November of 1990 "National American Indian Heritage Month", a tradition that has been continued every year since 1994.

KEY VALUES

The film industry's image of an American Indian living in a teepee and running around in a breech cloth gives a grossly inaccurate portrayal of American Indians in today's time. Rather, life in American Indian communities is a mix of contemporary lifestyles and traditional roots. Although values and lifestyles differ from tribe to tribe, many American Indians live in modern homes and carry on daily routines much the same as non-Natives. However, one major difference is the inclusion of different traditional tribal values and customs. This may be represented by the inclusion of daily prayers of thanks to mother Earth and her belongings, utmost respect for family and community, an emphasis on spirituality, following values laid down by elders, and looking ahead for future American Indian generations.

There is more variation among tribal groups than there are similarities. This variation extends to geographic areas, which are, in effect, distinct cultural areas as well: the Arctic, Sub-Arctic, Northwest Coast, Plateau, Plains, East, California, Great Basin, and Southwest (Driver, 1969; Manson, Shore, Barron, Ackerson, & Neligh, 1992). Tribes have different traditions, speak different languages, have different ceremonies, wear different clothes, eat different foods, and have different spiritual and religious customs. Some tribes have a matrilineal hierarchy, and some do not. It is important to keep these differences in mind when working with Native American populations, and it is always advisable to employ a dynamic and ever-evolving approach to understanding the culture and needs of the American Indian client.

Despite their diversity, most Native Americans are drawn together by core values such as an emphasis on spirituality, recognition of the sacredness of all living things, and respect for the land and the natural world in which they live. The American Indian worldview can be described as being based on contextual relationships – relationships with family, community, tribe, as well as the physical environment. The notion of balance is extremely important to understand, particularly for health or disaster response service providers. In the American Indian worldview, maladies and diseases are seen as the result of imbalance between vital forces and relationships. Traditional healing ceremonies, then, are aimed not at attacking symptoms, but at restoring an individual's balance with their culture and the natural world. Belief in the interconnectedness of all things reflects the non-linear worldview of American Indians. Don Coyhis (1999) has detailed a number of key American Indian values. These values and others are described below.

Cooperation

While competition and independence are valued in mainstream American culture, these values and their corresponding behaviors are not viewed in high esteem by Native Americans. Rather, cooperation, which encourages a state of being, as opposed to competition, which encourages a state of doing, is a cultural value. Cooperation among families, tribes and communities recognizes that it takes a combined effort to achieve harmony.

Harmony with Nature

Many American Indian culture 5 views relationships with the physical environment in a similar manner as relationships with other individuals. This means, in essence, that cooperation with nature is as important as cooperation with people. Native Americans show this by valuing animals, the earth, and understanding that everything is connected.

Non-linear Thinking

Within a non-linear cognitive framework, objects, feelings, knowledge, people, and events are viewed primarily within their context to each other. This contextual relationship is cyclical. Viewing life through a non-linear lens allows a person to view their relationship to both their past and their future as a continuum that includes both ancestors and legacies. All things are related, and everything is involved and interconnected. Groups become more important than individuals, and individuals are not left in isolation but related to all things around them. Thus, thinking and communication becomes inclusive, and not exclusive.

Group Emphasis

One distinction related to a value system is the interdependence between individuals and the citizens of a community. American Indian people may make their decisions based on what is in the best interests of the tribe, clan, group, or family rather than what is best for the individual. This reflects the non-linear worldview and the emphasis of American Indian culture on community. The individual's point of view does not come first. Placing too much emphasis on individual needs may embarrass the American Indian client, particularly if the client is deeply rooted in traditional Native culture. A more balanced approach would be to position the importance of the service or intervention within a more global framework, emphasizing not only the benefits to the individual, but also the advantages for the family, community, tribe, etc.

Sharing and Social Responsibility

Another property of the American Indian value system revolves around the concept of having social responsibility for one another and the responsibility of providing ways to overcome obstacles that cause disequilibrium between individual and environment. The value of sharing was not only an integral value of the American Indians of the past, it is an inherent feature that has been instilled in contemporary American Indian communities. The value of sharing may be represented by sharing food or meals with relatives or neighbors. Sharing may also be manifested in providing shelter for members of the family or other community members in time of need. Finally, the value of sharing may be seen in everyday activities such as sharing the responsibility of care giving to the elderly or watching over children while their parents are at work.

Family

For many American Indians, the concept of family often transcends the nuclear model and encompasses extended family as well as other close members of the community. Often times, when American Indian families speak of family they are not only referring to a nuclear family in one residential setting; rather, the definition of family may include the extended family in various communities. It is important to remember that American Indians may have broader notions of family, the family's role, and the individual's obligations and responsibilities to the family.

Honoring Elders

Generally speaking, American Indian cultures have great respect for the elders of their tribe and community. The elders are seen as wise, and typically assume a role of leadership within a tribe or community. It may be a good idea to involve or consult the elders when working within American Indian communities.

Religion and Spirituality

In the traditional American Indian worldview, spirituality or religion is an integral part of life. Spirituality is expressed through prayer, ceremony, or "ways". It may be important for the mental health provider or disaster response worker to gain an understanding of the role of religion in the client's life. However, this should be done slowly and with caution, as religious practices may be viewed as a private matter. There are many American Indians who continue to observe traditional spiritual practices and beliefs. However, the influx of European missionaries in early centuries has resulted in widespread conversion to Christianity by the ancestors of modern-day American Indians. However, even in cases where American Indians identify as Christians, they may not discard their traditional beliefs or cultural practices. Rather, these traditional values may be integrated into the Christian faith to varying degrees. Traditional ceremonies and observances may be practiced alongside another religion.

Because religion or spiritual belief can represent a powerful personal force in the lives of many American Indians, it is important to resist making unfounded assumptions about the importance, role, or structure of these beliefs in the client's life. Discussion of spirituality should be included only after a trusting relationship has been built; and even then counselors should await cues from the client to initiate discussion. Conversation of spirituality and religion should surface from the client rather than be initiated and probed by the counselor. Of course, this assumes the given situation allows time for a relationship with the client to be built and maintained. In real-world instances of disaster and trauma, however, this may not always be the case. Spirituality and religion are often maintained as sacred and intellectual property of the individual and tribe, and should thus be approached only when the client wishes to share, unless there is clear evidence that avoiding the subject would have a damaging effect on the client's outcomes.

The Circle and the Four Directions

The use of circles and cycles in many Native American cultures is indicative of how Native people view and interpret the world (Fixico, 2003). The "Four Directions" is an important symbol which typically appears as a cross within a circle. This can symbolize, literally, the four directions of north, east, south, and west. It is also the foundation of the "Medicine Wheel", which is part of some, though not all, Native American cultures. While the meaning attached to the four directions and the medicine wheel can vary between tribes, the four quadrants of the medicine wheel typically represent the mental, spiritual, emotional, and physical aspects of the individual, enclosed by a circle to emphasize the importance of balance between these forces and their mutual interdependence. The symbol of the circle and the four directions resonates with the American Indian worldview and provides a template through which to view concepts and phenomena.

Non-materialism

Contrary to the dominant society, materialism is typically not a key value for American Indians. Rather, importance is placed on living a value-oriented life, spiritual wholeness, and existing in harmony with the world. The popular notion that success is measured by material possessions may have little impact on traditional Native American people.

Names

A person's name is very important in most tribes. The linguistic name is a source of strength and identity. When the administrators at the Carlisle boarding school took the Indian children's names away and forced upon them new "white" names, they knew what they were doing in the long process of breaking and reshaping the childrens' cultural identities. Traditionally, Indian children did not have their names spoken often. When someone was referred to, it was usually either by relationship or by a nickname. But the children knew who they were: they belonged to the name, and the name belonged to them, and to no other. Most Native Americans introduced themselves by naming their tribe, and honoring their ancestors.

COMMUNICATION STYLES

In general, American Indian communication styles are very different from the communication styles of non-Indians in the United States. Of course, communication styles vary, but there are several common elements which the service provider should recognize when working with American Indian clients.

Silence and Patience

One form of communication that is often present in many American Indian cultures is the practice of silence. Silence is often mistaken for shyness. However, for American Indians it often represents a period of reading body language and non-verbal communications. It is also a time in which American Indian clients may evaluate and test the specialists attempting to assist them. Silence is also a derivative of patience, which is an important American Indian value and communication element.

Oral Tradition

Story telling is the cornerstone of the American Indian oral tradition, and it is the vehicle through which the actions and traditions of ancestors have been passed down through the generations. Stories can serve many different functions, from creation stories which help to explain the beginning of the physical and spiritual universe, to historical accounts which preserve knowledge of family lineage and tribal practices. Some stories are metaphors for explaining cultural values. American Indians typically are a visually- and orally-oriented culture, and use stories as a means of conveying information or teaching morals and values.

Turn-taking and Story-telling

Most American Indians do more listening and observing than talking. This can be a barrier for mental health and disaster recovery work at times when it is necessary to get information from the client in an expedient fashion. Whenever possible, it is a good idea to allow for sufficient time during the consultation or intervention for the client's ideas to surface. Another nuance of American Indian communication styles to be aware of may be defined as the process of "turn-taking". This process may have its origins in Native American talking circles, where people sit in a circle and pass an object around to indicate whose turn it is to speak.

American Indian clients may elaborate their concerns in a thoughtful and meaningful story. Permitting the client to complete their story without interrupting or probing for information too early allows the client to bring forth the meaningful end of a particular incident, thought, or story conclusion. At the end of a given story, the "turn-taking" then transfers to the specialist or counselor. Rather than providing information directly, American Indian clients may rely heavily on metaphor-rich storytelling to illuminate their feelings or situation.

Modesty and Eye Contact

In many Native cultures there are different behaviors with regards to eye contact during conversations, and Coyhis (1999) estimates that close to half of the Native cultures do not maintain eye contact. To be modest is to be polite, show respect, and honor the other person. This value of modesty may be manifested by not looking into the eyes of the other person, maintaining considerably less direct eye contact during dialogue than is typical in mainstream society. Health care specialists are often taught to maintain eye contact with the patient or client to convey attentiveness. When working with American Indians, however, this practice may decrease the person's comfort. Recommendations to positively increase the comfort level may include sitting to the side of the client, maintaining some eye contact but not constantly staring, and allowing the client to initiate, engage, and control the eye contact process.

¡'Indian Time"

A common phrase used across Indian Country is "Indian Time". In the non-Indian world, being late is often indicative of not being prepared or not being able to budget time. From an American Indian perspective it may be the result of respecting and honoring those you meet along the way. For example:

> Willard was on his way to an appointment, when his great grandmother asked him how his sister was doing. Respectfully, Willard answered his great grandmother. He did not say ¡'I've got to go, I will tell you tomorrow". After talking with his great grandmother, Willard traveled on to the building where his appointment was scheduled. Just before entering he ran into his Uncle. Willard respectfully carried out a conversation with his uncle. Unfortunately, Willard was 10 minutes late to the appointment.

As a specialist or counselor working with American Indian clients, it is important to take into consideration "Indian Time". To many American Indians, communicating with people along their travels is well warranted and being a little delayed is often commonplace. Therefore, some clients may come to appointments and meetings a little later than expected. It is important to recognize that this behavior does not necessarily indicate a lack of interest or commitment on the part of the client.

Humor

Humor is often a part of many American Indian cultures. However, a comfortable rapport should be established before attempting to include this during the intervention. American Indian clients may use humor in many ways. It can be a way to increase the comfort level with the specialist or counselor. Humor may also serve as part of the story telling process. Finally, humor may serve as a defense mechanism against pain, trauma, distress, or an embarrassing situation.

Therapeutic Styles

When working with American Indian populations, a non-confrontational approach may be more appropriate and effective. Lafromboise, Trimble, and Mohatt (1990) stated that attention to the life styles of American Indians is necessary for a shift away from conventional counseling techniques towards the design of therapies that build on the values and strengths of American Indian peoples, tribes, and societies.

One therapy that has showed promise for working with Native populations is narrative therapy (Lyness, 2002). Narrative therapy refers to a range of constructionist approaches that provide a process of personal change (Etchinson & Kleist, 2000). This type of therapy asks specialists and counselors to shift attention away from a search of pathology and move toward an appreciation of new stories that manage people's lives (Schwartz, 1999).

Monk et al. (cited in Etchinson & Kleist, 2000) commented that the primary goal of narrative therapy is to form an alliance with the client that promotes the ability to enhance relationships. As part of the narrative therapy framework, a therapist may also help the client separate past repetitious stories, develop different relationships to those stories, and help the client bring forth new life-improving actions and behaviors. This process positions the health care provider as a collaborator with the client and promotes particular attention to their unique values, customs, and rituals. Therefore, counselors are not telling the client what was wrong with a story in their past. Rather, the counselor is working side by side as a partner, helping the client look at old stories from different angles and ultimately bringing forth new preferred plots.

VALID ASSESSMENT INSTRUMENTS AND RESEARCH CONSIDERATIONS

Concern has been expressed regarding the use of conventional evaluation assessment techniques with Native Americans. Exclusive reliance on quantitative techniques may be too reductionistic to adequately portray Indian realities in a manner meaningful to Indian people. That is, if the purpose of assessment is expected to be useful to Native Americans, the purpose must reflect the values, beliefs and other epistemological assumptions of the Indian community. The assessment process itself should respect the wide range of linguistic, tribal, and cultural differences. There is very little in the literature that addresses measurement with American Indians, and most assessment does not concern itself with the diversity of the population. Very little assessment of American Indians focuses on specific tribal groups but instead has a generic race category for American Indian or Native American.

Trimble (1991) refers to this approach as an "ethnic gloss" and argues that it fails to capture the significant differences that exist within most racial and ethnic groups. Using ethnic glosses with American Indians is especially problematic because of the extreme diversity of the population. Nevertheless, ethnic gloss has been the dominant approach used in assessing American Indians. As a result, little refined work related to measurement is available for this population. Ethnic gloss can be minimized by elaborating on the population descriptions or sample through administering detailed demographic or ethnic identification measures. Another factor to consider is the level of assimilation into the dominant culture. In addition, assessing American Indians requires moving beyond a framework that uses an individualistic approach to one that utilizes a sociocultural framework that will focus on the individual in context.

American Indians might be classified as one racial or ethnic group, but culturally they are many. In the face of inadequate assessment, two steps can be taken to improve current instrumentation: 1) Improve existing standardized instruments to make them less culturally inappropriate for all cultural groups in which they are used. Careful attention to the translation and back-translation process is extremely important; 2) Draw upon qualitative/ethnographic research approaches in the development and administration of semi-structured assessment formats that permit flexibility in the way in which questions are framed and rephrased; 3) Serious attention needs to be given to the valid administration of assessments by skilled professionals who are familiar with the subject's culture and language.

Despite questions about the validity of existing tests for Native Americans, they endure a considerable amount of testing. But these standardized tests, often normed on the principles of Western culture, conflict with many aspects of Native American culture. For example:

- The content of standardized assessments measures experiences which may not be common to reservation Indians.
- Native Americans, who value patience in response, may be penalized by timed assessments merely because they are taught to take time when responding.
- Native Americans are a visually oriented culture, and tests relying on written or verbal responses may unduly penalize them.
- Native Americans may approach written tasks differently. Individuals who are accustomed to cooperating with each other and sharing information may not be able to proceed readily when faced with the solitary task of writing a response to a question.

A few studies have examined the use of standardized instruments with Native American youth and adults. McCullough, Walker, and Diessner (1985) used the Wechsler Scales of Intelligence with Native American youth in the Columbia River Basin and also reviewed the literature on intelligence testing with Native American youth. These studies found a large difference between verbal and performance scale tests, with performance scale scores being one to two standard deviations higher, calling into question the validity of the full scale IQ score. Self report personality inventories, such as the California Psychological Inventory (CPI) or the MMPI, are used extensively. Dahlstrom (1986) reviewed MMPI patterns of American Indians, but the data was too minimal to make any generalizations. Use of the CPI has been reported in a few studies (see Davis, Hoffman, & Nelson, 1990), suggesting a lower profile for American Indians, but these differences have been attributed to acculturation and role expectations.

Recent work on trauma among American Indians has resulted in the development of two important measurement scales which bear mentioning here.

Whitbeck, Adams, Hoyt, and Chen (2004) developed the Historical Loss Scale and the Historical Loss Associated Symptoms Scale. In their paper, the authors offer a cogent discussion of the multiple issues associated with conceptualization and measurement of historical trauma (see also Brave Heart & DeBruyn, 1998; Brave Heart, 2004). The Historical Loss Scale measures how often an individual thinks about a series of historical events such as "loss of our land" and "loss of our family ties because of boarding schools". The Historical Loss Associated Symptoms Scale refers back to the Historical Loss Scale to ordinally measure emotional reactions from these losses.

It can be reasonably argued that all assessment is essentially a culturally negotiated product and implies some degree of social compromise. At a practical level, these types of principles are articulated in the works of theorists like Patton (1990) and Guba and Lincoln (1989, 1981). Guba and Lincoln (1981) recommend using naturalistic inquiry methods in order to maintain the cultural integrity of the assessment process and to respect multiple perspectives. Naturalistic inquiry allows for and encourages all stakeholders in the enterprise to tell their story. They state that the standardized or survey interview does not take into account multiple worldviews. Wolf and Tymitz (1976–1977) suggest that naturalistic inquiry is aimed at understanding actualities, cultural realities, and perceptions that exist untainted by the obtrusiveness of formal measurement or preconceived questions. Naturalistic inquiry is a more valuable method for assessing Native Americans because it is geared to the uncovering of narratives told by real people, about real events, in real and natural ways.

In the absence of adequate standardized instruments, naturalistic inquiry has been a fruitful alternative. The use of participatory research methods (which lend themselves well to naturalistic inquiry) has been especially valuable in evaluation research and studies leading to intervention development (Caldwell, Davis, Du Bois, Echo-Hawk, Erickson, Goins et al., 2005). Participatory approaches have the advantage of including diverse voices within the community in the actual research process. Participatory research is collaborative and flexible in nature, and thus may be preferred over other methods in American Indian populations. Involving the community has numerous advantages over the traditional "detached investigator" research model (or, in the case of intervention, the "detached professional" model). These benefits include, among others, 1) helping to ensure that the true needs of the community are considered and 2) the ability to access subpopulations which are difficult to reach. Furthermore, the method can produce fertile ground for the development of trust between the researcher or practitioner and the subject.

Culturally responsive evaluation can employ semi-structured interviews that can be designed to allow each respondent to "tell their own story," in their own words, minimizing the bias imposed by the method. This means that in the actual conduct of data collection respondents would not be discouraged from offering whatever they considered important. Using storytelling as a means of assessment serves the purpose of recognizing that each respondent is, in a very meaningful way, a stakeholder in the process. Storytelling, dialogue, and metaphoric expression enable us to decipher and acknowledge the complexities of language and culture.

A metaphor is a kind of story that calls us to consider a radically different way of knowing. In her book, *The Sacred Hoop: Recovering the Feminine in American Indian Tradition*, Paula Gunn Allen (1992) contends that allowing people to "give voice" to their life journey, i.e., telling their story, allows a "holistic image to pervade and shape consciousness, thus providing a coherent and empowering matrix for action and relationship" (pp. 104–105). Zemke (1990) notes that stories can play a stabilizing role in culture. A story provides structure for our perceptions and assessments of reality. In many American Indian tribal groups, a story is seen as having a life of its own. Such stories carry an energy – a truth, a lesson, an insight, an evaluative reflection – that can enter our being and connect us to a powerful source of truth making and perceptual affirmation. Many Native healers have often viewed English words as being "cages for ideas" and become frustrated with their inability to authentically express the gestalt of their cultural reality and life experience when non-Native researchers probe for explanations that fit into a structuralist world view.

CONSIDERATIONS FOR SERVICE DELIVERY

Special Therapies and Healers

American Indian medicine is more oriented towards healing than it is to curing. The major distinction here is that healing entails the restoration of balance and harmony with the body and the world, whereas curing combats specific ailments or diseases. Traditional Native healers do not attempt to address symptoms or diseases. Rather, their role is to assist the individual in returning to a state of balance or equilibrium with themselves, their relations, and their environment. Native American approaches to healing emphasize the simultaneous treatment of the mind, body, and spirit. Healers, or medicine men or women, work with each individual using the herbs, ceremony, and power best for the person.

As with other cultural practices, the specific healing methods and philosophies of American Indians are not uniform across tribal lines. However, several common elements do emerge when examining traditional healing. Specifically, the underlying mechanisms by which ceremonies are believed to heal are based on the notion of restoration of harmony. Most Native American healing practices involve a combination of spirituality, herbalism, and ceremony. The traditional American Indian equivalent of the "intervention" does not have rigid prescribed rules for how it is administered. Practices differ among tribes, and even among individual healers. Examples of traditional healing practices or ceremonies include sweat lodges, talking circles, vision quests, or pipe ceremonies. Four practices are common to most tribes:

1. **The Involvement of Healers (Medicine Men, Medicine Women):**
   The healer (who may have inherited their powers from ancestors, who may have had their powers transferred from another healer, or who may have developed their powers through initiation and training) functions much as a western health practitioner would. They observe, question, intuit, and rely upon their past experience. The healer may use a single approach or a combination of approaches, but these approaches are what distinguish Native American medicine from western medical practices. The approaches will not just involve psychopharmacology or testing, but instead may involve prayer, meditation, symbolic healing rituals, and counseling. These techniques are to appease spirits, rid the individual of impurity, and restore spiritual balance.

2. **The Use of Herbal Remedies:**
   Even though many contemporary Native Americans consult western physicians for antibiotics or surgery, they supplant this with herbal remedies as well. Herbs prescribed vary from tribe to tribe and vary from ailment to ailment. Traditional herbal remedies are often used for healing specific symptoms, but not all remedies are used by all tribes. For example, the Winnebago and Dakota tribes use skunk cabbage to treat asthma. On the other hand, the Menominees smoked the pulverized, dried root of mullein for healing asthma. The Natchez drink a tea of boiled pleurisy root for healing bronchitis, while the Yokia Indians use a tea of boiled wormwood roots for the same ailment. American Indian ethnobotany is a thriving practice among traditional healers.

3. **Ritual Purification:**
   Cleansing of the body, mind, and spirit is essential to restore balance to the individual and this is typically accomplished in a sweat lodge. A sweat lodge is similar to a sauna, except it is done outdoors in a small structure. Stones heated in fire are placed in the structure, and water is ladled onto the stones to produce steam and encourage sweating. The patient and the healer will pray or sing together to cleanse the individual of spirits dampening the healing process. Sweat lodge ceremonies can be done with an individual or a group.

4. **Ceremony:**
   Ceremonies vary according to tribe, but most tribes have a rich collection of ceremonies for healing. Dancing, singing, drumming, sand painting, chanting, feathers, or rattles can be used in ceremony to remove the disease, the blockage, or the bad energy that is contributing to the illness of the individual.

Traditional Indian medicine people and healers have not disappeared in modern-day America. Many traditional practitioners now integrate their work with Western medicine. The combination of traditional techniques and western medicine is a complex process, and there are no accepted guidelines for how such a synthesis is best accomplished. Many western practitioners are unknowledgeable about traditional healing practices and their importance within the cultural context.

It is beyond the scope of this chapter to adequately address the healing practices, ceremonies, and beliefs of Native Americans. Many of these practices and ceremonies are not known to non-tribal members and are regarded as the property of the tribe. The Smithsonian Institute published a list of selected references on Native American healing and medicine through the Anthropology Outreach Office (http://www.nmnh.si.edu/anthro/outreach/Native_Americans.html). There are several specialists in the field. For example, William Lyon, a research associate at the University of Kansas, has studied Native American healing for the past 26 years (Lyon, 1998). Cohen (2003) has also examined these practices in great detail.

Considerations for Medications and Therapies

Native Americans tend to underutilize services, experience higher therapy drop-out rates, are less likely to respond to treatment, and may have negative opinions about non-Indian providers. Given this, disaster workers need to approach Native American communities with great care. It would be especially important to understand the particular tribal culture prior to the actual disaster event. For example, taking specialized training or classes in understanding Native American medicines and healing would be one aspect of preparedness that would go a long way. Native American physicians, while rare, do exist and should be used as part of the disaster response team whenever possible.

The Association of American Indian Physicians, a group dedicated to pursuing excellence in Native American health care by promoting education in the medical disciplines, honoring traditional healing practices and restoring the balance of mind, body, and spirit, should be consulted for advice on medicine and therapies. Because Native American healers are integral to healing in their tribe, disaster workers should try to seek out healers for consultation and advice. In urban areas, healers may not be so obvious, but many urban areas have Indian Centers that can serve as an important contact point for accessing elders or other community members for consultation.

Special Considerations for Disasters and Trauma

American Indians have a long history of involvement with outsiders, and this history has shown them that outsiders, at the very least, are not particularly trustworthy. Through force, cajoling, trickery, and outright brutality, outsiders have tried to take the land, the children, the clothes, and the food away from American Indians. Because of this, anybody entering any Native

American community needs to be sensitive to cultural differences and treat such differences with respect. In short, one must pay attention to the issue of cultural competency (Cardenas, 1989; Cross, 1988; Orlandi & Epstein, 1992). Green (1982) clarifies this concept by pointing out that being culturally competent means conducting one's professional work in a way that is congruent with the behaviors and expectations that members of a cultural group recognize as appropriate among themselves. He indicates that it does not mean that outsiders should attempt to conduct themselves as though they are members of the group. Rather, they must be able to engage the community on its own terms and demonstrate acceptance of cultural differences in an open, genuine manner. It should be noted that in urban American Indian communities, this task becomes even harder due to the presence of multiple tribal/cultural groups.

A basic step in this process is that strangers must become involved with the community in a manner that allows for the acquisition of meaningful cultural knowledge. Since the culture of each tribe and geographical area varies, there is no substitute for direct and extended involvement with the community of interest. This involvement does not need to occur in a vacuum; rather it can transpire as part of the helping process. In other words, in approaching a community in a respectful manner, an alert practitioner can gain some of the necessary cultural knowledge. To accomplish this, Beauvais and Trimble (1992) point out that the first step is to describe the intent, nature, and benefits of a possible project or intervention before the governing body. On reservations identification of the governing body is clear-cut and is usually the Tribal Council. However, urban Indian communities do not have a governing body. A parallel step might mean meeting with a group composed of representatives from the major Indian organizations. Recognizing that formal organizations do not necessarily represent all urban Indians, community meetings open to all Indian people could be utilized to explain the purpose, costs and benefits of the endeavor. The purpose of such meetings is to both show respect for the community by telling them about the proposed project or intervention and to obtain feedback from the community. If meeting with an organized group is impractical (either because such a group does not exist or cannot be assembled given the circumstances of a disaster event, if there are severe time restrictions in periods of crisis, or in cases where there are competing power structures and serious rifts within the community), accessing several key informants embedded in the community is usually an acceptable alternative. A key point in this process of community engagement is the recognition that the community's ideas and the practitioner's ideas are both important – the definition of problems and the goals of the intervention should involve the community in a meaningful way. An important point of this process is to gain the sanction of the community. Without it, whether formal or informal, practitioners will always be seen as outsiders and hence be frustrated in further attempts to establish credibility.

FINAL RECOMMENDATIONS

Recommendation 1: Service Delivery Needs to be Culturally Appropriate

Cultural barriers interfere with service delivery. When the culture is not known, assumptions are made that may interfere with service delivery. Western medicine sees problems as residing in the person. In the Native World View, interventions are not targeted to a particular symptom or cause, but rather are focused on bringing the person back into balance. Once harmony is restored, the problem dissipates. Fasting, sweating, or other kinds of Native interventions are used to bring about change, and to bring a person into balance. Understanding normative cultural responses to disasters is important for designing and implementing interventions which are accepted and utilized by the population. Cultural understanding and cultural competency are critical for providing effective service delivery in American Indian communities. To achieve their goals, academics, researchers, grassroots workers, health practitioners, disaster response workers, funding agencies, tribes, states, and the federal government must understand the cultural norms present in the communities in which they operate.

Recommendation 2: Outreach and Family Participation

The informal support network in the Native American community is a strong and viable resource. Families and elders would be an important part of service delivery effectiveness as they are the central focus of the Native American community. Family ties go beyond biology. Families make decisions about important issues together as a group, including medical care. Individuality is not the central organizing feature; families, communities, and tribes are the organizing theme of everyday life. Many people stay within their own family or community to solve a problem and do not go outside of that social network. Elders are respected and revered and taken care of by the family; they are honored. Individuals with disabilities are generally cared for by the family, and not sent to an outside agency. Thus, to influence a community, you must value and honor its' interconnection. Given the strong value of family and social connectedness in Native communities, a comprehensive program should integrate family, small group, and community-based activities into the range of individual services offered whenever possible.

Recommendation 3: Develop Partnerships

Finding functional ways to develop programs in American Indian communities is to *partner with local leadership* to shape and own the program (Davis & Keemer, 2002). This is a major component – one that is essentially *listening to what the people have to say*. This step may entail establishing dialogue and working relationships with local educators, elders, health service providers, and community people including youth.

The first step of any partnership is to develop a sense of trust and to foster an ongoing dialogue between all parties. This process does not happen over night. A major error in many failed programs is the lack of time in which to establish the groundwork for the project. Sufficient time must be allowed in which the disaster management team can meet with community members to discuss the plans for relief efforts and to encourage community involvement. Many Indian communities have developed a certain level of independence that is upheld by both formal and informal regulatory structures not found in non-Indian communities. It is necessary to gain approval for new programs and research from tribal or village councils. In larger tribes, this authority may be delegated to a council committee, a health committee, and/or a tribal institutional review board. In addition, one will often find that community gatekeepers must be well informed of the new partnership and their input must be sought (Baldwin, 1999).

The disaster response team would be well advised to consider establishing a community advisory board and partnering with existing change agents within the community. An advisory committee or board composed of community residents and leaders can play an extremely important role in continually monitoring the progress of the project and providing guidance to the project team. It is also very important to partner with *change agents within the community*. It is well accepted in the field of community development that the deepest and most lasting changes in community life are generated from within and not by outsiders who may not have lasting investment in the welfare of the community (Baldwin, 1999).

Recommendation 4. Be There

Being there is another important process for showing and building mutual respect, and proving the sincerity of the disaster response teams' commitment to local customs and ways of doing things. People who come and go at will in an Indian community will never be accepted, nor will their interventions or treatments be adopted.

Disaster response teams must engage in more personal involvement when working with American Indian communities and can learn a tremendous amount by actively immersing themselves in the culture. Demonstrating a genuine interest and willingness to participate in community-based social and cultural events (e.g., pow-wows, and traditional ceremonies when invited) that may not be directly related to the program's agenda are important ways of showing respect (Rolf, Nansel, Baldwin, Johnson, & Benally, 2002).

Recommendation 5. Employ Indigenous Staff

Davis and Keemer (2002) suggest that the hiring of indigenous staff has several benefits: It improves the local economy, teaches the indigenous staff members new skills, and improves the quality of the intervention. Among other benefits, hiring indigenous staff provides a non-invasive vehicle for the practitioner to participate in social and cultural events. However, the possibility exists that some Native Americans would prefer to utilize services at non-Native clinics and programs due to issues of confidentiality. In these cases, developing a robust referral network is essential. Outreach and peer prevention workers often play a pivotal role in Native communities. Rural clinics have utilized Community Health Representatives to provide services as part of the overall health system.

Recommendation 6. Utilize Key Informants and Local Channels of Delivery

Elders, cultural leaders, spiritual advisors, teachers, parents, and youth leaders can all be important and credible sources of information. The use of visual materials that reflect specific tribal images is a preferred communication strategy, because local music, images, and values can increase the community's identification with messages and materials (Native Communities HIV/STD Prevention Guidelines Task Force, 2004). The use of tribal legends and stories (where appropriate) can also be an important way to incorporate cultural knowledge into communication strategies. Traditional tribal stories and legends grounded in tribal language organize the world and lay out individual and communal responsibilities and obligations. Utilizing this local cultural knowledge is critically important to teach new skills and habits.

References

Annie E. Casey Foundation. (2003). *Kids Count pocket guide: American Indian children*. State-level measures of child well-being from the 2000 Census.

Allen, P. G. (1992). *The sacred hoop: Recovering the feminine in American Indian traditions*. Boston: Beacon Press.

Baldwin, J. (1999). Conducting drug abuse prevention in partnership with Native American Communities: Meeting challenges through collaborative approaches. *Drugs and Society*, 14(1/2), 77–92.

Beauvais, F., & Trimble, J. E. (1992). The role of the researcher on evaluating America Indian drug abuse prevention programs. In M. Orlandi & L. Epstein (Eds.), *Cultural competence for evaluators: A guide for alcohol and other drug abuse prevention practitioners working with ethnic/racial communities* (pp. 173–201), Monograph of the Office of Substance Abuse Prevention, Cultural Competence Series 1. Rockville, MD.

Berzok, L. M. (2005). *American Indian Food*. Westport, CT: Greenwood Publishing Company.

Biggs, V. (2002). Problems facing Indian youth. Testimony before the United States Senate, Committee on Indian Affairs on behalf of the American Association of Pediatricians. Accessed September 12, 2006 from: http://www.aap.org/advocacy/washing/scia.htm

Blackmore, W. (1869–1870). The North-American Indians: A sketch of some of the hostile tribes, together with a brief account of General Sheridan's campaign of 1868 against the Sioux, Cheyenne, Arapahoe, Kiowa, and Comanche Indians. *The Journal of the Ethnological Society of London*, 1(3), 287–320.

Brave Heart Yellow Horse, M., & DeBruyn, L. M. (1998). The American Indian holocaust: heal-
    ing historical unresolved grief. *American Indian and Alaska Native Mental Health Research,
    8*(2), 60–82.
Brave Heart Yellow Horse, M. (2004). The historical trauma response among Natives and its rela-
    tionship to substance abuse: A Lakota illustration. In E. Nebelkopf & M. Phillips (Eds.),
    Healing and mental health for native Americans: Speaking in red. Walnut Creek, California:
    AltaMira Press, pp. 7–18.
Brave Heart Yellow Horse, M. (2005). Cultural Trauma. Talk given at the 4th Wellbriety
    Conference: Denver, CO.
Bureau of Indian Affairs (BIA). (2003). 2001 youth risk behavior survey of high school students
    attending bureau funded schools. Office of Indian Education Programs. Retrieved on April
    13, 2005, from http://www.oiep.bia.edu/docs/hsyrbs_2001.pdf.
Burhansstipanov, L. (2000). Urban Native American health issues. *Cancer, 117*(supplement),
    207–1213.
Caldwell, J. Y., Davis, J. D., Du Bois, B., Echo-Hawk, M., Erickson, J. S., Goins, R. T., et al. (2005).
    Culturally competent research with American Indians and Alaska Natives: Findings and
    recommendations of the first symposium of the work group on American Indian research and
    program evaluation methodology. *American Indian and Alaska Native Mental Health Research,
    12*(1), 1–21.
Cardenas, P. (1989). *Culture and cultural competency: Youth focused prevention and intervention.*
    Monograph of the Colorado State Alcohol and Drug Division. Denver, CO.
Carlisle Industrial Indian School. (2005). Retrieved on March 3, 2005, from http://home.epix.
    net/~landis
Centers for Disease Control (CDC). (2005a). National diabetes fact sheet: General information
    and national estimates on diabetes in the United States. Atlanta, GA: U.S. Department of
    Health and Human Services, CDC.
Centers for Disease Control (CDC). (2005b). Deaths: Leading causes for 2002. *National Vital
    Statistics Reports, 53*(17), 1–90.
Center for Substance Abuse Treatment (CSAT). (1999). *Cultural issues in substance abuse treatment.*
    Substance Abuse and Mental Health Services Administration, Department of Health and
    Human Services.
Cheshire, T. C. (2001). Cultural transmission in urban American Indian families. *American
    Behavioral Scientist, 44*(9), 1528–1535.
Child, B. J. (1998). *Boarding school seasons: American Indian families, 1900–1940.* Lincoln: University
    of Nebraska Press.
Clark, S. L., & Weismantle, M. (2003). *Employment Status: 2000.* Census 2000 Brief (C2KBR-18).
    Washington, DC: U.S. Department of Commerce, Economics and Statistics Administration,
    U.S. Census Bureau.
Cohen, K. B. H. (2003). *Honoring the medicine: The essential guide to Native American healing.* New
    York, NY: Random House.
Coyhis, D. (1999). *Understanding Native American culture.* Colorado Springs, CO: Coyhis
    Publishing.
Crawford, J. (1995). Endangered Native American languages: what is to be done, and why? *The
    Bilingual Research Journal, 19*(1), 17–38.
Cross, T. (1988). Services to minority populations: Cultural competence continuum, *Focal Point,
    3*(1), 1–3.
Dahlstrom, W. (1986). Ethnic status and personality measurement. In W. G. Dahlstrom, D.
    Lacher, & L. E. Dahlstrom (Eds.), *MMPI patterns of American minorities.* (pp. 3–23). Min-
    neapolis: University of Minnesota Press.
Davis, J. D., & Keemer, K. (2002). A brief history of and future considerations for research in
    Native American and Alaska Native communities. In J. D. Davis, J. S. Erickson, S. R. John-
    son, C. A. Marshall, P. Running Wolf, & R. L. Santiago (Eds.), *Work group on Native American
    Research and Program Evaluation Methodology (AIRPEM), Symposium on research and evaluation*

methodology: Lifespan issues related to Native Americans/Alaska Natives with disabilities (pp. 9–18). Flagstaff: Northern Arizona University, Institute for Human Development, Arizona University Center on Disabilities, Native American Rehabilitation Research and Training Center.

Davis, G. L., Hoffman, R. G., & Nelson, K. S. (1990). Differences between Native Americans and Whites on the California Psychological Inventory. *Psychological Assessment: A Journal of Consulting and Clinical Psychology, 2*(3), 338–342.

Department of Veteran's Affairs. (2002). America's war. Retrieved August 29, 2006, from www1.va.gov/opa/fact/amwars.asp.

Driver, H. E. (1969). *Indians of North America.* Chicago, IL: University of Chicago Press.

Drug and Alcohol Services Information (DASIS). (2005). *The DASIS report: Substance abuse treatment admissions among Native Americans and Alaska Natives: 2002.* Retrieved February 9, 2005, from http://oas.samhsa.gov/2k5/IndianTX/IndianTX.htm

Durrett, D. (1998). *Unsung heroes of World War II: The story of the Navajo code talkers.* New York: Facts on File.

Etchinson, M., & Kleist, D.M. (2000). Review of narrative therapy: research and utility. *Family Journal, 8,* 61–66.

Fixico, D. L. (2003). *The American Indian mind in a linear world.* New York, NY: Routledge.

Forquera, R. (2001). *Urban Indian health.* Seattle, WA: Henry J. Kaiser Family Foundation.

Green, J. W. (1982). *Cultural awareness in the human services.* Englewood Cliffs, NJ: Prentice-Hall.

Grossman, D., Krieger, J., Sugarman, J., & Forquera, R. (1994). Health status of urban American Indians and Alaska Natives: A population based study. *Journal of the American Medical Association, 271*(11), 845–850.

Guba, E. G., & Lincoln, Y. S. (1989). *Fourth generation evaluation.* Newbury Park, CA: Sage.

Guba, E. G., & Lincoln, Y. S. (1981). *Effective evaluation: Improving the usefulness of evaluation results through responsive and naturalistic approaches.* San Francisco: Jossey-Bass.

Guerrero, M. (1979). Indian Child Welfare Act of 1978: A response to the threat to Indian culture caused by foster and adoptive placements of Indian children. *American Indian Law Review, 7,* 51–77.

Hirschfelder, A., & Montano, M. (1993). *The Native American almanac.* NJ: Prentice Hall.

Indian Health Service. (2005). *Fiscal year 2005 budget requests, justification of estimates for appropriations committees.* Retrieved on April 13, 2005, from www.ihs.gov/AdminMngrResources/Budget/FY_2005_Budget_Justification.asp

Jaimes, M. A. (1992). *The state of Native America: Genocide, colonization, and resistance.* Boston, MA: South End Press.

Johnson, J. L., & Cameron, M. (2001). Barriers to providing effective mental health services to American Indians. *Mental Health Services Research, 3*(4), 215–223.

Keppel, K. G., Pearcy, J. N., & Wagener, D. K. (2002). Trends in ethnic specific rates for health status indicators: United States, 1990–1998. *Healthy people statistical notes, no 23.* Hyattsville, MD: National Center for Health Statistics.

Kroeber, K. (1992). American Indian persistence and resurgence. *Boundary 2, 19*(3), 1–25.

Lafromboise, T.D., Trimble, J.E., & Mohatt, G.V. (1990). Counseling intervention and American Indian tradition: An integrative approach. *The Counseling Psychologist. 18*(4), 628–654.

Lyness, K.P. (2002). Alcohol problems in Alaska natives: risk, resiliency, and native treatment approaches. *Journal of Ethnicity in Substance Abuse, 1*(3), 39–56.

Lyon, W. S. (1998). *Encyclopedia of Native American healing.* New York, NY: Norton.

Manson, S. M., Shore, J., Barron, A., Ackerson, L., & Neligh, G. (1992). Alcohol abuse and dependence among American Indians. In J. Helzer & G. Canino (Eds.), *Alcoholism in North America, Europe, and Asia* (pp. 119–130). New York: Oxford University Press.

Markstrom, C. A., & Charley, P. H. (2003). Psychological effects of technological/ human-caused disasters: Examination of the Navajo and uranium. *American Indian & Alaska Native Mental Health Research, 11*(1), 19–45.

May, P. A., & Moran, J. R. (1995). Prevention of alcohol misuse: A review of health promotion efforts among American Indians. *American Journal of Health Promotion, 9*(4), 288–299.

McCullough, C. S., Walker, J. L., & Diessner, R. (1985). The use of Wechsler Scales in the assessment of Native Americans of the Columbia River basin. *Psychology in the Schools, 23*, 23–31.

Meriam, L. (1977). The effects of boarding schools on Indian family life. In S. Unger (Ed.), *The destruction of American Indian families* (pp. 14–17). New York, NY: Association on American Indian Affairs.

Nabokov, P. (1991). *Native American testimony: A chronicle of Indian-white relations from prophesy to the present, 1492–1992*. New York: Viking.

Native Communities HIV/STD Prevention Guidelines Task Force. (2004). *HIV/STD prevention guidelines for Native American communities: American Indians, Alaska Natives, and Native Hawaiians*. Bloomington, IN: Rural Center for HIV/STD Prevention.

Nelson, S., McCoy, G. F., Stetter, M., & Vanderwagen, W. C. (1992). An overview of mental health services for American Indians and Alaska Natives in the 1990s. *Hospital and Community Psychiatry, 43*(3), 257–261.

Nichols, R. L. (1986). *The American Indian: Past and present*. New York, NY: Alfred A. Knopf.

O'Brien, S. (1985). Federal Indian policies and the international protection of human rights. In V. Deloria (Ed.), *American policy in the twentieth century* (pp. 35–61). Norman, OK: University of Oklahoma Press.

Officer, J. (1971). The American Indian and federal policy. In J. Waddell & O. Watson (Eds.), *The American Indian in urban society* (pp. 8–65). Boston: Little, Brown, and Company.

Ogunwole, S. U. (2002). The American Indian and Alaska Native population: 2000. *Census 2000 Brief* (C2KBR/01-15). Washington, DC: U.S. Department of Commerce, Economics and Statistics Administration, U.S. Census Bureau,

Ogunwole, S. U. (2006). We the people: American Indians and Alaska Natives in the United States. *Census 2000 Special Reports* (CENSR-28). Washington, DC: U.S. Department of Commerce, Economics and Statistics Administration, U.S. Census Bureau.

Orlandi, R. W., & Epstein, L. G. (Eds.). (1992). *Cultural competence for evaluators: A guide for alcohol and other drug abuse prevention practitioners working with ethnic/racial communities*. Rockville, MD: Office for Substance Abuse Prevention.

Patton, M. (1990). *Qualitative evaluation and research methods, 2nd edition*. Newbury Park, CA: Sage.

Perry, S. W. (2004). *American Indians and crime: A BJS statistical profile, 1992–2002*. U.S. Department of Justice, Bureau of Justice Statistics (NCJ 203097).

Peterson, I. (2004). Would-be tribes entice investors. *New York Times*. March 29, 2004.

Peterson, N. J. (1999). Introduction – Native American literature: From the margins to the mainstream. *Modern Fiction Studies, 45*(1), 1–9.

Rolf, J. E., Nansel, T. R., Baldwin, J. A., Johnson, J. L., & Benally, C. C. (2002). HIV/AIDS and alcohol and other drug abuse prevention in American Indian communities: Behavioral and community effects. In P. D. Mail, S. Heurtin-Roberts, S. E. Martin, & J. Howard (Eds.), *Alcohol use among American Indians: Multiple perspectives on a complex problem*. National Institute on Alcohol Abuse and Alcoholism Research Monograph No. 37. Bethesda, MD: National Institute on Alcohol Abuse and Alcoholism.

Schwartz, R. C. (1999). Narrative therapy expands and contracts family therapy's horizons. *Journal of Marital and Family Therapy, 25*(2), 263–267.

Snipp, C. M. (1992). Sociological perspectives on American Indians. *Annual Review of Sociology, 18*, 351–371.

Snipp, C. M. (1996). The size and distribution of the American Indian population: Fertility, mortality, migration, and residence. In G. D. Sandefur, R. R. Rindfuss, & B. Cohen (Eds.), *Changing numbers, changing needs: American Indian demography and public health* (pp. 17–52). Washington, DC: National Academic Press.

Sorkin, A. (1978). *The urban American Indian*. Lexington, Massachusetts: DC Health and Company.

Standing Bear, L. (1928). *My people, the Sioux* (E. A. Brininstool, Ed.). Cambridge: The Riverside Press.

Stiffarm, L. (1992). The demography of Native North America: A question of American Indian survival. In M. A. Jaimes (Ed.), *The state of Native America: genocide, colonization, and resistance* (pp. 23–54). Boston, MA: South End Press.

Substance Abuse and Mental Health Services Administration (SAMHSA). (2003, May 16). *The NHSDA report: Substance use among Native Americans or Alaska Natives.* Rockville, MD: Office of Applied Studies.

Substance Abuse and Mental Health Services Administration (SAMHSA). (2006). *Results from the 2005 National Survey on Drug Use and Health: National findings.* (NSDUH Series H-30, DHHS Publication No. SMA 06-4194). Rockville, MD: Office of Applied Studies.

Trimble, J. E. (1991). Ethnic specification, validation prospects, and the future of drug use research. *The International Journal of the Addictions, 25,* 149–170.

Thornton, R. (1987). *American Indian holocaust and survival: A population history since 1492.* Norman, OK: University of Oklahoma Press.

Thornton, R. (1996). Tribal membership requirements and the demography of "old" and "new" Native Americans. In G. D. Sandefur, R. R. Rindfuss, & B. Cohen (Eds.), *Changing numbers, changing needs: American Indian demography and public health* (pp. 103–112). Washington, DC: National Academy Press.

United States Bureau of the Census. (1937). *Fifteenth census of the United States 1930: The Indian population of the United States and Alaska.* Washington, DC: Government Printing Office.

United States Commission on Civil Rights. (2003). *A quiet crisis: Federal funding and unmet needs in Indian country.* Retrieved July 12, 2005, from http://www.usccr.gov/pubs/na0703/na0204. pdf#search=%22civil%20rights%20quiet%20crisis%20unmet%20needs%20Indian%22

United States Commission on Civil Rights. (2004). *Broken promises: Evaluating the Native American health care system.* Retrieved March 29, 2005 from http://www.usccr.gov/pubs/nahealth/ nabroken.pdf

United States Department of Health and Human Services (DHHS). (2003). *Health, United States, 2003.* Washington, DC: Government Printing Office, Table 29.

United States Department of Health and Human Services (DHHS). (2005). *Culture, race, and ethnicity – A supplement to Mental Health: A Report of the Surgeon General.* Office of the Surgeon General, Substance Abuse and Mental Health Services Administration. Retrieved on March 15, 2005, from http://www.surgeongeneral.gov/library/mentalhealth/cre/

Urban Indian Health Institute. (2004). *The health status of urban American Indians and Alaska Natives: An analysis of select vital records and Census data sources.* Retrieved on April 3, 2005, from http://www.uihi.org/reports/2004HealthStatusReport.pdf

Walker, R. D. (1981). Treatment strategies in an urban Indian alcoholism program. *Journal of Studies on Alcohol, Supplement 9,* 171–184.

Wares, D., Wedel, K., Rosenthal, J., & Dobrec, A. (1994). Indian child welfare: A multicultural challenge. *Journal of Multicultural Social Work, 3*(3), 1–15.

Whitbeck, L. B., Adams, G. W., Hoyt, D. R., & Chen, X. (2004). Conceptualizing and measuring historical trauma among American Indian people. *American Journal of Community Psychology, 33*(3/4), 119–130.

Williams, D. R., & Collins, C. (1995). U.S. socioeconomic and racial differences in health: Patterns and explanations. *Annual Review of Sociology, 21,* 349–386.

Wilson, T. P. (1992). Blood quantum: Native American mixed bloods. In M. P. P. Root (Ed.), *Racially mixed people in America* (pp. 108–125). Newbury Park, CA: Sage Publication, Inc.

Wolf, R., & Tymitz, B. (1976–1977). Ethnography and reading: Matching inquiry mode to process. *Reading Research Quarterly, 12,* 5–11.

Wright, R. (1992). *Stolen continents: The ¡'New World" through Indian eyes since 1492.* New York, NY: Houghten-Mifflin.

Zemke, R. (1990). Storytelling: Back to basics. *Training Magazine, 27*(3), 44–50.

Chapter 5

Arab Americans: Understanding Their Challenges, Needs, and Struggles

Naji Abi-Hashem

INTRODUCTION

The presence of Arabs, Muslims, and Middle Easterners in North America is becoming more visible, active, and influential. This is especially true in recent years due to the convenience of international travel and cross-national migration. Some Middle Easterners are venturing on their own, others are joining their family members. Yet, others are undoubtedly escaping the ethnopolitical conflicts and sociopolitical pressures in their regions. Arabs and Muslims are spreading across the United States and Canada in large numbers, creating unique neighborhoods and vibrant communities. This phenomenon is also taking place in Europe, Africa, Australia, and Central and South America. Middle Easterners come from all backgrounds, heritages, nationalities, social classes, and religious traditions. They are migrating as separate individuals, as small family groups, as close friends and colleagues, or as extended families and relatives. Some of them obtain a student or work visa, others obtain a permanent residency or immigrant status, and with that, they join previous generations who have been already living and working in their new found homeland. The Arab population in the United States is growing and becoming well situated and established. According to El-Badry (2004),

> The vast majority of Arab Americans are citizens of the United States. They are very much like other Americans, except younger, more educated, more affluent and more likely to own a business. Like any other immigrant

115

group, Arab Americans want to enjoy America's riches while preserving the
important parts of their native culture (2004, p. 1).

  Similarly, Hendricks (2005) noted that, "People of Arab descent are a small
but growing slice of the multiethnic American pie and, with higher-than-
average levels of education and income, they are succeeding in the United
States, according to findings in a new report from the U.S. Census Bureau"
(p. A-7).
  Some of these immigrants are adjusting well and quickly. They are making
good progress at the personal and communal level and are making positive contributions to American society. They are businessmen and women,
scholars and academics, community leaders and politicians, physicians and
healthcare providers, artists and musicians, lawmakers and engineers, social
activists and journalists, military personnel and sportsmen, etc. (cf. Arab
American Institute, 2006a; Grande finale, n.d.; San Francisco, 2003). Others
continue to struggle and have major difficulty assimilating into the American
system of life. Therefore, these groups may not be able to function properly or live in harmony within the hosting culture despite efforts to do so.
Yet others, who may be a smaller minority, refuse to integrate fully but rather
insist on keeping their own subculture and mentality intact, demanding more
accommodations, compromises, and privileges than the Untied States or local
governments are willing to offer.
  In this chapter we will discuss the basic characteristics of Arab Americans,
their cultures, religious affiliations, and social life. We will discuss their background, migration history, multiple generations, and current demographics.
We will explore the various groups and communities, their family structure
and education, their challenges and contributions, and their psychosocial
adjustment and acculturation. We will explain the similarities and differences
among Arabs, Muslims, and Middle Easterners. We will try to correct some
misconceptions and stereotypes about Arab Americans, and explore their connection with the situation in the Middle East. We will highlight the mental
needs, emotional injuries, and coping styles of those migrating from troubled areas where they have been exposed to trauma, multiple losses, and war
tragedies. We will also examine their psychological conditions, diagnoses,
and responses.
  Special sections are devoted to ethical-moral values, social heritage and
traditions, mentality and worldview, communication and relational styles,
coping and survival modes, and personal habits and practices of the people in the Middle East and the Arabic Islamic world. Their strengths and
resiliency as well as their vulnerabilities and common disorders will be
explored. We will list and examine the available modern therapies and also
the use of folk remedies, traditional practices, religious interventions, popular
spiritualistic methods, and para-psychological approaches. At the end, several guidelines and practical suggestions are presented for better dealing with

Arab Americans and for conducting culturally relevant and sensitive clinical and counseling work among Arabs and Muslims, whether they reside in North America or in the Middle East.

GENERAL BACKGROUND

Arab Americans have their roots in the Middle East, in North Africa, and in the Arabic Peninsula. Each of these regions has its own unique characteristics, rich history, and long heritage. Due to the constant media attention on the ethnopolitical conflicts and wars in Iraq and Palestine/Israel, people who live outside these areas tend to have the impression that the Middle East is a huge war zone. In fact, most of the Middle East is stable, safe, and secure. Life in many corners of the Arab world is enjoyable, meaningful, and productive. By nature, most Arabic Middle Eastern people are quite friendly, warm, and hospitable.

The Arabic Language

Geographically, the Middle East covers a large and vast area. It is known for its many subcultures, landscapes, dialects, trades, accents, societies, and religions. It is characterized by its richness of heritage, the beauty of the land, and the friendliness of the people. It is important to note here that the majority of Middle Easterners are non-political, non-aggressive, and non-fanatic. The classical Arabic language, in its written or official spoken form, is common to all Arab countries. It is:

> "... one of the great unifying and distinguishing characteristics of Arab people. Even so, colloquial Arabic differs from place to place. There are several categories: Levantine dialect (Jordan, Syria, Palestine, Lebanon), Egyptian and North African dialect, and Khalijji, or Gulf, dialect. Modern Standard Arabic (MSA) is a pan-Arabic language used in formal letters, books and newspapers. It is also spoken at Middle East ... conferences and on [radio and] television news. Quaranic Arabic ... differs in style and lexicon from MSA. Not all Arab Americans know Arabic, of course, as many are second, third, and fourth-generation Americans" (Detroit Free Press, 2001, Overview, p. 5).

Thus, each region, community, or country has its own colloquial form, style, or accent of the daily spoken language. It is called the conversational style of Arabic, a lower and smoother form of the highly classical text. This is similar to the difference between high German and low German or old Greek and contemporary Greek. People from neighboring regions or countries understand each other much better than people from distant regions. For example, when comparing the far North African region (like Morocco) with the East Mediterranean region (like Lebanon) or with the deeper Gulf region (like Qatar), one finds a wide spectrum of spoken Arabic reflecting the local heritage, terrain, climate, subculture, religion, and socio-ethnic traits. Even within one country there are multiple variations and accents of Arabic due to the old traditions found in each community. In addition, private and public schools normally teach at least one foreign language besides the Arabic, commonly French or English.

Urban people in the Middle East usually use or speak more than one language in their daily work, study, communication and conversation. They are very familiar with foreign media. Most Westerners do not know that Arabic is an old Semitic language (like Aramaic or Hebrew) and is written from right to left, unlike Latin-derived languages. There are other non-Arabic speaking languages and dialects in different regions of the Middle East and North Africa, like the Berber, Assyrian, Chaldean, and Kurdish. Of course, Persian is found in Iran, Greek in Cyprus and Greece, Hebrew in Israel, and Turkish in Turkey.

It is worth noting here that the Middle East is the birthplace of several major civilizations and prominent world religions. Many places in the Middle East are the meeting grounds between the Far East and the Far West. In the Arab world, one also can find a wide spectrum of subcultures and mentalities. It is like a colorful mosaic of traditions. Most rural areas represent the simple, old, and rich ways of life, while most urban areas and cities represent the more complex, modern, and sophisticated lifestyle. At times, these subcultures and trends clash with each other, creating social tension and division of mentality and ideology (traditionalism & fundamentalism versus modernism & secularism). In most places, however, both of these polarities coexist together, creating a wealth of culture and a harmony of integrated functions (Abi-Hashem, 1992, 2004a; 2006).

Myths and Misunderstandings About the Arabic-Islamic World

Before we explore the needs and struggles of Arab Americans and consequently suggest certain practical socio-clinical ways to help and deal with them, there is a great need to clarify some facts and correct some misunderstandings (or stereotypes) about the Arabic-Islamic World and Middle Easterners in general (cf. Abi-Hashem, 1992, 2004a).

First, not all Arabs are Muslims. Although most Arabs are Muslims, there are considerable communities of non-Muslims in the Middle East and North Africa, like the Christians (all denominations), Druze, Jews, Alawites (Alawe'en), etc. In several places, the demographic equilibrium is rapidly shifting and these communities (such as the Christians), once large and established in may areas, are decreasing in number and influence and thus becoming smaller minorities. Presently, there is an increased trend in migration of these minorities (specifically among Christians – e.g., Palestinians, Egyptians, Iraqis, Lebanese, etc.) to the West in general and to the United States in particular. Likewise, not all Muslims are Arabs. Some Muslims are ethnically and culturally much different from Arabs. Large Muslim populations are found in countries like Indonesia, Iran, Pakistan, India, South Central Asia, Africa, and Eastern Europe. In addition, not all Arab Muslims are highly devout or practicing believers. Many are Muslims by affiliation or by name only. This is fairly common among other faiths as well – such as the nominal Jew or the cultural Hindu. Therefore, religious affiliation is an integral part of people's heritage and social identity.

Second, not all Arabs are Middle Easterners. North African nations like Tunisia, Algeria, Morocco, Egypt, and Libya are Arabic and Muslim nations but are not considered Middle Eastern. Most of them are moderate nations with strong exposure to Mediterranean Europe, particularly France. The French language is the second official language in most North African nations. Likewise, not all Middle Eastern countries are considered Arabic (e.g., Turkey, Iran, Cyprus, Israel, etc.). Many of these countries, along with the Western European seashore nations, do share similar Mediterranean characteristics in terms of mood, climate, nature, world view, food, family life, emotional expression, etc.

Third, not all Arabs or Muslims are fanatics with regard to their religion. With the rise of Islamic fundamentalism and religious radicalism in the world today, there is a tendency for other nations and media (non-Muslims ones, especially Western) to portray devout Muslims as radicals or fanatics, whether this happens intentionally or not. Incidentally, the word Arabic does not automatically mean Muslim even though the news media usually portrays the two as synonymous. The region known as Arabia has a long non-Muslim history and had a rich culture long before Islam evolved. Furthermore, as already seen in this chapter, there are many groups of Arabic origin and descent which are not associated with Islam as a religion or worldview except by sharing common language, geographical proximity, and cultural roots.

Fourth, not all Arabs are uncivilized or poorly educated. This is another misconception or stereotype. Actually, many Arab communities are highly cultured, educated, polished, rich, and well established. Although not all Arab countries have oil, money, or royal palaces, many countries also do not have camels, nomads, tents, or tribes. In addition, not all Muslim men marry several wives or have lots of children. Likewise, not all Arab women are restricted or bound to extreme roles and rigid living (see Abi-Hashem, 2003). A major section of Arabs and Muslims, especially the younger generation, are highly open, quite international, and culturally versatile. Many people from these groups migrate to the West and North America and, therefore, require little adjustment or adaptation in order to function well in their new environment. The major cities of the Middle East are becoming quite cosmopolitan centers at the gate of Asia, where Western technology, business, and education meets Eastern customs, lifestyles, and traditions.

Fifth, not all Arabs hate America or the West. Neither do all Arabs deeply identify with the Israeli-Palestinian conflict, though it is central to the dynamics of the region and its psyche. In the Arab-Muslim world, people both young and old adore Westerners and Americans even while they may be critical of the U.S.'s harmful policies towards them. They usually rejoice when they have a chance to meet some foreigners. Americans are generally very welcomed and treated with hospitality and open hearts in all corners of the Middle East. What Arab-Muslims generally do not like, and do particularly resent, is the foreign policies and biases of the government of the United States – especially those biases towards the nation of Israel and what it represents on the geo-political level as a Jewish state.

In many traditional circles, there is also a great cautiousness and hesitancy to accepting American products, influences, values, and ways of life. In fact, many societies and countries resist the American ego, its pop culture, its economic exploitation, and its military expansion. They perceive the West in general and the United States in particular as invading their societies, markets, moralities, and traditions. Although they realize that there are so many goods, professional helps, and humanitarian aids coming from the West, they are weary of the other products, dangers, corruptions, hidden agendas, and political manipulations that are being exported as well. Therefore, these Arabs and Muslims have become very self-protective and self-preserving of their culture, values, heritage, religions, and social norms.

It is worth noting here, that although radical groups and extremists are thriving in their power and fight against modernism and secularism and in their level of hate toward the West, the majority of Arabs and Muslims in the Middle East are not radical, aggressive, or extreme. Nor are they happy with the damage the radical Islamists are causing them and others. The extreme few are ultimately ruining the reputation of all Arabs, Muslims, and Middle Easterners alike.

Conversely, there are many critics of the Arabic-Islamic world who point out the weaknesses and passivity of the systems. Barakat (1993), for example, observed many positive and negative features that characterize several societies in the Middle East. Among them are the centrality of religion, duality of Westernization and Arabism, the attempt to integrate capitalism into some Islamic systems of government, signs of social and political fragmentation, certain repressive socialization and neopatriarchy, dominance of traditionalism over sociopolitical creativity, some disequilibrium in the Arabic ego, the prevalence of traditional mentality, and the absence of future-oriented rationalism. Some of these characteristics have created a certain splitting within the psyche of many Arab Americans, causing them to attempt to reconcile their old ways with the new ones. They are now soul-searching deeply to find a new profile, a new affiliation, and a new identity that authentically represents them (cf. Abou-El-Fadl, 2005).

Again, it is important here to remember that the Middle East is the birthplace of many ancient civilizations and most world religions. The urban cities are vibrant places where ancient traditions, customs, and faith meet modern and western lifestyles. Social appropriateness is emphasized in speech, behavior, and appearance. Titles, labels, and compliments are essential. Respect for the elderly is imperative. Families and communities are the primary venues where social roles are learned and personal identities are formed and maintained.

Religion

Religious identity is an important ingredient in the fabric of the Middle East. A person's religious branch or affiliation, such as Sunnii, Shiitte, Eastern Orthodox, Maronite, Latin, Greek Catholic, Jewish, or Druze, is actually written on their personal identification card in most countries and provinces. In most Arabic-Islamic nations, religion is inseparable from culture and social contexts. A sharp division between religion and government typically does not exist. All these aspects are intertwined together inside the region's socio-cultural and political systems. Unlike in the West, there is no clear-cut separation or divorce between politics, culture, and religion. Therefore, it is common to hear references to God and faith (using at times spiritual concepts or theological terms) among people of all levels – in general conversations or in formal settings, whether in private or in public, in business or in education, in medicine or in politics, etc.

In the Arabic and Islamic worlds, people are not afraid of mentioning God, referring to religious values, or using spiritual terms and concepts in public. They recognize and respect each other's customs, faiths, and practices. In certain countries, the mass media usually acknowledges the religious feasts and makes room for all predominant faiths among the audience. When people are experiencing pain, are in a crisis, or having a joyful occasion, they expect to hear from their friends and caring others something about God that is relevant to their situation. People are typically quite open to receiving spiritual encouragement, even in the generic sense, offered as part of social support and expressions of solidarity with them. For some, even blaming God and their fate in life can be a common dynamic in their personal coping and emotional expressiveness.

DEMOGRAPHICS

Population

There is some inconsistency in reports of how many Arab Americans live in the United States, with the 2000 U.S. Census indicating a figure of nearly 1.2 million people reporting Arab ancestry alone or in combination with another ancestry (Brittingham & de la Cruz, 2005), while other sources and monitoring groups have reported up to 4 million Arab Americans (Allied Media, 2004a, 2004b; Tolerance, 2001; Zogby, 1991). There has been some criticism of the official Census count for Arab Americans, specifically because of sampling methodology which undercounts ethnic minorities, intermarriage, and a possible lack of Arab respondents' willingness to take part in the Census or report their ancestry to the government (Allied Media, 2004b; El-Badry, 2004).

Because of this lack of consensus, demographic data will be presented from both the U.S. Census and other sources, noting any discrepancies in the estimates. The 2000 Census reported that 74.7% of Arab Americans were citizens and 46.4% were born in the U.S. (Brittingham & de la Cruz, 2005). Arab Americans can be Muslim, Christian, Jewish, Druze, non-religious, or followers of another faith or tradition. Arab Americans in the U.S. have origins in more than 20 countries from around the Middle East and Northern Africa.

A Closer Look at Variability

Religion. As with other population data for this group, there is some inconsistency in reporting the religious affiliation of Arab Americans. Most sources agree that the population is predominately Christian compared to Muslim. A few other sources say about one half of Arab Americans identify themselves as Muslims and the other half as Christians. It is possible that this discrepancy reflects the rapid growth of Muslim communities worldwide, since, on average, the Christian family-unit is smaller than that of Muslims. Inherently, most Arab Americans trace their ancestry to the Middle East. Non-Arab Middle Eastern populations, like the Turks, Iranians (Persians), Kurds, Israelis, and Berbers, are also present in North America. Arab-Christians from Iraq, known as Chaldeans, and from Egypt, known as Copts, constitute large communities in the United States as well.

According to World (2001), it is estimated that there are over seven million Muslims living in the USA. They are from a wide variety of national, ethnic, and cultural backgrounds. It is also estimated that Islam is among the fastest-growing religions in the United States and around the world. It is worth clarifying here that when we talk about a purely Muslim population in the United States, namely American-Muslims, we mean the broader base of diverse Muslims, most of whom do not have origins in the Arab World. They are from Asia (e.g., Indonesia, the largest Muslim nation), the former Soviet Union, Iran, Turkey, or various African nations. In addition, there is the American style of Islamic religion growing specifically among the African American community (i.e., The Nation of Islam).

Some White and Hispanic Americans are showing interest in joining the religion as well. Based on an editorial in the Islamic Society of North America (2005, pp. 3–4), there are about 40,000 strong Muslim Latinos. This fact gives hope and enthusiasm for those advocating the spread of American Islam:

> The need for outreach to Latinos becomes even more evident when we look at statistics concerning conversions to Islam in America. According to Dr. Ihsan Bagby's study 'The Mosque In America: A National Portrait' . . . the average number of American converts per mosque is approximately 16 per year. He estimates an annual growth of 20,000 reverts nationally each year. Of these,

63% of reverts are African American, 27% White, and only 6% are Hispanic. In a study conducted by Samantha Sanchez, many Latino converts stated that Islam offers a sense of spirituality that they did not attain in their former religious affiliation. The Latino community needs to be informed about Islam. Thankfully, many Latinos who have reverted to Islam are taking the initiative in reaching out to the Hispanic community. It is therefore imperative that all Muslim Americans join, support, and encourage such initiatives (Islamic Society of North America Editorial, 2005, pp. 3–4).

According to the Arab American Institute (2006b), the religious identification of Arab Americans (based on a survey conducted in 2002) is as follows: Roman/Eastern Catholic – 35%; Muslim – 24%; Eastern Orthodox – 18%; Other religion or no affiliation – 13%; and Protestant – 10%.

Population Estimates. Several groups and agencies, such as the *Arab American Institute* (AAI), monitor the affairs of the Arabic population and advocate their cause both in social and political circles. Interestingly, the AAI has higher counting figures and database numbers (3 to 4 million) than the Census Bureau of the U.S. Government (1.3 million). The AAI explained that discrepancy as follows:

Arab Americans were undercounted in the 1990 Census . . . . Because being of Arab heritage is an ethnicity, Arabs (like Hispanics) are not counted separately in the race question on the Census, but there is no separate ethnic question for Arabs. The long form of the Census includes an ancestry question . . . . most Arab Americans are of Lebanese or Syrian origin, but the population of Egyptian, Palestinian, and Iraqi Americans has been growing steadily

(Allied Media, 2004a, Demographics, p 1).

Every ten years, the US Census Bureau:

.... takes the demographic pulse of the population, collecting information ranging from family size and citizenship to education, income, and occupation. . . . Historically, only a portion of this population self-identifies with an Arab ancestry, resulting in a numeric undercount by a factor of about 3 . . . . While the 2000 Census accounted for some 1.25 million persons who self-identify with an Arabic-speaking origin, our estimates (based on research done by the Zogby International polling and marketing firm) place the population at more than 3.5 million (Arab American Institute, 2006b, Endnotes, pp. 1, 2).

In 2000, the Census asked respondents to identify their ancestry or ethnic origin, providing two lines for a write-in response. This practice may lead to undercounting of ethnicity in cases where people identify with more than two ancestries. The question for ancestry/ethnic origin was collected on the long form of the Census, as had been done in 1990. The long form was sent to about 1/6 of households, and about 19% of the surveyed population left this question unanswered (de la Cruz & Brittingham, 2003), which casts further doubt on accuracy.

Locations. From 1990–2000, the Arab American population increased in nearly every U.S. state, but approximately half of the Arab American population was concentrated in just five states – California, Florida, Michigan, New Jersey, and New York. The largest concentrations of Arab Americans in U.S. cities are in New York, Dearborn (Michigan), Los Angeles, Chicago, Houston, and Detroit. Large communities (total population over 100,000) with the greatest percentages of Arab Americans include Sterling Heights in Michigan, Jersey City in New Jersey, Warren in Michigan, Allentown in Pennsylvania, and Burbank in California. While the total population in Dearborn, Michigan was about 98,000, Arab Americans represented 30% of the population (de la Cruz & Brittingham, 2003).

The Arab American Institute has been studying Arab concentrations and demographics in the United States. Helen Samhan, the director of the Institute's Census Information Center (as quoted in Allied Media, 2004b), indicated that the population which identifies with one or more Arab ancestries and lives in New York, New Jersey, Illinois and Texas, has more than doubled since 1990. Samhan emphasized, "With so many stereotypes about Arabs and suspicions since 9/11, the Census helps us tell the true story of how rooted and accomplished we are as a community. We can see the fruits of generations of Arab immigrants who have made America their home and continue to make positive contributions to the welfare of the country" (Allied Media, 2004b, p. 4).

It is also of interest to note here that nearly half of foreign-born Arabs arrived in the U.S. during the 1990s, and the present median age of the entire Arab American population is around 33. Similar to California, the state of Michigan is a preferred destination for new immigrants to the U.S. According to a ranking of states from the American Arab Chamber of Commerce (n.d.), which was based on a sample year of 1997, the largest number of new Arab immigrants to Michigan came from the country of Iraq, principally after the first Gulf war in 1991, and from Lebanon and Jordan. Michigan has the highest proportion of Arab Americans of any U.S. state. The greater Detroit area's Arab community is known for its national diversity, institutional leadership, and cultural outreach. Arab Americans in Michigan constitute the most visible, highly organized, and politically influential Arab group of any other location.

Ancestral Countries. Table 5.1 provides data from the U.S. Census Bureau regarding ancestral origins indicated by Arab Americans (Brittingham & de la Cruz, 2005).

Table 5.1. Ancestral origins of Arab Americans as reported in Census 2000

Ancestral Origin	Percent
Lebanese	28.8
Egyptian	14.5
Syrian	8.9
Palestinian	7.3
Jordanian	4.2
Moroccan	3.6
Iraqi	3.5
"Arab" or "Arabic"	19.7
Other Arab	9.6

Gender, Marital Status, Language, and English Proficiency. According to the U.S. Census Bureau 2000 Summary File 4 (as quoted in Arab American, 2005, Population, p. 2), "Lebanese Americans constitute a greater part of the total number of Arab Americans residing in most states, except New Jersey, where Egyptian Americans are the largest Arab group." The Arab population was 57 percent male compared to 49 percent in the total US population in 2000. The proportion of male Arabs was also larger than that of female Arabs in all age groups through 64 years old. Men in the 20 to 49 age group represented a disproportionately large segment of the Arab population when compared with the sex distribution of the nation as a whole. Among Arab groups, Syrians and Lebanese were more likely than others to be aged 65 and older (Brittingham & de la Cruz, 2005).

According to data from the 2000 Census (Brittingham & de la Cruz, 2005), the Arab population was less likely to be divorced, separated, or widowed (13 percent) and more likely to be married (61 percent), compared with 18.5% and 54.4% for the total U.S. population, respectively. Female family householders, with no husband present, were less common among Arabs compared to all U.S. households. Around three out of four people of Arab ancestry spoke English very well or spoke it exclusively at home, with 24.4% reporting that they speak English "less than very well".

Educational and Economic Profile. Typically, the top five occupational categories for Arab Americans are: Executive (administrative-managerial), professional specialties, sales services, and precision repair. The main industries attracting Arab American appear also to be retail trade, construction, finances, insurance/real estate, and other industries (El-Badry, 2004). According to Arab American Business (n.d.), Arab Americans are more likely to be self-employed and in management and professional-specialty occupations than to work for local governments or other open job markets. In general, both native-born and immigrant Arabs have a higher economic achievement level than the U.S. population as a whole. "Arab Americans are twice as likely to be health professionals than the national population and more likely than other ethnic groups" (Arab American Business, n.d., p. 1). Data from the U.S. Census corroborates the occupational pattern for Arab Americans, with 42% employed in management, professional, or related fields (Brittingham & de la Cruz, 2005).

The labor force participation among Arab American women was lower compared to all women in the United States (46 percent versus 58 percent) (Brittingham & de la Cruz, 2005). This gender gap also reflects cultural values and social preferences. However, Arab American women had higher median earnings than U.S. women, even with significantly lower participation in the labor force (Brittingham & de la Cruz, 2005).

As a group, all women, regardless of ancestry, earn less than men. But Arab American women entrepreneurs earn more than non-Arab females in all regions of the U.S. except the West South Central and the Mountain region (El-Badry, 2004). According to the U.S. Census Bureau (Brittingham & de la Cruz, 2005), both Arab men and women earned more than their counterparts in the general population. The median family income among Arab Americans in 1999 was $52,318. Among the different Arab groups, Lebanese, Syrian, and Egyptian families had higher family incomes than other Arab groups – around $60,000 per year. Thus, in general, Arab families have a higher median family income than many other families in the U.S. However, 17 percent of Arab Americans were financially struggling or in a state of poverty as reported in the year 1999, compared with 12 percent of the total US population (Brittingham & de la Cruz, 2005).

Although "Arab Americans are the least-studied ethnic group in the United States, they receive considerable publicity associated with political and economic events, a good example of which has been the intense focus on the community in the aftermath of the Sept. 11 . . . . While this attention may be of grave political and diplomatic importance, it overshadows Arab Americans' financial and social impact in the United States" (El-Badry, 2004, p. 1). This group as a whole tends to be quite young, probably because younger people are more likely to travel and migrate. Many Arab American individuals are in their childbearing years, some have young children of their own, or are themselves native-born children and teenagers.

About two thirds of Arab Americans speak English fluently and about three quarters use Arabic media and news agencies to obtain vital information of interest to them. According to Allied Media (2004a), over 70% of Arab Americans say the best way to reach them is through broadcast outlets. More than 90% of them have close friends and family members in the Middle East. Only about 65% have traveled back to their original homelands at least once. As noted before, many Arab Americans are well-educated, diverse professionals, affluent, and entrepreneurial. They tend to assimilate well within the larger society. Oberman (2005) indicated that Arabs and Muslims, in general, integrate into the American mainstream better than they do in most European countries. "Experts say Arab Americans and Muslims integrate in the U.S.

with relative ease despite facing disenfranchisement . . . . 'There's no clear connection between the European and the American Muslim experience.' " (Oberman, 2005, pp 1, 8).

Arab Americans in general have high educational attainment. The proportion of Arab Americans with at least a bachelor's degree was significantly higher (41 percent) than that of the general U.S. population (24 percent) (Brittingham & de la Cruz, 2005). Allied Media (2004a, p. 1), a group dedicated to reaching the most affluent and fastest-growing segments of the U.S. population, affirmed that, "The Arab American population is estimated at 4 million and represents a loyal, young, educated and affluent market segment. The majority are American citizens who hold executive or sales positions or are entrepreneurs." The regional distribution of Arab American entrepreneurs, for example, is very similar to that of other ethnic or racial groups. Entrepreneurs of any kind in the United States tend to live and work mostly in the Pacific, South Atlantic, East North Central, and Mid-Atlantic regions.

However, despite the success of many Arab Americans, there remains a disparity between the well off and the struggling, as evidenced in the contrast between high income/educational attainment and high poverty rates for this population (Brittingham & de la Cruz, 2005). Many Arabs and Muslims remain undeserved, nonintegrated, and uneducated. These people may be struggling to make a living, learn the language, and settle down mentally, emotionally, and culturally. Unfortunately, they face serious challenges to survive and function well and, at times, they themselves represent certain challenges (and burdens) to the larger American society.

Arab American Publications. Various Arab-oriented publications are present in the top ten cities of the U.S., where large Arab concentrations exist. These publications cater to the local communities and reflect their mindset and diversity. They have also built an effective relationship with the international media and major Middle Eastern newspapers and magazines to stay posted with homeland news and developments. Their local periodicals deliver regional news, cultural events, and professional services as well as network their functions and resources (Allied Media, n.d.). Among such publications: *Al-Nashraa*, an Arab American newspaper launched in Washington DC, Virginia and Maryland; *Arab American Journal*, has been published in Denver, Colorado since 1994; *Beirut Times*, is the leading weekly newspaper for the Arab American communities in North America. These local media venues also serve as an advertising tool and as a bridge between the scattered immigrant groups and Arab Muslim communities in North America.

In addition, many stores carry daily or weekly newspapers and magazines imported directly from cities in the Middle East. Similarly, many households have access to Arabic media (like Al-Jazeera, Lebanese Broadcasting Corporation, or Al-Arabia) through satellite dish reception, cable television, and radio. Evidently, with the exponential use of the internet, there are countless websites and links that provide up-to-the hour news and analyses of events that are of special interest to the Arabic population in the United States.

BASIC MORALITIES AND KEY ETHICAL VALUES

Most cultures, across time and space, share similar values and basic social norms at the macro level. However, the hierarchy of these moral values or ethical beliefs differs clearly among societies and cultures, depending on their traditions, backgrounds, needs, social systems, and worldviews. While significant variations will exist in groups and individuals, the following list represents some of the key values and moral principles found among the people in the Middle East and the Arab World:

Family (*El Aa-ilah*)

The family occupies a high place for Middle Easterners. It probably ranks as one of the top values in the Arabic-Islamic world in terms of its central role and crucial influence. Family is meant to include both immediate and extended members of the household. It is like a small community within the larger community, which encompasses neighbors, relatives, elders, clergy, teachers, vendors, healers, mentors, children, etc. In many traditional circles, marriage is not an end in itself or a separation from the family. Unlike in the Western-industrialized societies, a new marriage does not float alone as an isolated or singular unit. Marriage becomes an integral part of the communal family and an extension of kin. In addition to creating new unions, marriages serve to enhance the status, bonds, and prosperity of the larger extended family.

Thus, total *separation-individuation* (to borrow a term from Object Relation theory) is not a strong value in the Middle East nor is it looked upon as a healthy quality or favorable import. It is actually seen as leading to fragmentation, isolation, and loneliness. Furthermore, total individuality and privacy can contribute to the disintegration of the larger family and the disappearance of the smaller community, as is the case in some places in the modern West.

On the other hand, the great emphasis on family closeness and solidarity leaves little room for personal space and can lead to the mixing of boundaries and constant outside interference. In most urban settings, people effectively manage the demands and pleasures of professional life with those of the family and community. They seem to navigate well between the business mode of modernism and the social warmth of traditionalism, like friendly connections, informal visitations, and bonded lifestyles. So, there is a special attachment to the family and to the kin in general and a special dedication and loyalty to the idea of *home*. Even though these types of social connections and obligations are time consuming, they are still very nurturing and emotionally assuring as they meet a great psychological need for warmth, connectivity, and belongingness. This type of lifestyle is what can make living in such communal areas very pleasant, rewarding, and meaningful. Mutual care, lots of sharing, frequent visits, and personal touch are greatly enjoyed activities. However, they are also expected in return among family members, relatives, and close friends. Simply put, relationships are a priority in the Middle East. They typically take precedence over any other function, project, or activity regardless of time or context.

Religious Involvement and Piety (*Tadayyon*) – Including faith (*Imaan*), prayer (*Salaat*), and Spiritual Practices

Arabs and Arab Americans often have strong values based on their religiosity. Fearing God and loyalty to moral-ethical values, as embedded in the culture, are basic qualities that reflect the individual's or family's character and social behavior. People are expected to be involved in the "faith of their fathers" and be aware of the religious mindset, landmarks, feasts, and worldviews of their time. They also should be able to use religious language in greetings, compliments, interactions and verbal exchanges. This is part of the religious etiquette and protocol. It is worth noting here, that religion in the Middle East and Arabic-Islamic world is not synonymous with individual spirituality. Mentioning God in public is very common both in serious or casual settings and, in many times, this practice is expected in proper daily exchanges – like when people inquire about your health or your family, when they say good bye, wish you well, thank you for a gesture, or make plans. Common phrases one can hear on a regular basis include, "Thanks be to God (*el-ham-dellah*); God be with you; God willing (*in-sha-allah*); May safety and protection be with you; May God prosper you; God's blessings be upon you."

Religious affiliation is a major part of the social identity of the people. It is intimately related to tradition, heritage, and culture. Culture can virtually be seen as a form of religion and religion as a substance of culture (Tillich, 1959). Unlike in the West, religion as a set of values, rituals, feasts, and common knowledge is an integral part of peoples' lives. This is different from religion as a theological set of doctrines, as interpretation of scriptures, as training for clergy, or as a deep knowledge of faith and spiritual practices. While many Arabs, Muslims, and Middle Easterners are more spiritually active and committed to their religious faiths (as practicing believers) than Westerners, many of them are religious only by affiliation and identity but not deeply committed to the faith (i.e., social Christian, cultural Muslim, or nominal Druze).

Being part of open religious activities appears to meet some basic existential needs for belonging, worship, celebration, and hope. In addition, being involved to some degree in religious circles and ceremonies can reflect one's role and good standing in the community. Refusal to participate could mean rejection of the heritage and alienation from society. Thus, there is a wide spectrum of religiosity and spirituality in the Middle East. Furthermore, religion is often like nationalism: it remains at the center of people's social fabric, psychological function, and cultural mindset.

Community (*Muheet el-gamaah*)

This value is the glue which holds the pieces of the immediate and extended families together, as well as the surrounding group of neighbors, friends, relatives, teachers, clergy, mentors, etc. It is also the bridge that links the family to the larger society. The outside observer will immediately notice several major societal characteristics in the Arabic-Islamic world: 1) a strong family bond, 2) a strong sense of community and belongingness, 3) a strong social identity, 4) a fondness of the historical heritage, and 5) rootedness in the land (Abi-Hashem, 2006).

The concept of *community* is a very significant factor and it operates as an organizing principle of life in the Middle East. It is different from the concept of society at large. It is the lively molecule of culture in action. It is best felt, lived, and experienced rather than defined, taught, or analyzed. Although one may find pockets of individualism, extreme privacy, and personal aloofness in the Arabic Middle Eastern world, especially in certain highly mobile and industrialized places, most people are open, warm, sociable, and communal. Those few who are not naturally engaged or sociable at least remain polite and appropriate during social encounters.

Hospitality (*Diyaafah*)

For many Arabs, honoring guests is a great virtue, a universal duty, and a source of joy on the part of the host. Hosts feel this sense of honor and obligation regardless of their social status or economic abilities. In some traditional settings, hospitality and provision to those entering your home, your property, or your village are a mandate, even if the guests are strangers or former enemies. Hospitality is expected from all and is equally extended to all. This habit of hospitality, manifested in social gatherings, leisurely visits, and sharing feasts of food, can have a great therapeutic effect on the psychological well-being. It is a natural therapeutic intervention and prevention at once, embedded within the rich Middle Eastern cultures from ancient times. Such occasions are remarkable opportunities for emotional bonding, deep sharing, nurturing, consulting, supporting, and healing, especially in difficult and stressful times. Immigrants and refugees, who are separated from their original families and communities, can miss this cultural experience a great deal. They may feel a tremendous void inside of them, and an intense longing for social warmth and deep connectivity. It is worth noting here that, if these needs are not met in a legitimate or healthy way, they may drive the individual immigrant or foreigner to some unhealthy patterns and damaging habits, which eventually can increase his or her maladjustment and further disturb their acculturation and social functioning.

Truthfulness (*Sodok*)

This refers to avoiding deceit and keeping one's word regardless of the circumstances. In the Arabic Islamic world, truthfulness has been an extremely important ethical quality and moral value manifested strongly in personal relationships. Many deals and contracts among friends, relatives, and acquaintances are still being made based solely on the spoken word and the honor system. In addition, a major aspect of the Arabic communication style is the use of metaphors and verbal exaggeration in order to describe a matter, make a point, express an emotion, and contrast two ideas or two events. The Arabic language is very poetic and rich in idioms and terminology. This colorful style can be confusing to foreigners. But when it comes to a verbal agreement, keeping the promise and delivering the pledge is absolutely essential to keep the personal honor and to preserve the valued relationship. It is a measure of dignity reflecting the caliber of character and reputation not only of the two individuals involved in the deal but also of the whole family and household connected with them.

Thankfulness (*Shukor*) & Gratitude (*Im-Tinaan*)

Thankfulness to God and to others for the many blessings and favors one is enjoying in life is an important value for many in the Arab world. At the onset of visiting with people, even those hurting or depressed, it is common to hear from them, first and foremost, thanksgiving and gratitude for the remaining goodness and mercy before hearing about the complaint or agony. They typically respond to questions like "how are you?", "how is life?", or "how is your health . . . your family . . . your affairs . . . etc.?" very graciously, acknowledging their blessings first. They normally begin by dwelling on the positive and what is good before mentioning the hardship, illness, stress, crisis, or whatever struggle they are experiencing, almost minimizing its significance and volume. Complaining is not seen as a virtue! Dwelling on the negative and the awful is perceived as lack of gratitude or as possessing a critical or cynical spirit. In many subcultures, the custom is to be first grateful to God's goodness even under extreme pressure, showing appreciation for what is still right, hoping for the best yet to come, and showing patience with self and others. Similarly, gifts and kind gestures are received warmly, yet also creating a sense of strong obligation toward the giver, to reciprocate likewise in the future.

Respect (*Ihti-Raam*) and Esteem (*Takdeer*)

Respect for other people, authority figures, parents, and elderly, especially in public, is imperative in the Arabic Islamic world. Politeness (*tah-theeb*) and showing regards and courtesy to others is greatly expected in formal encounters, in business meetings, in religious gatherings, in daily exchanges, in the market place, and especially with visitors and outsiders. Using appropriate labels is extremely important even in informal settings. Being kind and polite in dealing with others is the norm, i.e., when greeting, interacting, responding, and modeling (cf. Abi-Hashem, 2004b). In the Middle East, you will never hear a child call an adult by their first name. That is absolutely unacceptable! Children show respect towards adults, students towards teachers, lay people towards community leaders, parishioners towards clergy, etc. Older married people are called with a label reflecting their status as parents and in relation to their offspring – normally their first born son or daughter. For example, the mother of five children that include David (Dawood in Arabic) as the oldest boy (or the only boy) will be referred to as Umm Dawood. Similarly, the Father of Youssef will be called Abou Youssef. Such labels also reflect generational heritage and give the family a status that is rewarding and fulfilling to older people.

Thus, labels are extremely important to use: Uncle, Auntie, Mr., Mrs., Miss., Sheikh, Elder, Reverend, Doctor, Teacher, President, Master, etc. There are variations within each category as well – serious labels for formal occasions and endearing labels for informal, leisurely, or intimate occasions. In some situations, however, fancy labels can be overly used or misused (like in certain meetings, in mass media reports and news, in personal interviews and panel discussions, or in special encounters), making the setting potentially difficult to manage with the exaggerated, superficial, complicated, and lengthy titles.

Contentment (*Ridaah*) and Satisfaction (*Iktifaa*)

Contentment, like thankfulness, is a great virtue inspired from both religious tradition and cultural heritage. People in more rural areas, who have a special relationship with their land and fields, are more likely to be satisfied and content and therefore less anxious about life outcomes in general (similar to Native American Indians). However, in more urban settings, people may display more worries, anxiety, and stress. Of course, there are extremes in both of these human experiences: a high level of contentment can lead to a lack of vision and laziness, while a low level of contentment can lead to competition and greed. Both of these polarities, and the full spectrum in between, are strongly present in the Middle East. But broadly speaking, for the Middle Eastern mind and soul, contentment, satisfaction, and the simple joys of life appear to be experienced more easily and enjoyed more readily than in the West.

Generosity (*Karam*)

This is the virtue of giving and not withholding whatever is in your ability to share, especially to those within your circle. Giving includes precious gifts, attention and time, needed items, love and affection, money and loans, etc. Generosity is sharing materially, culturally, and psychologically. So often Westerners are alerted when traveling to the Middle East, not to admire an item or a belonging too much (e.g., a picture, a piece of clothing, a nice item, a watch, etc.) because the owner could feel obligated to offer that item to them as a present by saying *mokaddameh*, meaning "it is gracefully and gladly presented to you" or "it is totally yours!" This is often a full and complete offer and it is considered impolite for the guest to refuse the gift (United Arab, n.d.). Since you made it clear that you liked the item that much, the owner feels obliged to make the decision and relinquish it to your possession. It is part of good hospitality and the honor system, and is considered to fall under moral and cultural obligations. Now, such a gesture can be shocking to some. But, refusing to accept the offer, in return, becomes an even greater offense! The more traditional the Arabic person is, the more likely he or she will behave in this way. Thus, the matter requires a greater sensitivity on the part of the visitor.

On a personal note, this happened to me in the States as I once saw a former Iraqi client of mine wearing a nice jacket. It was a long green winter jacket and looked brand new. Without much thinking, I commented twice on its color and texture and how well it fit him. Without any hesitation, and to my utter surprise (though I was somewhat familiar with this custom but it never occurred to me that it would happen right then), he immediately took it off and pushed it into in my arms, and said, *mokaddameh*. Gently, I tried to decline, but in vain! We spent about half an hour debating, arguing, and pushing the jacket back and forth, with me complimenting him on his sense of generosity and dignity, yet endlessly assuring him that, even though morally and emotionally I do accept his generous gift, but practically I decline since I also have too many jackets and am unable to use them all . . . and convincing him that he needs it more than I do, knowing his financial struggles and conditions. He again would give it back and swear that he will never wear it because he already "pronounced" it as mine. Finally and reluctantly, and out of my firm insistence and his mere respect for me as his former therapy doctor, he took it back in his hand but never put it on in my presence (as a sign of honoring his word and intention). That was a very challenging, sensitive, and uncomfortable encounter, yet socially and culturally, it was a very rich moment, indeed.

Dignity (*Karameh*) and Honor (*Sharaf*)

Middle Easterners greatly prize their personal and familial honor. This is a part of the Arabic culture and its developmental values. Honor and dignity, whether they are achieved or prescribed, real or perceived, personal or tribal, represent a cultural tendency for preserving the name of the family, the group's identity, and the village's sense of community. Honor is an important factor in the psychosocial makeup of individuals and groups alike. This sense of dignity appears to guide social relationships and transactions. Middle Easterners place emphasis on their roots and treasure their history of belonging. They show loyalty to their lineage, including family and clan, communal and tribal leadership, familiar religious traditions, and sociopolitical norms and customs. These represent major sources from where people derive their identity (*hawiyyeh*) and sense of pride (*fakher*).

Arabs and Middle Easterners are, by nature, a proud people due to their long heritage, rootedness in the land, and generational continuity. Pride is not merely a matter of individualistic ego, grandiosity, or narcissistic quality, stemming solely from self-preservation by avoiding injury and humiliation (though it can be this way at times). It rather stems from a collective sense of existence and a deep inherent value of the people. Humans are not viewed as a mere collection of individuals (isolated or unrelated) but as a collective community. Dignity is experienced, expressed, and expected on several levels: Personal, familial, communal, social, and national.

Badolato (1984, The Bedouin, p. 2) affirmed that, "Honor (sharaf) has been highly valued since early Arab history because it was conducive to group cohesion and survival. Sharaf probably follows from the fact that shameful behavior or cowardice would weaken the group and endanger society." Hence, honor in the Middle East is greatly cherished as a strong moral-ethical and social value.

Gender Roles: Male (*Thakar*) and Female (*Unthaa*)

Unwritten laws and oral traditions are prominent and powerful in the Arabic-Islamic world. Many people who migrate to the West carry with them such unspoken codes and subtle expectations. Even some of those (married or single) who were previously moderate or progressive in their homeland may revert back to a more traditional role and conservative stance once they travel to a new country. This is especially true if they relocate within a concentrated Arab community in North America with specific in-group expectations. Men who marry an American or European woman and move back to their homeland in the Middle East often face pressures to conform to the norms and cultural traditions of their extended families. In many established and settled communities in the Arabic-Islamic world, the roles of men and women seem to be set and agreed upon in a broad cultural sense. So, each gender usually enters the courting and marriage relationship with a preconceived idea about their roles and parameters.

Yet, in other modern cities and vibrant circles in the Middle East, these roles are not agreed upon or clearly defined, just like in the West. They are rather fluid, evolving, dynamic, and open to negotiation. Young people especially discuss their roles and readily decide on a non-traditional function and mode of living. This phenomenon depends on many factors such as socioeconomic class, geographical location, professional education, and religious affiliation.

Generally speaking, individuals take their role in the family and in society seriously: The man as a breadwinner and provider and the woman as a capable homemaker, a responsible wife and caregiver, and a house manager. Roles are reinforced constantly, directly or indirectly. Family members and friends look after each other extensively. They rush to help in times of need and give necessary care, each in their capacity. Men and women, regardless of their age or circumstances, seem to take pride in their roles, family achievements, and social representations. They attempt to play their role and fulfill their duties to the best of their ability. Those roles seem also to give each gender a great sense of reward and satisfaction, not to mention the external praise and reinforcement from others in the circle of community.

In most Arab-Islamic societies, boys enjoy more favor than girls and girls are more restricted than boys. However, each gender is cherished on its own merit and is praised in special ways. In traditional communities, girls and women are especially protected. They are treasured and viewed as the vulnerable members of the family. Hence the idea of *Aard*, which represents all the females in the clan, pack, or kin. The value of women is part of the family's dignity and honor. It is the utmost duty of males to guard and protect them. Therefore, the harassing or bothering of a woman by an outsider is considered a great offense and could result in dishonoring or disgracing the family. Revenge acts and honor killings are still practiced in some rural areas and among traditional tribes in the Middle East as an attempt to restore the injured honor and undo the public shame. Serious tragedies and unfair crimes have been committed under this cause.

In most urban settings, where modern living is progressive and complex, the place and role of women is very similar to Western societies with respect to freedom of behavior, mechanism of personal decisions, and participation in social activities. Many women conduct themselves in dress and manner, in work and education, in relationships and public service almost like in Europe and North America. However, many Western lifestyle aspects remain unfitting and unacceptable in the Arab Islamic world, such as the extensive display of affection, romance, and physical intimacy in public (e.g., holding hands and kissing on the streets or during social gatherings). Though common on television programs and in special and limited gatherings, such behavior is not as accepted as in the West.

Again, depending on socioeconomic background, religious faith, and the traditions of the community, the roles within each family are set in a certain manner to reflect norms regarding parents and children, husbands and wives, boys and girls. Because older boys are often more privileged than girls in terms of status and freedom of actions and decisions, they are groomed to be the "man of the house." They are encouraged to follow their father's lead in taking care of the family and in supervising younger siblings. This practice has resulted in both remarkable and damaging outcomes – older boys at times show superior care and devotion to their families and clan yet, at other times, they practice oppression and abuse against their family and siblings.

Certainly, many women are repressed and mistreated in many corners of the Middle East. However, not all Arab-Muslim women want the total freedom or the modern lifestyle common in the West. Many women remain traditional by choice and are content in their lifestyle, role, and status. Actually, some Arab women are very powerful in their own ways, inside their own homes, and within their areas of influence. This is similar to many American women who prefer more traditional roles in their personal lives, marriages, and relationships. This is also similar to certain women in some African American communities, where they appear to be in charge inside the house (as the family boss and manager) while the man seems to be in charge of the affairs outside the home. Thus, in many apparent repressive societies in the Middle East, women remain in control and continue to enjoy power in their own spheres. Yet it is important to note that gender roles and norms differ widely across and within cultures.

Saving Face and Avoiding Public Shame (*Ayybb*)

The concept of saving face is an old tradition in the Arabic culture. Losing face is equated with experiencing shame and embarrassment. When people try to preserve their face it means they are preserving their personal dignity, moral integrity, public image, and honorable word. While *personal guilt* is a major psychological force in the West, affecting self-esteem and performance, *public shame* is a major driving force in the East and other non-western cultures, shaping group behavior, social attitudes, and the status of individuals in the community (cf. Peristiany, 1965). It is also worth noting here that, in terms of dealing with global business or political agreements, preserving dignity and saving face is often viewed as more important than preserving projects or saving deals. This is especially important when conflicts and disputes arise.

Western business leaders are primarily occupied with preserving their deals and focusing on the immediate task at hand, while Middle Eastern leaders are normally preoccupied with saving face and the status of the relationship. So, building warm and trustworthy relationships usually precedes any tasks or deals and eventually secures success. This is a major cross-cultural principle that should guide any communication across nations and ethnocultural groups. Differences in mentality, approach, and communication style could cause serious tension, conflicts, or even wars as has been the case in many parts of the world and, most recently, in the Middle East.

Gossip can be prominent in tight families and intimate circles. Therefore, people try to avoid public mistakes or questionable behaviors that may feed into rumors or blame. Personal and family reputations are extremely important to guard. Even children are taught from an early age to avoid what is considered shameful. So, on one hand, the concept of *ayybb* is helpful in regulating people's social behavior, expression, and attitudes and encouraging decency and civility. On the other hand, it could encourage secrecy, inhibition, restriction, cover up, and double standards in activities and relationships. Thus for some, the gap between their private self and their public self can be quite wide.

In addition, putting someone in a morally or ethically awkward position is usually referred to as blackening or darkening their face, of course in a figurative way. One could blacken his or her own face by acting foolishly, inconsiderately, or inappropriately in public or by breaking his or her own promises. On the other hand, when someone performs well, honors others, and shows them favor, this implies that he or she is "brightening" or "whitening" his or her own face. Thus, most people go the extra measure to appear favorable, in a good light. When disgraced, people suffer socially and psychologically. Therefore, they try to make every effort to repair their shame, restore their reputation, and reverse the darkening of their face.

Working Hard and Providing for Family

Good working habits and ethics are considered great social values. Although many people in the Arab-Islamic world take life too easily, are not highly motivated or suffer from laziness, especially in very poor areas (desert mentality) or in oil rich societies, the majority of people in the Middle East are industrious and very dedicated workers. Earning and providing is a moral virtue. Men usually are not ready to marry or even to propose by asking for a lady's hand, until they have proven themselves financially and socially (having a good job and reputation, a car, a furnished apartment, etc.). Sometimes, becoming rich and accumulating much money or property helps a person to earn better social status in the eyes of their extended family and surrounding community.

Social Obligations and Relational Duties (*Wagibaat*)

This is a practice that fulfills a set of social expectations, the need for remaining involved, and the pleasure of sharing and connecting. *Wagibaat* includes presenting congratulations for births, happy occasions, and successes, as well as offering sympathies for illnesses, losses, or death, wishing well before or after traveling, paying tribute and respect to authorities and the elderly, acknowledging feasts and religious celebrations inside and across religious lines, and so on. *Wagibaat* also implies returning social favors, invitations for home visits and meals, exchanging gifts, and checking on the sick and weak. Although this is one of the basic virtues and beautiful practices in the Middle East and Arabic world, it could leave the receiver-recipient feeling indebted to the initiator-giver. It creates a desire and a sense of obligation to return the favor(s).

Thus, people with limited financial resources often decline social invitations and miss on the warmth and joy of fellowship, knowing that they cannot present the host with an expensive gift nor can afford inviting the host back into their humble home. We have seen a significant decline in hospitality, *wagibaat*, and social exchanges in war torn areas due to financial hardships and the erosion of the middle class.

Patience (*Saber*) and Endurance (*Tahammol*)

In the face of difficulties and hardships, Middle Easterners value longsuffering, the ability to be patient, and to have a big heart – *sader waasih*, figuratively a "wide chest." Actually, people encourage each other to endure and wish the troubled or distraught patience. Many songs and poems have been written about endurance and patience. On one hand people are encouraged to try to do all they can in a difficult situation, however, they are also encouraged to accept and endure the things they cannot change. For some, the common belief in "fate and destiny" (*kadaa wa kadar*) is a very powerful mental tool that helps them cope with unpredictable accidents, unfortunate events, and unexpected tragedies.

A narrow view of this belief implies that each person would get his or her portion in life no matter what. So, it is better to make peace with that fate and submit to the ultimate will of the supernatural rather than fight it or resist it in vain. In some cases, this kind of belief helps bring a great relief and resolution to loss and tragedy. In other cases, it encourages disengagement, passivity, and apathy. Generally speaking, in traditional or non-industrialized societies people have a higher tolerance to hardship than in more affluent societies. This is largely due to experience. They expect that suffering, pain, disasters, illnesses, death, etc., are all integral and vital parts of living. People seem to be able to reconcile life's fragility with life's abundance. They have also learned to expect life's unpredictability, therefore they may not be as surprised or as resentful of struggles, disappointments, and tragedies as their counterparts in more affluent or comfortable societies.

Summary of Values

The hierarchy of the values listed above depends on the people, subculture, mentality, background, and particular setting, whether it is a traditional-rural or modern-urban region. It is worth noting here that the above list of values is described in general terms and does not appear in a special order. In addition, there are variations within each community and society as there are conceptual and lifestyle differences among families and groups. Therefore, it is wise not to expect that every Arabic, Muslim, or Middle Eastern person or family would hold to these moral characteristics and virtues, practice them, or express them in the same manner.

Some of these values can have a dark side or a shadow polarity to them, which results in a social and counter-culture effect that the observer and the caregiver need to keep in mind. Some of these negative side-effects are: (1) Being biased and showing favoritism to certain family members, bypassing moral-ethical principles for the sake of maintaining closeness; (2) secrecy resulting from avoiding public shame; (3) shaming others for minor behaviors, attitudes, or acts by using embarrassment as a powerful weapon (double edge sword); (4) gossip and blurred boundaries taking place within closed and intimate communities; (5) manipulating traditions and ethical norms to serve one's goals and benefits; (6) lack of a critical mind and objectivity; (7) loss of reading and learning habits due to intense socialization and a leisurely lifestyle; (8) double standards and discrepancy (even hypocrisy) between private versus public behavior; (9) interference in the affairs of others when there is minimal or no privacy; and (10) losing personal identity, autonomy, and future aspirations for the sake of the family or just to maintain the cohesiveness of the community.

Normally, value formation, expression, implementation, and manipulation are the function of the various socio-cultural forces, dynamics, and worldviews at play in Arabic culture. These processes are defined and shaped by the culture and, in turn, they shape and define the culture as well. According to Hodge (as quoted in Allied Media, 2004c, p. 12), "Cultures share the same values but they set different priorities for those values." Similarly, Zogby (as quoted in Allied Media, 2004c, p. 13) found that the top Saudi values polled were faith, family, justice, ambition, and knowledge. In contrast, "in the U.S., it's freedom, family, honesty, self-esteem and justice . . . 'the common ground we can work on,' he said, 'is family and children.' "

According to Lemawie (2005), the hierarchy of the same set of values is not the same across cultures. He compared six key values between the East and the West. In some Eastern and Arab-Islamic societies, these values are ranked as follows: 1) dignity and integrity, 2) courage and fearlessness, 3) generosity and hospitality, 4) honor and character, 5) truthfulness and honesty, and 6) passionate love. In some Western and Anglo-American cultures, these same values are ranked differently: 1) passionate love, 2) truthfulness and honesty, 3) honor and character, 4) generosity and hospitality, 5) courage and fearlessness, and 6) dignity and integrity.

Finally, the following are some additional moral characteristics that are very treasured in Middle Eastern societies and cultures – listed briefly:

- Quick mindedness, awareness, and a deep insight into a given situation (*futna*).
- Deep faithfulness and commitment (*amanah, wafaa'*) towards people for whom one feels a debt or an obligation. This includes relatives, spouses, children, as well as work, business, and relational covenants even when the person is not totally satisfied with the relationship.

- Readiness to help others and defend their rights (*muru-aah*). Courage, motivation, and eagerness shown to others.
- Esteeming mentors, respecting elders, and learning from oral tradition (*tak-leed*), which is the stored historic experiences, skills (*khibra*), and generational wisdom (*hek-meh*) that transcends school knowledge.

COMMUNICATION AND INTERPERSONAL STYLES

Arabs, Muslims, and Middle Easterners can be, simultaneously, open and closed, direct and indirect, expressive and cautious, tough and tender, outgoing and reluctant, polite and aggressive. It all depends on the context – their mood, their comfort level, their setting, or the pressures and influences surrounding them.

There is No Standard Approach

Communicating with Middle Easterners is not uniform and does not take one standard approach. When relating to Middle Easterners, we need to discover the particular style of that group, family, or person we are dealing with, whether young or old, traditional or modern, lay or educated, fluent in what languages, spiritually dedicated or simply nominal, etc. Normally, people's appearance and mannerisms tell a great deal about their background, subcultures, values, and styles. It is important however, to watch for cues and to ask what would be the best approaches to use, i.e., what is appropriate socially and what is not, before initiating contact or further connection (e.g., handshake, hug, kiss on the cheek, or just a smile or a nod of head).

The style of relationships in rural and traditional settings is different than the one practiced in urban and modern settings, especially regarding contact with the opposite sex. When relating to conservative women, for example, it is quite sufficient to make a simple gesture symbolizing acknowledgement and respect instead of risking the consequences of inappropriate physical contact.

Some children and young ladies are innately shy with strangers or unfamiliar people, but when they are among themselves, with familiar visitors, or in comfortable situations, they become very warm, friendly, inviting, and alive. People gather in close proximities (sitting or standing), frequently touching each other during conversations and discussions, especially during walks, leisure times, and meals. The exchange of best wishes, cheerful greetings, and good will is very habitual when they first meet. Then, when they part, they usually give each other extensive generic blessings.

Use of Metaphors, Proverbs, Sayings

Quite often people use metaphors, sayings, proverbs, and old liners, delivered in a poetic style. These sayings carry ancient wisdoms and apply well to daily living, to the subjects at hand, and to many social situations. The Arabic language and heritage are very rich and colorful. Many older people have beautifully mastered these verbal skills and oral traditions. This form of spoken art is quickly disappearing among the younger generations and city inhabitants, which is sadly an irreversible cultural loss.

According to Morrison (2003, p. 6), "Middle Easterners generally speak at much closer quarters than North Americans. Some feel uncomfortable being far away from others, even if they are among strangers. Eye contact can be intense and constant." Regarding the art of language communication and verbal styles, especially the use of the classical form of Arabic, Badolato (1984, Emotional impact, pp. 1–2) pointed out:

> The Arabs place a high value on the Arabic language, and it exerts an over-powering psychological influence over their behavior... Orators are prone to be carried away in verbal exaggeration when speaking before an audience. This exaggeration is called *mubalagha* in Arabic, but it is not considered to be a derogatory term by the Arabs. Rather it is considered to be an admirable capacity for oratorical eloquence . . . (Badolato, 1984, pp. 1–2).

Remarkably, most urban people in the Middle East are multi-cultural and multi-lingual. They are able to easily mix foreign terms and concepts with their daily conversations, business interactions, and routine expressions. They are very comfortable with both their highly Western-minded friends and colleagues and their highly traditional relatives and neighbors. Mixing languages, interrelating with other social classes, and incorporating various mindsets and approaches come quite naturally for urban and city people. They seem to enjoy a wider scope of social functioning, communal harmony, and cultural integration.

In the Arabic-Islamic world, relationships are shaped by the region, setting, age, gender, education, social context, religious affiliation, and general tradition. Labels are important. Respect of authority and strangers is a mandate. Verbal contracts and spoken words among friends, colleagues, and new acquaintances who have a good reputation and recommendation, are still valid agreements and honored bonds in many places and communities.

Relationships

Arabic people are often open about many areas of their lives which are considered broad and safe, but hesitant and even secretive about personal and family matters that may be considered negative or unconventional. They may be reluctant in discussing certain issues that could potentially raise doubts, gossip, or unfavorable judgment from others, given the moral standards and particular values of the society or community.

While for most Americans, *time is money* – a value derived from the industrial revolution and reinforced by the modern capitalist system and the mentality which arises from it – for most Arabs time is not money but a sheer vehicle. In the Middle East, relationships are more important than deals, serenity than schedules, and people than projects. Morrison (2003, pp. 5–7) noted that:

> . . . the perception of time is vastly different in the Middle East and in the U.S.A. Nothing happens at breakneck speed in Saudi Arabia or Kuwait. Relax and schedule one [major] appointment a day. . . Since trade was the foundation of the culture for thousands of years, most Arabs still consider themselves Bedouins at heart. They will be loyal first to their families, then to their tribes, then to friends. Many Middle Easterners are also exceedingly generous, and their hospitality is legendary. Never admire an item too intensely – they will often present it to you as a gift
>
> (Morrison, 2003, pp. 5–7).

Distressed and hurt people are, at times, uncomfortable describing others (even those who caused their agony) as bad, wrong, or evil. At other times, they are verbally punishing, sharp, and aggressive. They may utter wishful damnation on their adversaries and enemies. Some go to the extent of over-demonizing them as the source of their misery, swearing and cursing, which is a common way of releasing any stored anger or inner frustration. On one hand, we find Arab and Muslim people who display great politeness, sensitivity, and social awareness, and yet, on the other hand, those who possess a great sense of entitlement, grandiosity, and narcissism.

However, on average, Middle Easterners do not express certain negative emotions as quickly or as sharply as their North American counterparts. An example of these common and drastic statements would be, "I am angry with you," "I am scared to death," "I hate my mother," "Our president is bad (or corrupt)," etc. Westerners are used to hearing such expressions from their clients, students, children, colleagues, etc., but for non-Westerners this is blunt verbal language, which is outside the range of their repertoire. Such statements are not normative to use on a daily basis or in casual conversation.

Daawah: The Desire to Bestow Blessings upon Loved Ones

Daawah is a strong wish for wellness and a desire to bestow blessings upon the beloved. It can be positive, as a way of pronouncing favor on others, especially loved ones (may God prosper you in all your ventures and keep you wherever you go; may God have his favor on you, etc.). Conversely, it can be a negative utterance as a way of pronouncing curse and judgment (may their lives be always disturbed; may they fail continuously; may their days be short and full of trouble as they have caused us so much pain, etc.). People utter positive lines, usually in a poetic style, when they are served well and when they are in a happy mood or in the middle of a content moment. These seemingly automatic statements come out naturally as thanks, best wishes, and graces toward others.

When *daawa* is negative, it takes the form of a mild curse and it is most often expressed not on the spot but later on after the fact. When someone is upset, hurt, or frustrated he or she may utter a few *daawas* in front of trusted friends and family. It is a kind of reaction to other people's behavior, injustice, or mistreatment and also to some harmful events and unfortunate happenings at large. *Daawa* is different from the pop swearing or cursing we may hear on the street. Sometimes it is directed towards life in general, e.g., someone renouncing or cursing their bad luck in life. However, as a bestowed blessing, *daawa* is different from the generic prayers or spiritual rituals that people practice. Examples of such verbal expressions are found in the Old Testament and in Arabic literature.

Normally, when hurting people are asked about their own condition, either by a friend or a stranger, they reply with something like "thanks be to God" or "still surviving well" or "grateful to have many blessings left" or "God is granting me patience," etc. They tend to report on what is still good before reporting on their struggles, pain, frustration, or agony. They also frequently end their description positively, reflecting on their hope, faith, and endurance, as God's remaining special gifts to them.

It is very common for people of all walks of life and professions to mention God and to refer to divine providence in their daily interactions and social dealings. Regardless of the degree of their traditional life or religious heritage (a modern versus secular orientation), the many people in the Middle East make existential remarks about one's portion and fortune, fate and destiny, life and death, etc., referring to God often and wishing for His guidance in the matters discussed. They readily accept and refer to the notion of good faith and good will. Expressions like "As God Wills" (*allah bireed*), "Lord Willing" (*inshallah*), or "Thanks be to God" (*elham-dellah*), are very common and popular expressions.

It is very interesting to notice that Far Eastern people tend to look at the global picture first while the far Westerners tend to look at the details first. However, for the Easterners the whole is more important and more obvious than the segments or pieces. Even though the discussion is about details, at the end it is equally important to draw a global conclusion and put all matters in their grand perspective.

Improving Relational Style and Communicative Approaches

McCroskey and Richmond (1996 as quoted in Shaw 2005) suggested several ways for cross-cultural workers to improve their relational style and communicative approaches, among them: Demonstrate respect for other people's culture; Avoid criticizing any culture; Recognize your own ethnocentrism; Develop a higher tolerance for ambiguity; Reduce the level of evaluation in your talks and messages; Be empathetic and sensitive to relational needs; Be aware of cultural differences in non-verbal communication; Discover similarities and commonalities, not solely the differences; Work to build better stereotypes; Remember that meanings are in people not in cultures.

Shaw (2005) observed, "The two key world view understandings that drive the structure of Middle Eastern social institutions are 'relationships' and 'honour.' These stand in contrast to the West. . . where social institutions are driven by values of 'order' and 'individual... initiative'" (p. 5). Regarding the approach to living reality, Shaw also suggested that "the value the Middle Easterners give to building social relationships reflects a perspective on reality in which the group is more important than the individual, relationships are more important than tasks, and honour is more important than efficiency" (p. 5).

There is a great emphasis on *affiliative behavior* in the Middle East. Relaxed and personal relationships are fundamental to well-being and even to getting projects accomplished. Relationships take time and require setting priorities both in social and professional life, not only in casual encounters but also during business hours. This may sound chaotic and inefficient to Westerners. "People who come in inopportune times must be welcomed and cannot be put off" (Shaw, 2005, p. 11). Unlike in non-Arabic societies, one must never be seen as rushing others away or putting money, business, or other deals before cordial relationships and courteous personal contacts.

When talking, Arabs and Middle Easterners tend to use word pictures and imagery, communicating on a much closer level than typical Westerners. Do not back away even if you are unaccustomed to this level of personal space and physical closeness. "If you keep your distance, the perception might be that you find your counterpart's physical presence distasteful or that you are a very cold, unfeeling person" (Cross-cultural, n.d., Acceptable behavior, p. 1).

Practical Suggestions

The following are some additional guidelines and practical recommendations (i.e. do's & don'ts) for safe and valuable encounters, for a specific code of conduct, and for a favorable style of interpersonal communication with Arabs, Muslims, and Middle Easterners (see also Cross-cultural, n.d.; Morrison, 2003; United Arab, 2003):

1. Do not use your left hand when greeting, eating, or handling precious items. It is considered personally disrespectful, and poor conduct manner in general. Make sure that you use your right hand (not the left) when greeting others and when giving or receiving gifts. Using both hands, however, is even better – this gesture implies warmth and respect.
2. When sitting among others, keep both of your feet on the floor. Never cross your legs or display the sole of your shoes towards others. Exposing the bottom of your shoe is considered very offensive.

3. Outsiders who are visiting among conservative groups are expected to abide by the local standards of behavior, act in modesty, and respect their customs and code of morality.

4. Friday is the Muslim Holy Day or official weekend holiday in the Arabic Islamic countries (except for Lebanon). Sunday is a regular working business day.

5. Dedicated Muslims do not eat pork, drink alcohol, or discuss the female members of their group or clan in public. So, kindly ask before offering any potentially questionable items.

6. Do not eat or drink in front of Muslims during the month of Ramadan. The vast majority of Muslims of all persuasions observe its mandate of fasting. It is their special month of prayer, alms giving, and purification. Business hours are also shortened during Ramadan to facilitate religious preparations and social activities.

7. Never interrupt devout Muslims during their prayer rituals even if they engage in it five times a day, the required amount of the faithful. Do not be offended if they have to stop whatever they are doing and seek a quiet place (even in public) to recite their daily ritual prayer.

8. Westerners, both males and females, should always wear modest clothing when entering Arab Muslim homes, communities, or countries.

9. "Women business travelers are expected to dress modestly at all times . . . While a hat or scarf is not always required, it is wise to keep a scarf on hand" (Cross-cultural, n.d., Business attire, pp. 5, 6).

10. Business attire is important when having formal meetings or counseling sessions. This shows respect to the clients and their families, generates trust, and reflects professionalism on the part of the caregiver.

11. Interruption of meetings is normal. Do not expect rigid formalities or undivided focus when dealing with Arab Middle Easterners, especially in large settings like training sessions, classrooms, home gatherings, etc.

12. Body language and hand gestures are important. They have different meanings in different societies. Some common American gestures have an entirely different meaning in many Arab societies. For example, pointing with one finger toward someone in a meeting is considered impolite. The *thumbs up* can also be considered offensive.

13. "Some Muslims feel it is inappropriate for unrelated men and women to shake hands. Wait until the other person extends his or her hand before you extend your own" (Detroit Free, 2001, Customs, p. 51).

14. Before important visits or meetings, it is best to learn the names of people in English that you are going to be with, speak to, or introduce, so you know how to properly address them. Mispronouncing names or making fun of them because they are different is very inconsiderate and disrespectful. In many parts of the world, names have

precise meanings and they do represent the character of persons and families.

15. When visiting a traditional community, refrain from wearing their local costume or their traditional clothes right away. People may feel that you are not genuine or authentic, perhaps taking them lightly or making fun of their traditions.

16. Do not make jokes about Arab Americans' way of life or countries of origin, even when they themselves are joking about their culture, politicians, heritage, or lifestyle. As a case in point, "Cross-cultural" (n.d., Conversations, p. 1) elaborated by saying, "Egyptians like to joke around and make fun of themselves. For example, Egyptian bureaucracy is a favorite target. Nevertheless, no matter how self-deprecating their humor gets, you should not try to make fun of Egypt or the Egyptians."

17. Avoid discussing hot controversial topics with Arab Muslims and Middle Easterners, like sensitive and core religious values of fundamentalism and radical Islam, Israel, and U.S. policies in the region. Such polarizing subjects can affect your smooth relationship with them (many Arab-Muslims are highly critical of U.S. policies in the region and specifically of its bias and support to Israel).

18. Avoid discussing women with men, especially during early encounters with them. Realize that information about the female members of the family may be considered an internal matter.

19. Most Middle Easterners ought to be addressed using a label, title, or surname, but never by their first name alone. If there is no clear label or connotation, like sheikh, uncle, elder, reverend, master, umm (mother of . . .), abou (father of . . .), etc., then use generic titles like Mr., Mrs., Miss., etc., exactly as Westerners would like to be called when they are overseas. It is common to call the Easterner with a title and their first name as well. This reflects both due respect and personal endearment.

20. Most Arabs, Muslims, and Middle Easterners would welcome you at their home repeatedly. They will prepare all the entertainments and meals. Make sure to eat whatever food is presented to you without inappropriate questioning, wondering, or hesitation. Be polite and kind as you decline the many seconds they would keep putting on your plate. Also, during the first visit or two, you may hear a lot of repeated welcoming phrases, mainly the classical one, *Ahlan Wa Sahlan*. That is their tradition of showing hospitality and expressing their joy for having you. They would feel honored by your visit with them and in turn would like to honor you as their esteemed guest, even though they may be quite poor or live in a humble home. Such warmth should not be mistaken as superficial, flowery, insincere, or cheap talk. On the contrary, hosting you will give them a great source of warmth and satisfaction.

ASSESSMENT AND EVALUATION INSTRUMENTS

When psychological testing is involved or is necessary, it is recommended to use mostly projective instruments, especially with first generation and low educated immigrants. With the younger generations, who were born and raised in North America, are fluent in English, and are fairly acquainted with the American mentality and lifestyle, it is safer to administer more technical tests (intelligence, personality, etc.). It is essential to remember that the vast majority of available tests were originally designed and standardized in the West in general and for North American audiences in particular. They reflect the psycho-emotional structure and cognitive-mental views of this group. They have serious limitations and do not apply to all populations of the world. Some researchers and clinicians in the Arab World have translated English tests with little or no modifications. Some have developed their own but without proper standardization and validation. They tend to borrow concepts and theories from the Western literature without cultural screening or appropriation (cf. Khaleefa, 1999).

Eventually, the professional therapist will run the risk of having inappropriate testing which is partly irrelevant, at least, in terms of questioning methodologies, socio-cultural values, and subject contents. Consequently, this may produce a confusing testing process and inaccurate results, which complicates the matter for both the provider and the client. There are now more culturally sensitive instruments available from cross-cultural sources, but they require some effort to locate and become familiar with. Finally, regardless of the type or source of these testing instruments, it is essential to realize that such measures will shed only a narrow light into the world of an Arab American. Therefore, we must keep these endeavors in reasonable perspective.

SPECIAL DISORDERS AND COMMON THERAPIES

The mental and emotional disturbances found among Middle Easterners in the Arab-Islamic world are, to some degree, similar to those found in other developing or developed countries. However, their manifestation and impact may be different. There are also some distinctive characteristics and psychiatric severities that are more frequent or more dominant among this population due to the unique socio-cultural dynamics and religio-traditional climate in the region. Males are more prone to personality, behavioral, and addictive disorders (pathological traits, substance abuse, acting out, aggression, etc.) while females are more prone to mood, affective, and somatic disturbances (anxiety, depression, psychosomatic, obsessions, acute and chronic stress, etc.). This may partially reflect gender roles and gender-differentiated social acceptability of certain behaviors, disorders, or symptom manifestations.

Some struggling people would readily agree to seek help from physicians or mental health professionals available in their community and medical centers. Others would absolutely refuse to consult such professionals at any cost. However, many people are unaware of counseling or psychological services. Their level of awareness and acceptance of these services will depend to a large degree on their socioeconomic class, level and type of education, and exposure to the Western mindset and resources.

Historically, psychotherapy is not as popular, as known, or as needed in the Middle East as it is in the West. This is partly due to the social structure and communal living in the Middle East, which often meets the emotional needs of people and provides an outlet to their distress compared to the individualistic and relatively isolated lifestyle that is more common in the West. Therefore, several psychosocial features in the Arab-Islamic cultures are considered as healthy and natural therapy. Many customs there do have therapeutic benefits and mental health qualities without being labeled as such in modern terms.

According to Soliman (1986 as quoted in Haque, 1993), in Arab cultures, mentoring is a part of informal counseling and philosophies:

> Some counseling aspects, therefore, can be considered natural components of these cultures, though they may not always be formalized. In Middle Eastern Arab societies, 'informal counseling' is considered part of daily life, and takes place informally when people meet each other and share common interests and issues. . . People in Arab societies are always socializing with their relatives or friends in their houses, coffee houses, worship places, or work settings
>
> (Soliman, 1986, p. 33, Quoted in Haque, 1993).

Adults and adolescents alike share deep concerns and mobilize themselves to help each other and support the needy or distressed. However, along with the cultural advantages, there are serious limitations. Many severe cases remain unresolved and many troubled people continue to struggle deeply on emotional and relational levels. Yet, the stigma of visiting a mental health facility or a psychiatric hospital is still a major barrier. If obliged, some do it privately and secretly, trying to contain the publicity of their decision.

Consequently, the belief that seeking help for personal stress and troublesome matters from outside the family or social network is a sign of social weakness which may adversely cause disgraceful exposure and affect the individual's or family's esteem and worth (cf. Farina, Fischer, Boudreau, & Belt, 1996). Apparently, the fear of being perceived negatively by others prevents many people from potential benefits. According to Al-Rowaie (2001), who conducted a study in the Gulf region,

> . . . previous research suggests that individuals who embrace western values have more positive attitudes toward seeking psychological help than less western-acculturated individuals. Those individuals with less traditional and ideological cultural views express more positive attitudes toward psychological services than their culture-specific counterparts, who tend to

express stronger preference for seeking help from family ties or social network first and foremost (Brody, 1994, 1984; Fischer, Jome, & Atkinson, 1998;
Hill & O'Brien, 1999). Kuwait society has retained many traditional views
that can yield negative attitudes and perceptions relative to the seeking of
professional psychological services (Al-Rowaie, 2001, p. 73).

Haque (1993) also found that "liberal Arab students, who are more open to
western values, have significantly more positive attitudes toward counseling
than conservative Arab students" (p. 30).

A small segment of Arab Americans would take the initiative to seek psychological help on their own, specifically the younger generation and the
professionals. Another small segment would agree to seek such help only if
they receive real encouragement from others, like their educators, friends,
physicians, and clergy. The average Arab American would most likely not
seek counseling or mental health services on their own, due to a number of
reasons: Feeling intimidated by the system, the stigma attached to that profession, the critical language barrier, ignorance about the subject matter, lack
of experience in dealing with counselors, and in some cases, a negative experience with previous counselors, especially if the therapist was insensitive or
not adequately trained in cross-cultural services.

A certain proportion of Middle Easterners do not navigate well in North
America. The progress of their adjustment is slow and complicated. Their
acculturation process normally depends on many major factors, including
their background and tradition, mental exposure, emotional stability, and
previous coping experiences. Unfortunately, many face serious adjustment
challenges, mental confusion, emotional isolation, identity crises, family
conflicts, job struggles, relationship problems, and marriage and romantic
troubles, especially in cross-national relationships.

Many refugees and asylums carry with them scars of traumas and wars.
Some are escaping political unrest and religious persecution while others are
the victims of armed conflicts, violent conditions, and horrifying tragedies. In
many ways, the Middle East is unique with respect to disasters and trauma, in
that the disastrous events affecting the region in recent times are of a human
origin. The people in countries with fresh histories (and the continuing threat
of) war, conflict, and turbulent or unstable socio- and geo-political situations can face additional challenges with respect to mental health, trauma,
adaptation, and survival. Many have been deeply uprooted, geographically
displaced, and emotionally subjected to severe losses, grief, and disasters. The
accumulated agonies and psychological troubles of these people may quickly
become severe mental disorders ranging from clinical depression to psychotic
disorders. They require timely cross-cultural interventions with a thorough
understanding and appreciation of their background experience and cultural
heritage. This is the window to their minds and souls. Mechanical interventions, based on detached interpreters and mere "translation therapy" from/to
Arabic does not carry them far at all.

While in the West it is common to under-spiritualize existential matters and separate practical issues from philosophical issues of daily life, but this is not the case among Middle Easterners. In fact, it is very common to over-spiritualize matters and over amplify the religious-existential components of all sorrows and agonies, failures and disappointments, and even joys and successes. Therefore, empathizing with their worldviews, cultural heritage, and spiritual connotations is a major therapeutic tool in terms of alliance, understanding, and rapport, which can help to advance healing, recovery, and hope.

Major Disturbances, Symptoms, and Conditions

The following are some common symptoms, special disorders, and potentially problematic behaviors found among the average Arab, Muslim, and Middle Easterner population:

- Strong mixture of depressions and anxieties.
- Nervous breakdown.
- Substance use and abuse (all kinds of drugs and strong alcohol, local and imported).
- Anger and aggression: Quick temper, impulsivity, and controlling behavior.
- Social and general phobias.
- Religious suspiciousness and obsessions.
- Gambling – the sort depends on the local cultures and what is available in town.
- "Hysteria" or hysterical reactions as a way of releasing accumulated tensions and pressures and as a way of coping with acute stress and turmoil (internal, interpersonal, and external, i.e. national conflicts and wars).
- Acting out sexually or over-sexualizing behaviors.
- Family tension and domestic violence.
- Extramarital affairs are common and divorces are becoming somewhat more acceptable (though historically divorces are easier and more common among the Muslim population). The family home remains the central hub of meetings and activities to all members, but hidden affairs and cheating behaviors sometimes take place behind the scenes. Some countries are entertaining the idea of civil marriage as an option alongside or in place of religious marriages.
- Acute stress, chronic stress syndromes, Post Traumatic Stress Disorder and related conditions.
- Cognitive paranoia and Obsessive Compulsive tendencies.
- Dissociations of all types.
- Occult-related activities, involvements, and illusions.
- Somatization and psychosomatic symptoms.

- Other common medical conditions include: diabetes, cancer (increased cases lately), heart diseases, strokes, lung problems due to smoking, liver diseases due to drinking, thyroid and kidney problems, and the like.

Disabilities of all forms are present and common in the Middle East, yet, most societies are not prepared to handle the physically challenged, to accept the mentally disturbed, to accommodate the handicapped, or to help the emotionally troubled. Progress is being made in heightening the public's awareness of mental health and illness and in implementing facilities which are accessible to handicapped persons and their families. It is worth noting here, that many countries in the Middle East are considered to have low suicide rates. Death wishes may be average or equal to other countries, but the actual execution of a terminal death plan is rather below average (Weissman et al., 1999).

In dealing with an Arab American, especially with first generation immigrants, it is wiser not to rely solely on Western criteria for diagnosis or to lock them into one singular DSM-IV classification or disorder. Middle Easterners are usually multi-dimensional, multi-linguistic, multi-cultural people with a broad view and deep existential experience. Therefore, their struggles would also reflect that combination of conditions, dynamics, and worldviews. A broad evaluation and diagnosis, using a cluster of syndromes, with an open-ended prognosis, would in some cases be a more accurate description and a better psychosocial reading of their condition and psychosocial situation. It is also recommended here that the health care provider take a religious history or inventory of such clients to discover their degree of spiritual involvement, dedication, and practice. This will further reflect the individual's or family's belief system and the nature of their religiosity. Crises of faith are common during acute stress, trauma, or grief. Yet others draw from their faith a tremendous psychological strength and existential hope. Therefore, such inventories will help determine whether "faith" is a part of the problem, the solution, or irrelevant, and whether they can utilize the available support system richly found in their communities of faith.

Traditional Therapies: Popular and Folk Remedies

Religious Oaths (Nidir) *and Shrine Visitation* (Zeyaa-raat or Hajj). This is a very popular practice in the Middle East among all religions and faiths. In time of crisis, illness, or desperate needs, people make pledges, covert or overt, large or small, and travel distances to visit holy places. Some carry their own loved ones there as well. They promise to offer money, gifts, service, time, sacrifice, etc., to a particular saint, church, or shrine if their petition is answered and their wish comes true. This is a kind of personal covenant between them and God or the deity's representative – historic religious figures or divine places of worship and sacred spots. *Nidir* can serve both as intervention and also as prevention from harm, danger, failure, or injury. That means when a family or an individual is truly thankful for the great gift they received from heaven (like a newborn, a new house, a new success, etc.) they make an oath for thanksgiving and protection. Interestingly enough, some people pledge amounts they do not have. So, when their prayer or petition is answered, they boldly go around asking their neighbors, relatives, friends, distant acquaintances, and even strangers to participate in the fulfilling of their personal oath. This practice becomes, at times, a type of spiritual fund-raising, not in a collective sense for public goals but for a pure individualistic value that has a mystic nature.

Rakweh: *Purposeful Prayer.*   A folk-type of purposeful prayer over the suffering or disturbed soul, practiced by an elderly man or experienced lady to defuse and cast out sickness and ailment. The healer would repeat focal prayers and certain memorized statements out loud or softly over a cup of water or other drinking liquid, intentionally breathing into the cup. The healer would occasionally yawn over it as well in an attempt to instill in the substance a healthier mode and a divine intention, repeating the name of God, saint(s), or prophet(s). Then the cup of water or liquid is offered to the sick or troubled person to drink, believing it has been consecrated and empowered to overcome the illness. Another version of this practice, which is more conventional, is to bring holy water from a recognized church or temple and sprinkle it or drink from it several times during the course of sickness.

Evil Eye Protection.   Protection against the Black Eye, called in Arabic a "marked attack of the eye" (*sowbit el-ayin*). People use a blue precious stone or just a blue bead (made of glass) to repel any curse of bad intention known also as "the hit of a bad eye." These blue beads are made in different shapes and forms and are a very common sight across the whole Middle East. Usually, the stone's center is painted with a few circles or with the shape of an eye. People wear them around the neck, or attach them to clothes, key holders, and various objects. They hang them in cars, above the doors, at work, etc. They can be visible as a sign of overt and unconcealed protection form evil intentions. They are especially used on new items and newly born children.

The popular belief is that some individuals possess the ability to pronounce a curse or to reverse an already bestowed blessing. This is done by staring at the target and verbalizing a subtle message, which actually sounds like a compliment or an admiration at first, but in fact is loaded with bad intentions at the core, uttered in flat emotion. It is believed that the reason for a black eye could be envy, resentment, revenge, negative spirit, or just the desire to achieve cynical pleasure by inflicting pain on others.

Script Writings (**Kitaabi**).   Secretly seeking a guru, a clergy (mostly a sheikh), a folk healer, or a psychic (*arraaf*) for preparing a script veil (*hijaab*). This usually includes a prescribed statement or a written verdict regarding a specific person, a family, or a situation wrapped in a tiny piece of cloth. It is believed

that this practice can have a magic power or a supernatural influence to fulfill a wish (money, business, marriage, or romance), to disturb existing plans
(agreements, covenants, relationships), to tie a judgment against someone,
to inflict pain and suffering on certain enemies, or to pronounce condemna-
tion on another party. The process of writing such a script may be fast and
simple or prolonged and complex, depending on the type of request and the
dynamics of the people involved. It is believed also that once the script is
written and finalized it should remain secret to retain its power. However,
once discovered, it can be negated using similar approaches to counter its
effects. Thus, many troubled individuals (or their caregivers) seek experienced sheiks to untie any possible veil and unlock any curse that has been
part of the developmental life and history of the sick or troubled person.

The *hijaab* may contain constructive or destructive material with specific references, verses, or religious spells, written by hand, and occasionally
accompanied by drawings or profiles. It is tightly wrapped and stuffed into
a tiny piece of fabric, normally shaped like a triangle. Positive veil scripts
may be placed in purses, on clothes, or around the neck. Negative veil scripts
may be secretly placed into the possessions of the adversary, smuggled into
his or her house, or inserted into the surroundings outside their property.
The ceremony can be, at times, graphic and extreme. It may consist of rituals
similar to the ones practiced by occultist or satanic movements, like burning
images, pronouncing curses, punching pins and nails into dolls or photos,
and projecting harm and evil unto the target.

On the other hand, some people seek such interventional help to discover
any possible scripts written against them and uncover the curses pronounced
at them. They want any lead they can find in order to break their misery
and the root causes of their disorders. This tradition of *kitaabi* and *hijaab* is
especially common among rural people and folk Muslim communities. Some
sheikhs charge money for their services, either to tie or to break the scripts.
Those who believe in this practice or those who resort to it as an option of
last resort can become obsessed with its mystery and influence. For some
troubled people, the simple fact of hearing that the curse placed upon them is
now totally broken has a tremendous psychological effect on their recovery
and well-being. Charms and talismans are commonly used, thus, it is easy to
deceive the seekers and satisfy their naive curiosity, charging them extra fees
for these special items and services. The fact that veil-script writings rely on
religious symbols and include spiritual language or sacred Scriptures makes
vulnerable and needy people eager to accept the practice readily without
questioning or doubting its authenticity, hazards, and risks.

Psychic Activities.   Other unconventional means which people seek in times
of crisis, need, loss, disorders, and trauma include psychic activities (*tab-
seer*), spiritualism, parapsychology, sensationalism (*ulm el-hiss*), astrology
(*tan-geem*), telepathy, telekinesis, and other practices like reading palms, cups,
and crystal balls, using cards or boards, etc. Some people also seek these

approaches out of curiosity and suspiciousness regarding the future of the world and their own personal fate and destiny (obsession about end-times). These activities can range from the mild and simple practice to the complex and dangerous, often leaving the struggling individual(s) more vulnerable, confused, and disturbed than when they started.

Natural Therapies.   Natural therapies reflect oral traditions and unconventional treatments passed through the generations. At times and in simple cases, they are a good resource of relief and healing. However, in intense or severe cases they may complicate the situation or condition or, at least, cause significant delay in seeking professional help due to multiple attempts at these alternative ways and traditional methods.

Folk and natural therapies and remedies are very popular and common, like using herbs, honey, teas, oils, vinegar pads on the head, chest, or joints, treatment with pressure cups on the skin (especially on the back), Turkish baths, etc.

Modern and Contemporary Therapies in the Middle East

- Medical care and treatment. Health care clinics and medical centers are available, ranging from the basic to the sophisticated, providing all types of health services. The scope of services depends on the local setting.
- General practitioners. People seek their family physician, after consulting first with their friends, relatives, teachers, clergy, or colleagues. GPs are trusted and easily sought for all kinds of help. They are often acquainted with family affairs and dynamics as they maintain personal interest and close relationship with their patients. They serve as front-line consultants, bridges, counselors, and a broad referral source.
- Physical and massage therapy.
- Fast walking, picnics, and leisure activities.
- Sauna, swimming, and traditional or modern types of sports.
- Psychotherapy. Psychiatric and psychological services are usually attached to hospitals and medical centers in the Arab Middle Eastern world while guidance and counseling offices are more attached to educational institutions and religious agencies. People normally do not seek these treatment options readily unless their situation becomes absolutely critical. In some cities, private counseling offices and family guidance clinics are becoming available and more visible. Presently, the mass media is presenting more psychologically oriented topics, discussions, programs, and interviews to help the public gain awareness of the mental-emotional aspects, needs, and struggles facing all human beings.
- Vitamins, special diets, healthy nutrition, and exercise gymnasiums.
- Spirituality. Pastoral care and visitation and focused prayer over the troubled and the sick by recognized ministers and certified clergy is very

common and popular in the Middle East. Most people readily seek spiritual intervention from ministers, books, or sacred places during an illness or crisis. They readily receive spiritual help and prayer from friends and clergy alike. It is considered an integral part of the human psyche and therefore an essential part of recovery, healing, and comprehensive care. This includes conventional pastoral care like reading Scripture, reciting appropriate prayers, laying of hands, and anointing the sick with oil.

DISASTERS AND TRAGEDIES: WHEN GRIEF, LOSS, AND TRAUMA ARE SIMULTANEOUSLY PRESENT

The majority of the region in the Middle East is not an extremely high-risk area in terms of natural disasters (e.g., volcanoes, hurricanes, earthquakes, major floods, forest fires, etc.). However, it has its share of sociocultural tensions and ethnopolitical conflicts and wars. Currently, these conflicts are the main source of turmoil, grief, loss, and tragedy. Nevertheless, there is a certain level of natural disasters that occur in some places on a regular basis, like earthquakes (Iran, Turkey), soil drought and sand storms (North Africa, Gulf region), local floods (Egypt's Delta, sea coast cities), severe winter storms and freezing weather (the mountain ranges), and diseases and epidemics (refugee camps, heavily dense poor areas).

Although most Middle Easterners live in relatively stable regions, some of them dwell in rather highly stressful or volatile areas, where constant fighting and political tensions prevail (Iraq, Palestine, Israel, Sudan, Iran, Lebanon, etc.). They have endured multiple hardships, losses, and traumas, but still the agonies continue in many places.

Social Trauma and Collective Grief

When dealing with disasters or with the aftermath of wars, it is important to shift the therapeutic attention beyond individual trauma to *social trauma* and beyond personal grief to *collective grief*. The impact of trauma injury normally extends beyond the individual to affect the social matrix of the larger community, and at times the whole nation. Interestingly enough, in the midst of any war or conflict zone and following any major attack or invasion (e.g., September 11, 2001 in the USA) the whole nation responds, feels, acts, and reacts similar to an *Individual Self*. Virtually, there are parallel characteristics to "trauma responses" and "grief reactions" between a single person and a large community (Abi-Hashem, 2006).

The concept of social trauma is still being developed in the literature. This especially makes sense to disaster relief and mental health workers who are trying to help victims across cultural barriers. Naturally, psychological symptoms do not occur in a vacuum and are not limited to scattered individuals. Their experience is communal and existential in nature, and is the direct result of living together in a conflict zone. Actually, such symptoms are the manifestation of the ethno-political tensions, socio-cultural dynamics, and religious dimensions of people. Many immigrants carry these scars with them as they relocate in the hosting country. Therefore, applying culturally sensitive methods is absolutely essential for the success of any mediations or interventions.

Relying on theories and clinical approaches developed in the West and for Western use can be utterly unhelpful, irrelevant, and, at times, counterproductive for many groups, including the various Middle Eastern communities both in the Arabic-Islamic world and in North America (Abi-Hashem, 1997, 1998, 1999a, 2006; Marsella & Christopher, 2004; Summerfield, 1995).

Any significant loss could have elements of both trauma and grief, but not all losses are traumatic (e.g., the peaceful death of a loved one), nor are all traumas grief-laden (e.g., being shaken by a major explosion or watching a sudden terrifying event). However, traumatic stress and mourning bereavement do clearly overlap. When both elements are strongly present, their impact on the survivors is much greater. These combined symptoms can become highly intensified, thereby impairing the person, family, or group involved. Consequently, the steps toward healing, resolution, and recovery become more demanding, time consuming, and possibly complicated. This is especially true when there is no break in the cycle of stress, loss, conflict, or despair. Also, additional challenges are present when circumstances that provide time for personal reflection, communal grief, and emotional survival are rare, limited, or non-existent.

Prolonged Grief

Prolonged and unresolved grief can have strong negative consequences for individuals, communities, and even entire nations. Severe and extended mourning affects the emotional, mental, physical, and spiritual life conditions of the bereaved. It affects their mood, functioning, outlook, stability, and relationships. Any focused treatment approach or counseling method must target the twin goals of trauma mastery and grief resolution (Abi-Hashem, 1999b, 1999c, 2006; Meichenbaum, 1994; Rando, 1996). Similarly, Stroebe, Schut, and Stroebe (1998) suggested the dual model of coping, when therapeutic approaches ought to address both the manifestation of grief from major losses and the severe stress from traumatic events.

Many people in the troubled areas of the Middle East have suffered and continue to suffer from all types of losses, which often result in chronic cases of unresolved grief and complicated bereavement. They arrive in Europe, Canada, or United States with unanswered questions and open wounds. They have experienced major losses on many levels and at multiple times: Personal and communal, sudden and gradual, real and symbolic, private and public, existential and material, etc. Past and present losses are compounded by the apprehension of the "unknown" and the anticipation of upcoming future losses, causing a phenomenon known as *anticipatory grief*. This normally happens when all surrounding events give no sign of relief or possible ending in-sight to the ongoing tensions and conflicts. Rather, the only indication is the unrelenting deterioration of the situation with signs of further escalation.

> The idea, that any devastating conflict or war injury could be justified or satisfactorily explained, is usually essential to inspire any victimized person to cope with the war anguish and its aftermath. However, the more people perceive that war as meaningless or endless, the worse they will feel and eventually become (Abi-Hashem, 2006).

For example, the Lebanese people have suffered from all kinds of losses, civil unrest, and agonies in the 15 years of serious troubles triggered and transplanted on their land. Such difficulties have continued into the present, with the destruction of Lebanese infrastructure by Israeli forces in the summer of 2006. Likewise, the majority of the common people in Iraq, Palestine, Sudan, and Israel have been experiencing an intense combination of trauma and grief resulting from their regular exposure to violence. The survivors must undoubtedly endure a host of symptoms relative to the degree of their exposure. Sadly, they struggle with prolonged traumatic residuals and multiple grief reactions.

> Similarly, millions of victims have to live with the unfortunate consequences of devastating wars and strong urban conflicts. They may never be able to master their traumas or resolve their grief and perhaps never to experience any significant relief for years to come. Some deeply affected individuals try to medicate themselves to numb the pain and sense of terror. Others are more fortunate because they benefit from the social support, warmth, and network available around them in the community and from the closeness of friends and family members who care enough to prevent them from suffering alone (Abi-Hashem, 2006).

Therefore, at times, disturbed survivors do respond well to the natural therapeutic sources available to them among their people. And these therapies are embedded beautifully and naturally within their own communities and subcultures. At other times, however, these natural support systems may be disrupted in the course of war, conflict, or disaster.

COPING STRATEGIES AND SURVIVING MODES

Many Arabs and Muslims are moving to North America for a variety of reasons. Some of them arrive as regular immigrants and social refugees. They are foreign born, first generation, and are arriving in large numbers. Many are trying to escape political instabilities, conflict zones, and economic hardships. Several minorities are, in fact, escaping persecution and mistreatment.

They are constantly subject to political and religious pressure. They have endured war-related stress and socio-emotional disturbances and, therefore, carry with them traumas, serious loss, stored anger, affective depression, and mental confusion. They want to escape the seemingly endless stagnation, hopelessness, and life of despair. Yet, they still struggle deeply with lingering negative consequences. Others have developed better coping skills and have survived countless agonies, and despite the turmoil adjust well to their new environment. Now they are trying to navigate and establish themselves in a new society and move ahead with their limited resiliency.

Yet, another group migrates from stable areas of the Middle East for traditional reasons, like starting a business, pursuing further education, or joining family members. Historically, there have been large numbers of students (both undergraduate and graduate) who come from the Middle East on their own or who are sent from their governments as special delegates. Young people in particular like to travel, especially to Western nations, merely for pleasure and exploration and also for gaining a sense of international adventure. However, each group brings with them a host of psychological issues and cultural properties which require special consideration from all caregivers – mental health providers, public educators, spiritual mentors, social workers, physicians, and community leaders, to name a few.

In order to better understand Arab Americans and to adequately help those who are vulnerable, in need, or at risk, we have to discover their emotional background and learn about their coping strategies, namely as practiced back home, in their original settings and cultures, as well as how these strategies develop and change in the host culture.

General Coping Styles in Tragedies, Conflicts, and Wars

Since many Arab Americans directly originated from troubled areas within the Middle East, it is wise to examine how they respond during high stress crises and disasters that hit their communities. Pre-existing conditions, like war-related anxieties, vulnerabilities, and unresolved grief, can be easily reawakened inside many victims. Normally, people who have had previous exposure to traumas or who have had a history of psychological maladjustment and psychopathology become highly sensitized and at higher risk than others. However, the mere presence of certain "risk factors" does not necessarily result in negative emotional consequences or psychosomatic disturbances. According to Hobfoll et al. (1991), there are two major factors that put people at risk for developing mental health problems as a result of war and tragedy: First, the greater the threat of loss or the actual loss to which they are exposed, the greater their level of risk – threat to life being the primary fear. Second, the fewer coping resources people have, the more likely they will be overwhelmed by their losses.

Unfortunately, during any kind of civil unrest, political turmoil, or military conflict, daily living becomes unbearable and any psychological malfunction will surface and could easily multiply. Some individuals or families will react in a severe fashion while others cope well and show better tolerance. If the stress becomes traumatic and people develop a full measure of post-traumatic stress disorder (PTSD), then they will likely continue to react to current triggers that are reminiscent of the original trauma, displaying physiological reactions related only to the early traumatic event. If this occurs, one can expect to see (a) nightmares, (b) intrusive daytime images and bodily sensations related to the traumatic experience, (c) excessive physiological startle, (d) extreme anxiety states alternating with numbing and anhedonia, (e) difficulty modulating arousal in general and anger in particular, and (f) dissociative reactions (cf. Hobfoll et al., 1991).

Unhealthy Coping Methods

There are certain ways of coping in the Arab Middle Eastern world that are unhealthy and unproductive. These can lead to negative psychosocial consequences. The survivors of stress and tragedy can easily fall back again into dysfunction, apathy, and despair. That tendency is hard to resist, even for previously high functioning people, when the sources of fighting and instability continue. Loss of hope and the persistence of conflicts are major factors in negative coping styles and clinical depression. The following are some potentially unhealthy methods that Middle Eastern people may use to cope, especially in high tension and conflict zone areas:

Prolonged Avoidance and Withdrawal. Prolonged avoidance and withdrawal in the face of emerging stressors and serious troubles is a common problematic coping response.

> Absence of action can further lead into immobilization and mental paralysis. Of course, war related shocks and stressors can result in psychological numbness and marked helplessness. Individuals have to make a constant effort to remain active and alert and to break the emotional passivity. This is very difficult to achieve especially when every thing around the survivors is bleak, dark, hopeless, and violent with no end in sight (Abi-Hashem, 2006).

Fighting and civic unrest tend to force people to hide, wait, and wonder. However, some people tend to isolate not because they are loners by nature but because they are cut off physically due to the fighting or their experience causes them to become seriously anxious, self-protective, and fearful. Others are embarrassed due to the physical injury or material losses they have recently suffered. They cut down their social participation and tend to deal with their own fear, loss, uncertainty, and the unknown alone. At times, the isolation is suddenly broken when the disaster hits closer to them and they are obliged to evacuate home or share their residence with other survivors.

Therefore, prolonged social isolation is also another maladaptive way for coping.

Blaming and Cynicism.   Blaming the government, the parties, the local leaders, the militias, other family members, etc., is a common defense practice during troubled war times and social disorders. Cynicism and pessimism are powerful attitudes, which can lead the victims to believe that the worst is yet to come. They tend to amplify their problems into a catastrophic magnitude. This coping style is a self-protective measure used by low tolerance and bereaved people who have already experienced multiple losses and substantial disappointments. Eventually, cynical and pessimistic individuals drive others away, including their good friends and potential supporters, denying themselves the readily available and centralized emotional help they desperately need.

Irritation and Aggression.   Deep frustration, anger, and low tolerance are very common reactions during and after any major crisis or tragedy. Usually, poor sleep, inability to make clear decisions, living in crowded places, constant danger, enduring grief and mourning, and an endless wait for resolution, are all factors contributing to the rise of aggressive behaviors. It should come as no surprise that this inner frustration influences some individuals to become quite rebellious and join opposition groups, street gangs, or armed militias.

Overdependency on Tranquilizers.   Due to the high level of stress associated with turbulent times (wars, disasters, conflicts, tragedies, injuries, unemployment, traumas, losses, etc.), many survivors resort to tranquilizers to sedate their anxieties, pains, and fears. In many countries, legal drugs are easily obtained from regular pharmacies without formal prescriptions. Therefore, the public has access to serious medications and pain killers without medical screening or supervision. This easy availability has encouraged many distressed people to begin using and become highly dependent on tranquilizers. In some places, this type of addiction has become an epidemic with long-term consequences.

Alcohol and Drug Abuse.   An easy way to find solace for social troubles, ethnopolitical conflicts, war related stress, or severe personal problems, has been through alcohol and drug use. Chemical and substance abuse is a very common avenue for coping during such turbulent times. "Small amounts of chemicals may aid individuals by limiting very intense emotions, especially during initial periods of distress. However, prolonged usage or use of large amounts of illicit or prescriptive drugs or alcohol can be very destructive" (Hobfoll et al., 1991, Negative coping pathways, p. 6).

Gambling, Sexualizing, and Acting Out Behaviors.   With plenty of free time and lack of emotional outlets, many develop bad habits to occupy their time and release their internal pressures. Some give in to peer pressure, others follow their own impulses and indulge in practices to satisfy their drives. The results are destructive ways of coping, affecting one's life, stability, finances, relationships, and welfare and, on a larger scope, further disturbances and troubles for the immediate family and community.

Moving and Migration. At times, disaster survivors have to make last minute decisions without adequate information or resources (e.g., relocating, sending children away, selling the family home, switching businesses, quitting schooling, leaving the country, etc.). Later on, they may regret some of these hasty decisions and struggle with guilt and self-blame, a phenomenon that further demoralizes and paralyzes them and compounds their negative surviving style (Abi-Hashem, 2006). However, relocating does not always happen by choice. Due to the intensity of fighting in one area, residents must evacuate to another area. Therefore, many become displaced, second-class citizens, and actual immigrants and refugees within their own countries.

In addition to the factors mentioned above, the following symptoms and stress-related reactions are from the author's personal observation of the Lebanese people during and after the civil war (and serious troubles that were mostly imported and imposed on their country) from 1975 until the present time. The author typically spends several months per year in Lebanon. The following are very obvious to notice on a daily basis: Very low tolerance, marked impatience, being on edge, highly nervous, easily scared, feeling caged, venting anger, feeling crippled or immobilized, becoming pushy and irritable, quickly losing temper in public as evidenced by yelling, shouting, complaining, or cursing in public (even women do this now, which represents a totally new phenomenon).

With the increase in stressful events, economic hardship and extremely high inflation, political uncertainties, ongoing conflicts, struggling infrastructure, and the decrease of material resources and monthly income, many people have become tight with their money and very self-protective. Some have even become dishonest and manipulative in order to gain more. Consequently, this is contributing to the decline of hospitality and sociocultural values, like civility, politeness, and mutual care among friends, neighbors, and relatives. In some areas of the Arab-Islamic world, the middle class in society has been shrinking considerably due to the financial hardships and economic depressions experienced in the troubled regions, leaving the majority of the population depleted and poor.

Therefore, we have seen an increase in cheating, stealing, cursing, heavy smoking, substance use and abuse, egoism and self-centeredness, and acting out behaviors. Many have become quite materialistic, greedy, hedonistic, numb to danger and death, workaholic, and indifferent to the misery of others. Thus, such described symptoms and psychological maneuvers reflect common unconscious processes and reactive coping mechanisms. It is also interesting to note how certain traumas and stress-related events cause people to alter their attitudes, relationships, priorities, social values, and moral behaviors.

Factors Determining the Degree of Psychosocial Impacts

The severity of the symptoms and emotional outcomes usually depends on many additional factors (cf. Abi-Hashem, 2006, 1999b, 1999c, 1999d; Worden, 1991). Among them: The circumstances surrounding the event, conflict, disaster, or war-torn area; the emotional stability and resiliency of the survivors; the support systems available to the families or groups during and after the crisis (or crises); the age and gender of the survivors; the personality traits, temperaments, and any pre-existing conditions of people involved; the severity of the trauma (i.e., its timing, magnitude, duration, frequency, etc.); the problem solving skills, educational level, and financial abilities of the victims (as individuals, families, and community); the availability of any survival opportunity or escape option (exits in case of heavy fighting); the collective or group experience in handling previous traumas and tragedies; the cultural background and traditions of the survivors; the ability and freedom to practice common rituals and religious customs; and the spiritual faith and the degree of people's existential hope and optimism.

Healthy Traditional Coping

In times of trouble and turmoil, most people tend to gravitate around each other and create circles of friends and cells of neighborhoods, where they can share daily living and chores, frequently give and receive support, leisurely laugh and converse, prepare food and eat meals together, exchange needed encouragement and belonging, openly and passionately discuss the political issues of the day, share insights about their emotional struggles, freely nurture and compliment each other, and together help keep their perspectives realistic and clear.

Each population and subculture utilizes different variations of coping styles, depending on their background, education, tradition, political involvement, rootedness in the land, level of resiliency, spirituality, etc. Urban people utilize more sophisticated and modern ways while rural people utilize more traditional and simple ways. There is also a combination of styles as well. Certainly, each type has its own richness and psychosocial benefits.

In general, most urban people of the Middle East integrate the old methods with the new in order to form a balanced life reflecting a wide spectrum of functioning (including the use of several languages). Normally, they are able to navigate between lifestyles and cultural values without obvious tension or major conflict. They observe their local customs and traditional norms and, at the same time, function well in a business mode or professional context. In this way they enjoy the warmth of family and closeness of friends (tightness of kin and community) yet operate independently and freely (self-reliance and autonomy).

Traditionally, social support has been a strong feature in the Middle East. It is popular and readily available for the needy and struggling. Immediate and extended families as well as many friends and relatives normally gather around the weak, the ill, the victim, the vulnerable, and the bereaved in a marvelous way (at times to the degree of overbearing). Virtually, any traumatized individuals who receive and enjoy consistent long-term support, are more likely to adjust and heal better than those who do not receive such abundant support.

Eating meals together and social gatherings of family members and friends are powerful therapeutic ways to cope and unwind. Even poor hosts usually go to a great extent to prepare elaborate meals for their guests. That is part of the Middle Eastern culture and innate virtue of hospitality. "Preparing for such gatherings can reinforce communal bonds and alleviate anxiety and depression; eating together can also give a certain feeling of bliss, comfort, and solidarity" (Abi-Hashem, 2006).

Another prevalent custom of coping in the Middle East is the old-time habit of visiting friends, relatives, neighbors, and acquaintances. During troubled times, these practices increase and become the lifeline of the community. Spending long hours visiting together, recreating in a tribal atmosphere, and frequent overnight stays in the same household can have a strong bearing on the moods of survivors. It also facilitates mental relief and helps the heavyhearted reconcile the harsh realities of living in constant stress or danger. This type of communal gathering substantially nurtures the group's soul and mind and gives them a sense of calm, assurance, and solidarity. Thus, they can endure the dangers, face the unknown, and navigate through the endless pressures and traumas of wars and disasters (Abi-Hashem, 2006).

Individuals and families normally take turns caring for each other, especially during times of intense crisis. If someone becomes exhausted and depleted or falls into severe depression and despair, others typically rally around him/her, supporting, encouraging, challenging, and uplifting until he/she bounces back to a better mood and level of functioning. People may do this, all the while realizing their turn may come next.

Other forms of positive coping include both indoor and outdoor activities like group singing, folk dancing (rak-saat), celebrating religious feasts (even across faiths), playing cards and familiar games, evening group visitations and gatherings (sah-raat), strolling on safe roads and streets, intensely discussing the issues of the day, field picnics and road trips, playing local sports, gathering to work on a common neighborhood project or humanitarian mission, attending public prayers, visiting worship places, community problem solving, volunteering delivery of interrupted and crucial services (water, food, candles, batteries, etc.), assisting the elderly and the sick, watching popular television programs and documentaries together, etc.

Such natural and creative coping activities provide a positive distraction from the daily bombardments and worries of the dark season. Consequently, many show a high degree of survival skills, emotional resiliency, and stress tolerance in the face of such unfavorable and devastating events.

GUIDELINES FOR COUNSELING AND THERAPY

Conducting psychotherapy, clinical research, and regular counseling with Arab Americans are specialized activities that have their unique characteristics and challenges. Whether these approaches are in the form of empirical research, mental health surveys, therapeutic interventions, medical inventories, supportive counseling, or in-depth psychotherapy, they must be culturally sensitive, clinically accurate, socially appropriate, and humanly respectful. When a mental health professional embarks on conducting such psychosocial endeavors, it is recommended that he or she take the following guidelines and suggestions into consideration (cf. Abi-Hashem, 1999a, 2006):

- Be open, honest, and sensitive as you deal with Arab Americans and try to learn about their values, norms, faiths, customs, and traditions.
- Find common ground and build solid bridges with them. By earning their trust and confidence, you will increase your effectiveness and respect in their community as a caregiver.
- Acknowledge the obvious differences between you and the client. Gently ask if they have any concerns about relating to you or working with you on these personal matters.
- Appreciate their heritage as you offer to help, support, challenge, and serve them.
- If they belong to an ethnic or religious minority, acknowledge the reality of their situation and the possible hardship they may face, including being misunderstood, stereotyped, or even mistreated.
- Try to find out the degree of grief, trauma, and bereavement the person or the family is struggling with. Also, find out their level of adjustment and acculturation within the new hosting society and larger environment.
- Discover any unresolved issues and emotional residues carried over from their home country, which can be compounded by many additional challenges stirred up within the new culture.
- Apply appropriate Grief and Bereavement Counseling, Critical Incident Debriefing Techniques, or Trauma Mastery approaches (or a combination of these) according to the need and intensity of issues, especially following a major crisis, civil unrest, significant loss, war, disaster, or horrifying act.
- Do not be afraid of silence! Be careful not to misinterpret politeness, slow disclosure, repetition of information, indirectness, low expressiveness, or minimal eye contact as defensiveness, psychological resistance, emotional disturbance, or lack of interest in participating.

- Make an effort to be sensitive in your feedback and culturally relevant in your comments and interpretations. Be clear in your suggestions, guidance, and set of instructions.
- Avoid generalizations! Do not label or classify them, e.g., "You Arab people . . . All practicing Muslims can be fanatic . . . The Middle East is a male-dominated society . . . Your women are mistreated . . . Arab cultures are backwards and primitive", and so forth. These comments are hurtful and stereotypical, and may have potentially alienating and damaging effects for the therapeutic relationship.
- Realize that you are dealing with various backgrounds, social classes, education levels, mindsets, religious affiliations, and worldviews. They all reflect the complex mosaic of the Arabic world and Middle East.
- Inquire gently! Allow enough time for processing and be patient with them. Do not demand information or put pressure on them to quickly disclose their issues or completely describe their heritage, struggles, habits, pain, needs, etc.
- Watch the non-verbal cues. Listen to the signals, gestures, common phrases, and styles of communication used. Do not impose on them your ideas, solutions, values, or personal preferences. Only present those as another option.
- Be faithful to what you learn from them. They probably expect you to remember and honor their personal history and the private information they share with you.
- Allow yourself to grow and change as a result of these cultural encounters and rich experiences. Appreciate the depth and uniqueness of every individual, group, or community. Allow yourself to be creative, less rigid and non-conventional in dealing with them. Keeping a distant and too-high-professional profile, or relating to them only behind closed doors or on the phone is limiting. Some will probably bring you gifts and invite you to their home for meals. Most people from developing countries prefer less formal, less rigid types of counseling – where flexibility, friendliness, and spontaneity produce great results.
- Realize that people will usually appreciate the little you can offer, including yourself, and will respond accordingly, positively, and gratefully.

GUIDELINES FOR RESEARCH AND INTERVENTIONS

In-depth research studies and adequate specialized surveys are needed to understand the psychosocial functioning and coping strategies of the various Middle Eastern populations in North America. These investigations should be based on comprehensive observations, deep insights and awareness, new conceptual frameworks, carefully crafted designs, and friendly approaches. Research designs should include consultation with experts in cross-cultural psychology and/or communication, who possess intimate knowledge of the

Middle East and the Arabic-Islamic world. For some types of research activities, consulting an anthropologist or sociologist with concentrated expertise in Arabic or Middle Eastern studies may be called for. If warranted by the complexity of the research endeavor, consulting a range of relevant experts with diverse disciplinary orientations and perspectives would be ideal. Insensitive approaches or literally translated questionnaires from Western sources can be misleading and confusing, both to the participants and the researchers alike (cf. Khaleefa, 1999). In short, mere translations without consideration of context and culture can completely miss the point.

Thus far, the focus of research and intervention has been largely targeted towards individuals, couples, or small family units, but not much towards the whole community (which is larger than the extended family and smaller than the larger society). Given that most Arab Americans live in close human proximities and concentrated communities, those groups should be targeted for more observation and research. Lustig et al. (2004) pointed out, "More research is needed on interventions, specifically on efficacy and cultural relevance. Interventions that have an impact on multiple ecological levels need further development and evaluation" (p. 1). Even though the location and the type of population involved determine, to a large degree, the content and the phenomenology of the survey, investigation, or study, all research efforts among Middle Easterners should reflect certain characteristics and basic qualities.

In my opinion as well as in many others', any research study, academic endeavor, clinical intervention, or even humanitarian service to be conducted among Arab Americans, and in the Arabic-Islamic world at large, should take the following principles, qualities, and guidelines into serious consideration (cf. Abi-Hashem, 2006):

- It should be mostly non-western in nature. It must be culturally sensitive and basically relevant to the Eastern mentality and intergenerational culture. Although many concepts, theories, and approaches in psychology, counseling, and the social sciences are global and universal in their nature and application, many others simply are not. They need to be adapted, modified, changed, or completely omitted.
- It should be mostly non-pathological in orientation, trying to detect not only the malfunctions and disorders but also the strengths, positive qualities, and healthy aspects of the people. It should be able to detect the inter-generational wisdom, communal strength, psychological resiliency, and social support that keep them surviving and functioning well. It is very rewarding indeed to discover some of their hidden sources of hope, tolerance, and innovation as a stored capital of emotional energy.
- It should be both individualistic and collective in nature, focusing on the familial and communal entities of the large group and not exclusively limited to the isolated aspects of individuals. A shift in paradigm is necessary here from the purely *intrapsychic* approach to the *sociocultural*

dimensions of human beings. This is especially true when dealing with Middle Easterners, and non-Western populations in general, due to their ability to process and navigate life among several mindsets, languages, and subcultures.

- It should be mostly philosophical in nature. It should be non-superficial and non-mechanical, but rather able to detect the existential depth, the global perspective, and the communal presence. Foreigners and internationals living in North America normally speak two or three languages. With that ability comes a marvelous socio-cultural dimension and depth that mono-linguistic people do not naturally possess, share, or deeply understand. It seems that with every language comes a certain experiential level, a mental operation, a cultural adaptation, and a unique worldview.

  The human mind can be functioning on one or three-dimensional levels (similar to a 1D versus 3D object or picture). Thus, research studies and interventions should be able to detect not only the needs, struggles, and pathology of Arab Americans, but also their resiliency, strengths, and sources of endurance. It is also important to keep in mind that most people in developing countries have a different view of *time, space, place, hardships*, and *pain* than people in developed or more affluent countries.

- It should be non-rigid but comprehensive in its diagnostic scope, focusing on the global psychological picture rather than on merely the specifics of trying only to isolate one single DSM-IV criteria at a time. This seems to be limiting and superficial as it applies to many populations (e.g., targeting one type of Anxiety or one class of Depression or PSTD, etc.). Rather, it must remain open-ended, looking for underlying clusters, multiple features, and combinations of syndromes. Most people, even in western societies, do not fit either under one single diagnosis of the DSM-IV (which after all is based on Western settings and paradigms). It must fit a combination of paradigms and integrate many experiences, disturbances and diagnoses together. Virtually, what is considered pathological in one culture can be quite normal in another, and vice versa. Thus, the challenge is to capture the Arab Americans' global experience and condition rather than focus on only one small piece or slice of the psychosocial picture. This is true for therapy as well.

- It should be non-provincial, non-materialistic but broad in its approach to reality. That means non-linear and non-mechanical but circular (or even spiral) in its worldview and mode of thinking.

- It should be concerned, not only with details, pieces, or fragments, but also with the larger scope and global picture. It is essential to remember here that, while the parts are important to deal with separately at times for the sake of specific healing, functional recovery, harmony, and empowerment, the *whole* remains more vital and much greater than the sum of the little *parts*.

- It should be non-secular but spiritual. Communal heritage, religious affiliation, and spiritual faith are integral elements of many Middle Eastern group-identities and social functions. Many Arab Americans are simply non-religious in the devout sense. They are just socially religious or culturally spiritual (and some even secular). However, many others are highly dedicated and quite active in their faith. So, referring to faith, mentioning God, asking about religious background, and so forth can be important aspects of assessment, counseling and caregiving approaches. They are appropriate indicators of people's internal conditions and can be a great resource for help, hope, and support. For some Arab-Muslims, their social community is the same as their faith community. Therefore, it can be a double-edged sword: A source of support and identity or a source of pressure and conformity. Thus, including some theological themes and religious questions is at times very revealing, and can serve as an entry point to other substantial dynamics and private matters.
- It should be non-literal but meaning oriented! It should often not be mono-linguistic either! Many educated people in the Middle East, especially in large towns and cities, are fluent in more than one language. Therefore, it would be appropriate to use some terminologies in English or French in adjunction with the Arabic terms so the meaning can be clearer, richer, easy to grasp, and well integrated with the purpose of the instrument or intervention used.
- It should be non-intrusive but respectful! Avoiding embarrassment, revealing questions and conversations, and discussion of hot topics, sensitive material, or private issues (like eliciting detailed information about one's intimate or sexual life: Describe your *sexual* relationship . . . Report about your *guilt* and *shame* . . .), especially when done too quickly or too soon. It should also be non-provocative and topically-oriented, not promoting free wild expressions (Talk about your *anger* toward your father/mother . . . Describe your hate toward your boss or government . . . etc.).
- It should be non-artificial but realistic. Avoid presenting a quick fix to the problem or an easy way out of the situation. People do not typically expect you to offer a fast solution to their dilemma, pain, and struggle. As mentioned earlier, most people in still-developing countries are able to tolerate psychic agony and physical pain much better than their counterparts in more developed countries, as they usually experience more of it. To them, hardships are integral parts of life. Therefore, there is no need to exaggerate or amplify their problems beyond a reasonable volume or to feel the pressure to find them a quick solution to their agony. Let them set the tone of impact. Also, it is always helpful to first discover their perception of the situation before you describe it to them from your own perspective, especially when you are dealing with a set of cross-cultural mindsets, perceptions, and worldviews.

Finally, immigrants and refugees can teach us a great deal about endurance, survival, wisdom, community, contentment, and contribution to life if we have the humility and desire to learn from them with an open mind and friendly soul.

References

Abi-Hashem, N. (1992). The impact of the Gulf War on the churches in the Middle East: A sociocultural and spiritual analysis. *Pastoral Psychology, 41*(1), 4–26.

Abi-Hashem, N. (1997). Reflections on "International Perspectives in Psychology." *American Psychologist, 52*(5), 569–570.

Abi-Hashem, N. (1998). Returning to the fountains. *American Psychologist, 53*(1), 63–64.

Abi-Hashem, N. (1999a). Cross-cultural psychology. In D. G. Benner & P. C. Hill (Eds.), *Baker encyclopedia of psychology and counseling* (2nd ed.). Grand Rapids, MI: Baker, pp. 294–298.

Abi-Hashem, N. (1999b). Grief, loss, and bereavement: An overview. *Journal of Psychology and Christianity, 18*(4), 309–329.

Abi-Hashem, N. (1999c). Trauma. In D. G. Benner & P. C. Hill (Eds.), *Baker encyclopedia of psychology and counseling* (2nd ed.). Grand Rapids, MI: Baker, pp. 1229–1230.

Abi-Hashem, N. (1999d). Loss of function. In D. G. Benner & P. C. Hill (Eds.), *Baker encyclopedia of psychology and counseling* (2nd ed.). Grand Rapids, MI: Baker, p.705.

Abi-Hashem, N. (2003). Syria. In B. Sherif-Trask (Ed.), *The Greenwood encyclopedia of women's issues worldwide: The Middle East and North Africa* (pp. 355–380). Westport, CT: Greenwood Press.

Abi-Hashem, N. (2004a). Peace and war in the Middle East: A psychopolitical and sociocultural perspective. In F. M. Moghaddam & A. J. Marsella (Eds.), *Understanding terrorism: Psychosocial roots, consequences, and interventions* (pp. 69–89). Washington DC: American Psychological Association Press.

Abi-Hashem, N. (2004b, November). *Respect: A psychological, moral, and spiritual reflection.* International Network on Personal Meaning (INPM). Online publication at http://www.meaning.ca/articles04/hashem-respect.htm

Abi-Hashem, N. (2006). The agony, silent grief, and deep frustration of many communities in the Middle East: Challenges for coping and survival. In P. T. P. Wong & L. C. J. Wong (Eds.), *Handbook of multicultural perspectives on stress and coping.* New York, NY: Springer.

Abou-El-Fadl, K. (2005). *The great theft: Wrestling Islam from the extremists.* San Francisco, CA: Harper Collins.

Al-Rowaie, O. (2001). *Predictors of attitudes toward seeking professional psychological help among Kuwait university students* [Electronic version]. Unpublished doctoral dissertation. Virginia Polytechnic Institute and State University. Blacksburg, Virginia.

Allied Media. (2004a). Arab Americans: Introducing a niche market and the unique opportunity to tap its potential. Retrieved July 30, 2005, from http://www.allied-media.com/Arab American/default.htm

Allied Media. (2004b). Census figures on Arab population in US give partial glimpse at community. Retrieved July 30, 2005, from http://www.allied-media.com/Arab-American/census.htm

Allied Media (2004c). Muslim American Media. Can American values be marketed to Muslims? Retrieved August 15, 2005, from http://www.allied-media.com/marketing%20to%20muslims.htm

Allied Media. (n.d.). AMC Arab publications. Retrieved August 02, 2005, from http://www.allied-media.com/Arab-American/muslim-media.htm

American Arab Chamber of Commerce. (n.d.). State's Rank by Arab American Population. Retrieved on July 30, 2005 from http://www.americanarab.com/main.cfm?location=28

Arab American Business. (n.d.). Educational level of Arab Americans: Occupation of Arab Americans. Retrieved July 30, 2005, from http://www.arabamericanbusiness.com/Demogr04.pdf

Arab American Institute (2006a). Famous Arab Americans. Retrieved 11/17/2006 from: http://www.aaiusa.org/Arab Americans/23/famous-Arab Americans

Arab American Institute. (2006b). Arab American Demographics. Retrieved 11/18/2006 from: http://www.aaiusa.org/Arab-Americans/22/demographics

Badolato, E. V. (1984). *Learning to think like an Arab Muslim: A short guide to understanding the Arab mentality.* Retrieved August 15, 2005, from http://www.blackwaterusa.com/btw2004/articles/0503arabs.html

Barakat, H. (1993). *The Arab world: Society, culture, and states.* Los Angeles, CA: University of California Press.

Brittingham, A., & de la Cruz, G. P. (2005). We the people of Arab ancestry in the United States. *Census 2000 Special Reports* (CENSR-21). Washington, DC: U.S. Department of Commerce, Economics and Statistics Administration, U.S. Census Bureau.

Cross-cultural communication. (n.d.). Egypt. Retrieved September 15, 2005, from http://www.cba.uni.edu/buscomm/InternationalBusComm/world/africa/egypt/egypt.html

de la Cruz, G. P., & Brittingham, A. (2003). The Arab population: 2000. *Census 2000 Brief* (C2KBR-23). Washington, DC: U.S. Department of Commerce, Economics and Statistics Administration, U.S. Census Bureau.

Detroit Free Press. (2001). *100 questions and answers about Arab Americans: A journalist guide.* Retrieved July 30, 2005, from http://www.freep.com/jobspage/arabs/arab1.html

El-Badry, S. (2004). *Arab American demographics.* Arab Media–Allied Media Corp. Retrieved on August 02, 2005, from www.allied-media.com/ArabAmerican/Arab%20american%20Demographics.htm

Farina, A., Fischer, E., Boudreau, L., & Belt, W. (1996). Mode of target presentation in measuring the stigma of mental disorder. *Journal of Applied Social Psychology, 26,* 2147–2156.

Grande finale. (n.d.). Retrieved October 24, 2005 from http://mec.sas.upenn.edu/marhaba/finale.htm

Haque, A. (1993). *Attitudes toward and expectations about counseling: Cultural considerations regarding the Arab Middle-Eastern students* [Electronic version]. Unpublished master's thesis. Denton: Texas Woman's University.

Hendricks, T. (2005, March 9). Data show U.S. Arab population growing; Census report says education, income are above average. *San Francisco Chronicle,* A-7.

Hobfoll, S. E., Spielberger, C. D., Breznitz, S., Figley, C., Folkman, S., Lepper-Green, B., et al. (1991). War-related stress: Addressing the stress of war and other traumatic events [Electronic version]. *American Psychologist, 46*(8), 848–855.

Khaleefa, O. (1999). Research on creativity, intelligence, and giftedness: The case of the Arab world. *Gifted and Talented International, 14,* 21–29.

Lemawie, E. (2005, June 30). How to understand the different other? Lecture delivered at the Arab Theological Seminary during the conference on Christian-Muslim Relations. Beirut, Lebanon.

Lustig, S. L., Kia-Keating, M., Knight, W. G., Geltman, P., Ellis, H., Kinzie, J. D., et al. (2004). Review of child and adolescent refugee mental health [Electronic version]. *Journal of the American Academy of Child and Adolescent Psychiatry, 43*(1), 24–36.

Marsella, A. J., & Christopher, M. A. (2004). Ethnocultural considerations in disasters: An overview of research, issues, and directions. *Psychiatric Clinics of North America, 27*(30), 521–539.

Meichenbaum, D. (1994). *A clinical handbook/practical therapist manual for assessing and treating adults with PTSD.* Waterloo, Ontario: Institute Press.

Morrison, T. (2003). Doing business in the Middle East: Customs and culture. Network of the National Association of Realtors. Retrieved from http://www.realtor.org/IntUpdt.nsf/Pages/Doing_Business_in_the_Middle_East

Oberman, M. (2005). Arabs, Muslims more integrated in US than in France. [Middle East Online]. Retrieved November 12, 2005, from http://www.middle-east-online.com/english/?id=14971

Peristiany, J. G. (Ed.). (1965). *Honor and shame: The values of mediterranean society.* London: Weidenfeld & Nicolson.

Rando, T. A. (1996). On treating those bereaved by sudden, unanticipated death. In *session: Psychotherapy in practice*, 2, 49–71.

San Francisco Department of Public Health. (2003). Enviro-Times. Retrieved October 24, 2005, from http://www.dph.sf.ca.us/eh/enviro_times/series/cd_famous.htm

Shaw, P. (2005). Entrepreneurs and tribal leaders: A phenomenological approach to leadership and teamwork in the Middle East. *MEATE Journal*, 2, 2–17.

Stroebe, M. S., Schut, H., & Stroebe, W. (1998). Trauma and grief: A comparative analysis. In J. H. Harvey (Ed.), *Perspectives on loss: A sourcebook* (pp. 81–96). Philadelphia, PA: Bruner/Mazel.

Summerfield, D. (1995). Addressing human response to war and atrocity: Major challenges in research and practices and the limitations of Western psychiatric models. In J. Kleber, C. Figley, P. Berthold, & R. Gersons, *Beyond trauma: Cultural and social dynamics* (pp. 17–29). New York, NY: Plenum Press.

Tillich, P. (1959). *Theology of culture.* New York, NY: Oxford University Press.

Tolerance. (2001, September 13). Who are the Arab Americans? *Tolerance in the news.* Retrieved July 30, 2005 from http://www.tolerance.org/news/article_tol.jsp?id=274

United Arab Emirates. (2003). International Business Center. Retrieved August 15, 2005 from http://www.cyborlink.com/besite/uae.htm

Weissman, M. M., Bland, R. C., Canino, G. J., Greenwald, S., Hwu, H. -G., Joyce, P. R., et al. (1999). Prevalence of suicide ideation and suicide attempts in nine countries. *Psychological Medicine*, 29, 9–17.

Worden, J. W. (1991). *Grief counseling and grief therapy: A handbook for the mental health practitioner* (2nd ed.). New York, NY: Springer.

World: Q&A on Islam and Arab Americans. (2001, September 30). Retrieved July 28, 2005, from http://www.usatoday.com/news/world/islam.htm

Zogby, J. (1991). *Arab Americans today: A demographic profile of Arab Americans.* Washington, DC: Arab American Institute.

FURTHER READINGS AND RESOURCES

Abraham, N., & Shryock, A. (2000). *Arab Detroit: From margin to mainstream.* Detroit, MI: Wayne State University Press.

Abi-Hashem, N. (in press). The Children of Qatar. In G. Talhami (Ed.), *The Greenwood Encyclopedia of Childern's Issues Worldwide: North Africa and the Middle East.* Westport, CT: Greenwood Press.

Abi-Hashem, N. (2007). The psychology of religious conversion: A sociocultural and spiritual analysis. In D. McCarthy, R. B. VanderVennen, & J. McBride (Eds.), *Surprised by faith: Conversion and the academy: A collection of papers commemorating the 75th anniversary of the conversion of C. S. Lewis.* United Kingdom: Cambridge Scholars Publising.

Abu-Gharbieh, P. (1998). Arab Americans. In L. D. Purnell & B. J. Paulanka (Eds.), *Transcultural health care: A culturally competent approach* (pp. 137–162). Philadelphia, PA: FA Davis.

Al-Krenawi, A., & Graham, J. R. (2000). Culturally sensitive social work practice with Arab clients in mental health settings. *Health and Social Work*, 25 (1), 9–22.

Al-Mateen, C. S. (2004, January). The Muslim child, adolescent, and family. *Child and Adolescent Psychiatric clinics of North America*, 13(1), 183–200.

Alamuddin, R., & Zebian, S. (2005). *Psychology in the Arab World: A working annotated bibliography of works involving studies of a psychological nature conducted on Arab and Middle Eastern populations and/or by Arab social scientists, published in English.* Beirut, Lebanon: American University of Beirut.

Amin, Y., Hamdi, E., & AbouSalem, M. (2001). Depression in the Arab world. In A. Okasha & M. Maj (Eds.), *Images in psychiatry: An Arab perspective*. Cairo: World Psychiatric Association. Arab American Institute. http://www.aaiusa.org/about_arab_americans.htm

Axtel, R. E. (Ed.). (1998). *Gestures: The do's and taboos of body language around the world* (3rd ed.). New York: John Wiley & Sons.

Carter, D. J., & Rashidi, A. (2004, May–June). East meets West: Integrating psychotherapy approaches for Muslim women. *Holistic Nursing Practice, 18*(3), 152–159.

Chaleby, K. (1992). Psychotherapy with Arab patients: Towards a culturally oriented technique. *Arab Journal of Psychiatry, 3*(1), 16–27.

Culturally Competent Care for Arabs. (2004). A selected bibliography containing 170 citations, compiled by Jacquelyn Coughlan. Retrieved October 06, 2005 from http://www2.sunyit.edu/library/html/culturedmed/bib/arab/

Dwairy, M. (1998). *Cross-cultural counseling: The Arab-Palestinian case.* New York: The Haworth Press.

Dwairy, M. (1999). Toward psycho-cultural approach in Middle Eastern societies. *Clinical Psychology Review, 8,* 909–915.

Erickson, C. D., & Al-Tamimi, N. R. (2001). Providing mental health services to Arab Americans: Recommendations and considerations. *Cultural Diversity and Ethnic Minority Psychology, 4,* 61–71.

Gostin, L. O. (1995). Informed consent, cultural sensitivity, and respect for persons. *Journal of the American Medical Association, 274*(10), 844–845.

Gregg, G. (2005). *The Middle east: A cultural psychology.* Cambridge, UK: Oxford University Press.

Haddad, Y. Y. (2004). *Not quite American?: The shaping of Arab and Muslim identity in the United States.* Waco, TX: Baylor University Press.

Hammoud, M. M., & Siblani, M. K. (2003). Care of Arab Americans and American Muslims. In J. Bigby (Ed.), *Cross-cultural medicine* (pp. 161–194). Philadelphia: American College of Physicians.

Hamady, S. (1960). *Temperament and character of the Arabs.* New York: Twayne.

Hattar-Pollara, M. (2003). Arab Americans. In St. P. Hill, J. Lipson, & A. I. Meleis (Eds.), *Caring for women cross-culturally* (pp. 45–62). Philadelphia: F.A. Davis.

Hoogland, E. (1987). *Crossing the waters: Arabic speaking immigrants to the United States before 1940.* Washington, DC: Smithsonian Institutions Press.

Hourani, A. (1991). *A history of the Arab peoples.* New York: Warner Books.

Hunter, S. T. (1998). *The future of Islam and the West: Clash of civilizations or peaceful coexistence?* Westport, CT: Praeger.

Ijtihad: A Return to Enlightenment. http://ijtihad.org/

Islamic Society of North America (2005). The changing face of Islam in America [Editorial]. Retrieved August 18, 2005 from http://www.isna.net/services/horizons/current/TheChangingFace.html

Jackson, M. L. (1997). Counseling Arab Americans. In C. C. Lee, C. L. Bernard, & L. Richardson (Eds.), *Multicultural issues in counseling: New approaches to diversity* (2nd edition). Alexandria, VA: Association for Counseling and Development.

Kobeisy, A. N. (2004). *Counseling American Muslims: Understanding the faith and helping the people (contributions in psychology).* Westport, CT: Praeger.

Kulwicki, A., & Cass, P. S. (1994, Spring). An assessment of Arab American knowledge, attitudes, and beliefs about AIDS. *Image: the Journal of Nursing Scholarship, 26*(1), 13–17.

Kurzman, C. (1998). *Liberal Islam.* New York: Oxford University.

Lawrence, P., & Rosmus, C. (2001). Culturally sensitive care of the Muslim patient. *Journal of Transcultural Nursing, 12*(3), 228–233.

Lipson, J. G., & Meleis, A. I. (1989). Methodological issues in research with Middle Eastern immigrants. *Medical Anthropology, 12,* 103–115.

Meleis, A. I. (1981). The Arab American in the western health care system. *American Journal of Nursing, 6*, 1180–1183.

Meleis, A. I., & Hatter-Pollard, M. I. (1995). Arab Middle Eastern American women: Stereotyped, invisible, but powerful. In D. L. Adams (Ed.), *Health issues for women of color: A cultural diversity perspective* (pp. 133–163). Thousand Oaks, CA: Sage.

Marsella, A. J. (1998). Toward a global-community psychology: Meeting the needs of a changing world. *American Psychologist, 53*(12), 1282–1291.

Medved, M. (2001, October 15). Can Hollywood change its ugly version of USA? *USA Today,* A 17.

Nassar-McMillan, S., & Hakim-Larson, J. (2003). Counseling considerations among Arab Americans. *Journal of Counseling & Development, 81*(2), 150–159.

Nobles, A., & Sciarra, D. (2000). Cultural determinants in the treatment of Arab Americans: A primer for mainstream therapists. *American Journal of Orthopsychiatry, 2,* 182–191.

Nydell, M. K. (2002). *Understanding Arabs: A guide for Westerners* (3rd ed.). Yarmouth, Maine: Intercultural Press.

Reizian, A., & Meleis, A. I. (1986). Arab Americans' perceptions of and responses to pain. *Critical Care Nurse, 6*, 30–37.

Sayed, M. A. (2003). Psychotherapy of Arab patients in the West: Uniqueness, empathy, and "otherness." *American Journal of Psychotherapy, 57*(4), 445–460.

Sayed, M. (2003). Conceptualization of mental illness within Arab cultures: Meeting challenges in cross-cultural settings. Social Behaviour and Personality, 31, 333–342.

Suleiman, M. W. (2000). *Arabs in America: Building a new future.* Philadelphia, PA: Temple University Press.

Tobin, M. (2000). Developing mental health rehabilitation services in a culturally appropriate context: An action research project involving Arabic-speaking clients. *Australian Health Review, 23*(2), 177–184.

Chapter 6

Asian Indians: Cultural Considerations for Disaster Workers

B.J. Prashantham

INTRODUCTION

Introduction to India and Indian History

Despite the success of Asian Indian communities, some households suffer from poverty that remains well hidden to the larger society. During times of disaster, from rescue and relief to rehabilitation and the rebuilding of lives, Asian Indian culture provides support for these communities. Without undermining the diversity within the Indian community and the complexity of various stages of acculturation, this chapter discusses some of the issues that mental health professionals can keep in mind to provide more effective and acceptable services. The disaster relief efforts during the aftermath of the 2004 Tsunami have demonstrated the importance of cultural differences between patient and provider in disaster contexts. Accordingly, this chapter argues for a paradigm shift in disaster and relief work.

India occupies a third of the landmass of the United States, yet has three and a half times the population of the U.S. India has the largest democracy in the world and a rich 6000 year history. It has been the cradle of some of the world's important religions and ways of life, like Hinduism, Sikhism, Buddhism, and Jainism. Faiths such as Zoroastrianism, Christianity and Islam have also flourished in India. Beginning with the Aryans centuries before the birth of Christ, India has been colonized by the greatest of invaders, including Alexander the Great and Genghis Khan. Europeans like the French, Dutch, Danish, and the British also came to make India their home. India had great civilizations as seen in the Harappa and Mohenjo-Daro excavations, and had many successive empires promoting progress at home and trade abroad. After being ruled by the British for 200 years, India became free in 1947, accelerating the process of decolonization around the world. The country was the founder of the Non-Aligned Movement (NAM) and has been progressing steadily in all sectors since its Independence. India hopes to give its citizens continued opportunities for a high quality of life as it moves into the global economy of the 21st century.

Currently India has a high profile as an international hub for information technology and biotechnology. Twenty-five million of its 1 billion+ population are living outside of India, making India's contribution to multiple fields world-wide. In addition, many Indians living outside of India acquire education and engage in international business. Over 15 major languages are spoken in India, with more than 800 dialects. Six major religions are practiced in India, with approximately 82% of the population following Hinduism. Hinduism is a fundamental piece of the cultural framework for Indians, much like Confucianism influences the culture in China, Taiwan, Hong Kong, Japan and Korea.

In the following discussion, some issues specific to Indians are presented. Indian psychology has been characterized by a sense of transcendence, a holistic perception and a collectivist social relation. Self-realization and self-transformation are its values. Beliefs in karma are a central influence. Society is organized in a hierarchical fashion while individual human rights are also pursued vigorously. India is transitioning from an agrarian to a modern society, and major differences can be seen between urban and rural parts of the country. Among Indians living in the United States, the level of acculturation and orientation to American culture varies widely. Many Indians have lived in the U.S. for years and are assimilated into its culture, but may maintain Indian norms for domestic and personal issues to varying degrees. All of these factors have a bearing on coping with disaster and providing services to this community.

POPULATION DEMOGRAPHICS

Number

As of the 2000 Census, Asian Indians in the U.S. (reporting a single group) numbered at nearly 1.7 million. The Census collects data on a person's race and subgroups (Asian Indian is considered a subgroup of the Asian category), with a separate question for ancestry (ethnic origins). A brief population overview derived from official Census 2000 documents is provided below (Barnes & Bennet, 2002; Brittingham & de la Cruz, 2004; Reeves & Bennet, 2004).

- The 1990's saw a large influx of people claiming Asian Indian ancestry. The percent change for Asian Indians in the United States from 1990–2000 was 171.7%, the largest growth in the Asian American community.
- Individuals claiming Asian Indian as their race represented approximately 0.6 % of the United States population with over 1.65 million people.
- Individuals who reported Asian Indian alone or *in addition* to one or more other races or Asian groups numbered at nearly 1.9 million.
- Asian Indians comprised 16.2% of the Asian population in the United States at the time of Census 2000.
- Asian Indians are the 3rd largest constituency in the Asian American community behind Chinese and Filipinos.
- The majority of Asian Indians (88.4%) identified themselves as only Asian Indians, while the remaining 11.6% indicated Asian Indian *in combination* with one or more other races or Asian groups.
- The total United States population was estimated at 281,421,906 at the time of the 2000 Census, but the Census Bureau has indicated that in 2006 the total population exceeded 300 million.

Age Distribution

Asian Indians in the United States are relatively young, with a median age of 30.3 years, contrasted with 35.4 for the total population and 33 for all Asian groups. Among the Asian groups, Asian Indians have relatively fewer people who are age 65 or older. Only 3.8% of the Asian Indian population in the U.S. was aged 65 or older at the time of the 2000 Census, while 7.7% of Asians in general and 12.4% of the total U.S. population were in this age group (Reeves & Bennet, 2004).

Gender Distribution and Marriage

Approximately 46% of Asian Indians in the U.S. are female and 54% are male. This gender difference is primarily due to immigration. Many tend to marry within their community. There is some growth in the number of intercultural marriages both among Indians and between Indian and non-Indian American citizens. Asians in general have somewhat higher rates of marriage than the general population. Asian Indians have the highest percentage of married people among all Asian groups. Sixty-seven percent of Asian Indians were married in 2000, compared with only 54.4% for the total population in the United States. Asian Indians are also approximately three times less likely to be separated, divorced, or widowed than the population as a whole (Reeves & Bennet, 2004).

Language and Origins

Approximately 75% of Asian Indians in the U.S. were born in another country, and 39.3% of the foreign-born Asian Indians in the country are naturalized citizens. Over half of the foreign-born Asian Indian population arrived in the United States after 1990. While 80.7% of Asian Indians reported speaking a non-English language at home, 23.1% reported that English was spoken "less than very well" (Reeves & Bennet, 2004).

Geographical Location of the Population

The top ten states and top five cities with the largest Asian Indian populations are shown in Table 6.1 below.

Education

Of all the Asian groups, Asian Indians have the highest educational attainment, with about 64% of individuals aged 25 and older holding a bachelor's degree or higher. This was over 2.5 times the rate of the total population in the U.S. of the same age group. On the other end of the educational attainment spectrum, 13.3% of Asian Indians aged 25 and older had not completed high school (Reeves & Bennet, 2004).

Income and Occupation

Indian Americans are one of wealthiest and best educated communities in the United States. With a median family income of $70,708 in 2000, compared with $50,046 for the general population, there are few groups who have comparable income levels. It is important, however, not assume that all Indian Americans are doing well economically. The high numbers mask growing poverty, especially among the elderly and single female households. Moreover, there is a significant gap between male and female earnings and labor force participation for Asian Indians. To illustrate, 79.1% of Asian Indian males age 16 and older were in the labor force, while only 54% of Asian Indian women participated in the labor force in 1999. These disparities are even more marked when

Table 6.1. States and Cities in the United States with the Largest Asian Indian Populations

Top 10 States		Top 5 Cities
1. California	6. Florida	1. New York City, NY
2. New York	7. Michigan	2. Chicago, IL
3. New Jersey	8. Ohio	3. Los Angeles, CA
4. Illinois	9. Massachusetts	4. San Francisco, CA
5. Texas	10. Virginia	5. Washington, DC

one considers median earnings by sex. For full-time, year-round workers age 16 and over in 1999, Asian Indian males had a median yearly income of nearly $52,000. Asian Indian women, on the other hand, had median yearly earnings of $35,173. It is important to note, however, that this figure is still more than for women in the total population and Asian women as a whole (Reeves & Bennet, 2004).

Asian Indian economic success is reflected in the occupational distribution of the population. Asian Indians are more likely to be employed in management, professional, or related fields than any other Asian group or the population as a whole, with about 60% of the Asian Indian population working in these sectors. Asian Indians also had the lowest percentage of all the Asian groups to work in service positions (Reeves & Bennet, 2004).

Overshadowed by the apparent success of the population, poverty is a hidden and often ignored problem in the Indian American community. Poverty has an increased toll for immigrants over the age of 65 and female-headed households, as Asian Indian women have been shown to make significantly less than men. This problem has been exacerbated by the welfare reform laws passed in 1996, which made it more difficult for immigrants and the population as a whole to get aid. In 1999, the poverty rate for Asian Indians was 9.8%, which was lower than the poverty rate for the Asian groups combined (12.6%) and the total population (12.4%) (Reeves & Bennet, 2004). In times of disasters and trauma, the elderly and female-headed households can be quite vulnerable and hence special care may need to be taken to help them.

Religion

The majority of Asian Indians practice the Hindu religion. Others practice Sikhism, Buddhism, Jainism, Christianity, or Islam. A small number may be agnostic or atheistic, and may consider Hindu a term originally given by the British to refer to the people of the Indus Valley to differentiate them from Muslims. Hinduism represents a diverse set of ways of living. According to Hindu beliefs, Brahman is the principle and source of the universe. This divine intelligence pervades all beings, including the individual soul. Hence, the many Hindu deities are manifestations of the one Brahman. Hinduism is based on the concept of reincarnation, in which all living beings, from plants on earth to gods above, are caught in a cosmic cycle of becoming and perishing. The law of *karma* determines life – one is reborn to a higher level of existence based on moral behavior in a previous phase of existence. Life on earth is regarded as transient and burdensome. The goal of existence is liberation from the cycle of rebirth and death and entrance into the state of *moksha* (liberation).

The practice of Hinduism consists of rites and ceremonies centering on birth, marriage, and death. There are many Hindu temples, which are considered to be dwelling places of the deities and to which people bring offerings. Places of pilgrimage include Benares on the Ganges, the most sacred river in

India. Of the many Hindu deities, the most popular are the cults of Vishnu, Shiva, and Shakti, and their various incarnations. Also important is Brahma, the creator god. Hindus also venerate human saints. Orthodox Hindu society in India was divided into four major hereditary classes: (1) the Brahmin (priestly and learned class); (2) the Kshatriya (military, professional, ruling, and governing occupations); (3) the Vaishya (landowners, merchants, and business occupations); and (4) the Sudra (artisans, laborers, and peasants). Below the Sudra was a fifth group, the Untouchables (lowest menial occupations and no social standing). The Indian government banned discrimination against the Untouchables in the Constitution of India in 1950. Observance of class and caste distinctions varies throughout India. In the event of death the following are typically considered desirable:

- Cremation desired within 24 hours.
  - Male member to perform last ceremonies, ashes sent to India to be immersed in the holy river Ganges; Priests to officiate at ceremonies; Priests are addressed as Swamjiln (last name) or Gurujiln.
  - Death at home is preferable when at all possible.
  - White dress is appropriate.
- A mourning period of up to one year is appropriate.
- There may be resistance to autopsy unless legally necessary.
- Remove shoes when visiting home, respect rituals and amulets worn.

Importance of Generations

Older Asian Indian immigrants are often financially dependent on their children. They face the challenges of a culturally different society, such as a language barrier, culture mismatch, new lifestyle factors, and role reversal. In traditional Indian society, extended family members usually live together as a single-family unit. Often, the husband's parents will join the family after they have retired or when help is needed. The grandparents' role in raising the children is highly respected, and they form the linkage to the Indian culture, religion, and heritage.

Ethnic Identity

While there are more than three hundred languages and dialects spoken in India, Hindi, the national language is spoken by over 40% of the population. Other languages spoken are Telugu, Gujarati, Punjabi, Bengali, Urdu, Marathi, Oriya, Kannada, Tamil and Malayalam. However, English is becoming a popular second language in India. Older Indian immigrants to the United States may not speak English and may need a translator for various transactions. India is a country of racial diversity. The original inhabitants are said to be Dravidians who tend to be short and dark skinned. The Aryans who came from Europe and their descendents (who reside primarily in North

India) tend to be fairer in complexion and large in physical stature. In addition, there are large numbers of tribes in north-eastern India who have Mongoloid features, akin to Chinese. This diversity of linguistic, religious, and caste backgrounds makes India a very pluralistic society.

Eating habits of the people vary widely with more rice-eaters in the South to more wheat in the North. Certain communities have large numbers of vegetarians. There are degrees of strictness in vegetarianism from group to group. Due to the pre-dominance of vegetarianism in India, food is often classified as vegetarian and non-vegetarian in the course of conversation. Among those who are non-vegetarians, typically Hindus do not take beef and Muslims do not take pork. Even so, many non-vegetarians only eat meat a few times a week and stick to a primarily vegetarian diet. Sensitivity to people's food habits becomes critical in times of emergencies and disaster situations. In the recent tsunami many people refused cooked food in favor of rations so that they could make their own food.

It is said that Indians use between seven and 10 spices in their curry powder, giving Indian food its unique flavor. Even though there are shared values throughout India from Kashmir to Kanyakumari, the variations in foods, festivals, rituals, dress, folklore, and fine arts make India a multi-dimensional tapestry of plurality and co-existence. Therefore one cannot easily generalize about their food, dress, and culture.

A certain degree of restriction on inter-marriage is common, even though inter-marriages across ethnic barriers are common. This is primarily due to mobility, communication, urbanization and the inter-mingling of people in places of education, work and leisure. India has the distinction of being the country that produces the largest number of films in the world. The Indian Hollywood has been named "Bollywood", and is very influential in affecting the lifestyles of the Indian population, particularly the youth. Videos of movies and film songs are very popular. In the U.S., for example, many ethnic Indian stores devote considerable space to the Indian film industry, cinematic music, and videos. India is a lyrical society wherein information, education and vicarious ventilation occur through folk songs and poetic compositions. Consequently, songs can be a source of solace and strength to people.

Indians wear traditional garments of great variety from State to State. In the North men wear *kurta* pajamas and women wear *sarees* and *salwar kameez*. However, many educated men and women wear shirts and trousers in the Western style. In the South men wear shirts and *lungis*, while many wear Western clothes as well. Women mostly wear sarees and adorn their hair with flowers. Weddings are often arranged by parents, while there is also growing freedom for youth to have greater say in mate selection. Weddings are lavish events where guests numbering sometimes thousands are invited and provided hospitality, and hence they are often very expensive affairs. Marriages are a union of two families, not only two individuals.

The Alienation of Land Act in India under British rule prohibited certain non-farming castes from owning agricultural land and subsequently

Table 6.2.   Key Historical Dates for Asian Indians in the United States

TEN KEY HISTORICAL DATES

1790	First recorded arrival of an unnamed "man from Madras" in Salem, MA.
1899	7000 mostly unskilled laborers would migrate over the next 14 years, largely to the west coast and Pacific Northwest.
1907	Several hundred whites raided and demolished Indian living quarters in Bellingham and Everett, Washington and drove them out of the cities in opposition of their immigration.
1910	Restrictions were relaxed later in 1910, as demand for laborers increased for the construction of the Western Pacific Railroad.
1917	Congress passed an immigration law over Woodrow Wilson's veto placing a "barred zone" on immigration from Asia.
1940	By 1940, the number of Asian Indians had dropped in half, with only 2,405 remaining in the US.
1946	President Truman signed the Asian American Citizenship Act into law on July 3, 1946. The Act reversed the Third decision allowing naturalization and set an annual quota for Indian immigration at 100 per year.
1965	In 1965, Congress made massive reforms to immigration laws, equalizing quotas which allowed immigrants from many countries to enter, particularly from Asia.
1971	There was a multiple-fold increase in the size of the Indian population living in the Unites States over the next two decades.
2000	64% of Asian Indians living in the United States are found to have bachelor's or more advanced degrees, and about 60% of Indian Americans are employed in professional, managerial, and related fields. The prior decade saw a large influx of Asian Indian migration to the United States, with over half of all foreign-born Asian Indians in the United States arriving after 1990.

prompted 3000 people to move to the West Coast of the U.S. in 1908, many of whom were Sikh farmers. In 1946, legislation gave Asian Indians the right to become American citizens and bring relatives to the U.S., but the annual quota was small. More Indians immigrated when the door was opened by the 1965 Immigration Act that granted visas to people in certain professions and with more education. Elders continue to come to the U.S. as "followers of children". Table 6.2 shows key historical dates for Asian Indians in the United States.

KEY VALUES AND CULTURAL ISSUES

Novinger (2001), among others, points out certain differences between American (or Western) and non-American (or non-Western) cultures. Among the differences: monochronic versus polychronic perceptions of time, person-oriented versus task-oriented focus, independence versus interdependence, direct versus indirect communication, open entry versus networked entry, written agreements versus oral agreements, individuality versus cooperation, informal versus formal, and the like. The following are ten important values of Asian Indians that guide people's behavior and serve as models and ideals. It is important for the disaster response specialist or the mental health provider to be aware of these cultural values, but it is equally important to understand that there may be a great deal of variability with regard to the acceptance of these values and how the values may be manifested in people's cognition or behavior.

The ideals presented in Table 6.3 are followed to varying degrees. As in all cultures, lack of awareness can lead to incorrect assessment of the individual. Some useful models to understand cultural realities were proposed by Berry (1996), Hofstede (1997), Marsella (1998), Triandis (1999), Matsumoto (2000), and Marsella and Pedersen (2004), among others. These authors emphasize areas like individualism and collectivism (both vertical and horizontal), flexible ethnocentrism, and critical thinking to develop cultural empathy. Some authors advocate for a paradigm shift in the fundamental assumptions of counseling psychology and making multicultural and multi-disciplinary perspectives the main stream to advance positive dialogue in the U.S. and abroad.

Table 6.3. Descriptions of Key Values Common in Asian Indian Culture

Values	Descriptions
HUMILITY	Downplaying or displacing own importance or achievements. This should not be confused with lack of self-esteem.
RESPECT	For parents, teachers, elders, women, and authorities. This should not be confused with inferiority.
RESPONSIBILITY	Filial piety, protection for women and children. This is normal interdependence and considered to be responsible and mature. It should not be confused with dependency.
POLITENESS	Hesitation to disagree or say "no" or express anger. This should not be confused with intentional falsehood.
MORALITY	Dharma or duty based on stage of life, status, bio-psycho traits and environment. Epics of Ramayana and Mahabharata extol these virtues. This includes the concept of "word of honor" and caring for parents and family members, economically as well as emotionally.
TOLERANCE	Accepting differences in others' lifestyles and showing greater tolerance for paradox and contradictions. This is not considered illogical.
SPIRITUALITY	Belief in transcendental divine reality. Proof is not sought for such beliefs as the unseen world is considered more real than the seen.
HOLISTIC PERCEPTION	Seeing things as a whole. Hence, people may not be impressed by hair – splitting logic. Such a perceptual framework is not considered imprecise.
HOSPITALITY	Generous in treating friends and visitors with a belief that God may be coming to them in the disguise of guests. Hospitality is a higher priority value than punctuality.
NON-VIOLENCE (ahimsa)	Respect for and non-harm towards all beings. Gandhi used this principle with great effect. It is seen as a great strength.

In addition, some anthropological insights on reactions to crisis and the role of folk religion on facing disasters may be pertinent, and hence are mentioned below as well. This is in tune with the compelling need of the times for a better world for all.

Cultural Adjustment

Berry's (1996) four orientations to cultural group relations are based on two primary issues of *cultural maintenance* (the extent to which one's cultural identity and characteristics are considered important to maintain) and *contact and participation* (the extent that one should become involved with other cultural groups, vs. remaining primarily among one's own group members). This is illustrated in Figure 6.1. Berry (1996) proposes a very useful model to demonstrate the options given to different minorities, which is worth reflecting upon in understanding the social and political systems in which people live.

From this structure, there follows the processes of hierarchy, indirect communications, consensus, and spokesperson. Lack of this awareness of differences in cultural group relations can cause considerable misunderstanding, but this can be minimized through sensitivity. Communication style is considerably more context-laden in interdependent cultures.

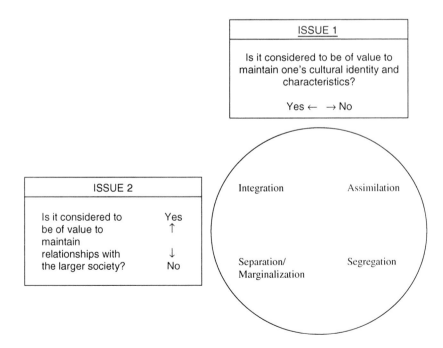

Figure 6.1. Four Orientations to Cultural Group Relations Based on Two Basic Issues (adapted from Berry, 1996)

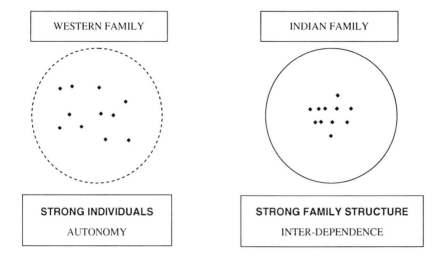

Figure 6.2. Graphic Depiction of Family Structure for Typical Western and Asian Indian Families

Independence and interdependence with respect to family and individuality may be viewed in the following diagrams shown in Figure 6.2.

Approaches to Crisis

Among many cultural values, Lingenfelter and Mayers (1986) show the difference between crisis and non-crisis orientation (Table 6.4). Table 6.5 shows examples of dichotomist and holistic thinking.

Many nonwestern-cultures, including Asian Indians, are known to be non-crisis oriented. Hence, understanding them could lead to helping them act with more sensitivity. By combining the previous insight on interdependence, it is important to get to know them before disasters, to share information, work with community leaders, and gain their trust and cooperation. According to Lingenfelter and Mayers (1986), many non-western cultures are also lean towards a holistic thinking and decision making.

Table 6.4. Differences Between Crisis and Non-crisis Orientations

Crisis Orientation	Non-crisis Orientation
Anticipates crisis	Downplays possibility of crisis
Emphasizes planning	Focuses on actual experience
Seeks quick resolution to avoid ambiguity	Avoids taking action
Pre-planned procedure	Ad hoc solutions from available options
Seeks expert advice	Distrust of expert advice

Table 6.5. Examples of Dichotomist and Holistic Thinking and Decision Making

Dichotomist	Holistic
Judgments are black and white	Judgments are open-ended
"Security from role clarity"	
Clear pattern of information organizing	Security from openness to multiple roles
	Seemingly disorganized but complete.

Thinking and Decision Making

Issues in India to be Aware of When Providing Services

- *Diversity*: People from India share Indian culture, however, there is significant diversity among the population. Religion is a key factor, and people may identify with any number of religious groups such as Hindu (majority), Muslim, Christian, or Sikh.
- *Multi-lingual*: They may speak different languages (18 major languages and 800 dialects in India). However, most living in the U.S. do speak English. Language barriers may still persist with some groups, such as visiting elders.
- *Family-centered*: Indians are very family centered. Communication through the family representative is appropriate.
- *Amulets*: May wear amulets like sacred thread, comb, scriptures, etc. Do not remove them without permission!
- *Diet*: Many are vegetarians. Many do not eat beef, and some will fast on a daily or weekly basis.
- *Attitudes towards tragedy*: Have a very accepting attitude towards tragedy, though they equally hurt and suffer.
- *Cremation*: Within 24 hours is preferred among Hindus.
- *Respect for religious beliefs and ceremonies*: Respect for religious rites and ceremonies are desired. Respected community leaders would be helpful consultants when in doubt.

Many who come to the US are highly educated and may belong to the middle or upper socioeconomic strata. Disaster workers should not hesitate to clarify the meaning of any gesture, accent, or expression that is not clearly communicated or comprehended. Indian families openly express grief. The social support of friends and family is their strength. Their concept of privacy may be very different from that of westerners.

Folk Religion

Religion in many societies is an integral part of the culture. There is a co-existence between local cultures with religious beliefs and practices. Thus, there can be a big difference between Chinese Buddhist and Western Buddhist practices towards daily life challenges. Hence, Hiebert, Shaw, and Tienou (1999) differentiate between high religion and low religion. They respectively refer to doctrinal versus pragmatic views. The former deals with the ultimate origin, purpose, and destiny of humans along with the entire universe. The latter, also labeled as folk religion, deals with four practical questions of existential significance for the common person. They are:

- meaning in this life and the problem of death
- well being in this life and the problem of misfortunes
- knowledge to guide decisions and the problem of the unknown
- righteousness and justice and the problem of evil and injustice

Folk religion has a *corporate anthropocentrism* whereby humans and their ancestors, the living and the unborn are all related in this life and events of this life such as birth, initiation, marriage, retirement, death (funerals) and ancestral anniversaries. Thus, transitional rites and rituals include the unborn. There is also the *spirit world* along with witchcraft, curses, and magic existing in a middle zone of reality between the natural and the supernatural world. This world view is thus composed of a three-tier reality. This is in contrast to the two-tier dualism of much of western religious thinking.

Holism or interconnectedness of all the three tiers of reality is important for disaster and mental health workers to understand because the world-view may have a bearing on how people cope with tragedy. Hiebert et al. (1999) emphasize that folk religious beliefs dominate the world. They suggests that most Christians in America are folk Christians, that most Hindus are folk Hindus, and that most Muslims in Arabia, Pakistan, and Malaysia are folk Muslims, and most religious believers in China are folk Buddhists. Hiebert et al. (1999) suggest that to cope with difficult experiences Hindus speak of fate (Karma), Muslims of Kismet (fate), and Koreans of Woon (fortune). When tragedies or good things occur, there is community participation because people find meaning in belonging and in being linked.

At a fundamental level, Hiebert and colleagues (1999) clarify a distinction in the ontology of the Western and the non-Western worldviews. The Western world holds a two-tier view of the world, with natural and supernatural levels, keeping a certain separation between the two. Science and religion have historically become increasingly separate in the Western world. In the non-Western world, reality is often viewed in a three-tier fashion, with a middle zone comprising of deities, demons, ancestors, the unborn and angels. This middle zone serves as the link between the natural and supernatural world.

Therefore, while a Westerner might think of the cause of the 2004 Tsunami as an earthquake in the ocean near Indonesia, a common Indian may see it as the anger of a deity unleashed on them due to some misdeeds of themselves (karma) or their kin or kith, committed in this life or the past one. Consequently, there may also be less interest in blaming and less thought to preparing for such calamities. The causes in both the Western and non-Western approaches can be either organic or mechanical (Hiebert et al., 1999).

Peoples' understanding of assessment and remedy may be influenced by their religious orientation (high vs. low). A number of people affected by the Tsunami talked about Karma, fate, and sin against God as an underlying cause for the disaster.

Patriarchy and Special Issues for Women

India is a patriarchal society by and large. Consequently there is a widespread preference for male children and a second class status for girls and women. Considerable social change efforts are afoot and are showing signs of progress. Laws are also being enacted to ensure less discrimination towards women, pushing the process for greater gender justice. It is important to be aware of the patriarchal society in India, and that women may face specific challenges because of their status in Indian society.

Challenges of Accelerated Change

It is important for the service provider to understand that, in many parts of the country, India is a nation in transition. This reality is reflected in the culture, and may have differentiated meaning for India's subgroups (e.g. the infusion of technology and industry in traditional tribal groups). There has been rapid industrialization and urbanization in India, and now India's leap into the age of information technology and economic globalization. Yet many challenges become evident with this social change, particularly where some rural and, especially, tribal groups may not be afforded the full benefits of these advances because of unequal resource distribution.

COMMUNICATION STYLES

Non-verbal

Communication via eye plays a very crucial role in ritual and other religious/mystic experiences. In the Hindu pantheon of gods, Siva is endowed with three eyes, and Indra has eyes all over his body. Some deities are described as having thousand eyes. Many Buddhist Temples exhibit an all-seeing eye on their towers. In the case of Siva, having three eyes signifies power; it also signifies knowledge of everything. Vishnu's eyes are half-closed in the sleeping posture, but they are wide awake within, aware of and regulating every object and phenomenon in all the worlds. Eyes play an important role in the worship of folk deities as well.

The study of nonverbal communication modes via the eyes in religious practices also provides insight into certain nonverbal communication at the secular social level. Physical touching in the course of social communication is less common in Indian cultures, and emotions are often expressed through the eyes and face. Body language is a very nuanced and important communication method, and it is important to be aware of what is considered acceptable and inappropriate when working across cultural lines. When working with Asian Indians, particularly those who are less familiar with the host culture, avoid beckoning people with the palm facing up. Palms facing down are considered respectful. The American style of beckoning with palms facing up may be considered disrespectful. In terms of toilet practices, many Asian Indians use water for cleaning after elimination and tend to use their left hand for this. Giving or receiving of presents with the left hand is normally avoided.

Gestures

The superior status of a person is indicated in certain instances by speakers not looking at the addressees. Respect is shown to the individual addressed in this manner. The individuals shown this respect may be close relatives, (males-in-law, elder to the speaker, for example), individuals of higher socioeconomic status, and employers. This form of communication posture is resorted to more by traditional women. This posture is achieved by looking away from the individual addressed, including looking down on the ground when the person addressed stands face to face. While this form of communication is generally adopted to show respect, there were also certain religious injunctions that proscribed individuals of lower castes to look upon superiors and on food and other objects offered to the deities. Sometimes these members of the so-called lower castes are also proscribed from seeing the idols/objects of worship. To carry out the above, it is enjoined upon the members of the so-called upper castes to conduct themselves and their religious acts in such a way that the members of the so-called lower castes would have no opportunity to cross the proscribed limits of vision and space. India has been changing and is becoming less rigid with regard to the status of women and those considered members of the lower castes.

Nonverbal communication is a key element in all negotiations. It is especially vital that its ramifications are fully understood in cross-cultural settings. What words fail to convey is told through gestures and body movements. Nonverbal communication therefore presents a context to the spoken word. Humans will often disregard the spoken word when physical expressions indicate otherwise. People in non-Western cultures are more prone to understand nonverbal implications than those in the West. Seemingly harmless and even mundane behavior as crossing one's leg and exposing the soles of one's shoes, or putting hands in one's pockets are, in India, often considered in poor taste, offensive, and insulting.

In relation to showing one's thoughts and feelings through behavior, a display of anger is particularly destructive in India and one should strive not to display it in any form. Anger disturbs harmony. Differences in body language between cultures are many. Americans, Germans and Russians shake hands forcefully; in some parts of Europe a handshake is usually quick and to the point; in Asia, it is often limp. An Asian might view an American as too abrupt and heavy-handed after a typical American handshake, while an American might view those with less firm handshakes as unassertive. Laughter and giggling in the West indicates humor; in Asia it more likely indicates embarrassment and humility. Many women do not shake hands with men, instead they greet with folded hands. Of course, if they offer their hand it is appropriate to shake hands. Those who have lived in the U.S. or other western cultures, or in more progressive parts of India, may be accustomed to more permissive gender norms for women.

Modesty is highly valued among Asian Indians, and patients usually feel more comfortable with same sex care providers. Direct eye contact from women to men may be limited. Sensitivity and care should be taken in situations that may cause the patient embarrassment, such as wearing an examination gown which the patient may consider too short or revealing. Hindu women often wear a thread around their necks *(mangalsutra)* and it should not be removed during the exam. The patient may expect the doctors to have all the answers and make all the decisions. As a result, the patient takes a passive role, answering but not asking questions, and waiting for physicians to impart their diagnosis and recommendations. Most of the time medical advice is accepted without question. Mental illness is considered as a stigma, so it is frequently concealed and presented to the physician as somatic complaints, such as headaches or stomach pain, instead of anxiety or depression.

Older Asian Indian immigrants often do not speak English and may need a health care interpreter or translator. Elderly patients may be stoic in the expression of pain. It is important to observe non-verbal behavior. An active and commanding doctor who takes charge and gives prescriptions for medications may be preferred. Physicians may be perceived as incompetent if they say something such as. "I do not know what is wrong, we need to do more tests," or "It is just a cold. There is no need for medicine." Because of the close-knit family structure, healthcare decisions are frequently discussed within the immediate family before seeking outside help. Women are more passive in the Indian Culture and men play a major role in health care decisions. These roles are slowly changing among immigrants now, as well as among Indians in some parts of India.

Metaphors

According to Dubois (2002), Brahmins in India have a peculiar way of talking and expressing themselves. Their language is generally concise, refined and elegant, and they enrich their vocabulary with many Sanskrit words. Thus there is a tendency for indirect, contextualized, and metaphoric speech which can lead to misunderstanding by others. Many normally speak in allegories to convey important truths. Proverbs, stories, and other forms of expression are typical vehicles through which complex concepts are elaborated. An example is a Hindi/Urdu couplet which states that ¡'. . . *people say that the world around changes a person, but only he/she can be called a person who changes the world around them" (Log kahethe hai dunia badaltha admi ko, magar admi wohi hai jo badaltha duniya ko).*

In terms of speaking style, many Asian Indians will start with pleasantries and generalities and come to the point afterwards. Their conversation is always interspersed with pedantic proverbs and allegories. Their idioms are so numerous and varied, that although you may think you know their language well, it is often the case that you will be unable to understand them when they are talking familiarly amongst themselves. In speaking and writing they make use of an assortment of polite and flattering terms, often very aptly. True understanding and cultural empathy requires far more than translation!

There is a tendency to seek advice and enlightenment. Hence non-directive methods may be less effective. Therapy as story telling, therapy as education, therapy that deals with systems and structures, and therapy as spiritual enlightenment is more accepted. Hence, nonprofessional, informal, holistic, interdisciplinary, family-centered and community-based approaches are accepted. Truly integrative bio-psycho-social-spiritual models can also be more effective in reaching Asian Indians.

ASSESSMENT INSTRUMENTS

There are far more instruments that are not normed to the Indian population than not. Some of the instruments for which Indian norms are available are Catell's 16 PF (Personality Factor), the Edwards Personal Preference Schedule (EPPS), the Eysenck Personality Inventory (EPI), Raven's Progressive Matrices (RPM) test, and the Impact of Event Scale (IES-8). The multiplicity of languages also makes it rather difficult to use these tests. There is also the tradition of clinical judgment over instrument-driven approaches. Tests are used but used cautiously. There are some Indian tests as well based on the personality variables of Rajas, Tamas, and Sattva. The World Health Organization has also validated some instruments like the General Health Questionnaire (GHQ). There are ongoing efforts to develop more culturally sensitive instruments. There are relatively few psychologists practicing and conducting research in India, but the numbers are growing.

CULTURAL ISSUES AND HEALTH

Special Disorders

Culture-specific conditions like possession state, koro and dhat syndrome have been reported from the Indian subcontinent. These and other culture-specific syndromes are noted in Table 6.6.

Table 6.6.   Examples of Culture-specific Syndromes

KORO:	A syndrome characterized by an acute anxiety reaction with partial depersonalization arising from a fear of shrinkage and dissolution of the penis.
DHAT:	A syndrome involving severe anxiety and hypochondriasis-preoccupation with excessive loss of semen by nocturnal emission. The genesis of the syndrome can be understood on the basis of the importance given to semen in Indian culture (dhat, from dhatu in Sanskrit literally meaning elixir as the source of potency in males, as described in the Ayurveda).
SPIRIT POSSESSION:	A condition in which a person feels that their personality has been taken over or possessed by a deity or the spirit of a dead person.

Studies in India (Varghese & Abraham, 1996) show that, compared to the West, there is greater manifestation of hysteria. They further show that first-borns and married persons in the East are more vulnerable to mental health problems than single persons and later-borns in the West. There is also evidence that the incidence of mental illness is higher among the poor. Further, a lot of mental abnormalities appear to be due to a number of preventable factors like injuries to the head during childbirth, malnutrition, and encephalitis. There appears to be greater tolerance for obsessive compulsive behavior, since rituals at various stages of life from birth to death are observed in abundance.

The Stigma Attached to Mental Illness

There is considerable stigma attached to mental illness. There are beliefs among the general public that demon possession may be a possible reason for mental illness. Public expression of hysterical behavior is more accepted from middle-aged women, particularly in the rural areas.

Traditional Therapy and Healing

Several traditional therapeutic practices used throughout India are described so that the service provider may become familiar with traditional healing which may be sought to act as a supplement or alternative to western-oriented services (Table 6.7).

Stigma for mental illness remains a significant barrier to treating people in India for psychological conditions. In the cities, however, there are increasing numbers of practicing mental health workers like psychiatrists, psychologists and social workers alongside lay counselors such as teachers, priests, and elders. Presented in Table 6.8 is an overview of beliefs about mental and physical illness and the type of healer consulted under each conceptualization.

Table 6.7.   Description of Traditional Asian Indian Therapeutic Approaches

Traditional Therapeutic Practice	Description
YOGA	Dates back nearly 5000 years, and was first inculcated and mastered by the Rishis, or sages, of India. The word "yoga" is derived from the Sanskrit word that means "yoke" or union. It has been suggested to have healing and revitalizing effects on a person's mind, body, and spirit. Yoga is of various types and involves the use of exercises, positions (asanas) and proper breathing to relieve stress and promote feelings of peace and serenity, both physically and mentally.
AYURVEDA	Originated in India over 5000 years ago. "Ayur" means life and "Ved" means knowledge. It includes in its consideration, longevity, rejuvenation and self-realization therapies through herbs, diets, exercise, yoga, massage, aromas, tantras, mantras and meditation. Ayurveda treats illness at its source, rather than at the level of symptoms and helps an individual to take responsibility for their own health and well being.
NATUROPATHY	Naturopathy uses a range of natural approaches including diet and herbs and encourages exposure to the sun and fresh air to maximize the body's natural responses.
SIDDHA TREATMENT	The Siddha system of medicine is the oldest and was derived from the vegetable kingdom. The word "Siddha" means an "object to be attained" or "achievement". It used medicine coupled with essential portions of alchemy, astrology, philosophy, magic, etc. towards elimination of diseases and their symptoms in order to rejuvenate and revitalize persons.
HOMEOPATHY	German physician Samuel Hahneman established homeopathy 200 years ago. It aims to stimulate the body's own defense and immune processes. Homeopathic medicines are derived from plants, animal materials, and minerals. Homeopathy is popular in some Indian communities.
UNANI TREATMENT	The Unani System of medicine is based on the Humoural theory, which presupposes the presence of 4 humours in the body – blood (Dam), Phlegm (Balgham), Yellow bile (Safra), and Black bile (Sauda). Humoural imbalance can be corrected by correct diet and digestion. Its main emphasis is on diagnosis of a disease through Nabz (pulse), Baul (urine), Baraz (stool), etc.
TANTRA	Tantra is a rich and diverse spiritual tradition of the Indian subcontinent. It is the art and science of receiving, conserving, and transacting energy from cosmic resources; it encompasses every activity of life. Tantra aims to release a person's dormant energy to unleash a fountain of active energy.
SHAMANS	Shamans are folk religious practitioners and traditional healers. They rely on their mastery of the spirit world and healing to assist people in need.
REIKI	Reiki is a healing approach that uses light touch from the practitioner to channel healing for the recipient. It is used to relieve physical and emotional pain and to promote spiritual clarity. Reiki is said to speed the healing process and balance the body's energy.

(Continued)

Table 6.7.   (Continued)

Traditional Therapeutic Practice	Description
PRANIC HEALING	Pranic healing using Prana (or Life Force) is based on the overall structure of the human body, working on a theory that it is composed of a visible physical body and an invisible energy body (or the etheric body). The underlying assumption is that illnesses are caused by incorrect proportions of prana. The technique brings the prana in the energy body to a desired level.
KALARI and MARMA	In this approach, the practitioner does treatments like bone setting and massages. Marma Chikitsa is an offshoot of the Kalarippayattu, Kerala's martial art. It involves oil therapy or snehana in which medicated oils are applied in large amounts to specific trouble spots and the body is then massaged using these oils. The underlying principle here is that an abnormality to any system of the human body can happen only if any one or more of 107 spots called marmas are bruised. The treatment is about detecting the vital spots affected and curing them to normalcy.

Table 6.8.   Traditional Conceptualizations of Illness and Appropriate Healers

Beliefs about illnesses	Types of healers
Illness as an imbalance between the natural elements leading to an excess of heat, cold, bile, wind or fluid secretions in the body.	VAID – trained in Indian Medicine
Illness as the consequence of past misdeeds – karma (breach of the community's customs or taboos), individual or collective, committed by the suffering person or their near kin, in their present or past life.	MANTARVADI – making use of potent holy verses (mantras) and astrologyPATRI – a medium acting with the authority of the possessing spirit
Illness based on astrological convictions using the idea of the influence of inter-planetary movements on the lives of people based on their exact time, date, and place of birth.	THE TEMPLE PRIEST
Illness due to objects placed in a person's body by witches or enemies, mental illness is caused by possession	SHAMAN – making use of séances
Belief in traditional home remedies for different condition.	FAMILY ELDER – know and dispense remedies passed on to them by their ancestors
Western conceptualization of disease. Doctors trained in Western medicine who have a good reputation can be trusted for medical and surgical needs.	DOCTOR – trained in Western Medicine

Considerations for Medication and Therapy

According to the Surgeon General's report (1999) on mental health, ethnopsy-chopharmacology points to the interaction between a patient's culture and psychiatric medicine. This report indicates that due to the racial and ethnic variation in pharmacokinetics, Asians with schizophrenia may require lower doses of antipsychotics than Caucasians to achieve the comparable blood levels of the drug. Biological differences among cultural groups (such as differences in metabolism) should be considered when providing medications. It is also important to consider how disease is conceptualized within a culture's worldview.

VIGNETTES

The following are a few case examples that may help illuminate the complexities of culture and the need for cultural competence and understanding when providing services.

Case #1: The Role of Culture and Religion

On the West Coast of the U.S., a 40 year old Indian woman was brought to the emergency room for having attempted suicide by swallowing some pesticide. After a bowel wash she was shifted to the regular ward for continuing treatment. The notation in the chart that the patient attempted suicide because her 13 year old son cut his hair baffled the health professionals. When consulted, the author was teaching a seminar on cross-cultural counseling and asked for the name of the person. Unenthusiastically they gave the name as Mrs. Kaur. They did not know the significance of the name. The author brought to their notice that such a name belonged only to a person of the Sikh religion (the names of all men end with Singh and all women end with Kaur). He further pointed out to them that in the Sikh religion, one of the important tenets is not to cut one's hair. This is why Sikhs wear the turban. The health professionals were wondering as to what type of therapy might be indicated.

Discussion.   It was suggested to them that a family conference without even calling it psychotherapy be called for. It was suggested that the Sikh priest from the gurudwara where they worship also be invited to help. This resulted in the priest showing understanding of the peer pressures to which the young Sikh boy succumbed. The priest encouraged the family both to take it easy and to calmly acquaint the young boy with the tenets of the Sikh religion.

Case # 2: Somatization

A 70-year-old woman lived in India for most of her life and moved to the United States two years ago. She came into the doctor's office with a complaint of generalized tiredness. On questioning, she also revealed problems with sleeping. No active medical problems were found, and she was not on any medications. When she was asked whether she feels depressed she said "No". On further questioning, she expressed some dissatisfaction with her life and pointed out that life here in the U.S. is lonely. Her weekdays are confined to the four walls of the house. What should the physician do?

Discussion.   Since there is stigma to mental illness, most Asian Indian elders will present their psychological problems with physical complaints. The treating physician should understand this cultural reason and information should be obtained sensitively and addressed carefully. To get better compliance, it may be better to treat the issue as a psychosomatic medical illness, rather than a mood disorder.

Case # 3: The Place of Diet

A 70-year-old Indian Muslim was admitted to the hospital for pneumonia. Speech therapy evaluation revealed swallowing dysfunction. A modified diet containing gelatin was recommended. However, the patient refused to eat gelatin.

Discussion.   Muslims who follow the kosher diet may reject this food. This person has come from an ethnocultural tradition that prohibits the eating of pork. Gelatin is made from pig bones. Therefore, the dietitian should understand this cultural reason for avoiding such food items and offer alternatives.

Case # 4: Gender Relations

The family of an Indian scientist was distressed over the low academic performance of the older daughter of 15 years of age due to self-esteem. The school counselor recommended longer counseling for the girl and the family. They went to a counselor and dropped out because the counselor shook hands with the mother. They saw another one who wanted to talk to the daughter alone.

Finally, they contacted the author who felt that first trust needs to be built in the counseling relationship, as well as an accurate understanding of what counseling entails. After three sessions of clarifying what counseling is and what it is not, another referral was suggested which this time was carried through with the girl. This achieved outstanding results commensurate with her talents, as well some changes in the attitudes of the parents such as ceasing to compare their children unfavorably.

Discussion.   Trust building and cultural sensitivity in greetings with these Indians seemed to be the major barrier to overcome before counseling could take place. Cultural competence needed to precede clinical competence. This is one example of the perceptions of Indian Americans about mental health. Cultural adjustability varies between newly arrived persons and persons who have lived in the U.S. for some time. A lot of people adapt to host cultures in work-related matters while maintaining varying degrees of association with the culture of their country of origin.

Case # 5: Community-based Interventions

In a community-based treatment program for alcoholics, the author and his team found a high level of sobriety after one year of initial treatment consisting of detoxification, counseling interventions, peer support and rehabilitation. Datta, Prashantham, and Kuruvilla (1991) attribute the higher sobriety rate compared to other hospital-based studies to several factors. An overview of these factors is given in the discussion below. Pre-treatment motivation helped to increase trust, awareness and openness to treatment. The patients, having been taken in groups for detoxification, developed social bonds and did not want to let their group down. The active participation of the patients' spouses in treatment helped a great deal. Finally, the multi-disciplinary nature of the treatment group, with a psychiatrist, psychotherapist and psychologist (two of them women) was helpful as they functioned as a cohesive team and could address a complex problem from multiple perspectives.

Discussion.   Here is a longer-term observation: Going to where the people are made accessibility to the service real. Prior to offering the intervention, we clarified to the community the purpose of the program and established the credibility of the team. By looking into patients' economic rehabilitation through referrals to Rotary and the bank, six patients were able to get some sheep to rear, a shop to repair bicycles, two cows to sell milk, and a bullock cart to carry freight from the railway station to the marketplace. After one year and more, the sobriety rate remained beyond 75% and a couple of successful patients came forward to help others in need. Recent oral reports indicate a huge transformation in the village. The cultural rural appropriateness of women therapists working with women was highly acceptable to the community. Thus, a combination of cultural competence and clinical competence led to the implementation of an effective program. Since post-disaster situations are fraught with possibilities of palliative measures by some through the use of alcohol or drugs, this case study is mentioned to consider a community-based model for rehabilitation when appropriate.

CONSIDERATIONS FOR TREATMENT

Role of Family in Treatment

India is a very family-centered society in all its manifestations of nuclear, extended, and joint modes. In psychiatric centers in Agra, Bangalore and Vellore it has been demonstrated that families rooming with the patient lead to better patient improvement. In these places, admission of family members along with the patient is mandatory. They are given small quarters where they can cook their own food, help with medication compliance, and provide a supportive milieu.

Culturally-rooted Preferences in Treatment

Health is usually conceptualized in relation to the connectedness of body, mind and spirit. Hospital food can present a problem for Asian Indians, particularly those who strictly observe religious dietary restrictions. Hospital meals may also be too bland for many Asian Indians in terms of flavor. Many will prefer to know whether the food served to them contains any beef, as beef is forbidden for Asian Hindus. Foods containing pork are prohibited for Muslims who follow a religiously prescribed diet. Some patients may hesitate to wear clothing that others have worn before them, even though it has been washed and sterilized. When a patient is in the hospital, the sacred thread across the chest in men and around the neck in women should not be removed or cut without the permission of the patient or family. Sikh men do not cut their hair and wear a bracelet and kirpan. If the hair must be cut, it is important to explain the need to the patient and family.

If procedures such as an enema or bladder catheterization must be done, many Asian Indians would probably prefer that someone of the same sex perform it. Family and friends will likely want to stay with a hospitalized person and be included in performing personal care. It is often not enough to drop in briefly, but instead visitors may be expected to sit and spend time with the patient. For many Indians, hospital visits are a very important way to provide support for the sick person and the family.

Older Asian Indians often recommend home treatment for those who are ill. Home remedies such as massage, bathing, and herbal medicines may be used first, while a physician is sought out only for serious illness. Some behaviors that may be preferred, particularly by elders, include ritual chanting by a priest; tying a thread around the sick person's wrist; and writing a protective verse to be worn in a metal cylinder on a chain around the neck or wrist. Sick persons may also promise gifts to the temple god if they recover. For many Asian Indian elders, the activities of social workers and home care nurses are unfamiliar and often not welcomed. Home visits by these providers are not always acceptable.

Role of Religion and Indigenous Methods

Yoga is widely practiced as a stress-reducing activity. The insights of ayurveda, siddha and unani approaches to medicine and healing are in vogue. Psychospiritual therapies offered by Godmen and Godwomen are often sought by the public. Many also make periodical pilgrimages to temples, churches, mosques, and gurudwaras in search of not only a cure for specific ailments, but holistic spiritual healing. Spirituality pervades Indian society, with generally tolerant attitudes towards different faiths and the occasional non-observer. For many, religion encompasses all aspects of life. Peoples' lifestyles are often guided by messages handed down through oral tradition, such as traditions regarding dietary feasting and fasting, hygiene and health, and interpersonal and socially-sanctioned celebrations.

Ayurveda is an intricate system of healing that originated in India thousands of years ago. Ayurveda is made up of two Sanskrit words, "Ayu" meaning life and "veda" meaning the knowledge of. Ayurveda is not merely a medical system of dealing with physical disorders. It is an approach to healing that relates to the complete human being (body, mind, senses and soul). It explains how balance can be attained physically, mentally and spiritually. According to Ayurveda, each individual is made up of three doshas (vata, pitta or kapha). Each Dosha represents certain bodily activity. The ratio of the doshas varies in each individual. When any of the doshas becomes accumulated, Ayurveda practitioners will suggest specific lifestyle and nutritional guidelines to assist the individual in reducing the dosha that has become excessive. They may also suggest herbal supplements to hasten the healing process.

There are aspects of the Hindu religion that commonly affect health care decisions. Hinduism is a social system as well as a religion; therefore customs and practices are closely interwoven. "Karma" is a law of behavior and consequences in which actions in a past life affect a person's circumstances and station in this life. Even for people with a thorough understanding of biological causes of illness, it is often believed that an illness is caused by "Karma".

Somatization of Symptoms

Asian Indians may present greater somatization of symptoms for mental health issues than people in the west. This calls for a careful assessment as to whether these complaints are masking underlying psychopathology. Psychotherapists and physicians alike need to be alert to this possibility. Continuing education programs focusing on culture and somatization can be valuable tools for the practitioner.

Issues in End-of-life and Death

The cultural and religious backgrounds of Asian Indians often influence end of life care decisions. Older patients may subscribe more to family-centered decision making rather than being autonomous. Sometimes family members may ask the physician not to tell patients their diagnosis or other important information. Open-ended questions and dialogue as to why the family does not want the patient to know may be helpful in alleviating the family's concerns. Many patients prefer to die at home, and there are specific rituals and practices in each religious community. Many believe suffering is due to karma, which is inevitable. When close to death, family members are likely to be present in large numbers. A dying person may wish to be moved to the floor, with the idea of being closer to the mother earth. Family members will typically prefer to wash the body after death and before cremation. The mourning Hindu family may prefer to have a Hindu priest perform a prayer and blessing. It is very important to provide privacy to the family after the death of a family member and to allow for the religious rites to be performed. It is an accepted practice for family members and others to display expressions of grief openly. After cremation there is a traditional mourning period of 10 to 40 days, though the times of course vary widely. Many Indians will not readily agree to a postmortem examination or organ donation.

Special Considerations for Disasters and Trauma

In general, Asian-Indians tend to be reactive rather than proactive: There is a tendency to be laid back and less prepared. Culture may have an impact on how people respond to disasters and trauma. There have been instances in the U.S. where persons of Indian origin were stopped by the police and opened the door and came out of the car as they would do in India. To their shock, they found the police officer pointing a gun at them and asking them to get back into the car as the regulations in the United States require. This has caused needless and unintentional misunderstandings between the police and the Indians concerned. Likewise, during the 2001 earthquake in Seattle several Indians were seen running out of buildings as they do in India rather than getting under a table or door frame as is recommended in the U.S. Below is an outline of some cultural traits which may impact Asian Indians' responses to disaster situations and influence the process of service provision.

- Asian Indians typically accept help from family and friends only. This attitude when present can be an impediment and needs to be addressed.
- The in-group, out-group concept is stronger in India (due in part to the historical caste system) than in the West and can affect help behavior (receiving and extending).
- Asian Indians are typically willing to take on responsibility for relatives outside the nuclear family. This can be a resiliency factor.
- Elements of trust or distrust in the governmental machinery and bureaucracy can influence attitudes, expectations, and acceptance of help and responsibility.
- Underlying belief in karma could lead to quicker acceptance of the inevitable and less desire to challenge and fight.

CULTURAL INSIGHTS FROM THE 2004 TSUNAMI

Who sets the rehabilitation priorities? Soon after agreeing to write this chapter, I came to India only to be confronted with the unprecedented disaster of the tsunami in the Southern part of India and other countries like Sri Lanka, Maldives and Indonesia. I got involved in providing trauma counseling training as a vital component of disaster management throughout its lifecycle of rescue, relief, and temporary shelters to permanent settlements and socio-economic rehabilitation. I conducted several training courses and observed the crescendo of generous responses from the Government, non-government agencies, international organizations and concerned individuals. In this process I noticed a number of culturally-significant issues that had a major bearing on helping people rebuild their lives with dignity.

Help Receiving Behavior

During the very first week it was found that the affected people, while appreciating the assistance, rejected outright donations of used clothing, much of which was not even the kind of clothes they wear. They felt insulted by such giving. It was also found that after 2–3 days of accepting cooked food they wished to have rations, so that they could cook their own food. In addition, one community also reacted negatively by rejecting rations sent for only a section of the village, as the fisher community are especially united and "live or die together", unlike other communities which may not be so collectivist. Therefore, many Indians trying to help began to realize that they were dealing with the fisher folk subculture, which has its own unique characteristics as a community. At times, understanding subcultural differences may be as important as understanding the macro-culture.

Cultural and Subcultural Complexities: The Case of the Fisher Folk

Many did not realize that the fisher folk lived a comfortable life with many of the amenities of an urban middle class family, possessing a television, VCR, refrigerator, cell phones and other comforts in a less attractive dwelling closer to the sea. Their major economic equipment consisted of fishing boats and fishing nets. When the tsunami hit they lost homes and their means of livelihood (namely boats and nets), along with family, friends, and neighbors. The fisher community had been largely self-sufficient, and people were not accustomed to receiving help from outsiders. The reality of seasonal variations in income made many use their savings for the proverbial rainy day, which occurred with annual regularity for some of the months when fish were in short supply. Many were liable to make loan payments on boats and nets, leaving them in a difficult position to save.

On top of all this, the land-based rescue and rehabilitation workers descended on them, offering to build shelters away from the sea and expecting them to look after their own economic recovery. This made many of the fisher folk angry that while their priorities are for boats and nets, the donors' priorities were for housing away from the economic lifeline, namely the sea. Fortunately the government mandated consulting the affected people in relief efforts, refusing any measures to be permitted which are donor-driven and disturb the way of life of the people. While interacting with the affected persons it became clear that some of the cultural values of the fisher folk had potential implications for rehabilitation:

- The strong in-group inclinations of this community resulted in a tendency to divert aid coming in to their group rather than other affected minorities who were not fisher folk. Moreover, their sense of pride made them less accepting of outside assistance. The close-knit nature of their community meant that Indians not directly in the subculture were also viewed as outsiders. This was a barrier to overcome, and establishing the community's consent, input, and support was necessary.
- Decisions for the community in the village are made by their panchayat (village council), consisting of 12 elders. Any aid coming into the village had to be cleared by them in advance. This meant that those agencies or individuals who worked through this proper channel were able to deliver services and be accepted by the community. Other helpers who ignored this protocol were suspect, stopped, or refused.
- There is a belief that the behavior of women at home affected the safety of the men at sea. This provided for a certain amount of fidelity and social control. It also gave certain restraints on the social movements of women outside of the home. This aspect was seen in some women feeling guilty and responsible for what happened. In addition, voluntary agencies who did not have women workers found it difficult to reach out to women. Hence gender issues can certainly play a role in extending services and the victim's willingness to use them.
- The rehabilitation priorities for the fisher folk seemed to be boats and nets, followed by shelter. For most of the aid workers, the priorities were temporary shelter and rations. This disparity was discovered gradually and had a significant negative effect in the sense that disaster response workers, both domestic and international, delayed providing for the acquisition of boats and nets for the affected fisher folk. This has caused frustration and anguish among the fisher folk. The question of whose priorities we serve becomes an important one. Some of the local voluntary agencies found that the needs of the affected people were changing from day to day, resulting in the need for quite a lot of flexibility in resource allocation.
- Girls are normally married after achieving the age of 16+, with ample dowry in the form of two-wheelers, gold, and cash to the bridegroom's family. With the loss of homes and everything they had, there has been a significant delay in marriages.

A Psycho-social Intervention Model

In the course of disaster relief efforts, the approach this author and his colleagues in India took was to engage voluntary agencies that have been in the community and who are committed to remaining there. We trained some of their childcare and adult workers in trauma counseling, using their mother tongue (*Tamil* language), emphasizing:

- The importance of peer support to people and communities – human support for normal individuals going through an extraordinary situation.
- The lay counselors were given a 5-day residential training in understanding emotional reactions to the Tsunami using simple language rather than professional jargon. Training included elements of rapport-building, resiliency promotion, relaxation methods, graded exposure, and cognitive methods. Professional community workers were trained to monitor, streamline, network, and facilitate this work. A team of professional counselors and a consulting psychiatrist provided consultation and oversaw data collection for understanding the prevalence of disorders and the impact of interventions.
- A survey was conducted before the training to determine the extent of post-traumatic reactions beyond one month such as anxiety disorders, PTSD, depression, traumatic grief, and psychotic episodes.
- Non-improvement within one month of intervention, as well as cases of suicidal risk and psychotic breakdown, were to be referred to available medical and mental health facilities.
- Age-appropriate unstructured, semi-structured, and structured games and drawing work were to be used with children and adolescents.
- Regular debriefing was also encouraged for the caregivers.

RECOMMENDATIONS

Resiliency and Prevention

Sue and Sue (1999) have described that many minorities in the U.S. do not trust the mental healthcare system, which can results in low retention and fewer people seeking services. Less permissive help-seeking behavior, rules regarding the display of emotion, and the stigma attached to mental illness are factors that need to be taken seriously. While cross-cultural counseling can be difficult, it is not impossible. While trust can sometimes come more easily for persons with the same background, it is possible for persons from diverse backgrounds to develop mutual trust and cultural empathy. Benson and Proctor (2003) have demonstrated that the meditations of the Hindu and Buddhist cultures and religions have beneficial effects on combating stress and anxiety related problems. It is generally good practice to encourage people to use what they feel works for them, provided of course that it is not harmful.

The complexity of diverse subcultures within cultural groups also needs to be kept in mind. Second generation immigrants tend to be more acculturated to the host society. Hence, treating them as new arrivals can be unhelpful. The fact that many Indians use the host cultural norms for work and native norms for domestic issues and relationships is another factor to be taken into account. I have found a four-tier model to work for me over the last three decades of my work in India. It consists of a community-based and approach oriented towards social change (Prashantham, 2001). Its components are peer counseling aided by lay counseling, supported by professional counseling for training, and consultancy, with hospitalization as the last resort. There are efforts in India to integrate mental health with primary health. Review of training of psychologists and social workers and medical folk is underway.

The following are some practical suggestions for working more effectively with Asian Indian clients, particularly in the aftermath of disasters or trauma.

- Get to know people outside of professional and academic relationships. Participate in cultural events and celebrations like Diwali (festival of lights), Ugadi (New Year), etc. This will help to become more familiar with their culture.
- Learn about their day to day lives.
- Attempt to interpret issues from the cultural perspective of the clients.
- Recognize the role of religious leaders and community elders, and utilize their resources to communicate in times of crisis.
- Have more women volunteers and helpers.
- Rice and dhal (lentil soup) is the most common food in an emergency. Add more options after finding out preferences.
- Avoid psychological labels, as there may be great stigma attached to them.
- Modernity and tradition go hand in hand among many – they are not mutually exclusive!
- Be aware that there is a certain amount of domestic violence in the community. There may also be conflicts among the generations.

Final Recommendations

1. Meet and become acquainted with persons of other faith communities as neighbors and friends and learn what religion means to them their lives.
2. Attend training classes on world religions to better understand them.
3. Work through community and religious leaders to help with prepared-ness.
4. Remember that ignorance of culture can lead to a wrong diagnosis, especially among cultural groups that differ dramatically from Western cultural views.
5. It is important to remember that many non-western people speak English after translating in their minds from their native language. The English language has a grammatical structure of subject, verb

and object. However, in Indian languages the grammatical structure sequence is often object, subject and verb. This has a potential to lead to misunderstandings. Colloquialism is another source of not finding identical shared meaning, consequently leading to misunderstanding. For example: An American who came to live in Bangalore and admitted her eight year old son in an International school was given a list of things that the mother should buy for the child. This included books, notebooks, covers, pens, pencils and rubber. The American was confused by the words cover and rubber, which to her meant bed sheets and a condom. For the International school they meant brown paper covering for the books and an eraser. Another aspect of language that can cause confusion is the style of Westerners stating the main point first and describing it later versus Indians, like other Asians, giving general comments first and stating the main point later. This has been a source of frustration in many an Indo-American conversations.

6. Mandatory cultural immersion training for all mental health workers in different cultural settings including India could be made part of internships. Longer internships rather than shorter ones are preferred, meaning at least a couple of months rather than a few days.

7. Establish connections with International specialists in cultural psychology on a reciprocal basis.

8. Review the issues surrounding the philosophy of science, especially the questions of epistemology regarding the assumptions of mainstream psychology.

9. All of this will naturally lead to a review of the curriculum a serious examination of the suggestions of Marsella and Pedersen (2004) regarding these issues.

10. Regular conferences on this theme with mental health professionals around the world would be an important step.

11. Research collaborations for deeper investigations of cultural issues and their impact within a multidisciplinary approach would be very valuable.

12. Capitalize on the globalisation and openness developing for multicultural and multidisciplinary approaches in various academic and professional fields.

13. As a practising psychotherapist in India and the U.S., I feel the need for a paradigm shift in psychology and counselling from individualistic to relational, from adjustment to social change, from uni-disciplinary to multidisciplinary, from limited focus to a multidimensional focus.

14. I endorse the practical suggestions of Marsella and Pedersen (2004) on 50 ways to internationalize psychology and the call for a deeper dialogue among all psychologists around the world for a necessary paradigm shift.

Saukhyam. I would like to close with the Sanskrit word *Saukhyam,* which is a popular greeting throughout India. It conveys a wish for health, happiness, comfort, felicity, enjoyment, and a quality of life that is not only free from stress and strain, but also one that reflects inner peace and repose, enabling a person to function at their maximum potential.

References

Barnes, J. S., & Bennet, C. E. (2002). The Asian population: 2000. *Census 2000 Brief.* (C2KBR/01-16). U.S. Department of Commerce, Economics and Statistics Administration.

Berry, J. W. (1996). Individual and group relations in plural societies. In C. S. Granrose & S. Oskams (Eds.), *Cross-cultural work groups* (pp. 17–35).Thousand Oaks, CA: Sage Publications.

Benson, H., & Proctor, W. (2003). *The break-out Principle: How to activate the natural trigger that maximizes creativity, athletic performance, productivity, and personal well being.* New York: Scribner.

Brittingham, A., & de la Cruz, G. P. (2004). Ancestry: 2000. Census 2000 Brief. (C2KBR-35). U.S. Department of Commerce, Economics and Statistics Administration.

Datta, S., Prashantham B. J., & Kuruvilla, K. (1991). Community treatment for alcoholism. *Indian Journal of Psychiatry, 33,* 305–306.

Dubois, A. J. A. (2002). *Hindu manners, customs and ceremonies* (3rd ed.). Clarendon, UK: Oxford.

Hiebert, P., Shaw, D., & Tienou, T. (1999). *Understanding folk religion: A Christian response to popular beliefs and practices.* Grand Rapids, MI: Baker Books.

Hofstede, G. (1997). *Culture and organizations.* New York: McGraw Hill.

Lingenfelter, S., & Mayers, M. (1986). *Ministering cross-culturally.* Grand Rapids, MI: Baker Book House.

Matsumoto, D. (2000). *Culture and psychology: People around the world* (2nd ed.). Delmar, CA: Wadsworth

Marsella, A. J. (1998). Toward a global psychology: Meeting the needs of a changing world. *American Psychologist, 53,* 1282–1291.

Marsella, A. J., & Pedersen, P. (2004). Internationalizing the counseling psychology curriculum: Toward new values, competencies, and directions. *Counseling Psychology Quarterly, 17,* 413–424.

Novinger, T. (2001). *Intercultural communication: A practical guide.* Austin: University of Texas Press.

Prashantham, B. J. (2001). *Indian case studies in therapeutic counseling.* Vellore, India: Christian Counseling Center.

Reeves, T. J., & Bennet, C. E. (2004). We the People: Asians in the United States. *Census 2000 Special Reports.* (CENSR-17). U.S. Department of Commerce, Economics and Statistics Administration.

Surgeon General's Report on Mental Health. (1999). Rockville, MD: Department of Health and Human Services.

Sue, D. W., & Sue, D. (1999). *Counseling the culturally different: Theory and practice.* (3rd ed.). New York: John Wiley & Sons.

Triandis, H. C. (1999). Vertical and horizontal individualism and collectivism: Theory and research implications for international comparative management. In L. Joseph, C. Cheng, & R. Peterson (Eds.), *Advances in international comparative management, Vol. 12* (pp. 7–35). Stamford, CT: JAI Press, Inc.

Varghese, A., & Abraham, A. (1996). *Introduction to psychiatry.* Madras, India: BI Publication Pvt. Ltd.

ADDITIONAL READING AND RESOURCES

Alagiakrishnan, K., & Chopra, A. (2001). Health and health care of Asian Indian American elders. *Curriculum in Ethnogeriatrics* (2nd ed.). [Electronic version]. Retrieved May 15, 2005: http://www.stanford.edu/group/ethnoger/asianindian.html

Ananth, J. (1984). Treatment of immigrant Indian patients. *Canadian Journal of Psychiatry, 29*, 490–493.

Bardi, A., & Schwartz, S. H. (2003). Values and behavior: Strength and structure of relations. *Personality and Social Psychology Bulletin, 29*, 1207–1220.

Barr, M. D. (2004). Cultural politics and Asian values. *Journal of Southeast Asian Studies, 5*, 159–160.

Bhopal, R., Unwin, N., White, M., et al. (1999). Heterogeneity of coronary heart disease risk factors in Indian, Bangladeshi, and European origin population: A cross sectional study. *British Medical Journal, 319*, 215–220.

Carstairs G. M., & Kapur R. L. (1976). *The great universe of Kota: Stress change and mental disorder in an Indian village.* London, UK: The Hogarth Press.

Datta, D., & Chatterjee, S. (1968). *An introduction to Indian philosophy* (7th ed.). Calcutta, India: University of Calcutta Press.

Dave, I. (1989). *The basic essentials of counseling.* New Delhi, India: Sterling Publishers Private Limited.

Enas, E., Garg, A., Davidson, M., et al. (1996). Coronary heart disease and its risk factors in first-generation immigrant Asian Indians to the United States of America. *Indian Heart Journal, 48*, 343–353.

Hiriyanna, M. (1968). *Outlines of Indian philosophy.* London, UK: George Allen and Unwin.

Kakar, S. (1996). *The Indian psyche.* New Delhi, India: Oxford University Press.

Kavalar, J. M. (1999). Intergenerational relations and service utilization: The experience of Asian Indian elderly in the United States (Research Abstract).Bethesda, MD: National Institute on Aging, Summer Institute on Aging Research, July 10–16.

Khare, R. (1998). *Cultural diversity and social discontent: Anthropological studies on contemporary India.* London: Sage Publications.

Marsella, A. J., & Christopher, M. (2004). Culture, disasters, and mental health: An overview of findings and issues. In C. Katz & A. Pandy (Eds.), *Disaster psychiatry* (pp. 521–539). *Psychiatric Clinics of North America, Vol. 27, No. 3.* Philadelphia: WB Saunders.

Murthy, S. R. (2001). Community mental health in India: People's action for mental health. In S. R. Murthy (Ed.), *Mental health in India: 1950–2000.* Bangalore, India: People's Action for Mental Health (PAMH).

Negus, K., & Pickering, M. (2004). *Creativity, communication, and cultural values.* Thousand Oaks, CA: Sage Publications.

Panganamala, N., & Plummer, D. (1998). Attitudes toward counseling among Asian Indians in the United States. *Cultural Diversity and Mental Health, 4*, 55–63.

Samovar, L., & Porter, E. (Eds.). (2000). Intercultural communication: A reader (9th ed.). Los Angeles, CA: Wadsworth.

Sinha, J. (1986). *Indian psychology* (3 vols.). New Delhi, India: Mothilal Banarsidas.

Sinha, D., & Kao, H. (Eds.). (1988). *Social values and development.* New Delhi: Sage India.

Smith, P., Peterson, M., & Schwartz, S. (2002). Cultural values, sources of guidance, and their relevance to managerial behavior: A 47-nation study. *Journal of Cross-Cultural Psychology, 33*, 188–208.

Sriram, S., & Chaudhary, N. (2004). An ethnography of love in a Tamil family. *Culture & Psychology, 10*, 111–127.

Weiss, D., & Marmar, C (1997). The Impact of event scale-revised. In J. Wilson & T. Keane (Eds.), *Assessing psychological trauma and PTSD.* (pp. 168–190). New York: Guilford Press.

Chapter 7

Caribbean Blacks: (Haitiains, Jamaicans, Virgin Islanders, Eastern Caribbean) Responses to Disasters in Cultural Context

G. Rita Dudley-Grant and Wayne Etheridge

INTRODUCTION

This chapter is being completed in the shadow of the worst natural disaster in United States history. Hurricane Katrina hit the Gulf Coast of the United States on August 29, 2005, but the disaster's legacy remains with us. Large stretches of the Gulf Coast were destroyed. Subsequently the levees broke and flooded the city of New Orleans, destroying the city and taking hundreds of lives and causing billions of dollars in damage. Most heart wrenching in this catastrophe was the incredible delay in response on the part of federal and state officials. It was immediately clear that the vast majority of the victims shared a deadly set of demographics, they were black and poor. One cannot help but hypothesize that underlying racist attitudes and social systems/institutions played significant roles in the inadequate prevention and intervention which resulted in so many avoidable deaths. Hurricane Katrina and the events that followed brought issues of race and class to the forefront of the public consciousness, revealing the stark realities of inequality and prejudice embedded within American society.

Yet as Dovidio, Gaertner, Kawakami, and Hodson (2002) have taught over the past two decades, this is a new form of racism, much more subtle, and below the consciousness of those who hold these beliefs. Those with subtle prejudice believe that racism is bad and want to deny its existence in our society. In order to maintain this denial, they avoid addressing issues of inequality, in order to avoid their own discomfort.

209

It is these pervasive attitudes that are hidden within the established social structure that prompted Dr. Carl Bell, MD, President and C.E.O. of the Community Mental Health Council in Chicago, to write the following email. An excerpt of the email is copied below. On Sep 3, 2005, at 7:31 AM, Carl C. Bell, M.D. (personal communication) wrote:

> *While I too am miffed at the stereotyping and demonization of our brothers and sisters, I am more concerned with the reality that the U.S. has absolutely no idea how many poor people of color there are living in the country's cities nor how to adequately meet their needs during a disaster.*
>
> *We have no idea how many poor people of color there are (not to mention illegal immigrants) in our cities as the census does not count them, they have fallen off unemployment rolls, they may or may not be registered to vote, etc. - thus they are invisible.*
>
> *At some point the nation will need to realize from strictly a public health perspective, it is the health status of the poorest in the country that will determine the health status of all of us. As Dr. David Satcher (former U.S. Surgeon General) reminds us, the diseases that develop in other countries do not need passports to come to the U.S., and the diseases that will develop in the southern gulf coast region will be able to migrate through the country as well. . . .*
>
> *The planning for the unknown numbers of poor people of color and immigrants needs to be vastly improved if the U.S. is going to respond to disasters any better in the future.*

Carl C. Bell, M.D. President and C.E.O.,
Community Mental Health Council

It is with these thoughts in mind, and a heavy heart for all of the losses resulting from Hurricane Katrina, that we offer the following information on the immigrant (first and second generation) population from the English- and French-speaking Caribbean. It is hoped that this information will assist disaster workers in providing services to this population in a manner that honors their culture, their self image, and their untold wellspring of resilience. Disasters are no longer issues for a single country or a single community. As Russian President Vladimir Putin informed America on CNN a week after Hurricane Katrina, it was a disaster for the world. Moreover, as Marsella and Christopher (2004) point out, the collective response to trauma can be a "coming together, rebuilding and reaffirmation of identity". Culturally competent disaster metal health workers can play a key role in preventing social collapse and enhancing resilience.

ENGLISH AND FRENCH SPEAKING CARIBBEAN BLACKS

People from the Caribbean have been characterized as some of the warmest, most jovial and embracing individuals that one can encounter. From spicy foods to Calypso and Reggae music, from indigenous spirituality to deeply held religious beliefs and practices, tenacious and fiercely independent while also a truly communal society, Caribbean culture represents a unique blend of the African Diaspora in the West Indies, and as immigrants to the United States and other colonizing countries. They are a significant percentage of the southern American population, and have a presence in major cities on the East Coast. Their values and life experiences in immigrating to the United States will unquestionably play a role in their resilience in handling disasters. Various writers have characterized Caribbean Blacks as the "model minority within the black community" although more recently this reputation has been tarnished by Caribbean involvement in the drug trafficking trade (Kalmijn, 1996; Reed, 2005). This "model minority" status had been achieved in large part due to the economic success achieved primarily by immigrants from the British-speaking Caribbean. In order to understand this rich culture, it is helpful to understand the history of the islands and the various cultures that have contributed to the shape of the Caribbean Black cultures of today.

The area referred to in this chapter as the Caribbean is encompassed by many different independent countries and people, who while having some common historical similarities, can be quite different in terms of their language, customs, and traditions (Table 7.1). The term Caribbean and West Indian will be used interchangeably throughout this chapter. The Spanish-speaking Caribbean, including Puerto Rico, Cuba, and the Dominican Republic, are different enough in language and culture that they will not be addressed in this chapter.

It is essential to realize that each island is a unique entity, with variations in cultural practices that can be quite minor, such as across the forty miles of water that separate St. Thomas from St. Croix, both in the American Virgin Islands. In contrast, the same distance of forty miles can produce a difference that is quite dramatic, such as that which separates St. Croix from Puerto Rico, two completely different languages and cultural experiences. This chapter

Table 7.1.   Overview of English, French, and Dutch Speaking Islands in the Caribbean

English Speaking Caribbean	*French Speaking Caribbean*
Cayman Islands	Haiti
Jamaica	St. Martin
U.S. Virgin Islands	Guadeloupe
British Virgin Islands	Martinique
Anguilla	St. Lucia
St. Kitts and Nevis	
Antigua and Barbuda	*Dutch Speaking Caribbean*
Montserrat	Aruba
Barbados	Curacao
St. Vincent and the Grenadines	Saba
Grenada	St. Maarten
Dominica	
Trinidad and Tobago	

will consider the primary cultural commonalities that are shared among the English- and French-speaking West Indian island nations, always cautioning the provider to consider individual differences first.

A brief look at the geography of the region is helpful. The northern perimeter within the Caribbean Sea is called the Greater Antilles and includes Cuba, Hispaniola, Jamaica, and Puerto Rico. The eastern boundary is outlined by an island chain running almost 1500 miles from the Tropic of Cancer in the north to approximately 10 degrees latitude above the equator and just off the coast of Venezuela and Colombia. The islands of the Greater Antilles are those towards the northwest of the Caribbean Sea – Cuba, Haiti, the Dominican Republic and Jamaica. The Lesser Antilles are comprised of the current and former American, British, French and Dutch colonies, from Puerto Rico to Trinidad. This chain is further divided into the Leeward Islands from Anguilla in the north to Dominica in the south, and the Windward Islands from Martinique to Trinidad. There is also an island chain which runs parallel to the coast of South America, including Aruba, Bonaire, and Curacao which are referred to as the Netherlands Antilles, due to their common Dutch colonial past.

There are approximately 2000 islands strung between the U.S. and the primary sources of illegal drug production. It is not surprising then, that one of the major law enforcement issues in the region is the use of the islands as a transshipment point of illegal drugs from Colombia and other South American Countries to the United States. With this comes the concomitant explosion in drug use and its attendant ill effects on the various communities of the islands. Thus, drug abuse and addiction should be considered as one of the major mental health issues facing Caribbean people today. The associated criminal activity has also contributed to the loss of status as a "model minority" due to the role of some Caribbean people in the drug trade. Nevertheless, economically, United States trade is dependent on the security of the Caribbean. All thirteen sea-lanes in the Caribbean are included in the thirty-one sea-lanes around the world designated "essential" by the United States government. A lifeline of seaborne commerce and communication, the Caribbean is both a convergence of major interoceanic trade routes and a logistical and supply route for the United States (Griffith, 1997).

While a large subsection of Afro Caribbean people living in the U.S. originate from Jamaica and Haiti, it is helpful to realize that the individual that one is working with might come from one of many island nations in the Caribbean. Sociologists have written about the "trans-Caribbean identity", which is formed by people of Caribbean origin residing outside of the Caribbean. It is made up of the shared history, values and beliefs shared by much of the Caribbean (Premdas, 1996). Yet language and the influences of the colonizing country maintain a significant impact on Caribbean expatriates. Indeed, while there is some cross-island identification among the English speaking Caribbean people living abroad, those from other islands such as Aruba or Haiti tend to go their own way. For example, the relationship between the large Haitian community and the many Jamaicans living in Miami tends to be cordial but distant (Stepick, Stepick, & Kretsedemas, 2001).

The major colonizers and hence European cultural influences in the Caribbean were the Spanish, from the time of Columbus, the English and French who followed soon after seeking religious freedom and economic development, and to a lesser extent the Dutch and the Danish. Colonists met several tribes of Indigenous Indians – most notably the Caribs, a fierce war-like people, and the Arawaks or Tainos, a more gentle and welcoming group. The genocide of these individuals was accomplished by the diseases brought from Europe, as well as the failed attempt at enslavement to have the Indigenous people work in the goldmines. Their death and virtual extinction necessitated the slave trade which lasted about 300 years until the mid-1800's. Although slavery has ended, the American and European power structure continues to be upheld through unequal distribution of wealth and the economic control exerted by the small 5 to 10% of mostly white American and European inhabitants.

The racial portrait of the population in the Caribbean is unique in that it reflects one of the most multicultural communities found anywhere on the planet. Once slavery was abolished, workers from India and Asia were imported to continue working on the plantations. These workers remained and raised their families, and became integrated into the communities. Many maintained certain aspects of their culture, such as the Moslems from India still sprinkled throughout the Caribbean, but primarily in Trinidad and Jamaica. Caribbean white refers to the primarily white or extremely light-skinned West Indians of European descent who remain in the upper echelons of Caribbean society both academically and economically. Inroads have been made by the darker West Indian populations into the political arena. However, economic control is still heavily vested in the hands of the American- and European-dominated businesses, particularly tourism which is the major foundation of the West Indian economy.

It has sometimes been stated that racism does not exist in the Caribbean. It is more accurate to state that racism as it exists in the United States is less evident in the West Indies, in large part due to the demographic differences (Bowser, 1995). Ninety to ninety-five percent of the population is made up of black and other "ethnically different" individuals. Whites make up a small percentage of the population; hence overt racism is very rare. Rather, classism is the frequent tool of those in power. It has been said that with enough money, the "blackest of men can turn white". Intraracial prejudice, primarily based on skin color, is the most frequently observed method of discrimination.

Gopaul-McNicol (1993) reported that in her own study of 144 U.S. based Caribbean children, the vast majority chose white dolls over those with darker skin tones. Similar studies were replicated with children residing in the Caribbean with the same results. Nevertheless, acquisition of money and education can elevate one into the dominant sections of the community. It is these very values which are the primary motivation for persons from the

Caribbean to migrate to the United States, Great Britain and Canada, with the espoused intention of one day returning to claim their enhanced status in their island society. Hence, due to the ongoing poverty that is an unfortunate hallmark of the Caribbean, migration to Britain and the United States has been seen as the best means of improving one's economic and social standing.

POPULATION DEMOGRAPHICS

Caribbeans in the United States

Caribbean people in the United States are colloquially referred to as exceeding the number of Caribbean people remaining in the West Indies. This is in large part due to the poor economy of the West Indies which has resulted in over 100 years of migration. Traditionally these immigrants will send money back to family members, particularly for children left behind to be raised by grandparents and other extended family members. This phenomenon is known as serial migration and can have a very negative impact on family structure and parent-child bonding, and will be discussed later in this chapter. However, the benefit of this migration is the provision of significant economic benefit to the islands.

For example, according to Jamaica's Minister of State for Finance, Errol Ennice, between January and November of 1994, Jamaicans residing in the U.S. alone remitted some U.S. $278 million to the Jamaican economy. It was reported that 2.5 million Jamaicans living in New York, Miami, Hartford, Washington DC, Toronto, London, and Philadelphia sent close to U.S. $600 million to Jamaica during that same year. Similarly, money from expatriate residents of the Dominican Republic is reported to reach U.S. $1.2 billion per year, the second largest source of foreign exchange after tourism. Moreover, the growth of the informal economy created by remittances by the U.S. and other colonial countries has been expanded to such an extent that countries such as Guyana, Haiti, Surinam, and the entire Eastern Caribbean, are equally or more dependant on it than they are on the formal economy (Griffith, 1997).

The U.S. Census Bureau (Larsen, 2004) reports that there are 28.4 million foreign-born residents in the United States, comprising 10.4% of the population. Of those, about 10% are from the Caribbean – about 3 million people (Larsen, 2004). In addition, it is estimated that there may be just as many second and third generation Afro-Caribbeans residing in the country, as well as a 1:1 ratio of documented to undocumented individuals. This suggests that there may be as many as 8 or 9 million persons of Caribbean descent currently residing in the United States. Given that the UNECSCO World Education Report of 1998 suggests that there are about 12.5 million persons residing in the Caribbean, it can be seen that Caribbean persons living in the United States play a major role in Caribbean affairs. In fact, the Interamerican Development Bank Study (2004) reported that people of Caribbean heritage contribute 1.6 billion in remittances to economies in the Caribbean each year. The largest majority reside in Haiti (over seven million), and the second largest population resides in Jamaica (2.4 million). These percentages are reflected in the numbers that have immigrated to the United States.

It is also important to consider changes in the typical profile of immigrants over the past several decades. Early immigrants tended to be upwardly mobile, seeking to better their economic well being, but frequently having come from some level of education and accomplishment (Bibb & Casimir, 1996). More recent immigrants have often been refugees, such as those coming from Haiti seeking political and economic asylum. These individuals tend to be more economically distressed in their own country, and more vulnerable to fall prey to the inadequate services, poor housing, lack of employment and job opportunities, and the inevitable prejudice inherent in the American culture (Perez Foster, 2001).

There are significant differences between the Jamaican and Haitian cultures, and hence how they fare in the United States. Jamaica is one of the most multicultural of the islands, with a rainbow of ethnicities and individuals. Those who emigrate tend to represent a cross section – highly educated individuals as well as those from the lower classes seeking to better their life conditions. Jamaican integration into American culture tends to be a true success story, with one of the best examples being Former Secretary of State Colin Powell. Hence, these and other persons from the English-speaking Caribbean tend to be well integrated and acculturated to the U.S., while maintaining Caribbean-based values (Brice-Baker, 1996).

Jamaicans

Historically, Jamaican emigration has been heavy. In the 1950s and 1960s the destination was Britain. Since the United Kingdom restricted immigration in 1967, the major flow has been to the United States and Canada. About 20,000 Jamaicans immigrate to the United States each year; another 200,000 visit annually. Since 1970, approximately 481,000 have legally immigrated to the United States. New York, Miami, Chicago, and Hartford are among the U.S. cities with a significant Jamaican population. Remittances from the expatriate communities in the United States, United Kingdom, and Canada make increasingly significant contributions to Jamaica's economy (History of Jamaica, 2005).

It is difficult to estimate the number of Jamaicans or other Caribbean nationals residing in the United States, as the Census provides a category which only partially identifies the individual. For example, a Jamaican or Haitian is forced to choose "Black American", although there are significant cultural differences from the Americanized black population. However, it is estimated that there are about half a million Jamaicans residing in the New York area (Gopaul-McNicol, 1993). Next to New York, the greatest concentrations of Jamaicans can be found in the Miami/Ft. Lauderdale area. For example, it is reported that there are 70,000 documented Jamaicans living in Broward County (Dinham, 2002). It appears that the majority are younger adults of employment age between the ages of 22 to 34, although the traditional population emigrating from the West Indies overall tended to be young males until the 1960's when it shifted to females due to the types of jobs available. Approximately 50% tend to be married with men slightly more likely to be so than women. Upper class parents will frequently send their children "abroad" to be educated, and often they then settle in the United States. However, the majority of immigrants are less educated upon arrival, but many seek to educate themselves. They tend to start out in the service industries and in employment sector areas designated as "precision, craft, and repair", and "operator, fabricator and laborer" (Gopaul-McNicol, 1993).

Rastafari Culture: No discussion of Jamaican culture would be complete without consideration of that aspect of Jamaica which is perhaps the most influential and well known. The Rastafarian movement became internationally recognized with Jamaica where it had its roots. It began as a "religious counteraction to the imperialistic outcomes of Eurocentric Christendom" (Semaj, 1979, p. 8 cited in Gopaul-McNicol (1993, p. 43). Four major tenets stressing the means to positive change have been recognized as basic to the Rastafari religious movement, again as cited in GoPaul-McNicol (1993 p. 43):

- Awareness by black people of their African Heritage
- Recognition of the former emperor of Ethiopia, Haile Selassie, as the black reincarnated Christ.
- Repatriation to Ethiopia/Africa, the true home of all blacks.
- The apocalyptic fall of Jamaica as Babylon, the corrupt world of the white man.

Since then the movement, which has both religious and social connotations, has spread throughout the West Indies. Through its music, promoted most prominently by Bob Marley, the "Reggae" beat has catapulted Jamaica onto the international stage. Besides the music, another aspect of the Rastafari culture which has now gained worldwide recognition is the hair style. Dreadlocks (or the "Crown of Glory") were uniquely Rastafari, setting them apart from others. The hair style has now become popular in a variety of cultures. It was said to come from the Old Testament, allowing the hair to grow, without cutting it, and plaiting it, following the Lord's admonition to "never take scissor to his hair nor razor to his face", a common practice among Ethiopian warriors. The hairstyles no longer distinguish the true practitioners of Rastafari religion. The culture also uses the "heavenly colors" gold, green, and red, the colors of Ethiopia.

The Rastas eat neither pork nor shellfish, and many are vegetarian, preferring "Ital foods", foods grown organically and chemically untreated. They avoid strong liquor seeing it as another means of oppression by the ruling class. They have a strong patriarchal family structure, taking their fathering roles very seriously. Their love of children is universally acknowledged and one can frequently see Rasta fathers with their children, attempting to raise them in the "African ways". This can pose significant problems for Rastas in America, as the women can frequently be the more successful breadwinner and higher wage earner. There is a strong belief in formal education, and Rastas typically encourage their "youths" to attend school, while closely attending to what is taught – marking the concern that the government educational system helps to colonize the minds of young people. They will frequently refuse to work for the government, preferring to engage in agricultural or sea-based entrepreneurship, due to the "Babylonian attitudes" of the ruling power structure.

Perhaps the most controversial aspect to the Rastafarian religion is the use of marijuana in their religious ceremonies. Interestingly, unlike the wider West Indian society, there is no formal profession of faith in obeah or other traditional spiritual practices. Rather, their religious tradition is anthropomorphic: they believe in God, a black visage with African features which some have seen as symbolic of the struggle of the black man for self respect. The use of marijuana or ganja as it is called is accorded religious significance, supported by God's exhortation to smoke it as quoted from passages of the Bible including Genesis 8, Psalms 18 and Revelations 22. It is also used medicinally and in daily rituals by some Rastafari.

In their communities in Jamaica it may be given in tea to children, indicating that it is not seen as harmful. This attitude plays an important role in marijuana use, as it is seen as "natural", making substance abuse intervention for marijuana particularly difficult with this population. However, the true practitioners of the Rastafari religion are equally concerned about the drug dealers who would exploit their beliefs and practices to further the narcotics trade. They are eager to distinguish themselves from the drug lords who are the managers and beneficiaries of drug trafficking, but who benefit from the public perception that ascribes it to Rastafari. While the Rastafari influence has lessened in Jamaica, it continues to spread world wide primarily by the music, the method of hairstyle and dress, and the adherence to a "natural" life style (GoPaul-McNicol, 1993). When interviewing persons that might be of this persuasion, it is important to understand the extent of their practice and participation in the Rasta culture. The belief of being close to God and the soil can serve as a source of resilience in times of disaster, both natural and man-made.

Haitians

Unlike the Jamaicans, the recent Haitian immigrant experience in the U.S. has not been as successful, nor have they fared as well economically or socially as their English-speaking counterparts. The history of Haitian immigration to the United States is in part based on the U.S. relationship with that country. From 1915–1934 the United States occupied Haiti due in part to their

G.R. Dudley-Grant, W. Etheridge

fears over the impact of World War I on that strategic country. The occupation by the United States had several effects on Haiti. An early period of unrest culminated in a 1918 rebellion by up to 40,000 former *cacos* and other disgruntled people. The scale of the uprising overwhelmed the Gendarmerie, but marine reinforcements helped put down the revolt at the estimated cost of 2,000 Haitian lives. Thereafter, order prevailed to a degree that most Haitians had never witnessed. The order, however, was imposed largely by white foreigners with deep-seeded racial prejudices and a disdain for the notion of self-determination by inhabitants of less-developed nations. Still, as Haitians united in their reaction to the racism of the occupying forces, the mulatto elite managed to dominate the country's bureaucracy and to strengthen its role in national affairs (Factbites, n. d.). However, Haiti has continued to have long periods of unrest and political upheaval.

These attitudes particularly dismayed the mulatto elite, who had heretofore believed in their innate superiority over the black masses. The whites from North America, however, did not distinguish among Haitians, regardless of their skin tone, level of education, or sophistication. This intolerance caused indignation, resentment, and eventually a racial pride that was reflected in the work of a new generation of Haitian historians, ethnologists, writers, artists, and others, many of whom later became active in politics and government. Still, as Haitians united in their reaction to the racism of the occupying forces, the mulatto elite managed to dominate the country's bureaucracy and to strengthen its role in national affairs. However, Haiti has continued to have long periods of unrest and political upheaval. Hence, numerous Haitians have sought political asylum in the United States. Unfortunately, political asylum has frequently been denied. There was a notable emigration of elite Haitians to the United States in the late 1950's as they fled the Francois Duvalier repressive regime. At that point New York was the epicenter of Haitian immigration. However, starting in the 1970's and 1980's the Haitian population in Florida started growing (Bibb & Casimir, 1996).

Presently, the largest population of Haitians resides within the Miami, Florida area, although there are other large Haitian communities in major urban areas on the east coast (Phelps, 2003). They are reported to comprise about one third of all of the Haitians living in the United States and doubled to at least 267,689 between 1990 and 2000 in the Miami Dade and North Miami area. Haitians continue to struggle in the United States against discriminatory immigration policies and anti-Haitian prejudice. The Haitians unfortunately do not comprise harmonious, united communities. There is significant mistrust between "Haitian" Haitians and Americanized Haitians. There is also tension between social classes, language differences, and ambivalent attitudes towards the Black American community. Accordingly, many Haitians mistrust outsiders and each other and do not believe that involvement in civic affairs will make a difference. Their basic needs tend to be housing, youth mentorship programs, and education. The biggest hindrance to empowerment and integration into the American community is the lack of trust, based on two centuries of corruption and broken promises. Building trust in these individuals requires close attention to meeting their basic needs and ensuring a lack of self serving, corrupt actions which can undermine their budding but tenuous faith in the system (Stepick, Stepick, & Kretsedemas, 2001).

Eastern Caribbean Island Nations

The United States maintained a diplomatic presence in the Eastern Caribbean, as well as a small military one as well, including the purchase of the United States Virgin Islands and the conquest of the Commonwealth of Puerto Rico (Willocks, 1995).

The ethnic identities of the English-speaking Caribbean are predicated on the colonial influences of the major European countries, including Spain,

Table 7.2. Key Historical Dates and Events

1492:	Columbus lands in the Caribbean, bringing disease and destruction to the indigenous Indian peoples.
1690's:	Amelioration policies preceding emancipation allowed slave trade to show positive growth.
1801:	A former slave, Toussaint L'Ouverture, conquered the whole island and abolished slavery. Then in 1804 Haiti became the second independent nation and first island state in the Americas and the Caribbean (US Occupation 1915–1934).
1920's:	First major immigration wave to the U.S., in part due to changes in immigration laws.
1940:	The death of Marcus Garvey and the birth of the Rastafarian movement.
1962:	The first call for a regional Caribbean community was made in a January 1962 speech by Eric Williams, former prime minister and first head of state of independent Trinidad and Tobago. T&T achieved independence August 31, 1962.
1964:	Caribbean immigrants formed their own subcultures within Harlem, but they were not geographically segregated from other Harlem residents. "Given the stiff competition for space in the zone of black settlement, the formation of a distinct Caribbean enclave within the black community would have been difficult, even if West Indian immigrants had desired it" (Kasinitz, 1992, p. 43).
	Harlem was something of a black metropolis, and West Indians became in some ways part of a larger, more Pan-African, demographic group. Caribbean immigrants from different countries and different classes found themselves being considered part of the same homogeneous group in the Harlem community. Their struggle for freedom, their history and heritage, and the prejudice they encountered in the U.S. both united them to one another and differentiated them from the broader African American population.
	The Virgin Islander, especially, found his problem complicated by failures to make the distinction between him (as an American citizen) and immigrants from foreign countries. West Indians worshipped in different churches, practiced different religious customs, had a different family structure, dressed differently, had a different accent, and were generally noticeably different from native blacks (Kasinitz, 1992).
1980's:	A new wave of Haitian immigrants escaping political as well as economic devastation enter legally and illegally, primarily through the southern United States.
1983:	The United States invades Grenada on October 25, 1983.
2004:	America intervenes as President Aristede of Haiti is ousted by a military coup and a transitional government is formed awaiting "democratic" elections.

England, France, Holland, Denmark, and the United States. In addition, slavery played a major role by importing millions of Africans into the Caribbean over its 400 year history. When slavery was abolished in the mid-1800's, indentured workers were imported from China and India. All of these cultural influences along with more recent immigrants from the Middle East, the Phillipines, and South America have resulted in a very international mixture of ethnic identities and cultural practices. In the U.S., persons from the Caribbean can reflect one or any combination of these sub-cultures. Sub-cultural identity takes preeminence over skin color and plays a role in the common West-Indian rejection of "minority status". Table 7.2 shows ten key historical dates for the Caribbean Black population.

Nevaer (2003) reports four common mistakes when considering attempts to market services of any kind to Caribbean people:

- Stereotyping all Caribbean people as one. Each island nation is quite independent with fierce loyalties from their expatriate citizens.
- Pooling Caribbean people with Black Americans – they prefer Caribbean American or a reference to the country of the birth (i.e. Haitian American).
- Not using local Caribbean press and other media to publicize mental health and related messages.
- Community involvement and visibility. Caribbean people support their community and are deeply committed to sending their children to college to enable them to participate in the "American Dream" achievement ideology.

TEN KEY HISTORICAL DATES (CHRONOLOGY)

TEN KEY VALUES

The Eastern Caribbean has been heavily colonized, with European and more recently American influences. These relationships have had an impact on the values of West Indian people throughout the Diaspora, intermingled with those retained from the cultures of their homelands.

Extended Family

From the earliest times of Caribbean interaction with the Western world in the fifteenth century, the family has traditionally been communal in nature, based on its roots in indigenous Carib and African cultures. Gopaul-McNicol (1993) describes the West Indian family as "usually an extended family that encompasses not only those related by marriage and blood, but also godparents, adopted children whose adoption is informal ("child lending"), and in some cases even friends" (p. 22).

Work Ethic

The Caribbean Black is known to be a hard worker upon immigration to the United States. This activity reflects the immigrant status which is known to be determined in their pursuit of success (Boneva, Frieze, Ferligoj, Pauknerova, & Orgocka, 1998). There is also the same expectation of hard work within the home, however it occurs at a slower pace (Dudley-Grant, 1998). It is believed by most Caribbean immigrants that the key to success in America is hard work and education. Moreover, the expectation that funds will be sent to support family members in the West Indies is an even more powerful motivator to gain and maintain employment at all costs (Dudley-Grant, Mendez & Zinn, 2000).

Multiculturalism and Caribbean Blacks' Experiences with Racism

The Caribbean Black is not always suspicious of racism or on guard since racism is much more subtle within the Caribbean culture (Heath, 2005; Mintz, 1974). While this openness can be harmful, it can also be liberating in that the Caribbean Black is often slightly more willing to take risks and to accept offers of assistance from Whites, while the American Black might mistrust the white person based on historical and/or personal experiences. Many Caribbean Blacks are also willing to take the most menial jobs, a common practice among immigrants, as there is a strong belief that the job does not define the person.This psychological distinction is much more easily made when one has not grown up with constant images and experiences of prejudice and discrimination.

Many Caribbean Blacks will argue heatedly that racism does not exist in their country and that their strategy for dealing with it in America is to ignore it as long as possible. Thus, it appears that racism is experienced by some Caribbean Blacks as an evil that is outside of them, which does not define who they are or how they must operate in the world. This attitude may alleviate some of the stress placed on psychological functioning, which can be experienced by Blacks raised in America. There is one group of Blacks in America who can claim a similar experience, and that is those who have been raised in a virtually all Black environment, such as the small or mid-sized Black towns found frequently in the South and parts of the Midwest. With adequate role models and a safe environment, the Blacks who grow up under these circumstances often feel more empowered and less burdened by the need for the "protective paranoia" which is a frequent characterization of the psychology of Blacks in America.

It is important to qualify that none of these statements imply that Caribbean Blacks are any less prone to encountering racism once in America. While one can be caught off guard and unwittingly become the victim of racism, the decreased sensitivity can also serve as a protective factor for one's self image. Milton Vickerman, author of *Crosscurrents: West Indian Immigrants and Race*, documents the complex relationship between race and ethnic identity among

New York Jamaicans. "West Indians come from societies where blacks are the majority, so they have a different life experience, one in which they are not a minority but part of society's majority," says Vickerman. "And 'race' is downplayed" (as quoted in Nevaer, 2003).

Education

Education is valued throughout West Indian society. Education is typically seen as the surest means of upward mobility, and a key distinguishing factor between the classes (Bibb & Casimir, 1996; Brice-Baker, 1996; Reed, 2005). Universal access to education is being established throughout the region. Immigrants to this country can experience discrimination particularly when moving from the British system, causing youngsters to be forced to repeat a grade. Nevertheless, a common practice (for those who can) is to send the youngster abroad for a part of high school and their college education. For first generation immigrants from the Eastern Caribbean, a key difficulty is moving from the British to the American system. Due to the differences in education, as well as difficulty in understanding the language, youngsters may be retained in a lower grade, or even mislabeled as having a learning disability (Gopaul-McNicol & Armour-Thomas, 2001).

Spirituality

Religion and spirituality are key aspects of the Caribbean culture (Dudley-Grant, 2003). The people of the West Indies are predominantly Christian, with the East Indians in Trinidad and Guyana primarily Hindus or Muslims. These mainstream faiths are practiced alongside traditional beliefs from the Vodoun in Haiti to the Obea in the Eastern Caribbean.

Respect

The Caribbean culture tends to be fairly authoritarian in nature. There are both paternalistic and maternalistic orientations, but respect for elders and for authority are key aspects of the community. Children are taught to avoid direct eye contact as a sign of respect, as well as to greet all adults upon encountering them, which can be unusual and even place them in danger when initially migrating to the inner cities of the United States.

Ancestors and Elders

Another aspect of respect is the veneration of elders and ancestors. The Caribbean culture maintains basic Afrocentric values by respecting those who have gone before and maintaining them in the family. Extended families will include the elders who will rarely be placed outside of the family for caretaking as they age. In addition, most Caribbean people will "talk to the ancestors" which can appear to be a sign of hallucinatory activity but is in fact a normal part of Caribbean culture.

Community

The West Indies is known to have a communal culture, based on the African values of extended family and community above self. This value can be quite helpful when one is experiencing emotional disturbance or trauma as it can be particularly supportive. Cognitive dissonance can occur with second generation youngsters who are more "Americanized" into individualistic Western values. Parents may have difficulty understanding and managing apparently self-centered behavior of their children in a culture that does not necessarily support their authority and value systems.

Disaster as a Result of Negative Actions

West Indians may see disasters as the result of negative actions that are taken individually and collectively. Hence one can perceive a natural disaster as retribution for actions, engendering excessive guilt and anxiety.

Creativity

Caribbean people are by character warm and lively, manifesting their creativity in dance, art, and rhythm. Musical celebrations such as carnivals are replete in most Caribbean islands and these festivals have been recreated in the United States, most notably in the Labor Day Carnival in Brooklyn, and the Carnival in Miami. These events are seen as a celebration of the culture and the heritage, and are highly valued within all aspects of Caribbean society.

COMMUNICATION STYLES

The base language in the English-speaking Caribbean is heavily accented English commonly called "Creole". French speaking Caribbean islands include Haiti, Guadeloupe, Martinique and French St. Martin. There is also Dutch St. Martin, Saba and Curacao. Each European language (English, French, Dutch, etc.) has been modified sufficiently so that it has formed a new language, such as Creole (English), Papiamento (Spanish) or Patios, which is the officially recognized second language of Haiti and is a modified blend of French with African words and phraseology.

Not all of these languages are officially recognized in the academic system. For example, in the U.S. Virgin Islands, heavily accented English, termed "calypso" is frequently spoken (to be distinguished from the musical art form of Calypso). Yet school children are frequently cautioned to "speak properly" or "speak English". While calypso is not considered a separate language it has recognizable features. It is American English (as distinguished from British English), and is heavily accented with frequent colloquialisms. For example, the plural of child can be children or "child-dem". Differences in syntax, intonation, and meanings of words are prevalent. For example, "me'n know" means "I don't know" rather than "I do know" (Dudley-Grant et al., 2000).

In the West Indian culture, respect is a primary value among all levels of society. One shows respect in many ways, nonverbal as well as verbal. Interpersonal interactions tend to be more formal, particularly in the middle and working classes. One can tell the level of acculturation as determined by the formality of address when meeting a West Indian in a foreign country such as the United States, Britain or Canada. West Indians do not look steadily into someone's eyes, as this is seen as a sign of disrespect, or even aggression. However, the culture tends to be rather warm and open, hence touching and hugging is an acceptable form of address when greeting persons that are little known. Nonverbal interpersonal distance tends to be slightly closer than is experienced in the United States. Hence an American may feel uncomfortably "crowded" when interacting with West Indian clients, particularly those from the rural cultures.

The West Indian culture tends to be a very physically expressive one. One sociological study of a small village in St. Vincent gave the following descriptions (Young, 1993):

> The women of Windward Valley have a great talent for joking and laughing. Laughter in women often permeates their bodies, weakens their limbs, and sends them into sweeping contractions at mid-body. Men laugh heartily with postures similar but less deeply collapsed, Laughter is a household and friendship bond (p. 138).
>
> The erotic dancing style of young adults, of "shaking" the pelvis in syncopated rhythm, loosely extending the arms and bending the knees to one side as though the body is suspended, is performed by children as well as adults. Gestures from this dance style communicate exuberance in public interpersonal behavior and are frequently seen. The gestures may be encouraged, allowed, or restricted and are handled differently in childhood, adolescence, and adulthood (p. 142).

The latter description of the suggestive dancing of the West Indian culture is reflective of a truly culturally based exuberance that can be seen particularly during the carnival or festival celebrations. These celebratory practices are an important part of the cultural link with the Caribbean's African heritage, and have been maintained in the larger communities of the host countries, such as the Labor Day Celebration in Brooklyn, which is a continuation of the carnival celebrations from the West Indies.

Feelings are valued and tend to be more freely expressed. It is not uncommon to hear heated discussions among friends that might be misconstrued as arguments, but in fact are strongly stated opinions that carry no lasting implications past the current interaction. This is particularly true of political discussions, which are a favorite pastime of West Indians regardless of the specific island or cultural orientation.

Anthropomorphism is common, and storms are very much referred to and thought of as living things (Joseph & Rowe, 1990). Indeed, fighting against a disaster such as a hurricane can be seen as a spiritual battle. The following excerpt exemplifies this point:

> The howling of the wind in my bedroom was very intense and it just didn't seem secure. Somehow the kids slept until 11 pm. I was a wreck and we were alone. I was saying a prayer when the first loud crash startled me. The kids woke up and asked about the noise. I went to investigate the noise and was not prepared for what I saw! There was a hazy mist hovering in my living room, and my front door had been forced open. My natural reaction was to go and close the door. However, when I attempted to do so a force, the strength of 10 men, pushed me back about 15 feet. My fear turned to anger and I cursed it, and told it that it was not getting into this house. I proceeded to step on a nail that had fallen from a gaping hole in the kitchen roof. I gathered my courage and hobbled over to the couch and pushed it against the door. All night we were haunted by the door rattling against the couch.
>
> In fact, the noises grew in intensity as the long night creeped on. The wind's different voices, cooing, rattling, buzzing and groaning, were all experienced. I turned to my Bible for comfort through that night. After hearing the fear in General Moorhead's voice on the radio I realized that no rescue squad was going to come and save my family. I said a long prayer because the frightening reality was that I had to handle this alone, with God. (Gereau, 1993, p. 117).

Mental Illness within Cultural Context

Diagnosing mental illness can be challenging as the symptoms of emotional disturbance can be confounded by culturally consonant behavior which is considered normal and acceptable cognitive and emotional functioning in the West Indies. For example, it is standard practice to use the mental status exam to determine the presence of hallucinations by asking whether the individual "hears voices or sees things". Frequently, due to spiritual and cultural values and experiences, many West Indians do report seeing and hearing their dead grandparents or other significant figures on a fairly regular basis, with no indication of thought disorder. Cultural adaptation to the country of immigration can also result in post traumatic stress disorder symptoms which mimic major cognitive or mood disorders. It is essential to familiarize oneself with these cultural experiences prior to making a definitive diagnosis.

When persons from the Caribbean immigrate to the mainland, they carry their beliefs with them. It is not at all unusual for a Caribbean person who is emotionally distressed to seek assistance from a traditional healer first, or concurrently with the modern mental health establishment. This is significant, as often disasters can be personalized as retribution for past sins which must be expiated and atoned for, hence the use of a faith healing approach. This belief system also helps to manage the inevitable stigma that is associated with mental illness. In the West Indian community it is easier to accept that a family member is "possessed" than that they are "crazy". Due to the attitude of the mainstream culture to such activities, the individual may be very reluctant to reveal information regarding their work with the natural healer. Once a therapeutic relationship is established, it may be helpful to inquire whether "other" approaches to intervention have been sought by the family. In some cases, it is also important to be willing to explore what directives have been given and are being followed by the individual, as avoidance of contradictory interventions will greatly enhance treatment. It is also important not to reject the beliefs of the client, which the profession historically has tended to do. In another chapter this author wrote:

> Thus psychology like medicine has been no less rejecting of the notion of "faith healers". Those who were exhibiting emotional distress, changes in personality, loss of weight, and believed themselves to be possessed by spirits, were diagnosed as being delusional or frankly psychotic. Even worse, the practitioners, the witch doctors, Espiritistas or Spriritists, or Obeah men or women, were viewed as mentally ill at best or charlatans at worst (depending on your perspective), particularly when in a trance state or speaking with the spirits. Yet these traditional healers have saved many lives, healed illnesses, rescued marriages and relationships, counseled community and world leaders and brought hope to a sea of despair.
>
> One example of this comes from medical science as related by Dr. Anduze (1993). "As the story goes . . . there was once a Nigerian prince attending a prestigious London university. He became quite ill and all the top English doctors and scientific minds failed to diagnose or cure him. The family sent home for the local tribal doctor who came with a bunch of rauwolfia roots to cure the "moon madness" (mental illness). After receiving the appropriate dosage, the prince was up and around and none the worse in no time. The English quickly seized the remaining roots and upon analysis "invented" the first synthetic tranquilizer, Reserpine— the basis for many antihypertensives, (p1). This story characterizes how western medicine has taken the knowledge of traditional healers without crediting or legitimizing its source (Dudley-Grant, 2003, pp. 343–344).

VALIDITY OF ASSESSMENT INSTRUMENTS

The major concerns when using standardized instruments to assess persons from the Caribbean culture is the lack of standardization on that culture, as well as the Caribbean dialects which can make comprehension of the speaker quite difficult. Both the literature on appropriate standardization and that for dialect and language difficulties needs to be considered (Gopaul-McNicol & Armour-Thomas, 2001). Very little has been done to develop tests that would accurately assess the Afro Caribbean American. Psychologists have found that mere translations are insufficient (Gopaul-McNicol, 1993, Group for the Advancement of Psychiatry, 2002). However, there are three levels of assessment that need to be considered.

Clinical Interviewing and the Mental Status Exam

Due to the lack of accurate standardized tests, it is helpful for the clinician to use their interviewing skills, keeping in mind the many cultural factors presented in this chapter. It is frequently helpful to assess behavioral anomalies with family members or consult with others from the culture to determine when a behavior is truly disordered vs. culturally consonant (Gopaul-McNicol & Armour-Thomas, 2001). The mental status exam has shown that it can be a robust tool for assessing acute emotional distress, particularly if the examiner is cautioned about ascribing too much pathology to areas such as "hearing voices and seeing things". Collaborating with culturally different colleagues or others from the patient community can significantly enhance the accuracy of clinical judgment.

Cognitive Assessments

While the Wechsler Scales remain the standard in evaluating intelligence level, the same cautions must be made in terms of applicability to the cultural reality. Some psychologists will recommend elimination of certain aspects of the test, such as the General Information Subtest which is perceived to be the most culturally biased of the verbal scales (GoPaul-McNicol, 1993). Other screenings, such as the Kaufman tests of intelligence may be somewhat less biased, however the clinician is cautioned to consider such factors as length of time in the country, academic level of the parents, generation (first, second, etc), and other environmental factors which might play a role in the individual's acculturation (Russo & Lewis, 1999; Sternberg, 1987). Nonverbal testing, such as the Human Figure Drawings and the Bender Gestalt Test of Visual Motor Integration have been successfully used by practitioners to gauge the basic intelligence level of the client.

Personality and Psychopathology

Again, the practitioner is at a disadvantage in that projective testing is highly sensitive to culture. While personality traits are increasingly reported to have universality (McCrae & Terracciano, 2005), psychopathology is acknowledged to have significant aspects of culture in its manifestation (DSM IV, 1994). Studies have shown that racial identity measures can function as predictors of selected MMPI scale scores. A study by Whatley, Allen, and Dana (2003) found that those with heightened participation and socialization into African American cultural practices and experiences, along with the adoption of a more Afrocentric orientation and worldview, demonstrated less distrust and manifest psychopathology. Many studies have indicated that the MMPI is affected by cultural factors (Dahlstrom & Gynther, 1986). There are a plethora of tests that have been developed to test psychopathology, however very few have included standardization on West Indian clients. Dr. Sharon GoPaul-McNicol (1993) has developed several surveys including the West Indian Comprehensive Assessment Battery, and subsets of attitude surveys to determine the level of acculturation and distress within the American culture. These surveys, used in conjunction with more traditional instruments, are better able to provide an overall picture of the individual's level of emotional functioning.

Knowing and Recognizing Special Disorders

Major mental illness presents in the traditional forms found world wide, as well as in illnesses peculiar to the Caribbean-in-America experience. Lu, Lim, and Mezzich (1995) have coined the term "idioms of distress" as a reflection of how one's culture shapes the way in which mental illness is manifested. For the Afro-Caribbean population, as for all other ethnic groups, culture is a major factor that imprints mental health by influencing whether and how individuals experience the discomfort associated with mental illness. When conveyed by tradition and sanctioned by cultural norms, symptoms are ego syntonic and individuals can seek help. However, when symptoms fall outside of acceptable behavior, then the individual will deny, avoid, or attempt to manage their emotional issues within the context of what is familiar. Awareness of the idioms of distress is essential in accurately diagnosing and effectively treating culturally different individuals. A number of idioms of distress are well recognized as culture-bound syndromes and have been included in an appendix to the DSM-IV. Those diagnoses most relevant to the Caribbean population that a treating individual might encounter in the United States are presented below (DSM IV, 1994).

Boufee Delirante (Brief Psychosis).   A syndrome observed in the Haitian population as well as West Africa. The name of the syndrome is a French term with behavior characterized by sudden outbursts of agitated and aggressive behavior, marked confusion and psychomotor excitement. Paranoid or other delusional experiences may occur. The symptoms are similar to a Brief Psychotic Disorder.

Falling out or Blacking out.   These episodes are found primarily in persons from the southern United States and the Caribbean. The individual experiences a sudden collapse, with or without dizziness. The person is unable to see even if their eyes are open and feels paralyzed, but can hear what is happening around them. Symptoms are similar to Conversion Reaction or a Dissociative Disorder.

Rootwork. Illness is believed to result from being the victim of some version of black magic inflicted by another individual directly or through the intercession of a practitioner (i.e. witchdoctor or Obeah woman). Symptoms include generalized anxiety and gastrointestinal complaints (nausea, vomiting, and diarrhea), weakness, dizziness and the fear of being poisoned. The outcome can be fatal ("voodoo death"). The person may remain compromised until the root has been "taken off" (eliminated) usually through the intercession of a similar practitioner or healer in the tradition working on behalf of the victim. Symptoms may mimic Major Depressive Disorder, Paranoid Disorder and Posttraumatic Stress Disorder.

Susto (Soul Loss). This folk illness, while more prevalent thoughout the Latino Caribbean, is also gaining ground within the Afro Caribbean cultures. Susto is an illness attributed to a frightening event or trauma often in childhood, but may be in adulthood as well. It is believed that this causes the soul to leave the body, resulting in chronic dysphoria and psychosomatic illness. Disturbance in social relationships is also experienced, along with chronic dissatisfaction in one's own life, both personal and professional. Interventions can include ritual healings where one calls the soul back to the body, and cleansing the person to restore physical, emotional, and spiritual balance. These symptoms, similar to rootwork, may be related to Major Depressive Disorder, Posttraumatic Stress Disorder and Somatoform Disorders.

Zombie (Possession). Possession, and the more extreme being made into a "Zombie", are experiences that are most frequently attributed to the Haitian culture. For a person who has been made into a Zombie, which is reported to be accomplished by artificially inducing a trance state and then burying the individual alive, a misdiagnosis of catatonic schizophrenia can be given by the mental health professional. Regarding possession, folk belief says that when a person is "possessed" a spirit enters the individual's body and the behavior of the person becomes the behavior of the spirit. It is felt that the more easily influenced a person is, the more likely he or she is to become "possessed". There is a gender difference that has been noted where females are more likely than males to have the "possession" experience. These beliefs are widespread and transcend class, gender and geographical location. It is important for the mental health professional to be respectful of these beliefs (Gopaul-McNicol, 1993).

Differential diagnosis between one who is "possessed" and one who is suffering from a major mental illness can be difficult. A possessed person can exhibit symptoms and behaviors similar to several common diagnostic categories, including schizophrenia, epilepsy, hysteria or Tourette's syndrome. Unlike the persistent state of hallucinatory and delusional behavior of the schizophrenic, possession is a reflection of a socio-culturally accepted set of behaviors and beliefs (often learned from childhood) which are situationally based, and may even be reminiscent of traditional fundamentalist Christian experience, i.e. the Spiritual Baptists who offer possession experiences (Young, 1993). For a more detailed account of the differential diagnostic categories, the reader is referred to the excellent volume *Working with West Indian Families* by Sharon Gopaul-McNicol (1993).

Ethnocultural Allodynia.   A repetitive exposure to racial discrimination and the development of dysfunctional reactions to racism can compromise people of color's resilience. Because of the pervasiveness of racism, many people of color are socialized to be vigilant in ambiguous social situations. Ethnocultural Allodynia is the abnormally increased sensitivity to relatively innocuous or neutral stimuli resulting from previous exposure to painful racially and culturally based situations (Comas-Diaz & Jacobsen, 2001). As a risk factor, Ethnocultural Allodynia limits the person's ability to discern between a racist act and a neutral situation.

Serial Emigration.   In addition to identifiable syndromes, certain life experiences common to Afro Caribbean people can result in a unique set of significant mental health issues. One such circumstance that can play a pivotal role in the emotional well being of Caribbean immigrants is the serial emigration to a host country, most commonly the United States, Canada or Great Britain. This is an extremely common practice among West Indian families, dating back to the 1920's when economic devastation resulted in the need to seek a better life in the colonizing country.

Smith, Lalonde, and Johnson (2004) studied this phenomenon to determine the long term impact on the Caribbean children and families who had moved consecutively to the mainland. Children may be separated from their families anywhere from one or two to as long as ten or more years prior to reunification. The child or children are left with family members such as grandparents or aunts, kinship relatives such as Godparents or in some instances a friend or neighbor. They are then reunited with the parent or parents who may have since had children born in the new country, or may have taken younger siblings with them, leaving the older ones to come when financially able. This longitudinal study used survey methods to assess the mental health of individuals who had experienced this type of immigration. Their findings indicate a significantly greater identification with the caregiver than with the biological parent(s). Moreover, the youngsters had decreased self esteem upon reunification in the foreign country. Researchers found lower self esteem, lower family cohesion at the time of reunification and when the study was administered, and less identification with family members and caregivers. Boys were significantly more likely than girls to display lower self esteem and to engage in deviant behavior and not conform to the desires of their parents/caregivers (Smith, Lalonde, & Johnson, 2004).

Misdiagnosis and Labeling of Learning Disabilities.   As previously mentioned, another factor of major concern is the diagnosis and misdiagnosis of Caribbean school-aged children. Labels of "learning disability" and "mild mental retardation" can be placed on children who are more likely suffering from "educational deprivation" (Gopaul-McNicol, 1993). Natural disasters also play a role in compromised school functioning. When the islands suffer a major disaster, the school system can be shut down for weeks or months at a time. Parents with means often decide to send their children abroad to continue their education. These youngsters are uprooted in the middle of their academic year, and can be sent to a foreign school system. Adjustment can be a retarding experience for what would otherwise be an average student. Moreover, the separation from family members can create separation anxiety and may even result in acting out behavior in an attempt to force reunification with family and culture.

Substance Abuse and Addiction.   No discussion of special disorders within the Caribbean population is complete without consideration of the high prevalence of substance abuse disorders. This issue has burgeoned within the past several years due to the Caribbean's increasing role as a transshipment lane for illegal substances, primarily cocaine and marijuana. The use of Caribbeans as "mules" or smugglers exposes them to these substances. Upon their arrival in the United States, they may find a culture that promotes drug use among a variety of classes. The incidence of drug use among the Afro Caribbean population of the U.S. has had a deleterious effect on their overall status as the "Model Black Minority". Jamaicans are as likely to be associated with a gang or "Posse" in the public mind as persons of high accomplishment. In addition, the prevailing attitude of marijuana as a "natural" herb, and a part of the Rastafari religious culture, tends to enhance the use of this substance among many Afro Caribbean teens.

It is an economic reality that drug production and distribution are important sources of income for the Jamaican economy, and less so for the Haitian economy (Griffith, 1997). The increasingly widespread use of these substances continues to wreak havoc on the once closely interconnected communities and the communal structure of the Caribbean. There has been an enormous increase in drug-affected newborns over the past twenty years. These children may grow up to be neurologically, emotionally and socially impaired, experiencing dysfunctional family structures and chronic school failure. The overwhelming impact of chronic poverty and generational dysfunction has had a deleterious effect on a significant subsection of the Caribbean Black community and their ability to succeed in mainstream America.

SPECIAL THERAPIES AND HEALERS

Traditional Healers

Traditional healers are an essential part of the overall treatment community for many persons of Caribbean descent. While all cultures within the West Indian Diaspora have the traditional healer, some are more open and accepting of their presence than others. In the English-speaking Caribbean there are two primary practices identified as those of indigenous healers, although there are many more subgroups and branches within the three main areas. There are the Obeah practitioners primarily of the Eastern Caribbean and the Voodoo or Witch doctors who originate in Haiti (Black, 1996). However, within the theology and practice of VooDoo found in Haiti, Obeah in the English Caribbean, and other traditional spiritual practices found throughout the Caribbean, many African Gods in the pantheon of traditionally Catholic deities are also included (Dudley-Grant, 1999).

For example, Voodoo originated in Haiti, and has been described as "a conglomeration of beliefs and rites of African origin, which having been closely mixed with Catholic practice, has come to be the religion of the greater part of the peasants and the urban proletariat of the black republic of Haiti. Its devotees ask of it what men have always asked of religion: remedy of ills, satisfaction of needs and the hope of survival" (Metraux, 1959, p. 27). One could suggest that the difference between prayer to saints and to spirits is simply a matter of class and culture rather than a true distinction of experience. In addition, within the Spanish-speaking Caribbean, there are the *Espiritistas, Spiritists* or *Curanderos* who primarily perform the same faith healing and intervening functions found in the English-speaking Caribbean.

It is important to note that these indigenous faiths are practiced concomitantly with active participation in traditional Christian religions. Thus, in this author's collaboration with an Espiritista, it was revealed that several members of the prominent middle and upper class of the community, quite active in the church, also came regularly to her for guidance on problems ranging from relationships to success in political careers (Dudley-Grant, 1999). What is extremely interesting is that when one considers the rituals of the Catholic and High Anglican or Episcopal Church, the worship of this or that patron saint is very akin to homage paid to the Voodoo gods. Furthermore, the priests of each sect or practice can be held in the same awe and reverence, with the expectation of a closer connection with God, however that may be conceptualized.

Religious Counselors

Of the 15% of the U.S. population that use mental health services in a given year, about 2.8% receive care only from members of the clergy (Larson, Hohmann, Kessler, Meador, Boyd, & McSherry 1988). The Afro Caribbean community does tend to be a highly spiritual one, varying from high Roman Catholic or Episcopal, to the more fundamentalist such as the Rosicrucians or the Charismatics. The fastest growing religions throughout the Caribbean tend to be the Seventh Day Adventists, and the many newly formed religious sects such as the "Speak the Word Ministries" imported from the southern United States. These newer faiths tend to make attempts at meeting the multiple needs of the community, and will often include counseling services as well as gender specific programming for young people. Persons with emotional disturbances and their families will most often seek out intervention from their spiritual leaders, as this is the approach with the least stigma attached.

Thus, collaboration with spiritual leaders can be a highly effective approach to culturally competent delivery of mental health services (Richards & Bergin, 2000). Providing workshops at church gatherings and school functions on topics such as early detection of mental illness, stress management, and substance abuse prevention helps to place the message and the messenger in a normalized setting.

Extended Family Therapy

The communally oriented culture of the Caribbean American is frequently more responsive to family based interventions than to individual treatment. This is particularly true in times of disaster when the natural response results in a banding together to care for each other. Nancy Boyd-Franklin (1989) has identified multimodal family therapy as most effective for working with African Americans in treatment. This form of intervention also meets the highly integrated extended family system found within the Caribbean American family and community structure.

Herbal Baths or Sea Baths

Bathing as a ritual form of healing tends to be an often utilized traditional intervention. Parents or spiritual healers will bathe their children in "bush" such as Bay leaves or St. John's bush, to cure everything from allergies to anxiety. Sea Baths are seen as the ultimate cure, and one is often referred to "Dr. Neptune" to address all manner of maladies, emotional as well as physical.

Meditation and Other Nontraditional Practices

Other therapies that are culturally responsive for Afro Caribbean Americans are those that build on the convergence of eastern and western philosophies, found in practices such as mindfulness meditation, soul retrieval practices, workshops on stress management and reduction, and cultural hegemony. As has been previously emphasized, the Caribbean culture represents a unique blend of many ethnicities, languages, values and religious beliefs and practices. Therefore, the Afro Caribbean is more open to nontraditional interventions, or those that are reflective of other than the western culture.

Considerations for Medications and Therapies

Thirty three percent of African Americans and 37% of Asians are slow metabolizers of several antipsychotic medications and antidepressants (such as tricyclic antidepressants and selective serotonin reuptake inhibitors) (Lin et al., 1997, cited in Reports of the Surgeon General, Chapter 2, 2001). This awareness should lead to more cautious prescribing practices, which usually entails starting patients at lower doses in the beginning of treatment.

Reliance on psychoactive traditional and alternative healing methods (such as medicinal plants and herbs) may result in interactions with prescribed pharmacotherapies. The result could be greater side effects and enhanced or reduced effectiveness of the pharmacotherapy, depending on the agents involved and their concentrations (Lin et al., 1997, cited in Reports of the Surgeon General, Chapter 2, 2001).

High salt and high fat diets must be considered in prescribing medications. Like African people throughout the Diaspora, Caribbean Blacks may be at increased risk for hypertension and diabetes. The counselor is especially cautioned when treating a person for stress or anxiety related ailments, as there is a higher likelihood of undetected hypertension. The high carbohydrate diet found in "provisions" (potato and rice based foods, the dietary staple of the Caribbean) also results in a tendency towards obesity, particularly in women (and to a lesser extent men) from the lower income strata of the community. A major disease that is found in this ethnic group is sickle cell anemia. The emotional toll on the individual and the family is enormous. While the disease is not the virtual death sentence in childhood that it once was, it still carries enormous challenges for all aspects of treatment.

Talk therapies are not popular among older generations as they tend to be more private. Consider the use of family based interventions, and collaboration with religious or indigenous healers. Excessive screaming or emotional displays are not necessarily a sign of an acute psychotic episode. This highly demonstrative culture is more comfortable with excessive displays of emotion, both positive and negative, than is usually expressed within the dominant culture.

Practice of rituals, such as full moon ceremonies, ritual cleansing of doorways and objects, and other behaviors need to be clearly evaluated before being labeled as symptomatic of mental illness such as Obsessive Compulsive Disorder or Paranoia.

SPECIAL CONSIDERATIONS FOR DISASTERS AND TRAUMA

There is the potential for retraumatization in a disaster situation for those immigrants who have escaped devastation in their homeland, with both political and natural disasters as a common life experience (Bibb & Casimir, 1996). Perez Foster (2001) has identified the stages of immigrant trauma which can lead to greater vulnerability and can present psychiatric symptomatology.

Stages of Immigrant Trauma

As noted above, the formidable immigrant mental health literature that has emerged in the last decade attests to the complex psychosocial stressors that appear to be endemic to the immigrant experience. However, the most recent reports in this area have begun to identify specific stressors and their cumulative effects as precipitants of the symptoms of distress – i.e., PTSD and clinical levels of anxiety and depression – associated with immigrant trauma. Desjarlais et al. (1995, as reported in Perez Foster, 2001) concluded that it is not migration alone but, rather, traumatic or derailing events before, during, or after dislocation that lead to psychological distress of clinical proportions.

This new literature identifies four migration stages at which there is significant potential for traumatogenic experiences that may lead to serious psychological distress:

- Pre-Migration Trauma: events experienced just prior to migration that were a chief determinant of the relocation;
- Traumatic events experienced during transit to the new country;
- Continuing traumatogenic experiences during the process of asylum-seeking and resettlement;
- Substandard living conditions in the host country resulting from unemployment, inadequate supports, and minority persecution (Perez Foster, 2001).

While much has been written regarding the trauma of immigration, it is essential to herald the innate strengths in being a survivor in a new country. Boneva et al. (1998) studied migration attitudes in part of the former Soviet Union. Their premise was that those who choose to leave their country of origin have higher achievement and power motivation and lower affiliation motivation than those who want to stay.

The model was tested with 1050 college students in Albania, the Czech Republic, and Slovenia, with data collected between 1993 and 1996. They also tested the model in migration attitudes in students in Pittsburg, Pennsylvania. They found that those who wanted to leave the region of their university after graduation scored significantly higher on achievement and power motivation than those who wanted to stay, as did the Eastern European students. This study supports the personal experience of this author, herself a Caribbean immigrant who found that the motivation to migrate has proven to be a strong symbol of the psychological resilience of the individual.

Hesitancy to Use External Assistance

Cultural factors tend to encourage the use of family, traditional healers, and informal sources of care rather than treatment-seeking behavior, as noted earlier. In general, African Americans tend to deny the threat of mental illness and strive to overcome mental health problems through self-reliance and determination (Snowden, 1998). This may particularly be the case for Caribbean populations, especially if the individual's status is questionable or the natural mistrust of the "system" frequently found in the immigrant population has not yet abated. Stepick et al. (2001) identified a lack of connection to the larger community resulting from a lack of information about resources, as well as past disappointments which reaffirmed the distrust of government brought from their island nation. Moreover, there may be a hesitancy to seek external assistance born of shame and avoidance to reveal the extent of the subjugation and vulnerability experienced in the country of origin to an ethnic stranger (Perez Foster, 2001). In a time of disaster, when the sense of security is lost, one tends to turn away from the unfamiliar to attempt to put some pieces of known reality back together. This "turning inwards" can be used to strengthen bonds as well as foster empowerment. Hence it is essential that disaster response workers, service providers, and disaster policy makers respect the values and wishes of the Afro Caribbean people, allowing the offered assistance to build on the natural resourcefulness and resilience that is inherent in the community.

Generational Variations

The older generations tend to have more trauma due to more difficult migration experiences and difficulties in acculturation. Two responses to trauma are possible. On the one hand, the individual can call on existing resources to manage the trauma. On the other hand, posttraumatic stress disorder can result in greater difficulty in managing the disaster and response (Dudley-Grant et al., 2000).

Variations in the Expression of Mental and Behavioral Disorders

The "response to trauma" literature has emphasized the importance of normalizing stress based on emotional dysfunction when providing mental health interventions in disasters (American Red Cross, 1995). In Haiti, one can be surrounded by overwhelming poverty and suffering, and yet live a joyous life, buoyed by the hopefulness of the human spirit (O'Keeffe, 1999). Similarly, in Jamaica as elsewhere, a strong sense of self has been associated with ability to manage in the face of adversity. Hence, in the face of disasters or major trauma, it could be expected that the Afro Caribbean individual can attempt to minimize their emotional distress and take a more optimistic view of their future ability to recover. While this posture can cover more deep seeded emotional issues, strengthening self efficacy and family ties can be essential aspects of culturally competent intervention (GoPaul-McNicol, 1993).

Bilingual immigrants may have specific needs for a bilingual and/or bicultural clinician to help them articulate their needs. One of these is the use of religion to assist in overcoming the effects of the disaster. This behavior appears to be true of Southern Blacks as well as Caribbean peoples. In a survey conducted immediately after Hurricane Katrina with evacuees in the Houston Astro Dome, 92% of the 680 randomly selected adults over 18 reported that religion played an important role in helping them get through the first two weeks after the storm (Vickie M. Mays, personal communication via email sent to Division 45 list serve, generated 9/17/05). Due to the high level of spiritual beliefs and practices within the Caribbean Black community, it is essential that the role of religion in the victim's life be assessed. It may be necessary to assist the individual in accessing faith-based social support or interventions as needed.

SOME CLOSING RECOMMENDATIONS

The Caribbean culture provides a rich opportunity to observe the potential for movement towards intercultural functioning. The inherent resilience and pride of Caribbean people, whatever their level of economic, academic or social achievement must be recognized and respected. There are significant challenges in migrating and integrating into the American culture. While the Afro Caribbean makes great strides in achieving their objectives, they do so in the face of the inherent racism of the American culture, which serves as a further barrier to those inherent in the immigrant experience.

Culturally competent disaster interventions must be mindful of the current needs of the individual. However, they must also avoid stereotyping and offering assistance in ways which are not culturally appropriate. Respect for the level of acculturation of the individual, their personal and family resources, and their sense of self, are key ingredients in a successful intervention.

Ultimately, it is the sincerity of the provider and their authentic willingness to interface with a culturally different individual that can transcend the inevitable barriers of race, dialect, language and culture. The willingness to learn as much from the client as they are receiving from you, will ultimately determine the success of the intervention. An open mind, a sincere heart, and a respectful demeanor are the most important tools that any clinician, service provider, or responder can utilize to engage the Afro Caribbean client in the process of recovery from disaster and trauma.

References

American Red Cross. (1995). *Disaster mental health services: Participants' workbook.* Washington, DC: Author.

Anduze, A. (1993, May). *Controversy in the use of non-conventional medicines in the Caribbean.* Paper presented at 18th annual conference of the Caribbean Studies Association, Jamaica.

Bibb, A. & Casimir, G. J. (1996). Haitian families. In M. McGoldrick, J. Pearce, & J. Giordano (Eds.), *Ethnicity and family therapy* (pp. 97–111). New York: Guilford Press.

Black, L. (1996). Families of African origin: An overview. In M. McGoldrick, J. Giordano & J. K. Pearce. *Ethnicity & family therapy* (2nd ed.) (pp. 57–65). New York: Guilford.

Boneva, B., Frieze, I. H., Ferligoj, A., Pauknerová, D., & Orgocka, A. (1998). Achievement, power, and affiliation motives as clues to emigration desires: A four-countries comparison. *European Psychologist, 3,* 247–254.

Boyd-Franklin, N. (1989). *Black families in therapy: A multisystems approach.* New York: Guilford Press.

Bowser, B. (1995). *Racism and anti-racism in world perspective.* Thousand Oaks, CA: Sage Publications.

Brice-Baker, J. (1996). Jamaican families. In M. McGoldrick, J. Pearce, & J. Giordano (Eds.), *Ethnicity and family therapy* (pp. 85–96). New York: Guildford Press.

Comas-Diaz, L., & Jacobsen, F. M. (2001). Ethnocultural allodynia. *Journal of Psychotherapy Practice and Research, 10,* 246–252.

Dahlstrom, W. G., & Gynther, M. D. (1986). Previous MMPI research on Black Americans. In W. G. Dahlstrom, D. Lachar, & L. E. Dahlstrom (Eds.), *MMPI patterns of American minorities* (pp. 24–49). Minneapolis: University of Minnesota Press.

DSM IV – Diagnostic and Statistical Manual of Mental Disorders, Fourth edition (1994). Washington, DC: American Psychiatric Association.

Dinham, P. (2002). Life in south Florida, Posted Saturday Oct. 5, 2002. Retrieved September 9, 2005, from jamaicans.com electronic newsletter. http://www.jamaicans.com/jamaicansoverseas/miami/sociallife-2.shtml

Dovidio, J. F., Gaertner, S. E., Kawakami, K., & Hodson, G. (2002). Why can't we just get along? Interpersonal biases and interracial distrust. *Cultural Diversity & Ethnic Minority Psychology, 8,* 88–102.

Dudley-Grant, G. R. (1998). Disaster response in cultural context: "Slow, not stupid". In A. Barnard, G. R. Dudley-Grant, G. Mendez, I. Rothgeb, & J. Zinn, (Eds.). *Hurricane stress handbook.* St. Thomas, U.S. Virgin Islands: Association of Virgin Islands Psychologists, published with a Grant from the Committee for the Advancement of Professional Psychology, American Psychological Association.

Dudley-Grant, G. R. (1999, August). Psychologists and indigenous healers in the Caribbean. In M. A. Garcia (Chair), *Collaboration between traditional healers and psychologists.* Symposium conducted at the 107th annual convention of the American Psychological Association, Boston, MA.

Dudley-Grant, G. R., Mendez, G. I., & Zinn, J. (2000). Strategies for anticipating and preventing psychological trauma of hurricanes through community education. *Professional Psychology: Research and Practice, 31,* 387–392.

Dudley-Grant, G. R. (2003). Perspectives on spirituality and psychology in ethnic populations. In J.S. Mio & G.Y. Iwamasa (Eds.), *Culturally diverse mental health: The challenges of research and resistance* (pp. 341–359).New York: Brunner-Routledge.

Factbites: Where results make sense: Factbites. (n.d.). Retrieved September 5, 2005, from: http://www.factbites.com/topics/Haiti 9/5/05

Gereau, L. K. (1993). HUGO – A spiritual battle. In G. I. Joseph & H. Rowe (Eds.), *Hell under God's orders* (pp. 116–119). St. Croix, VI: Winds of Change Press.

Gopaul-McNicol, S. (1993). *Working with West Indian families.* New York: Guilford Press.

Gopaul-McNicol, S., & Armour-Thomas, E. (2001). *Assessment and culture.* New York: Academic Press.

Griffith, I. L. (1997). *Drugs and security in the Caribbean: Sovereignty under siege.* Pennsylvania: Pennsylvania State University Press.

Group for the Advancement of Psychiatry. (2002). *Cultural assessment in clinical psychiatry.* Washington, DC: American Psychiatric Publishing.

Heath, C. D. (n.d.) Womanist ethics and inequality in women's mental health: A transcultural analysis of race, class, and gender. Retrieved September 6, 2005, from: http://www.peoplewho.org/documents/heath.ppt#256

History of Jamaica. Retrieved September 9, 2005, from: http://www.absoluteastronomy.com/encyclopedia/h/hi/history_of_jamaica.htm

Interamerican Development Bank Study (2004). *Sending money home: Remittance to Latin America and the Caribbean.* Interamerican Development Bank: Multilateral Investment Fund (Author). Retrieved September 15, 2005, from: http://www.iadb.org/mif/v2/files/StudyPE2004eng.pdf

Joseph, G. I., & Rowe, H. (1990). *Hell under God's orders*. St. Croix, VI: Winds of Change Press.

Kalmijn, M. (1996). The socioeconomic assimilation of Caribbean American blacks. *Social Forces, 74,* 911–930.

Kasinitz, P. (1992). *Caribbean New York: Black immigrants and the politics of race.* Ithaca, NY: Cornell University Press.

Larsen, L. J. (2004). The foreign-born population in the United States: 2003. *U.S. Census Current Population Reports.* (P20–551). U.S. Census Bureau, Department of Commerce, Economics and Statistics Administration.

Larson, D. B., Hohmann, A. A., Kessler, L. G., Meador, K. G., Boyd, J. H., & McScherry, E. (1988). The couch and the cloth: The need for linkage. *Hospital and Community Psychiatry, 39,* 1064–1069.

Lu, F. G., Lim, R. F., & Mezzich, J. E. (1995). Issues in the assessment and diagnosis of culturally diverse individuals. In J. Oldham & M. Riba (Eds.), *Review of Psychiatry* (Vol. 14, pp. 477–510). Washington, DC: American Psychiatric Press.

Marsella, A. J., & Christopher, M. A. (2004). Ethnocultural considerations in disasters: an overview of research, issues and directions. *Psychiatric Clinics of North America, 27,* 521–539.

McCrae, R. R., & Terracciano, A. (2005). Universal features of personality traits from the observer's perspective: Data from 50 cultures. *Journal of Personality & Social Psychology,* 88(3), 547–561.

Metraux, A. (1959). *Voodoo in Haiti.* Translated by Hugo Charteries. New York: Schocken Books.

Mintz, S. W. (1974). The Caribbean region. In S. W. Mintz (Ed.), *Slavery, colonialism and racism.* (pp. 45–71). New York: W. W. Norton.

Nevaer, L. E. V. (2003). In *Black-Hispanic debate, West Indians side with Hispanics news feature.* Pacific News Service, Dec 04, 2003.

O'Keeffe, K. (July, 1999). Apparent sorrow, contagious joy. *The Other Side* (Vol. 35(4) p. 18.) Retrieved April 9, 2005, from: thurn.ggsrv.com ([165.193.106.28]) by prserv.net (in8) with ESMTP <200504091626561080gvpgeme>

Perez Foster, R. (2001). When immigration is trauma: Guidelines for the individual and family clinician. *American Journal of Orthopsychiatry, 71,* 153–170.

Phelps, L. D. (2003). *Cultural competency, Haitian immigrants, and rural Sussex County, Delaware.* Retrieved August 23, 2005 from: http://www.salisbury.edu/Schools/Henson/ NursingDept/haitiancultcomp/begin.htm

Premdas, R. R. (1996). The Caribbean: Diversity and a typology of identities. *Caribbean perspectives.* Annual Publication of the UVI Eastern Caribbean Center, University of the Virgin Islands, December, 3–7.

Reed, A. (June, 2005). *New scholarship in race and ethnicity, black ethnic options: Afro-Caribbean immigrants and the politics of incorporation.* Reuel Rogers, Northwestern University, speaker; commentators Andrea Simpson, University of Richmond; Rogers Smith, University of Pennsylvania. Retrieved September 10, 2005, from Woodrow Wilson International Center for Scholars, Washington, DC website: http://www.wilsoncenter.org/index.cfm?fuseaction= events.event_summary&event_id=121481

Reports of the Surgeon General, US Public Health Service. (2001). *Mental Health: A report of the surgeon general. Chapter 2, Overview of cultural diversity and mental health services.* Retrieved September 13, 2005 from: http://www.surgeongeneral.gov/library/mentalhealth/ chapter2/sec8.html#family

Richards, P. S., & Bergin, A. E. (2000). *Handbook of psychotherapy and religious diversity.* Washington, DC: American Psychological Association.

Russo, S. A., & Lewis, J. E. (1999). The cross-cultural applications of the KAIT: Case studies with three differentially acculturated women. *Cultural Diversity & Ethnic Minority Psychology, 5,* 76–85.

Smith, A., Lalonde, R. N., & Johnson, S. (2004, May). Serial migration and its implications for the parent-child relationship: A retrospective analysis of the experiences of the children of Caribbean immigrants. *Cultural Diversity & Ethnic Minority Psychology,* 10(2), 107–122.

Snowden, L. R. (1998). Racial differences in informal help seeking for mental health problems. *Journal of Community Psychology, 26*, 429–438.

Sternberg, R. J. (1987). *Beyond I.Q.* Cambridge, England: Cambridge University Press.

Stepick, A., Stepick, C. D., & Kretsedemas, P. (2001). Civic engagement of Haitian immigrants & Haitian Americans in Miami Dade County. Haiti – Immigration and Ethnicity Institute of South Florida, Retrieved November 16, 2006 from the Haitian American Foundation, Inc., Human Services Coalition of Miami-Dade County, Kellogg Foundation Web site: http://www.wkkf.org/pubs/Devolution/Pub3670.pdf

Whatley, P. R., Allen, J., & Dana, R. H., (2003), Racial identity and the MMPI in African American male college students. *Cultural Diversity and Ethnic Minority Psychology, 9*, 345–353.

Willocks, H. W. L. (1995). *The umbilical cord: The history of the United States Virgin Islands from pre-Columbian era to the present.* St. Croix, USVI: Author.

Young, V. H. (1993). *Becoming West Indian: Culture, self and nation in St. Vincent.* Washington, DC: Smithsonian Institution Press.

Chapter 8

Chinese Americans: Guidelines for Disaster Mental Health Workers

Frederick T. L. Leong and Szu-Hui Lee

INTRODUCTION

The purpose of the present chapter is to provide disaster mental health counselors with some baseline information about Chinese Americans so that they may work more effectively with this group of clients. In 2002, the American Psychological Association adopted the multicultural counseling competency guidelines. Multicultural counseling competence is defined as counselors' attitudes/beliefs, knowledge, and skills in working with culturally diverse clients (see Sue, Bernier, Durran, et al., 1982; Sue, Arredondo, & McDavis, 1992). Even before the adoption of these guidelines, the need for mental health providers to move beyond "cultural sensitivity" (i.e., the attitudes and beliefs component of the competency guidelines) to "culture-specific knowledge" (i.e., the knowledge component of competency guidelines) has been noted as an important factor to consider when working with clients (Leong & Kim, 1991). In keeping with this movement towards increasing specificity in cross-cultural counseling and the shift from purely consciousness-raising activities to actual prescriptive knowledge, this chapter is intended to provide culture-specific information about Chinese Americans with a particular focus on disaster assistance efforts.

The multicultural counseling competency guidelines outline three areas of competencies for the culturally-skilled counseling psychologist. The first area, which concerns *belief and attitudes*, requires that the culturally-skilled counseling psychologist be culturally aware, in touch with his or her own biases about minority clients, comfortable with such differences, and sensitive to circumstances which may require the referral of minority clients to a same-culture counselor. The second area consists of *knowledge* (i.e., information sets) which the culturally-skilled counseling psychologist should have, including an understanding of the effects of the sociopolitical system within the United States on minorities, culture-specific knowledge about the particular group being counseled, an understanding of the generic characteristics of counseling and psychotherapy, and knowledge of institutional barriers to the minority's utilization of mental health services. Finally, the culturally-skilled counseling psychologist should have the following *skills*: a wide repertoire of verbal and nonverbal responses to send messages accurately and appropriately, with the ability to use appropriate institutional interventions where needed. The importance and viability of this tripartite training framework was reaffirmed when the model was incorporated in another landmark paper calling for the development of multicultural counseling competencies within the counseling profession (Sue et al., 1992).

For the purposes of the present chapter, it is the second dimension of this tripartite training model, namely *knowledge*, which is most relevant. In the multicultural counseling competency guidelines, Sue, Arredondo, and McDavis (1992) proposed that "culturally skilled counselors possess specific knowledge and information about the particular group that they are working with. They are aware of the life experiences, cultural heritage, and historical background of their culturally different clients..." (p. 482). We will use this training framework in providing culture-specific information about Chinese Americans which would enable counselors to work more effectively with this ethnic group. However, it should be pointed out that there are varying levels of cultural "specificity" in information. While it would be useful for counselors to learn about Asian Americans as an ethnic minority group, there is sufficient heterogeneity within the Asian American groups that sub-group or within-group information is also highly valuable. At the same time, it should also be recognized that given the historical trend in the counseling field, much more of our existing knowledge-base has been focused on larger ethnic groups (e.g., Asian Americans) rather than specific subgroups (e.g., Chinese Americans).

To achieve the purpose outlined above, this chapter will be divided into four parts. In the first part, we will provide a demographic profile of Chinese Americans in the United States. The second part will cover the key culturally relevant factors mental health provides should pay special attention to when working with Chinese Americans. This review will provide a more holistic understanding of Chinese Americans, beyond demographics. The third part will focus on clinical issues based on empirical knowledge for treating Chinese Americans. Due to the brevity of the current chapter, the final section of this chapter will end with an overview of additional resources, including assessment instruments that have shown valuable clinical utility, to which the reader can refer in order to gain a deeper understanding of Chinese Americans.

DEMOGRAPHIC PROFILE OF CHINESE AMERICANS

According to 2000 Census data, Asian Americans make up 4.2% of the United States population. Chinese Americans are 23.8% of all Asian Americans, making them the largest Asian group in the United States (Reeves & Bennet, 2004). In 1990, Chinese Americans, numbering approximately 1.65 million, made up 0.7% of the United States population (Barringer, Gardner, & Levin, 1993). By 2000, the population increased to over 2.4 million, or 0.86% of the population. People who reported their race as Chinese in addition to one or more races numbered at 2.86 million, or 1.02% of the total U.S. population. Chinese Americans have approximately the same median age as the nation overall: 35 years (Reeves & Bennet, 2004). They are heavily concentrated on the West Coast (54.1%), but are sparse in the Midwest. The vast majority of Chinese Americans live in urban areas. As a group, they have very low divorce rates. Out-marriage rates to people of other races are 22.5% for males and 10.9% for females (Barringer et al., 1993). Although Chinese in the United States have a slightly greater proportion of people who have less than a high school education (23%) compared to the total population (19.6%), they also have four-year college completion rates (48%) that are nearly twice as high as national averages (Reeves & Bennet, 2004). However, there is evidence that Chinese Americans do not benefit as much economically from high levels of educational attainment as other groups (Huang, 1991).

There are significant within group differences such that some Chinese Americans are well educated and highly acculturated, but others have very low educational levels and are more traditional (Sue & Sue, 1991). Chinese Americans are clustered in the technical/professional fields like engineering or medicine, as well as the service industry and sales or office positions. They are significantly more likely to be employed in management, professional, or related fields (52.3%) than all workers in the U.S. (33.6%). Finally, in 1999, median family income for Chinese Americans ($60,058) was significantly higher than the national median ($50,046). However, the poverty rate of Chinese Americans (13.5%) was higher than that of the general population (12.4%) (Reeves & Bennet, 2004), a phenomenon that is indicative of wide income disparities among Chinese Americans in the United States. Please refer to Tables 8.1 through 8.7 for more detailed data regarding the demographic profile of Chinese Americans.

Table 8.1.   Chinese American Population, 1960–2000

Year	Number	Percent Increase Per Year
1960	237,292	5.8
1970	436,062	8.4
1980	812,178	8.6
1990	1,645,472	10.2
2000	2,422,970	4.7

Source: U.S. Census Bureau (2000).

Table 8.2. Chinese Immigrant Arrivals to the United States by Decade

Decade	Number of Chinese Immigrants
1820–1850	43
1851–1860	41,397
1861–1870	64,301
1871–1880	123,201
1881–1890	61,711
1891–1900	14,799
1901–1910	20,605
1911–1920	21,278
1921–1930	29,907
1931–1940	4,928
1941–1950	16,709
1951–1960	25,198
1961–1970	109,771
1971–1980	237,793
1981–1990	444,962
1991–2000	528,893

Source: U. S. Office of Immigration Statistics (2000).

Table 8.3. Chinese Population in the United States, 1860–2000

Year	Total	Male	Female	Sex Ratio (males per 100 females)	Foreign Born (%)	% Under Age 14
1860	34,933	33,149	1,784	1,858		
1870	63,199	58,633	4,566	1,284	99.8	
1880	105,465	100,686	4,779	2,106	99.0	
1890	107,475	103,607	3,868	2,679	99.3	
1900	87,863	85,341	4,522	1,887	90.7	3.4
1910	71,531	66,856	4,675	1,430	79.3	
1920	61,639	53,891	7,748	696	69.9	12.0
1930	74,954	59,802	15,152	395	58.8	20.4
1940	77,504	57,389	20,115	286	48.1	21.1
1950	117,140	76,725	40,415	190	47.0	23.3
1960	236,084	135,430	100,654	135	39.5	33.0
1970	431,538	226,733	204,850	111	46.9	26.6
1980	812,178	410,936	401,246	102	63.3	21.1
1990	1,645,472	818,542	827,154	99	69.3	19.3
2000	2,422,970				37.5	21.4

Source: Adapted from Glenn (1983); U.S. Census Bureau (2000).

Table 8.4.   Chinese Population in the United States by Major States, 1990 and 2000

	1990		2000	
State	Number	Percent	Number	Percent
California	704,850	42.8	1,222,187	50.4
New York	284,144	17.3	451,859	18.6
Hawaii	68,804	4.2	170,803	7.0
Texas	63,232	3.8	121,588	5.1
New Jersey	59,084	3.6	110,263	4.6
Massachusetts	53,792	3.3	92,380	3.8
Illinois	49,936	3.0	86,095	3.6
Washington	33,962	2.1	75,884	3.1
Rest of U.S.	327,668	19.9	91,911	3.8
Total	1,645,472	100.0	2,422,970	100.0

Source: U.S. Census Bureau (2000).

Table 8.5.   Occupational Characteristics of the Chinese and White Populations, Ages 25–64, in the United States, 2000 (in percentages)

Occupations	Chinese Total	White Total
Professional, Management, and related	52.3	36.6
Service	13.9	13.4
Sales and office	20.8	27.0
Farming, fishing, and forestry	0.1	0.6
Construction, extraction, and maintenance	2.6	9.8
Production, transportation, and material moving	10.4	13.6

Source: U.S. Census Bureau (2000); see also Reeves & Bennet (2004).

Table 8.6.   Educational Attainment of Chinese and White Populations in the United States, 2000 (in percentages)

Education	Chinese	White
Less than High School	23.0	10.5
High School Graduate	13.2	29.5
Some College or Associate's Degree	15.8	28.0
Bachelor's Degree or More	48.1	26.1

Source: U.S. Census Bureau (2000); see also Reeves & Bennet (2004).

Table 8.7. Indicators of Economic Status for Asian Ethnic Groups in Comparison to Other Groups (1999)

Group Level	Median Family Income	Percent in Poverty
White	$53,356	6.3
Black	$33,255	21.6
Hispanic	$34,397	20.0
Asian and Pacific Islander	$59,324	12.6
Chinese	$60,058	13.5
Japanese	$70,849	9.7
Filipino	$65,189	6.3
Korean	$47,624	14.8
Asian Indian	$70,708	9.8
Vietnamese	$47,103	16.0

Source: U.S. Bureau of the Census (2000).

GOING BEYOND DEMOGRAPHICS TOWARDS A DEEPER UNDERSTANDING OF CHINESE AMERICANS

Historical Context

Historically, Chinese Americans have faced discrimination in the form of immigration exclusion acts. They have been stereotyped as exotic, unassimilable, and immoral. More recently, stereotypes portray them as law-abiding, quiet, intelligent, and hardworking (Gaw, 1982). Gaw suggests that both kinds of stereotypes are harmful because they ignore individual differences and prevent accurate assessments of the mental health needs of Chinese Americans.

According to Huang (1991), some of the social and psychological issues Chinese Americans face relate to their interaction with U.S. society. These include the immigration experience and its stresses (e.g., culture shock, alienation), racism, and discrimination. One could also add to this list anti-immigrant sentiment and harassment, which may be compounded by language barriers that some Chinese Americans face. Taking into consideration the historical context of the Chinese American experience in the U.S. would help mental health providers to obtain a fuller and more holistic understanding of their Chinese American clients. Please refer to Table 8.8 for more detailed listing of the historical dates exemplifying the Chinese experience in the United States.

BELIEF SYSTEMS AND WORLDVIEWS

As with all cultural groups, it is important to understand Chinese Americans' belief systems and worldviews. Historically, Chinese conceptions of mental health and mental illness have moved from supernatural beliefs, to emphasis

Table 8.8. The Chinese Experience in the United States: Key Historical Dates

19th Century	Soon after the first Chinese immigrants arrive in the United States, racially grounded bias surfaces and restrictive laws are enacted.
1848–49	Large numbers of Chinese come to the United States to strike it rich in the California gold rush.
1854	In *The People v. George W. Hall*, the California Supreme Court states that "Chinese, and all other people not white, are included in the prohibition from being witnesses against whites."
1868	Under the Burlingame Treaty, Chinese laborers are encouraged to enter the United States to help build the transcontinental railroads but are denied citizenship.
Oct. 16, 1876	The Workingman's Party of California, advocating an end to Chinese immigration, asserts: "To an American death is preferable to life on a par with the Chinaman. Treason is better than to labor beside a Chinese slave."
1882	The Chinese Exclusion Act bans immigration of all Chinese laborers and miners for 10 years. The law is extended for 10 years in 1892, for two years in 1902 and indefinitely in 1904, until its eventual repeal nearly four decades later.
1884	The Democratic National Platform declares, "American civilization demands that against the immigration of Mongolians to these shores our gates be closed."
1920's	With one notable exception, the prohibition against immigration from Asia remains firmly in place during the decade following World War I.
1924	Congress Passes the National Origins Act, prohibiting nearly all immigration by Asians.
1940's	Americans of Japanese descent are persecuted during World War II, but there is new respect for China, a U.S. ally in the war.
1943	Congress repeals the Chinese Exclusion Act and also permits Chinese residents to become naturalized U.S. citizens.
Postwar Era	Legal barriers to Asian immigration are dismantled after World War II. A residue of anti-Asian prejudice, however, remains.
1952	The Immigration and Nationality (McCarran-Walter) Act makes foreign-born persons of all Asian groups eligible for U.S. citizenship.
1957	Tsung Dao Lee of Columbia University and Chen Ning Yang of Princeton's Institute Advanced Study are awarded the Nobel Prize in physics. Both were born in China and became naturalized U.S. citizens.
1965	The Immigration Act opens the way to large-scale immigration from Asian countries for the first time.
June 19, 1982	Vincent Chin, a Chinese American, is fatally beaten in Detroit by two white autoworkers. Many Asian Americans are outraged when the two are sentenced to only three years' probation.
Feb. 15, 1990	Professor Chang-Lin Tien, a mechanical engineer born in China, is named chancellor of the University of California at Berkeley. He is the first Asian American chosen to head a University of California campus.
Nov. 29, 1990	President George H. W. Bush signs into law a bill allowing immigration to climb from about 500,000 persons annually to about 700,000 for the first three years of the act.
Contemporary	1. Numerous illegal Chinese immigrant workers enter the U.S. to work in low paying jobs.
	2. China emerges as a major global economic power, eliciting mixed responses from the government and U.S. population because of perceived threats to the economy.
	3. Chinese Americans are perceived as "high achievers" in school and in the workplace, eliciting some resentment.
	4. Continued physical assaults on Asians in major cities.

on natural forces (e.g., wind), to a somatic focus on the human body as a source of abnormality. Since the 19th century, psychological causes for mental illness have been accepted, although in some cases the preferred method of treatment is still herbs and medicine (Lum, 1982).

Huang (1991) suggests the traditional Chinese worldview revolves around interconnections between mind and body, parent and child, and neighbor and neighbor. While Westerners value autonomy and independence, Chinese traditionally value harmony, togetherness, and unity. Chinese culture was traditionally a shame-based culture that emphasized public disgrace as punishment, as opposed to the Western guilt-oriented culture's emphasis on self-blame as punishment. The four primary coping strategies in Chinese culture were endurance, looking the other way, not thinking too much, and activity.

Modern Chinese American values still retain some traditional aspects. According to Sue and Sue (1991), these values include: filial piety, stress on family bonds and unity, importance of roles and status, somatization of mental problems, control over strong emotions, emphasis on academic achievement, and low assertiveness. Huang (1991) points out that emotional problems still tend to be expressed in somatic ways. As such, most Chinese Americans do not view "talk therapy" as particularly helpful and seek therapy only as a last resort.

Finally, Chinese American culture values self-control and inhibition of strong emotions, and individuals learn that their behavior is very significant in that it reflects upon the entire family. If one has feelings that might disrupt family harmony, one is expected to restrain those feelings (Sue & Sue, 1972). Lin (1958; cited in Huang, 1991, p. 86) comments, "The Chinese worldview emphasizes the interpersonal to such an extent that the Chinese look to their relationships with people instead of to themselves as the cause of their stress."

Acculturation and Ethnic Identity

Sue and Sue (1972, 1990) describe three ways in which Chinese Americans may adjust to the conflicting demands of Asian and American cultures: "traditionalists" retain traditional values and live up to their families' expectations, "marginal persons" become over-westernized by rejecting traditional Asian values and existing in the margin of the two cultures, and "Asian Americans" formulate a new identity that integrates Asian and American cultures without completely rejecting one or the other. Many studies have been devoted to understanding acculturation and its relationship with cultural identity. As Leong and Chou (1994) described, the question of racial and ethnic identity is essentially a two-dimensional problem: how do members of a racial or ethnic minority group view their own culture and how do they view their dominant host culture? These viewpoints towards the original and the host culture can both be either positive or negative, thus the relationship can be illustrated with a two-by-two table (own: positive/negative; host: positive/negative).

Through acculturation models, we are able to identify the different levels of acculturation using such a framework.

It has been consistently recognized that acculturation is a major moderator of the counseling attitudes and experiences of Asian Americans in general, and Chinese Americans in particular (e.g., Sue & Sue, 1972; Leong, 1986; Uba, 1994). According to this viewpoint, highly acculturated Chinese Americans, who are quite Americanized, are more likely to use the western-based mental health and counseling services available in their communities. Relatively little modifications to these western-oriented counseling approaches are needed in order to be successful with these Chinese Americans.

As for the middle group of Chinese Americans who exhibit a medium level of acculturation, some of them may be like their highly acculturated counterparts and be quite willing to use western-oriented services. However, since they are not highly acculturated, they may bring with them certain traditional Chinese values, beliefs, and customs which may interfere with western-oriented services (see Sue & Sue, 1990). Counselors and therapists working with these groups of Chinese Americans need to be flexible and be willing to modify their counseling approaches in order to be helpful to their clients.

On the other hand, Chinese Americans who exhibit a very low level of acculturation are quite likely to resist counseling from these western-oriented mental health agencies. For these Chinese Americans, two types of alternative programs have been suggested to be particularly helpful. First, owing to the high level of stigma associated with mental health problems for Chinese Americans, Sue and Sue (1990) have suggested that counseling may be offered indirectly by targeting problem areas that are much more acceptable to Chinese Americans as initial points of entry. For example, given the high value placed on academic achievement among Chinese Americans, they would be more likely to seek academic and vocational counseling. Within the context of these academic and vocational counseling services, any mental health problems which surface may be addressed in a culturally acceptable manner. The importance of indirectness and subtlety in communication among Asian Americans has been consistently pointed out by investigators (e.g., Leong, 1986; Sue & Sue, 1990). Chinese American clients may also be more motivated to complete the counseling if the interventions were linked to issues that are highly salient to them (e.g., you will be much more able to concentrate on your studies once we have begun to address your depression).

Individualism/Collectivism

Another important dimension of cultural identity and cultural values is the existence of various types of societies – specifically, individualistic and collectivistic societies. Simply put, members of individualistic societies are those whose needs are often put before the needs of the group in which they belong, whereas members of collectivistic societies generally place the needs of their group before their individual needs. It is typical to describe Western societies as being individualistic and Eastern societies as being collectivistic (Hofstede, 1980). Another way to illustrate the differences between these two societies was presented by Hofstede in his research. Hofstede (1980) defined Individualism as a loosely knit social framework in which individuals take care of themselves and their immediate families only; whereas Collectivism is defined as a tightly knit social framework in which individuals are emotionally integrated into an extended family, clan, or other in-group which will protect them in exchange for unquestioned loyalty (pp. 295–296). The societal orientation of a culture certainly affects how its members communicate, make life decisions, and cope with distress. Thus, it is important for psychologists and disaster mental health workers to not overlook such group differences and attend to the needs of clients hailing from diverse groups and societies.

Another concept pivotal to gaining an understanding of Chinese Americans is concerned with self-construal. According to Markus and Kitayama (1991), within each of us there exists the self, and this self is perceived to be either independent or dependent. Having more collectivistic values, which we will discuss later in the chapter, Chinese Americans often conceive of the self as interdependent. Persons from individualistic cultures on the other hand, often view the self within them as independent. As Markus and Kitayama (1991) pointed out, the independent self finds it necessary to strategically express the internal attributes it contains, whereas the interdependent self places importance on relations with others. In other words, the independent self strives to be unique while the interdependent self strives to fit in.

The foundation of self-esteem in individuals with independent selves is the ability to express the self and attain validation for those internal attributes. For the interdependent self, self-esteem is built upon the ability to adjust, restrain the self, and maintain harmony with the social context (Markus & Kitayama, 1991). In order for an assessment to be culturally-appropriate for Chinese Americans, the notion of self-construal must be incorporated into the evaluation process. Psychologists and disaster mental health workers must not make quick generalizing assumptions about Asian Americans. Value differences can cause psychologists and disaster mental health workers to foster inappropriate and ineffective counseling relationships. It is evident that self-construal is an important culture-specific variable affecting both the psychology of Asian Americans and the cultural validity of therapeutic theories.

Communication: High Context vs. Low Context

Cultural competence is defined by Hall (1976) as "the ability to establish interpersonal relationships with persons from different cultures by developing understanding through effective exchange of both verbal and non-verbal levels of behavior." While the thought of communication is simple, how to communicate effectively is the difficult task. As Chan (1992) described, problems with intercultural communication are not simply due to language barriers, they are also the result of differences in thought patterns, values, and communication styles. In fact, the communication styles of Chinese Americans are drastically different from the Eurocentric cultures. Chinese Americans communicate in a high-context style, with context being the primary channel for communication. Direct and specific references to the meaning of the message are not given and receivers must rely on their knowledge of nonverbal cues as well as other subtle affects for interpreting message meaning. In the dominant American culture, however, people communicate via a low-context style where words are the primary channel for communication. Direct, precise, and clear information is delivered verbally and receivers in this case can simply take what is said at face value.

In the high-context style of communication found in Asian cultures, the most meaningful information is conveyed within the physical context which receivers acknowledge and internalize. Unlike the low-context style of typical American communication, comparatively little of the meaningful message is contained in the actual spoken words. Considering the collectivistic culture and interdependent self-construal of Chinese Americans, it is not surprising to find that some of the goals sought by communication are mutual satisfaction of both parties and face saving outcomes (Chan, 1992). The purpose of communication is not merely to achieve goals and attain personal satisfaction. In order to meet their communication goals, Asians have developed an elaborate, subtle, and complex form of interpersonal communication. Such a style enables them to avoid causing shame or loss of face to themselves and others, maintaining harmonious relations between the parties involved in the dialogue. In fact, any form of direct confrontation and verbal assertiveness is considered rude, disrespectful, and in direct opposition to the Asian American preferred way of communication (Chu & Sue, 1984).

Another characteristic of high context communication styles is the reliance on shared experiences/history, formal interpersonal relations, and greater stability with slow changes. Contrary to this, low context communication styles rely on expression of individual experiences, informal interpersonal relations, and less stability and continuity in what is communicated. The preference one has for a communication style (high or low context) certainly influences how one perceives others who use the opposite style. Those that prefer high context communication may perceive those that use low context styles to be too direct and insensitive to context. Those that use low context communication styles may, in turn, perceive high context communicators as indirect, lacking in verbal skills, and even untrustworthy.

Chan (1992) also highlighted several crucial elements found in high context communication styles. First of all, silence is considered valuable and a way to express not only interest but also respect, either from the speaker or receiver's perspective. The use of eye contact is seldom found due to the belief that direct eye contact may imply hostility and aggression. Too much eye contact during communication may thus be perceived as a rude gesture. Similarly, use of body language is selective and some gestures that hint hostility and rudeness are not appreciated. An example of this given by Chan (1992) is the gesture used by Americans to signal "come here", in which the pointing finger is waved with hand raised and palm inward. This particular signal is considered to be hostile and projects superiority. The emphasis on avoidance of conflict in communicative exchange illustrates Asian Americans' focus on achieving and maintaining collective group harmony.

Psychologists and disaster mental health workers must be able to acknowledge such communication style differences and understand how their clients communicate in order to appropriately interpret the messages being delivered. Not doing so would inevitably hinder the development of a therapeutic relationship and, in a way, justify Chinese Americans' reluctance to seek counseling and the premature withdrawal from services typically seen in this population. An implication of this is provided by Leong (1986) and Sue and Morishima (1982): Because Chinese Americans much prefer structured, problem-focused, and task oriented approaches to solving problems, open-ended and ambiguous approaches can be uncomfortable for them. For the counselor, difficulty in understanding the client and obtaining direct and accurate feedback could also cause discomfort. The underlying point is that it is important to recognize elements of the high-context communication style and appreciate the cultural differences that exist. Te (1989) cleverly reminds us that "not all people smile in the same language."

Losing Face

It is also important to consider the notion of loss of face within interpersonal relationships when working with Chinese Americans. The notion of loss of face is consistent with Chinese Americans' collective and interdependent self-construal. In order to maintain harmony with others, one must behave in ways that would not bring shame upon oneself, one's family, and upon others. Any disruption to the harmony is considered a loss of face. Chinese Americans hold great pride in the honor of their families and are taught at an early age to uphold that honor by maintaining and enhancing the family face rather than bringing shame to it. Finally, it is important to note the importance of interpersonal relationships. In American culture, interpersonal relationships can be characterized as informal and collaborative. In Asian American cultures, interpersonal relations tend to be hierarchical with very strong respect and loyalty toward elders and authority (Sue & Sue, 1990). This interpretation of interpersonal relations may play a part in how Asian Americans interact with their counselor or disaster worker. For example, while a counselor may invite the Chinese American client to collaborate in solution seeking by encouraging the client to give their own opinions and suggestions, the Chinese American, seeing the counselor as an authority figure, may feel uncomfortable with collaborating side by side and would much prefer the counselor to give directions and provide steps towards a solution. Psychologists and disaster mental health workers must access the client and understand their preferences for different approaches before a successful therapeutic relationship can be developed.

Personality

Chinese Americans have been found to have high external locus of control and value authoritarianism, filial piety, and traditionalism. In comparing Chinese Americans to European Americans, Vernon (1982) reported that Chinese Americans show greater modesty, humility, self-depreciation, anxiety, immaturity, conformity, inhibition, sensitivity to group pressure, and introversion. Vernon (1982) also noted that Chinese Americans displayed a greater tendency to give socially desirable responses. Compared to European Americans, Chinese Americans have also been found to be less sexually permissive and less condoning of premarital sex. Uba (1994), in her review of studies on Chinese American personalities, agrees with these findings and adds that Chinese Americans tend to be less autonomous, less independent, more inhibited, and more obedient to authority figures than European Americans.

It is interesting to note that many of these contrasts between Chinese American and European American personalities also highlight the differences between collectivistic and individualistic cultures. For many Chinese American clients, these personality traits may cause difficulties in interactions with mainstream culture. It is important to note, however, that they are nevertheless Americans, and therefore will also have similar personality traits to many European American clients. The level of the client's acculturation into the American mainstream is important to keep in mind. Thus, many Chinese Americans function within a marginal area that seeks to balance the similarities and differences they have with mainstream Americans. This "balancing act" alone may be sufficient cause for seeking counseling. Counselors can help their Chinese American clients develop their skills toward expressing their Chinese traits when appropriate (e.g., when spending time with their family members) and employing their American traits when called for (e.g., in a work setting or when interacting with non-Asian friends).

Assertiveness. The clinical literature has long pointed to the lack of assertiveness among Chinese Americans as a potential personality problem. In one of two empirical studies concerned with this hypothesis, Sue, Ino, and Sue (1983) tested the view that Asian Americans are nonassertive and the possibility that they display differential assertiveness depending on situational variables. They were interested in determining if the race of the individual with whom they are interacting is an influential variable on assertion in Asian Americans. The results indicated that Chinese Americans were as assertive as Caucasians on all objective behavioral measures and that the race of experimenter was not an important variable in the performance of Asians. The authors also pointed out that, consistent with previous studies, significant differences on self-report measures were obtained. Chinese Americans were more likely to report anxiety in social situations, greater apprehension in evaluative situations, and lower assertiveness than Caucasians.

In the second study on assertiveness, Sue, Sue, and Ino (1990) used several self-report and behavioral measures to examine the notion that Chinese Americans are passive and nonassertive compared to Caucasian Americans. The findings indicated that Chinese American students were as assertive as the Caucasian participants on all behavioral measures. However, Chinese American students were more apprehensive about social situations than Caucasian students. Hence, the empirical literature does not seem to support the clinical literature that Chinese Americans have problems with assertiveness, and there appears to be a discrepancy between self-report and behavioral measures of assertiveness in this population.

Locus of Control. Another personality dimension that has received some empirical attention among Chinese Americans is Rotter's (1966) concept of locus of control. For example, Hsieh, Shybut, and Lotsof (1969) investigated the relationship between internal versus external control and ethnic group membership among 3 groups of high school participants (Chinese, American-born Chinese, and Anglo-American) using the Internal-External Control Scale. The authors' hypothesis that a belief in internal versus external control is significantly related to ethnic group membership was confirmed, with the Chinese attributing the most control to external forces.

In another study, Cook and Chi (1984) investigated cooperative behavior and the effect of locus of control in American (n = 64) and Chinese American (n = 75) boys aged 8–10 years. Participants from two ethnically homogeneous, lower middle class, urban Catholic schools were administered the Nowicki-Strickland Locus of Control Scale for Children. Nineteen external and 12 internal American participants and 15 external and 15 internal Chinese American participants were randomly paired into groups of internal, external, and mixed locus-of-control dyads, yielding a 2 x 3 between-Ss design. Each pair played a cooperative board game, with latency to achieve a goal as the major dependent measure. The results indicate that (a) overall, Chinese Americans were significantly more external in control attribution than Americans and, when matched on locus of control, were significantly more cooperative than Americans; (b) external dyads were significantly more cooperative than internal or mixed dyads; and (c) in mixed dyads, Chinese Americans took significantly less time, indicating they were more cooperative than Americans. According to the authors, the findings underscore the importance that cultural context plays in the socialization process.

Childrearing Practices. It has been suggested that many of the values and personality traits of Chinese Americans are a product of the way they were raised. In reviewing empirical research on Asian Americans, Uba (1994) found that Chinese Americans are very similar to other Asian American ethnic groups in their childrearing practices. Chinese American mothers tend to emphasize conformity and family cohesion. In addition, they maintain social control primarily by the use of guilt and shame. Chinese American children have been found to remain dependent upon their parents longer than European American children. They are raised such that the older members of the family make all the decisions. This can lead to inhibited assertiveness and awkward interactions with non-family members. On the other hand, Uba (1994) is quick to point out that studies have shown Chinese Americans are not necessarily less assertive than European Americans. Instead, they show assertiveness differently and in ways that are not tapped by existing measures.

Clients may benefit from understanding the relationship between the childrearing practices of their families and the development of their values and personality traits. Thus, a client who may feel comfortable expressing him or herself assertively with family members or other Chinese Americans may not understand why he or she is unable to do so among other groups of people. Conversely, clients may feel that they are expressing themselves assertively, but their behavior may be misinterpreted.

IMPORTANT CLINICAL ISSUES TO CONSIDER

Depression

A quick review of the empirical literature on Chinese American mental health will reveal that depression is the most commonly studied psychological problem among Chinese Americans. Marsella, Sanborn, Kameoka, Shizuru, and Brennan (1975) compared different measures of depression on normal populations across different ethnic samples including Chinese Americans. In this study, 5 self-report measures of depression (Beck Depression Inventory, KASHogarty Depression Scale, MMPI D-scale, Multiple Affect Adjective Check List, and Zung Depression Scale) were administered to 50 male and 50 female Japanese-Americans, 36 male and 37 female Chinese Americans, and 39 male and 37 female Anglo-Americans who were residing in Hawaii. The results indicated that the measures yield different levels of depression as a function of ethnicity and gender variables. Interestingly, the different measures correlated highly for certain groups, but not for others. Marsella and his colleagues speculated that different assessment techniques and varying response styles by ethnocultural groups may account for the results that they found. They concluded that both of these factors indicated that alternative self-report measures of depression may be differentially sensitive to the detection of depression. They also called for new measures to be developed that consider frequency, intensity, and duration attributes of symptoms as well as the use of varying response styles which reflect cultural norms.

In one of the rare field epidemiological studies, Kuo (1984) examined the prevalence of depression among Asian Americans, including Chinese Americans. In this study, the Center for Epidemiological Studies Depression Scale (CES-D) was administered to 499 Chinese-, Japanese-, Filipino-, and Korean-Americans. The findings indicated that the prevalence of depression among Asian Americans is at least as high as that of the White population. Findings also supported the interpretation that Asian American underutilization of mental health services is not a reflection of lesser need for these services. Factor analysis revealed a pattern of symptoms that was similar among the Koreans, Japanese, and Chinese. Kuo (1984) discovered four factors within the data, accounting for 53% of the variance. The factors identified were: Positive Affect, Depressed Affect, Somatic and Retarded Activity, and Interpersonal Problems. Kuo (1984) observed that participants tended to express depression through a combination of mood and somatic descriptors. He also noted that the newer immigrants, notably the Koreans, were more likely to show adjustment problems.

In another study of depression, Ying (1988) examined the level of depressive symptomatology in a community-based Chinese American sample by using the Center for Epidemiological Studies-Depression Scale (CES-D). The CES-D was administered to 360 Chinese American adults on the telephone. Ying observed that the CES-D's internal reliability was good. Further analyses revealed inseparability of affective and somatic structures in this sample. Ying concluded that this may reflect the nature of experience and manifestation of depression in Chinese culture. When comparing the data to previous studies, Ying found that the level of depressive symptomatology of the present sample was higher than previously reported in both White and Asian samples (Kuo, 1984). In addition, participants who belonged to a lower socioeconomic status (SES) (as measured by education and occupation) scored as significantly more depressed than participants with higher SES.

In a related study, Ying (1989) examined the phenomenon of nonresponse on the Center for Epidemiological Studies Depression Scale (CES-D) among 403 Chinese Americans. She found that 43 participants had missed 1–4 items and 43 participants had missed over 4 items. In her analyses, she found that test completers were likely to be younger, better educated, and male. Conversely, the participants who missed 1–4 items were likely to be middle-aged and male, and missed positive items (e.g., feeling good, hopeful) most frequently. Participants who missed more than 4 items were likely to be older women. For these participants, Ying observed that nonresponse may be a result of unfamiliarity with survey research and reluctance to share personal experiences with strangers.

In another study that attempted to examine the potential relationship between depression and other mental health variables, Marsella, Shizuru,

Brennan, and Kameoka (1981) investigated the relationship between depression and body-image satisfaction in different ethnic groups by comparing 256 depressed and non-depressed (as measured by the Zung Self-Rating Depression Scale) Caucasian American, Chinese American, and Japanese-American undergraduates. They hypothesized that depressed participants would manifest significantly higher levels of body-image dissatisfaction than nondepressed respondents, regardless of ethnicity and gender. The results supported their hypothesis. As a function of the depression condition, however, there were numerous ethnic and gender differences with regard to dissatisfaction with specific body parts. They concluded that depression exacerbates levels of existing body-image dissatisfaction for some groups, introduces new areas of body-image dissatisfaction for others, and does not alter the image for others.

In another study of depression in relation to other psychological variables, Ying (1990) explored explanatory models of major depression and the relationship between problem conceptualization and help-seeking behavior in a sample of 40 recently immigrated Chinese American women (mean age 29.5 yrs). The participants were presented with a vignette depicting a woman experiencing major depression and were then asked to conceptualize the problem and answer questions regarding its cause, impact, and potential sources for help seeking. Ying (1990) found that participants who provided a psychological conceptualization were more likely to turn to themselves, family and friends for assistance than to suggest professional services. On the other hand, participants who held a physical conceptualization were likely to seek out medical services. Ying (1990) went on to discuss implications for effective mental health service delivery to this population in light of their explanatory models of depression.

Suicide

It may be necessary to conduct a suicide assessment on Chinese American clients. As in other areas, it is important that counselors be aware of the similarities and differences between Chinese and European Americans. Uba (1994) looks at the scant literature on suicide among Asian Americans. Research shows that, overall, suicide rates for Chinese Americans are generally lower than for European Americans. However, when broken down by age group, suicide rates are higher than those of European Americans after age 64. In addition, the 15–24 year age group shows a greater proportion of deaths due to suicide for Chinese Americans than for European Americans. Thus, it may be important for counselors to be aware of these patterns when assessing suicide. As noted above, Chinese American clients may be more verbally reticent, show deference to authority, and tend to provide socially desirable responses. It is important to take these factors into consideration when assessing the client for suicide risk.

Stress

In one of the earliest studies of Chinese Americans, Lin, Simeone, Ensel, and Kuo (1979) examined the effects of social support and stressors (stressful life events) on illness (psychiatric symptoms) in a model with data from a representative sample of the Chinese American adult population in Washington, DC. The participants (n = 170) were given the Social Readjustment Rating Scale and a psychiatric symptom checklist. The analysis revealed that, as expected, stressors were positively related to the incidence of psychiatric symptoms, and social support was negatively related to psychiatric symptoms. In addition, they found that the contribution of social support to predicting symptoms was greater in magnitude than that of stressful life events. When the authors incorporated marital status and occupational prestige into the model, the significant (negative) contribution of social support to symptoms was not reduced. Hence, the stressful life-events model seems to be culturally valid for Chinese Americans as well as for White Americans.

Given the importance of acculturation to Chinese Americans' adjustment, Yu's (1984) study provides useful information by exploring the effects of acculturation on stress levels for 277 male and 233 female Chinese Americans living in the Midwest United States. Participants in the study completed a bilingual questionnaire. Acculturation was assessed by grouping participants by the number of years they had been in the United States. Stress was measured by 4 indicators: number of psychological stress symptoms, number of negative life events, life dissatisfaction, and discomfort levels. Yu (1984) chose three major components of filial piety for exploration: concern for parental health, financial support of parents, and housing needs of parents. Results indicated that for males, the number of psychological stress symptoms and life dissatisfaction decreased as the level of acculturation increased. Results were similar (but not statistically significant) for females. Females belonging to the least and the most acculturated groups reported the highest level of discomfort regarding financial support to aged parents.

In another study examining the relationship between acculturation and stress, Yu and Harburg (1980) studied the effects of filial responsibility on adult Chinese Americans. Over 500 Chinese Americans in a Midwestern university town completed a bilingual questionnaire used to measure 4 levels of acculturation with 4 stress indicators (psychological stress symptoms, negative life events, life dissatisfaction and discomfort levels in a) taking care of aged parents' health, b) financially supporting parents, and c) meeting parents' housing needs). An ANOVA was computed using acculturation as the independent variable and stress as the dependent variable. Results showed that the most acculturated group responded with the lowest number of psychological stress symptoms and the lowest level of discomfort regarding their filial responsibility to their aged parents. The US-born reported more psychological stress symptoms than the most-acculturated group, the least-acculturated group reported the highest negative life events among the 4 acculturation groups, and the totally acculturated group reported the lowest level of life dissatisfaction. Within immigrant groups, acculturation was associated with decreased number of negative life events and decreased discomfort when participants did not fulfill their filial responsibility. Yu and Harburg (1980) interpreted the findings as suggesting that US-born Chinese are more susceptible to stress because they lack support from the Chinese American subculture.

RESOURCES FOR TREATMENT

Parallel Mental Health Approach

An important alternative to mainstream western-oriented mental health services is that of parallel services (Sue, 1977). Sue has noted that the mental health needs of Asian Americans can be more effectively met by the development and implementation of counseling services which are offered in parallel to mainstream agencies. These parallel mental health service agencies would consist of certain characteristics making them much more culturally relevant and appropriate for Asian Americans. For example, these parallel services would be located directly in the ethnic neighborhoods where the majority of Asian Americans live and would consist of bicultural and bilingual professionals who can more easily understand and identify with the problems of their clients. These mental health professionals would also be able to modify existing evidence-based interventions to fit with the values, customs and expectations of their clients. Indeed, research has shown that parallel services are much more effective than mainstream western-oriented services alone in meeting the counseling and mental health needs of many Asian Americans (e.g., Zane, Hatanaka, Park, & Akutsu, 1994).

As indicated above, highly acculturated Chinese Americans are quite likely to benefit from mainstream western-oriented counseling services. It is the low acculturation Chinese Americans who are in need of special programs to meet their mental health needs. It would be valuable for mainstream mental health agencies to employ more indirect service approaches in order to reach more Chinese Americans (e.g., health fairs and academic and vocational assistance programs). In addition, given their success and effectiveness, many more parallel agencies are needed in those cities with high concentrations of Chinese Americans. Both of these approaches would go a long way towards improving counseling services for Chinese Americans.

Chinese Americans with a medium level of acculturation are most likely to benefit from modifications of western-oriented counseling approaches. In order to increase actual utilization rates and to minimize premature dropout, counselors and therapists need to be trained (either in their original training programs or as part of their continuing education) to make promising and culturally-sensitive modifications to their western-oriented approaches.

These modifications would involve integrating the cultural values, beliefs, and attitudes of Chinese Americans into the actual interventions. In other words, interventions may need to be restructured to resonate more with the Chinese culture, with an emphasis on cultural appropriateness and program or intervention acceptability. For low acculturation Chinese Americans, even more drastic modifications to western-oriented services may be needed before they are acceptable to this group. For some low acculturation Chinese Americans, practitioners may have to discard their western models altogether and start from scratch. Some of the important cultural values, beliefs and attitudes to consider have been described above. In addition, given the brevity of this chapter, the referenced material listed at the end provides a resource for the reader to explore Chinese American culture in greater depth.

Counselors who work with Chinese American clients need to be aware of how they are similar to and different from not only European Americans, but also other Asian Americans. Although there are many similarities between Chinese Americans and other Asian American ethnic groups, there are also substantial differences. The more detailed understanding and skill a counselor has in working with clients from specific Asian American ethnic groups, the better able they will be to serve the unique needs of their clients.

Example of a Parallel Mental Health Approach: CBT and Chinese Americans. In response to the call to move beyond "cultural sensitivity" and towards "culture-specific knowledge" by adhering to the multicultural counseling competency guidelines, some researchers and practitioners are beginning to explore ways to implement parallel approaches in treatment. In their recent article, Chen and Davenport (2005) proposed a modified application of cognitive-behavioral therapy (CBT) which they argue draws parallels between the philosophy of CBT (e.g., reframing of one's cognition, structured and educational nature) and the cultural norms and values of Chinese Americans (e.g., influences of Confucianism, collectivism, restraint of strong emotions). For example, in Chinese culture, people are taught the powerful influence of one's mind and are encouraged to think prior to taking action (Chen, 1995). This worldview and belief system parallels some of the foundations of CBT, which states that one's cognition causes emotional reactions and consequent behaviors. The authors argued that by drawing such parallels, use of CBT within the Chinese American cultural context would be a viable and culturally-sensitive model, and one that relies on the incorporation of culture-specific knowledge.

ADDITIONAL RESOURCES

There is an old Chinese proverb that states that: "If you give someone a fish, they eat for a day; if you give them several fishes, they may eat for a week; but if you teach them to fish, they will eat for a lifetime". In keeping with the spirit of that Chinese proverb, we would like to end our review by "teaching the readers to fish for themselves" (i.e., sharing some additional resources that the reader is encouraged to use in their quest to work with Chinese American clients more effectively). Beginning with books, the classic is of course Francis Hsu's (1970) *Americans and Chinese: Purpose and Fulfillment in Great Civilizations*, which provides a thorough psychological and anthropological analysis of Chinese and American lifestyles. A much more accessible and textbook version of Hsu's classic was published within the Wadsworth's "Minorities in American Life" series. This text version is entitled, *The Challenge of the American Dream: The Chinese in the United States* (Hsu, 1971). Another comprehensive review of the Chinese experience in the United States can be found in Rose Hum Lee's (1960), *The Chinese in the United States of America*. Betty Lee Sung's (1967) *Mountain of Gold: The story of the Chinese in America* provides a historical review of the Chinese experience in the United States from the Gold Rush to the mid 1960s. A more focused history related to prejudice and discrimination against Chinese Americans is provided by Cheng-Tsu Wu's (1972) *Chink: A Documentary History of Anti-Chinese Prejudice in America*. A more recent book concerned with the hardships experienced by Chinese Americans is Chalsa Loo's (1991) *Chinatown: Most Times, Hard Times*. For more information about the demographics of Chinese Americans, Barringer et al. (1993) *Asians and Pacific Islanders in the United States* would be a valuable resource.

In terms of book chapters, one of the earliest volumes with chapters devoted to psychological issues of Chinese Americans is Stanley Sue and Nathaniel Wagner's (1973) *Asian Americans: Psychological Perspectives*. Eight of the 27 chapters in this book were devoted specifically to Chinese Americans. In volume 2, Endo, Sue, and Wagner's (1980) *Asian Americans: Social Psychological Perspectives* contained 4 chapters devoted to Chinese Americans. In several other volumes related to counseling and mental health, there are chapters devoted to Chinese Americans. For example, in McDermott, Tseng, and Maretzki's (1980) *People and Cultures of Hawaii: A Psychocultural Profile*, a chapter on the Chinese was written by Char, Tseng, Lum, and Hsu. Lee and Richardson's (1991) *Multicultural Issues in Counseling: New Approaches to Diversity* contains a chapter by David Sue and Derald Sue on "Counseling strategies for Chinese Americans." Karen Huang has a chapter on Chinese Americans in Noreen Mokuau's (1991) *Handbook of Social Services for Asian and Pacific Islanders* and Albert Gaw has a chapter on Chinese Americans in his book (Gaw, 1982) *Cross-Cultural Psychiatry*.

In terms of empirical studies on the psychology and mental health of Chinese Americans, several bibliographies are available. Each bibliography is annotated and contains a significant number of entries related to Chinese Americans which can be accessed through the index. The earliest is Morishima, Sue, Teng, Zane and Cram's (1979) National Institutes of Mental Health (NIMH) bibliography entitled, *Handbook of Asian/Pacific Islander Mental Health, Volume 1*. Another useful bibliography is Doi, Lin, and

Vohra-Sahu's (1981) *Pacific/Asian American research: An Annotated Bibliography* which was published when the NIMH-funded Pacific/Asian American Mental Health Research Center was at the University of Illinois-Chicago Circle. Finally, Leong and Whitfield's (1992) APA bibliography entitled, *Asians in the United States: Abstracts of the Psychological and Behavioral Literature, 1967–1991* is the most recent bibliographic resource on empirical studies of Chinese Americans.

VALID ASSESSMENT INSTRUMENTS

Several assessment instruments which have been found to have clinical utility in addressing the various culturally-relevant factors outlined in this chapter are available and described below.

Self-Construal Scale (SCS) (Singelis, 1994)

Purpose: This scale measures an individual's independent and interdependent self-construal, as defined by Markus and Kitayama (1991). Consistent with the idea that independence and interdependence are two separate dimensions, rather than opposite ends of a single dimension, the SCS provides separate scores for the strength of an individual's interdependent and independent self-construal.

Respondents indicate their agreement with each of the 30 statements on a 7-point Likert-type scale, ranging from 1 (strongly disagree) to 7 (strongly agree). An example of an independent item is, "I'd rather say 'No' directly, than risk being misunderstood." An example of an interdependent item is, "I should take into consideration my parents' advice when making education/career plans."

Clinical Utility: Self-construal has been found to be an important construct that reliably differs among individuals from Western and Eastern cultures and has important effects on motivation, cognition, emotion, and behavior.

Family Acculturation Conflict Scale (FACTS) (Lee, Choe, Kim & Ngo, 2000)

Purpose: The Family Acculturation Conflicts Scale (FACTS) was developed to assess the likelihood and seriousness of various family conflicts that are typical of an acculturation gap.

The FACTS consists of 10 items. These items were developed based on the existing literature and focus groups conducted by the authors about typical acculturation conflicts in Asian American families. An example of one of the FACTS items is, "You have done well in school, but your parents' academic expectations always exceed your performance." Respondents rate the likelihood of the occurrence of each situation on a 5-point Likert-type scale from 1 (almost never) to 5 (almost always). Respondents also rate the seriousness of each situation in their family on a similar 5-point scale from 1 (not at all) to 5 (extremely).

Clinical Utility: High levels of family conflict are a risk factor for behaviors such as alcohol, tobacco, and other drug (ATOD) abuse, and this relationship between family conflict and ATOD abuse has been found for Asian Americans. The FACTS is an important measure of this risk factor because it taps into an area of family conflict common among Chinese American families but one that is not typically found in majority culture families.

Center for Epidemiological Studies Depression Scale (CES-D) (Radloff, 1977)

Purpose: The CES-D is a 20-item self-report measure designed to assess the current level of depressive symptoms, with an emphasis on affective symptoms. The CES-D is intended to assess symptoms of depression in a normal population but is not meant to identify cases of clinical or pathological depression, although the items were chosen to "isolate the major components of depressive symptomatology identified by the clinical literature and factor analytic studies," (Kuo, 1984, p. 451).

Clinical Utility: The CES-D has been successfully used with Chinese American individuals in numerous studies, and there is accumulated evidence supporting its validity with this population. Although the CES-D is not designed to diagnose clinical depression, it may be particularly useful in identifying Chinese Americans who experience strong symptoms of depression.

Brief Symptom Inventory (BSI) (Lyn and Leong, 1992)

Purpose: The BSI is a 53 item self-report psychological symptom inventory that could be completed in less than 10 minutes. The BSI is essentially a brief form of the SCL-90-R. The SCL-90-R is composed of 90 items and can be completed within 15–20 minutes. In order to devise a symptom inventory which would be compatible with the SCL-90-R but which could be utilized in clinical and research settings where even the above administration time was too long, the five to six highest loading items from each of the nine primary symptom dimensions on the SCL-90-R were selected and compiled. The result was the BSI, a 53 item self-report psychological symptom inventory which could be completed in less than 10 minutes.

The format of the BSI is such that respondents rate their degree of distress on each BSI item according to a five point (0 to 4) Likert scale ranging from "not at all" to "extremely." Each of the 53 BSI items is linked to one of nine primary symptom dimensions: somatization, obsessive-compulsive, interpersonal sensitivity, depression, anxiety, hostility, phobic anxiety, paranoid ideation, and psychoticism. The inventory itself is scored and profiled according to these dimensions.

Clinical Utility: The primary asset of the BSI is its brevity. It could be included with other assessment inventories to provide reliable information about symptoms of psychological distress without significantly lengthening testing time.

The Ethnocultural Identity Behavioral Index (EIBI) (Yamada, Marsella, Yamada, 1998)

Purpose: "The EIBI is a behavioral index of ethnocultural identity that can be used with persons of all ethnocultural backgrounds," (p. 37). "Ethnocultural identity focuses on the extent to which an individual endorses and practices a way of life associated with a particular cultural tradition," (p. 36). The EIBI is composed of 19 items reflecting various behaviors. Respondents report how frequently they engage in the behaviors.

Clinical Utility: As discussed above, both acculturation and ethnic identity are associated with several mental health issues. The EIBI, because it assess the behavioral component of these constructs, may be particularly useful in identifying specific behaviors exhibited by clients.

Measure of Individualism-Collectivism (Triandis, Bontempo, Villareal, Asai, & Lucca, 1988)

Purpose: To operationalize the constructs of individualism and collectivism and find a way to best measure them. In the process of developing this measure researchers found that U.S. individualism is reflected in three main factors.

Clinical Utility: Individualism and collectivism are culture/group level constructs similar to the individual level constructs of independence and interdependence discussed above under self-construal. Just as Independence and Interdependence have been found to differ meaningfully between individuals from Western and Eastern cultures, individualism and collectivism also varies between Western and Eastern cultures.

Loss of Face Scale (LOF) (Zane, 1991)

Purpose: The Loss of Face Scale is a self-report instrument consisting of 21 items developed to measure individuals' attitudes toward losing face in public and their behavioral attempts to maintain face for themselves or others. Response categories for the items are presented on a 7-point Likert scale (1 = Strongly Disagree, 7 = Strongly Agree). Scores are obtained by summing responses to individual items, with higher scores indicating greater sensitivity toward losing face.

Clinical Utility: Loss of Face is an important concept in Chinese culture, affecting social relationships and interaction in a variety of domains.

Chinese Personality Assessment Inventory (CPAI) (Cheung, Leung, Fan, Song, Zhang, & Zhang, 1996)

Purpose: A multiphasic personality inventory for assessment of both normal and clinical populations that incorporates emic constructs relevant to the Chinese people. Using Chinese novels, books of Chinese proverbs, surveys of students and professionals, and a review of the literature, the research team identified 26 normal personality and 12 clinical constructs, including several emic constructs: Harmony, *Ren Qin*, Modernization, Thrift, *Ah-Q* Mentality (Defensiveness), Graciousness, Veraciousness-slickness, Face, Family orientation, and Somatization.

Clinical Utility: The CPAI is the first comprehensive measure of Chinese personality, and, as such, is an important tool in understanding and predicting culturally-specific risk and protective factors for mental health. Since the CPAI is specifically designed for use with persons of Chinese cultural origin, it is likely to more fully capture relevant personality factors, leading to neither under-nor over-estimation of risk and protective factors.

FINAL RECOMMENDATIONS FOR DISASTER WORKERS

For our final recommendations, we would like to conclude with a summary of Leong's (1996) multidimensional and integrative model of cross-cultural counseling and psychotherapy. In that model, using Kluckhohn and Murray's (1950) tripartite framework, Leong (1996) proposed that cross-cultural counselors and therapists need to attend to all three major dimensions of human personality and identity: namely the Universal, the Group, and the Individual dimensions. The Universal dimension is based on the knowledge-base generated by mainstream psychology and the "universal laws" of human behavior that have been identified (e.g., the universal "fight or flight" response in humans to physical threat). The Group dimension has been the domain of both cross-cultural psychology as well as ethnic minority psychology and the study of gender differences. Much of our chapter has focused on this group dimension by providing culture-specific information for Chinese Americans.

The third and final dimension concerns unique Individual differences and characteristics. The Individual dimension is more often covered by behavioral and existential theories where individual learning histories and personal phenomenology are proposed as critical elements in the understanding of human behavior. Leong's (1996) integrative model proposes that all three dimensions are equally important in understanding human experiences and should be attended to by the counselor in an holistic fashion.

The integrative model of cross-cultural counseling proposed by Leong (1996) has as one of its cornerstones the notion that the client must exist at three levels, the universal, the group, and the individual. The problem with much of the previous research conducted in the field of multicultural counseling is that there has been focus on only one of the three levels, ignoring the influence of the other levels in the counseling situation. Leong's (1996) integrative model includes all three dimensions of personality as well as their dynamic interactions, and thus will have better incremental validity than any model that only focuses on one of the three levels. The integrative model for cross-cultural counseling and psychotherapy was conceived to provide a more complex conception of a very dynamic enterprise in counseling.

In cross-cultural counseling and psychotherapy, the same variables that have been found to be important in mainstream counseling and psychotherapy are also important when the client and counselor come from different cultural backgrounds. By mainstream counseling and psychotherapy, we are referring to the body of literature on psychotherapy research that has been reviewed in the *Handbook of Psychotherapy and Behavior Change* (Bergin & Garfield, 1994). These same variables happen to interact with cultural variables in cross-cultural counseling and psychotherapy. This represents the interaction of the Universal and Group dimensions in the integrative model (Leong, 1996). At the same time, the Universal dimension also interacts with the Individual dimension, just as the Group dimension would be expected to interact with the Individual dimension.

In a sense, the three dimensions of Universal, Group and Individual factors exert their influence in cross-cultural counseling encounters as both main effects and as interaction effects. This is precisely why Leong (1996) proposed that it is important to include complexity theory in analyzing and understanding the cross-cultural counseling relationship. We propose that a culturally competent therapist or counselor needs to attend to all three dimensions when working with their clients. Each Chinese American is a human being who possesses various group identities and at the same time is also a unique individual unlike other Chinese Americans in certain respects.

References

Barringer, H. R., Gardner, R. W., & Levin, M. J. (1993). *Asians and Pacific Islanders in the United States*. New York, NY: Russell Sage Foundation.

Bergin, A. E., & Garfield, S. L. (1994). *Handbook of psychotherapy and behavior change* (4th ed.). New York, NY: John Wiley & Sons, Inc.

Chan, S. (1992). Families with Asian roots. In Lynch, E. W. & Hanson, M. J. (Eds.), *Developing cross-cultural competence* (pp. 181–257). Baltimore, MD: Paul H. Brookes Publishing.

Chen, D. (1995). Cultural and psychological influences on mental health issues for Chinese Americans. In L. L. Adler, B. R. Mukherji, et al. (Eds.), *Spirit versus Scalpel: Traditional healing and modern psychotherapy* (pp. 185–196). Westport, CT, USA: Bergin & Garvey/Greenwood Publishing Group, Inc.

Chen, S. W. H., & Davenport, D. S. (2005). Cognitive-behavioral therapy with Chinese American clients: Cautions and modifications. *Psychotherapy: Theory, research, practice, training*, 42, 101–110.

Cheung, F. M., Leung, K., Fan, R. M., Song, W. Z., Zhang, J. X., & Zhang, J. P. (1996). Development of the Chinese personality assessment inventory. *Journal of Cross-cultural Psychology*, 27, 181–199.

Chu, J., & Sue, S. (1984). Asian-Pacific-Americans and group practice. *Social Work with Groups*, 7, 23–36.

Cook, H., & Chi, C. (1984). Cooperative behavior and locus of control among American and Chinese American boys. *Journal of Psychology*, 118(2), 169–177.

Doi, M. L., Lin, C., & Vohra-Sahu I. (1981). *Pacific/Asian American research: An annotated bibliography*. Chicago: Pacific/Asian American Mental Health Research Center.

Endo, R., Sue, S., & Wagner, N. N. (Eds.). (1980). *Asian Americans social and psychological perspectives*: *Vol. II*. Palo Alto, CA: Science and Behavior Books.

Gaw, A. (1982). Chinese Americans. In A. Gaw (Ed.), *Cross-cultural psychiatry* (pp. 1–29). Littleton, MA: PSG Publishing Co.

Glenn, E. N. (1983). Split household, small producer and dual wage earner: An analysis of Chinese American family strategies. *Journal of Marriage and the Family*, 45(1), 35–46.

Hall, E. (1976). *Beyond culture*. Garden city, NY: Anchor.

Hofstede, G. H. (1980). *Culture's consequences: International differences in work related values*. Beverly Hills, CA: Sage.

Hsieh, T. T., Shybut, J., & Lotsof, E. J. (1969). Internal versus external control and ethnic group membership: A cross-cultural comparison. *Journal of Consulting & Clinical Psychology*, 33(1), 122–124.

Hsu, F. L. K. (1970). *Americans and Chinese: Purpose and fulfillment in great civilizations*. New York: Natural History Press.

Hsu, F. L. K. (1971). *The challenge of the American dream: The Chinese in the United States*. Belmont, CA: Wadsorth Publishing Company.

Huang, K. (1991). Chinese Americans. In N. Mokuau (Ed.), Handbook of social services for Asian and Pacific Islanders (pp. 79–96). New York, NY: Greenwood Press.

Kluckhohn, C., & Murray, H. A. (1950). Personality formation: The determinants. In C. Kluckhohn & H. A. Murray (Eds.), *Personality in nature, society, and culture* (pp. 35–48). New York: Alfred A. Knopf.

Kuo, W. H. (1984). Prevalence of depression among Asian Americans. *Journal of Nervous & Mental Disease*, 172(8), 449–457.

Lee, C., & Richardson, B. L. (1991). *Multicultural issues in Counseling: New approaches to diversity*. Alexandria, VA: American Association for Counseling and Development.

Lee, R. H. (1960). *The Chinese in the United States of America*. Hong Kong: Hong Kong University Press.

Lee, R. M., Choe, J., Kim, G., & Ngo, V. (2000). Construction of the Asian American family acculturation conflicts scale. *Journal of Counseling Psychology*, 47(2), 211–222.

Leong, F. T. L. (1986). Counseling and psychotherapy with Asian Americans: Review of the literature. *Journal of Counseling Psychology*, 33, 196–206.

Leong, F. T. L. (1996). Toward an integrative model for cross-cultural counseling and psychotherapy. *Applied and Preventive Psychology*, 5, 189–209.

Leong, F. T. L., & Chou, E. L. (1994). The role of ethnic identity and acculturation in the vocational behavior of Asian Americans: An integrative review. *Journal of Vocational Behavior*, 44, 155–172.

Leong, F. T. L., & Kim, H. H. W. (1991). Going beyond cultural sensitivity on the road to multiculturalism: Using the intercultural sensitizer as a counselor training tool. *Journal of Counseling & Development*, 70, 112–118.

Leong, F. T. L., & Whitfield, J. R. (Eds.). (1992). *Asians in the United States: Abstracts of the psychological and behavioral literature: 1967–1991*. (Bibliographies in psychology, no. ll). Washington, DC: American Psychological Association.

Lin, N., Simeone, R. S., Ensel, W. M., & Kuo, W. (1979). Social support, stressful life events, and illness: A model and an empirical test. *Journal of Health & Social Behavior*, 20(2), 108–119.

Loo, C. M. (1991). *Chinatown: Most time, hard time*. New York, NY: Praeger Publishers.

Lum, R. C. (1982). Mental health attitudes and opinions of Chinese. In E. E. Jones & S. J. Korchin (Eds.), *Minority mental health* (pp. 165–189). New York, NY: Praeger.

Lyn, L., & Leong, F. T. L. (1992). Review of the brief symptom inventory. Unpublished manuscript.

Markus, H. R., & Kitayama, S. (1991). Culture and the self: Implications for cognition, emotion, and motivation. *Psychological Review*, 98, 224–253

Marsella, A. J., Shizuru, L. S., Brennan, J. M., & Kameoka, V. (1981). Depression and body image satisfaction. *Journal of Cross-cultural Psychology*, 12(3), 360–371.

Marsella, A. J., Sanborn, K. O., Kameoka, V., Shizuru, L., & Brennan, J. (1975). Cross-validation of self-report measures of depression among normal populations of Japanese, Chinese, and Caucasian ancestry. *Journal of Clinical Psychology*, 3(2), 281–287.

McDermott, J. F., Jr., Tseng, W. S., & Maretzki, T. W. (Eds.). (1980). *People and cultures of Hawaii: A psychocultural profile*. Honolulu, HI: University of Hawaii Press.

Mokuana, N. (1991). *Handbook of Social Services for Asian and Pacific Islanders*. Greenwood Press: New York.

Morishima, J. K., Sue, S., Teng, L. N., Zane, N. W. S., & Cram, J. R. (1979) *Handbook of Asian/Pacific Islander mental health, Vol. 1*. Rockville, MD: National Institute of Mental Health, DHHS Publication No. 80–754.

Radloff, L. (1977). The CES-D Scale: A self-report depression scale for research in the general population. *Applied Psychological Measurement*, 1, 385–401.

Reeves, T. J., & Bennet, C. E. (2004). *We the People: Asians in the United States. Census 2000 Special Reports*. U. S. Census Bureau (CENSR-17). U.S. Department of Commerce, Economics and Statistics Administration.

Rotter, J. B. (1966). Generalized expectancies for internal versus external control of reinforcement. *Psychological Monographs*, 33(1), 300–303.

Singelis, T. M. (1994). The measurement of independent and interdependent self-construal. *Personality and Social Psychology Bulletin*, 20, 580–591.

Sue, D., Ino, S., & Sue, D. M. (1983). Nonassertiveness of Asian Americans: An inaccurate assumption? *Journal of Counseling Psychology*, 30(4), 581–588.

Sue, D., Sue, D. M., & Ino, S. (1990). Assertiveness and social anxiety in Chinese American women. *Journal of Psychology*, 124(2), 155–163.

Sue, D., & Sue, D. W. (1991). Counseling strategies for Chinese Americans. In C. C. Lee & B. L. Richardson (Eds.), *Multicultural issues in counseling: New approaches to diversity* (pp. 79–90). Alexandria, VA: American Association for Counseling and Development.

Sue, D. W., Arredondo, P., & McDavis, R. J. (1992). Multicultural counseling competencies and standards: A call to the profession. *Journal of Counseling & Development*, 70, 477–486.

Sue, D. W., Bernier, J. E., Durran, A., Feinberg, L., Pedersen, P. B, E. J., & Vasquez-Nuttal, E. (1982). Position paper: Cross-cultural counseling competencies. *The Counseling Psychologist*, 10(2), 45–52.

Sue, D. W., & Sue, D. (1990). *Counseling the Culturally-Different*. (Second Edition). New York: Wiley.

Sue, D. W., & Sue, S. (1972). Counseling Chinese Americans. *Personnel and Guidance Journal*, 50(8), 637–644.

Sue, S. (1977). Community mental health services to minority groups: Some optimism, some pessimism. *American Psychologist*, 32, 616–624.

Sue, S., & Morishima, J. K. (1982). *The Mental health of Asian Americans*. San Francisco: Jossey-Bass.

Sue, S., & Wagner, N. N. (Eds.). (1973). *Asian Americans: Psychological perspectives*. Palo Alto, CA: Science and Behavior Books.

Sung, B. L. (1967) *Mountain of gold: The story of the Chinese in America*. New York: Macmillan Co.

Te, H. D. (1989). *The Indochinese and their cultures*. San Diego: San Diego State University, Multifunctional Resource Center.

Triandis, H. C., Bontempo, R., Villareal, M. J., Asai, M., & Lucca, N. (1988). Individualism and collectivism: Cross cultural perspectives on self-ingroup relationships. *Journal of Personality and Social Psychology, 54*, 323–338.

Uba, L. (1994). *Asian Americans: Personality patterns, identity, and mental health.* New York, NY: The Guilford Press.

U.S. Census Bureau. (2000). *Census 2000, Summary File 1.* Generated by J. Smith using American FactFinder. Retrieved February 15, 2005, from http://factfinder.census.gov

U. S. Office of Immigration Statistics. (2000). *Yearbook of immigration statistics.* Retrieved February 15, 2005, from http://www.uscis.gov/graphics/shared/statistics/yearbook/index.htm

Vernon, P. E. (1982). *The abilities and achievements of Orientals in North America.* New York: Academic Press.

Wu, C. T. (1972). *Chink: A documentary history of Anti-Chinese prejudice in America.* New York: World Publishing.

Yamada, A. M., Marsella, A. J., & Yamada, S. Y. (1998). The development of the ethnocultural identity behavioral index: Psychometric properties and validation with Asian Americans and Pacific Islanders. *Asian American and Pacific Islander Journal of Health, 6*, 35–45.

Ying, Y. (1988). Depressive symptomatology among Chinese Americans as measured by the CES-D. *Journal of Clinical Psychology, 44*(5), 739–746.

Ying, Y. (1989). Nonresponse on the center for epidemiological studies-depression scale in Chinese Americans. *International Journal of Social Psychology, 35*(2), 156–193.

Ying, Y. (1990). Explanatory models of major depression and implications for help-seeking among immigrant Chinese American women. *Culture, Medicine & Psychiatry, 14*(3), 393–408.

Yu, L. C. (1984). Acculturation and stress within Chinese American families. *Journal of Comparative Family Studies, 15*(1), 77–94.

Yu, L. C., & Harburg, E. (1980). Acculturation and stress among Chinese Americans in a university town. *International Journal of Group Tensions, 10*(1–4), 99–119.

Zane, N. (1991). An empirical examination of loss of face among Asian Americans. Unpublished manuscript, Graduate School of Education, University of California, Santa Barbara.

Zane, N., Hatanaka, H., Park, S. S., & Akutsu, P. (1994). Ethnic-specific mental health services: Evaluation of the parallel approach for Asian American clients. *Journal of Community Psychology, 22*, 68–81.

Chapter 9

The *Kanaka Maoli*: Native Hawaiians and Their Testimony of Trauma and Resilience

Laurie D. McCubbin, Michele E. Ishikawa, and Hamilton I. McCubbin

Mark Twain on Hawaii (1868)

". . . the Sandwich Islands – to this day the peacefullest, restfullest, suniest, balmiest, dreamiest haven of refuge for a worn and weary spirit the surface of the earth can offer. . . . There they lie, the divine islands, forever shining in the sun, forever smiling out of the sparkling sea, with its soft mottling drifting cloud shadows and vagrant cat's paws of wind, forever inviting you."

(Frear, 1969, Quoted in Nordyke, 1989, p. xix).

INTRODUCTION

Mark Twain's words describing the Hawaiian Islands are an accurate description of the Islands' natural physical beauty. But, they do not tell of the beauty of the Native Hawaiian people who first came to these islands more than 2000 years ago, and of the beautiful culture they created, nor their subsequent struggle for survival against the destructive forces of Westernization brought to their sandy shores by British ships, whalers, missionaries, and a host of other commercial and military forces. In this chapter, we will try to offer the reader a more detailed understanding of the Native Hawaiian people (*Kanaka Maoli*), their culture, and their way of being.

The 1959 Statehood Admissions Act of Hawai'i defines a Native Hawaiian person as "...any descendant of the aboriginal peoples inhabiting the

Hawaiian Islands in 1778." Native Hawaiians have been referred to as any-one with any quantum of ancestral Hawaiian blood, i.e., ancestors who were indigenous to the land prior to 1778. The 1990 U.S. Census provided an esti-mated 310,747 people of Native Hawaiian ancestry who live in the United States with roughly one-third living on the mainland (e.g., continental U.S.) and two-thirds living on the Hawaiian islands (Marsella, Oliveira, Plummer, & Crabbe, 1995).

According to the 2000 U.S. Census, an estimated 401,162 people identified their race as Native Hawaiian, with approximately 60% of Native Hawaiians living in the state of Hawai'i and 40% on the "mainland" or continental U.S. Of this total number of Native Hawaiians living in the U.S., slightly over a third (35.1%) declared Native Hawaiian as their only race (Grieco, 2001). These figures demonstrate a significant growth in the Native Hawaiian population within the past ten years. These statistics gain significance when contrasted with the fact that the Native Hawaiians were nearly extinct, a condition which many historians refer to as the "cultural genocide" of Native Hawaiian peo-ple. Following western contact in 1778, the Hawaiian population declined by 90% within the first one hundred years due to diseases, infertility, war, and despair (Marsella et al., 1995). The lowest number of Native Hawaiians living in the Kingdom of Hawai'i was estimated to be 53,900 in 1876. Since 1876 to 2000, there has been an estimated increase of 750% in the population within a 124-year period of time!

A report published by the Pacific American Foundation (2004) based on 2000 Census data provides a "snapshot" of the current demographic profile of Native Hawaiians in the U.S. Among the Native Hawaiians, (including Hawaiians and part-Hawaiians), 49.9% are male and 50.1% are female, which is similar to the national population distribution (49.1% male and 50.9% female, respectively; U.S. Census, 2000). The average age of Native Hawai-ians is 25.6 years, which is significantly younger than the average age of the U.S. population (35.3 years old). Slightly over 40% of Native Hawaiians are 19 years of age or younger. This profile is prominent when contrasted with the national distribution of 28.6% in the same age group. It should be noted that official Census documents have produced different population demograph-ics, likely because they considered only individuals who identified with a sole race of Native Hawaiian. A report by Harris and Jones (2005) for the Census Bureau shows a Native Hawaiian age group distribution that is more similar to that of the general U.S. population, with a median age of 31.8 compared with 35.4 for the general population.

The vast majority (80%) of Native Hawaiians reside in Hawaii and the states of Washington, California and Oregon. When contrasted with the national percentage of 9.2%, Native Hawaiian families are more likely to be classi-fied as poor (12%) (Pacific American Foundation, 2004). The poverty rate for sole race Native Hawaiians was 15.6%, compared to 12.4% for the total U.S. population (Harris & Jones, 2005). Moreover, Native Hawaiian women (5.7%) and men (7.0%) are more likely to be unemployed, compared to the national average of 3.3% for women and 4.0% for men (Pacific American Foundation, 2004). Native Hawaiians are slightly more likely to graduate from high school (83.2%) compared to the national rate (80.4%). While these results are promising, the data also show that Native Hawaiians are less likely to have a bachelor's degree or higher (15.2%) compared to the total U.S. population (Harris & Jones, 2005) (24.4%).

Census reports often group Native Hawaiians with other Pacific Islander groups such as Samoans and Guamanians, and Fijians. This can lead to confusion when assessing demographic profiles as there are some important variations among the groups. Statistics are often reported for "Native Hawaiians or other Pacific Islander" as a single racial grouping, and prior to 2000 Pacific Islanders were grouped with Asians. Native Hawaiians are the largest Pacific Islander group in terms of population size. In addition to the report on Native Hawaiian demographics by the Pacific Islander Foundation (2004), the reader is referred to the Census report by Harris and Jones (2005), which provides detailed profiles for the major Pacific Islander groups, including Native Hawaiians. An earlier Census report by Grieco (2001) provides more general demographic information on Native Hawaiians and other Pacific Islanders.

NATIVE HAWAIIAN HISTORY: CULTURAL GENOCIDE AND REBIRTH

Early History

It is believed that the Native Hawaiian (*Kanaka Maoli*) people came to the Hawaiian Islands around 350 A.D. from Polynesia. By the 18th century, the Hawaiian cultural traditions were strong and well established with the population of the islands estimated at anywhere from 400,000 (Schmitt, 1968) to 800,000 (Kane, 1997) to 875,000 (Stannard, 1989). On January 18, 1778, Captain James Cook arrived in the Hawaiian Islands from Britain, signifying Native Hawaiians' first contact with Western culture. This initial contact led to tragedy for the Native Hawaiian people. The Hawaiian population declined by 90% within the first one hundred years following Western contact.

The first missionaries arrived on March 20, 1820, from New England in order to spread Christianity among the Native Hawaiians. These missionaries also took much of the land of Hawai'i in the process and assumed much of the power on the islands (Marsella et al., 1995). In the 1860's Reverend Rufus Anderson witnessed the decline of the native population; however, he declined to see this as a tragedy. He saw this potential extinction of a race as "only natural" and equated it to "the amputation of diseased members of the body" (Stannard, 1992).

On January 16, 1893, the U.S. Minister to Hawai'i, John Stevens, with a group of American businessmen and the help of the U.S. navy, invaded the sovereign Hawaiian nation without the permission or approval of the U.S.

government. On January 17, 1893, the Hawaiian monarchy collapsed with the overthrow of the last queen, Queen Lili'uokalani. The queen was tried and convicted for treason on January 7, 1895, in an act designed to humiliate her and her people. On July 7, 1898, Hawai'i became a territory of the United States without a single vote from the Native Hawaiians. As a testimony of her struggle to save the Native Hawaiian Kingdom and her resilience drawn from her heritage, a sense of balance, and spirituality, Queen Lili'uokalani wrote to her adopted daughter:

> "I could not turn back the time for political change but there is still time to save our heritage. You must remember never to cease to act because you fear you may fail. The way to lose any earthly kingdom is to be inflexible, intolerant and prejudicial. Another way is to be too flexible, tolerant of too many wrongs and without judgment at all. It is a razor's edge, it is the width of a blade of pili grass." (Lili'uokalani, 1917).

In an attempt to make amends of the illegal overthrow, in 1921 Congress passed the Hawaiian Homes Commission Act which set aside 200,000 acres of the land to be used to establish homelands for Native Hawaiians with 50% or more Hawaiian blood (Akau et al., 1998; Hawaii Advisory Committee to the U.S. Commission on Civil Rights, 2001; Council for Native Hawaiian Advancement, 2005). In 1959, Hawai'i became the 50th state with the federal government returning the ceded lands (i.e., the lands that were once property of the Hawaiian monarchy, which is approximately 1.8 million acres) to the state. One of the purposes of these ceded lands was for the "betterment of the conditions of Native Hawaiians." The Office of Hawaiian Affairs was created in 1978 to manage this share of the ceded land revenues (Bolante, 2003) with the mission:

> ". . . to malama (protect) Hawaii's people and environmental resources and OHA's assets, toward ensuring the perpetuation of the culture, the enhance-ment of lifestyle and the protection of entitlements of Native Hawaiians, while enabling the building of a strong and healthy Hawaiian people and nation, recognized nationally and internationally" (Office of Hawaiian Affairs, 2003).

Cultural Revival and Rebirth

Current events have also occurred that demonstrate the resilience and recov-ery of the Native Hawaiian people and the Hawaiian culture, including practices, language and values. The 1970's brought a revival of the Hawaiian culture and Native Hawaiians began a renewed interest in and commitment to their traditional language, music (mele), dance (hula), arts, and crafts (McCubbin & McCubbin, 1997). One of the major events that affected the Native Hawaiian people was the maiden voyage of the Hokule'a, a Poly-nesian voyaging canoe, to Tahiti, which proved advanced navigation skills of the Polynesian people (Polynesian Voyaging Society, 2005). Finney (2004) stated: "the Hokule'a emerged as a cultural icon credited with helping spark a general cultural renaissance among the Hawaiians." In addition, the history of oppression has been recognized by the United States and the state of Hawai'i, acknowledging the unique status of Native Hawaiians, which has been viewed as similar to Native Americans and Alaska Natives – politically, legally and culturally (Hawaii Advisory Committee to the U.S. Commission on Civil Rights, 2001).

In 1993, Congress passed a resolution and President Clinton signed Public Law 103–150, which acknowledged the 100th year commemoration of the overthrow of the Kingdom of Hawai'i and a formal apology to Native Hawaiians for the improper role of the U.S. military in support of the overthrow (Hawaii Advisory Committee, 2001). What this provided was an acknowledgement by the U.S. government of the ramifications of the "illegal overthrow" of 1893, and for the government to engage in a process for policy development on the reconciliation between the U.S. and the Native Hawaiian people (Hawaii Advisory Committee to the U.S. Commission on Civil Rights, 2001). This created a sense of optimism and renewed energy in the sovereignty movement and motion towards reconciliation. In 2000, Senator Daniel Akaka introduced a bill, the Native Hawaiian Restoration Act (also called the Akaka Bill), which would allow for federal recognition of Native Hawaiian people as a distinct indigenous entity, similar to the Native American tribal status. The bill did not pass, but the struggles and challenges for the Native Hawaiians continue to the present day. Despite the multiple stressors and adversity Native Hawaiian culture has faced and continues to face, it is a time of renewal, growth and prosperity. It is important for the Native Hawaiians' struggles to be documented; however, it is just as important to demonstrate their resilience.

A brief chronology of Native Hawaiian history is presented in Table 9.1 (McCubbin & Marsella, under review). This chronology provides a brief overview that begins with the arrival of Native Hawaiians in Hawaii and proceeds to modern times. A fuller and more complete version can be found in the original reference (i.e., McCubbin & Marsella, under review).

VALUES OF NATIVE HAWAIIANS

Knowledge of the cultural values of Native Hawaiians is essential to understanding these indigenous peoples' worldview, communication styles, culture-based definitions of positive and negative psychological functioning, and culturally defined diagnoses, therapies and treatment. Ten key values will be discussed to help guide clinicians in understanding some of the basic premises underlying the Native Hawaiian culture. However, it should be noted that this is not a comprehensive view of the multiple values that exist in Hawaiian culture. These values are part of the Native Hawaiian conception

Table 9.1.   Chronological History of Native Hawaiians (*Kanaka Maoli*)

1 A.D.	The first Native Hawaiian People arrive in the Hawaiian Islands from the Marquesas, Tahiti, or the Society Islands sailing double-hulled canoes.
1–1400	Migration between Polynesia and the Hawaiian Islands continues and the Islands grow in population. Settlement occurs across all major islands (i.e., Hawaii [Owhyhee], Maui [Mowee], Molokai [Morotoi], Lanai [Renai], Oahu [Woahoo], & Kauai [Atooi]. Different kingdoms led by various chiefs or royal families (alii) are established across the islands. Land is cultivated and hierarchical societies are established. Around 1400, travel between Polynesia and Hawaii ceases.
1778	Captain James Cook arrives in the Hawaiian Islands with two ships: HMS Resolute and HMS Discovery. This is the first contact of the Native Hawaiians with Europeans. Captain Cook names the Hawaiian Islands the "Sandwich Islands" in honor of his patron and sponsor, John Montagu, Earl of Sandwich. Population estimates at the time of Captain Cook's arrival vary from 300,000 to 850,000.
1778–1878	Many Native Hawaiians become ill and die from diseases spread by Captain Cook's men (e.g., tuberculosis, measles, smallpox, syphilis). Within 100 years from Cook's arrival, it is estimated that less than 10% of the Native Hawaiians remain.
1810	All the Hawaiian Islands are united for the first time under the leadership of Kamehameha I. Prior to this time, different islands were separate kingdoms. A Hawaiian monarchy is established.
1819	First whaling ships arrive in Kealakekua, Hawaii, signaling the beginning of a thriving whaling industry and the further demise of the Native Hawaiian people.
1820	First American missionaries arrive in Hawaii to spread Christianity and to further destroy Native Hawaiian cultural traditions. Missionary families soon join with Caucasian businessmen in taking ownership of land, politics, and the economy. Hawaiian language use and cultural practices are discouraged as pagan and primitive.
1850	Because there are so few Native Hawaiian men (i.e., estimates of less than 3000) during this period, the Legislature approves the hiring of foreign laborers from China, Japan, and Portugal to work in the growing sugar and pineapple industries. Floods of workers from these countries come to Hawai'i. They are followed by workers from Puerto Rico and the Philippines. In combination with the Caucasians (from America and Europe), these populations soon outnumber the Native Hawaiian people, who are rapidly dying from disease and who are now intermarrying.
1876	One of the lowest points in the population decline of the Native Hawaiian people was reached in 1876 when only 53,900 Native Hawaiian people were reported to be living in the Kingdom of Hawai'i. Assuming a compromise figure of 500,000 Native Hawaiians at the time of Cook's arrival (an estimate somewhere between 200,000 and 875,000 that have been the extremes of the population debate), the first one hundred years following contact (1778–1878) resulted in a 90% population decline (see Nordyke, 1989). King David Kalakaua states of his people: "One day their words will be heard no more forever."
1893	January 16, 1893, the U.S. Minister to Hawai'i, John Stevens, with a group of American businessmen and the help of the U.S. navy invaded the sovereign Hawaiian nation without the permission or approval of the U.S. government. On January 17, 1893, Queen Lili'uokalani, the last queen, and the Hawaiian monarchy were overthrown by a group of American businessmen. This tragic event is called the Onipaa by Native Hawaiians.
1893	President Grover Cleveland investigated the overthrow of the monarchy, declared it an "act of war" and called for restoration of the Hawaiian monarchy (Osborne, 1998). However, Cleveland's words went unheeded and the Provisional government declared itself as the Republic of Hawai'i (Hawaii Advisory Committee to the U.S. Commission on Civil Rights, 2001).

1895	Queen Lili'okulani is sentenced to jail. In a show of force and discontent, the annexationists put down a Native Hawaiian rebellion to restore the Queen and tried and convicted her for treason on January 7, 1895. She was sentenced to five years in jail (she actually served 21 months) in an act designed to humiliate her and her people.
1898	On July 7 Hawai'i became a territory of the United States without a single vote from the Native Hawaiians. The United States annexes the former Kingdom of Hawai'i. American population increases.
1959	Hawai'i becomes the 50th State.
1970-pres	Resurgence of activism among Native Hawaiian people including numerous civil protests. Cries for Native Hawaiian sovereignty and nationhood. Opening of many schools to teach Hawaiian languages. Native Hawaiian activists are calling for the preservation of Native Hawaiian culture and are pushing for various kinds of national and international recognition of Hawaiian people.
1972	Congress included Native Hawaiians in American Indian/Alaskan Native legislation; first grantee from the Administration for Native Americans was Alu Like, Inc.
1973	The *Hokule'a*, a Polynesian voyaging canoe, was launched and becomes a symbol of Native Hawaiian pride and navigational skills. Many young Hawaiians develop interest in traditional Native Hawaiian culture and begin studying Hawaiian arts and skills. Vessel sails to Marquesas and Tahiti using traditional navigation methods repeating historic voyages.
1980s	The Bishop Estate, an educational, cultural, and financial trust created at the turn of the century as the legacy of Princess Bernice Pauhi Bishop, emerges as a major social force in Hawai'i through its ownership of leased land. Its purpose is to promote the educational development of students of Native Hawaiian ancestry. By the 1990s, it becomes the wealthiest private trust in the U.S. with more than eight billion dollars of net worth.
1983	United States Congress Native Hawaiians Study Commission Report – a 21-month study of the culture, needs, and concerns of Native Hawaiians.
1985	*E Ola Mau* Native Hawaiian Health Needs Study Report (*E Ola Mau*) published by Alu Like, Inc., identifies the physical, mental, spiritual, and dental health needs of Native Hawaiians. The mental health report documents mental health status and major issues and stressors facing Native Hawaiians.
1988	U.S. Congress Native Hawaiian Health Care Improvement Act (PL 100-597), Section 2(3)–42 USC 11701 is passed. The purpose is to raise the health status of the Native Hawaiians (Oneha, 2001). *Papa Ola Lokahi* was formed with representatives from 25 public agencies and private organizations, representing the first effort to establish an infrastructure to address Native Hawaiian health issues.
1989	*Papa Ola Lokahi's* Native Hawaiian Health Master Plan to develop appropriate and culturally acceptable health care programs and delivery for Native Hawaiians (Akau et al., 1998).
1990	Population of State of Hawai'i exceeds 1,100,000 people distributed across the following islands: Oah'u (836,207), Hawai'i (120,317), Maui (91,361), Kaua'i (50,947), Moloka'i (6,717), Lana'i (2,426), and Ni'ihau (230). Ethnocultural minorities make up more than 75% of the State's population: Caucasian (262,604), Japanese (222,014), Part-Hawaiian (196,367), Other Mixed Race (190,789), Filipino (123,642), Chinese (51,293), African American (16,180), Korean (11,597), Pure-Hawaiian (8,711), Samoans (3,235), and Puerto Ricans (3,140).
	These population figures are inaccurate for 1996. Rapid influxes of legal immigrants into Hawai'i (e.g., Filipino, Korean, and Vietnamese populations) and illegal immigrants by other groups (e.g., Chinese, Mexican) have resulted in sizeable increases in the population of these groups and proportionate reductions in the population distribution of other groups.

Table 9.1   (Continued)

1990s	Federal government returns the Island of Kaho'olawe to the State of Hawaii along with a congressional appropriation exceeding 400 million dollars for its restoration following decades of military use/abuse including constant practice bombing operations.
	Sizeable Federal Government grants and entitlement funds for health, education, economic, and social demonstration projects are available to the Hawaiian people and the State of Hawaii.
	The Sovereignty Movement grows in strength and determination. Office of Hawaii Affairs manages an election procedure to determine Native Hawaiian interest in various forms of self-government.
1991	Office of Hawaiian Health declared a serious health crisis for the indigenous people of Hawai'i.
1992	Legislation amended and reauthorized the Native Hawaiian Health Care Improvement Act (Public Law 1 02-396).
1993	Congress passed a resolution and President Clinton signed Public Law 103-150 which acknowledged the 100th year commemoration of the overthrow of the Kingdom of Hawai'i and a formal apology to Native Hawaiians for the improper role of the United States military in support of the overthrow (Hawaii Advisory Committee to the U.S. Commission on Civil Rights, 2001). What this provided was an acknowledgement by the US government of the ramifications of the "illegal overthrow" of 1893 and for the government to engage in a process for policy development on the reconciliation between the US and the Native Hawaiian people (Hawaii Advisory Committee to the U.S. Commission on Civil Rights, 2001).
1998	The first Native Hawaiian Health and Wellness Summit was held which emphasized that land, water, ocean, and air are inseparable from the health of the Hawaiian people (Oneha, 2001).
	September – Publication of the Special Issue: The Health of Native Hawaiians in the *Pacific Health Dialog: Journal of Community Health and Clinical Medicine for the Pacific.*
2000	Senator Daniel Akaka introduced a bill, the U.S. Senate Bill 344 called the Native Hawaiian Recognition Act (also referred to as the "Akaka Bill", Bolante, 2003), which would allow for federal recognition of Native Hawaiian people as a distinct indigenous entity similar to the tribal status of Native Americans. Attorneys had been leading a campaign against Native Hawaiian entitlements, including challenging the funding of the Office of Hawaiian Affairs and the Native Hawaiian Homelands, and also planned to challenge this bill if it had passed.
2006	The Akaka Bill (Native Hawaiian federal recognition legislation) was voted down by the US Senate. The vote was 56-41 in favor of the move. However, that total was short of the 60 votes needed to advance this bill to the next level. The Bush administration made a statement prior to the vote strongly opposing this bill.

Source: McCubbin, L., & Marsella, A. J. (under review). Native Hawaiian psychology: The cultural, historical, and situational context of indigenous ways of knowing. *Cultural Diversity & Ethnic Minority Psychology.*

of being – that is their psyche. Figure 9.1 displays the Native Hawaiian psyche graphically (McCubbin & Marsella, under review).

1. *Aloha (affectionate, compassionate, and loving sentiments)*
   The value that captures the Hawaiian spirit is *aloha*, which describes affectionate, compassionate, and loving sentiments (Kanahele, 1986; Rezentes, 1996). *Aloha* has many meanings, including affection, love,

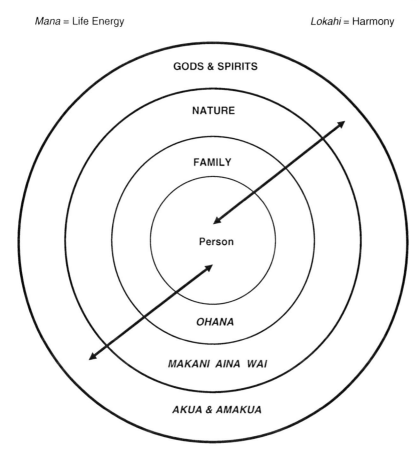

Mana = Life Energy   *Lokahi* = Harmony

GODS & SPIRITS

NATURE

FAMILY

Person

OHANA

MAKANI AINA WAI

AKUA & AMAKUA

Figure 9.1. Traditional Native Hawaiian Conception of Psyche: Person, Family, Nature, and Spiritual World
Source: McCubbin, L., & Marsella, A. J. (under review). Native Hawaiian psychology: The cultural, historical, and situational context of indigenous ways of knowing. *Cultural Diversity & Ethnic Minority Psychology.*

kindness, mercy, and sympathy (Pukui & Elbert, 1986). The term *aloha* is employed both in greeting and in parting, and conveys a message of community and goodwill (Kanahele, 1986; Pukui & Elbert, 1986; Rezentes, 1996). However, *aloha* has multiple meanings and can be applied to systems as well as individuals, including a philosophy of mutual kindness in a community (Kanahele, 1986; Rezentes, 1996). *Aloha* can also encompass the realm of the divine and can have a spiritual essence. According to Queen Lili'uokalani in a letter written to her *hanai'ed* (culturally and informally adopted) daughter after the overthrow of her monarchy, she stated: "To gain the kingdom of heaven is to hear what is not said, to see what can not be seen, and to know the unknowable. That is aloha" (Lili'uokalani, 1917).

2. *'Aina (the environment nourishing the body, mental health, and relationships with the spiritual world)*
Another value is the concept of *'aina. 'Aina* can be translated to refer to the earth, land, or nature (Kanahele, 1986; Pukui & Elbert, 1986; Rezentes, 1996). *'Aina* has three dimensions: physical, psychological, and spiritual (Kanahele, 1986; Rezentes, 1996). The environment embodies physical *'aina*, indicating both ancestral homelands and the substance required to nourish the body. Psychological *'aina* is related to mental health, particularly in regard to positive and negative thinking. Spiritual *'aina* speaks to daily relationships between Native Hawaiians and the spiritual world. Traditionally, the spiritual world has been – and continues to be – a source of great guidance and strength for Native Hawaiian people.

3. *Ha'aha'a (modesty or humility, interconnectedness, respect, and caring)*
Ha'aha'a refers to modesty or humility, and the values of interconnectedness, respect, and caring for the welfare of one's people (Kanahele, 1986; Rezentes, 1996). This stems from humility and sensitivity, as opposed to arrogance or a feeling of superiority (Kanahele, 1986; Rezentes, 1996). Pukui and Elbert (1986) describe *ha'aha'a* as an adjective meaning humble, modest, unassuming, or unpretentious. *Ha'aha'a* is a characteristic found in leaders who acknowledge their power and can surrender this power as an act of humility and honor. However, *ha'aha'a* has been misinterpreted by Western culture as submissiveness or weakness. It is important to understand that *ha'aha'a* refers to a balance between humility and self-respect as well as between humility and confidence. It is this balance that marks a good Hawaiian leader.

4. *Kokua (helping others)*
The value *of kokua* refers to help. The word *kokua* means to assist or relieve (Kanahele, 1986, Pukui & Elbert, 1986; Rezentes, 1996), and this value is demonstrated by empathic exchanges when one's family, friends, and neighbors have been in need of help. In modern day Hawaii, this value continues to serve a purpose, as values such as *aloha* can only survive with a balance of mutual give-and-take, as defined by *kokua.*

5. *Lokahi (harmony)*
Lokahi, or harmony (Kanahele, 1986; Rezentes, 1996), is a core Native Hawaiian value and a driving force guiding the other values such as *aloha, ha'aha'a*, and *kokua*. Pukui and Elbert (1986) further describe *lokahi* as meaning unity. According to Rezentes (1996), *lokahi* can be understood as a triangle formed by *'aina* (nature), *kanaka* (humankind), and *ke akua* (god(s)). Native Hawaiian health requires *lokahi* or a sense of harmony between mind, body, spirit and land. As U.S. Senator Daniel Inouye stated, "one's physical health is only one aspect of a whole

system that includes one's spiritual, emotional and mental well-being"
(Look, Mackura, & Spoehr, 1998). Unlike Western perspectives that
tend to compartmentalize areas of health (e.g., physical versus mental), Native Hawaiians tend to view the person holistically. This value
of *lokahi* is important when listening to Native people's stories and
allowing the space for them to express these interconnections, thus
incorporating this into the treatment plan. For example, Casken (2001)
points out the need for Native Hawaiians to protect the land and the
ocean as these aspects of *'aina* are key to the health of the *kanaka*.

6. ***Mana*** *(divine or spiritual power)*
   Mana means divine or spiritual power (Kanahele, 1986; Rezentes, 1996)
   and evokes respect for gods and their role in *lokahi*. *Mana* is a power
   and quantifiable energy bestowed by a spiritual source onto someone
   or something (Oneha, 2001). *Mana* emanating from ecological elements
   or nature has the power to calm, energize, heal, and relax (Oneha,
   2001), and therefore is important in understanding indigenous healing
   practices and traditions as well as certain cultural behaviors.

7. ***'Ohana*** (family)
   'Ohana, or family (Kanahele, 1986; Pukui & Elbert, 1986; Rezentes, 1996)
   is a primary Native Hawaiian value, and relates to the community values of *aloha*, *ha'aha'a* and *kokua*. ¡*Ohana* continues to be a strong source
   of support and identity in Hawaiian culture today. A person's ¡*ohana*
   can consist of extended family as well as informal relationships such
   as friends and family members of friends. Therefore ¡*ohana* encompasses not only kin but also those members who are closely tied to the
   extended family who provide support or that the ¡*ohana* is currently
   supporting emotionally, physically, and/or financially.

8. ***Alaka'i*** *(leadership)*
   The value of leadership or *alaka'i* is integral to the survival and the
   resilience of the Native Hawaiian people. *Alaka'i* means to direct, guide,
   or lead (Kanahele, 1986; Pukui & Elbert, 1986; Rezentes, 1996), and
   is necessarily accompanied by *ha'aha'a*. Today, *alaka'i* is very important in light of the Hawaiian renaissance movement and sovereignty
   (Kanahele, 1986). In general, the values of *aloha* (love), expertise, loyalty, *mana*, and *pono* (goodness) are characteristics necessary in a leader.
   Expertise includes competence, knowledge, judgment and *kela* (excellence), which are very important in Native Hawaiian culture. Loyalty
   means that leaders would band together no matter what hardships
   their people face. *Mana* flows from relationships and status, and is considered appropriate only under the conditions of good relationships
   and true status.

9. ***Pono*** *(justice)*
   Another key value is *pono*, which refers to goodness, or "right," "just"
   and "fair" (Pukui & Elbert, 1986). This value can refer to interpersonal
   relationships and behaving in a *pono* way, meaning that the individual

is acting properly or what is good and right for one's *'ohana*. *Pono* can also refer to the relationship between Native Hawaiians and the land. This value is demonstrated in the state motto, "Ua mau ke ea o ka aina i ka pono" which translates to "The life of the land is perpetuated in righteousness."

10. **Kela** *(excellence)*

   Kela means excellence or exceeding beyond (Pukui & Elbert, 1986; Rezentes, 1996), and refers to achievement or striving for positive performance. *Kela* is just one of many Native Hawaiian values challenging the stereotype of Hawaiians as community oriented to the point of lacking any sense of competition with either others or the self, in search of accomplishments or excellence (Shook, 1985).

In light of these values, general guidelines may be employed by mental health practitioners in order to ensure cultural sensitivity when working with Native Hawaiian clients. First, awareness of the importance of community, as evidenced by the values of *aloha* and *'ohana*, among others, will allow mental health professionals to avoid pushing a Western agenda of individualism, or misinterpret and misdiagnose Native Hawaiians as being enmeshed with their families. Furthermore, understanding Hawaiian culture, history, and values will assist mental health workers and disaster responders by helping them to be more aware of interrelated factors that affect psychological health and Native Hawaiians' ability to heal from trauma. Also, it is essential to understand Hawaiian values to gain insight into the strengths of Native Hawaiian people today, as well as to guide mental health practices to maintain these values and sources of resilience for future generations.

Communication Styles

It is a commonly stated truism that the Native Hawaiian people communicate on the basis of "relationships." That is, interactions and transactions which are grounded on the premise of developing, maintaining, nurturing, building, strengthening and utilizing interpersonal linkages which have a prior history and/or have a probability of leading to future relationships. Underlying this pattern of communication is the cornerstone of trust, loyalty, harmony and predictability in present and future interactions.

Essentially, the Hawaiian concept of self is grounded in social relationships (Pukui, Haertig, & Lee, 1972) and tied to the belief that the individual, society and nature are inseparable as demonstrated by the value of *lokahi*. Such bonds of emotional affect are expected to support and protect each member (Ito, 1985).

Consistent with the self-portrayal as generous, gregarious and hospitable people, the Hawaiians are characterized as altruistic, giving and helpful, which is consistent with the value of *kokua*. The "easy going" self-portrayal is consistent with the Hawaiian's cultural foundation of expansive release, letting go, and a caring personality. Consequently, interpersonal exchanges are grounded in the preservation of harmony. Howard (1974), in his study of the Hawaiian community, noted the strong emphasis on "Ain't No Big Thing" as a way for the Hawaiian people to minimize conflict and open the door to a resolution or common ground for mutual understanding and acceptance.

Historically, the Hawaiian people were storytellers, transferring information across generations through storytelling. As noted in the writings of Cook, Withy, and Tarallo-Jensen (2003), the Hawaiian people, prior to the introduction of printed materials, depended upon oral communication as a way to develop shared concerns and beliefs, and to resolve issues (Gallimore & Howard, 1968; Gallimore, Whitehorn Boggs, & Jordan, 1974; Howard, 1974). All relationships are expressions of bonds of kinship involving the exchange of emotions. In this context hurt feelings are salient and leave the Hawaiians sensitive to rejection or disregard (Pukui et al., 1972). Thus it is the underlying intent of communication to keep rational bonds clear and free from entanglements of conflict.

Such openness in sharing information and feelings, however, does not generalize to the expectation that the Hawaiians would find comfort and seek refuge in the office of professional therapists and counselors. The elements of trust and prior relationships take on added importance and are expected to precede participation in professional counseling. Therefore it is important for mental health professionals to participate in organizations such as civic clubs, church groups and community activism organizations to assist in building a prior relationship with Native Hawaiians and demonstrating a commitment to community involvement.

This emphasis on sense of self in social relationships can also be seen in the conceptualization of mental illness. The inability to "let it go" or hold a grudge can lead to emotional retaliations. The reciprocal relationships and emotional bonds include not only altruistic indebtedness but can also refer to hurtful indebtedness and revenge (Ito, 1985). A transgression against another can lead to symptoms of illness. For example, *ma'i ma loko* refers to sickness from within (*loko*) which can be caused by *hihia* or unresolved, unforgiven hostilities (Pukui, et al., 1972). It is important to be aware that while Native Hawaiians may minimize conflicts and misunderstandings, the flip side is that the inability to let go or find resolution can lead to disharmony, which may manifest itself into symptoms of mental illness, injury or misfortune.

VALID ASSESSMENT INSTRUMENTS

One of the potential barriers to working with Native Hawaiians in trauma contexts is the possible misuse of measurements and assessments that have not been validated for Native Hawaiians. By using "Western" measures and not examining whether the constructs being measured fit for an indigenous population, errors can occur in diagnoses and treatment. Therefore it is important to be aware of the psychological measures that have proven to be valid with this particular population.

The E Ola Mau: The Native Hawaiian Health Needs study published in 1985 pointed out the need for culturally sensitive measurement instruments for Native Hawaiians. Given the alarming statistics regarding Native Hawaiian health, one needs to consider the cultural validity of measurement and assessment of mental health factors among Native Hawaiians. The reporting of discrepancies on mental health among Native Hawaiians may also be affected by the measurements used to explain mental health symptoms and the prevalence of certain disorders.

The Native Hawaiian Mental Health Research Development Program (NHMHRDP) at the University of Hawai'i at Manoa in the Department of Psychiatry has taken on the challenge of "Kukuli-I-Na-Hulili" or "bridging the gap" (Choi-Misailidis & Kaulukukui, 2004) between the knowledge regarding Native Hawaiian health, including developing a measure on Native Hawaiian identity and examining the validity of measures on psychological adjustment for this population.

Studies on the validity of instruments on Native Hawaiians fall into two categories: (a) Native Hawaiian cultural identity, and (b) measurement of psychological factors. Two measures of Hawaiian cultural identity were developed and empirically tested in 2000 and 2002, the Hawaiian Culture Scale–Adolescent Version (HCS; Hishinuma et al., 2000a) and the He'ana'mana'o o na mo'omeheu Hawai'i, called the Hawaiian Ethnocultural Inventory (HEI) of cultural practices (Crabbe, 2002).

The NHMHRDP took up the challenge of developing a measure of cultural constructs within the Native Hawaiian community and to discern the effects of a valid cultural identity and affiliation measure on psychological adjustment among Native Hawaiian adolescents. With this mission, the NHMHRDP developed the 50-item Hawaiian Culture Scale – Adolescent version which includes measures of the following constructs: (a) source of learning the Hawaiian way of life, (b) value and maintenance of Hawaiian beliefs, (c) value of non-Hawaiian beliefs, (d) Hawaiian blood quantum, and (e) specific cultural traditions with 7 subscales (i.e., lifestyles, customs-beliefs, activities-social events, folklore-legends, causes-locations, causes-access, and language proficiency). Various analyses were conducted from a large dataset which consisted of 2,272 Native Hawaiians and 1,170 non-Hawaiian adolescent participants (age range 14 to 17). The overall scale demonstrated internal consistency for both Native Hawaiian and non-Hawaiian participants. The seven subscales were also found to have satisfactory internal consistency for both Hawaiian and non-Hawaiian adolescents, ranging from .82 to .96 and .76 to .96, respectively.

The 243-item Hawaiian Ethnocultural Inventory (Crabbe, 2002) also measured cultural identification and affiliation. This measure consists of three aspects of Hawaiian cultural identity: (a) knowledge of a particular cultural practice, (b) belief in a cultural practice, and (c) the frequency in which a person engages in a cultural activity. In a study with 427 participants (55.7% Native Hawaiian and 44.3% non-Hawaiian; age range from 21 to 86), five factors on Hawaiian cultural identity were found via factor analysis from this inventory: (a) beliefs in Hawaiian cultural practices (internal consistency = .97); (b) knowledge of Hawaiian cultural practices (internal consistency = .95); (c) frequency of performing arts (internal consistency = .96); (d) frequency of ocean traditions (internal consistency = .89); and (e) frequency of spiritual and family customs (internal consistency = .85). Native Hawaiians consistently scored higher compared to Non-Hawaiians on belief in cultural practices, knowledge of Hawaiian practices, and frequency of performing arts, ocean traditions and frequency of spiritual and family customs. Further investigation is needed to determine how this valid measure of Hawaiian cultural identity is related to psychological outcomes.

The NHMHRDP has also tested and validated current measures on psychological factors and outcomes among Native Hawaiian adolescents. These measures are: (a) the Rosenberg Self-Esteem Scale (Rosenberg, 1965), (b) the Major Life Events checklist (Andrews, Lewinsohn, & Hops, 1993), (c) the State-Trait Anxiety Inventory (STAI; Spielberger, Gorsuch, & Lushene, 1970), (d) the Center for Epidemiologic Studies Depression Inventory (CES-D; Radloff, 1977), and (e) selected items from the Substance Abuse Subtle Screening Inventory-Adolescent (SASSI-A; Miller, 1990) in the prediction of substance abuse and dependence. Miyamoto and colleagues (2001) assessed the construct, scalar, and functional equivalences for the Rosenberg (1965) Self-Esteem Scale (RSES) and the Major Life Events checklist (MLE; Andrews et al., 1993) among Native Hawaiians. The RSES consists of two factors, positive and negative self esteem. The Major Life Events checklist measures the presence of 6 negative life events that have been experienced in the past six months by oneself (the participant), a family member, and a close friend. With a sample of 696 adolescents, including Native Hawaiian adolescents, this study found construct, scalar, and functional equivalences for the RSES and the MLE.

Hishinuma and colleagues (2000b; Hishinuma, Miyamoto, Nishimura, & Nahulu, 2000c) tested the psychometric properties of the State-Trait Anxiety Inventory among Asian and Pacific Islander adolescents, which included a subsample of Native Hawaiians. With a sample of 3,019 adolescents including Caucasians, Filipinos, Hawaiians, Japanese and mixed race Non-Hawaiians, this study found cross-cultural equivalence of the STAI and supported a four factor model (State-Anxiety Absent, State-Anxiety Present, Trait-Anxiety Absent and Trait-Anxiety Present) using confirmatory factor analyses. Also, this study found the STAI to have satisfactory internal consistency and concurrent validity of the different factors and subscale measures. Prescott and colleagues (1998) examined the predictive validity of the CES-D scale on major depression and dysthymic disorder among Native Hawaiians and other minority groups. The sample consisted of 556 adolescents (58% were Native

Hawaiian) randomly selected from a large database of over 7,000 students. The study supported the validity of the CES-D for screening of depression among Native Hawaiian adolescents.

Nishimura and associates (2001) from the NHMHRDP team also examined items from the Substance Abuse Subtle Screening Inventory-Adolescent (SASSI-A; Miller, 1990) version to determine their predictive validity of substance abuse and dependency among Native Hawaiian and non-Native Hawaiian adolescents. This study included 542 adolescents (57.4% were Native Hawaiian) who were randomly selected from a database of over 7,000 adolescents. Six items from the SASSI-A were used. This study found that these selected items may prove to be useful as screener questions for Hawaiian adolescents and identifying those at risk for substance abuse and dependence.

It should be noted that the majority of these instruments have only been tested on Native Hawaiian adolescents and therefore caution is needed when using these assessments with older adults.

CULTURALLY DEFINED SYMPTOMS AND DISORDERS

Given the traumatic history and the stress that Native Hawaiians face, these multiple burdens can lead to the manifestation of symptoms that can be categorized as disorders. However, to be congruent with the *Kanaka Maoli*, it is important to consider how Native Hawaiians define mental health issues and their etiology, which may be similar to Western categorizations or particularly unique to the culture.

Using Native Hawaiian concepts and definitions provided by Pukui and associates (1972) in their landmark work *"Ku Kanaka: Look to the Source,"* mental health issues will be presented in terms of their etiology, various symptoms, and culturally defined syndromes.

Ma'i mai waho (Sickness from Outside Forces) and Ma'i ma loko Sickness from Within

The diagnosis of an illness from a Hawaiian cultural perspective can encompass the body, mind and spirit (Judd, 1998). Native Hawaiian healers have two different etiologies of illness: *ma' i mai waho* and *ma' i ma loko* (Pukui, Handy, & Livermore, 1934). *Ma'i mai waho* refers to sickness caused by outside (*waho*) forces such as spirits or gods. For these illnesses a traditional healing practice would be *la'au kahea* or faith healing, which would involve prayer and restoration of *lokahi* of the body, mind and spirit (Judd, 1998). *Ma' i ma loko* refers to sickness from within (*loko*), not originating from the body but from the family, as in grudges, *hihia* (unresolved, unforgiven hostilities), *hukihuki* (hostile power struggles), and unpleasantness (Pukui et al., 1972). This may be prompted by negative feelings due to interpersonal conflicts (Boggs & Chun, 1990).

Disorders of Family Relationships. Pukui and associates (1972) described different symptoms similar to those found in depression or anxiety attributed to interpersonal interactions. Some examples of these symptoms connected to relational and intrapsychic discord are *waia, ike hewa, loha* and *manawai*. Waia refers to an intense lasting shame and an inability to face people, and is typically accompanied by disgrace to the family. *'Ike hewa* means a private worry or feelings of guilt over a transgression that is unwitnessed by others; however, a person is worried about punishment from god(s). This guilt can lead to mental anguish and can lead to rumination. *Loha* and *manawai* can refer to feelings of depression, being beaten down or spiritless, possibly stemming from guilt. Sickness or illness can occur from interpersonal disturbances or disharmony. *I loko o ka'ohana* translates to an illness that is caused by disturbed relationships within one's family.

Cultural Loss Syndrome – Kaumaha. Rezentes (1996), in his work on Hawaiian psychology, outlined two cultural syndromes that affect Native Hawaiians: the *Kaumaha Syndrome* and the *Ha'ole Syndrome. Kaumaha* in Hawaiian refers to grief or sorrow (Pukui et al., 1972) and feelings of sadness and depression. According to Rezentes (1996), this syndrome is rooted in the "collective sadness and moral outrage" that Native Hawaiians have felt due to historical events and trauma. This has also been referred to as the Cultural Loss/Stress Hypothesis (Hammond, 1988), which describes the effects of two centuries of culture loss for Native Hawaiians on health and educational outcomes.

It is similar to the concept of historical trauma (Whitbeck, Adams, Hoyt, & Chen, 2004) among American Indians who have suffered from multiple losses such as religion, language, traditional family systems, traditional healing practices and generations of people due to the colonization process in the U.S. Historical trauma has similar symptoms found in Post Traumatic Stress Disorder and can encompass a range of psychopathology such as depression, anxiety and grief (Whitbeck et al., 2004). Noyes (1996) draws parallels of the dynamics of abuse suffered by sexual and physical abuse survivors to the physical and emotional abuse that Native Hawaiians have suffered for the past 200 years. This historical trauma has been discussed in the literature; however, there remains a paucity of research on the distal and proximal effects of this trauma on Native Hawaiians across generations.

Ha'ole Syndrome *(Spiritual Sickness)*

The *Ha'ole Syndrome* (Rezentes, 1996) refers to the phenomenon when an individual lacks *aloha*. In essence, this means that one has lost their breath, essence, life, or spirit. Symptoms of this syndrome include superficial or dissatisfying relationships (may be abusive), low self-esteem, depression, and feelings of emptiness, along with a distorted sense of self-importance. When a person lacks "aloha" that is key to Native Hawaiian culture, emotional discord and disharmony can occur, which may lead to mental illness. Table 9.2 provides a more detailed listing of Native Hawaiian mental/spiritual disorders (McCubbin & Marsella, under review; Marsella et al., 1985).

The etiology of these syndromes, the expression of symptoms and the descriptions of these disorders are embedded in Hawaiian cultural values. Therefore, treatment of these cultural symptoms and disorders may involve Native Hawaiian healing practices.

Native Hawaiian Healing Practices   The Native Hawaiian Health Research Consortium in 1985 pointed out the need to look at the underlying sociocultural stressors and imbalances that Native Hawaiians have had to face, and pointed out the need for legislative action towards improving the health status of Native Hawaiians. In 1988, U.S. Congress passed the Native Hawaiian Health Care Act, which represents the first federal legislation to acknowledge and support traditional healing (Judd, 1998). With federal funding, Papa Ola Lokahi was developed to set up a system of Native Hawaiian health centers on each of the major islands. This system was designed to deliver health care services that were based on native values, indigenous health-seeking behaviors, Native Hawaiian problem-solving methods and Hawaiian

Table 9.2   Native Hawaiian Terms for Mental Illness

'a 'a	Panic stricken. Made dumb by anger and fury
'a aia	Demented
'a ala'ioa	Wild, uncontrolled
Hehena	Insane, lunatic, crazy
ho'ohewahewa	Deranged (not as strong as hehena or pupule)
Kaumaha	Sad, heavily burdened
Kuloloa	Idiotic
Loha	Sullen, spiritlessness
lu'ulu'u	Heavily burdened, sorrowful, troubled
Ma'ina loko	Sickness from within (caused by misdeeds, family troubles)
Ma'ina waho	Sickness from outside (evil forces, external cause)
Ohewa	Delirious, incoherent, drunk
Opulepule	Moronic, imbecilic
Pupule	Crazy, insane, wild, uncontrolled
Uluahewa	Crazy, sometimes due to evil spirit
Uluhia	Possessed by evil spirits
Uluhua	Irritated, vexed, annoyed
Uluku	Disturbed, agitated, nervous
'uhane noho:	Possessed by a spirit
wela:	Angry (hot)

(see Marsella et al., 1985 for an extensive glossary of mental health terms that were prepared by members of the E Ola Mau Mental Health Task Force). From McCubbin, L. & Marsella, A.J. (under review). Native Hawaiian psychology: The cultural, historical, and situational context of indigenous ways of knowing. *Cultural Diversity & Ethnic Minority Psychology.*

treatment modalities for Native people suffering from physical and mental illness (Casken, 2001). Handy (1927) offered this brief overview of the complex mind-body-spirit approaches of the Native Hawaiians:

> When it was a case of demons in the sick body, various modes of exorcism were resorted to, including the recitation of potent spells, the application of heat, the use of evil smelling herbs. Spells of black magic were capable of being counteracted by a powerful magician who attempted usually to cause the trouble to revert upon the sender. . . Finally there were various types of spells and rites designed to restore health and life to the sick body, and practices resorted to for the purpose of bringing back into the body the soul that was believed to have left it (p. 233).

Ho'olomilomi and La'au Lapa'au (Massage and Herbal Medicine)

Native Hawaiian indigenous healing practices consist of four significant modalities of treatment: *la'au kahea* (faith healing; also referred to as the "calling" medicine; Pukui et al., 1972), *ho'olomilomi* (massage), *la'au lapa'au* (herbal medicine), and *ho'oponopono* (conflict resolution; Chang, 2001; Judd, 1998). Native Hawaiian healers using indigenous healing practices emphasize the critical component of spirituality or some form of *la'au kahea* in treatment and that all healing begins with spiritual cleansing or prayer (Judd, 1998). Spiritual blessings are offered both before and after each healing session (Chang, 2001).

According to Chang (2001) *ho'olomilomi*, which refers to healing through massage, is a hands-on practice that is employed to ease back pain and muscle strain, as well as induce relaxation and relieve stress. It is also a common treatment for boils, cuts, gastric distress, scrapes, and sores (Chang, 2001), and can be used for anxiety and other mental health issues.

La'au lapa'au, or Hawaiian herbal healing refers to the use of common *la'au* (plant, animal or products from ocean and the sea) for healing various symptoms and illnesses. There are many herbal remedies that are used for a variety of symptoms, and the Hawaiian community has worked towards maintaining and preserving this knowledge and traditional healing practice. Judd (1998) interviewed Native Hawaiian healers and found common *la'au* used by these healers such as *popolo, uhaloa, hauoi, kukui, olena*. These *la'au* are used primarily for physical ailments rather than psychological illnesses. Another herbal remedy that has gained increasing attention is *noni*, which has been used to treat physical ailments (i.e., urinary disorders, respiratory conditions, diabetes, hypertension, diarrhea and arthritis, and cancer) and one psychological issue, drug addiction (Elkins, 1997). Empirical research still needs to be conducted to understand the contribution these *la'au* have on healing. There has been increased interest by the medical and pharmaceutical communities on the ethnobotanical component of Hawaiian traditional healing practices (Boyd, Maunakea, Mordan, & Csiszar, 1998).

Ho'oponopono

The fourth treatment modality is *ho'oponopono*, the healing practice aimed at achieving *lokahi*, which can be equated with harmony (Chang, 2001). The meaning of *ho'oponopono* is to "set things right," (Pukui et al., 1972) and it was traditionally practiced in order to resolve interpersonal problems or to prevent illness (Boggs & Chun, 1990; McDermott, Tseng, & Maretzki, 1980; Pukui et al., 1972; Shook, 1985). *Ho'oponopono* can be used to restore harmony and maintain good relations in the face of unresolved problems in the *johana* (family; McDermott et al., 1980). Regular practice of *ho'oponopono* resolves hostility, thereby preventing the accumulation of negative feelings, resentment, or *hilia* (entanglement) (Ito, 1985). In households containing individuals of Hawaiian ancestry, over one-third engages in *ho'oponopono*, (Boggs & Chun, 1990). A version of *ho'oponopono* has been approved by the Hawaiian Cultural Committee of the Queen Lili'uokalani Children's Center as culturally appropriate for therapy with families of Hawaiian descent (Ito, 1985).

Ho'oponopono is essentially Hawaiian family therapy that involves restoration and maintenance of positive relations within the family and spiritual world through acts of restitution and forgiveness that foster spiritual cleansing (Boggs & Chun, 1990; Rezentes, 1996). The process is usually directed by a *kahuna* or senior family member (Rezentes, 1996). Participants in *ho'oponopono* are members of an immediate family, with the exception of the leader, who is usually a relation or known to at least one participant (Boggs & Chun, 1990; McDermott et al., 1980; Shook, 1985). Confidentiality is a condition of *ho'oponopono* (Rezentes, 1996). Other conditions include commitment by all family members to the process, to be honest and sincere, to embody *aloha*, and to agree on the selected *haku*, or leader (McDermott et al., 1980; Rezentes, 1996).

The following list of the Native Hawaiian Healing Arts (*La'au Kahea*) demonstrates the broad spectrum of approaches available for restoring health and harmony:

1. Herbal treatments
2. Purification baths (*kapu kai*)
3. Massage (*lomi lomi*)
4. Special diets and fasting
5. Confession and apology (*mihi*)
6. Dream interpretation (*moe 'uhane*)
7. Clairvoyance (*hihi'o*)
8. Prayer (*pule ho'onoa*)
9. Transfer of thought (*Ho 'olulu ia*)
10. Possession (*noho*)
11. Water blessings (*pi kai*)
12. Spirit mediumship (*haka*)

SPECIAL CONSIDERATIONS FOR DISASTERS AND TRAUMA

The plight of Native Hawaiians in the state of Hawaii has been well documented. Research has found Native Hawaiian adults are either at the top or close to the top of every category of medical disease, social pathology, and psychological maladaption (e.g., Blaisdell, 1993; E Ola Mau, 1985; Goebert & Kanoa, 1992; Hammond, 1988; Marsella et al., 1985; Native Hawaiian Educational Assessment Project, 1983; Papa O Lokahi, 1987; United States Congress, 1987; White & Landis, 1982). Native Hawaiian adults have the highest rates in the state of Hawai'i for cancer deaths, diabetes, high blood pressure, gout, bronchitis, asthma, emphysema, and obesity, in addition to the shortest life expectancy for any racial/ethnic group in the state.

Native Hawaiians also have the highest rate of suicide, especially among young men and the elderly. Native Hawaiians also have high rates of substance abuse, depression and anxiety disorders compared to non-Hawaiians (Guerrero, Hishinuma, Andrade, & Bell, 2003; Marsella et al., 1995; Prescott et al., 1998). Despite ongoing efforts to infuse mental health care with cultural awareness, Native Hawaiians continue to experience poor mental health compared to many other minority ethnic groups (Bell et al., 2001).

Native Hawaiians' overrepresentation on most physical health, mental health and social dysfunction profiles and statistics has been causally linked to the residual trauma emanating from historical and cultural traumatic experiences (Native Hawaiian "Educational" Assessment Project, 1983). It is argued that the in-migration of foreign cultures into the Hawaiian archipelago forced changes in the life of the *Kanaka Maoli* people, and thus poor health status may be attributed to the maladaptive responses of the Hawaiian people over the past 200 years. The cultural trauma has contributed to a condition of long-term psychosocial cultural trauma similar to that experienced by other colonized indigenous peoples (Salzman, 2001). The native people were subjected to persistent ridicule and discrimination. Hawaiians were viewed as "stupid" and "lazy" people. Cook et al. (2003) characterized this adverse situation as "cultural wounding". And this wounding, it is argued, is related to the present day negative health status of *Kanaka Maoli*.

The decline in the health and well-being of the *Kanaka Maoli* flows from the impact of several traumatic events, each contributing to the gradual but notable deterioration in the fabric of the Hawaiian culture. Cook and associates (2003) offer the thesis that the Hawaiian culture was built on the concept of the *Maoli* philosophical truth. This "truth" reflected a defined way of life with divine laws initiated to protect and to perpetuate the physical and metaphysical health of all beings. "All life," Cook and colleagues (2003) argued, "all elements within that life, all ritual and prayer, all Ancestral dogma, all the mundane and spiritual disciplines – everything relevant to body and soul was ruled by an awareness of this Maoli philosophical truth."

In this worldview, humankind in the *Kanaka Maoli* worldview was the species with the duty to protect all other species. Thus at the core of the

Hawaiian culture was spirituality which in turn was built on two belief structures: (a) the *Ihi Kapu* or the consecrated law that enabled the Hawaiian people to live in harmony with one another, with nature and the spiritual realm; and (b) the *Huikala*, the psycho-spiritual process of untangling oneself (involving the *mihikala* protocol of repentance of error) and healing which allows a person to "elevate their earthly presence to a place where their divine self can express itself in this material world, allowing its influence to bring about conditions of health and prosperity for all" (Cook et al., 2003, p. 12).

This spiritual-cultural foundation gains significance in the context of historical trauma brought about in 1819 when the Hawaiian *Alii* (ruling) class introduced dramatic changes in religious practices, an act which removed the *Maoli* from their established practices, which defined the culture and its underlying spiritual base. The *Ihi Kapu*, which balanced the physical with the metaphysical and the celestial with the terrestrial, was replaced by Western epistemological dogma. The cultural healing process practiced for generations lost its meaning and purpose. These changes, driven by Western influences, amounted to dramatic shifts in the normative social order of the Hawaiian people.

The change was accelerated with the edict from the regent Ka'ahumanu announcing a ban on all traditional spiritual practices, thus bringing to an end the indigenous religious system. The new system legitimized the personal superiority of the Hawaiian leaders at the time, all of which introduced the end of the traditional social fabric of the Hawaiian society. Of importance in the loss of the *Maoli* were the philosophical and social system changes in cultural roles afforded to men and women, and "the name of *Kanaka Maoli* no longer substantiated the identity of the indigenous people" (Cook et al., 2003: p. 6). The resulting egalitarianism, which removed the class distinction, introduced ambiguity and confusion regarding the boundaries and responsibilities in the Hawaiian social order. A fact overlooked in the dialogue about the contemporary Hawaiian is the perception of disorder and chaos in the harmony between the physical, spiritual world, cosmological and temporal world, which was a fundamental part of the Hawaiian culture and social structure.

This discourse on historical trauma is essential in our efforts to shed light on the process that unveiled itself in the history of the Hawaiian people. Only recently has it been discussed in a meaningful way to explain the variability in vulnerability, health disparities and well-being of the Hawaiian people.

In drawing from the Native American writings of Brave Heart (Brave Heart, 2001) we can infer the possible resulting violations to the selfhood of the Hawaiian people. She introduced the concept of Historical Trauma Response (HTR), which may well apply to the Hawaiian people (Brave Heart, 2001). HTR is accompanied by symptoms of depression, self-destructive behavior, substance abuse, fixation to trauma, somatic symptoms without a medical reason, anxiety, guilt, and chronic grief. Cultural Wounding is a concept used to describe the psychological/spiritual/cultural injury to the Hawaiian people. Cook and associates (2003) reason that cultural wounds trigger a Post Traumatic Stress Disorder (PTSD) response in the present context and thus lead to clinical reactions that may appear as out of the ordinary.

As documented, PTSD has been linked to depression and other symptoms associated with the Historical Trauma Response. The works of McBride (2002) on PTSD responses to unresolved spiritual issues, Williams and Berry's (1991) study of stress reactions found in immigrant populations and native people removed from their indigenous culture, and Duran and Duran's (1995) reference to the Hawaiian male's loss of cultural roles in contemporary society, are offered as cumulative evidence of Historical Trauma across time (Cook et al., 2003).

RESILIENCE OF THE HAWAIIAN PEOPLE AND FUTURE DIRECTIONS

In this chapter we have discussed the plight of the Hawaiian people from the period before the arrival of explorers and missionaries to the present. In so doing we revealed and highlighted the host of tragedies, which undermined the integrity of an educated and strong nation of Polynesians committed to the maintenance of harmony in the collective group, and harmony with the land, sea and the skies. Clearly, the Hawaiian people were endowed with strengths, values, beliefs, practices, laws and capabilities, which were nurtured and cultivated to insure the longevity, stability, and continued growth of a sovereign nation. This foundation of strengths, however, was disrupted and, some argued, destroyed by the influx of foreigners who, with the aid of the Native people, introduced new values, beliefs, practices, and laws, thus rendering the Hawaiian people without their identity which was rooted in their past, their language and way of life.

Contrary to predications of the demise of the Hawaiian people as passive and of feeble strength in the resistance to the onslaught of change (Daws, 1968), the people of this chain of islands endured hardships and historical defeats to find meaning in a new way of life. Obviously, this pattern of resilience was, and continues to be, at a cost to a pronounced section of Hawaiian people.

Rene Dubos (1974), the renowned biologist and Pulitzer Prize winner, in his lecture to scientists at the Heinz Werner Lecture in 1972, made the poignant argument that "social groups, like individuals, never react passively with environmental situations, instead they respond in a purposive manner" (1974). In this chapter, the authors emphasize this profound observation in shaping their belief that Native people responded to the intrusion of explorers and missionaries by not only integrating and changing their way of life, but also the life of the foreign visitors who established their home among the Hawaiian people who received them.

The resilience of the Hawaiian people can be discovered and understood through the study of those persons of Hawaiian ancestry who negotiated the trauma and change, and found a way of life which promoted the growth and well-being of themselves as individuals, their *¡ohana*, and the community. Resilience is a process of recovery and bouncing back (McCubbin and McCubbin, 2005a) which when examined, reveals the interaction of strengths with the situation, the modification of strengths and capabilities, and the introduction of new and testable patterns of functioning which become a new repertoire of strengths for the Hawaiian people (McCubbin & McCubbin, 2005b).

The research literature begins to shed light on those resilience factors which appear to have some currency in facilitating the well-being and development of Native Hawaiian people and their families. In examining resilience in Native Hawaiian families, Thompson, McCubbin, Thompson, and Elver (1995) found three patterns of functioning which served these families well in the face of adversity: **Coherence**, the family's capability of developing a sense of trust, predictability, and manageability, demonstrating a higher probability of promoting the wellbeing of its members. **Problem-solving communication**, the capability to emphasize positive affirmation and confirmation in the face of adversity in contrast to being incendiary and provocative, emerged as critical to the promotion of wellbeing. The family's **Schema,** the family's shared ethnic identity through which the family defined their world and the problems and solutions presented to them, was not only positively related to well-being (McCubbin, 2006) but also to the family's sense of coherence.

Werner and Smith (1977, 1982, 1992), in their landmark study on the resilience of the children of Kauai, began the journey towards understanding the strengths and resilience of Hawai'i's children. With this foundation, the direction of this continued excursion is in understanding cultural resilience among Native Hawaiian adults, children, families and communities. This will lead to new experiments and interventions to isolate the impact and contributions of resilience research. In turn, the process of prevention and treatment of trauma among indigenous people in the Pacific awaits the influence of this and other research.

ACKNOWLEDGEMENT

The authors would like to extend their deep appreciation to Anthony J. Marsella for his many contributions to the completion of this chapter.

References

Akau, M., Akutagawa, W., Birnie, K., Change, M., Kinney, E. S., Nissanka, S., et al. (1998). Ke ala ola pono: The Native Hawaiian community's effort to heal itself. *Pacific Health Dialog*, 5(2), 232–238.

Andrews, J. A., Lewinsohn, P. M., & Hops, H. (1993). Psychometric properties of scales for the measurement of psychosocial variables associated with depression in adolescence. *Psychological Reports, 73,* 1019–1046.

Bell, C. K., Goebert, D. A., Miyamoto, R. H., Hishinuma, E. S., Andrade, N. N., Johnson, R. C., et al. (2001). Sociocultural and community factors influencing the use of Native Hawaiian healers and healing practices among adolescents in Hawaii. *Pacific Health Dialog, 8*(2), 249–259.

Blaisdell, K. (1993). The health status of the indigenous Hawaiians. *Asian American and Pacific Islander Journal of Health, 1,* 116–160.

Boggs, S. T., & Chun, M. N. (1990). Ho'oponopono: A Hawaiian method of solving interpersonal problems. In K. A. Watson-Gegeo & G. M. White (Eds.), *Disentangling: Conflict discourse in Pacific societies.* Stanford, CA: Stanford University Press.

Bolante, R. (2003). What happened to sovereignty? *Honolulu, 116*(3), 94–97.

Boyd, C. D., Maunakea, A., Mordan, L. J., & Csiszar, K. (1998). Polynesian ethnobotanicals: A critical role in new drug discovery. *Pacific Health Dialog, 5,* 337–340.

Brave Heart, M. (2001). Historical trauma response. *The Circle News, 22*(1), 8–9.

Casken, J. (2001). Improved health status for Native Hawaiians: Not just what the doctor ordered. *Wicazo SA Review, 16,* 75–89.

Chang, H. K. (2001). Hawaiian health practitioners in contemporary society. *Pacific Health Dialog, 8*(2), 260–273.

Choi-Misailidis, S. J., & Kaulukukui, C. M. (2004). Kukulu I na hulili: Building bridges to the understanding of Native Hawaiian mental health. *Multidisciplinary Research on Hawaiian Well-Being, 1*(1), 223–239.

Cook, B. P., Withy, K., & Tarallo-Jensen, L. (2003). Cultural trauma, Hawaiian spirituality and contemporary health status. *California Journal of Health Promotion, 1,* 10–24.

Council for Native Hawaiian Advancement. (2005). *The Akaka bill and current lawsuits: National policies for native needs.* Honolulu, HI: Author.

Crabbe, K. M. (2002). *Initial psychometric validation of He'ana'mana'o o na mo'omeheu hawai'i: A Hawaiian ethnocultural inventory (HEI) of cultural practices.* Unpublished dissertation. University of Hawaii, Manoa.

Daws, G. (1968). *Shoal of time: A history of the Hawaiian Islands.* Honolulu, HI: University of Hawai'i Press.

Dubos, R. (1974). *Of human diversity.* Barre, MA: Barre Publishers.

Duran, E., & Duran, B. (1995). *Native Americana postcolonial psychology.* Albany, NY: State University of New York Press.

Elkins, R. M. H. (1997). *Noni, the prize herb of the South Pacific.* Pleasant Grove, UT: Woodland Publishing.

Finney, B. (2004). Playing with canoes. In B.V. Lal (Ed.), *Pacific places, Pacific histories.* Honolulu, HI: University of Hawai'i Press.

Gallimore, R., & Howard, A. (Eds.). (1968). *Studies in Hawaiian community: Na Makamaka o Nanakuli.* Honolulu, HI: Pacific Anthropological Records, No. 1, Bishop Museum.

Gallimore, R., Whitehorn Boggs, J., & Jordan, C. (1974). *Culture, behavior, and education: A study of Hawaiian Americans.* Beverly Hills, CA: Sage Publications.

Goebert, D., & Kanoa, K. (1992). Injury mortality in Hawai'i: *The Rehab Journal, 8,* 4–6.

Grieco, E. M. (2001). The Native Hawaiian and other Pacific Islander population: 2000. *Census 2000 Brief.* (C2KBR/01-14). U.S. Census Bureau. U.S. Department of Commerce. Economics and Statistics Administration.

Guerrero, A. P. S., Hishinuma, E. S., Andrade, N. N., & Bell, C. K. (2003). Demographic and clinical characteristics of adolescents in Hawaii with obsessive-compulsive disorder. *Archives of Pediatrics & Adolescent Medicine, 157*(7), 665–670.

Hammond, O. (1988). Needs assessment and policy development: Native Hawaiians as Native Americans. *American Psychologist, 43,* 383–387.

Handy, E. (1927). Polynesian religion. *Bernice P. Bishop Museum Bulletin* #24. Honolulu, Hawaii.

Harris, P. M., & Jones, N. A. (2005). We the People: Pacific Islanders in the United States. *Census 2000 Special Reports*. (CENSR-26). U.S. Census Bureau. U.S. Department of Commerce. Economics and Statistics Administration.

Hawaii Advisory Committee to the U.S. Commission on Civil Rights. (2001). *Reconciliation at a crossroads: The implications of the Apology Resolution and Rice v. Cayetano for federal and state programs benefiting Native Hawaiians.* Summary report of the August 1998 and September 2000 community forums in Honolulu, Hawaii: Author.

Hishinuma, E. S., Andrade, N. N., Johnson, R. C., McArdle, J. J., Miyamoto, R. H., Nahulu, L. B., et al. (2000a). Psychometric properties of the Hawaiian culture scale – Adolescent Version, *Assessment, 6*, 1–18.

Hishinuma, E. S., Miyamoto, R. H., Nishimura, S. T., Nahulu, L. B., Andrade, N. N., Makini, G. K., et al. (2000b). Psychometric properties of the State-Trait anxiety inventory for Asian/Pacific Islander adolescents. *Assessment, 7*, 17–36.

Hishinuma, E. S., Miyamoto, R. H., Nishimura, S. T., & Nahulu, L. B. (2000c). Differences in state-trait anxiety inventory scores for ethnically diverse adolescents in Hawaii. *Cultural Diversity and Ethnic Minority Psychology, 6*, 73–83.

Howard, A. (1974). *Ain't no big thing: Coping strategies in a Hawaiian American Community.* Honolulu, HI: University Press of Hawai'i.

Ito, K. L. (1985). Affective bonds: Hawaiian interrelationships of self. In G. M. White & J. Kirkpatrick (Eds.), *Person, self, and experience: Exploring Pacific ethnopsychologies.* Berkeley, CA: University of California Press.

Judd, N. L. K. (1998). La'au Lapaau: Herbal healing among contemporary Hawaiian healers. *Pacific Health Dialog, 5*, 239–245.

Kanahele, G. H. S. (1986). *Ku kanaka: Stand tall.* Honolulu, HI: University of Hawaii Press.

Kane, H. K. (1997). *Ancient Hawai'i.* Honolulu, HI: Kawainu Press.

Lili'uokalani. (1917). Retrieved April 12, 2005 from http://www.oha.org/content_list.asp?contentid=150&contenttypeid=5.

Look, M. A., Mackura, G., & Spoehr, H. (1998). Native Hawaiian health and wellness summit: Ka 'Uhane Lokahi. *Pacific Health Dialog, 5*(2), 271–272.

Marsella, A. J., Gomes, K., Higginbotham, N., Kwan, L., Ostrowski, B., Roche, B., et al. (1985). E *Ola Mau: The Native Hawaiian health needs study. Volume 2 – Mental health.* Honolulu, HI: Alu Like, Inc.

Marsella, A. J., Oliveira, J. M., Plummer, C. M., & Crabbe, K. M. (1995). Native Hawaiian (Kanaka Maoli) culture, mind, and well-being. In H. I. McCubbin, E. A. Thompson, A. I. Thompson, & J. E. Frommer (Eds.), *Resiliency in ethnic minority families: Native and immigrant American families,* (pp. 93–113). Madison, WI: The University of Wisconsin System Center for Excellence in Family Studies.

McBride, J. L. (2002). Spiritual component of patients who experience psychological trauma: Family physician intervention. *Journal of the American Board of Family Practice, 15*(2), 168–169.

McCubbin, L., & Marsella, A. (under review). Native Hawaiian Psychology: The cultural, historical, and situational context of Indigenous Ways of Knowing. *Cultural Diversity and Ethnic Minority Psychology.*

McCubbin, H. I., & McCubbin, L. D. (1997). Hawaiian American families. In M. K. DeGenova (Ed.), *Families in cultural context: Strengths and challenges in diversity,* (pp. 239–266). Mountain View, CA: Mayfield Publishing Company.

McCubbin, L. & McCubbin, H. (2005a). Culture and ethnic identity in family resilience: Dynamic processes in trauma an transformation of indigenous people. In M. Unger(ed.), *Handbook for working with children and youth: Pathways to resilience across cultures and contexts* (pp. 27–44). Thousand Oaks: Sage.

McCubbin, H., & McCubbin, L. (2005b, April). *Pathways to illness and health: Vulnerability and Resilience of the Hawaiian people.* Paper presented at the Groves Conference on Marriage and Family: Native Americans Dealing with Change: Identity, Economics, Environment, Washington, DC.

McCubbin, L. (2006). The role of Indigenous family ethnic schema on well-being among Native Hawaiian families. *Contemporary Nursing Journal: Special Issue: Community & Family Health, 23(2)*, 170–180.

McDermott, J. F., Tseng, W. S., & Maretzki, T. W. (Eds.). (1980). *Peoples and cultures of Hawai'i: A psychocultural profile*. Honolulu, HI: University of Hawai'i.

Miller, G. (1990). *The SASSI adolescent manual*. Spencer, Indiana: The Spencer Evening World.

Miyamoto, R. H., Hishinuma, E. S., Nishimura, S. T., Nahulu, L. B., Andrade, N. N., Johnson, R. C., et al. (2001). Equivalencies regarding the measurement and constructs of self-esteem and major life events in an Asian/Pacific Islander sample. *Cultural Diversity and Ethnic Minority Psychology, 7*, 152–163.

Native Hawaiian Educational Assessment Project. (1983). *Final report*. Honolulu, Hawai'i: The Kamehameha Schools/Bernice Pauahi Bishop Estate.

Nishimura, S. T., Hishinuma, E. S., Miyamoto, R. H., Goebert, D. A., Johnson, R. C., Yuen, N. Y. C., et al. (2001). Prediction of DISC substance abuse and dependency for ethnically diverse adolescents. *Journal of Substance Abuse, 13*, 597–607.

Nordyke, E. C. (1989). *The peopling of Hawai'i* (2nd ed.). Honolulu, HI: University of Hawai'i Press.

Noyes, M. (1996, November). Cultural abuse. *Honolulu Magazine, 31*(5), 38.

Office of Hawaiian Affairs. (2003). *OHA Mission*. Retrieved April 12, 2005 from http://www.oha.org/cat_content.asp?contentid=20&catid=22.

Ola Mau, E. (1985). *The Native Hawaiian health needs study. Vol. 1 – Physical and medical health*. Honolulu, Hawaii: Alu Like, Inc.

Oneha, M. F. M. (2001). Ka mauli o ka 'oina a he mauli kanaka: An ethnographic study from a Hawaiian sense of place. *Pacific Health Dialog, 8*(2), 299–311.

Osborne, T. J. (1998). *Annexation Hawaii, fighting American imperialism*. Waimanalo, HI: Island Style Press.

Pacific American Foundation. (2004). *A snapshot of native Hawaiians in the United States* (Native Hawaiian Research Center Rep. No. 04-01). Honolulu, HI: Author.

Papa O Lokahi. (1987). *The Native Hawaiian health data book*. Papa O Lokahi: Honolulu, HI.

Polynesian Voyaging Society. (2005). *History of the Polynesian Voyaging Society, 1973–1998*. Retrieved April 12, 2005 from http://pvs.kcc.hawaii.edu/aboutpvs.html#briefhistory.

Prescott, C. A., McArdle, J. J., Hishinuma, E. S., Johnson, R. C., Miyamoto, R. H., Andrade, N. N., et al. (1998). Prediction of major depression and dysthymia from CES-D scores among ethnic minority adolescents. *Journal of the American Academy of Child and Adolescent Psychiatry, 37*(5), 495–503.

Pukui, M. K., & Elbert, S. H. (1986). *Hawaiian dictionary: Hawaiian-English, English-Hawaiian* (Rev. ed.). Honolulu, HI: University of Hawaii Press.

Pukui, M. K., Haertig, E. W., & Lee, C. A., (1972). *Nana I Ke Kumu (Look to the source)* (Vol. 2). Honolulu, HI: Queen Lili'uokalani Children's Center.

Pukui, M. K., Handy, E. S. C., & Livermore, K. (1934). Outline of Hawaiian physical therapeutics (Bulletin 126). Honolulu, HI: Bishop Museum.

Radloff, L. S. (1977). The CES-D Scale: A self-report depression scale for research in the general population. *Applied Psychological Measurement, 1*, 385–401.

Rezentes, W. C. (1996). *Ka Lama Kukui (Hawaiian Psychology): An Introduction*. Honolulu, HI: 'A'ali'i Books.

Rosenberg, M. (1965). *Society and the adolescent self-image*. Princeton, NJ: Princeton University Press.

Salzman, M. B. (2001). Cultural trauma and recovery: Perspectives from terror. *Trauma, Violence & Abuse, 2*, 172–191.

Schmitt, R. C. (1968). *Demographic statistics of Hawai'i: 1778–1965*. Honolulu, HI: University of Hawai'i Press.

Shook, E. V. (1985). *Ho'oponopono*. Honolulu, HI: University of Hawai'i Press.

Spielberger, C. D., Gorsuch, R. L., & Lushene, R. E. (1970). *Manual for the state trait anxiety inventory*. Palo Alto, CA: Consulting Psychologist Press.

Stannard, D. E. (1989). *Before the horror: The population of Hawai'i on the eve of western contact.* Honolulu, HI: Social Science Research Institute, University of Hawai'i at Manoa.

Stannard, D. E. (1992). *The conquest of the New World: American holocaust.* New York, NY: Oxford University Press.

Thompson, E. A., McCubbin, H. I., Thompson, A. I., & Elver, K. M. (1995). Vulnerability and resiliency in Native Hawaiian families under stress. In H. I. McCubbin, E. A. Thompson, A. I. Thompson, & J. E. Frommer (Eds.), *Resiliency in ethnic minority families: Native and immigrant American families.* Madison, WI: The University of Wisconsin System Center for Excellence in Family Studies.

U.S. Census. (2000). Racial or Ethnic Grouping: Native Hawaiian alone or in any combination for Data Set: Census 2000 Summary File 2 (SF 2) 100-Percent Data. Retrieved on November 30, 2006 at http://factfinder.census.gov/servlet/DTCharIterationServlet?_lang=en&_ts=182956554500

United States Congress. (1987). *Office of technology assessment annual report of national health status.* Washington, DC: United States Congress.

Werner, E. E., & Smith, R. S. (1977). *Kauai's children come of age.* Honolulu: University Press of Hawaii.

Werner, E. E., & Smith, R. S. (1982). *Vulnerable but Invincible: A longitudinal study of Resilient Children and Youth.* New York, NY: Cambridge University Press.

Werner, E. E., & Smith, R. S. (1992). *Overcoming the odds: High risk children from birth to adulthood.* Ithaca, NY: Cornell University Press.

Whitbeck, L. B., Adams, G. W., Hoyt, D. R., & Chen, X. (2004). Conceptualizing and measuring historical trauma among American Indian people. *American Journal of Community Psychology, 33,* 119–130.

White, A., & Landis, M. (1982). *The mental health of Native Hawaiians.* Honolulu, HI: Alu Like, Inc.

Williams, C., & Berry, J. (1991). Primary prevention of acculturalization stress among refugees: Application of psychological theory and practice. *American Psychologist, 46,* 632–641.

Chapter 10

Mexicans, Mexican Americans, Caribbean, and Other Latin Americans

Patricia Arredondo, Veronica Bordes, and Freddy A. Paniagua

INTRODUCTION

This chapter provides a comprehensive discussion about delivering disaster and trauma relief services for persons of Latin American heritage. This includes people from parts of the Caribbean, Mexico, Central, and South America. The aim of this chapter is to present the reader with information about Latin American cultures, with the idea that a thorough understanding of the victim's culture will lead to more appropriate and effective service approaches. In order to familiarize the reader with the Latin American population, this chapter includes an overview of population statistics, history, and culture. We conclude with recommendations for culture-centered interventions.

Clinicians, practitioners, and service providers working with Latin American populations in various disaster and trauma relief contexts should find the information presented here useful. It is important to keep in mind, however, that the information presented is, by necessity, selective and of a broad nature. There is a great deal of diversity among people of Latin American heritage, and it is therefore advisable to keep an open mind towards subgroup variations and to remember that, in practice, there may be any number of deviations from generalized information. The reader is urged to use the information in this chapter as a platform upon which to develop a more specific understanding of the population served.

POPULATION DEMOGRAPHICS

Demographics for Persons of Spanish-speaking Origin

The Census data and other reports that track population growth and change are referenced in this section. Data sources in particular include the World Health Organization and the U.S. Census Bureau. The greatest contributor to population growth in all Latin American countries is the birth rate, whereas in the U.S., the contributing factors are births and immigration. The greatest percentage of Latin American immigration is from Mexico.

To provide a portrait of the size of the Latino population outside of U.S. borders, population figures for different Latin American countries are reported in Table 10.1 (U. S. Census Bureau, 2000a World Health Organization, 2005).

Latinos in the United States

It should be noted that Hispanic is the term used by the U.S. Census Bureau, but many persons of Latino heritage prefer the terms Latina/o or Latinos. Currently the largest minority group in the United States, Hispanics/Latinos accounted for one-half of the national population growth of 2.9 million between July 1, 2003 and July 1, 2004 (U.S. Census Bureau, 2005). The Hispanic/Latino growth rate of 3.6 percent over the 22-month period was more than three times that of the total population (1.0 percent). In addition, as of July 1, 2004, the nation's Hispanic/Latino population reached 41.3 million.

In 2003, Latinos composed 13.85% of the nation's population (U.S. Census Bureau, 2003) with the following breakdowns:

- 25.3 million Mexican
- 3.7 million Puerto Rican
- 1.36 million Cuban.

Table 10.1. Populations of Latin American Countries

Mexico:	101,965,000
Venezuela:	25,226,000
Ecuador:	12,810,000
Guatemala:	12,036,000
Dominican Republic:	8,616,000
Honduras:	6,781,000
El Salvador:	6,415,000
Nicaragua:	5,335,000
Puerto Rico:	3,808,610

Additionally, at the time of the 2000 U.S. Census (Guzman, 2001), there were:

- 1.69 million Central Americans,
- 1.35 million South Americans, and
- 0.77 million Dominicans.

Immigration Patterns. As will be discussed later in this chapter, generational differences among Latina/os are important to consider. Based on 1990 Census data of Latinos living in the United States, Table 10.2 shows immigration patterns for different Latino groups from 1970 to 1990. Of all Latinos living in the U.S., Mexicans have the largest percentage of individuals born in the U.S. (65.3%), followed closely by Puerto Ricans with 53.9%. The greatest majority of Latinos immigrated between 1970 and 1990.

It is worth noting that the majority of Cubans (33.3%) immigrated between 1960 and 1969. Additionally, prior to 1950, Puerto Ricans had the largest percentage with 4.9% immigrating before that time (Boswell, 1994; U.S. Census Bureau, 1990).

Since 2000, there has been increasing focus on undocumented immigrants, primarily from Latin America. This is coincidental with the dramatic increase in the overall Latino population in the United States. When data about immigrants are reported, there are typically references to a possible undercount because of undocumented immigrants. Because these individuals do not have refugee or other legal standing, they can be subject to workplace abuse and can become targets of vigilante groups along the Mexican and U.S. border. While some non-immigrants consider new and even undocumented immigrants as benefiting the U.S. economy, the great majority believe that they have made no difference or even have been bad for the economy.

Findings from a national study indicate that 51% of non-immigrants fear that new immigrants may be taking jobs away from Americans (National Public Radio, 2004). Conversely, in the same survey report, immigrants stated that they believe that they strengthen the U.S. through their values of hard work and determination.

The use of wages and earnings to support their family "back home" is typical among Latino immigrants. In a report released by the Tomás Rivera Policy Institute, it was stated that over $30 billion was sent from the U.S. to Mexico and Latin America in 2004 (Cortina, de la Graza, Bejarano, & Wainer,

Table 10.2. Immigration to the United States by Selected Latino Groups

	Between 1970–1980	Between 1980–1990
Mexicans	10.6%	17.6%
Cubans	13.2%	19.7%
Dominicans	20.5%	37.8%
Central Americans	16.4%	57.2%
South Americans	21.9%	39.1%

2005). These funds are primarily the earnings of new and undocumented immigrants.

Primary Locations.   Hispanics/Latinos emigrate from various countries in Latin America. We will primarily discuss those from Mexico, Puerto Rico, El Salvador, Ecuador, Venezuela, Guatemala, Nicaragua, the Dominican Republic, Honduras, and Brazil. Throughout the U.S., Latinos can be found in many places, while the majority continue to live in California (11.0 million), Texas (6.7 million), New York (2.9 million), Florida (2.7 million), Illinois (1.5 million), Arizona (1.3 million), New Jersey (1.1 million), Colorado (765,000), and Washington State (442,000) (Paniagua, 2005; U.S. Census Bureau, 2000b). The U.S. cities with the largest percentage of Hispanic/Latinos include: East Los Angeles, California (97%), Laredo, Texas (94%), Brownsville, Texas (91%), Hialeah, Florida (90%), McAllen, Texas (80%), El Paso, Texas (77%), Santa Ana, California (77%), El Monte, California (72%), Oxnard, California (66%), and Miami, Florida (66%) (Paniagua, 2005).

Age Distribution.   When compared to the overall U.S. population, Latinos are much younger, with a median age of 25.9 years compared to 35.3 years for the U.S. population (Guzman, 2001).

- 39% of Latinos are under 19, representing 5% of the U.S. population.
- 19% of Latinos are in the 20–29 age group, representing 2% of the U.S. population.
- Both Latinos and the U.S. population as a whole have 24% of individuals between 30 and 44.
- There are 14% of Latinos between 45 and 64, representing 2% of the U.S. population.
- 12% of the U.S. population is 65 and over, compared to only 5% of Latinos (Therrien & Ramirez, 2001).

Age differences among the various Latino groups:

- Cubans are the oldest with a median age of 40.7 years.
- South Americans follow with a median age of 33.1 years.
- Dominicans and Central Americans are the next youngest with a median age of 29.5 and 29.2, respectively.
- Puerto Ricans and Mexicans are the youngest with a median age of 27.3 and 24.2, respectively (Guzman, 2001).

Gender Distribution for Latinas/Latinos.   The gender distribution for Hispanics/Latinos in the U.S. during the 2000 U.S. Census (2000d) indicates that there were slightly more males (18.16 million) than females (17.14 million). Gender differences seem to diminish as reported in Table 10.3. The data show that there are approximately equal percentages of both males and females in each age group.

Table 10.3. Age Distribution by Gender for Latinas/Latinos Living in the United States

Age	Males (%)	Females (%)
0–4	5.2	5.1
5–9	5.1	4.9
10–14	4.8	4.5
15–19	4.3	4.0
20–24	5.1	4.4
25–29	5.2	4.3
30–34	4.8	4.4
35–39	4.2	3.7
40–44	3.4	3.2
45–49	2.5	2.7
50–54	1.9	2.0
55–59	1.4	1.6
60–64	1.1	1.2
65–69	0.8	1.0
70–74	0.6	0.7
75–79	0.4	0.6
80–84	0.2	0.3
85 +	0.1	0.3

Source: U.S. Census Bureau, 2000c

Education.   Latinos vary in their educational attainment by group more than by gender. Interestingly, Latinas and Latinos have about the same percentages attaining the same levels of education:

- 27% of both Latinas and Latinos have less than a 9th grade education.
- About 15% have a 9–12th grade education with no diploma.
- 28% have a high school diploma.
- About 19% have some college or associate's degree.
- 7% have a bachelor's degree.
- About 3.5% have an advanced degree.

Looking at the differences among the different Latino groups, Mexicans have the highest percentage (32%) of individuals with less than a 9th grade education, and Cubans have the highest percentage (9%) of individuals with an advanced degree. All five groups (Mexicans, Puerto Ricans, Cubans, and Central and South Americans) have about a third of individuals with a high school diploma (Therrien & Ramirez, 2001).

Economics.   Just as Latinos vary in their educational attainment, Latinos also vary in occupational fields (Therrien & Ramirez, 2001).

- For individuals 16 years and older, the greatest number of Latinos (36%) work in skilled jobs such as transportation, inspectors, precision work, repair, laborers, and machine operators.

- There are also a large number of Latinos that work in service positions (19%).
- 14% work in executive, administrative/managerial and professional specialties.
- 13% work in clerical and administrative support positions.
- 10% work in sales positions.
- 6% work in farming, fishing and forestry.
- 2% work in technical support fields.

Income.   Reflecting this variety in occupations, Latinos also vary in their annual income. According the U.S. Census Bureau (Therrien & Ramirez, 2001), in 1999:

- 37% of Latinos earned between $10,000 and $19,000.
- 32% made between $20,000 and $35,000.
- 21% between $35,000 and $75,000.
- A small number (7%) made $9,000 or less.
- 3% made $75,000 thousand or more.

Among all cultural groups in the U.S., Latinos have one of the greatest percentages of people in poverty. As of 2003, 22.5% of Latinos were in poverty, just under Blacks (24.4%) and greatly above non Hispanic Whites (8.2%) and Asians (11.8%). For Latinos, this percent does not represent an increase from 2002, but the actual number in poverty increased to 9.1 million from 8.6 million in 2002. In 2003, the median income for Hispanic households declined by 2.6 percent. The median household income for these families was about $33,000, representing only 69% of the median income for non-Hispanic White households (DeNavas-Walt, Proctor, & Mills, 2004).

Religion.   Religion has historically been a large part of the Latino culture. To date, 43% of the world's Catholics live in Latin America (Campo-Flores, 2005). However, even though the majority of Latina/os are Catholic, many belong to other religions. In fact, the longer Latina/os live in the U.S., the less likely they are to identify as Catholic.

- 72% of first-generation Latinos are Catholic
- Only 52% of third-generation Latinos are Catholic. Latinos are not only are the the the fastest-growing ethnic group of Catholics, but they are also the fastest-growing ethnic group among most other denominations, including Mormon (Campo-Flores, 2005).

Cultural/Ethnic identity.   Marsella and Yamada (2000) define cultural/ethnic identity (or ethnocultural identity) in terms of the "extent to which an individual endorses and manifests the cultural traditions and practices of the particular group" (p. 13). An important cultural/ethnic identity variable in the Hispanic/Latino population is the selection of the appropriate term to refer to Hispanics/Latinos. As noted by Paniagua (2005), the current literature "suggests that most scholars prefer the term Hispanics and define it widely to include any person who labels him or herself as such because he or she is from, or descended from others who were from, Spain, any South American Country, any Central American Country, or the Caribbean" (p. 52). Comas-Diaz (2001), however, suggested that it is extremely important to avoid the use of the term "Hispanic" across all members of the Hispanic/Latino population because "self-designation [is] gaining a voice and power to name one's identity and define one's reality" (p. 116).

For this reason, when providing services to the Hispanic/Latino population (e.g., during disaster and/or trauma situations), it is important to use the self-designation that most closely reflects the cultural/ethnic identity of the individual in need of help. For example, as noted by Comas-Diaz (2001) some Hispanics/Latinos would prefer to be referred to as "La Raza," "Hispano/a," "Hispanic American," or "Americano/a" (for those Hispanics/Latinos who believe that they belong to the American Continent and not to the United States of America).

In addition to these generic terms, it is important also to consider "specific or national terms" in that self-designation (see Comas-Diaz, 2001, pp. 117–119). Examples of such specific or national terms include "Mexican," "Mexican American," "Chicano/a," "Boricua," "Nuyorican," "Chicagorican," "Rican," "Latinegro/a," and "Caribeño."

Comas-Diaz (2001) provided an extensive description of the use of these self-designations in the Hispanic/Latino population and their implications when serving members from this population (see also Paniagua, 2005, pp. 53–54). For example, many individuals of Mexican descent residing in the Southwest portion of this country would be offended if they are referred to as "Mexican American," preferring to refer to themselves as "Chicano/a" because they do not believe that they are members "of the mainstream U.S. culture and want to maintain their own cultural/ethnic identity in the United States" (Paniagua, 2005, p. 54).

Another example is the case of individuals residing in this country who would prefer to be referred to as "Boricua," which originated from the word "Borinquen", that is in itself the original name of the island that today is known as Puerto Rico. On the other hand, some Puerto Rican descendents who were born in New York or Chicago would prefer to be referred to as "Nuyoricans" and "Chicagoricans." A final example is the individual that self-designates him or herself as "Caribeño." This term reflects the ethnic/cultural identity of many individuals from any of the Caribbean Islands (e.g., Puerto Rico, Cuba, the Dominican Republic, and Jamaica). For example, a person of Puerto Rican descent may prefer to be referred to as "Caribeño" instead of "Puerto Rican" or "Boricua."

KEY HISTORICAL DATES AND VALUES FOR HISPANICS/LATINOS

"The following Table (10.4) illustrates a chronology of historical events that have shaped the worldview and values of Hispanics/Latinos as a whole. Determining the influence of these on an individual's worldview can be done by using the Latino Dimensions of Personal Identity Model (Arredondo & Santiago-Rivera, 2000)."

Table 10.4. Key Historical Dates and Events

1519	Colonization of Mexico by Spain. Hernán Cortez, sent by the king and queen of Spain, and Moctezuma, chief of the Aztec Indians, meet in Mexico City.
1848	Treaty of Guadalupe Hidalgo, ending the Mexican American War. Mexico ceded parts of Nevada, Colorado, Utah, Wyoming, New Mexico, Arizona, and California to the U.S. The treaty theoretically protected the property rights of Mexicans choosing to remain and become U.S. citizens.
1868–1898	Spanish American War in Cuba was fought against slavery and independence from Spanish rule. Resulted in the U.S. and Spain signing the Treaty of Peace in Paris, in which Spain renounced the right to Cuba and Cuba became independent. Spain ceded Puerto Rico and Guam to the United States and sold the Philippines to the U.S. in return for $20 million (Library of Congress, 1998).
1952	Puerto Rico becomes a commonwealth as a result of a movement toward self governance and being ceded to the U.S. following the Spanish-American war.
1967	The population of Puerto Rico voted to become independent, or stay a commonwealth. The majority decided for no change.
1968	First federal Bilingual Education Act passed to provide funding for school districts to serve the special needs of those with limited English proficiency. It mandated instruction in the native language of students. The first program was established in Dade County, Florida, as an initiative to support the educational needs of Cuban refugees.
1992	NAFTA signed by Mexico, Canada, and the U.S., establishing a free-trade zone for North America. It took effect in 1994 with immediate lifting of tariffs on goods produced by both nations.
1998	Proposition 227 in California banned bilingual education except under special conditions. It established a one-year immersion program for students with limited English proficiency.
2000	Proposition 203 in Arizona, like proposition 227, required the end of bilingual education with a one year immersion program for students with limited English proficiency.
2004	Proposition 200 in Arizona required proof of citizenship when registering to vote and proof of legal status when asking for non-federally mandated public health benefits (e.g., education and healthcare).
2005	Growing antagonism against Latino immigrants and "illegal" workers. Calls for building a wall across the US-Mexican border. Latino countries point out that the workers provide a cheap and essential workforce for the US and that the resentment and anger are unwarranted. Abuse and exploitation of "illegal" workers continues, especially for farm workers, sweatshop laborers, construction laborers, and female sex workers.

Importance of Generations

Historic colonization experiences and subsequent migration patterns affect the desire for cohesiveness across generations. When faced with possible extinction, indigenous people had to find ways to survive and maintain their cultural group. The disappearance of entire villages has often been a mystery to anthropologists and other social scientists, however, at face value, it should not be surprising that tribes and their extended kinship systems moved to safer spaces for self-preservation.

The importance of *familia* and extended kinship systems for Latinos speaks to the values of allocentrism, interdependence, and collectivism. Multigenerational families living together are not uncommon and a reflection of historic practices in rural areas. Divorce rates among Latino couples are the lowest among all cultural groups, largely influenced by Catholicism and other religious beliefs that marriage is a lifelong commitment. Understandably, Latinos view marriage for the purpose of childbearing, "making the children a central motivating force in family dynamics" (Santiago-Rivera, Arredondo, & Gallardo-Cooper, 2002, p. 70). In couples, the pressure to keep the family together is greater for the woman and a more common reason for a couple to stay together.

Families in agrarian societies have always had to depend on the entire family for economic reasons. The larger the family, the more individuals are available to contribute to the family welfare. In the U.S., migrant farm workers or agricultural families are an example of the importance of generations. Children as young as 10 or 12 would be found in the fields because everything they made was essential to the economic viability of their parents and siblings. As families emigrate to the U.S., it is very common to have cousins living with cousins, an adult with another sibling who arrived earlier, and couples who leave their children with extended family in their homeland so that they can establish themselves economically.

There is a high degree of mobility for Latinos in the U.S. However, the central importance of generations and extended kinship systems persists even in the face of secondary migration in this country. Sometimes a church group becomes the reference point, substituting for relatives. The tendency to emphasize social relations among Latinos is evidenced through continued generational interactions and the development of relationships within ethnic-specific neighborhoods. Cultural familiarity is a nutrient for the immigrant who has been displaced.

Although cultural values generally shift the longer one resides in the U.S., the *familia* is still viewed by many second and third generation immigrants and their descendants as a safe haven. Latinos will often bring their aging or ill parents to live with them rather than place them in a nursing home. Family members depend on one another, and in times of a disaster, family relations become even more critical. Togetherness for family members who are used to seeing one another on a daily basis may engender separation anxiety and a collapse of the individual's social support system if contact to family is cut off as a result of a disaster.

Family Centered Values

Like all cultural groups, there are many values that Latinos hold that service providers need to be aware of when working with Latinos in general, and in special circumstances such as disaster situations. Three of these are family-centered values, described by Santiago-Rivera et al. (2002) as *familismo*, *compadrazco*, and *personalismo*.

1. *Familismo (Family Ties)*

   Familismo is a value of maintaining close relations and ties to the family. This stems from a collectivistic worldview, but is often confused with seeing Latinos as enmeshed from a mainstream perspective worldview. For example, when a family member becomes ill, it is not unusual to see both immediate and extended family members make hospital visits. The presence of 6 or more relatives is common. Collective behavior is a sign of support, concern, and care. Therefore, it is important to realize that this is culturally appropriate, and that it is important to value these connections and interdependent tendencies when working with Latino families.

2. *Compadrazco (Friendship)*

   Another family-centered value is *compadrazco*. This has several applications. It may refer to a family's network of close friends, not necessarily blood relatives. *Comadres* and *compadres* (derived from the concept of *compadrazgo*) hold special status in the *compadrazco* system because of historical friendships and/or because they are godparents for the children in particular religious benchmarks including baptism and first Holy Communion. Thus the network of special relations is generational and extends beyond the immediate, and even extended, family.

3. *Personalismo (Warm Personal Relationships)*

   Finally, there is *personalismo*, which is a valuing of warm and personal relationships. This is essential when working with Latinos. One must work to have a sense *personalismo* with their clients in order to build rapport and trust, and to help the client work through the trauma. A way of demonstrating *personalismo* and building rapport is through *platica* or small talk (e.g. "What hurts?" or "Would you like some water?").

Other Relationship Values

1. *Respeto (Respect)*

   Two other values that can help in relationship-building are *respeto* and *confianza*. For Latinos, having and showing respect for others is an important value. When working with Latinos, showing *respeto* entails acceptance of the clients' values and worldview. For example, this may mean honoring a person's request to have a bible or a rosary to have comfort in the midst of a disaster.

2. *Confianza (Trust)*

   Confianza is a value of developing trust in a relationship. When the client has *confianza* in the counselor, the relationship becomes stronger and the client will feel more willing to be open in the relationship (Santiago-Rivera et al., 2002).

   During and following a disaster, survivors may experience various levels and manifestations of trauma. Thus, they can be highly dependent on the helpers. Defensive behavior such as denial that anything hurts, or projections of fear onto one's children or parents, needs to be anticipated. Individuals (survivors) in the crossfire of a natural disaster such as an earthquake, hurricane, or human-made disaster such as war, may experience shock and paralysis, both physically and emotionally. Thus, therapists will need to anticipate defensive reactions as they intervene with calmness, reassurance, and hope.

3. *Caridad (Caring)*

   Other Latino values that may manifest following a disaster include *caridad, teniendo valor, fortalezas, esperanza,* and *fé.* The value of *caridad* is a value of caring for others. Latino individuals, especially women, will be concerned with caring for others following a disaster, so much so that they may care for others before they take care of themselves. It may be difficult for the women to understand that they also need to take care of themselves for their own sake and in order to be better caregivers.

4. *Tener Valor* and *Fortaleza (Courage and Fortitude)*

   Tener valor is a Latino value of being brave even in difficult situations, including disasters. This is especially the case for the men who are taught that they must be strong and in control at all times, a sign of *machismo.* Therefore, when working with men following a disaster, it is important to realize that they may not want to open up emotionally for fear of showing weakness, of not being "manly". They may also not want to show that they are scared or troubled because of their need to be brave and strong for others who depend on them. This is strongly related to *fortalezas.* This is a value of strength and fortitude. Just like with *tener valor,* this value teaches Latinos to always be strong and not show weakness. Crying is sometimes seen as a sign of weakness. Both men and women may refuse to cry so that they can show that they are strong for the sake of their children and parents.

Spiritual Values

1. *Esperanza (Hope)*

   The final two values are related to spirituality. *Esperanza* means hope and hopefulness. When Latinos have a sense of *esperanza,* they may be hesitant to talk about the negative aspects of the disaster because they are praying for a positive outcome. This is likely related to religious and spiritual beliefs that their needs and well-being will be taken care of if it is God's will.

2. *Fé (Faith)*

Finally, *fé* is the value of having faith. This is a faith in a higher power. Therefore, when working with Latinos after a disaster, responders need to be aware of and respectful of religious beliefs. An assumption often voiced is that Latinos are fatalistic. Negative attributions to acceptance of the will of God or of another higher power may lead to miscommunications and culturally inappropriate interventions.

Gender-based Socialization Values

In the section on the importance of generations, a reference was made regarding the continued pressure on woman to maintain family cohesiveness. In Latino families, there are guidelines for gender role socialization that continue to persist, particularly for immigrant families. Two concepts that inform the socialization process are *marianismo* and *machismo.*

The root of the term *marianismo* is "María", in reference to the Virgin Mary, mother of Jesus Christ. The term engenders expectations of purity, passivity, piety, long-suffering, care-taking, generosity, and of course, motherhood. For most Latinas, being a mother is the major identity achievement and married women without children or unmarried women are often pitied. While there is a glorification of motherhood, there is also a downside for women who find themselves in relationships with philandering or abusive men. In these situations, women *se aguantan,* that is they engage in behavior whereby they suppress their true feelings of disagreement, disappointment, or unhappiness. Women who choose to stop *aguntandose,* are often viewed negatively from traditional or *machista* perspectives.

For male gender socialization, *machismo* is the norm. There are both positive and negative behaviors associated with machismo. On the positive side, men are expected to be "machos" – manly, responsible for their family, reliable breadwinners. The negative behavior is more often portrayed in contemporary media. These men are controlling and oppressing, particularly of women. *Machistas* engage in self-centered and often abusive patterns of behavior, diminishing women's worth, and expecting total allegiance to their wishes. It should be noted that the negative and positive behaviors associated with machismo are cross cultural.

In families where traditional gender roles manifest, the man is more likely to have the last word on decisions for everyone. This will occur in "normal", and perhaps even more so, in crisis situations. Although the woman many know what is best for her family, she may defer to her *machista* husband, helping him to save face.

Communication Styles

The Latino communication style is considered "high context." This means that individuals rely on nuances, non-verbal behavior, and other environmental conditions to communicate meaning. Thus, the exactness or directness of communication is not all that counts. Affect also plays an important role.

Latino value orientations of *respeto* and formality are also evident in patterns of communication. Lines of authority and hierarchy within a family must be considered. It is important to address someone older in age with the salutation of "Señor" or "Señora" or "Don" or Doña." When speaking with a professional such as a teacher or a doctor, titles are also used. Adults are the authority, not the children.

The previous discussion on gender role socialization and expectations is relevant to communication practices. The formal, hierarchical nature of family relationships suggests a power differential between women and men. Thus, directing questions or comments to the man would be expected. Additionally, depending on the internal family communication patterns, it may be necessary to address the man before the woman. In some families, decisions are left to the men, a sign of respect for their role.

It is also important to understand non-verbal behavior, particularly expressions of touch. People of the Latino culture are often (stereotypically) described as highly emotional, both verbally and non-verbally. All cultures have non-verbal gestures, ones that may not be generalizeable across other cultures. Assumptions should not be made about nodding to agree or disagree, hand gestures, or other behaviors. In these situations, it is best to ask about the meaning of the gesture.

MENTAL HEALTH AND CULTURE

Special Disorders

There are a few culture-bound disorders explained in the DSM-IV-R that Latinos may experience in a crisis (American Psychiatric Association, 2000, henceforth APA, 2000).

1. *Ataque de Nervios (Somatic and Emotional Distress)*

   One of the most well known disorders is *ataque de nervios*, which primarily occurs as a result of a stressful event, particularly those relating to family members. The symptoms include uncontrollable shouting, crying, and trembling. Verbal and physical aggression, and dissociative or seizure-like experiences may accompany the episode. The individual may feel as though they are out of control.

   Another disorder related to multiple and difficult life stressors is a general state of vulnerability called *nervios*. This includes somatic and emotional distress, and general inability to function. Trauma will likely precipitate anxiety and "irrational" fears, such as that an earthquake will reoccur. Though not necessarily based on unfounded fears, *nervios* lead to sleep disturbances, nausea, trembling, loss of appetite, and general suspicion of even those who may want to help.

2. *Bilis/Colera/Muina (Anger / Rage)*

Another culture-bound disorder is *bilis/colera/muina*, which is the result of strong anger or rage in the individual that disrupts the individual's bodily balance. The symptoms include nervous tension, stomach problems, headaches, screaming, trembling, and occasionally a loss of consciousness.

3. *Mal de Ojo (Curse)*

Mal de ojo is a belief that someone has cast a spell on another individual. The consequences of this bad karma are possible illness or other misfortunes to oneself or one's family. An example is one that occurred in a Salvadoran refugee family in the mid-1990s. The civil war in El Salvador led to mistrust among neighbors and even family members who then resettled in the same community in the Boston area. The 7 year old daughter of a refugee family began to have epileptic seizures. In spite of treatment by a western-trained physician, the seizures continued. Convinced that someone had cast a *mal de ojo* on the child, the parents insisted on finding an espiritista to "cure" the child.

4. *Locura (Psychosis)*

Locura is another disorder, which is a severe and chronic psychosis, usually attributed to inheritance, having many life difficulties, or both. The symptoms include visual and auditory hallucinations, agitation, incoherence, inability to follow social norms, unpredictable behavior, and sometimes, violent outbursts.

5. *Susto (Fright)*

Susto is a state of unhappiness and sickness brought on by a frightening event after which, according to the belief, the soul leaves the body. In the case of trauma, *susto* is a typical response. Symptoms include appetite and sleep disturbances, lack of motivation, low self-esteem, sadness, and somatic symptoms (e.g., headaches, and physical maladies). On the extreme end of the continuum, if the symptoms are not dealt with, they may even cause death.

A failure to consider culture-bound disorders when assessing victims of disasters and/or traumas could lead to errors in diagnosing mental disorders in those cases when symptoms are the results of "locally specific troubling experiences that are limited to certain societies or cultural areas" (Smart & Smart, 1997, p. 394) such as, for example, the case of *susto, mal de ojo*, and *ataques de nervios* in the Hispanic or Latino community.

As noted by Paniagua (2005), however, rescue workers involved in the assessment of mental disorders among victims of disasters or traumas (e.g., psychologists, psychiatrists, social workers) should be "aware that the

symptoms associated with a given mental disorder may be related to a particular cultural context without being part of a culture-bound disorder per se"
(p. 140). For example, *ataques de nervios* resemble the symptoms of Dissociative
Identity Disorder (APA, 2000), but the first is generally considered an example
of culture-bound disorders whereas the latter is a disorder often considered
"as particularly specific to the American culture because of the relatively high
rate of the disorder in the United States" (Paniagua, 2005, p. 140).

Special Therapies and Healers

While there is wide variation in actual beliefs, many Hispanics/Latinos might
consider the causes of disasters and/or trauma associated with "bad spirits,"
"divine force," or "fatalism." For this reason, Hispanics/Latinos with these
beliefs would expect help from the *espiritista, curandero/a,* or "healer." During
the first encounter with Hispanics/Latinos who have experienced a disaster
(e.g., hurricane, earthquake), it is important to explore the individual's magical or spiritual explanatory model around the particular disaster and/or
trauma for two reasons (see Paniagua, 2005, p. 63).

First, the efforts of first line responders (e.g., rescuer workers, medical staff,
etc.) to understand and accept a victim's magical or spiritual interpretation
of the particular disaster may enhance that person's willingness to follow
instructions in order to prevent further injuries. Second, acknowledging the
victim's supernatural beliefs could help to engage the individual in behaviors
that could prevent diseases and additional complications resulting from the
after-effects of the particular disaster. For example, an *espiritista* or *curandero*
could be part of the rescuer team, giving instructions to victims regarding
what specific self-care skills they should display after the disaster to protect
themselves from diseases, such as taking medication, boiling the water before
drinking it, and so forth. This particular example is important to remember
because many Hispanics/Latinos believe in *fatalismo* (fatalism), and this belief
might prevent them from displaying the self-care skills necessary to prevent
diseases following a disaster. Paniagua (2005) defined *fatalismo* in terms of "a
sense of vulnerability and lack of control in the presence of adverse events,
as well as the individual's feelings that such events are [just waiting] to affect
his or her life" (p. 59). Therefore, victims of disasters who believe in *fatalismo*
might also believe that those self-care skills are not necessary because they
would not protect them from diseases resulting from the "divine providence"
that brought a given disaster in the first place (see Paniagua, 2005, pp. 58–59).

CONSIDERATIONS FOR COUNSELING AND MEDICATION

When counseling Latinos who have experienced a disaster or trauma as
individuals and/or among family members, counselors must take into
consideration sociocultural, physical, and political circumstances. For example, undocumented victims may decline involvement with rescue workers

because they fear they will be turned into *la migra* (immigration authorities). This is also a double-edged sword for helpers who may find themselves working in states (e.g., Arizona) that outlaw public medical assistance to undocumented persons.

Unaddressed Health Needs

Another consideration relates to victims' unaddressed health needs. For example, many migrant farm workers and their families have been exposed to toxins and diseases that have been untreated. Therefore, helpers in disaster areas populated by farm workers should ensure that there are a range of medical services available.

In the intervention process with Latino victims of disaster, helpers are encouraged to be mindful of cultural variables that could greatly enhance the effectiveness of the process (Cuellar & Paniagua, 2000). For example, many Hispanics or Latinos believe that a divine providence controls the world and that one cannot prevent or control adversity. As noted earlier, this cultural belief is known as *fatalismo* (fatalism). Therefore, Latinos who are victims of disasters would reject help from rescuer workers or may not perceive preventative measures as something that could assist the community because of that sense of vulnerability.

Role of the Family

Another key cultural variable to consider in the context of a disaster or trauma is the impact of *familismo* (familism) and the extended family on decision-making during a disaster or trauma situation. Any attempt to provide counseling to victims of disasters or traumas in the Latino community would not be effective without considering the role of the victim's biological family (nuclear family) and the victim's extended family (e.g., nuclear family plus other individuals the victim considers as members of his or her family, such as the priest, the minister, godmother, godfather, friends, etc.). Hispanics or Latinos may not consult with professionals before consulting with members of the nuclear family or the extended family about how to deal with stressors and economic difficulties; two crucial variables during and after a disaster or trauma.

Therefore, when providing counseling in this context, clinicians assigned to assist victims with their emotional and economic difficulties might make efforts to assure that the victim understands that both their nuclear and extended family members will be consulted and included in the counseling process.

Recognition of Religion

Recognition of the importance of religious and folk beliefs is a third critical cultural variable that may impact the counseling process for victims of disasters or trauma from the Hispanic/Latino community. Many Hispanics or Latinos affected by natural disasters or trauma may believe that these events are the result of evil spirits or punishment from God, and so also believe that religious leaders such as the priest (for Hispanics who are Roman Catholic), or brujo/a (witch doctor) are the individuals with the power to assist the victims rather than the counselor or therapist (Paniagua, 2005). In this context, victims of disasters or traumas holding those beliefs would consider prayers and folk remedies as their first choice in seeking a cure for their emotional (e.g., anxiety and depression) and physical (e.g., broken legs) problems resulting from those disasters or traumas.

Use of Indigenous Resources

To be more culturally responsive, therapists working from a Western perspective are encouraged to consult with healers from the community, including priests, curanderos, and brujos/as (witch doctors). A collaborative approach with a healer in whom the victims already have trust will likely facilitate increased receptiveness to the non-native therapist. However, this should also be done with caution as not all native healers may be viewed with the same respect and high regard. Further, not all Latinos would necessarily want to be treated by a curandero or other native healer. In all cases, it is best to ask the victims what might be of help.

Consulting with healers from the community could also prevent mental health professionals serving victims of disasters and/or traumas from over-diagnosing, underdiagnosing, or misdiagnosing. As noted above, this is particularly important to remember in those cases when symptoms of mental disorders resemble culture-bound disorders, as well as when making the distinction between "locally troubling experiences that are limited to certain societies" (Smart & Smart, 1997, p. 394), i.e., the culture-bound disorder per se and cultural variations leading to similar symptoms (e.g., the case of *ataques de nervios* versus Dissociative Identity Disorder discussed above).

Use of Medications

As noted by Paniagua (2005), "many mental health professionals do not like to recommend the use of medication [because they] simply do not believe in the effectiveness of drug therapy [in the management of emotional problems]" (Paniagua, 2005, p. 70). Paniagua (2005) also suggested that in the case of those mental health professionals (who are not medical doctors) who believe in the use of medication to treat emotional disorders, the need to depend on a physician to prescribe and monitor the effect of the particular medication often prevents them from considering medications as a treatment choice in the management of their clients.

Regardless of the reason for rejecting the use of medication, it is important to note that many Hispanics or Latinos would expect to receive medication during treatment of their emotional problems and not only during the treatment of their physical (medically-related) problems (e.g., back pain, broken legs, etc.). For this reason, the counseling process used with Hispanic or Latino victims of disasters or traumas should carefully explore the victim's expectancy for receiving medication to treat not only his or her physical problems but also mental problems or emotional disorders (e.g., depression) that resulted from the same disaster or traumatic event.

As noted by Simon and Gorman (2004), although pharmacological interventions have been extensively investigated in many controlled trials, both in outpatient and inpatient settings, little evidence exists to demonstrate the effectiveness of these interventions in disasters or trauma contexts. The main reason for this observation is "the difficulty in performing randomized, double-blind, and placebo controlled studies" (p. 425) with people affected by disasters or trauma events. Despite this conclusion, however, the use of pharmacological interventions should be considered with Latinos who have experienced a disaster or trauma because, as noted early, many members of the Latino community would expect medication for the treatment of their emotional problems resulting from those events.

CONSIDERATIONS FOR DISASTER AND TRAUMA

A well-known organization that provides disaster aid is the Federal Emergency Management Agency (FEMA). In their training manual (2003), they do not discuss special implications for different ethnic/cultural groups. However, they do describe techniques to use with survivors, some of which could be especially helpful with Latinos. The first of these is to include uninjured individuals in small tasks. This fits in with the Latino value of *caridad*. It is important for FEMA workers to recognize cultural differences when working with disaster survivors and for FEMA to include instruction on culture-specific practices when training rescue volunteers.

Consideration must also be given to individual differences based on age, gender, and language difference. Not all Latinos are necessarily fluent in Spanish. Indigenous immigrants often speak Spanish as their second language and may require additional attention when help is being rendered. As has been noted previously, women often defer to men and their children. Service providers and relief workers in disaster situations need to be attuned to gender differences. Finally, special consideration must be given to the elderly. If these individuals emigrated at an older age, they are likely less familiar with U.S. society and less likely to speak English. Helpers need to be prepared to respond to individuals not only based on cultural and language differences, but also based on age and gender differences.

For those professionals working with disaster and trauma survivors, it is important to consider not only disasters that happen here in the U.S., but also disasters that happen in Latino countries. Many Latino immigrants continue

Table 10.5. Contagious Diseases in Selected Latin American Countries

2000	Brazil	61 suspected cases of yellow fever in Brazil.
2001	Brazil	33 confirmed cases of yellow fever in Brazil, including 9 deaths.
2002	El Salvador	2249 cases of dengue including 6 deaths, and 156 cases of hemorrhagic fever.
2002	Ecuador	5833 cases of dengue and 158 cases of hemorrhagic fever.
2002	Honduras	3993 cases of dengue and 8 deaths from hemorrhagic fever.
2002	Brazil	317,787 cases of dengue and 57 deaths in Brazil. 41% of the cases were in the Rio de Janeiro State.
2003	Brazil	24 cases of yellow fever, including 5 deaths.
2004	Venezuela	2 cases of yellow fever, including 1 death.

to have family in their country of origin. They maintain close ties to their family "back home" because of the value of *familismo*. This means they may feel as though they are experiencing the disaster as well. Additionally, they may have feelings of survivor's guilt because they could not be there to help their family or because they feel that they have abandoned their family. Counselors should remain apprised of disasters happening in Latin America and check-in with clients from those countries to see how they are dealing with the situation. As part of this section, we will discuss some historical disasters in Latin America.

Table 10.5 shows recent contagious disease figures from the World Health Organization (2005). Note the high incidence of Dengue and dengue hemorrhagic fever across various Latin American countries in 2002. When reaching epidemic or pandemic proportions, outbreaks of disease can be highly disruptive disaster events.

Examples of Earthquakes from the U.S. Geological Survey (2005)

1985 Michoacan, Mexico. This earthquake reached a magnitude 8.0. More than 9,500 people were killed, more than 30,000 were injured, and more than 100,000 people were left homeless. The death toll was projected at 35,000 by the end of the rescues. The earthquake was felt as far away as Guatemala City, Guatemala and Houston, Texas, and caused approximately 3–4 billion U.S. dollars worth of damage. It was one of the ten worst earthquakes in the twentieth century.

2003 Colima, Mexico. This earthquake reached a magnitude 7.6. Approximately 29 people were killed, 300 injured, and 10,000 left homeless. The earthquake was felt as far away as Dallas and Houston, Texas.

318 P. Arredondo et al.

Examples of Hurricanes

1998 Hurricane Mitch in Central America.   This was a category 5 hurricane and was, "one of the most destructive hurricanes in the recorded history of the western hemisphere" (U.S. Geological Survey, 2005, p. 1).

2005 Hurricane Wilma in Mexico.   Shortly following the devastation of Hurricane Katrina in New Orleans, Louisiana, Hurricane Wilma ravaged the Yucatan Peninsula in Mexico, causing significant damage in its path. It was the strongest hurricane recorded to date.

FINAL RECOMMENDATIONS

Our final recommendations were developed with input from individuals who have worked with Latino survivors of disasters, and also from an individual who found herself in two roles, first as a victim and then as a helper. Contributing to this listing of recommendations are Dr. Joseph Ralph Ortiz, of the San Bernardino County Department of Behavioral Health, David Luna of the Texas Health and Human Services Department, and Ms. Enriqueta Chipana-Appel, M.S.

According to Dr. Ortiz, language is a key issue. Being able to talk to someone in their first language about what they have gone through allows them the opportunity to more fully express their emotions. The cultural competency literature reminds us that one's first language is the language of emotions (Santiago-Rivera et al., 2002). Agencies who are offering assistance are also encouraged to consider the involvement of a community liaison person. Providing a reputable individual from the community can help the rapport building process because helpers are usually "strangers" to local residents. To engage victims of a disaster in the process that ministers to their various needs, rapport and trust are essential. Dr. Ortiz also suggests that meetings with survivors be held at a community site. Because this is a more familiar locale, residents will likely feel safer and more comfortable, particularly if some members of the community may fear deportation due to their immigrant status.

To these recommendations, Ms. Chipana-Appel, a disaster victim herself, adds the importance of a psychosocial assessment. In order to begin to help victims plan for reconstruction, a comprehensive assessment of physical, medical, and emotional needs is essential. Another recommendation is to refer to the Kubler-Ross (1997) model of loss and grief. Most likely, victims will be in the first stage of this 5-step model, the shock stage. Shock may manifest in numerous ways such as paralysis, inability to carry out normal tasks, and what may appear to be a lack of emotions. Counselors need to be prepared for responses based on shock and denial.

Ms. Chipana-Appel also notes that during disasters people tend to get isolated due to moving around because of the loss of their home. Relocation means a loss of neighborhood and a loss of neighbors. In many cases, the counselors will have to play a very proactive role, making calls on behalf of the victims, not just giving them numbers to call. It is important to assess the level of shock because when one is in a state of shock, normal behaviors and tasks may be impossible to carry out.

Finally, counselors are encouraged to work with Latino disaster victims by following a cultural competency framework. That is, counselors need to be mindful of the myriad of ways culture affects all people, including themselves. Because counselors are cultural beings, they too have beliefs about how people "should" react during a disaster.

Everyone will have a different set of reactions, usually culturally influenced as well as affected by variables of age, gender, and socioeconomic status. The multicultural counseling competencies literature (Sue, Arredondo & McDavis, 1992) specifies three areas of competence: 1) counselor awareness of own biases and assumptions of others who one perceives to be culturally different; 2) counselor awareness of other cultural worldviews and how these affect people's behaviors; and 3) the application of culturally responsive and ethical interventions. Working with victims of disaster requires personal fortitude and selflessness. The focus on culture-specific knowledge will serve to strengthen one's good intentions to assist people under extreme life conditions.

References

American Psychiatric Association (2000). *Diagnostic and statistical manual of mental disorders* (4th ed.). Washington, DC: Author.

Arredondo, P., & Santiago-Rivera, A. (2000). *Latino dimensions of personal identity* (adapted from Personal Dimensions of Identity Model). Unpublished manuscript.

Boswell, T. (1994). *A demographic profile of Cuban Americans.* Miami, FL: Cuban American Policy Center, Cuban American National Council.

Campo-Flores, A. (2005). *The battle for Latino souls.* New York, NY: Newsweek.

Comas-Diaz, L. (2001). Hispanics, Latinos, or Americanos: The evolution of identity. *Cultural Diversity and Ethnic Minority Psychology, 7,* 115–120.

Cortina, J., de la Graza, R., Bejarano, S., & Wainer, A. (2005). *The economic impact of the Mexico-California relationship.* Los Angeles, CA: Tomas Rivera Policy Institute.

Cuellar, I., & Paniagua, F. A. (Eds.). (2000). *Handbook of multicultural mental health: Assessment and treatment of diverse populations.* New York: Academic Press.

DeNavas-Walt, C., Proctor, B. D., & Mills, R. J. (2004). Income, poverty and health insurance coverage in the United States: 2003. *Census Current Population Reports* (pp. 60–226). U.S. Department of Commerce, Economics and Statistics Administration. Washington, DC: Government Printing Office.

Federal Emergency Management Agency. (2003). *Community emergency response team: Instructor guide.* Retrieved April 4, 2005, from https://www.citizencorps.gov/cert/training_mat.shtm#CERTIG

Guzman, B. (2001). The Hispanic population. *Census 2000 Brief* (C2KBR/01-3). U.S. Department of Commerce, Economics and Statistics Administration. Washington, DC: Government Printing Office.

Kubler-Ross, E. (1997). *On death and dying* [Reprint Edition].New York: Scribner.

Library of Congress, Hispanic Division. (1998). The world of 1898: The Spanish-American war. Retrieved March 28, 2005, from http://www.loc.gov/rr/hispanic/1898/chronology.html

Marsella, A. J., & Yamada, A. M. (2000). Culture and mental health: An introduction and overview of foundations, concepts, and issues. In I. Cuellar & F. A. Paniagua (Eds.), *Handbook of multicultural mental health: Assessment and treatment of diverse populations* (pp. 3–24). New York: Academic Press.

National Public Radio, Kaiser Family Foundation, & Harvard's Kennedy School of Government. (2004). *NPR/Kaiser/Kennedy School Immigration Study*. Retrieved March 30, 2005, from www.npr.org/news/specials/polls/2004/immigration/summary.pdf

Paniagua, F. A. (2005). *Assessing and treating culturally diverse clients: A practical guide*. Thousand Oaks, CA: Sage.

Santiago-Rivera, A. L., Arredondo, P., & Gallardo-Cooper, M. (2002). *Counseling Latinos and la familia: A practical guide*. Thousand Oaks, CA: Sage.

Simon, A., & Gorman, J. (2004). Psychopharmacological possibilities in the acute disaster setting. *Psychiatric Clinics of North America, 27*, 425–458.

Smart, D. W., & Smart, F. F. (1997). DSM-IV and culturally sensitive diagnosis: Some observations for counselors. Journal of Counseling and Development, 75, 392–398.

Sue, D. W., Arredondo, P., & McDavis, R. M. (1992). Multicultural counseling competencies and standards: A call to the profession. *Journal of Counseling and Development, 20*, 64–88.

Therrien, M., & Ramirez, R. R. (2001). The Hispanic population in the United States. *Census Population characteristics: March 2000* (pp. 20–535). U.S. Department of Commerce, Economics and Statistics Administration. Washington, DC: Government Printing Office.

United States Census Bureau. (1990). *1990 census population* (Public use microdata sample). Washington, DC: Government Printing Office.

United States Census Bureau. (2000a). *Census 2000 demographic profile highlights*. Retrieved March 26, 2005, from http://factfinder.census.gov/servlet/SAFFFacts?_event=Search&geo_id=_geoContext=&_street=&_county=&_cityTown=&_state=04000US72&_zip=&_lang=en&_sse=on

United States Census Bureau (2000b). *Mapping census 2000: The geography of U.S. diversity*. Retrieved March 20, 2005, from http://www.census.gov/population/cen2000/atlas/censr01-111.pdf

United States Census Bureau. (2000c). *Race and Hispanic or Latino origin by age and sex for the United States: 2000 (PHC-T-8)*. Retrieved March 26, 2005, from http://www.census.gov/population/cen2000/phc-t08/tab08.pdf

United States Census Bureau.(2000d). *Sex by age (Hispanic or Latino) [49]–universe: People who are Hispanic or Latino* (Table No. P12H). Retrieved August 7, 2007, from http://factfinder.census.gov/servlet/DTTable?_bm=y&-geo_id=01000US&-ds_name=DEC_2000_SFI_U&-_lang=en&-redoLog=false&-mt_name=DEC_2000_SFI_U_P012H &-format=&-CONTEXT=dt

United States Census Bureau. (2003). *General demographic characteristics: 2003 American community survey summary tables*. Retrieved March 24, 2005, from http://factfinder.census.gov/servlet/ADPTable?_bm=y&-geo_id=01000US&-qr_name=ACS_2003_EST_G00_DP1&-ds_name=ACS_2003_EST_G00_&-redoLog=false&-_scrollToRow=29&-format=

United States Census Bureau. (2005). *Hispanic population passed 40 million, Census Bureau reports*. U.S. Department of Commerce. Washington, DC: Author.

United States Geological Survey. (2005) Earthquakes hazards program. Retrieved March 15, 2005, from http://neic.usgs.gov/neis/world/

World Health Organization. (2005). Communicable disease surveillance & response (CSR). Retrieved March 10, 2005, from http://www.who.int/countries/en/

Chapter 11

Working with Vietnamese Americans in Disasters

Aaron S. Kaplan and Uyen Kim Huynh

INTRODUCTION

The story of Vietnamese immigration and integration into the American landscape is a compelling story of tragedy and hope, and ultimately of the enduring human spirit for survival amidst destruction and despair. Before the Vietnam War (early 1960's–1975) few Vietnamese were living in the U.S. After the war, Vietnamese immigrated to the U.S. in large numbers, especially during four distinct waves of immigration (see Key Historical Events below).

Because of the relatively recent mass immigration to the U.S., the Vietnamese American population is a mix of older, foreign-born individuals and younger, American born children. This mix has led to interesting intergenerational dynamics within the Vietnamese American community. It is not uncommon, for example, for a Vietnamese American family to include adult family members who fled Vietnam as refugees, children who were born in Vietnam and arrived with their parents, and even younger children who were born in the U.S. after arrival. Furthermore, relatives in Vietnam often reunite with families in the U.S. years later after struggling to obtain exit visas (Montero, 1979).

This chapter focuses on Vietnamese culture and belief systems that are important in understanding how to best work with Vietnamese American clients in the aftermath of a disaster. We begin with brief descriptions of population demographics and cultural factors to paint a picture of Vietnamese American life.

The authors believe that it is impossible to fully appreciate the Vietnamese American experience without an understanding of the impact of the traumatic disruption of lives that occurred for many families who immigrated to the U.S. after the Vietnam War. Thus, we describe the circumstances surrounding four primary waves of Vietnamese immigration to the U.S. following the Vietnam War.

Next, we discuss the importance of traditional values and belief systems for Vietnamese family structure, dynamics, and behavior. Buddhist, Confucian, and Taoist influences on traditional Vietnamese beliefs and values are also discussed.

The next sections focus on considerations for mental health treatment, specific communication styles, assessment tools used for screening depression, anxiety, and trauma in Vietnamese populations, cultural beliefs and practices around illness and treatment, and recommendations for treating Vietnamese Americans in the aftermath of a disaster.

POPULATION AND CULTURAL DEMOGRAPHICS

Population Overview

According to U.S. Census data from 2000, approximately 1.1 million Vietnamese live in the United States. This marks an 82% increase in population over the past decade. Of those reflected in the 2000 census, 88.9% were foreign born, making Vietnamese the 5th largest foreign-born ethnic group in the United States. Furthermore, Vietnamese were the third fastest growing Asian-American group in the U.S.

More than 50% of all Vietnamese Americans live in California (43%) and Texas (11%). The largest population of Vietnamese Americans lives in the Los Angeles/Orange County area. An area known as "Little Saigon," located across the cities of Westminster and Garden Grove, California, is one of the best known and earliest established Vietnamese communities in the United States (U.S. Census Bureau, 2000).

The second largest concentration of Vietnamese Americans is located in the San Francisco Bay area, with a large population living in San Jose. Outside of California and Texas, there are sizable Vietnamese populations in the Washington D.C., Seattle, Boston, Philadelphia, and Atlanta areas (U.S. Census Bureau, 2000).

The percentage of adults (25 years and older) with at least a high school degree is 62%, and 19.5% attained a bachelor's degree or higher (U.S. Census Bureau, 2000). As of 2000, 14.3% of Vietnamese American families fell below the poverty level. Nearly 60% of Vietnamese Americans live in owner occupied housing (U.S. Census Bureau, 2000).

Religion

Under the current communist regime, Vietnam does not recognize a state religion. While the majority of Vietnamese in recent centuries practiced Buddhism, Vietnamese culture is influenced by values and beliefs of several religions (Bechert & Gombrich, 1991). These primarily include Buddhism, Taoism, and Confucianism, and will be described further in the Key Cultural Values section below because of their historical importance to the development of Vietnamese values.

A sizeable Christian community has grown in Vietnam over the past five centuries. Christianity was first introduced to Vietnam in the 16th century by the Catholic missionaries (Jamieson, 1995). It was not uncommon for entire communities of Vietnamese to convert at once, so that enclaves of Christians could be found throughout the country. It is estimated that by the beginning of the Vietnam War (mid 1960's), approximately 10% of the population in South Vietnam was Christian. Christians in Vietnam experienced differing degrees of tolerance and persecution over the centuries, depending on the ruling government and the leaders' fears of Christianity disrupting the established social order (Jamieson, 1995). Today, a sizeable number of Vietnamese refugees and immigrants to the U.S. are Christian and worship in both predominantly Vietnamese and in English speaking churches around the country.

Two other interesting religious sects, known as Cao Dai and Hoa Hao, combine elements of other religious and philosophical teachings. Cao Dai was organized in 1919 and is a mixture of Taoism, Confucianism, Buddhism, and Christianity. It was formed in an attempt to create a universally acceptable religion (Jamieson, 1995). Hoa Hao (named after the village of the founder, Prophet Huynh Phu So), formed in 1939, is believed to have over two million followers. Hoa Hao focuses on simplifying Buddhist doctrine and practice, and focuses on bringing Buddhist principles to farmers and laypeople (Jamieson, 1995).

Vietnam has experienced periods of religious persecution toward worshippers, particularly under the communist regime. Religious freedom has improved somewhat in recent years. However, a combination of philosophical and religious systems has greatly influenced the intellectual, cultural, and behavioral development of the Vietnamese people.

Religious life for Vietnamese Americans varies between families and across generations. In most Vietnamese American communities, worshipers are able to find Catholic or Protestant churches or Buddhist temples, where services are conducted in Vietnamese. For many Vietnamese Americans, religious communities play an important role in their social lives and sense of connection to others (Vuong, 1976). Acculturated Vietnamese Americans, especially the younger generations who are fluent in English, are more likely to become affiliated with English speaking congregations (Vuong, 1976).

Language

The Vietnamese speak a single, distinct language that includes northern, central, and southern dialects. Vietnamese borrows many words from Chinese dialects because of Vietnam's close proximity and historical connection to China (Ruhlen, 1987).

Vietnamese is monosyllabic and polytonal. Each vowel conveys a different meaning to the word when it is pronounced with a different tone, making the language sound musical and flowing. Vietnamese is the only language of the Asian mainland that is written with the Roman alphabet, which was adopted during the period of French colonization from the mid-1800's to 1900's (Ruhlen, 1987).

There are several ethnic groups that reside in Vietnam (and neighboring countries) who are ethnically and culturally different from the Vietnamese, and who speak their own languages. These include groups such as the Hmong and Mien, both of which have immigrated to the U.S. in large numbers in recent decades (U.S. Census Bureau, 2000).

Holidays

Aside from celebrating the typical religious holidays (e.g., Christmas), the most important non-religious Vietnamese holiday is *Tet*, or Lunar New Year, which is also celebrated by the Chinese (Chinese New Year). *Tet* is widely celebrated among Vietnamese American communities, often with several days of preparation before the actual date. It symbolizes a time for paying debts, forgiving others, correcting faults, and for wishing each other happiness, luck and prosperity (Nguyen, 1967).

Vietnamese believe that the fortune or misfortune experienced during *Tet* will set the tone for the rest of the year. Families honor their ancestors, and then spend time with friends and relatives. Children often look forward to *Tet* because they receive gifts of money wrapped in red envelopes called *li xi* or "lucky money", symbolizing prosperity and good fortune. During the festival of *Tet*, Vietnamese families traditionally light firecrackers to frighten away evil spirits (Nguyen, 1967).

Food

Vietnamese cuisine is considered one of the healthiest ethnic cuisines (Kittler & Schuer, 1989). Vietnamese dishes are generally not rich and heavy, and often favor simmering in broth to frying in oil. Vietnamese cuisine is influenced by French cuisine due to French colonization of Indochina. Due to Vietnam's proximity to China, Northern cuisine is particularly influenced by Chinese cooking, and is especially known for stir-fries and noodle-based soups. Central Vietnam boasts fresh produce because of the cooler mountain region, and it is also known for more elaborate dishes due to previous imperial rule in that region. As a result of the more tropical climate of the South, Southern cuisine is known to use more spices and coconuts. Seafood is also abundantly available and important to Vietnamese cuisine due to Vietnam's lengthy coastline (Kittler & Schuer, 1989).

Vietnamese meals are usually eaten "family style", where all dishes are served at once and shared from the center of the table. The various dishes are usually served with rice, or sometimes noodles. Meals often include soup, stir fry, another main dish, and a light salad that sometimes contains shrimp or beef. Vietnamese food is eaten with chopsticks (Nguyen, 1967).

KEY HISTORICAL EVENTS

Vietnamese immigration and resettlement in the United States is relatively recent, and stems from the aftermath of the Vietnam War (1964–1975). Between the end of the Vietnam War (1975) and 1990, more than 615,000 refugees and immigrants had arrived in the United States from Vietnam (Jamieson, 1995). Immigration to the United States is often viewed as occurring in four significant waves.

First Wave

The First Wave occurred at the end of the Vietnam War when approximately 130,000 immigrants entered the United States between 1975–1977 (Montero, 1979). These immigrants were primarily individuals and their families who were ex-military and government officials of South Vietnam, and Vietnamese who had worked for the U.S. during the war. They feared persecution by the new communist regime; a fear which was in fact warranted given the fate of many who did not leave and ended up in prison or forced labor camps. During the final days of the South Vietnamese government, dramatic film footage has documented the chaotic scene as many Vietnamese desperately attempted to leave the country by military transport. Many of these first wave refugees arrived with intact families and were dispersed throughout the U.S., often living with American families who sponsored them (Montero, 1979).

Vietnamese initially arrived at one of four primary military bases in the U.S., located in California, Arkansas, Pennsylvania, and Florida. They were subsequently dispersed across the U.S. with the assistance of several voluntary agencies working with the U.S. State Department (Montero, 1979). Most Vietnamese initially lived with American families who served as sponsors until Vietnamese families got their feet on the ground. Approximately 90% of the adults who arrived in the First Wave were employed within the first year of their arrival (Montero, 1979).

The First wave of Vietnamese immigrants seemed to adapt better to life in America compared to subsequent waves of refugees. This may be partially attributed to the fact that First Wave immigrants were generally of a higher educational level and socioeconomic status, as they had professional or business ties with the U.S. government and military. Furthermore, individuals arriving in the First Wave generally did not experience the same degree of trauma that subsequent immigrants experienced after the communist regime gained power. Finally, the U.S. had less difficulty absorbing the relatively small number of immigrants arriving in the First Wave, so that it was easier for families in this group to be placed in housing and obtain social services.

Second Wave

After the war, many people who were associated with the government of South Vietnam remained in Vietnam hoping to rebuild their war-torn country. Unfortunately, many faced retaliation by the new government, especially those who were associated with the South Vietnamese regime. The new government also singled out classes of people they considered to be potentially subversive, such as religious figures, intellectuals, and entrepreneurs. Furthermore, because of escalating conflict with China after the Americans departed, the Vietnamese government persecuted individuals believed to belong to the Chinese merchant class, including many farmers and fisherman. Punishment of political prisoners included torture, imprisonment, harassment, property confiscation, forced labor, denial of official identification documents, and limited access to employment, education, health care and legal protection.

By 1977, the lives of many Vietnamese had become so desperate and intolerable that they sought to escape Vietnam at any cost. Sometimes referred to as the "boat people", the Second Wave (1977–1978) of immigrants escaped Vietnam through long, arduous, and dangerous journeys (Hauff & Vaglum, 1993). Some journeyed across war torn Cambodia to reach refugee camps in Thailand. Others were smuggled out of the country on boats. During their escape, many Vietnamese refugees witnessed or were subjected to horrible and traumatic experiences (Hauff & Vaglum, 1993). For example, pirates or military forces sometimes attacked refugee boats. Refugees report experiences of rape, theft, starvation, cannibalism, and murder. Many immigrants of the Second Wave experienced symptoms of post-traumatic stress disorder upon arriving in the U.S., which only made it more difficult to adjust to life in a new country (Montero, 1979).

Life in refugee camps in countries such as Hong Kong, Thailand, and Malaysia was not easy, as conditions were often cramped and refugees were not permitted to leave the camps until they were repatriated. Some looked forward to joining relatives elsewhere in the world. Others remained in a state of uncertainty for periods of months to sometimes years, waiting to immigrate to another country with little knowledge about what to expect.

Third Wave

The Third Wave resulted, in part, as a response to the plight of the "boat people". The U.S. initiated the Orderly Departure Program (ODP) in 1979 to provide a safe, controlled, and legal means of immigrating to the U.S. Under an agreement between the Vietnamese government and the U.S., Vietnamese with family members in the U.S. were allowed to immigrate provided they met specific criteria. Unfortunately, the ODP was often stymied by bureaucratic red tape, especially by the Vietnamese government, around eligibility issues.

Fourth Wave

A Fourth Wave of immigration began around 1987 as a result of a policy known as the Amerasian Homecoming Act (United States General Accounting Office, 1994). Amerasians are the children of Vietnamese women and U.S. military and civilian personnel. During the 1980's, stories began to emerge from Vietnam about the sad plight of Amerasian children who were generally rejected by the Vietnamese and were often found begging in streets and in poor health. The U.S. and Vietnamese governments had bitterly disagreed for years about who was responsible for the Amerasian Children, each side insisting the children were the responsibility of the other. The U.S. eventually acknowledged responsibility for the children. Under the Amerasian Homecoming Act, Amerasian children and close relatives were given special priority status under the ODP. The Amerasian Homecoming Act provided funds for transportation and repatriation, and ensured post-arrival refugee benefits such as food stamps, welfare, housing, health care and employment assistance (United States General Accounting Office, 1994).

Under the Act, Amerasians and their relatives flooded into the U.S. to escape the poverty and degradation they experienced in war torn Vietnam. Unfortunately, some Vietnamese exploited the "golden passports" to America by marrying themselves or their children to Amerasians, or by bribing, threatening or persuading Amerasians to claim them as "relatives." Partially because of the abuse, the resettlement program was terminated, leaving behind an unknown number of Amerasians who will likely never have the opportunity to be repatriated (United States General Accounting Office, 1994).

There were also a sizeable number of individuals who were associated with the U.S. or South Vietnamese government and were imprisoned by the communist regime after the fall of Saigon. Many were detained in "reeducation camps" for many years under harsh conditions. Finally, in 1988, the U.S. State Department reached an agreement with the Vietnamese government to allow many detainees to leave through the ODP. Approximately

100,000 former detainees were repatriated to the U.S. under the program (Montero, 1979).

In recent years, the Vietnamese government has been warming to the return of Vietnamese ex-patriots. These returnees, known as *viet kieu*, are beginning to play an important role in bringing foreign currency into Vietnam and stimulating business and the economy. The return of Vietnamese has increased since the U.S. reestablished diplomatic ties with Vietnam under the Clinton Administration.

KEY CULTURAL VALUES

The Cultural Context of Beliefs and Practices

Traditional Vietnamese values are strongly influenced by the philosophical underpinnings of Confucianism, Buddhism, and Taoism. These belief systems impact Vietnamese culture at all levels, including family/social dynamics, communication, and behavioral patterns in every day life.

Confucianism is more of a social philosophy and code of ethical and moral behavior than a religion (Jamieson, 1995). Confucianism was imported from China when Vietnam was under Chinese rule (approx. 939–1404 A.D.). Confucianism stresses the importance of a personal code of ethics and conduct, especially as they relate to one's duties towards family and society (Jamieson, 1995).

Buddhism was first introduced to Vietnam around the 1st Century A.D. by Indian scholars (Bechert & Gombrich, 1991; Jamieson, 1995). According to Buddhism, people suffer when they become attached material wealth, or to expectations about the way things should be in life. To alleviate suffering, one must learn to suppress desire and expectation. A person gains clarity of mind through meditation and introspection.

Buddhism places importance on practicing compassion and good deeds toward. An important tenet of Buddhism is that a person repeatedly cycles through stages of existence until he or she attains spiritual enlightenment, and becomes free of worldly suffering (Bechert & Gombrich, 1991).

Taoism is concerned with harmony between man and nature, especially regarding the balance of opposites (e.g., rest/motion, liquid/solid, darkness/light, spiritual/material). The most notable duality is between the forces of *yin* (female) and *yang* (male), and all dualities can be viewed as containing elements of these (Bechert & Gombrich, 1991; Jamieson, 1995). When *yin* and *yang* are in balance, a natural order is achieved, and we experience a sense of harmony. Inaction, conformity, and passivity are often viewed within a Taoist framework as important to achieving a sense of well being. This concept is exemplified by the famous Taoist maxim: "Do nothing and everything will be accomplished spontaneously."

In working with Vietnamese clients, it is helpful to understand how the deeply entrenched beliefs and values of Buddhism, Confucianism and Taoism influence Vietnamese values, beliefs, and cultural practices. For example, the Vietnamese practice of ancestor worship, and importance placed on family piety and hierarchy, stem from a combination of Buddhist, Taoist, and Confusion beliefs. Other key traditional values and beliefs, such as karma, harmony, and moral duty, also share commonalities between the religions. It should be noted that the key values described below are not necessarily ascribed to any one religious or philosophical belief system, and may share elements between them.

Family Piety (*hieu*)

A key reason Vietnamese society has survived for thousands of years, despite numerous wars and foreign occupations, is due to *hieu*, or family piety (Jackson, 1987; Jamieson, 1995). The family is at the core of Vietnamese culture and society, and the needs of the family outweigh the needs of the individual. When a family member enjoys success or achievement, the whole family celebrates the accomplishment. His or her achievement is "owned" by the family, and the entire family experiences a sense of pride and expects to share in the benefits of success. Similarly, failure is believed to reflect badly upon the family. Family members may experience shame if one family member fails to live up to expectations. Vietnamese children are encouraged to view their achievements as a means of contributing to the well being of the family (Jackson, 1987).

The importance of family is apparent in how Vietnamese individuals identify themselves. Traditionally, Vietnamese present their last name before their first name (e.g., Smith John), suggesting that family affiliation is more important than individual identity (Nguyen, 1967).

Moral Duty (*on*)

Consistent with the values of family piety, Vietnamese demonstrate respect according to age hierarchy (Jackson, 1987; Jamieson, 1995). Vietnamese believe they have a duty (*on*) to respect and serve their elders. Younger children are expected to show deference to older siblings, and older siblings are expected to help care for younger ones.

At the top of the hierarchy are the parents. Children learn that they must show the utmost duty and respect toward their parents. They must abide by strict cultural and religious practices that reflect discipline, perseverance, commitment, and unconditional loyalty to elders in the family. Furthermore, children are taught caretaking responsibilities at an early age, both for parents and for younger siblings (Jackson, 1987; Jamieson, 1995).

The importance of respect for elders and caring for family members is crucial to family structure. As parents become elderly, children and grand-children are expected to care for them. Thus, in traditional Vietnamese culture, elderly parents never fear being alone and unable to care for themselves (Vuong, 1976).

Continuity of Family Lineage

Many Asian cultures emphasize the importance of ancestor worship as a central focus of the family (Jamieson, 1995). Traditional Vietnamese families believe the spirits of ancestors exist at the heart of the household, and family members must continue to pay respects to them. Furthermore, Vietnamese believe that physical proximity to the tombs of their ancestors is important for maintaining communication with them. During important dates or festivals, offerings of food or gifts are made to ancestors first. Children are reminded to behave in a manner that would not bring shame to their ancestors (Leung, Boehnlein, & Kinzie, 1997).

Vietnamese immigrants are forced to separate from the physical proximity to their ancestors. This separation may cause some to experience a heightened sense of loneliners and guilt because they no longer feel they are able to com-municate with their ancestors. A sense of connection with ancestors may serve as a source of comfort, reassurance, and guidance. When one is physically sep-arated from ancestors, he or she may feel isolated and unsure of themselves without the guidance of ancestors for comfort (Leung et al., 1997).

Gender Roles

Vietnamese families traditionally are patriarchal in nature (Nguyen, 1967; Vuong, 1976). Prior to World War II, it was not uncommon for a man to take more than one wife. After World War II, laws prohibited polygamy. However, men commonly "socialized" with women in entertainment settings, (Leung et al., 1997). Girls were raised to acknowledge "Three Obediences": respect for father, husband, and eldest son.

Furthermore, girls learned they were supposed to obey the "Four Virtues": a dignified or serious expression, a reserved manner of speaking, a chaste temperament, and industriousness (Jamieson, 1995).

Traditionally, Vietnamese women are expected to marry early, produce children, and look after the household. They are also expected to help carry out duties in worshipping the husband's family's ancestors (Vuong, 1976). While the husband is generally viewed as the primary provider, it is not uncommon for Vietnamese women to earn additional income through a small business. In the U.S., many Vietnamese women supplement the family income through a small business, especially in the food or beauty industries.

The blurring of traditional gender roles is a byproduct of American accul-turation and changing times (Freeman, 1995). Older Vietnamese men and women may experience discomfort when women are viewed by American authorities or service providers as sharing an equal role in the family decision-making process. Men may feel that their traditional gender role is threatened or undermined. Women may not feel comfortable when asked to assume power beyond what is traditionally sanctioned.

Similarly, younger and more acculturated Vietnamese Americans may adopt contemporary American values of gender equality in role expectations. Parents may have difficulty accepting their acculturated children's behavior, especially around dating, communication, lack of "modesty," and non-traditional career goals (Zhou & Bankston, 1998).

Karma (*Nghiep*)

Karma is a Buddhist concept that expresses a belief in a metaphysical law of causality (Bechert & Gombrich, 1991). According to karma, a person's life situation is determined by one's deeds and behavior in previous lives. Similarly, the way a person chooses to live his or her life in the present will determine his or her situation in a future life.

An awareness of karma may have practical implications for the way a person chooses to behave. The actions one chooses may have a direct result on the well being of another, which in turn may affect the other's subsequent behavior. Thus, a person with an awareness of the laws of karma understands the interconnected nature of the world. Living a moral and ethical life is only possible when one realizes he or she is directly connected to everyone else (Bechert & Gombrich, 1991).

One's behavior may lead to karmic retribution or karmic benefit. Vietnamese believe that one's actions will also affect the karmic outcome for the rest of the family. Thus, Vietnamese are keenly aware of the impact of individual behavior on the rest of the family (Bechert & Gombrich, 1991; Jamieson, 1995).

An acceptance of life conditions due to karma should not be mistaken for passivity or fatalism. One may not have control over the occurrence of an adverse event, but the manner in which an individual or family meets a challenge may affect the outcome and one's karmic disposition. Therefore, Vietnamese may prefer to solve problems on their own rather than rely on others for help so that they may perceive they are taking an active role in determining their outcomes (Bechert & Gombrich, 1991).

Harmony (*Dieu*)

The concept of *dieu* may be attributed to the Taoist belief in the importance of harmony between man and nature (Jamieson, 1995). Being reasonable is a prerequisite for achieving harmony for a Vietnamese person. *Dieu* is achieved only as a result of doing things the "right" way and conforming to the natural order that includes the physical, social, and natural worlds. Individuals, families, and institutions that are "reasonable" are rewarded because they achieve harmony. When one violates natural order, and *dieu* is disrupted, it is believed that he or she is inviting disaster upon themselves or their family (Jamieson, 1995).

The Righteous Path (*Nghia*)

The primacy of social obligation is known as "righteousness," or *nghia* (Jamieson, 1995). It implies duty, justice, and obligation. *Nghia* emphasizes a willingness to do what one must to fulfill one's social obligations, to repay one's moral debt, and to meet the demands of filial piety. To live by principles of *nghia*, one must employ a calm rationality and live scrupulously by rules of morality and duty. A person following principles of *nghia* must not waver according to circumstances, personal preferences, or potential consequences to oneself. Examples of *nghia* can be highlighted by expectations of hierarchical social behavior, such as relational behavior between elders and youth, parents and children, husband and wife, living and ancestors, etc. (Jamieson, 1995).

CONSIDERATIONS FOR MENTAL HEALTH TREATMENT

Trauma and PTSD

The Vietnam War raised awareness within the mental health community about the psychological distress caused by war-related traumatic experiences. Because of years of clinical work and research on post-traumatic stress disorder (PTSD), the present generation of mental health practitioners is more aware of the clinical implications of trauma and PTSD on the well-being of refugees.

After the Vietnam War, numerous PTSD research programs were initiated (especially within the Department of Veteran's Affairs) when it was apparent that high numbers of returning Vietnam veterans were experiencing severe psychological and emotional distress from their military experiences. Stemming from the work with Vietnam Veterans, researchers examined the effects of trauma on victims experiencing a wide variety of traumatic events. Concern for the welfare of refugees has emerged as an important field of research and practice, as refugee populations are often exposed to significant numbers and varieties of trauma.

The Vietnamese people began experiencing the impact of American involvement in Vietnam by the early 1960's (Karnow, 1984). Vietnamese soldiers and their families experienced the types of psychological distress and loss typically experienced during times of war. Similar to the American Civil War, in the Vietnam War, Vietnamese fought against Vietnamese, and families and communities were sometimes pitted against each other. There were many civilian casualties, especially because Vietcong guerrilla fighters in the South were often indistinguishable from civilians. In some areas, the U.S. used dioxin (Agent Orange) to defoliate strategic jungle areas. Dioxin is believed to be linked to skin disease and cancer in U.S. soldiers exposed during the war. While there is a lack of data on its effects on Vietnamese villagers, some Vietnamese doctors believe there is a link between exposure and elevated cancer rates and birth defects.

Many refugees suffered severe traumatic experiences in post-war Vietnam. Some were political prisoners who suffered prolonged periods of torture and abuse while in prison or "re-education" camps following the end of the war (Karnow, 1984). Others suffered trauma during the process of escaping Vietnam. Because of these factors, many Vietnamese individuals have come to the U.S. with a history of trauma either directly or indirectly related to the war (Hauff & Vaglum, 1993). While acculturation is often difficult for immigrants in the best of circumstances, traumatized refugees may experience a disruption in their ability to function at a level necessary to perform their basic roles (Kinzie et al., 1990; Tran, 1993).

Although it was estimated that 10% of Vietnamese immigrants who arrived in the first four waves suffered from PTSD, the disorder may be under diagnosed (Kinzie et al., 1990).Many survivors may avoid disclosing their trauma histories because they do not wish to re-experience the trauma. Vietnamese refugees may also not disclose because of feelings of shame and guilt around the stigma associated with mental illness (Tran, 1993). Instead, Vietnamese refugees may complain of somatic symptoms, (i.e., backaches, headaches, loss of appetite and poor sleep), or problems with depression and anxiety, resisting a full disclosure of their traumatic experiences (Kinzie et al., 1990; Purnell & Paulanka, 1998).

Recommendations to Clinicians Regarding Trauma.   In the aftermath of a disaster, many survivors will experience exacerbations of psychiatric symptomatology, especially related to depression, anxiety, and PTSD. For many Vietnamese immigrants who experienced significant trauma histories prior to arriving in the U.S., a disaster experience may remind immigrants of previous traumas and re-trigger PTSD symptoms. Health care providers should be aware of the potential impact of prior trauma on an individual's reaction to a disaster.

Aside from experiencing typical symptoms of PTSD, an immigrant with a prior trauma history may express concern about their family's safety in the U.S. after a disaster. A trauma survivor may ask, "After leaving my traumatic experiences behind in Vietnam, if I am not safe in the U.S., where can I be safe?" The author (AK) recalls interviewing Hmong refugees shortly after 9/11, who were concerned that they didn't know where to find caves to hide in, or which berries and nuts to pick for survival, if terrorists attacked California. Hiding from attackers, and surviving off the land, had become a way of life for the Hmong until they reached "safety" in the U.S.

Health care providers should not assume that a patient's psychological and emotional distress is entirely related to the present traumatic event. It may be advisable to assess for prior history of trauma and mental health problems.

Acculturation and Adjustment

Strangers in a Strange Land. Upon arriving in the United States, many Vietnamese refugees struggled to rebuild their lives from scratch. With the experiences of the Vietnam War not far behind, refugees embarked on an uphill battle to build economic prosperity and develop a sense of security.

Vietnamese refugees are faced with new values, norms, laws, language, climate, housing, work, and cultural customs. Many face financial worries, difficulty finding jobs, prejudice, discrimination, stress, and intergenerational conflicts with their children. Difficulty adapting to the ways and demands of the new culture, and in utilizing effective coping strategies, often leads to avoidance and isolation as well as difficulty forming meaningful relationships with "natives" (Roysircar-Sodowsky & Maestas, 2000). For example, when refugees are not able to learn English, they become more socially isolated and alienated from the new host society. This may contribute to barriers in accessing health and social services, and makes it more difficult to find work or advance in a career.

Like many newly arrived immigrant groups, Vietnamese immigrants often initially settled in low-income neighborhoods with typical community problems, including inferior schools, gangs, drugs, and crime (Freeman, 1995; Rutledge, 1992). They faced challenges in learning to navigate through the bureaucracy and customs of a foreign society. It is likely that acculturative stresses increased the likelihood of Vietnamese immigrants developing anxiety, depression, and other symptoms of psychological, emotional, and physical distress (Lin, Masuda, & Tazuma, 1984; Sodowsky & Lai, 1997).

Besides psychological and emotional distress, Vietnamese refugees suffer from high rates of physical illness (Muecke, 1983a). While refugees are believed to suffer from high rates of psychiatric problems (UNHCR, 1998), there is a lack of reliable epidemiological data to accurately assess the magnitude of mental health problems. Southeast Asian refugees are commonly reported to suffer from higher rates of anxiety and depressive disorders, thought disorders, and PTSD (Buchwald, Manson, Dinges, Keane, & Kinzie, 1993; Gold, 1992; Mollica et al., 1990). Major Depressive Disorder and Generalized Anxiety Disorder have been found to be the most commonly diagnosed mental health problems among refugees exposed to war trauma (Buchwald et al., 1993; Kinzie et al., 1990; Lin, Masuda, & Tazuma, 1984). Lin et al. (1984) reported that anxiety and depression had greater prevalence among Vietnamese and Hmong refugees than among other subgroups.

Stigma of Mental Illness and Somatization of Symptoms.   There is a significant stigma associated with mental illness in traditional Vietnamese families (Nguyen, 1985). It is difficult to even discuss mental health issues without provoking feelings of shame. The term typically used for psychiatrist is *bac si tam than* (lit. mental doctor), and implies a Western concept mental illness based on a biologically based disease model. When mental health problems are attributed to "brain disease" or "organic brain dysfunction", individuals tend to generate more negative associations with the problem and are less likely to seek treatment because of shame (Kaplan, 2000).

There is no historically equivalent word in the Vietnamese language for the terms "counselor" or "therapist". Many non-acculturated Vietnamese are unfamiliar with the concept of talking with a therapist to gain psychological insight and decrease psychological and emotional distress. Instead, many Vietnamese clients may initially seek help for somatic complaints, such as headaches, before revealing emotional problems (Fabreg & Nguyen, 1992; Gold, 1992).

Victims of a natural disaster are likely to experience a range of psychologically distressing symptoms, including symptoms related to anxiety and depression. In order to de-emphasize the concept of "mental illness", clinicians may approach Vietnamese clients by putting their psychological and emotional reactions into a situational context. Essentially, it is important to "normalize" the post-traumatic experience rather than label the problems as psychological or emotional maladjustment.

Clinicians should demonstrate to their Vietnamese clients that they take their somatic complaints seriously, and resist the urge to overtly draw connections between emotional distress and somatic problems. As rapport is established, the client's somatic complaints may become a metaphorical representation of the client's psychological and emotional distress, even if this is never directly discussed. On the other hand, once rapport is established, many Vietnamese trauma survivors are willing and able to discuss their traumatic experiences and address the psychological and emotional sequalae of trauma. The topic should be treated sensitively, with individuals varying in the degree to which they feel comfortable acknowledging and disclosing psychological and emotional distress.

Intergenerational Dynamics: A Source of Conflict and Support.   Since the Vietnam War, there has been a major influx of Vietnamese immigrants and refugees to the U.S., and the majority of Vietnamese Americans were born in Vietnam at the time of this writing. The Vietnamese American population is a mix of older, foreign born individuals and younger, American born children, leading to interesting intergenerational dynamics within the Vietnamese American community. Vietnamese American families may include family members who fled Vietnam as refugees, children who were born in Vietnam and arrived with their parents, and younger children who were born in the U.S (Montero, 1979). Many families also contain relatives who later immigrated to the U.S. to join their families.

Intergenerational dynamics can be both a source of support and a source of conflict within Vietnamese families. Younger family members support their parents and grandparents by helping care for them, and by carrying on the honor of the family and household over generations. Adult immigrants often have more difficulty with acculturation than children (Liebkind, 1996). They may have had occupations, community affiliations, and social status in Vietnman that were stripped away and rendered irrelevant in an unfamiliar American culture. Children, on the other hand, may be free of such expectations and experiences, enabling them to adapt better to a new environment. Children often become the "spokesperson" or "go between" for the family and institutions within the new culture (Liebkind, 1996). Immigrant children often learn English more quickly than adults because they have the opportunity to attend American schools, and are able to interact with American children. Therefore, children often play an important role in the functioning of the immigrant family.

As Vietnamese American children become acculturated, they adopt traditional American values, such as the importance placed on individual achievement and behavioral expression (Zhou & Bankston, 1998). Vietnamese American children may find themselves straddling two social worlds, wanting to "fit in" to American culture and at the same time maintain Vietnamese cultural values. Older family members may experience distress and dismay as they witness their children's behavioral changes. They may be concerned that if their children forget about traditional Vietnamese values, the children may not care for them when they are old, or honor them after they die (Zhou & Bankston, 1998).

Recommendations to Clinicians Regarding Acculturation and Adjustment.
Vietnamese culture places the family at the center of importance to an individual's happiness and well-being (Vuong, 1976). In the event of a disaster, clinicians working with Vietnamese Americans should consider that Vietnamese individuals might view their own health and well being as less important than the welfare of their families. They may downplay the significance or severity of their own problems. Clinicians should acknowledge the importance of the welfare of the individual's family while treating the individual, and view treatment of the individual as occurring within the context of the family system.

Clinicians should be aware of respecting appropriate boundaries of family hierarchy. This may include working or communicating with elders first to acknowledge the importance of family hierarchy, and then asking permission to speak with younger family members after rapport is established.

Though Western trained counselors may feel the urge to "empower" their clients by nurturing independence and individuality, they should be careful not to underestimate the importance of family hierarchy, even to those who appear disempowered. Clinicians may face difficult cultural/ethical dilemmas, such as cases involving domestic violence, childhood physical abuse, and extreme emotional distress within the family, where the family may resist outside intervention. Furthermore, Vietnamese children, even those who are relatively acculturated to American society, may not feel comfortable with therapeutic modalities that may appear geared towards "blaming" the parents.

Clinicians should be aware of gender role expectations of clients and their families, and the potential for conflict within families around these issues. Gender role issues are especially likely to occur between generations, where more acculturated younger Vietnamese Americans adopt American values and behaviors which are incongruent with traditional Vietnamese culture and behavioral roles.

Barriers in Accessing Mental Health Services

Like immigrants from many Asian countries, Vietnamese Americans often do not seek mental health services because of the stigma associated with mental illness within their culture (Nguyen, 1985). Even those who do seek a psychiatrist for treatment often suffer from other barriers that contribute to vast health disparities (Collins et al., 2002). Potential barriers include lack of medical insurance, language barriers, lack of access to culturally sensitive services for them, and a lack of understanding of the purpose of mental health treatment (Collins et al., 2002; Nguyen, 1985). Furthersome, when professionals do not speak Vietnamese, and translators are not available, the likelihood of treatment compliance (e.g., keeping appointments) is significantly diminished (Nguyen, 1985).

Prior to immigrating to the U.S., most Vietnamese obtained substandard health care services on an episodic basis. Clinics in Vietnam typically provide treatment on a walk-in basis, focusing on treating immediate physical symptoms, and de-emphasizing a long-term therapeutic relationship between doctor and patient (Liebkind, 1996). Consequently, Vietnamese immigrants are not accustomed to aspects of the Western practices of medicine, such as preventive care, active participation in disease management and treatment planning, and scheduling/following up with appointments (D'Avanzo, 1992; Nguyen, 1985). Western practitioners may feel frustrated when they perceive Vietnamese patients as being resistant, non-compliant, or non-participatory in the treatment process.

Medical and mental health treatment compliance may improve when patients are able to establish an ongoing relationship with a health care provider (D'Avanzo, 1992; Nguyen, 1985). Clinicians who understand the importance Vietnamese place on interpersonal relationships may find significantly improved success in treating Vietnamese clients. For example, Vietnamese clients may appreciate when practitioners show an interest in their culture, family and immigration histories. Similarly, Vietnamese clients may show their appreciation and trust in their health care providers by bringing food or small gifts.

Compliance to treatment will be greatly enhanced when Vietnamese clients feel a sense of interpersonal connection, rapport, and trust with their providers (Purnell & Paulanka, 1998). Vietnamese Americans will be more likely to comply with treatment when they have a clear understanding of what to expect with regard to diagnostic and treatment procedures. Without a clear understanding of procedures and a good rapport with their providers, it is much more likely that Vietnamese Americans will discontinue treatment or miss follow-up appointments (Purnell & Paulanka, 1998).

There are other practical barriers to receiving mental health care among Vietnamese immigrants. Many lack transportation, health insurance, and access to social service resources (D'Avanzo, 1992). Because of the barriers many Vietnamese Americans face in obtaining health services, health care is often not considered a high priority to them. Many immigrants identify other goals they consider to be more important than attending to their health, such as maintaining home and family stability, earning an income, gaining an education or training, and caring for children. As a result, Vietnamese immigrants are often at a higher risk of developing health complications because of neglecting to adequately address health problems.

Many Vietnamese Americans, especially those living below or near the poverty line, cannot afford health insurance. This is consistent with findings that a disproportionately high number of Southeast Asian Americans lack health insurance (Collins et al., 2002). In addition, Vietnamese immigrants frequently are unaware of free legal, medical, and social services in their communities (Die & Selbach, 1988; Gold, 1992). Furthermore, Vietnamese Americans may feel intimidated dealing with complicated U.S. bureaucracies, such as social service and health care agencies. Instead, Vietnamese Americans may choose to rely on family, friends, and religious organizations within their communities to meet their needs.

An individual's degree of acculturation may be the best predictor of his or her utilization of social services (Muecke, 1983a). Vietnamese immigrants who speak little English and have limited familiarity with American culture and customs are far less likely to access beneficial social services.

Recommendations to Clinicians Regarding Barriers to Services.   Because of barriers to accessing and utilizing mental health services, clinicians and social service agencies should make special efforts to reach Vietnamese victims of disaster. The following are suggestions for improving access and utilization of services:

- Availability of translators and practitioners familiar with traditional Vietnamese culture.
- Outreach to Vietnamese community organizations, such as churches and temples, through respected leaders in the community.

- Efforts to explain the complexities of the American social service and benefits systems, and assistance in navigating through these systems.
- Build rapport by acknowledging and involving family members whenever possible (while respecting age and gender hierarchies).
- Improve treatment compliance by educating patients about the purpose of diagnostic and treatment procedures.

COMMUNICATION STYLES

Indirectness

Vietnamese possess a well-developed ability to keep their true feelings hidden. Within Vietnamese culture, it is believed that a person should not be in a hurry to reveal his or her feelings, because to do so may seem impolite, self-centered, and disrespectful. Instead, Vietnamese individuals may express their feelings or desires indirectly, at times by hinting or talking around subjects important to them (Rutledge, 1992).

It may take time and sensitivity to understand the "inner life" of a Vietnamese person. Because Vietnamese individuals are better able to understand the indirect communication style, they are more attuned to the underlying complexity of meaning in communication. When culturally unaware practitioners work with Vietnamese clients, they may make serious errors in understanding if they take the meaning of verbal communication at face value. Worse, they may view Vietnamese clients as suspicious or resistant, and purposely not forthcoming with information because of an intentional lack of cooperation.

Similarly, Vietnamese individuals may not understand the American style of "speaking one's mind." American straightforwardness may be considered impolite. In Vietnamese culture, it is often considered rude to come directly to the point (Rutledge, 1992). It is possible that a Vietnamese client may discontinue services with a provider if he or she feels uncomfortable with a provider's straightforwardness on sensitive topics, before adequate rapport has been established.

Service providers should be aware that sometimes Vietnamese individuals may verbally respond in a manner consistent with their cultural values, even when the response may not appear accurate, forthcoming, or truthful. For example, a Vietnamese individual may respond in a way that facilitates interpersonal harmony and respect for gender and age hierarchies. When asked to provide a list of problems or complaints, a Vietnamese person may feel uncomfortable responding directly, following values such as modesty, self-sacrifice, and enduring hardship.

Indirect communication styles may stem from cultural factors rooted in the Easter philosophies and religions previously discussed. It should also be noted that some Vietnamese immigrants may have learned the importance of exercising caution with strangers because of their experiences with internal wars in Vietnam and oppressive political rule.

Non-verbal Communication

Similar to other Asian cultures, Vietnamese place importance on the meaning of non-verbal communication (Vuong, 1976). In many instances, the subtlety involved in non-verbal communication is based on interpersonal respect. Especially in hierarchical relationships (e.g., teacher/student, doctor/patient, elder/youngster), individuals may demonstrate respectful boundaries through non-verbal means (Vuong, 1976).

Given the nature of the relationship, an individual may not speak unless spoken to, and may avoid eye contact. Similarly, direct eye contact may be considered rude between individuals of the opposite sex. While adherence to these behaviors is considered appropriate within Vietnamese culture, Westerners may misinterpret them as passive, elusive, or suspicious (Vuong, 1976).

The smile is another common non-verbal communication behavior that is often misunderstood by Westerners (Vuong, 1976). Instead of verbal explanations, Vietnamese often smile as a means of non-verbally conveying a variety of uncomfortable feelings. For example, a smile may be used as an apology for a minor offence, or to acknowledge embarrassment over a mistake. A smile may also be used to express enthusiasm, as opposed to an emphatic verbal response that may appear rude (Vuong, 1976).

Hierarchical Communication in Families

Vietnamese family structure is hierarchical, with respect and deference paid in order of age and position in family (Jackson, 1987). Providers should be aware that younger clients might feel uncomfortable communicating with mental health professionals when their older siblings or parents are present. It may be considered rude for younger clients not to defer to parents or older siblings in such situations. Similarly, younger clients may be less forthcoming with information, such as what they really think or feel, in the presence of elders.

Many Vietnamese clients may feel uncomfortable criticizing their parents or elders (Sue & Morishima, 1982; Tran, 1993). They may feel uncomfortable attributing psychological distress to their childhood upbringing and resist "blaming" parents or elders for their problems. Similarly, women may feel uncomfortable "blaming" their husbands for marital distress. They may deny having marital problems (even in the case of domestic violence), or even accept blame for the abusive behavior of their husbands.

Recommendations to Clinicians on Awareness of Non-verbal Communication. It is important for providers to recognize the importance of non-verbal communication behaviors. During times of disaster or tragedy, mental health workers may express a genuine desire to help disaster victims, and may feel frustrated if they perceive resistance or unwillingness to cooperate with relief efforts.

Providers should be aware that if a Vietnamese client does not overtly state his or her wishes verbally, it does not necessarily mean that he or she agrees or disagrees with the provider. Providers should be careful not to take the person's initial response at face value regarding how he or she is feeling, or what he or she wants. As a Vietnamese client becomes more comfortable with the provider, and a sense of connection and rapport is established, he or she may be more verbally forthcoming regarding his or her internal experience, thoughts, and wishes. It may be helpful to view the family as a system, and include other family members in the treatment process to best learn the sentiments of the identified individual.

Providers should be aware that sometimes non-verbal communication may be meant to convey a different message than what appears at face value. For example, while a smile may be interpreted as sign of "pleasant agreement," it could also signify feelings of embarrassment, shame, or respectful disagreement. Similarly, avoidance of eye contact is often a sign of respect in Vietnamese culture. Providers should not assume that if a Vietnamese client avoids eye contact, he or she is not listening or taking the matter seriously. When providers understand the potential meaning of non-verbal communication, and they understand the importance of key Vietnamese values, they are more likely to develop trusting relationships with clients. Over time, clients may begin to feel comfortable expressing themselves more directly.

OVERVIEW OF ASSESSMENT INSTRUMENTS

Researchers at the Harvard Program in Refugee Trauma (HPRT) developed psychometric instruments to measure anxiety and depression symptomatology, and to assess trauma history in a primary care setting. Designed for survivors of torture, there are several language versions of each instrument. Two instruments have Vietnamese translations and have been used in primary care settings among Vietnamese refugees and survivors of torture. All of HPRT's instruments have undergone extensive translation processes in order to maintain linguistic and cultural validity, including back translation procedures to ensure that Vietnamese idioms of distress were accurately captured.

Hopkins Symptom Checklist-25 (HSCL-25)

The Hopkins Symptoms Checklist-25 (HSCL-25) was translated by HPRT for use with torture survivors. There are several language versions of the instrument. The HSCL-25 is a short version of the Hopkins Symptom Checklist (HCSL), which is a well known and widely used instrument used to assess psychiatric symptomatology originally developed in the 1950s (Parloff, Kelman & Frank, 1954). The developers of the HSCL demonstrated the usefulness of the HSCL-25 in a family practice or a family planning service.

The HSCL-25 measures symptoms of anxiety and depression. It consists of 25 items: Part I contains 10 items covering anxiety symptoms, and Part II contains 15 items for symptoms of depression. Items on the scale are rated from 1–4 based on severity of the symptom (i.e., "Not at all", "A little", "Quite a bit", and "Extremely.") Total Score is calculated by averaging of all 25 items, and Depression and Anxiety subscale scores are calculated by averaging of the 15 depression items and 10 anxiety items, respectively. It has been consistently demonstrated in several populations that the Total Score is highly correlated with general emotional distress, and the depression score is correlated with Major Depressive Disorder.

The HPRT screening instruments are administered through interview format by health care workers under the supervision and support of a mental health professional. The instrument was not designed to be completed by individuals on their own.

Simple Depression Screening

The Simple Depression Screening instrument was translated into Vietnamese and Kru/Khmer. This brief screening instrument was adapted from the Hopkins Symptom Checklist-25 (HSCL-25) and the Harvard Trauma Questionnaire (HTQ) to screen for histories of torture and depression. The instrument consists of the 15 Depression Scale items from the HSCL-25 (described above), and six items related to torture.

The screening instrument is administered in a brief 15-minute interview that can be conducted by the primary health care workers, including a Vietnamese interpreter. It is used to quickly screen for torture survivors who may be in need of more extensive psychiatric evaluation and mental health treatment. The instrument was originally developed for the U.S. Office of Refugee Resettlement, and is intended to provide health care providers with a brief, self-report inventory used to detect symptoms of depression and PTSD among Southeast Asian refugees.

The second half of the instrument asks "Yes/No" questions related to exposure to torture and symptoms of PTSD. For example:

- Do you suffer from reoccurring nightmares? If yes, how often?
- Have you experienced torture?
- While in captivity, did you ever receive a deliberate or systematic infliction of physical or mental suffering, from an agent of a government or, of an armed political group, or any person acting with the government's approval?

The Vietnamese Health and Social Adjustment Scales

These scales were developed as part of larger study of Vietnamese immigrants and refugees in Hawaii. Hawaii was a major port of entry for Vietnamese immigrants and refugees following the end of the war and efforts were made by a group of researchers (Marsella, Fox, Butler, & Truong, 1995) to document the adaptation and adjustment patterns of refugees. The researchers developed a series of seven scales that assessed a number of dimensions including ethnic identity, life stress, acculturation and mental health.

CULTURAL BELIEFS AND PRACTICES AROUND ILLNESS AND TREATMENT

Thuac Bac

Traditional beliefs about health, illness, and treatment are greatly influenced by Chinese beliefs and practices (Purnell & Paulanka, 1998). A traditional system of medicine derived from Chinese health concepts is called *thuac bac* (Northern medicine). *Thuac bac* views disease as stemming from imbalance between external (e.g., climate, time of year, food/drink), internal (e.g., physical or emotional strain), and moral forces. Practitioners of *thuac bac* prescribe medications derived from natural ingredients to induce a bodily reaction (e.g., sweating), or to excite or soothe specific organs. This system is based on the premise that living things are composed of four basic elements: air, fire, water and earth with the respective associated characteristics of cold, hot, wet and dry.

Thuac Nam

Another system of medicine, called *thuac nam* (Southern medicine), relies on traditional herbal remedies, tonics, avoidance of excess, and massage to maintain good health and treat ailments (Chow, 1976; Muecke, 1983a,b; Purnell & Paulanka, 1998). Remedies used in *thuac nam* generally consist of ingredients, such as roots, herbs, or vegetables, easily found or produced in a typical village.

Chinese Medicine

Practices with origins in China, such as moxibustion (the burning of moxa or other substances on the skin to treat diseases or to produce analgesia) and acupuncture are also common among the Vietnamese (Chow, 1976; Purnell & Paulanka, 1998). These practices are most often administered to treat common maladies, such as colds, nausea, headaches, backaches, and motion sickness. For a Vietnamese villager, these "symptoms" are often accepted as a natural part of one's life rather than illness warranting a visit to a doctor.

Because of the stigma associated with mental illness, a Vietnamese person may not care to view their psychosomatic symptoms (i.e., somatic complaints that may arise from psychological distress) as an indicator of psychological problems (Chow, 1976; Purnell & Paulanka, 1998). Therefore, home remedies and traditional healing practices are likely to focus on the manifestation of somatic and physical symptoms of illness, and de-emphasize the psychological.

CONCLUSION

This chapter presented information about Vietnamese Americans that may be helpful in understanding how to work with this population in the event of a natural disaster. Because the cultural landscape of Vietnamese Americans has changed dramatically over the past thirty years, issues related to immigration, acculturation, and adaptation to American culture were discussed. The Four Waves of recent Vietnamese immigration to the U.S. were described, including the impact that circumstances of immigration have had on Vietnamese adjustment in the U.S. Key traditional Vietnamese values and beliefs were discussed, including important influences stemming from Buddhism, Taoism, and Confucianism.

The chapter discussed of factors in working with Vietnamese Americans, including special considerations for mental health treatment, barriers in accessing mental health services, issues regarding verbal and non-verbal communication, cultural beliefs and practices around illness and treatment, and assessment tools. A basic understanding of the Vietnamese American experience will greatly enhance the clinician's effectiveness and enjoyment in working with this interesting and dynamic population.

References

Bechert, J., & Gombrich, D. (1991). *The World of Buddhism.* London: Thames & Hudson.

Buchwald, D., Manson, S. M., Dinges, N. G., Keane, E. M., & Kinzie, J. D. (1993). Prevalence of depressive symptoms among established Vietnamese refugees in the United States. *Journal of General International Medicine, 8,* 76–81.

Chow, E. (1976). *Cultural health traditions: Asian perspectives.* In M. F. Brance & P. P. Paxton (Eds.), *Providing safe nursing care for ethnic people of color* (pp. 210–221). New York, NY: Appleton-Century-Crofts.

Collins, K. S., Hughes, D. L., Doty, M. M., Ives, B. I., Edwards, J. N., & Tenney, K. (2002). *Diverse communities, common concerns: Assessing health care quality for minority Americans: Finding from the Commonwealth Fund 2001 health care quality survey.* Washington, DC: Author.

D'Avanzo, C. E. (1992). Barriers to health care for Vietnamese refugees. *Journal of Professional Nursing, 8,* 245–253.

Die, A. H., & Selbach, W. C. (1988). Problems, sources of assistance and knowledge of services among elderly Vietnamese immigrants. *Gerontologist, 28,* 448–452.

Fabreg, H., & Nguyen, H. (1992). Culture, social structure, and quandaries of psychiatric diagnosis: A Vietnamese case study. *Psychiatry, 55,* 230–249.

Freeman, James M. (1995). *Changing identities: Vietnamese Americans, 1975–1995*. Boston, MA: Allyn and Bacon.

Gold, S. J. (1992). Mental health and illness in Vietnamese refugees. *Western Journal of Medicine, 157*, 290–294.

Hauff, E., & Vaglum, P. (1993). Vietnamese boat refugees: The influence of war and flight traumatization on mental health on arrival in the country of resettlement. A community cohort study of Vietnamese refugees in Norway. *Acta Psychiatrica Scandinavica, 88*, 162–168.

Jackson, H. M. (1987). Vietnamese social relationships: Hierarchy, structure, intimacy and equality. *Interculture, 20*, 2–17.

Jamieson, N. L. (1995). *Understanding Vietnam*. Berkeley, CA: University of California Press.

Kaplan, A. (2000). *An exploration of the meaning of psychiatric symptomatology in rural Nepal*. Ann Arbor, MI: Bell & Howell Information and Learning Center.

Karnow, S. (1984). *Vietnam: A history*. New York, NY: Penguin Books.

Kinzie, J. D., Boehnlein, J. K., Leung, P. K., Moore, L. J., Riley, C., & Smith, D. (1990). The prevalence of posttraumatic stress disorder and its clinical significance among Southeast Asian refugees. *American Journal of Psychiatry, 147*, 913–917.

Kittler, P., & Schuer, K. (1989). *Food and culture in America*. NY: Van Nostrand & Reinhold.

Leung, P. K., Boehnlein, J. K., & Kinzie, J. D. (1997). Vietnamese American families. In E. Lee (Ed.), *Working with Asian Americans: A Guide for Clinicians*. New York: Guilford Press.

Liebkind, K. (1996). Acculturation and stress: Vietnamese refugees in Finland. *Journal of Cross-Cultural Psychology, 27*(2), 161–180.

Lin, K. M., Masuda, M., & Tazuma, L. (1984). Adaptational problems of Vietnamese refugees IV: Three-year comparison. *Psychiatric Journal of the University of Ottawa, 9*, 79–84.

Marsella, A. J., Fox, S., Butler, N., & Truong, D. (1995). *Vietnamese immigrant adaptation and adjustment scales*. In A. J. Marsella (Ed.), Department of Psychology, University of Hawaii, Honolulu, Hawaii, 96822.

Mollica, R. F., Wyshak, G., Lavelle, J., Truong, T., Tor, S., & Yang, T. (1990). Assessing symptom change in Southeast Asian refugee survivors of mass violence and torture. *American Journal of Psychiatry, 147*, 83–88.

Montero, D. (1979). *Vietnamese Americans: Patterns of resettlement and socioeconomic adaptation in the United States*. Boulder, CO: Westview Press.

Muecke, M. A. (1983a). Caring for Southeast Asian refugee patients. *American Journal of Public Health, 73*, 431–439.

Muecke, M. A. (1983b). In search of healers: Southeast Asian refugees in the American health care system. *Western Journal of Medicine, 139*, 835–840.

Nguyen, D. (1985). Culture shock: A review of Vietnamese culture and its concepts of health and disease. *Western Journal of Medicine, 142*, 409–412.

Nguyen, K. (1967). *An introduction to Vietnamese culture*. Saigon: Vietnam Council on Foreign Relations.

Parloff, M. B, Kelman H. C., & Frank, J. D. (1954). Comfort, effectiveness, and self-awareness as criteria for improvement in psychotherapy. *American Journal of Psychiatry, 3*, 343–351.

Purnell, L., & Paulanka, B. (1998). *Transcultural health care: A culturally competent approach*. Philadelphia, PA: F.A. Davis Company.

Roysircar-Sodowsky, G., & Maestas, M. V. (2000). Acculturation, ethnic identity, and acculturative stress: Evidence and measurement. In R. H. Dana (Ed.), *Handbook of cross-cultural and multicultural personality assessment* (pp. 131–172). Mahwah, NJ: Lawrence Erlbaum.

Ruhlen, M. (1987). *A guide to the world's languages, vol. 1: Classification*. Stanford, CA: Stanford University Press.

Rutledge, P. (1992). *The Vietnamese experience in America*. Bloomington, IN: Indiana University Press.

Sodowsky, G. R., & Lai, E. W. M. (1997). Asian immigrant variables and structural models of cross-cultural distress. In A. Booth, A. C. Crouter, & N. Landale (Eds.), *Immigration and the family: Research and policy on U.S. immigrants* (pp. 211–234). Mahwah, NJ: Lawrence Erlbaum.

Sue, S., & Morishima, J. K. (1982). *The mental health of Asian Americans.* San Francisco, CA: Jossey-Bass.

Tran, T. V. (1993). Psychological trauma and depression in a sample of Vietnamese people in the United States. *Health and Social Work, 18,* 184–194.

United Nations High Commission on Refugees. (1998). *The state of the world's refugees 1997–1998. A humanitarian agenda.* Washington, DC: Oxford University Press.

United States Bureau of the Census (2000). *Statistical abstract of the United States Population.* Washington, DC: Author.

United States General Accounting Office. (1994). *Vietnamese Amerasian resettlement: Education, employment, and family outcomes in the United States.* Washington, DC: United States General Accounting Office.

Vuong G. T. (1976). *Getting to know the Vietnamese and their culture.* New York, NY: Unger.

Zhou, M., & Bankston, C. (1998). *Growing up American: How Vietnamese children adapt to life in the United States.* New York, NY: Russell Sage Foundation.

APPENDIX: VIETNAMESE ADJUSTMENT SCALES

(Marsella, Fox, Butler, &Truong, 1995)
#1 Vietnamese Ethnic Identity Questionnaire

How much do you participate in the following activities and behaviors associated with Vietnamese ethnocultural traditions?

		Very much	Somewhat	A little	None
A	Eat Vietnamese food at home	—	—	—	—
B	Watch Vietnamese movies	—	—	—	—
C	Watch Vietnamese TV program	—	—	—	—
D	Shop at Vietnamese stores (e.g. Chinatown, Asian market)	—	—	—	—
E	Visit Vietnam	—	—	—	—
F	Belong to at least one Vietnamese cultural organization	—	—	—	—
G	Speak Vietnamese	—	—	—	—
H	Understand Vietnamese	—	—	—	—
I	Read Vietnamese	—	—	—	—
J	Dress in Vietnamese clothes	—	—	—	—
K	Listen to Vietnamese Music	—	—	—	—
L	Read Vietnamese newspapers	—	—	—	—
M	Observe Vietnamese Holidays	—	—	—	—
N	Have Vietnamese hobbies	—	—	—	—
O	Attend Vietnamese religious services (e. g. Buddhist, Catholics)	—	—	—	—
P	Learn Vietnamese dances and music	—	—	—	—

Q	Use Vietnamese traditional medicine	—		—	—	—
R	Furnish house with Vietnamese furniture and artifacts	—		—	—	—
S	Play Vietnamese games	—		—	—	—
T	Go to physicians, hairstylists, lawyers, or dentists who are Vietnamese	—		—	—	—
U	Go to Vietnamese restaurants	—		—	—	—
V	Participate in ancestor worship	—		—	—	—
W	Have Vietnamese friends	—		—	—	—

2 TRADITIONAL VALUES ASSESSMENT SURVEY (TVAS)

Please place the letter of your choice in before each statement

Strongly agree	Agree	Agree a little	Disagree a little	Disagree	Strongly disagree
A	B	C	D	E	F

1 __ Children should always obey their parents wishes and desires

2 __ Females should be responsible for family affairs and house works (e. g. cooking, cleaning, childrearing, etc)

3 __ One should never make another family member lose face in public

4 __ Family relationships are the most important part of a person's life

5 __ One should always support an immediate family member and be able to depend on the family for support

6 __ A parent's obligation is to care for their children to the very best of their abilities (e.g. education, housing medicine)

7 __ A child's obligation is to care for his/her parents when they reach old age up to the time of death

8 __ Suffering is a part of life and should be endured and accepted

9 __ All things in life can be overcome through persistence, hard work, and meeting one's obligations

10 __ It is the responsibility of each person to contribute to the family in accord with age and ability

11 __ One must make personal sacrifices for the betterment of the family

12 __ Women should be encouraged to earn extra income to help the family

Strongly agree	Agree	Agree a little	Disagree a little	Disagree	Strongly disagree
A	B	C	D	E	F

13 __ One should always strive to overcome adversity and to pursue individual/family achievement and success

14 __ One should maintain respect for family ancestors and heritage

15 __ One should strive to maintain traditional Vietnamese values

---

T.V.A.S.

Xin làm ơn viết chữ cái thích hợp nhất theo sự hiểu biết của bạn vào chỗ trống

Rất đồng ý	Đồng ý	Đồng ý chút đỉnh	Không đồng ý chút ít	Không đồng ý	Hoàn toàn không đồng ý
(A)	(B)	(C)	(D)	(E)	(F)

_____1. Con cái phải luôn luôn vân lời sự mong muốn và đoài hỏi của cha mẹ

_____2. Phụ nữ có nhiệm vụ lo công việc ở nhà (e.g. nấu ăn, dọn nhà, nuôi con, v.v.)

_____3. Không bao giờ làm người nhà (sấu hổ) mất mặc ngoài xã hội

_____4. Sự liên hệ giữa bà con thân thuộc là rất quan trọng trong đời sống của con người

_____5. Người trong nhà phải luôn luôn ủng hộ anh em bà con ruột thịt của mình và người ấy cũng có thể tin cậy đến người trong gia đình để ủng hộ

_____6. Bổn phận của cha mẹ là phải hết sức trông nom chăm sóc cho con cái của mình (e.g. giáo dục, thuốc men, nhà của)

_____7. Bổn phận của người con là chăm sóc cho cha mẹ lúc cha mẹ già yếu đến lúc chết

_____8. Sự đau khổ là một phần của đời sống và phải cam chịu và chấp nhận

_____9. Mọi điều trên đời có thể vượt qua bằng cách kiên nhẫn, bền chí, hết sức cố gán làm việc và đạt được mục đích của mình

_____10. Bổn phận của mọi người là đóng góp cho gia đình đúng theo tuổi và khả năng của mình

_____11. Người nhà phải hy sinh lợi riên cá nhân để làm cho gia đình cải tiến hơn

_____12. Nên khuyến khích đàn bà đi làm phụ và thu nhập tiền thêm để giúp gia đình

_____13. Phải luôn luôn cố gắng vượt qua vận nghịch và theo đuổi đạt đến thành công và kết qủa tốt cho mình/gia đình

_____14. Phải duy trì sự tôn kính cho ông bà tổ tiên và (truyền thống) giòng họ

_____15. Phải cố gắng duy trì truyền thống qúy trọng của người Việt

#3 VIETNAMESE WELL-BEING CHECKLIST
Please read each statement carefully and place a nember in the appropriate blank.

1 Not at all
2 A little
3 Quite a bit
4 Extremely

	In Vietnam	Now (in US)	
1	—	—	The idea that someone else is controlling your thoughts
2	—	—	The idea that something is wrong with your mind
3	—	—	Feeling easily annoyed or irritated
4	—	—	Temper outbursts that you could not control'
5	—	—	Having urges to beat, injure or harm someone
6	—	—	Getting into frequent arguments
7	—	—	Hearing voices
8	—	—	The feeling that something bad is going to happen to you
9	—	—	Feeling that people are unfriendly
10	—	—	Trouble remembering things
11	—	—	Having frequent bad dreams and nightmares
12	—	—	Difficulty making decisions
13	—	—	Your mind going blank
14	—	—	Trouble concentrating
15	—	—	Unhappy much of the time
16	—	—	Having thoughts that are not your own
17	—	—	Feel that the future is completely hopeless and nothing can improve
18	—	—	Feel that you don't have anything to expect
19	—	—	Often have the feeling that you are going crazy
20	—	—	Often feel sad
21	—	—	Often feel bothered
22	—	—	Often feel low-spirited and bored, not wanting to do anything anymore
23	—	—	Often feel exhausted, completely tired
24	—	—	Often feel desperate (completely hopeless)
25	—	—	Often feel downhearted and low-spirited, losing excitement and enjoyment in work and life

Culture, Trauma, and the Treatment of Post-Traumatic Syndromes: A Global Perspective[1]

John P. Wilson[2]

INTRODUCTION

Culture and Trauma

The relation of trauma and culture is an important one because traumatic experiences are part of the life cycle, universal in manifestation and occurrence, and typically demand a response from culture in terms of healing, treatment, interventions, counseling and medical care. To understand the relationship between trauma and culture requires a "big picture" overview of both concepts (Marsella, Friedman, Gerrity, & Scurfield, 1996; Marsella & White, 1982). What are the dimensions of psychological trauma and what are the dimensions of cultural systems as they govern patterns of daily living? How do cultures create social-psychological mechanisms to assist its members who have suffered significant traumatic events?

Empirical research has shown that there are different typologies of traumatic experiences (e.g., natural disasters, warfare, ethnic cleansing, childhood

---

[1] This chapter is based on a paper presented at the 1st meeting of the Asian Society for Traumatic Stress, Chinese University of Hong Kong, November 12, 2005, and an article in the Asian Journal of Counseling, 2006, Vol. 13 No. 1, 107–144.

[2] Correspondence concerning this article should be addressed to John P. Wilson, Department of Psychology, Cleveland State University, 2300 Chester, Cleveland, OH 22115, U.S.A. E-mail: j.p.wilson@csuohio.edu

abuse, domestic violence, terrorism, etc.) that contain specific stressors (e.g., physical or psychological injuries) that tax coping resources and challenge personality dynamics (e.g., ego strength, personal identity, self-dimensions) and the capacity for normal developmental growth (Green, 1993; Wilson, 2006; Wilson & Lindy, 1994). Traumatic life events can be simple or complex in nature and result in simple or complex forms of posttraumatic adaptation (Wilson, 1989, 2006). Similarly, cultures can be simple or complex in nature with different roles, social structures, authority systems and mechanisms for dealing with individual and collective forms of trauma. For example, dealing with an accidental death of one person is significantly different than coping with the aftermath of the worst tsunami disaster in humankind's history in 2004, which caused the death of thousands, as well as destruction of the environment and societal infrastructure. Hence, it is important to know how cultures utilize different mechanisms to assist those injured by different forms of extreme stress experiences.

The injuries generated by trauma include the full spectrum of physical and psychological injuries. Problems that require mental health and counseling interventions involve a broad range of posttraumatic adaptations that include posttraumatic stress disorder (PTSD), mood disorders (e.g., major depression), anxiety disorders, dissociative phenomena (Spiegel, 1994) and substance use disorders. In terms of mental health care, cultures provide many alternative pathways to healing (Marsella et al., 1996; Moodley & West, 2005). The integration of extreme stress experiences can be provided by shamans, medicine men and women, traditional healers, culture-specific rituals, conventional medical practices, and community-based practices that offer forms of social and emotional support for the person suffering the adverse, maladaptive aspects of a trauma. It is therefore essential to understand the psychology of trauma and trauma recovery in a broad sense.

This article begins with a discussion of issues in trauma intervention in the global context, including cultural assumptions and other operating principles in the treatment of posttraumatic syndromes. The discussion is followed by a review of the literature on culture as it relates to trauma recovery, with conceptual, research and practice implications for the advancement of the trauma field.

The Treatment of Traumatic Stress in Global Context

The ubiquity of traumatic events throughout the world has raised global awareness of posttraumatic reactions as an important psychological condition that results from a broad range of traumatic experiences (e.g., war, ethnic cleansings, terrorism, tsunamis, hurricanes, catastrophic earthquakes, etc.). Economic globalization has "flattened the world" (Friedman, 2005) as technologies have changed the face of commerce and the international marketplace. In a real sense, globalization has generated trends towards the homogenization of cultures and at the same time heightened awareness of distinct cultural differences. However, when it comes to the issue of cultural differences and posttraumatic syndromes, it cannot automatically be assumed that advances in Western psychotherapeutic techniques can be exported and applied to non-Western cultures.

In an influential and important critique of mental health programs in war-affected areas (e.g., Bosnia, Rwanda, etc.), Derek Summerfield (1999) explicated seven fundamental operational principles that many of these programs embrace, with programs derived from research and clinical efforts on psychotherapy in Western cultures, primarily the United States and Western Europe. These seven operational principles are stated as follows:

> (1) Experience of war and atrocity are so extreme and distinctive that they do not just cause suffering, they 'cause' traumatization; (2) there is basically a universal human response to highly stressful events, captured by Western psychological frameworks [cf. PTSD]; (3) large numbers of victims traumatized by war need professional help; (4) Western psychological approaches are relevant to violent conflict worldwide; victims do better if they emotionally ventilate and 'work through' their experiences; (5) there are vulnerable groups and individuals who need to be specifically targeted for psychological help; (6) wars represent a mental health emergency: rapid intervention can prevent the development of serious mental problems, as well as subsequent violence and wars; and (7) local workers are overwhelmed and may themselves be traumatized (pp. 1452–1457).

This same set of principles, it is assumed, could safely be generalized to non-warzone countries in which there are catastrophic natural disasters (e.g., tsunami; earthquake) or other conditions of human rights violations by political regimes: "the humanitarian field should go where the concerns of survivor groups direct them, towards their devastated communities and ways of life, and urgent questions about rights and justice" (p. 1461). Moreover, he notes that:

> . . . the medicalization of distress, a significant trend within Western culture and now globalizing, entails a missed identification between the individual and the social world, and a tendency to transform the social into the biological . . . consultants . . . have portrayed war as a mental health emergency writ large, with claims that there was an epidemic of 'posttraumatic stress' to be treated, and also that early intervention could prevent mental disorders, alcoholism, criminal and domestic violence and new wars in subsequent generations by nipping brutalization in the bud (p. 1461).

These observations by Summerfield raise a number of critical points when it comes to the proper and efficacious treatment of posttraumatic syndromes in simple and complex cultures in the world.

The term post-traumatic syndrome should not be regarded as synonymous with PTSD, although it certainly includes the narrow, diagnostic definition of the disorder. Rather, posttraumatic syndromes involve a broad array of phenomena that include trauma complexes, trauma archetypes, post-traumatic self-disorders (Parsons, 1988), posttraumatic alterations in core personality processes (e.g., five-factor model); identity alterations (e.g., identity confusion) and alterations in systems of morality, beliefs, attitudes, ideology and values (Wilson, 2006). The experience of psychological trauma can have differential effects to personality, self, and developmental processes, including the epigenesis of identity within culturally-shaped parameters (Wilson, 2006).

Given the capacity of traumatic events to impact adaptive functioning, including the inner and outer worlds of psychic activity (Wilson, 2004), it is critically important to look beyond simple diagnostic criteria such as PTSD (Summerfield, 1999) to identify both pathogenic and salutogenic outcomes as individuals cope with the effects of trauma in their lives. As argued elsewhere (Wilson, 2006), the history of scientific research on PTSD is badly skewed (perhaps for reasons of historical necessity) towards the study of psychopathology rather than on human growth, self-transformation, resilience and optimal functioning. We need to understand both functional and dysfunctional reintegration in trauma recovery.

Knowledge of healing practices for traumatized persons poses challenging questions to anthropological and Western empirical approaches to diagnosis, assessment and criteria of behavioral change. It cannot be assumed that psychotherapeutic techniques scientifically validated for use in Western cultures have generalizability to non-Western cultures, despite the fact that in terms of PTSD treatment, in particular, evidence suggests that "exposure" treatments designed to desensitize the disruptive effects of distressing traumatic memories, are useful in ameliorating anxiety, depression and states of emotional liability associated with PTSD (Wilson, Friedman, & Lindy, 2001).

In non-Western cultures, such therapeutic techniques, the customary settings in which they are utilized with patients (e.g., office, hospital, clinic), and their dependence on verbal expressions in response to the service provider's questions could be asynchronous with cultural norms or traditional cultural healing practices. The understanding of global applications of different therapeutic procedures to assist persons suffering from posttraumatic syndromes requires clarity and knowledge (clinical and empirical) of what "works best" to restore integrative psychological functioning – to enable persons to continue healthy, normal and adaptive coping within the cultural contexts of such parameters. The assumption is that by examining empirical and clinical knowledge, it becomes possible to further identify useful, pragmatic and communally validated practices to alleviate suffering among persons adversely impacted by trauma. Moreover, native or indigenous healing practices require evaluation and respect as to reports of efficacy in treating a broad range of posttraumatic symptoms and phenomena (Wilson, 1989).

Thus, the extension of Western PTSD practices to non-Western people must be done with great care and sensitivity. The following steps may be helpful in this process. First, local clinical knowledge in certain parts of the world is also folk knowledge, accumulated wisdom about the types of experiences that facilitate the restoration of well being and recovery from posttraumatic syndromes. Second, empirical knowledge in the Western context is that which typically uses controlled experimental research designs to determine treatment effects on clinical outcomes. Western cultures place a premium on the merits of tightly controlled research designs, especially randomized clinical trials (RCT), double-blind studies, manualized treatment protocols (e.g., cognitive behavior therapy) and similar techniques. However, in non-Western cultures such studies may not be possible, intelligible, or acceptable within the culture itself in terms of its prevailing religious, ideological or indigenous belief systems. The accumulation of global knowledge about the treatment of posttraumatic syndromes will require the convergence of empirical and clinical information so as to develop a conceptual matrix of therapeutic techniques that identifies what interventions work for whom and under what conditions, in response to different types of traumatic events. Such a conceptual matrix would identify such categories as: (1) the client population; (2) traditional healing practices; (3) therapeutic contexts; (4) medical practices; (5) shamanic practices; (6) assumptive belief systems about illness and health; (7) perspectives on the psychobiology of traumatic stress (i.e., mind-body relationships); (8) the implicit psychological and behavioral principles; (9) the range of healer roles and practices; (10) individual vs. collective practices; and (11) religious and spiritual involvement in healing and recovery. In writing about the complexities of cross-cultural treatment in general, Marcella (2005) listed a series of healing principles that are found across different cultures. He considers these principles to be both therapeutic and salutogenic:

- Beliefs (Instill new beliefs or reinforce and reward others)
- Catharsis (Anger, hate, fear)
- Confession and release of guilt
- Cultural re-embeddedness or separation
- Redefinition of problems and of self
- Empathy (Communicate shared feeling and understanding in dyad)
- Expression and verbalization of problems
- Faith
- Forgiveness
- Hope
- Identity development and awareness
- Information Exchange
- Insight
- Interpretation of events
- Locus of control alterations
- Mobilization of endorphin and immune system
- Propitiation

- Reduction of uncertainty, anxiety, fear through increased confidence and control
- Re-socialization and acquisition of new social skills
- Reduction of guilt and shame through approval and forgiveness
- Social supports and network development and strengthening
- Suggestion and persuasion
- Unconscious (Making the unconscious conscious)

Culture and the Treatment of Post-Traumatic Symptoms

The literature on cultural competence has brought awareness of the need for knowledge, sensitivity and innovation when it comes to mental health treatment in non-Western cultures (Marsella & White, 1982). More recently, Moodley and West (2005) discussed the limitations of verbal therapies and presented a rationale for the integration of traditional healing practices into counseling and psychotherapy. While a discussion of the types of traditional healing practices (e.g., shamanism, medicine healing in aboriginal nations) is beyond the scope of this article, it is worthwhile to point out that there are culture-specific healing practices as well as overlaps in conceptual viewpoints about the assumptions underlying traditional healing practices across different cultural groups. Consider for a moment four very different cultural views of healing: Native American; African – Zulu; Indian (Ayurveda); and traditional Chinese medicine (TCM). What does each of these cultures assume about traditional healing and the cosmological (cf. one could also say mythological) assumptions they hold about physical and mental health?

Native American.   In most North American aboriginal nations, healing is considered from the perspective of relations – balanced relations – between individuals and environment and the world at large (Mails, 1991). When sickness occurs it is generally assumed that there is an imbalance in the nature of "relations to all things"; that a loss of balance and harmony has occurred within the person. Healing, then, is the empowerment of the individual spirit with the great circle of life; to restore balance and harmony with nature, others and the Great Spirit (God). The medicine wheel and traditional shamanic (i.e., medicine) practices are used as a guide to understanding. Through traditional healing practices, rituals and ceremonies, the designated "medicine" person facilitates the restoration of a person's spirit and inner strength in order to restore the person's vital power to be in good balance (i.e., to have good relations of balance and harmony). More specifically, trauma can cause a loss of centeredness in the person and lead to a loss of "spirit", resulting in various forms of "dispiritedness" which include depression, PTSD, dissociation, and altered maladaptive states of consciousness and being (Jilek, 1982; Mails, 1991; Wilson, 1989; Poonwassie & Charter, 2005).

South African (Zulu).   The Zulu culture in South Africa employs a view of mental and spiritual life that is intricately interconnected. Bojuwoye (2005) states: "The interconnectedness of the phenomenal world and spirituality are two major aspects of traditional African world views. The world view holds that the universe is not a void but filled with different elements that are held together in unity, harmony, and the totality of life forces, which maintain firm balance or equilibrium, between them. A traditional Zulu cosmology is an individual universe in which plants, animals, humans, ancestors, the earth, sky and universe exist in unifying states of balance between order and disorder, harmony and chaos" (p. 63). In Zulu culture, then, traditional healing practices have respect for this view and attempt to facilitate the restoration of a harmonious state of being in relation to these dimensions of the persons' phenomenal world.

Indian (Ayurveda).   Indian healing in the Ayurvedic tradition views restorative practices as unifying mind, body and spirit within the context of social conditions. Kumar, Bhurga and Singh (2005) state: "According to Ayurvedal principles, perfect health can be achieved only when body, mind and soul are in harmony with each other and with cosmic surroundings. The second dimension in this holistic view of Ayurveda is the social level, where the system describes the ways and means of establishing harmony within and in the society. Mental equilibrium is sought by bringing in harmony three qualities of the mind in sattva, vajas and tamas" (p. 115). Thus, traditional Indian healers use time-honored practices (e.g., touching, laying of hands) to facilitate helping a person restore unity in the psyche. After the 2004 tsunami, such practices were used with success by local healers to aid victims who suffered from the stress-related effects of the disaster in India (Shah, 2007).

Traditional Chinese Medicine.   In traditional Chinese medicine (TCM), "mental illnesses are said to result from an imbalance of yin and yang forces, a stagnation of the qi and blood in various organs, or both" (So, 2005, p. 101). Furthermore, "the driving forces behind this relationship are the entities of qi (virtual energy) and li (order). The oft-cited concepts of yin and yang, oppositional yet complementary in nature, are characteristics along the meridian channels of that compound to the specific organ of the body" (p. 101). Thus, TCM views health and illness as related to a balance of vital forces, and that disruptions which affect their critical balance can result in physical or mental illness.

    Table 12.1 summarizes and compares these four different cultural approaches to healing across six basic dimensions that represent assumptions about the nature of illness and health: (1) harmony in relations (e.g., with earth, others, nature, society); (2) personal vulnerability within the person due to imbalance caused by external forces or inner conflict; (3) the importance of balance in biological and mental processes; (4) causation of illness from imbalance and loss of harmony; and (5) health as the restoration of balance

Table 12.1. Cultural Convergence: Similar Principles?

Principles	Native American	African (Zulu)	India (Ayurveda)	Chinese (TCM)
1. Harmony in relations (earth, people, society)	Yes	Yes	Yes	Yes
2. Vulnerability within person	Yes	Yes	Yes	Yes
3. Balance of biological and mental forms	Yes	Yes	Yes	Yes
4. Illness is imbalance, loss of harmony	Yes	Yes	Yes	Yes
5. Health is restoration of balance, harmony	Yes	Yes	Yes	Yes
6. Healing empowers vital energy	Yes	Yes	Yes	Yes

(Wilson, 2006)

and harmony in mind, body and spirit. Thus, (6) healing empowers vital energies contained within the person. By comparing different traditional cultural views and their underlying assumptions, we can go further and ask how it is that culture deals with those who are severely traumatized by events of human design or acts of nature. The practical question remains as to what posttraumatic interventions should be applied in culturally different contexts and under what conditions.

What Works Best for Whom and Under What Conditions?

To focus the central issues rather sharply, what types of counseling, interventions, treatments, practices, rituals, medicines, ceremonies and therapies work best for whom and under what set of conditions? This seemingly simple and straightforward question turns out to be extraordinarily complex and multifaceted for several key reasons:

- **First**, we do not have sufficient scientific studies across cultures to begin to answer this question.
- **Second**, cultural competence requires us to explore assessment, diagnosis and treatment within a sensitive cultural framework that reflects knowledge and understanding of a culture. Indeed, the World Health Organization (WHO) published a global plan for culturally competent practices that included mandates to ensure the availability of traditional and alternative medical practices in safe and therapeutically useful ways (World Health Organization, 2002).
- **Third**, it cannot be assumed that well-documented Western psychotherapies for PTSD, for example, are necessarily useful in non-Western cultures, especially therapies that rely heavily on verbal self-reports (e.g., CBT, psychodynamic).

- **Fourth**, there is a broad range of individual responses to traumatic events. It cannot be assumed "a priori" that PTSD is an inevitable outcome of exposure to extremely stressful life-events. It is entirely possible that the concept of PTSD (cf. Western in conceptualization) is foreign and not readily understood in many cultures that do not utilize psychobiological explanations of illness or human behavior.
- **Fifth**, to understand "maladaptive" behavioral consequences of trauma (and therefore traumatization), such behaviors can only be meaningfully defined by cultural norms and expectations about what is "normal" and "abnormal". Human grief reactions for example are universal to death and loss but that does not make them pathological (Raphael, Martinek & Wooding, 2004). Acute adjustment reactions for a short period of time are entirely expected after a tsunami that destroyed towns, cities, and more than 250,000 people. But that does not make adaptational requirements pathological or posttraumatic symptoms of an illness *per se* for the survivors.
- **Sixth**, it can be justifiably assumed that throughout centuries of human evolution, adaptive mechanisms and wisdom have existed in culture to deal with the human effects of extreme trauma. The great mythologies of the world chronicle such events and the adaptational dilemmas they present for survivors. Such mythical themes point to the necessity of framing culture-sensitive perspectives on human resilience versus psychopathology (Wilson, 2006).

These considerations allow us to now explore a number of hypotheses about the relation of culture to trauma and posttraumatic adaptations, and how mental health "treatments" can be construed in culturally-competent ways.

TEN HYPOTHESES CONCERNING TRAUMA, CULTURE, AND POST-TRAUMATIC MENTAL HEALTH INTERVENTIONS

1. Each person's posttraumatic syndrome, state of psychological distress or adaptational pattern is a variation on *culturally sanctioned* modalities of behavioral-emotional expression.
2. Healing and recovery from psychic trauma is *person-specific*. There are multiple pathways and forms of treatment within a culture.
3. Each culture develops specific forms and mechanisms for posttraumatic recovery, stabilization and healing (e.g., rituals, counseling practices, treatment protocols, medications, etc.). At any given time, cultures may not have available certain types of treatments that would be beneficial to people. These will either evolve in time or be adapted from other cultures.
4. Based on Trauma Archetypes, cultures contain the wisdom to develop mechanisms to facilitate the processing and integration of psychic

trauma. Empathy, as a universal psychobiological capacity, underlies the development and evolution of culture-specific forms of healing (Wilson & Thomas, 2004; Wilson & Drozdek, 2004).

5. The concept of "mindfulness" in states of consciousness (traditionally associated with Buddhism) is a key mental process to self-transcendence and the integration of extreme psychic trauma into higher states of consciousness and personal knowledge. Mindfulness, in this regard, is personal awareness of the impact of trauma to living in one's culture of origin and how trauma has impacted one's quality of life.

6. There is no individual experience of psychological trauma without a cultural history, grounding or background. Similarly, there is no individual sense of personal identity without a cultural reference point. Anomie and alienation are commonly produced by severely traumatizing experiences and are associated with forms of anxiety, distress and depression (Wilson & Drozdek, 2004).

7. The rapid growth of globalization in the 21st Century is creating new evolutions in a "world/universal" culture and the possibility of fusing cross-cultural modalities of treatment and recovery.

8. Posttraumatic therapies and traditional healing practices, in *culturally-specific forms*, can facilitate resilience, personal growth and self-transcendence in the wake of trauma (Wilson, 2006).

9. The pathways to healing are idiosyncratic and universal in nature. The pathways of healing vary in nature, purpose, duration, social complexity and utilization by a culture.

10. Healing rituals are an integral part of highly cohesive cultures. Healing rituals evolve in situations of crisis, emergency and threat to the social structure of society and culture. Healing rituals demand special roles and skills (e.g., shaman, crisis counselor, psychologist, medicine person, priest, etc.) to facilitate efforts for recovery and the psychic metabolism of trauma.

These ten hypotheses concerning the relationship of culture and trauma provide a framework for understanding the diversity of posttraumatic psychological outcomes. As Summerfield (1999) noted, it is prejudicial and scientifically unwarranted to assume that traumatic events at the individual or cultural (collective) level will always produce PTSD and the clinical need to intervene with programs and procedures developed primarily in Western cultures. For example, cognitive behavioral therapy (CBT) is the most validated psychotherapy for PTSD in the USA (Foa, Keane & Friedman, 2000). But is CBT applicable to assisting victims of the 2004 tsunami who live in a non-English speaking culture in Aceh, Indonesia? Or the survivors of the 2003 catastrophic earthquake in Bam, Iran which killed over 30,000 people? Or the mothers whose children were murdered or starved to death in the genocidal warfare of the Sudan in 2005? Or Native American Vietnam War veterans living in traditional ways on the Navajo reservation in Arizona? Or even recent immigrants to the U.S. who happened to settle in New Orleans before Hurricane Katrina pounded the city?

These questions bring into focus critical assumptions that each person's posttraumatic adaptational pattern is a variation on culturally-sanctioned modalities of coping with extreme stress experiences that impact the psychobiology of the organism. Clearly, posttraumatic adaptations fall along a continuum from pathological to resilient (Wilson, 2006). At the pathological end of the continuum we find PTSD, dissociative reactions, brief psychosis, depressive disorder and disabling anxiety states. In contrast, the resilient end of the continuum includes optimal forms of healthy adaptation, manifestations of behavioral resiliency in the face of adversity, and the resumption of normal psychosocial functioning (Wilson, 2006).

By examining the continuum of culturally sanctioned modalities of posttraumatic adaptation, the second and third assumptive principles can be understood more precisely. Healing and recovery is *person-specific* and there are *multiple pathways* to posttraumatic recovery, if they are needed. Considered from an evolutionary and adaptational perspective, cultures develop rituals, helper roles (e.g., shaman, mental health specialists, herbalist, medicine persons, physician), ceremonies and other modalities to facilitate recovery from distressing psychological conditions, including those produced by trauma. Where such modalities of treatment do not exist or are inadequate, they will be developed and implemented as it is critical for a culture to have functional and healthy members to carry out the critical activities necessary to sustain commerce, family life and the functions that define the identity and essence of the culture itself. A culture that is sick, self-destructive and dissolving due to warfare, political conflicts and revolution, massive natural disaster, or illness will be less able to thrive or maintain itself in a viable way.

The viability of culture in the face of collective trauma illustrates the sixth assumptive principle that there can be no experience of psychological trauma without a cultural history, grounding or continuity of background. There is no individual sense of personal identity without a cultural reference point (Wilson, 2006). Personal identity within a cultural context includes a sense of continuity and discontinuity in life-course development that shapes personality and the coherency of the self-structure. Thus, there is no sense of personal identity without a cultural reference marker to counterpoint and define those events that seemed to shape the formation of identity for the person. As an extension of this viewpoint, it can readily be seen that anomie and alienation (e.g., feeling detached, separate, cut off, divorced, estranged, distanced, removed) from mainstream cultural processes is a potential consequence of severely traumatizing experiences and typically associated with anxiety, distress and depression since the traumatic experience can "push" the person "outside" the customary boundaries of daily living.

The potential of trauma to dysregulate emotions and set-up complex patterns of prolonged stress cannot be dismissed as statistically infrequent. As

Wilson and Drozdek (2004) have noted, this is particularly true when: (1) the trauma is massive and damages the entire culture, (2) the nature of trauma causes the person to challenge the existing moral and political adequacy of prevailing cultural norms and values, (3) the trauma causes the individual to become marginalized within the culture and to be viewed as problematic, stigmatized, "damaged goods", or tainted by their experiences or posttraumatic consequences (e.g., physically disabled, disease infected, atomic radiation exposure, mentally ill, etc.).

The question of how cultures deal with the social, political and psychological consequences of trauma raises the issue of the availability of therapeutic modalities of healing and recovery. Stated simply, what does the culture provide to assist persons in recovering from different types of trauma? Examining this question is instructive since one can analyze the nature of formal, organized and institutionalized mechanisms for recovery from trauma as well as informal, non-institutionalized or officially sanctioned modalities of care and service provisions. While a detailed analysis of these issues is beyond the scope of this article, it is nonetheless important when using a "crows nest" or "helicopter aerial" view of how cultures deal with those who suffer significant posttraumatic consequences of trauma, which include being displaced, homeless, unemployed, physically injured, and emotionally traumatized.

Clearly, there are levels of posttraumatic impact to the social structures of culture and to the inner-psychological world of the trauma survivor. There are primary, secondary, and tertiary sets of stressors associated with trauma. In the "big view" of traumatic consequences, they intersect to varying degrees in affecting the patterns of recovery, stabilization and resumption of normal living (Wilson, 1995). A further understanding of the relation of culture and trauma can be analyzed with knowledge of the Trauma Archetype (Wilson, 2004, 2006). The Trauma Archetype represents universal forms of traumatic experiences across time, space, culture and history.

Table 12.2 presents a summary of the dimensions of the Trauma Archetype that has eleven separate but interrelated dimensions. The Trauma Archetype is a primordial type of human experience in which a psychological experience is encoded into personality dynamics. It gives birth to Trauma Complexes (see Table 12.3) which, in turn, represent how traumatic experiences are encapsulated in individualized ways in the psyche. Moreover, Trauma Complexes (1) develop in accordance with the trauma archetype; (2) are comprised of affects, images and perceptions of the trauma experience; (3) are mythological in form, symbolic in nature, and shaped by culture; (4) contain the specter of the extreme threat of annihilation; (5) articulate with other psychological complexes; (6) may become central in the self-structure; (7) contain motivational power; (8) are expressed in personality dynamics; (9) are primarily unconscious phenomena; and (10) contain forms of prolonged stress reactions, such as PTSD, dissociative and anxiety disorders.

Table 12.2.   Trauma Archetype (Universal Forms of Traumatic Experience)

1.	The Trauma Archetype is a prototypical stress response pattern present in all human cultures, universal in its effects and is manifest in overt behavioral patterns and internal intrapsychic processes, especially the Trauma Complex.
2.	The Trauma Archetype evokes altered psychological states, which include changes in consciousness, memory, orientation to time, space and person and appears in the Trauma Complex.
3.	The Trauma Archetype evokes allostatic changes in the organism (posttraumatic impacts, e.g., personality change, PTSD, allostatic dysregulation) which are expressed in common neurobiological pathways.
4.	The Trauma Archetype contains the experience of threat to psychological and physical well being, typically manifest in the Abyss and Inversion Experiences.
5.	The Trauma Archetype involves confrontation with the fear of death.
6.	The Trauma Archetype evokes the specter of self-de-integration, dissolution and soul (psychic) death (i.e., loss of identity), and is expressed in the Trauma Complex.
7.	The Trauma Archetype is a manifestation of overwhelmingly stressful experience to the organization of self, identity and belief systems, and appears as part of the structure of the Trauma Complex.
8.	The Trauma Archetype stimulates cognitive attributions of meaning and causality for injury, suffering, loss, death (i.e., altered core beliefs) which appear in the Trauma Complex.
9.	The Trauma Archetype energizes posttraumatic tasks of defense, recovery, healing and growth, which include the development of PTSD as a Trauma Complex.
10.	The Trauma Archetype activates polarities of meaning attribution; the formulation of pro-social – humanitarian morality vs. abject despair and meaninglessness paradigm.
11.	The Trauma Archetype may evoke spiritual transformation: individual journey / encounter with darkness: return / transformation / re-emergence, healing (Campbell, 1949). The evocation of a "spiritual" transformation is manifest in the Trauma Complex as part of the Transcendent Experience and the drive toward unification.

(Wilson, 2004)

The conceptualization of Trauma Archetypes and Trauma Complexes has much utility when looking at trauma and culture, as these concepts are universal in nature and not "wedded" to the concept of PTSD per se or Western perspectives of psychiatric illness. While a more extensive analysis of Trauma Archetypes and Complexes is not possible here due to page limitations, their relevance to the other assumptions about healing, recovery and culture-specific forms of counseling, psychotherapy or treatment is transparent and critical (Wilson, 2006).

First, it is necessary to understand, in culture-specific ways, the phenomenal reality of a person. Wilson and Thomas (2004) have presented evidence that sustained empathy, as part of any treatment modality, is essential to facilitate posttraumatic recovery. Among other consequences of sustained empathic attunement, it helps the individual develop states of "mindfulness" as self-awareness of how a traumatic experience has affected all levels of functioning, especially affect dysregulation (Schore, 2003). Mindfulness

Table 12.3.   The Trauma Complex

1.	The Trauma Complex is a feeling-toned complex which develops in accordance with the Trauma Archetype.
2.	The Trauma Complex is comprised of affects, images, perceptions and cognitions associated with the trauma experience.
3.	The Trauma Complex is mythological in nature and takes form in accordance with culture and symbolic, mythological representations of reality.
4.	The Trauma Complex contains the affective responses of the abyss experience: fear, terror, horror, helplessness, dissociation.
5.	The Trauma Complex articulates with other psychological complexes and innate archetypes in a "cogwheeling", interactive manner. This includes the Abyss, Inversion and Transcendent forms of traumatic encounters.
6.	The Trauma Complex may become central in the self-structure and reflect alterations in identity, ego-processes, the self-structure, and systems of personal meaning.
7.	The Trauma Complex contains motivational power and predisposition to behavior.
8.	The Trauma Complex is expressed in personality processes (e.g., traits, motives, altered personality characteristics, memory and cognition, etc.).
9.	The Trauma Complex is primarily unconscious but discernible by posttraumatic alterations in the self and personality.
10.	The Trauma Complex contains the polarities of the abyss experience: diabolic vs. transcendent which are universal variants in the search for meaning in the trauma experience.

(Wilson, 2004)

as a process of meditation is facilitative of higher states of consciousness and personal awareness of how a traumatic event may have impacted pre-existing beliefs about self, others and nature. We can consider posttraumatic interventions, treatments, traditional healing practices, etc., as *culture-specific* forms designed to facilitate recovery, resilience, and the resumption of healthy living.

The pathways to healing are idiosyncratic and universal in nature and may vary greatly in their contexts, purpose, length, social desirability and utilization within the culture. In highly cohesive cultures, there will be the use and prescription of rituals, practices, traditional methods of healing, etc. as they reflect archetypal forms of healing. Where such rituals and treatments do not exist, they will be developed by the culture in response to crises and threats to social structures vital to cultural continuity. Hence the need for multiple modalities of treatment and specialists (e.g., counselor, shaman, medicine person, priest, doctor, etc.) who, "through the lens of culture," can assist in recognition of how a person has been affected by psychological trauma.

The Development of Culture-Sensitive Trauma Theory, Research, and Practice

The concept of posttraumatic stress and the multidimensional nature of cultures require a conceptual framework by which to address core issues that have direct relevance to understanding the nature of trauma as embedded within a culture and its assumptive belief systems and patterns of behavioral regulation. Marsella (2005) has noted that all healing sub-cultures have at least five distinct elements: "(1) a set of assumptions about the nature and causes of problems specific to their world view and construction of reality; (2) a set of assumptions about the context, settings, and requirements for healing to occur; (3) a set of assumptions and procedures to elicit particular expectations, emotions, and behaviors; (4) a set of requirements for activity and participation levels and/or roles for patient, family, and therapist; and (5) specific requirements for therapist training and skills expertise criteria" (p. 3). These sets of assumptions are useful as they define a necessary conceptual matrix for examining how different cultures handle psychopathology, behavioral disorders and complex posttraumatic syndromes.

When addressing the question of how individual cultures deal with psychological trauma in its diverse forms, it is useful to examine commonalities and differences among approaches to counseling, healing, psychotherapies, treatments and traditional practices. If traumatic stress is universal in its psychobiological effects (Friedman, 2000; Wilson et al., 2001), are therapeutic interventions, in turn, designed in culture-specific ways to ameliorate the maladaptive consequences of dysregulated systems of affect, cognition and coping efforts (Wilson, 2006; Wilson & Drozdek, 2004; Marsella et al., 1996)? If so, what are the differences and commonalities in therapeutic approaches to dealing with trauma?

Table 12.4 presents 21 core questions concerning the relation of culture to traumatic life experiences and post-traumatic adaptation. These core questions serve to frame future conceptual and research work toward a culture-sensitive trauma psychology.

1. **Is the Experience of Psychological Trauma the Same in All Cultures?**
   This question addresses the issues of how cultural belief systems influence the perception and processing of trauma. For example, Kinsie (1988; 1993) noted that among Cambodian refugees who had suffered multiple life-threatening traumas during the Khmer Rouge regime, many who suffered from PTSD and depression understood their symptoms within the framework of their Buddhist beliefs in karma as a station in life, an incarnate level of being and fate. Hence, Western psychiatric views of suffering and depression may not exist within a Buddhist ideology per se. Personal suffering may be seen from a religious-cosmological perspective of the meaning of life. If a culture does not have linguistic connotations of a pathogenic nature (e.g., PTSD), how then does the person construe acute or prolonged effects of extreme stress experiences? In a discussion of depression and Buddhism in Sri Lanka, Obeyesekere (1985) stated: "How is the Western diagnostic term depression expressed in society whose predominant ideology of Buddhism states that life is suffering and sorrow, that the cause of

Table 12.4. Core Questions for Understanding Culture, Trauma and Posttraumatic Syndromes

1. Is the experience of psychobiological trauma the same in all cultures?
2. Are the emotional reactions to trauma the same in all cultures?
3. Is the psychobiology of trauma the same in all cultures?
4. Does culture act as a filter for psychic trauma? If so, how do internalized beliefs and culturally shaped patterns of coping and adaptation govern the posttraumatic processing of traumatic experiences?
5. Are traumatic experiences universal in nature across cultures? Are traumatic experiences archetypal for the specter?
6. If trauma is archetypal for humankind, what are the universal characteristics across all cultures?
7. Does culture determine how individuals respond to archetypal forms of trauma? Are posttraumatic syndromes and trauma complexes culture-specific in nature?
8. Are there cultural-based syndromes (not necessarily PTSD) of posttraumatic adaptation? If yes, what do they look like? What is their psychological status?
9. How do cultures develop rituals, medical-psychological treatments, religious practices and other institutionalized mechanisms to assist persons who experience psychic trauma?
10. Are there culture-specific and universal mechanisms to help persons recover from trauma?
11. What does cultural mythology tell us about the experience of trauma?
12. What are the great myths in cultural literature that concern individual and collective trauma?
13. What are the psychological and cultural functions of mythology? How do they relate to the cross-cultural understanding of trauma?
14. What is the Abyss Experience in mythology and how does it relate to the psychological study of trauma?
15. What does mythology tell us about culture-specific rituals of psychic trauma?
16. How do forms of traumatic experiences relate to the universal myth of the Hero as protagonist?
17. How does modern psychology standardize the assessment and treatment of trauma across cultural boundaries?
18. Do pharmacological treatments of posttraumatic syndromes work equally well in all cultures?
19. Is the unconscious manifestation of posttraumatic states the same in all cultures?
20. What are the mythological images of the life-cycle and the transformation of consciousness by trauma?
21. What cultural belief systems underlie cultural approaches to healing and recovery from trauma?

(Wilson, 2006)

sorrow is attachment or desire or craving, that there is a way (generally through meditation) of understanding and overcoming suffering and achieving the final goal of cessation from suffering or nirvana?" (p. 134). Hence, sorrow, suffering, depressive symptoms, traumatic memories, disruptions in sleep patterns, and other trauma-related symptoms will likely be construed in a similar manner, especially since depression is a component of posttraumatic stress disorder (Breslau, 1999).

2. **Are the Emotional Reactions to Psychological Trauma the Same in All Cultures?**

   Scientific evidence, especially neurobiological studies, have documented that affect dysregulation, right hemisphere alterations in brain functioning, and strong kindling phenomena are universal in PTSD (Schore, 2003; Friedman, 2000). If there is a common set of psychobiological changes associated with either PTSD or prolonged stress reactions, is the emotional experience universal in nature (e.g., hyperarousal, startle, anger, irritability, depressive reactions) or do cultural belief systems "override" or attenuate the magnitude or severity and intensity of dysregulated emotional states?

3. **Is the Psychobiology of Trauma the Same in All Cultures?**

   This question is similar to the one above. If extreme stress impacts the human organism in the same manner irrespective of culture, does the organism react in exactly the same way? Or, do cultural belief systems act as perceptual filters to the cognitive appraisal and interpretation of traumatic stressors? For example, in the 1988 Yunnan earthquake in a rural, peasant area of China, over 400,000 people were impacted by the event, the likes of which had not been previously experienced by most inhabitants. However, among the common explanations for the earthquake was that a mythical great dragon was moving beneath the earth because he was angry with the people (McFarlane & Hua, 1993). Does such a mythical attribution influence the subsequent psychobiological responses to the disaster once it terminates? What if the dragon metaphorically returns to his "rest" and "sleep"?

4. **Does Culture (i.e., cognitive-affective belief systems) Act as a Filter for Psychic Trauma? If So, How Do Internalized Belief Systems and Culturally Shaped Patterns of Coping and Adaptation Govern the Posttraumatic Processing of Traumatic Experiences?**

   This question goes to the heart of the culture-trauma relationship. First, how does a culture define trauma? Is a trauma in one culture (e.g., natural disaster, incestual relations; torture; political oppression; motor-vehicle accidents; murder, etc.) necessarily viewed as a trauma in another culture? Second, what sets of expectations for resiliency in coping does the culture possess? For example, after the July, 2005 terrorist bombings to transit systems in London, the general media and political leaders noted that the British people immediately returned to work the next day, rode the buses and subways, and manifested high levels of resilience. The Prime Minister, Tony Blair, made reference to how British resolve was evident during the bombing raids in WWII and that in 2005 such resilient resolve was once again transparent. The people of Mumbai, India showed similar resiliency following the coordinated train bombings in July of 2006, and media reports were filled with stories of people "coming together" to resume normal operations in the city. Is this a cultural norm or expectation? How do cultural beliefs and values influence the post-event processing and cognitive interpretation of the traumatic stressor itself?

5. **Are Traumatic Experiences Universal in Nature Across Cultures? Are Traumatic Experiences Archetypal for the Species?**

   Research on PTSD has identified categories and typologies of traumatic life-events and the specific stressors they contain (Green, 1993; Wilson & Lindy, 1994). While there is agreement on the nature and types of traumatic events, a more fundamental question is whether or not they are archetypal in nature. Elsewhere, I have discussed the unique nature of trauma archetypes and trauma complexes (Wilson, 2006; Wilson, 2004) and suggested that the experience of trauma is both universal and archetypal for the human species. However, culture shapes the way that individuals form trauma complexes and, once formed, how they articulate them with other psychic complexities.

6. **If Trauma is Archetypal for Humankind, What are the Universal Characteristics across All Cultures?**

   This question is a corollary to the one above. Given that traumatic experiences are archetypal for the species, what are the defining characteristics of the trauma archetype? I have delineated eleven dimensions (see Table 12.2) of the Trauma Archetype and how they influence posttraumatic personality dynamics and adaptive behavior (Wilson, 2006).

7. **Does Culture Determine (i.e., shape, influence, design) How Individuals Respond to Archetypal Forms of Trauma? Are Posttraumatic Syndromes and Trauma Complexes Culture-Specific in Nature?**

   Culture serves as a powerful socializing force, creating and shaping beliefs and regulating patterns of behavior and adaptation. For example, among many Native American people a "good world" is one defined by harmony and balance in "all things" and "all relations" in the environment and amongst people (Mails, 1991). Illness is thought to result from imbalance, loss of harmony and being dispirited within oneself due to a loss of vital connectedness. Among some aboriginal native people, trauma is simply defined as that which causes one to lose balance in living with positive relations with nature and the human-made world. Moreover, within this cosmology, it was well known that certain events, such as warfare, could cause profoundly altered states of well being (i.e., dispiritedness) and necessitated healing rituals for the restoration of wholeness (Wilson, 1989, 2006).

8. **Are There Cultural-Based Syndromes (cf. not necessarily PTSD) of Posttraumatic Adaptation? If Yes, What Do They Look Like? What is Their Psychological Structure?**

   This core issue is among the most fascinating to consider and interesting to conceptualize since there may be unique ways that posttraumatic adaptations occur within a culture or sub-culture (e.g., trance

states, dissociative phenomena, somatic illnesses, mythical attributions, etc.). How does culture provide awareness for posttraumatic
syndromes to exist and be expressed? Are these forms of adaptation
pathogenic or salutogenic in nature (Marsella & White, 1982)? What
are the implications of culture-specific posttraumatic adaptations for
culture-specific interventions?

9. **How Do Cultures Develop Rituals, Medical-Psychological Treat-
ments, Religious Practices and Other Forms of Institutionalized
Mechanisms to Assist Persons Who Experience Psychological
Trauma?**

   This question attempts to identify the specific ways that cultures
evolve and develop institutionalized and non-institutionalized mechanisms and treatments for victims of trauma. This question is of
significant research interest as it defines the areas in which commonalities overlap and in which culture-specific differences exit. It is possible
that each person's posttraumatic syndrome is a variation on a culturally sanctioned modality of adaptation which can then be "treated" by
either generic or culturally-specific practices.

10. **Are There Culture-Specific and Universal Mechanisms to Help
Persons Recover from Psychological Trauma?**

   How have cultures evolved specific rituals, treatments or ceremonies to facilitate recovery from psychic trauma? For example, most
Native American nations use the Sweat Lodge Purification Ceremony
to "treat" states of dispiritedness, mental illness, alcohol abuse, and
depression, as well as to instill spiritual strength (Wilson, 1989). The
Sweat Lodge purification ritual has a unique structure and process and
is embedded within the traditional cosmology of a tribe (e.g., Lakota
Sioux). Under the guidance of a trained and experienced medicine
person, the Sweat Lodge is used to restore "balance" through purification, sweating and emotional catharsis (Wilson, 1989; Mails, 1991).
This is just one example of many that exist among and between cultures to facilitate "stress reduction" and to alleviate suffering, including
prolonged stress reactions after traumatic life events. Marsella (2005)
describes the range of healing forces used around the world.

11. **What Does Cultural Mythology Tell Us About the Experience of
Trauma?**

   The discovery of how cultures deal with trauma can be found in
the great mythologies of the world (Campbell, 1949, 2004). Mythology
contains themes that converge across cultures, literary forms (e.g.,
epochs) and style. While it is the case that modern science, especially in the study of PTSD, has generated an impressive body of
knowledge, it lacks carefully crafted cross-cultural studies of trauma,
healing and human adaptation (Wilson, 2006). However, from the pre-
Greeks to the middle ages to our present time, the great mythologies
of the world have chronicled the trials and tribulations of simple,

ordinary, "heroic" figures and their individual journeys which present profound challenges to life, spirit, body and human integrity. Joseph Campbell's (1949) study of mythology has identified universal themes of the heroic figure whose journey of self-transformation in the life-cycle is also about the universal stories of trauma survivors. Analysis of the great mythologies is a rich source of inquiry as to the interplay between culture, traumatic events and their transformation by facing challenges to existence itself.

12. **What Are the Great Myths in Cultural Literature That Concern Individuals and Collective Trauma?**

There are many great mythologies in cultures throughout the world (Campbell, 2004). The Great Mythologies are themes and stories about the human condition: adversity, jealousy, confrontation with powerful "zones of danger", the prospect of death, the process of individual transformation by confrontation with unconscious and external forces, and the difficult task of re-entry into society after an adverse journey into the abyss of trauma (Wilson, 2006). Analysis of these myths thus illuminates the archetypal nature of trauma and the challenges it sets up for human development, healing and the maintenance of personal integrity.

13. **What Are the Psychological and Cultural Functions of Mythology? How do they Relate to the Cross-Cultural Understanding of Trauma?**

In his book, *Pathways to Bliss*, Joseph Campbell (2004) outlines the four functions of mythology as follows: (a) spiritual-mystical; (b) cosmological; (c) sociological; and (d) psychological. Each of these functions are revealed within mythology and have direct parallels to the nature of psychological requirements in dealing with the impact of trauma to self and psychological functioning. For example, trauma and traumatic life-experiences form a reconciliation with unconsciousness and the meaning of life. This issue concerns directly the mythology of one's own life and the role trauma has played in it.

For example, novels and autobiographies of war trauma of former combat soldiers typically characterize the horrific encounter with death, the existential questioning of the purpose of war and how such experiences subsequently shape life-course trajectory (Caputo, 1977). Traumatic experiences often force a self-effacing look at personal identity and consciousness. Trauma serves to put the individual in touch with their unconscious processes, including the disavowed, dark or "shadowy" side of personality. By carefully analyzing the functions of mythology within a culture we can understand how it is that culture shapes posttraumatic adaptation, growth and the challenges of self-transformation.

14. **What is the Abyss Experience in Mythology and How Does it Relate to the Psychological Study of Trauma?**

The Abyss Experience is a term I have coined to describe the "black hole" of psychological trauma: a vast chasm of dark, empty space in which terror and fear of annihilation exists (Wilson, 2004, 2006). There are five dimensions of the Abyss Experience which include: (1) the confrontation with evil and death; (2) the experience of soul death with non-being; (3) a sense of abandonment by humanity; (4) ultimate aloneness and despairing; and (5) cosmic challenge of meaning. For each of these five dimensions there are corresponding posttraumatic phenomena: (i) the trauma experience: (ii) self/identity; (iii) loss of connection; (iv) separation and isolation; and (v) spirituality and sense of the numinous. In the mythology of cultures, these themes and aspects of the Abyss Experiences are always present and yet played out within the unique tapestry of a particular culture.

15. **What Does Mythology Tell Us About Culture-Specific Rituals for Psychological Trauma?**

   The awareness of the Abyss Experience and the zones of danger through which the mythical hero figure traverses suggest that upon return to society from the zone of danger (i.e., trauma), the individual crosses a threshold of re-entry that often includes being ignored or rejected because of the overwhelming and often horrifying nature of his experience. Mythology suggests that there may exist a "guide" or nurturant person, who helps "cast light" as to the meaning of the trauma experience and provides clues as to how to recover and integrate the experience without prolonged suffering or maladaptive avoidance behaviors (e.g., excessive drinking, alienation, anomie, emotional detachment and numbing). It can be seen that cultures have built-in wisdom as to the pathways to healing, and the literature of mythology describes the nature and character of these life pathways.

16. **How Do Forms of Traumatic Experiences Relate to the Universal Myth of the Hero as Protagonist?**

   The mythical hero traverses a journey and encounters powerful forces (e.g., trauma) which challenge mind, spirit, body and sense of personhood. The travails of the protagonist are universal images of how psychic trauma creates hurdles in the process of living and finding meaning in life.

17. **What Are the Mythological Images of the Life-Cycle and the Transformation of Consciousness by Trauma?**

   In mythology the challenges of trauma can occur anywhere in the life-span, from infancy to old age. However, no matter where trauma occurs in epigenetic development, it can influence the configuration of ego-identity and transform personal consciousness about oneself, others, the meaning of death and the task of self-transformation. Elsewhere, I have described in detail the process of traumatogenic experiences with an ontogenetic framework of self-metamorphosis (Wilson, 2006). Understanding mythological and epigenetic frameworks of how trauma alters the trajectory of the life-cycle has important implications for counseling and psychotherapy.

18. **How Does Modern Psychology Standardize the Assessment and Treatment of Trauma Across Cultural Boundaries?**

   This is a core issue in terms of the "globalization" of knowledge about the relation of trauma to culture. At present, we have no standardized etic (universal) measurements of trauma and PTSD (Dana, 2000). Similarly, we do not have standardized cross-cultural treatment protocols for persons suffering from posttraumatic syndromes. There exist empirical and clinical voids in the knowledge base as to what "treatments" work best for what kinds of person and under what set of circumstances. Marsella et al. (1996) provide an extensive review of the issues and concerns in this area.

19. **Do Pharmacological Treatments of Posttraumatic Syndromes Work Equally Well in All Cultures?**

   This question is intriguing because it posts the controversy as to whether or not the psychobiology of trauma is the same across cultures and therefore treatable by pharmacological agents designed to stabilize the dysregulation in neurobiological functioning caused by extreme stress experiences. However, to date, there are few comparative randomized clinical trials (RCT) of medications to treat PTSD in culturally diverse populations (Friedman, 2001). Yet, studies have shown that some anti-depressant medications are more efficacious in symptom reduction than others for non-Western populations with severe PTSD (Kinsie, 1988; Lin, Poland, Anderson & Lesser, 1996).

20. **Is the Unconscious Manifestation of Posttraumatic States the Same Across Cultural Boundaries?**

   This core question is complex and fascinating because it demands a method to assess unconscious processes cross-culturally (Dana, 2000) and to discern if unconscious memory encodes trauma experiences in similar ways, perhaps in trauma complexes that are, in turn, shaped by cultural factors (Wilson, 2006).

21. **What Conceptual Belief Systems Underlie Cultural Approaches to Healing and Recovery from Trauma?**

   In many respects, this issue deals with the most "pure" consideration of the trauma-culture relationship. How does the culture view "trauma" and employ methods to facilitate healthy forms of posttraumatic adaptation? What set of assumptive beliefs does the culture "bring" to the understanding of trauma? Within a culture, is trauma idiosyncratic or synergistic in nature? Are there differences between individual and cultural trauma? What does damage to the structure of a culture mean in terms of posttraumatic interventions? For example, Erikson (1950) noted that among the Lakota Sioux Indians in the United States, the loss of their nomadic mystical culture oriented around the Buffalo meant a loss of historical continuity and collective identity, which was profoundly traumatic once the Lakota were interned on federal reservation lands that deprived them of their cherished patterns of living (Wilson, 2006).

CONCLUDING COMMENTS

So what does globalization portend for trauma treatment in the 21st Century as the world "flattens" due to technological advances and commercial homogenization? In brief, the ready availability of scientific data on international databases for posttraumatic stress disorders (e.g., P.I.L.O.T.S.@ncptsd.org) may enable clinicians, researchers and patients to have instant access to information about PTSD, complex PTSD, treatment advances, pharmacotherapies, and much more.

Second, the spread of knowledge has spurned unprecedented levels of international cooperation and the formation of international professional societies (e.g., International Society for Traumatic Stress Studies in 1985; Asian Society for Traumatic Stress in 2005) to share scientific data and clinical wisdom and to lobby for political and legislative changes on behalf of trauma victims.

Third, globalization, to a certain extent, allows for homogenization, fusion and experimentation with different modalities of counseling, psychotherapy, traditional healing practices and modern medicine. In a related way, globalization, driven by economic and political forces, is creating the emergence of a "global culture" which enables the prospect of fusing cross-cultural modalities of treatment and subjecting them to scientific measures of efficacy. As this occurs, the answer to the question, "What works for whom and under what conditions?" will take on new meaning in terms of how we conceptualize the prolonged effects of extreme stress experiences to the human psyche and as a holistically integrated organism.

Beyond doubt, 19th and 20th Century conceptualizations of counseling and psychotherapy are culture-bound in nature and origin. The 21st Century will witness the development and emergence of global conceptualizations of what constitutes trauma and how it gets healed. There will be developed a matrix of databases which cross-list cultures and the diversity of techniques employed to cope with states of traumatization. Moreover, as this convergence begins to occur, the scientific "gold standards" of what works for whom under what circumstances will take on meaning that transcends culture but not persons whose suffering impels humanitarian care.

References

Bojuwoye, O. (2005). Traditional healing practices in South Africa: Ancestral spirits, ritual ceremonies and holistic healing. In R. Moodley & W. West (Eds.), *Integrating traditional healing practices into counseling and psychotherapy* (pp. 61–73). Thousand Oaks, CA: Sage Publications.

Breslau, N. (1999). Psychological trauma, epidemiology of trauma and PTSD. In R. Yehuda (Ed.), *Psychological trauma, epidemiology of trauma and posttraumatic stress disorder* (pp. 1–27). Washington, DC: American Psychiatric Press, Inc.

Campbell, J. (1949). *The hero with a thousand faces.* New York. Penguin Books.

Campbell, J. (2004). *Pathways to bliss: Mythology and personal transformation.* New York: Harper.

Caputo, P. (1977). *A rumor of war.* New York: Holt, Rinehart & Winston.

Dana, R. H. (2000). *Handbook of cross-cultural and multicultural personality assessment.* Matwah, NJ: L. E. Erlbaum Associates.

Erikson, E. (1950). *Childhood and society.* New York: Norton.

Foa, E. B., Keane, T. M., & Friedman, M. J. (Eds.). (2000). *Effective treatments for PTSD*: Practice guidelines from the International Society for Traumatic Stress Studies. New York: Guilford Press.

Friedman, L. J. (2000). *Identities architect: A biography of Erik Erikson.* Cambridge: Harvard University Press.

Friedman, M. J. (2001). Allostatic versus empirical perspectives on pharmacotherapy. In J. P. Wilson, M. J. Friedman, & J. D. Lindy (Eds.), *Treating psychological trauma and PTSD* (pp. 94–125). New York: Guilford Press.

Friedman, T. (2005). *The world is flat: A brief history of the twenty-first century.* New York: Girraux, Strauss & Co.

Green, B. (1993). Identifying survivors at risk: Trauma and stressors across events. In J. P. Wilson & B. Raphael (eds.). *International handbook of traumatic stress syndromes.* New York: Plenum Press.

Jilek, W. G. (1982). Altered states of consciousness in North American Indian ceremonies. *Ethos, 10*(6), 326–343.

Kinsie, J. D. (1988). The psychiatric effects of massive trauma on Cambodian refugees. In J. P. Wilson, Z. Harel, & B. Kahana (Eds.), *Human adaptation to extreme stress* (pp. 305–319). New York: Plenum Press.

Kinsie, J. D. (1993). Posttraumatic effects and their treatment among Southeast Asian refugees. In J. P. Wilson & B. Raphael (Eds.), *International handbook of traumatic stress syndromes* (pp. 311–321). New York: Plenum Press.

Kumar, M., Bhurga, D., & Singh, J. (2005). South Asian (Indian) traditional healing: Ayurvedic, shamanic, and sahaja therapy. In R. Moodley & W. West (Eds.), *Integrating traditional healing practices in counseling and psychotherapy* (pp. 112–123). Thousand Oaks, CA: Sage Publications.

Lin, K. L., Poland, R. E., Anderson, D., & Lesser, I. M. (1996). Ethnopharmacology and the treatment of PTSD. In A. J. Marsella, M. J. Friedman, E. T. Gerrity, & R. M. Scurfield (Eds.), *Ethnocultural aspects of posttraumatic stress disorder* (pp. 509–529). Washington, DC: American Psychological Association.

Mails, T. E. (1991). *Fools crow.* San Francisco, CA: Council Oaks Books.

Marsella, A. J. (2005). Rethinking the "talking cures" in a global era. *Contemporary Psychology (PsyCritiques – Amercian Psychological Association),* November, 2–12.

Marsella, A. J., Friedman, M. J., Gerrity, E., & Scurfield, R. M. (Eds.). (1996). *Ethnocultural aspects of posttraumatic stress disorder: Issues, research and applications.* Washington, DC: American Psychological Association Press.

Marsella, A. J., & White, G. M. (1982). *Cultural conceptions of mental health and therapy.* Boston, MA: Springer.

McFarlane, A. C., & Hua, C. (1993). Study of a major disaster in the Peoples Republic of China: The Yunan earthquake. In J. P. Wilson & B. Raphael (Eds.), *International handbook of traumatic stress studies* (pp. 493–499). New York: Plenum Press.

Moodley, R., & West, W. (Eds.). (2005). *Integrating traditional healing practice into counseling and psychotherapy.* Thousand Oaks, CA: Sage Productions.

Obeyesekere, G. (1985). Depression, Buddhism and the work of culture in Sri Lanka. In A. Kleinman & B. Good (Eds.), *Culture and depression: Studies in anthropology and cross-cultural psychiatry of affect and disorder* (pp. 134–152). Berkeley, CA: University of California Press.

Parsons, E. (1988). Post-traumatic self-disorders. In J. P. Wilson, Z. Harel, & B. Kahana (Eds.), *Human adaptation to extreme stress: From the Holocaust to Vietnam* (pp. 245–279). New York: Plenum Press.

Poonwassie, A., & Charter, A. (2005). Aboriginal worldview of healing: Inclusion, blending and bridging. In R. Moodley & W. West (Eds.), *Integrating traditional healing practices into counseling and psychotherapy* (pp. 15–26). Thousand Oaks, CA: Sage Publications.

Raphael, B., Martinek, N., & Wooding, S. (2004). Assessing traumatic bereavement. In J. P. Wilson & T. M. Keane (Eds.), *Assessing psychological trauma and PTSD* (pp. 492–513). New York: Guilford Press.

Schore, A. N. (2003). *Affect dysregulation and the repair of the self*. New York: Norton.

Shah, S. A. (2007). Ethnomedical best practices for international psychosocial efforts in disaster and trauma. In J. P. Wilson and C. Tang (Eds.). *Cross-cultural assessment of psychological trauma and PTSD* (pp. 51–64). New York: Springer.

So, J. K. (2005). Traditional and cultural healing among the Chinese. In R. Moodley & W. West (Eds.), *Integrating traditional healing practices in counseling and psychotherapy* (pp. 100–112). Thousand Oaks, CA: Sage Publications.

Spiegel, D. E. (1994). *Dissociation*. Washington, DC: American Psychiatric Association Press.

Summerfield, D. (1999). A critique of seven assumptions behind psychological trauma programs in war-affected areas. *Social Science and Medicine*, 48, 1449–1462.

Wilson, J. P. (1989). *Trauma, transformation and healing: An integration approach to theory, research and posttraumatic theory*. New York: Brunner/Mazel.

Wilson, J. P. (1995). Traumatic events and PTSD prevention. In B. Raphael & E. D. Barrows (Eds.), *The handbook of preventative psychiatry* (pp. 281–296). Amsterdam: Elsevier Press.

Wilson, J. P. (2004). The abyss experience and the trauma complex: A Jungian perspective of PTSD and dissociation. *Journal of Trauma in Dissociation*, 5(3), 43–68.

Wilson, J. P. (2006). *The posttraumatic self: Restoring meaning and wholeness to personality*. New York: Brunner-Routledge.

Wilson, J. P., & Drozdek, B. (2004). *Broken spirits: The treatment of traumatized asylum seekers, refugees and war and torture victims*. New York: Brunner-Routledge.

Wilson, J. P., Friedman, M. J., & Lindy, J. D. (2001). An overview of clinical considerations and principles in the treatment of PTSD. In J. P. Wilson, M. J. Friedman, & J. D. Lindy (Eds.), *Treating psychological trauma and PTSD* (pp. 59–94). New York: Guilford Press.

Wilson, J. P., & Lindy, J. (Eds.). (1994). *Counter-transference in the treatment of PTSD*. New York: Guilford Press.

Wilson, J. P., & Thomas, R. (2004). *Empathy in the treatment of trauma and PTSD*. New York: Brunner-Routledge.

World Health Organization (2002). *Traditional medicine strategy 2002–2005*. WHO Publication, WHO/EDM/2002.1. Geneva: Switzerland.

Section III

Appendices

Appendix A
A Brief List of Disaster-related Vocabulary Terms

The following list represents a collection of vocabulary terms that are often used during the course of disaster preparation, response, and recovery phases. This list will familiarize disaster workers with words they will hear and use during all phases of a disaster.

Acute Stress Disorder
Advocacy
American Psychiatric Association
American Psychological Association
Burnout
Catastrophic Disaster Response Group
Center for Mental Health Services
Community-Based Intervention
Community-Based Organizations
Community Emergency Response Team (CERT)
Compassion Fatigue
Complex Humanitarian Emergencies
Complicated Grief
Crisis Management
Critical Incident Stress Debriefing
Cultural Differences
Cultural Competence
Debriefing
Defusing
Disaster(s)
Disaster Assessment and Evaluation
Disaster Phases
Disaster Monitoring Agencies (Examples for Natural Disasters)

    Federal Emergency Management Agency (FEMA)
    National Aeronautics and Space Administration (NASA)
    National Oceanic and Atmospheric Administration (NOAA)
    National Weather Service (NWS)
    United States Geological Survey (USGS)

Disaster Relief and Response Organizations (Examples)

> Centers for Disease Control (CDC)
> Department of Homeland Security
> Doctors Without Borders (Medicin Sans Frontiere)
> Federal Emergency Management Agency (FEMA)
> Red Cross/Red Crescent

Disaster Types

> *Natural Disasters*
> > Avalanches
> > Catastrophic Disasters (i.e., Massive destruction)
> > Droughts
> > Earthquakes
> > Floods
> > Hurricanes
> > Ice and Hail Storms
> > Insects (e.g., Locusts)
> > Mudslides
> > Tsunami (Tidal Wave)
> > Typhoons
> > Volcanic Eruptions
> *Human Caused Disasters*
> > Bombs
> > Nuclear Leaks and Meltdowns
> > Oil Spills (Wells and Ships)
> > Secondary Disasters (e.g., unemployment, violence, rioting)
> > Terrorist Attacks
> > Toxic Waste Spills
> > Transportation Accidents (e.g., Air, Sea, Train)
> > War

Disaster Responders

> Clergy
> Emergency Medical Technicians
> Nursing
> Paraprofessionals
> Public Health
> Psychiatry
> Psychology
> Social Workers
> Trauma Physicians
> Volunteers

Diseases (Communicable/Non Communicable)
Disillusionment Phases

Early Intervention
Emergency
Emergency Response Team
Emergency Response Vehicle (ERV)
Epidemiology
Ethnic Groups
Hazards
Heroic Phase
Honeymoon Phase
Incident Command System
International Critical Incident Stress Foundation
International Society for Traumatic Stress Studies
Key Informant
Memorandum of Understanding
Mental Illness
Morbidity
Mortality
National Association of Social Workers
National Center for Post-Traumatic Stress Disorder
National Organization for Victims Assistance
Outreach
Post-Traumatic Stress Disorders
Preparedness Plan
Presidential Declaration
Psychological First-Aid
Public Affairs of Public Information Officer
Public Health Service
Referral
Refugees/Internally Displaced People
Risk Factors
Search and Rescue
Secondary Traumatization
Social Networks
Social Support
Staffing
Staging Area
Standard Operating Procedure
State Coordinating Officer
Stress
Stressors
Stress Reaction
Substance Abuse and Mental Health Services Administration (SAMHSA)
Support System
Trauma
Traumatic Grief

Traumatic Reactivation
Triage
Uncomplicated grief
United Nations

> High Commissioner for Refugees (UNHCR)
> Department of Humanitarian Affairs
> World Health Organization (WHO)

Victim
Victims Rights
Weapons of Mass Destruction

Appendix B

Summary and Overview of Disasters in Developing Countries

Fran H. Norris

Psychosocial Consequences of Natural Disasters in Developing Countries: What Does Past Research Tell us About the Potential Effects of the 2004 Tsunami?[1]

- *Purpose.* This fact sheet presents a review of the empirical research on the mental health consequences of natural disasters, with a focus on findings for disasters that occurred in the developing world. Findings for human-caused disasters are not included in this summary. First, I describe the characteristics of the studies that have been conducted to date and summarize the range and magnitude of the effects that have been observed in the samples, often by comparing results for developing countries to those for developed countries. Then, I discuss the experiential, demographic, and psychosocial factors that most often have influenced individual-level outcomes across these studies. All articles reviewed were quantitative in method and published, in English, between 1981 and 2004.
- *The Data.* As part of a larger database on disaster research, data were available for 121 distinct samples composed of 52,061 individuals who experienced 62 different natural disasters around the world.

---

[1] Reprinted with permission of the author. National Center for PTSD Fact Sheet, posted on the NC-PTSD website (www.ncptsd.va.gov) January, 2005. Downloaded March, 2006. Copyright retained by author.

- Of these samples, 63 (52%) resided in the *USA*, 21 (17%) resided in *other developed countries*, and 37 (31%) resided in *developing countries*. See Table A.1 for a list of the studies in the third category. Fifteen of these samples were located in Southeast or South Central Asia (China, India, the Philippines, Taiwan, Thailand), with the remainder residing in Turkey ($n = 4$), Latin America ($n = 11$), and Eastern

Table B.1.   Studies of Natural Disasters in Developing Countries

First Author and Year of Publication	PILOTS ID	Country	Agent	Event Year	Sample Type
Armenian, 2000	22383	Armenia	Earthquake	1988	Adult
Assanangkornchai, 2004	18298	Thailand	Flood	2000	Adult
Basoglu, 2002	16884	Turkey	Earthquake	1999	Adult
Basoglu, 2004	18243	Turkey	Earthquake	1999	Adult
Bokszczanin, 2002	25273	Poland	Flood	1997	Youth
Caldera, 2001	23340	Nicaragua	Hurricane	1998	Adult
Chang, 2002	24456	Taiwan	Earthquake	1999	Adult
Chang, 2003	25728	Taiwan	Earthquake	1999	Rescue
Chen, 2002	25283	Taiwan	Earthquake	1999	Youth
De la Fuente, 1990	10822	Mexico	Earthquake	1985	Adult
Durkin, 1993	04377	Chile	Earthquake	1985	Adult
Goenjian, 1995	06107	Armenia	Earthquake	1988	Youth
Goenjian, 2001	23393	Nicaragua	Hurricane	1998	Youth
Howard, 1999	21740	Philippines	Volcano	1991	Adult
Karanci, 1999	24481	Turkey	Earthquake	1999	Adult
Kuo, 2003	25373	Taiwan	Earthquake	1999	Adult
Laor, 2002	25373	Turkey	Earthquake	1999	Youth
Liao, 2002	24574	Taiwan	Earthquake	1999	Rescue
Liao, 2004	26279	Taiwan	Earthquake	1999	Adult
Lima, 1990	10741	Colombia	Volcano	1985	Adult
Lima, 1990	10821	Ecuador	Earthquake	1987	Adult
Lima, 1991	02281	Colombia	Volcano	1985	Adult
McFarlane, 1993	11535	China	Earthquake	1988	Adult
Najarian, 1996	07041	Armenia	Earthquake	1988	Youth
Najarian, 2001	06091	Armenia	Earthquake	1988	Adult
Norris, 2001	15858	Mexico	Hurricane	1997	Adult
Norris, 2002	24927	Poland	Flood	1997	Adult
Norris, 2004	18521	Mexico	Flood/mudslides	1999	Adult
Sattler, 2002	16997	Dom. Rep.	Hurricane	1998	Adult
Scott, 2003	17168	Colombia	Earthquake	1999	Youth
Sharan, 1996	07053	India	Earthquake	1993	Adult
Suar, 2002	16889	India	Earthquake	1998	Adult
Wang, 2000	22485	China	Earthquake	1998	Adult
Watanabe, 2004	18116	Taiwan	Earthquake	1999	Adult
Yang, 2003	25846	Taiwan	Earthquake	1999	Adult
Yeh, 2002	25191	Taiwan	Earthquake	1999	Rescue

Rescue includes recovery workers as well as first responders. PILOTS ID is the identification number for the abstract and citation in the PILOTS database, which can be accessed at www.ncptsd.org. Full citations follow.

Europe ($n = 7$). Japanese samples ($n = 5$) were classified in the second group (other developed countries).

- By far, most of the samples experiencing natural disasters in developing countries were composed of *adult survivors* ($n = 27, 76\%$), with smaller proportions composed of *youth* ($n = 7, 19\%$) and *rescue/recovery workers* ($n = 3, 8\%$). Proportionally, the distribution of sample types for these countries was the same as in developed countries, although the numbers are fewer.

- Four types of natural disasters have been studied in developing countries. Earthquakes composed 68% of the agents, hurricanes/cyclones 14%, floods 11%, and volcanoes 8%. No tsunamis have been studied. However, many of these events (e.g., the Armenian earthquake, Marmara Turkey earthquake, Mexican mudslides) occurred suddenly without warning and resulted in high death tolls and massive displacements and thus are relevant to understanding the potential consequences of the impact of the 2004 Indian Ocean tsunami.

- Each sample was coded on several methodological variables to provide a crude accounting of the quality of the studies.
  - Procedures used to draw the sample of participants influence the validity of a study, especially in terms of how well the sample represents the afflicted population. Probability and census samples are high in representativeness and thus are preferred. Only 19% of the samples studied in developing countries were high in representativeness, compared to 42% and 47% of the samples studied in the USA and other developed countries, respectively.
  - Larger samples provide greater power and precision than smaller samples and allow for more advanced multivariate analyses, and thus are preferred. The median N of the samples in developing countries was 218, intermediate to the median $N's$ for the USA (162) and other developed countries (240). Mean $N's$ (423, 442, 436 for USA, other developed countries, and developing countries, respectively) did not differ.
  - On average, studies in developing countries began 10 months postevent (median= 6), compared to 7 months in the USA (median = 4) and 14 months in other developed countries (median = 6). Seven (19%) of the developing-country studies provided information on the acute aftermath by beginning data collection no later than 2 months postevent. Four of these studies described consequences of the 1999 earthquake in Taiwan (Kuo et al., 2003; Liao et al., 2002; Liao, Lee, Lee, & Huang, 2004; Yeh, Leckman, Wan, Shiah, Lu, 2002), a fifth an earthquake in India (Sharan, Chaudhary, Kavathekar, & Saxena, 1996). Comparatively, 35% and 25% of the samples residing in

the USA and other developed countries were studied within the first two months.

- Longitudinal studies involving multiple timepoints provide information on the course of recovery that cross-sectional studies cannot and thus are generally preferred. Only 4 (11%) of the studies conducted in developing countries were longitudinal in design. Liao et al. (2004) studied outcomes 1 and 18 months after the 1999 earthquake in Taiwan, Watanabe et al. (2004) studied the same event at 6 and 12 months, and Wang et al. (2000) studied outcomes 3 and 9 months after an earthquake in China. In what appears to be the only study in a developing country with more than two waves of data collection, Norris, Murphy, Baker, and Perilla (2004) studied outcomes at 6,12, 18, and 24 months after floods and deadly mudslides in Mexico. Longitudinal studies composed a higher proportion of studies in the USA (27%) and other developed countries (38%), although they were less common than cross-sectional studies in all locations. On average, longitudinal studies collected their last data at 14, 21, and 16 months, respectively, in the three locations.

- *Outcomes*. These frequencies reflect the extent to which these outcomes were examined as well as the extent to which they were observed.
    - *Specific psychological problems* were identified in 89% of the developing-country samples after natural disasters. Posttraumatic stress or PTSD was found in 81% of these samples, depressive symptoms or major depressive disorder were found in 57% of the samples, and anxiety or generalized anxiety disorder was found in 19% of the samples.
    - *Non-specific distress*, assessed by means of global indices of psychological and psychosomatic symptoms, was identified in 35% of the same samples.
    - *Health problems and concerns*, such as self-reported somatic complaints, verified medical conditions, increased taking of sick leave, elevations in physiological indicators of stress, declines in immune functioning, sleep disruption, increased use of substances (primarily if previously a problem drinker), and (if previously disabled) relapse and illness burden, were identified in 22% of the same samples.

- *Magnitude of Effects*. To provide a rough estimate of the overall impact of the disasters studied, each sample's results were classified on a 4-point scale of severity from *minmal* (1) to *very severe* (4).
    - The 37 samples in developing countries showed more severe effects overall ($M = 2.9$, $SD = 0.8$) than did samples from the USA ($M = 2.1$, $SD = 0.8$) and other developed countries ($M = 2.5$, $SD = 0.8$). Disaster location alone explained 15% of the variance in severity of

effects, which is quite substantial. The mean for natural disasters in developing countries was higher, in fact, than the mean for disasters of mass violence in the USA and other developed countries ($M = 2.6$, $SD = 0.9$).

- A more specific breakdown of the results for samples experiencing natural disasters in developing countries follows.
  - **3% showed** *minimal impairment*, meaning that the majority of the sample experienced only transient stress reactions. This one study was Yeh et al.'s (2002) study of Taiwan earthquake rescue workers.
  - **32% showed** *moderate impairment*, wherein prolonged but subclinical distress was the predominant result.
  - **41% showed** *severe impairment*, meaning that 25% to 49% of the sample suffered from clinically significant distress or criterion-level psychopathology.
  - **24 % showed** *very severe impairment*, meaning that 50% or more of the sample suffered from clinically significant distress or criterion level psychopathology.
- Comparatively, 14% and 0% of the samples from the USA and other developed countries, respectively, showed minimal effects; 65% and 67% showed moderate effects; 13% and 19% showed severe effects; and 8% and 14% showed very severe effects. Thus the modal outcomes after natural disasters were *moderate* in developed countries and *severe* in developing countries.
- **Risk Factors for Adverse Outcomes.** This section focuses on within-sample factors that have been found in previous studies to influence who is most likely to experience serious and lasting psychological distress. For these results, the entire database was used, not only those studies from developing countries. More detail about these risk factors can be found in Norris, Friedman, Watson, Byrne et al. (2002).
- *Individual-level severity of exposure* was almost universally important in predicting postdisaster outcomes. Important stressors included bereavement, injury to self or another family member, life threat, panic or similar emotions during the disaster, horror, separation from family (especially among youth), extensive loss of property, and displacement. In general, injury and life threat were most predictive of long term adverse consequences, especially PTSD. As the number of these stressors increased, the likelihood of psychological impairment increased in many studies. The relevance of this fact for victims of the tsunami should be self-evident.
- *Neighborhood- or community-level severity of exposure* was assessed only occasionally but had modest outcomes, as follows. Personal loss was more strongly related to increases in negative affect, but community destruction was more strongly related to

decreases in positive affect, reflecting a community-wide tendency for people to feel less positive about their surroundings, less enthusiastic, less energetic, and less able to enjoy life. Such findings are an excellent reminder that disasters impact whole communities, not just selected individuals.

- *Gender* influenced postdisaster outcomes in many samples; almost always, women or girls were affected more adversely than were men or boys. The effects occurred across a broad range of outcomes, but the strongest effects were for PTSD, for which women's rates often exceeded men's by a ratio of 2:1. The effects of gender appeared to be greatest within samples from traditional cultures and in the context of severe exposure.

- *Age* often influenced disaster victims' outcomes. Samples of children generally exhibit more severe distress after disasters than do adults. Older adults were at greater risk than were other adults in only a small minority of adult samples where age differences were observed. In every American sample where they were differentiated from older and younger adults, middle-aged adults were most adversely affected. Some research suggests that middle-aged adults are most at risk because they have greater stress and burden even before the disaster strikes and assume even greater obligations afterwards. Cross-cultural research suggests that the effects of age may differ across countries according to the social, political, economic, and historical context of the setting involved.

- *Ethnicity* shaped the outcomes of disaster victims in several USA and Australian samples. Among youth, results for ethnicity were not entirely consistent, but among adults, minority status was associated with greater risk for adverse outcomes. There is little explanatory research available, but the disproportionate risk of ethnic minorities appears to follow both from differential exposure to more severe aspects of the disaster and from culturally specific attitudes and beliefs that may impede seeking help.

- *Socioeconomic Status (SES),* as manifest in education, income, literacy, or occupational prestige, has often affected outcomes of disaster victims, with lower SES most often being associated with poorer outcomes.

- *Family Factors* influenced outcomes in several different ways.
  - *Married status* was a risk factor for women in a few studies. Husbands' symptom severity predicted wives' symptoms more strongly than wives' symptom severity predicted husbands'. Marital stress has been found to increase after disasters.
  - *Being a parent* also adds to the stressfulness of disaster recovery and, especially for events involving uncertain threats, mothers were especially at risk for substantial distress.

- *Family environment* is critical for children, who tend to be highly sensitive to postdisaster distress and conflict in the family. Parental psychopathology was typically the best predictor of child psychopathology in child studies. Less irritable, more supportive, and healthier parents had healthier children.
- *Predisaster Functioning and Personality* influenced outcomes in many samples. Persons with predisaster psychiatric histories were disproportionately likely to develop disaster-specific PTSD and to be diagnosed with some type of postdisaster disorder. Other research suggests that a "neurotic," as opposed to stable and calm, personality increases the likelihood of postdisaster distress and that "hardiness" decreases the likelihood of postdisaster distress.
- *Secondary Stressors,* when measured, were almost always important. Both life-event stress (discrete changes) and chronic stress have been strong predictors of survivors' health outcomes. In part, the long-term effects of *acute* stressors (the individual-level aspects of exposure outlined above) on psychological distress operate through their effects on *chronic* stressors, such as marital stress, financial stress, and ecological stress. Attention needs to be paid to stress levels in stricken communities long after the disaster has happened and passed.
- *Psychosocial resources* were likewise important in all relevant studies.
  - *Ways of coping* influenced symptom outcomes in several studies, but the findings were not always consistent across them. Avoidance coping and blame assignment were consistently problematic, but other ways of coping were sometimes helpful and sometimes not.
  - *Beliefs about coping* were far more important than ways of coping. What matters, apparently, is not how individuals actually cope but rather how they perceive their capabilities to cope.
  - *Self-efficacy, mastery, perceived control, self-esteem, hope, and optimism* were all related positively, strongly, and consistently to mental health.
  - *Social support* appears to be especially important for disaster recovery.
    - *Social embeddedness* – the size, activeness, and closeness of the survivor's network – is related strongly and consistently to mental health.
    - *Received social support* is the actual helping behavior that emerges in response to stress. Although it usually is related positively to mental health, the findings are not entirely consistent, in part because levels of help received are confounded with need. Received support is

important primarily because it protects and replenishes other resources, such as perceived social support.

- *Perceived social support* is the most thoroughly researched social resource. With few exceptions, disaster survivors who subsequently believed that they were cared for by others and that help would be available, if needed, have fared better psychologically than disaster survivors who believed they were unloved and alone.

- *The Social Support Deterioration Model*, which has been tested across several disasters, indicates that declines in perceived social support account for a large share of victims' subsequent declines in mental health. A variant of the original model showed that support *received* after the disaster offset the detrimental effects of disaster exposure on subsequent levels of *perceived* (expected) social support. Attending to the social needs of disaster victims could go a long way towards protecting them from long-term adverse psychological consequences.

- *Summary and Conclusions.*
  - *More and better research on disasters in developing countries is needed.* A substantial amount of research pertinent to understanding the range, magnitude and duration of the effects of disasters has been published over the past 25 years. Many of the samples included in this review of the research on natural disasters (37 of 119) resided in developing countries, such as Taiwan, India, the Philippines, and Thailand. This accumulating research base, especially given the recent studies on the 1999 earthquakes in Taiwan and Turkey, allows the effects of catastrophic disasters in these regions to be understood better than ever before. A list of these studies may be found in Table A.1.
    - Progress notwithstanding, research on natural disasters in developing countries is rare relative to the frequency with which such disasters occur in those countries. Averaging almost 200 incidents annually, Asia dramatically leads the rest of the world in disaster frequency, followed by the Americas (111 events annually, on average). There is a critical need for additional research in such areas of the world, especially on children, for which too few studies exist to even begin to extrapolate general principles. We know little about how culture shapes the psychological impact of disasters.
    - Mechanisms for supporting international researchers financially are also advised, as are approaches for mentoring them. Many of the studies conducted in developing countries were not optimal in terms of their sampling strategies and designs. A plethora of tsunami studies of questionable quality will do little to advance knowledge.

- That only four of the identified studies in developing countries were longitudinal in design points to a critical need for longitudinal research that can inform us about the course of recovery under low-resource conditions. Longitudinal research on natural disasters in the developed world predicts strong recovery for most people, but we know very little about recovery under more harsh conditions.
- *The effects of the tsunami on mental health are likely to be quite severe.* The research to date strongly suggests that natural disasters in developing countries often produce severe effects on the public's mental health. In fact, the modal sample-level outcome after natural disasters in developing countries was *severe*, whereas the modal outcome after natural disasters in developed countries was *moderate*. This general finding from the research base may reflect the fact that disasters tend to be more destructive when they occur in the developing world. Many of the samples from developing countries survived disasters where death tolls were measured in thousands or even tens of thousands. The difference may also attest to the ability of government services and other resources to make a difference in the lives of disaster victims. Moreover, the victims of the 2004 tsunami are likely to have experienced multiple intense stressors that have been found to predict adverse outcomes, such as bereavement, threat to life, extensive property damage, financial loss, and displacement.
- *Even after very serious disasters, individuals differ in the risk for adverse psychological outcomes.*
  - Risk factors for adults include: severe exposure to the disaster, especially injury, threat to life, and extreme loss; living in a highly disrupted or traumatized community; female gender; age in the middle years of 40 to 60; little previous experience relevant to coping with the disaster; ethnic minority group membership; poverty or low socioeconomic status; the presence of children in the home; psychiatric history; secondary stress; and weak or deteriorating psychosocial resources.
  - With a few modifications – primarily the deletion of age – this risk-factor model holds reasonably well for children and adolescents.
- *Implications for intervention.* Several implications for intervention can be drawn from the research on disasters. There is a critical need for research that tests the impact of postdisaster psychosocial interventions.
  - Families are extremely important systems and constitute the most important unit for postdisaster treatment and intervention efforts, especially with children. Interventions for children may be of limited effectiveness if the family is not considered as a whole. In fact, providing care and support to their overly

stressed parents might be among the most effective ways to provide care and support to the children affected by disaster.

- We should educate survivors, and those who come into contact with them, that avoidance and blame assignment are rarely effective coping strategies. Otherwise, however, the specific ways of coping matter much less than do people's perceptions of themselves as able to cope and control outcomes. It may be more important for disaster workers to reassure survivors that they do, in fact, have what it takes to meet the demands faced.
- A focus on self-efficacy does not mean that mental health services are not needed, but rather that such services should be delivered in a way that provides resources without threatening them. Some people are more likely to accept help for "problems in living" than to accept help for "mental health problems." In exercising our good intentions to help victims, we must not inadvertently rob them of the very psychological resources they need to persevere over the long term.
- Naturally occurring social resources are particularly vital for disaster victims. Professionals and outsiders are important sources of assistance when the level of need is high, but they must not and cannot supplant natural helping networks. People should not abandon their routine social activities because these keep people informed about the relative needs of network members, provide natural forums for sharing experiences, and preserve a sense of social embeddedness. It also might be helpful to educate the public about the reasons significant others may not always be able to provide them with the quality or quantity of interpersonal support they expect.
- Individual-focused interventions are not always necessary. They should be reserved for those persons who are most distressed, who had weak psychological and social resources to begin with, or who suffered particularly dire resource losses. Resources must be invested in order to acquire new ones, and thus people who need such services the most may be least likely to seek them. Outreach to such persons, and to the communities in which they are most likely to live, is essential.

References

Armenian, H. K., Morikawa, M., Melkonian, A. K., Hovanesian, A. P., Haroutunian, N., Saigh, P. A., et al. (2000). Loss as a determinant of PTSD in a cohort of adult survivors of the 1988 earthquake in Armenia: Implications for policy. *Acta Psychiatrica Scandinavica, 102,* 58–64.

Assanangkornchai, S., Tangboonngam, S., & Edwards, J. G. (2004). The flooding of Hat Yai: Predictors of adverse emotional responses to a natural disaster. *Stress and Health, 20,* 81–89.

Basoglu, M., Salcioglu, E., & Livanou, M. (2002). Traumatic stress responses in earthquake survivors in Turkey. *Journal of Traumatic Stress, 15,* 269–276.

Basoglu, M., Kiliç, C., Salcioglu, E., & Livanou, M. (2004). Prevalence of posttraumatic stress disorder and comorbid depression in earthquake survivors in Turkey: An epidemiological study. *Journal of Traumatic Stress, 17,* 133–141

Bokszczanin, A. (2002). Long-term negative psychological effects of a flood on adolescents. *Polish Psychological Bulletin, 33,* 55–61.

Caldera, T., Palma, L., Penayo, U., & Kullgren, G. (2001). Psychological impact of the hurricane Mitch in Nicaragua in a one-year perspective. *Social Psychiatry and Psychiatric Epidemiology, 36,* 108–114.

Chang, H., Chang, T., Lin, T., & Kuo, S. (2002). Psychiatric morbidity and pregnancy outcome in a disaster area of Taiwan 921 earthquake. *Psychiatry and Clinical Neurosciences, 56,* 139–144.

Chang, C., Lee, L., Connor, K. M., Davidson, J. R. T., Jeffries, K., & Lai, T. (2003). Posttraumatic distress and coping strategies among rescue workers after an earthquake. *Journal of Nervous and Mental Disease, 191,* 391–398.

Chen, S., Lin, Y., Tseng, H., & Wu, Y. (2002). Posttraumatic stress reactions in children and adolescents one year after the 1999 Taiwan Chi-Chi Earthquake. *Journal of the Chinese Institute of Engineers, 25,* 597–608.

De la Fuente, J. R. (1990). The mental health consequences of the 1985 earthquakes in Mexico. *International Journal of Mental Health, 19,* 21–29.

Durkin, M. E. (1993). Major depression and post-traumatic stress disorder following the Coalinga and Chile earthquakes: A cross-cultural comparison. *Journal of Social Behavior and Personality, 8,* 405–420.

Goenjian, A. K., Pynoos, R. S., Steinberg, A. M., Najarian, L. M., Asarnow, J. R., Karayan, I, et al. (1995). Psychiatric comorbidity in children after the 1988 earthquake in Armenia. *Journal of the American Academy of Child and Adolescent Psychiatry, 34,* 1174–1184.

Goenjian, A. K., Molina, L., Steinberg, A. M., Fairbanks, L. A., Alvarez, M. L., Goenjian, H. A., et al. (2001). Posttraumatic stress and depressive reactions among Nicaraguan adolescents after Hurricane Mitch. *American Journal of Psychiatry, 158,* 788–794.

Howard, W. T, Loberiza, F. R., Pfohl, B. M., Thorne, P. S., Magpantay, R. L., & Woolson, R. F. (1999). Initial results, reliability, and validity of a mental health survey of Mount Pinatubo disaster victims. *Journal of Nervous and Mental Disease, 187,* 661–672.

Karanci, A. N., Alkan, N., Aksit, B., Sucuoglu, H., & Balta, E. (1999). Gender differences in psychological distress, coping, social support and related variables following the 1995 Dinar (Turkey) earthquake. *North American Journal of Psychology, 1,* 189–204.

Kuo, C., Tang, H., Tsay, C., Lin, S., Hu, W., & Chen, C. (2003). Prevalence of psychiatric disorders among bereaved survivors of a disastrous earthquake in Taiwan. *Psychiatric Services, 54,* 249–251.

Laor, N., Wolmer, L., Kora, M., Yucel, D., Spiriman, S., & Yazgan, Y. (2002). Posttraumatic, dissociative and grief symptoms in Turkish children exposed to the 1999 earthquakes. *Journal of Nervous and Mental Disease, 190,* 824–832.

Liao, S. C., Lee, M., Lee, Y., Weng, T., Shih, F., Ma, M. H. M. (2002). Association of psychological distress with psychological factors in rescue workers within two months after a major earthquake. *Journal of the Formosan Medical Association, 101,* 169–176.

Liao, S., Lee, M., Lee, Y., & Huang, T. (2004). Hyperleptinemia in subjects with persistent partial posttraumatic stress disorder after a major earthquake. *Psychosomatic Medicine, 66,* 23–28.

Lima, B. R., Pai, S., Lozano Guillén, J., & Santacruz Oleas, H. (1990). The stability of emotional symptoms among disaster victims in a developing country. *Journal of Traumatic Stress, 3,* 497–505.

Lima, B. R., Santacruz Oleas, H., Lozano Guillén, J., Chávez Oleas, H., Samaniego, N., Pompei, M. S., et al. (1990). Disasters and mental health: Experience in Colombia and Ecuador and its relevance for primary care in mental health in Latin America. *International Journal of Mental Health, 19,* 3–20.

Lima, B., Pai, S., Santacruz Oleas, H., & Lozano Guillén, J. (1991). Psychiatric disorders among poor victims following a major disaster: Armero, Colombia. *Journal of Nervous and Mental Disease, 179*, 420–427.

McFarlane, A. C., & Cao, H. (1993). Study of a major disaster in the People's Republic of China: The Yunnan earthquake. In J. P. Wilson & B. Raphael's *International handbook of traumatic stress syndromes* (pp. 493–498). New York: Plenum Press.

Najarian, L. M., Goenjian, A. K., Pelcovitz, D., Mandel, F. S., & Najarian, B. (1996). Relocation after a disaster: Posttraumatic stress disorder in Armenia after the earthquake. *Journal of the American Academy of Child and Adolescent Psychiatry, 35*, 374–383.

Najarian, B., Goenjian, A. K., Pelcovitz, D., Mandel, F. S., & Najarian, B. (2001). The effect of relocation after a natural disaster. *Journal of Traumatic Stress, 14*, 511–526.

Norris, F., Friedman, M., Watson, P., Byrne, C., Diaz, E., & Kaniasty, K. (2002). 60,000 disaster victims speak, Part I: An empirical review of the empirical literature, 1981–2001. *Psychiatry, 65*, 207–239.

Norris, F., Friedman, M., & Watson, P. (2002). 60,000 disaster victims speak, Part II: Summary and implications of the disaster mental health research. *Psychiatry, 65*, 240–260.

Norris, F. H., Kaniasty, D. Z., Conrad, M. L., Inman, G. L., & Murphy, A. D. (2002). Placing age differences in cultural context: a comparison of the effects of age on PTSD after disasters in the United States, Mexico, and Poland. *Journal of Clinical Geropsychology, 8*, 153–173.

Norris, F. H., Murphy, A. D., Baker, C. K., & Perilla, J. L. (2004). Postdisaster PTSD over four waves of a panel study of Mexico's 1999 flood. *Journal of Traumatic Stress, 17*, 283–292.

Norris, F., Perilla, J., Ibañez G., & Murphy, A. (2001). Sex differences in symptoms of post-traumatic stress: Does culture play a role? *Journal of Traumatic Stress, 14*, 7–28.

Sattler, D. N., Preston, A. J., Kaiser, C. F., Olivera, V. E., Valdez, J., & Schlueter, S. (2002). Hurricane Georges: A cross-national study examining preparedness, resource loss, and psychological distress in the U.S. Virgin Islands, Puerto Rico, Dominican Republic, and the United States. *Journal of Traumatic Stress, 15*, 339–350.

Scott, R. L., Knoth, R. L., Beltran-Quiones, M., & Gomez, N. (2003). Assessment of psychological functioning in adolescent earthquake victims in Colombia using the MMPI-A. *Journal of Traumatic Stress, 16*, 49–57.

Sharan, P., Chaudhary, G., Kavathekar, S. A., & Saxena, S. (1996). Preliminary report of psychiatric disorders in survivors of a severe earthquake. *American Journal of Psychiatry, 153*, 556–558.

Suar, D., Mandal, M. K., & Khuntia, R. (2002). Supercyclone in Orissa: An assessment of psychological status of survivors. *Journal of Traumatic Stress, 15*, 313–319.

Wang, X., Gao, L., Shinfuku, N., Zhang, H., Zhao, C., & Shen, Y. (2000). Longitudinal study of earthquake-related PTSD in a randomly selected community sample in North China. *American Journal of Psychiatry, 157*, 1260–1266.

Watanabe, C., Okumura, J., Chiu, T., & Wakai, S. (2004). Social support and depressive symptoms among displaced older adults following the 1999 Taiwan earthquake. *Journal of Traumatic Stress, 17*, 63–67.

Yang, Y. K., Yeh, T. L., Chen, C. C., Lee, C. K., Lee, I. H., Lee, L., et al. (2003). Psychiatric morbidity and posttraumatic symptoms among earthquake victims in primary care clinics. *General Hospital Psychiatry, 25*, 253–261.

Yeh, C., Leckman, J. F., Wan, F., Shiah, I., Lu, R. (2002). Characteristics of acute stress symptoms and nitric oxide concentration in young rescue workers in Taiwan. *Psychiatry Research, 112*, 59–68.

Appendix C

Disaster Rescue and Response Workers
A National Center for PTSD Fact Sheet[1]

Bruce H. Young, Julian D. Ford, and Patricia Watson

The terrorist attacks on New York and Washington are, together, the greatest man-made disaster in America since the Civil War. Lessons learned from natural and human-caused disasters can help us understand the unique stressors faced by rescue workers such as police and firefighters, National Guard members, emergency medical technicians, and volunteers. Past experience may also help us recognize how these stressors may *affect* response workers. Rescue workers face the danger of death or physical injury, the potential loss of their coworkers and friends, and devastating effects on their communities. In addition to physical danger, rescue workers are at risk for behavioral and emotional readjustment problems.

WHAT PSYCHOLOGICAL PROBLEMS CAN RESULT FOR RESCUE WORKERS FOLLOWING DISASTER EXPERIENCES?

The psychological problems for workers that may result from disaster experiences include:

- Emotional reactions: temporary (i.e., for several days or a couple of weeks) feelings of shock, fear, grief, anger, resentment, guilt, shame, helplessness, hopelessness, or emotional numbness (difficulty feeling

---

[1] Reprinted with permission of the authors. National Center for PTSD Fact Sheet, posted on the NC-PTSD website (www.ncptsd.va.gov) March, 2006. Downloaded February, 2007. Copyright retained by authors.

love and intimacy or difficulty taking interest and pleasure in day-to-day activities)
- Cognitive reactions: confusion, disorientation, indecisiveness, worry, shortened attention span, difficulty concentrating, memory loss, unwanted memories, self-blame
- Physical reactions: tension, fatigue, edginess, difficulty sleeping, bodily aches or pain, startling easily, racing heartbeat, nausea, change in appetite, change in sex drive
- Interpersonal reactions in relationships at school, work, in friendships, in marriage, or as a parent: distrust; irritability; conflict; withdrawal; isolation; feeling rejected or abandoned; being distant, judgmental, or over-controlling

WHAT SEVERE STRESS SYMPTOMS CAN RESULT FOR DISASTER WORKERS?

Most disaster rescue workers only experience mild, normal stress reactions, and disaster experiences may even promote personal growth and strengthen relationships. However, as many as one out of every three rescue workers experience some or all of the following severe stress symptoms, which may lead to lasting Posttraumatic Stress Disorder (PTSD), anxiety disorders, or depression:

- Dissociation (feeling completely unreal or outside yourself, like in a dream; having "blank" periods of time you cannot remember)
- Intrusive reexperiencing (terrifying memories, nightmares, or flashbacks)
- Extreme attempts to avoid disturbing memories (such as through substance use)
- Extreme emotional numbing (completely unable to feel emotion, as if empty)
- Hyper-arousal (panic attacks, rage, extreme irritability, intense agitation)
- Severe anxiety (paralyzing worry, extreme helplessness, compulsions or obsessions)
- Severe depression (complete loss of hope, self-worth, motivation, or purpose in life)

WHO IS AT GREATEST RISK FOR SEVERE STRESS SYMPTOMS?

Rescue workers who directly experience or witness any of the following during or after the disaster are at greatest risk for severe stress symptoms and lasting readjustment problems:

- Life threatening danger or physical harm (especially to children)
- Exposure to gruesome death, bodily injury, or dead or maimed bodies
- Extreme environmental or human violence or destruction
- Loss of home, valued possessions, neighborhood, or community
- Loss of communication with or support from close relations
- Intense emotional demands (such as searching for possibly dying survivors or interacting with bereaved family members)
- Extreme fatigue, weather exposure, hunger, or sleep deprivation
- Extended exposure to danger, loss, emotional/physical strain
- Exposure to toxic contamination (such as gas or fumes, chemicals, radioactivity)

Studies also show that some individuals are at a higher than typical risk for severe stress symptoms and lasting PTSD if they have a history of:

- Exposure to other traumas (such as severe accidents, abuse, assault, combat, rescue work)
- Chronic medical illness or psychological disorders
- Chronic poverty, homelessness, unemployment, or discrimination
- Recent or subsequent major life stressors or emotional strain (such as single parenting)

Disaster stress may revive memories of prior trauma and may intensify preexisting social, economic, spiritual, psychological, or medical problems.

HOW CAN YOU MANAGE STRESS DURING A DISASTER OPERATION?

Here are some ways to manage stress during a disaster operation:

Develop a "buddy" system with a coworker.
Encourage and support your coworkers.
Take care of yourself physically by exercising regularly and eating small quantities of food frequently.
Take a break when you feel your stamina, coordination, or tolerance for irritation diminishing.
Stay in touch with family and friends.
Defuse briefly whenever you experience troubling incidents and after each work shift.

HOW CAN YOU MANAGE STRESS AFTER THE DISASTER?

After the disaster:

- Attend a debriefing if one is offered, or try to get one organized 2 to 5 days after leaving the scene.

- Talk about feelings as they arise, and be a good listener to your coworkers.
- Don't take anger too personally – it's often an expression of frustration, guilt, or worry.
- Give your coworkers recognition and appreciation for a job well done.
- Eat well and try to get adequate sleep in the days following the event.
- Maintain as normal a routine as possible, but take several days to "decompress" gradually.

HOW CAN YOU MANAGE STRESS
AFTER RETURNING HOME?

After returning home:

- Catch up on your rest (this may take several days).
- Slow down – get back to a normal pace in your daily life.
- Understand that it's perfectly normal to want to talk about the disaster and equally normal not to want to talk about it; but remember that those who haven't been through it might not be interested in hearing all about it – they might find it frightening or simply be satisfied that you returned safely.
- Expect disappointment, frustration, and conflict – sometimes coming home doesn't live up to what you imagined it would be – but keep recalling what's really important in your life and relationships so that small stressors don't lead to major conflicts.
- Don't be surprised if you experience mood swings; they will diminish with time.
- Don't overwhelm children with your experiences; be sure to talk about what happened in their lives while you were gone.
- If talking doesn't feel natural, other forms of expression or stress relief such as journal writing, hobbies, and exercise are recommended.

Taking each day one at a time is essential in disaster's wake. Each day provides a new opportunity to **FILL-UP**:

- **F**ocus **I**nwardly on what's most important to you and your family today;
- **L**ook and **L**isten to learn what you and your significant others are experiencing, so you'll remember what is important and let go of what's not;
- **U**nderstand **P**ersonally what these experiences mean to you, so that you will feel able to go on with your life and even grow personally

Index